STATISTICS
IN THE
BEHAVIORAL
SCIENCES
A Conceptual Introduction

STATISTICS IN THE BEHAVIORAL SCIENCES

A Conceptual Introduction

RICHARD S. LEHMAN
Franklin & Marshall College

Brooks/Cole Publishing Company
I(T)P™ An International Thomson Publishing Company

Pacific Grove • Albany • Bonn • Boston • Cincinnati • Detroit • London • Madrid • Melbourne
Mexico City • New York • Paris • San Francisco • Singapore • Tokyo • Toronto • Washington

Sponsoring Editor: *Jim Brace-Thompson*
Marketing Team: *Kathleen Bowers and Carolyn Crockett*
Marketing Representative: *Barbara Stein*
Editorial Associates: *Cathleen S. Collins and Patsy Vienneau*
Production Editor: *Marjorie Z. Sanders*
Manuscript Editor: *Carol Dondrea*
Permissions Editor: *Elaine Jones*
Interior Design: *Terri Wright*

Interior Illustration: *MacArt Design*
Cover Design: *Roy R. Neuhaus*
Cover Photo: *Ed Young*
Art Coordinator: *Lisa Torri*
Indexer: *Andrea Olshevsky*
Typesetting: *Asco Trade Typesetting Ltd.*
Cover Printing: *Color Dot Graphics, Inc.*
Printing and Binding: *Quebecor Printing Fairfield*

For more information, contact:

BROOKS/COLE PUBLISHING COMPANY
511 Forest Lodge Road
Pacific Grove, CA 93950
USA

International Thomson Publishing Europe
Berkshire House 168–173
High Holborn
London WC1V 7AA
England

Thomas Nelson Australia
102 Dodds Street
South Melbourne, 3205
Victoria, Australia

Nelson Canada
1120 Birchmount Road
Scarborough, Ontario
Canada M1K 5G4

International Thomson Editores
Campos Eliseos 385, Piso 7
Col. Polanco
11560 México D. F. México

International Thomson Publishing GmbH
Königswinterer Strasse 418
53227 Bonn
Germany

International Thomson Publishing Asia
221 Henderson Road
#05–10 Henderson Building
Singapore 0315

International Thomson Publishing Japan
Hirakawacho Kyowa Building, 3F
2-2-1 Hirakawacho
Chiyoda-ku, Tokyo 102
Japan

Printed in the United States of America

10 9 8 7 6 5 4 3 2 1

Library of Congress Cataloging-in-Publication Data

Lehman, Richard S.
  Statistics in the behavioral sciences: a conceptual introduction / Richard S. Lehman.
       p.   cm.
  Includes bibliographical references and index.
  ISBN 0534253202
  1. Social sciences—Statistical methods.   2. Statistics.
I. Title.
  HA29.L34 1994   94-22175
  519.5—dc20   CIP

For my parents,
from whom I learned to think

Brief Contents

Contents

3

DESCRIBING DATA NUMERICALLY 59

4

STANDARDIZED VARIABLES AND THE NORMAL DISTRIBUTION 96

5

BIVARIATE DESCRIPTIVE STATISTICS 120

* Optional section.

10   HYPOTHESIS TESTING IN EXPERIMENTS WITH TWO CONDITIONS   263

11   DEALING WITH CATEGORY AND FREQUENCY DATA   295

* Optional section.

* Optional section.

Preface

THE WORLD OF STATISTICS FOR THE BEHAVIORAL SCIENCES IS CHANGING, AND the computer is largely responsible. Behavioral scientists use inexpensive, approachable, and readily available computer facilities in both teaching and research. Instructors find that their students are computer literate before they begin a statistics course and, in many cases, anxious to learn more about how to use the computers that they already own.

In the recent past, textbook authors have addressed the growing use of computers by including computer illustrations in the text, along with examples of hand calculation. Although this approach seems to cover all bases—and several excellent books follow this model—it has some inherent problems.

The first problem is software selection. An author who includes, say, Minitab and SPSS as the example programs runs the risk of having his or her book rejected by an instructor because it doesn't use SYSTAT or SAS or Data Desk or Statistica or JMP. Yet including a large collection of software examples is impractical. A second and related problem is software obsolescence. Books that assume a particular computer instruction, output format, or way of solving a problem may suddenly become obsolete when the software changes.

Finally, no author (including the present one) wants to assume that each and every student has access to a computer. However, in an age when many students *are* computer users, detailed descriptions of hand calculations often get in the way of the text and obscure the logic of the material.

Although the author would like to assume that all readers have ready access to a computer with appropriate software (and thus abolish computations completely), that's just not a reasonable way to write a book. Not yet, anyway. What *is* reasonable is to move the computations out of the way of the exposition of the statistical material. In this way, the important parts of the content—logic, definitions, interpretation, and the like—can proceed without the interruption caused by computational formulas and extended examples. The presentation in this book of necessity includes some numbers and some definitional formulas, but all major computational methods and illustrations are removed from the body of the text. They appear in computational supplements to the chapters, easily available (and printed in gray for easy identification) should they be needed—but also easy to omit should an instructor want students to use computers only. In their place within the text are expanded discussions of the logic, meaning, and interpretation of statistical results, as well as several topics usually not presented in a book at this level.

In addition, no specific computation method is assumed, leaving the instructor and the student free to handle the computational detail in whichever way best suits their situation. No computer outputs are shown in the text, but the student is shown what to look for in output and how to interpret it. Instructors are free to use whatever software they feel is most appropriate for their teaching (including none at all!) without the limitations imposed by a text that includes specific software illustrations. (The exception to this approach occurs in Chapter 13, where multiple regression is presented. In that chapter, the author makes the reasonable assumption that students learning multiple regression will use a computer for the arithmetic.)

With the ready availability of computing comes two kinds of change to statistics: more extensive data analysis and exploration, and the increasing use of regression-based methods for hypothesis testing. The growing use of exploratory data analysis techniques and highly interactive computer programs testifies to the first, while the second is reflected in the increasing number of books and courses featuring the general linear model and its use in the analysis of variance and other hypothesis testing situations. The phrase "building models," a term from regression, is showing up regularly in the literature.

This book recognizes these changes in several ways. The first and most obvious is the separation between computation and logic in the presentation that allows the development of the statistical logic to proceed without getting unnecessarily involved in detail. Computational detail can be handled either by computer or by using the computational supplements that appear in most chapters. Appendix N gives a description of what a statistical program should do to be maximally useful with this text.

The trend toward more extensive data analysis has not displaced the traditional procedures. Certainly, descriptive statistics continue to be taught and used—the classical one- and two-condition experimental designs remain with us, and so do all of the analysis of variance designs. But exploring the data using graphical techniques and data summaries, and describing the meaning of the data in words and pictures, is assuming a much greater importance. Hypothesis tests are still used, of course, but more often they are viewed as yet another way of learning what is important in a set of data. Data analysis is a search for meaning in data; any technique that helps to shed light on the research question is useful and valuable. This is especially true when a computer is available. Looking at a single frequency distribution of, say, 1000 cases used to be a time-consuming matter. With a computer we can look at a number of them using different interval widths, along with box plots and stem-and-leaf displays, in a matter of minutes, and in the process get a much better feel for the data.

But this is not an "exploratory data analysis (EDA)" text—most assuredly not. This book's content is very traditional, as a glance at the table of contents will reveal. Nevertheless, it does try to incorporate the exploratory attitude toward data handling. All the expected descriptive and inferential statistics for a first course in the behavioral sciences are covered here, but with an emphasis on using them to understand data. The computational methods are still here, too; they're just moved out of the way.

In addition to an increased emphasis on exploring data, this book introduces multiple regression and the general linear model. And this introduction is the one place where the computer is assumed to be available. No computational formulas for regression are illustrated. But the multiple regression chapter can easily be made computations-optional as well if students are unlikely to have computer access. Even if they never actually compute a multiple regression, students can come to understand that a single "model," most readily visible in multiple regression, underlies much contemporary data analysis in the behavioral sciences.

A consequence of introducing multiple regression and the general linear model is the treatment of the analysis of variance with unequal group sizes. In the past, the difficulties inherent in this situation were simply bypassed in the first course by either showing only equal-group examples, or by introducing the unweighted means approximation procedure. But now we can introduce, in an optional section, the correct way of doing the computations using effect coding and regression. With computations handled externally by computer, the analysis is straightforward and within the reach of undergraduates.

This book represents what I feel to be a reasonable approach to a first course in statistics for the behavioral sciences, and most particularly for psychology. I would be very interested in receiving feedback on the book from students and instructors alike. Any suggestions, comments, errors, or ambiguities can be sent to me in care of Brooks/Cole, or directly to me via electronic mail at R_LEHMAN@ACAD.FandM.EDU.

Much of the first draft of this book was completed while I was on sabbatical leave. I thank Franklin & Marshall College for providing the leave, and for providing the supportive environment where I can both teach and complete this text at the same time. I spent the bulk of my sabbatical as a Visiting Fellow in the Psychology Department and the Institute for Statistics and Operations Research at Victoria University in Wellington, New Zealand. I thank those two departments for providing the necessary facilities, and for stimulating conversations. I must express special thanks to David Vere-Jones and Frank Walkey for inviting me and arranging the fellowship, to Ross Renner for making all kinds of arrangements for this foreign visitor, to Ray Brownrigg for keeping the electronic mail links open, and to Shirley Pledger for helping me to clarify my thinking on ANOVA. And to New Zealand, just for being there!

The following publishers deserve thanks and acknowledgment for granting their permission to use materials in the tables, or for providing various sets of data that have appeared through the book: American Statistical Association, Biometrika Trustees, Cambridge University Press, and Wadsworth Publishing Company.

This book would be very different were it not for a number of helpful people. Ken King, my former editor at Wadsworth, had enough faith in the concept of a "stat without (much) arithmetic" book that he signed it and encouraged the writing. His replacement and my old friend, Jim Brace-Thompson at Brooks/Cole, picked up Ken's enthusiasm for the book (along with much of Ken's psychology list!) and has been a terrific editor during a difficult transition in the publishing business. Drake Bradley of Bates College gave me a helpful early reaction to a preliminary outline. A number of reviewers have been valuable in shaping the book as it developed, and for that I thank Allan Bateson, Towson State University; Catherine Clement, Eastern Kentucky University; Dale Dinnel, Western Washington University; George Domino, University of Arizona; Douglas Eamon, University of Wisconsin–Whitewater; Frederick G. Fidura, State University of New York at Geneseo; Gary R. Francois, Knox College; Nickie L. Golden, University of Mississippi; Tim Goldsmith, University of New Mexico; Stephen Guastello, Marquette University; Jane Halpert, DePaul University; Donald Kendrick, Middle Tennessee State University; Katherine Klein, North Carolina State University; Gary McClelland, University of Colorado at Boulder; Lee Sechrest, University of Arizona; Kirk H. Smith, Bowling Green State University; Dianne Winn, Colby College; and George Wolford, Dartmouth College. Robert B. Stewart of Oakland University, my on-call reviewer and critic, has been valuable throughout the writing, and I thank him especially. Of course, I wish I might blame these reviewers and helpers for any errors or misstatements in the finished book. But that's not the way the game is played. If there are any, they're my fault.

This is my fourth "solo" book. In the three preceding volumes, N. John Castellan's name appeared in the acknowledgments because we always suggested each other as a reviewer on our various writing projects. His presence is here, too, in a clarification of the computations for the Wilcoxon Test in Chapter 10. My old friend and colleague died while I was finishing the manuscript. I miss him.

Finally, I want to thank my wife Jean and daughter Barbara for their love, support, and encouragement. They suffer through deadlines with me, prod, coax, and tolerate, and generally offer the support that a writer in the house needs.

Richard Lehman

PART 1 STATISTICS AND MEASUREMENT

tudents approach this statistics course with mixed (usually negative) emotions. They often see it as a requirement—a hurdle—to be passed before they can get to the "interesting stuff." In addition, they often fear the course as being difficult, mathematical, irrelevant, and boring. And—let's admit it—sometimes it is all of these. But it need not be any of them, and most especially it need not be feared. It's also certainly not irrelevant to the "interesting stuff."

Statistics is important in behavioral sciences because it provides the framework in which research is done, facts determined, and the "interesting stuff" discovered and described to others. In fact, without statistics, you might never learn any of the "interesting stuff" at all. Without statistics, you'd never be able to determine trends, draw explicit conclusions, or describe results. You couldn't communicate precisely with friends and colleagues (not to mention instructors), or even read the research literature in your chosen field. Some facility in statistics is essential for all psychology students, regardless of their career goals. For those with professional aspirations within the field, a knowledge of statistics at a high level is a requirement. For those who plan on careers in an area other than the behavioral sciences, statistics is a skill that is highly valued by future employers and colleagues.

This book is arranged in 15 chapters, organized into four sections or parts. Each part begins with a short overview, like this one, that tells you something about the nature of the material to follow. Their intent is to give you a bird's-eye view of how the coming material fits into the bigger picture that is the entire text.

This first section of the text contains a single chapter, whose goal is to provide a context and foundation for the study of statistics. It describes the fundamental roles that statistics play in behavioral science research. Because all scientific observation necessarily begins with measurement, it discusses the nature of measurement and the limitations that measurement places on what we may conclude. Finally, the first chapter looks at the kinds of research designs used in the behavioral sciences.

The chapter concludes, as do all of the chapters, with a review of important concepts, a list of key terms, and, very important, a set of exercises. An effective study technique is to read the chapter, and then test yourself to make sure you understand the important words and concepts. Then do the exercises, referring back into the chapter when you need help. Answers to roughly half the exercises appear in the back of the book.

1 Introduction and Overview

The American Psychological Association (APA) has rules designed to prevent therapists from becoming involved with their clients in roles other than the therapeutic one. The *Ethical Principles of Psychologists* (APA, 1981) includes the following statement: "Examples of such dual roles include, but are not limited to, research with and treatment of employees, students, supervisees, close friends, or relatives" (p. 636).

The rules are clear and are intended to protect clients from any possible harm that might result from such relationships. But dual roles often may be difficult to avoid. Borys and Pope (1989) conducted a national survey of 4800 therapists (psychologists, psychiatrists, and social workers) to ask how ethical dual relationships were and how often the therapists had actually found themselves in such relationships. To determine if the results would be different if the survey were limited to that group of therapists practicing on college and university campuses, the author and two of his colleagues (John, Forbes, & Lehman, in preparation) surveyed nearly 700 such therapists. We hypothesized that the frequency of dual relationships of therapists at college and university counseling centers might be greater than that of their more "public" counterparts. We reasoned that, because they are often in a smaller community, and student and counselor are more likely to encounter each other on campus. In addition, such therapists may teach or serve on various committees where they are likely to come into contact with potential or actual clients.

In the John et al. (in preparation) study, each individual surveyed responded to a total of 81 questions. Many of the questions asked the respondent to rate situations such as "Becoming friends with a female client," "Accepting a gift from a male supervisee," "Providing therapy to a female student," "Having a former student become a client," and so forth. Of the total respondents, 329 received a form of the survey that asked for a rating (on a 1–5 scale) of how ethical each hypothetical situation was, and 366 received an alternate form that asked how frequently each situation had occurred in the therapist's professional life. Because nearly 700 people responded, the survey resulted in a set of data containing roughly $81 \times 700 = 56,700$ pieces of numeric information. The answers to a large number of questions ("Do male and female therapists differ in their ethics ratings of having former students as clients?" "Do therapists at large and small institutions differ in how often they have served on committee with former clients?" and so forth) are in those 56,700 numerical values. But how do you find them? Certainly, it's impossible to inspect nearly 60,000 numbers by eye to find any answers. Even if you could actually see all the original questionnaires at once, the responses that would provide such answers would be nearly impossible to detect. We need help to find answers in data, and the help is available in the methods presented in this book. The methods given here let us use various summaries to help find the answers in the data more easily. For example, one way to answer the question about male–female differences in ratings on the ethics of having a former student as a client might be to show, in a graph like that in Figure 1.1, the number of male and female therapists making each ethics rating.

From the figure, it appears that males and females rate very much the same. There are slight differences, but both male and female therapists view the ethics of the situation as either "in the middle" or toward the "Always ethical" end of the rating scale. On balance, females seem to rate the situation as slightly more ethical.

Numerically, the average rating was 3.20 for males and 3.37 for females. These values are quite close, leading us to say that females rate the situation as only slightly more ethical—the same conclusion we reached based on Figure 1.1.

All research in psychology involves collecting data and interpreting the results, as we just illustrated. A number of methods are used in psychologi-

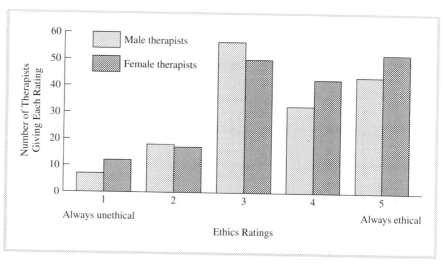

Figure 1.1

cal research; a survey method led to the John et al. (in preparation) data. You may have already completed a course in research methods, or you may be required to take such a course after this statistics course. Throughout this book, we'll encounter several different kinds of research procedures. Not all will be surveys like the one we've been discussing. Although we may comment briefly on the methods, our aim is not to teach research methods but rather to analyze and understand the data that come from them.

Whatever the method, though, research is directed at answering questions, and it does so by collecting data. Although the form of the data varies according to the questions being addressed and the methods chosen, data are always the end product of research. Statistical methods like the graphical and numeric illustrations just used in the example are tools for handling those data so the answers to the questions can be found.

More specifically, statistics has three purposes in research: description, inference, and communication.

DESCRIPTION

Descriptive statistics make the results of a research investigation understandable. It's usually very difficult to draw conclusions from a mass of raw numbers. Descriptive statistics offer ways to condense raw data so their important features stand out clearly. Without descriptive statistics, we would have to rely on hunches and "impressions" derived from a subjective and inefficient inspection of the data.

There are two varieties of descriptive procedures: graphical methods and numerical methods. Figure 1.1 represents a common graphical method, the frequency distribution, which summarizes the data by replacing therapists' individual ratings with simple counts of how many of each rating were made. The averages represent another form of data summary. They collapse a mass of data (the ratings of the 150 male and 172 female therapists who responded to this question) into two summary numbers. Both methods lead to roughly the same conclusion—males and females don't differ much, though females tend to rate the situation as a little more ethical. Chapters 2 through 6 present a variety of descriptive statistical methods.

INFERENCE

We might conclude from our earlier example that male and female therapists differ on the basis of either the frequency distribution or the averages in their ethics ratings of having former male students as clients. But how confident are we that we'd come to roughly the same conclusion if we repeated the survey with another group of therapists? And another? And another? In short, we not only want to know that the therapists in the survey hold differing opinions, but we would like to have some confidence that the same result would be found with a different set of therapists. That is, we're rarely interested in only the particular set of data that comes from a single research project. Instead, we hope that the results of one project will apply to other, similar situations and groups of subjects. The purpose of **inferential statistics** is to provide that confidence.

The particular group of observations in a research project is usually thought of as a **sample** of the much larger group of potential observations that we didn't observe. The data from the 700 subjects in one research project is a sample from all the possible sets of such data that might ever be available—that's a very large set of observations. The large set of potential observations is called the **population**, and it's normally the real interest in research.

The population in a particular research project might be the ethics ratings of all therapists, past, present, and future. Or it might be the scores of all third-grade children who have ever, and who will ever, take a reading achievement test. Or it might be the amounts of several liquids consumed by all rats (past, present, and future) in a particular taste preference study. Obviously, we can't hope to ever be able to determine the performance of any of the populations by actual test. But it's almost always the population that's most important. We don't want the results to be limited only to the particular people or animals who participated in a single research study; we want to have some confidence that the results will hold *in general*. We draw these kinds of conclusions based on inferential statistics.

The inferential methods, which we begin to introduce in Chapter 7, allow us to make estimates of **parameters** (characteristics of populations) on the basis of **statistics** (characteristics of samples). Inferential statistics are normally more complex than descriptive statistics, partly because of the slightly convoluted logic involved in inference. But their aim is simple enough: to use a sample statistic to make an inference about the probable value of a corresponding population parameter.

Science uses both descriptive and inferential statistics in communications. The literature of psychology is filled with research results (and the theory derived from them, of course). Those results are communicated by descriptive and inferential statistics. The figures, tables, and other data presentations in the literature are intended for communication with other scholars. Along with the written word, they communicate the findings of research.

MEASUREMENT IN PSYCHOLOGY

Data to be analyzed in research come from **measurement**. In its simplest form, "measurement is the assignment of numerals to objects or events according to rules" (Stevens, 1951, p. 1). We might also add that the aim of measurement is to assign the numerals in such a way that they represent the quantity of some attribute in the object being measured. Strictly speaking, we don't ever really *measure* an object, person, or animal, but instead measure its properties. We don't really measure Fred, Peter, or Sara, but we can measure their height, weight, IQ, running speed, or perhaps their recall of definitions in a statistics course.

The items just listed (height, weight, IQ, running speed, etc.) are all examples of what are known as **variables**, an important concept in measurement. A variable is a quantity that can vary. That is, if we were to obtain the weights of Fred, Peter, and Sara, we would have three numerals, each representing the weight of a different person. Or we might say that we have a set of three values of the variable named "weight." Measurement, then, is the way in which we obtain values of variables. John et al. (in preparation) measured a large number of different variables in their survey, each variable measuring an attitude toward some specific situation.

The "rules" by which numerals are assigned define the process of measurement and vary from very simple to complex. The rules for measuring the length of a table with a steel tape can be explained easily, as can those for weighing fruit in a grocery store. But the rules an experimenter might use to measure the amount of water consumed by an animal are a bit more complicated. And the rules used for measuring introversion/extroversion using a personality test are even more complex. The point of the rules is to ensure objectivity in research. In measuring personality traits, for example, the investigator needs to be sure that all the participants are treated the same so that differences in measurement don't become an unintended source of variation in the project. In addition, much research uses standard measurement procedures, so that following each test's rules exactly ensures that the new scores will be comparable to those of some other researcher who uses the same measurement rules.

The result of any measurement operation is a numeral. But the meaning of that numeral is not always clear—for at least two reasons. First, numerals carry with them certain properties that we're familiar with, and invite certain operations like addition and subtraction, but those operations and properties may not always be meaningful. And second, we're not always sure that the numbers actually measure what they purport to measure. The latter problem is that of validity, a topic we address later in this chapter. The first concern, though, leads us directly to consider the several "measurement scales" and their properties.

◆ Scales of Measurement

You may have never thought much about it, but variables representing some of the most common measurements of everyday objects are really quite different. Consider the weather and sports reports on the evening news. Suppose that the news tells you that the high temperature for the day was 62°, that a high wind was clocked at 46 miles per hour, and that your friend Fred finished third in a race. Think about those three numbers—temperature, wind speed, and place of finish in the race—for a moment. They are different variables measuring different phenomena and in different units, but they differ in several other important ways as well. These differences have an effect on what we may do sensibly with the numbers. The race results contain only the order of finish, and the "measurement" of the runners was accomplished by applying the rule "Assign '1' to the first person across the line, assign '2' to the second, and so on." (Does that rule constitute a measurement procedure? Certainly it does, according to Stevens's definition.) Notice that there is no information in the finish-position numbers to tell you the length of the interval between Fred and the person ahead of or behind him, only that there were two people ahead of him. The differences in finish tell you the order but not the spacing. There could have been 1 sec between the first- and the second-place runners, and 30 sec between the second-place runner and Fred. Or they could have all been very close. Fred could tell you more, but just knowing the position in the race tells you nothing about differences between the runners.

The use of the numerals 0, 1, 2, 3, and so on implies an order, because we know that the numbers are in that order. But notice that the race finish order doesn't use the zero value even though it's implied in the use of the values 1, 2, 3, ... What would the "0th" position in the race mean, anyway?

The two other numbers from the news report—wind speed and temperature—differ from the order-of-finish numbers. At least with a temperature report, you know that today's 62° is exactly 10° colder than yesterday's high of 72°, and that that 10° difference is the same as the difference between 90° and 100° (although it may not seem the same!). And as for wind speed, you also know that 46 mph is 10 mph harder than a wind clocked at a breezy 36 mph; you also know that a 10-mph difference in wind speed is the same whether it's between 36 and 46, or between 0 and 10.

In addition, you know that a wind speed of 36 mph means a breezy day, and that a wind speed of 0 mph means that there is no wind at all. You also know that a high temperature of 62° means a relatively cool day. But does a 0 on either the Fahrenheit or the Celsius temperature scale indicate that there was no temperature at all? No, because the zero on both of the these commonly used temperature scales doesn't correspond to the absence of the property being measured.

What have we just suggested? That the measurement rules, and the scales of measurement that come from them, differ in how they assign numerals. It also suggests that there are differences between the scales in how they use some of the properties of numbers, and in how we should interpret the meanings of the values.

SAME–DIFFERENT (NOMINAL) MEASUREMENT. John et al. (in preparation) devised a simple scheme for one of their questions. Psychotherapists differ in their orientation and approach to therapy, some preferring psychodynamic approaches, others preferring behavior modification, and so forth. The specific question was "What is your theoretical orientation?" The respondents were given five possible responses: psychodynamic, existential/humanistic, cognitive, behavioral, and other. The questionnaires were scored as

1   Psychodynamic
2   Existential/humanistic
3   Cognitive
4   Behavioral
5   Other

When the questionnaires were scored, each individual was "measured" by assigning the numeral shown for the response that was given. The process is certainly a measurement operation; it assigns numerals to objects (therapists, in this case) according to rules, and it does so in such a way as to let the numerals represent an important property of each object. But just what do the numerals mean? Only that a therapist assigned a "2" subscribes to a different theoretical orientation from one assigned a "4." It certainly does not mean that a "4" therapist is necessarily a larger, heavier, older, or better therapist than a "2" person. All it means is that "2" and "4" people have different theoretical viewpoints.

We have just described what is usually known as a **nominal measurement** scale. The numbers are really nothing more than names (hence the designation "nominal") for the various groups or categories into which the objects may be placed. In fact, we'll sometimes refer to nominal measure as **category measurement**.

John et al. (in preparation) measured all 700 of their respondents on the nominal measurement scale for theoretical orientation. Suppose you were to compute the average of those 700 values. What kind of sense could you make of the result? If the "average" theoretical orientation was 3.4, what could you do with that number? Actually, it means almost nothing, except that (if you did the computation right) it represents the average of a set of 700 numbers. But beyond that, knowing the value doesn't help you understand anything about the therapists. Are there any arithmetic operations that make sense on category data? In fact, about the only operation that can be meaningfully applied to nominal data is counting—but sometimes that in itself is quite informative. Suppose that we found that the theoretical orientations occurred with different frequencies, such as

CATEGORY	OUTLOOK	NUMBER OF THERAPISTS
1	Psychodynamic	179
2	Existential/humanistic	137
3	Cognitive	121
4	Behavioral	23
5	Other	236

The counting operation reveals a pattern: There are more people in the "Other" category than in any other, and there are very few behavioral therapists. So counting is a useful and meaningful thing to do to nominal data.

MORE-OF (ORDINAL) MEASUREMENT. The order of finish in a race assigns numerals in the order in which racers cross the finish line. The first person across receives a "1," the second a "2," and so forth. In this kind of measurement, called **ordinal measurement**, the larger value implies more of the quantity being measured (in a race, it's the time taken to complete the prescribed distance).

When we have measured on the ordinal scale, we can tell which objects have more and less of the property, but not how much more or less. If we were to line up in order from shortest to tallest, all the members of a high school gym class and give the number "1" to the shortest, then all we know for sure is that "18" is taller than "10" and shorter than "22." But we don't know whether the difference between scores of "16" and "18" is the same as the difference between "6" and "8."

A common ordinal value is high school rank in class, a value often used by college admissions officers. Other than rank in class, several common psychological procedures also produce ordinal scales. In aesthetic research, subjects are frequently asked to arrange artistic stimuli in order from most preferred to least preferred, or from least to most beautiful. Most subjects can handle such tasks easily. For example, you probably could arrange the food items broiled steak, baked fish, fried chicken, baked meat loaf, steamed shrimp, and roast turkey in order of preference without much difficulty. You might have more trouble if asked to assign each a number reflecting your choice, other than merely an order-of-preference number ("my first choice, my second choice, ..."). The ease with which humans can produce preference orderings among stimulus items has led to the rapid development of procedures for dealing with ordinal data within the past decade or so. We'll introduce a few of the descriptive measures for ordinal data in the next several chapters.

HOW-MUCH-MORE (INTERVAL) MEASUREMENT. The Fahrenheit and Celsius temperature scales represent **interval measurement**. In this form of measurement, the intervals between values may themselves be arranged in order, but a zero value doesn't necessarily represent the absence of the property being measured. Neither of the two common temperature scales align the zero value with absence of temperature as defined by a physicist, although the Kelvin (or absolute) temperature scale does. On both the Fahrenheit and the Celsius scales, though, differences between pairs of temperatures can be compared. Thus, on a day when it's 95° Fahrenheit, it's 10° warmer than when it's 85°. That difference of 10° is the same 10° difference as that between 20° and 30°. That kind of statement might or might not be true if the measurement had been made on an ordinal scale.

When the measurement procedure offers equal spacing along the numeric scale, then the measurement is interval. Interval measurement is probably the most common scale in psychology (although some writers claim that we really can measure only orders). The great bulk of the tests and scales that psychologists use appear to be interval scales.

Note the use of the word *appear* in the previous paragraph. It's there because it's often difficult to determine whether the intervals are actually equal. Consider an experiment in human learning, where a common measurement is the number of words recalled. When a subject in a learning experiment recalls 10 words from a list one time, and 14 words the next, we normally use those numbers to indicate a difference in the amount of learning that has occurred. Of course, we have no real way to know whether, in fact, the difference between 10 and 14 words recalled is *really* the same difference in amount learned as for a subject who recalled 5 words on one trial and 9 on the next. Are those equivalent amounts of actual *learning*? Is there any way that we can really know the answer to that question? No—until we can develop a way to measure the true basis of learning, we can't really know. But in the absence of clear evidence to the contrary, psychologists frequently assume that such measurements are at an interval level.

A common measurement technique for some areas in psychology is the rating scale. John et al. (in preparation) had their responding therapists rate the ethicality or frequency of various situations along a scale like the following, which is similar to that shown in Figure 1.1:

The researchers then scored the ratings by using the numeric scale equivalents:

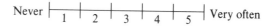

Naturally, the ethics items were scored on a slightly different scale, such as

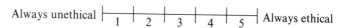

Many measurement authorities would agree that John et al. (in preparation) had measured with an interval procedure, because when the subjects made the ratings, they would have subjectively defined the intervals along the scale as equal. Note that only the extremes of the scale are labeled. That labeling avoids the difficulty of trying to develop verbal descriptions for a five-point scale that everyone would agree represents equal steps in attitude. This technique, known as the **equal-appearing intervals** scaling procedure, is widely used in psychology and the behavioral sciences.

With interval measurement, we can talk about the equality or difference in differences along the scale. With an IQ test, for example, we can feel confident that the difference of 10 points between 75 and 85 represents roughly the same difference in intelligence as the 10 points between 100 and 110. We can also talk about relative differences, indicating, for example, that the difference between two children with IQ scores of 95 and 103 is less than the difference between two other children with scores of 110 and 125. (As we'll note shortly, although it's meaningful to talk about differences, and even ratios of differences, it's not meaningful to talk about ratios of the scores themselves; Johnny, with an IQ of 120, is not twice as intelligent as his brother Sam, who has an IQ of 60.)

PROPORTIONS OF SCORES (RATIO MEASUREMENT). IQ tests are normally constructed so that a child who scores average for his or her age group will receive an IQ score of 100. The anchor point of an IQ scale is thus the "normal," or average, individual, and the performance of that individual is equated with a score of 100 on the test. Does an interval measuring scale like IQ have a meaningful or "true" zero point? That is, is zero aligned with "absence" of the property being measured? No, the fact that zero exists in a series of numbers doesn't mean that it corresponds to "0" quantity. Just what does an IQ score of 0 mean? Nothing, actually—the scale doesn't go down that far. A zero could mean only that the individual taking the test was so far off the scale as to be untestable, but it would not mean that there was no intelligence to be measured.

When measurement rules yield equal intervals and also align the zero point with absence of the property being measured, then we are measuring on a **ratio measurement** scale. The Kelvin (absolute) temperature scale is a ratio scale because a 0° temperature can be applied to a substance only when there is no molecular motion (that's the physical definition of absence of heat). Distance is another ratio measurement. When the measurement is ratio, we can speak meaningfully of ratios of measured values. It's correct to say, for example, that 10 miles is exactly one-half as far as 20 miles, or that an object with a temperature of 100° on the Kelvin scale has exactly twice the physical heat of an object with a temperature of 50°. Proportions of this sort make sense with a ratio scale, but not with any of the others. As noted earlier, we wouldn't say, for example, that an individual with an IQ of 150 is twice as intelligent as one with an IQ of 75.

Psychologists have comparatively few ratio measurement scales. Elapsed time is a ratio scale, as are such countable variables as trials to criterion, numbers of errors or correct responses, and so on, as well as clearly physical variables such as body weight or stimulus distance. And even for those few ratio scales that we do have, it's not at all clear that the measurement represents the underlying process adequately, or that the underlying process itself is a continuous process.

Most psychological variables yield measurement that is either ordinal or interval. And, in fact, that's probably appropriate in most instances. Do we have any concept of what no intelligence really means? Does it matter that the number zero doesn't line up with "no intelligence," even if we could understand what that meant? No, it really makes little difference. What's important generally in IQ measurement is to establish differences in level of IQ between groups or individuals, and interval measurement is certainly satisfactory for that purpose. But even at that, we don't know whether the underlying process that is presumably measured is even continuous. (In fact, there's considerable debate as to whether "intelligence" is a single property or a cluster of related intellectual abilities.)

THE IMPORTANCE OF MEASUREMENT SCALES

Why is all of this consideration of measurement scales important? Because the scale of measurement for a variable has an important effect on the kinds of operations that we can meaningfully apply to the data. And that, in turn, influences the choice of descriptive and inferential measures that we may use.

ARITHMETIC OPERATIONS. During data analysis, it's sometimes convenient or necessary to apply various arithmetic operations to the data. Sometimes we might want to add or subtract a value from every data value (for example, to make them all positive), or to multiply or divide each value by some other value (to change some characteristics of the data). Although the data we have are always "just numbers" and we can do any arithmetic operation to any numbers, some operations are sensible with some kinds of measurement and some are not. We already mentioned the possibility of calculating the average of a set of numbers; for any collection of numbers, we can compute the average, but whether the average has an interpretable meaning is quite another matter.

For nominal data, the only aspect of the number system that matters is uniqueness. We may do anything we like to the numbers from nominal measurement as long as we preserve the uniqueness. In the example of categories of theoretical orientation, it really doesn't matter whether we call the psychodynamic category 1, 63, or 528, just as long as we don't use the same number for any other category.

Ordinal measurement takes advantage of the fact that the numbers have an order defined for them. When the measurement is ordinal, assigning a large value indicates that more of the property is being measured. With data that represent ordinal measurement, we may do any operation that preserves the order property of the value without losing the meaning of the measurement. All that is required for meaning to be preserved is that a larger value is assigned to the object with more of the property being measured. In fact, most of the techniques for handling ordinal data simply convert the data from their original measured values to the values 1, 2, 3, ... for analysis. But it makes no difference whether we use the values 1, 2, 3, 4, 5, and 6 to describe food preferences, or values of 3, 8, 12, 13, 22, and 53. All that's important for interpreting the data is that a higher value indicate greater preference.

For interval data, any operations that are done must preserve the relationships among the intervals between data values. For example, if we had the interval measurement values 34, 42, and 46, a change in values must maintain the relationships between pairs. For these three values, the difference between the smallest pair (42 − 34 = 8) is twice the difference between the largest pair (46 − 42 = 4), and any changes must preserve that relationship or the interval property of the measurement scale is lost.

When the measurement is ratio, the value "0" is applied to the absence of the property measured. Numerous physical scales represent ratio measures—elapsed time, mass, and length are three examples. On a ratio scale, ratios between data values themselves are meaningful. Thus, if Dan takes 10 minutes to complete a problem-solving task, and Sara requires 15 minutes, then we may meaningfully say that Dan completed the task in two-thirds the time it took Sara. If we were to arbitrarily add 20 to both time scores, then we would have Dan measured at 30 and Sara at 35. It's still true that Dan completed the problem 5 minutes faster than Sara did, but Dan's score would no longer be two-thirds of Sara's. With ratio data, then, we may meaningfully apply any scale change that preserves both the interval ratios and the meaning of the zero point.

STATISTICAL OPERATIONS. Over the years, statisticians and writers of books like this one have taken varying positions on the importance, or lack of importance, of the measurement scale on the kinds of statistical operations that may be performed on data. Lord (1953), in a classic paper, pointed out that the numbers don't know or care what operations are done to them. His example uses the numbers on football jerseys. Football numbers are best regarded as coming from a nominal scale in that they serve primarily to distinguish one player from another. If we want to, Lord points out, we could calculate the average of the football numbers; nothing prevents us from doing so. The numbers that come from football jerseys follow the properties of the number system, and statistics based on those numbers follow known properties of the statistics.

However, the problem is in the meaning of the average we compute, not in whether the operation is "permitted" by the system of numbers. If we calculate a value based on a nominal measurement scale, any change that preserves the scores' uniqueness is permissible, but could change the statistic dramatically. Thus, the interpretation of the average becomes meaningless.

For ordinal data, the average also doesn't make much sense. Suppose that Fred, Barb, and Peter run a race, and we record their order of finish. It doesn't matter whether we assign the values 1, 2, and 3 to the first, second, and third finishers, or 21, 28, and 44—the lowest number is still the lowest, the highest is still the highest, and the score in the middle is still in the middle. But the average changes from 2 to 31 after making the change. Again, the mathematics gods can't complain about finding the average. But we can—the change, which is permissible for ordinal data, has made computing an average a nonsensical operation as far as interpretation is concerned.

On the other hand, with interval and ratio measurement, we can meaningfully talk about ratios of differences, and the average makes a great deal of sense, as do many other common statistical operations. As we proceed, we'll be alert to the measurement characteristics of the data, because they influence the choice of procedures that we might use for describing the data.

Lord's (1953) paper was called to mind recently by Velleman and Wilkinson (1993). They argue that, although the distinctions among the measurement scales are important in *interpreting data*, as just discussed, they need not be too stringently applied in selecting analyses. For example, the descriptive statistics for correlation normally assume that variables are measured on interval or ratio scales. But, later in this book, we discuss a correlation coefficient between interval and nominal values. The arithmetic gods will not strike us dead, but we should understand what we are doing in calculating that statistic, and, most important, how we should interpret the value.

VALIDITY AND RELIABILITY

Two important characteristics of any measurement procedure are **validity** and **reliability**. A valid measurement procedure is one that measures the property that it claims to measure. When we say that a measuring instrument is reliable, we mean that we can count on it to assign the same numeric value each time we measure the same object. A reliable yardstick will measure the length of your desk the same today as it did yesterday, and the same as it will tomorrow. Validity and reliability are related topics, but they address rather separate aspects of the measurement process. You might decide to measure an individual's intelligence by recording the number of words that person reads per minute. You'd probably find that the number of words read was fairly constant over time, assuming you gave the individual similar material each time; in other words, the number of words per minute is a reliable measurement, because you tend to get similar measurements every time. But does the number of words read per minute really provide a good measure of intelligence? Probably not; the relationship between them is likely quite weak. In this case, the number of words read per minute isn't a valid measure of intelligence. And that is the case even if the measurement of words per minute is reliable.

◆ Assessing Validity

Earlier in this chapter we quoted Stevens (1951) as saying that "measurement is the assignment of numerals to objects or events according to rules." We added that the aim of measurement is to assign the numerals so they represent the quantity of some attribute. This relationship between the measured value and its underlying attribute is important in research. Naturally, we want any measured value to reflect the underlying dimension. Evaluating the validity of a measurement means assessing how accurate the relationship between measure and underlying trait actually is.

Validity is often confined to a particular context. If a personality theorist were to measure introversion/extroversion, for example, validity would be confined to that specific research context, and the investigator would probably be content to establish the validity of measurement in that setting. Whether the scores correspond to the more "popular" meanings of introversion and extroversion as they are used to describe an individual's style of relating to others may not be important. Of course, a social psychologist might want to establish the validity of the same introversion/extroversion scale in another context, this time most likely attending to the interpersonal implications of the measure.

Some attributes that we might want to measure are readily available for validity checks. To assure ourselves that a timer is valid, we can check it against external standards. Establishing the validity of a timer is a simple matter of comparing its measurements to known time intervals or to the measurements from other timers that are known to be accurate. For some other variables that psychologists use, establishing validity is also a straightforward matter. But for many psychological variables, there is no "Bureau of Standards" to provide external validation; for this reason, psychology has probably directed more attention to the development of validation procedures than has any other scientific discipline.

A first consideration for many people is whether a measurement procedure "looks like" it's measuring what it should. That is, a test of introversion/extroversion should contain items that ask whether the person is outgoing and sociable, a test of reading ability should require reading, and so forth. In other words, does the measuring device look, on the face of it, to be measuring the correct characteristics? This criterion, called **face validity**, usually isn't considered important by measurement experts. Measurement procedures that meet the other criteria of validity often have face validity, but they need not. A valid measure of introversion/extroversion might not even ask about sociability, for example, but might instead ask about hobbies or even about leisure-reading habits. Although those kinds of questions might not *seem* closely related to introversion/extroversion, other criteria might well establish that they are better measures than they appear. These other, more useful, criteria for validity are those involving prediction, content, and theoretical relationships. More specifically, the most important aspects of validity are predictive validity, content validity, and construct validity.

The term **predictive validity** means that a measurement should predict other measures of the same thing. If a test is designed to select good candidates for a particular job, then it should be able to predict how well employees will succeed in the job. If you're developing a test to predict how well a word processor operator will succeed, you'll want your test to predict standard measures of job success. Establishing the validity of a measurement scale is of special importance in applied settings when just such predictions are routinely needed. Industrial placement and education are two of the situations where predictive validity is important. In those situations, it is also relatively easy to assess a test's validity, because there are known criteria for success.

For some variables, it's possible to define a set of behaviors that are characteristic of situations or knowledge relevant to the behavior being measured. The **content validity** of the measurement then is established by the extent to which it adequately samples that set of behaviors. The most obvious situations where content validity is useful are those where knowledge of a particular set of information is to be measured, as in an achievement test or course examination. When an instructor develops an examination for a course, he or she first defines what the students are expected to know (that is, the domain of knowledge to be covered by the test). Then the instructor samples from the content of the domain and develops the test items themselves. The test may be said to have content validity if it samples the domain representatively. The students' scores on the test are then regarded as valid measurements of the knowledge of the material.

Construct validation is the technique applied to most measurement in psychology, and is the area in which psychology has contributed the most to the theory of measurement. **Construct validity** looks for patterns of relationships among variables that are expected on the basis of theory. For example, a theory of introversion and extroversion suggests that those individuals who score toward the introversion end of the scale derive much of their stimulation internally, while those who score at the opposite end of the scale seek external stimulation. That suggestion, coming from theory, has prompted investigators to measure two variables, one an introversion/extroversion test and the other a measure of sensation seeking. When they find a relationship between those two variables, they are validating not only the theory but also the measures of introversion/extroversion and sensation seeking, because the variables relate as predicted.

◆ Assessing Reliability

Reliability is the degree to which you may expect to find the same result if you repeat the measurement. Thus, it is a measure of "repeatability," the extent to which we find that repeated measurements of the same individual or object will give essentially the same results. A classical definition of reliability is the test–retest definition: If the measurement results in the same answer upon retest, then the test is reliable. This form of reliability is established by measuring the same objects twice and correlating the results.

It's very difficult to actually obtain test–retest reliability directly, because once a human (or animal) subject has been tested or subjected to some measurement procedure, it's not the "same" organism any longer. Certainly your instructor couldn't establish the reliability of the final examination by giving it to the class twice! Several techniques have been devised to assess reliability in ways other than the classical test–retest manner. One procedure involves the use of *parallel forms* of the same test, in which two tests are given that contain different but equivalent items. Another procedure, the *split half* procedure, divides a test into two halves and checks them against each other. The result is the same as a parallel forms reliability check except that the two forms are given together.

◆ The Importance of Validity and Reliability

When you listen to the evening news and hear reports of temperature, wind speed, and race results, you now know that, in interpreting the reports, you need to take account of two features of those numbers. First, the numbers represent different measurement scales, and, second, you need to be concerned about their reliability and validity.

Perhaps you wouldn't make the mistake of trying to interpret the average of the order-of-finish positions in the races that are reported, but you might be tempted to conclude that today's high of 90° is twice the record low for this date of 45°. In addition to the interpretations you might make of the numbers, you can also think about the reliability and validity of the newscaster's values. Although weather values have probably been measured with accurate (that is, reliable and valid) instruments, and although the order in which racers cross the finish line is probably valid, how about statements like "9 out of 10 doctors surveyed …" or "72.6 percent of those questioned …" or "The polls show …"?

Earlier we used an example of measuring intelligence by counting the number of words read per minute. It's likely that the number of words per minute would be a reliable measurement. That is, if we kept the reading material fairly constant, an individual would probably read at roughly the same rate. But reading rate wouldn't meet most criteria for a valid measure of intelligence. It probably correlates only weakly with academic success or teacher ratings of ability (predictive validity). It doesn't sample the broad domain of activities that we would regard as "intelligent" behaviors (content validity). And it doesn't fit well with the current theoretical understanding of intelligence (construct validity). In short, just because a measurement (like reading speed, for example) is reliable, it's not necessarily valid.

Just as it's important to understand whether variables are measured on an interval or ordinal scale, it is important to understand that measurements used in research should be evaluated for their reliability and validity. If invalid measures are used, then any conclusion that might be drawn is meaningless, just as if an inappropriate descriptive procedure were used for ordinal data. Likewise, if measurements are unreliable, we have little confidence that the same results would be obtained if the research were repeated.

EXPERIMENTAL DESIGN

Much of the research in psychology is conducted by experiment. An experiment is an investigation that follows a strict set of rules, which we outline briefly here.

The word *experiment*, in psychology as in the other sciences, means a systematic investigation of the relationship between two or more variables. In an experiment there are at least two variables, one of which is measured and the other of which is controlled. For example, to establish the effect of a drug on ability to learn, we might establish two groups of experimental animals. We could inject one group with the drug and do nothing at all to the other group. Then we could measure the learning ability of the two groups by recording, for instance, how many tries it takes them to learn a simple maze. If we observed a difference in the average number of trials taken by the two groups, we might be tempted to infer that the drug caused the difference.

In this simple experiment, there are two distinct variables—the amount of drug given (some versus none) and the trials required to learn. These are called, respectively, the **independent variable** and the **dependent variable**. The dependent variable is measured to determine the result of the experiment; the independent variable is manipulated by the experimenter. An experiment *always* contains at least one independent variable and one dependent variable. Some experiments may contain more than one of either or both kinds of variables, but at least one of each must be there or it's not an experiment.

The experiment just sketched is incomplete—it's missing a third critical element in an experiment—namely, **control**. Suppose that one of the two groups of animals happened to be all male and the other all female. Could we conclude that it was the drug that caused an observed difference? No, because there are two differences between the groups: They differ in both sex and in drug. Suppose that the males were given the drug and that we observed that the drug group (the males) learn in fewer trials. What are we to conclude? It could be that males learn faster than females and that the drug had no effect, or it could just as likely be that the drug caused the difference and the sex of the animal made no difference. You simply cannot tell.

How can the problem be avoided? By recognizing that there was an **extraneous variable** in the experiment—namely, sex. Any variable in an experiment that is neither an independent variable nor a dependent variable is called an extraneous variable, and it can complicate interpretation of the results (or, as in this case, make the results completely meaningless!). To overcome this problem, an experiment uses control. In the example, the extraneous variable of sex could be controlled by using only males (or only females), or perhaps by having equal numbers of males and females in each group. In either case, the independent variable—drug—is separated from the extraneous variable of sex.

But if we control sex, are the results now clear? No. What if the drug group contained older animals and the nondrug group contained younger animals? We've just added another extraneous variable to the story—but it can also be controlled, perhaps by using animals all the same age or by making sure that each group is balanced by age of the animals. Even if we controlled a large number of variables in this way, are we still in the clear? Not the way the procedure was described. There's still an extraneous variable—the injection. Maybe animals that receive *any* injection learn faster than those who don't! How do we solve this problem? We do it by giving all of the animals an injection, in the same way, of the same amount of solution, and so on. Only the one group has the drug; the other group receives an inert solution. (The latter treatment is known as a **placebo**—a treatment that should have no effect.).

An experiment, then, is defined by three things: an independent variable, a dependent variable, and the control of extraneous variables. Ideally, the *only* difference between the two experimental conditions is in the independent variable. It is manipulated by the experimenter and the dependent variable is measured. Because all extraneous variables are controlled, any observed difference can probably be attributed to the independent variable.

Independent variables can be handled in several ways in an experiment. In the example, the independent variable was manipulated in two different amounts: "some" and "none." This experimental design is illustrated in Figure 1.2a, where the rectangles represent groups of animals treated in the same way. An experimental arrangement of this sort is often called a *two-condition experiment*, for obvious reasons.

Notice that there's no reason why the independent variable couldn't have several conditions or treatments (Figure 1.2b). We could choose to have multiple groups of experimental animals, each group receiving a different drug dosage. This experimental design could be called a *multiple-condition experiment*, again for obvious reasons. Note that there is still only a single independent variable—drug—but in varying amounts. In each case, we manipulate the amount of the drug (the independent variable) and observe the effect on the time taken to learn to press a bar (the dependent variable). Chapters 9, 10, and 12 discuss the inferential statistics used for these kinds of experiments.

We may also consider adding a second independent variable to an experiment. Using the two-condition experiment (Figure 1.2a), we could, for example, add age as a second independent variable, using both young and old animals. Now we have four groups of animals (Figure 1.2c): young animals that receive the drug, young animals that do not receive the drug, old animals that receive the drug, and old animals that do not receive the drug. This kind of experiment, having two separate independent variables, or **factors**, is called a **factorial experiment**. In a factorial experimental design, there

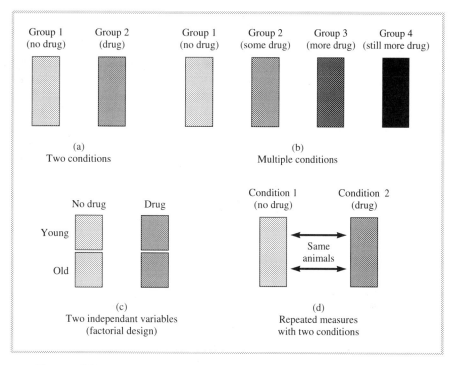

Figure 1.2

are two independent variables (there could be more) manipulated in all possible combinations, resulting in several distinct ways of treating the subjects. Factorial analysis is presented in Chapter 15.

In all of the experimental designs discussed so far, each treatment coincided with exactly one group of animals. In the experiment illustrated in Figure 1.2a, one group of animals got a drug and another received the placebo. In Figures 1.2b and 1.2c, four groups of animals received four separate treatments. It's important to note that differences between averages that might be observed between the treatment conditions are also differences between groups of subjects. For this reason, an experimental design where each treatment is administered to a separate group of subjects is called a **between-subjects experiment**.

As an additional modification to the simple two-condition experiment, consider using the *same* animals in both the drug and the nondrug conditions (Figure 1.2d). This arrangement is called a **repeated measures experiment**. There are two major advantages to using repeated measures. First, there is only a single group of animals to feed and house. Second, many issues of control are solved—there's no risk of having all the males (or young animals, or smart animals, or fast animals, and so forth) in one experimental condition. This increase in control makes the repeated measures experiment a powerful and popular design in psychological research. Inference in repeated measures experiments is discussed in Chapters 10 and 14.

Of course, there are disadvantages to using a repeated measures experiment. Most importantly, it cannot be used on every occasion. Suppose that instead of using the number of trials to learn a maze as the dependent variable, we had chosen how many minutes it takes animals to learn to press a bar to obtain a food pellet. However, once an animal has learned that "trick," we can't use that dependent variable again, and so that rules out a repeated measures experiment. If we use, as the dependent variable, the trials required to learn a maze, we have a different problem: We'd better have a different (but equally difficult) maze for the animal to learn the second time. But there's an even more troublesome extraneous variable, and that concerns the order in which the animals are tested. You have to be careful not to have the drug condition be the second (or the first) condition for every animal because then you couldn't tell whether the drug was causing the difference or whether the drug being the second (or first) condition was causing the difference.

Finally, in a repeated measures experiment, differences between the experimental conditions are differences *within* the same group of experimental subjects. Thus, you will not be surprised to learn that a repeated measures experiment is also called a **within-subjects experiment**.

A NOTE ON EXERCISES

As with most subjects, mastery of the skills in this book requires practice. To help you toward mastery, exercises are given at the end of each chapter. Your instructor will probably assign some of the chapter exercises for you to complete, or may provide you with separate problem sets. However, it's to your benefit to do *all* of the problems provided—those in the book and those given by your instructor. Every statistics instructor has stories of the students who claimed that they had mastered the material by reading, only to find that they couldn't apply their "knowledge" on an exam or when confronted with "real" data. The solutions to roughly half of the exercises appear in the back of the book.

Your instructor may expect you to do the calculations in this course by hand or perhaps by computer. Although it's not relevant to the exercises in this chapter, you should know your instructor's preference before you start to do computational exercises in the later chapters. If you do them by hand, you'll find a computational appendix for each chapter immediately following the exercises. The by-hand computations for all procedures discussed in a chapter are presented and illustrated in the supplements. They are placed at the end of each chapter so they don't interfere with the development of the text material and the conceptual explanation. The solutions at the back of the book to odd-numbered exercises were done using the hand computation procedures as illustrated.

If you will be doing all of your computations by computer, you may skip the computational supplements in each chapter unless your instructor expects you to do them by hand as well as by computer. If you are using a computer, you should check your answers with those in the back of the book. Your results may not agree to the last decimal with those in the book, but they should be "close." Computer programs normally use different formulas for the statistics than you would use doing the problems by hand; they're also likely to round off differently. If your computer's answers are far different from those in the book, check with your instructor.

It's possible that your instructor may not specify any particular computer program. In that case, you may want to buy one. Many good statistics programs for personal computers are available, and it would be impossible to develop a computer supplement for each one. Instead, Appendix N lists the characteristics that a program should have to be useful with this book. Only a few programs completely meet the specifications listed there; most do not, so you'll have to use hand computations for some things.

However you complete them, computational exercises are intended to give you practice in the skills needed to analyze and describe the results of a research investigation. Their goals are to help you understand the text material and give you practice in applying the techniques. Some of the exercises use simple values and are intended to help you to understand the definitional formulas given in the chapter. Other exercises use several sets of actual data that are presented throughout the book. When the data set is large [like that in John et al. (in preparation) discussed earlier, where there were nearly 700 individual subjects], the data given will be only a small part of the actual data set.

In the chapter exercises, many of the questions ask you to summarize conclusions in words as well as in numbers. This reflects the author's belief that if you can't state the results of a data analysis in words, then perhaps you haven't understood either the question being asked in the research or the answer provided by the data.

AND A NOTE ON READING AND STUDY HABITS

Reading a statistics textbook is not like reading a novel or a short story. With a fiction work, you may be able to skip sections and still be able to pick up the remainder of the plot. Not so with this material. You'll have to read slowly and carefully, making sure you understand one concept before you move on to the next. The material is highly cumulative, and it is essential that you understand it as you go.

Although mathematics underlies statistical methods, the presentation is not particularly mathematical. Students who go into a panic at the first mathematical symbol (a $\sum$, for example) may be reassured to know that, although symbols will be unavoidable, there is nothing particularly difficult about them. Understanding sentences containing Greek letters and formulas is not hard, but reading the material will take longer than if it were ordinary prose. The symbols are there because they represent a very convenient and compact notation for certain operations and definitions. The $\sum$, for example, appears often throughout the book. Whenever it does, it means only one thing—add 'em up. Thus, the simple formula $\sum X$ merely says to add all the things called X, and X is always a set of numbers. In other words, $\sum X$ says to sum all of the values called X.

This book is written in simple, direct, English sentences. Even symbols and formulas can be read as part of a sentence. Consider the following sentence: "Most students know that the formula for the arithmetic mean,

$$\frac{\sum X}{N}$$

says to add all the values and divide by the number of values summed." For clarity, the formula is shown in the middle of the page, but it's still a part of the sentence that surrounds it. The full sentence reads "Most students know that the formula for the arithmetic mean, 'sigma X over N,' says to add all the values and divide by the number of values summed." Formulas in this book are usually presented in just this way and invite being read as a part of a sentence. As you're reading, don't skip over the symbols; they're a part of the sentence, and the sentence usually explains the symbol.

Summary

- *There are two general kinds of statistics:*
  Descriptive statistics *summarize data and may help us see an answer in the research results.*
  Inferential statistics *let us generalize beyond a particular set of data.*
- *Both descriptive and inferential statistics are used to communicate the results of a research project.*
- *A* population *is a large set of observations; a* sample *is a small set of observations taken from a population.*
- *A* parameter *is a characteristic of a population; a* statistic *is a characteristic of a sample.*
- *A* variable *is a quantity that can vary.*
- Measurement *means to attach numerals to objects or events according to rules, thereby obtaining the values of variables.*
- *Measurement scales are usually categorized as* nominal, ordinal, interval, *and* ratio.
  Nominal scales *use numerals merely to differentiate among different objects.*
  Ordinal scales *take advantage of the order property of numbers and assign values so that a larger value means more of the attribute being measured.*

Interval scales *allow you to compare differences between pairs of values.*

Ratio measurement *aligns the zero with absence of the property and lets you meaningfully compute ratios of scores.*

◆ *Many psychologists regard the data from equal-appearing intervals measurement as interval data.*

◆ Reliability *refers to the ability of the measurement to assign the same value on different occasions.*

◆ Validity *refers to a measurement's ability to truly reflect the property that it claims to measure.*

◆ *A* two-condition *experiment has a single independent variable that is manipulated in two distinct ways.*

◆ *A* multiple-condition *experiment has a single independent variable with more than two different conditions.*

◆ *A* placebo *is a treatment that has no effect.*

◆ *A* factorial experiment *has two (or more) independent variables.*

◆ *In a* between-subjects experiment, *each treatment is administered to a separate group of subjects.*

◆ *A* within-subjects experiment *uses the same subjects in each condition.*

◆ *A* within-subjects experiment *is very powerful in that it provides a simple way to control many possible extraneous variables.*

Key Terms

BETWEEN-SUBJECTS EXPERIMENT
CATEGORY MEASUREMENT
CONSTRUCT VALIDITY
CONTENT VALIDITY
CONTROL
DEPENDENT VARIABLE
DESCRIPTIVE STATISTICS
EQUAL-APPEARING INTERVALS
EXTRANEOUS VARIABLE
FACE VALIDITY
FACTOR
FACTORIAL EXPERIMENT
INDEPENDENT VARIABLE
INFERENTIAL STATISTICS
INTERVAL MEASUREMENT

MEASUREMENT
NOMINAL MEASUREMENT
ORDINAL MEASUREMENT
PARAMETER
PLACEBO
POPULATION
PREDICTIVE VALIDITY
RATIO MEASUREMENT
RELIABILITY
REPEATED MEASURES EXPERIMENT
SAMPLE
STATISTIC
VALIDITY
VARIABLE
WITHIN-SUBJECTS EXPERIMENT

1. The following list gives some measurement rules. For each, indicate what scale of measurement (nominal, ordinal, interval, or ratio) is represented.

   a. The experimenter starts a stopwatch when the subject begins a task and stops it when the task is completed.

   b. A child is given an IQ test.

   c. Subjects are asked to arrange a set of five soft drinks in order of preference.

   d. Subjects are asked to indicate whether they agree or disagree with each of a series of statements. The experimenter then counts how many statements are checked for agreement.

   e. Subjects are shown a pattern of letters for a brief flash and asked to recall as many as possible; the experimenter counts how many are correctly recalled.

   f. A rat is placed in a Skinner box; the number of bar presses per minute is recorded.

   g. People are asked to indicate their political party preference.

   h. Participants in an experiment are asked to indicate their degree of agreement/disagreement with various political statements on a -10 to $+10$ scale.

   i. Subjects manipulate a switch that moves a visual pattern back and forth until it appears clearest. The experimenter measures the distance between the stimulus and the subject's eyes using a steel tape measure.

   j. Observers classify the behavior patterns of free-ranging gorillas into 15 categories.

   k. Students are asked to estimate the percent of their time spent in different activities during a typical week.

   l. Participants are asked to arrange a series of photographs of people in order of attractiveness.

   m. Animals are given a choice of two substances to eat. The food items are weighed before being placed in the cages. After a 2-hour period, the food is weighed again and the amount of each consumed is determined.

2. Some athletic events (for example, diving in the Olympics) are scored by having a panel of expert judges rate each performance on a 0–10 scale, where a 10 represents a perfect performance. What scale of measurement does each judge's rating represent?

3. In exercise 1.2, the score for each contestant is computed by dropping the highest and the lowest of the individual ratings and then summing the remaining values. Based on your answer to exercise 1.2, is that a reasonable operation to do with the ratings? Why or why not?

4. In some events (diving, for example), the judges' total (from exercise 1.3) is multiplied by a "difficulty rating" for the particular performance; the product becomes the final score. Based on your answer to exercise 1.2, is that a reasonable operation to do with the ratings? Why or why not?

5. You have developed a test that you claim can predict final grades in a statistics class. How would you convince someone that your test is valid using:

   a. Content validation

   b. Construct validation

6. Using the test from exercise 1.5, how might you establish that your test is reliable?

7. Try to think of a way to measure each of the following, so that the resulting scale is ordinal:

   a. The height of your classmates

   b. The walking speed of five of your favorite professors

   c. How long it takes the students in your English class to complete an essay examination

   d. The temperature in your statistics classroom on the first day of spring

8. For each item in exercise 1.7, invent a way to measure so that the resulting scale is interval.

9. For each item in exercise 1.7, invent a way to measure so that the resulting scale is ratio.

10. How could you establish the validity of each measurement in exercise 1.9? Name the kind of validation procedure you use.

PART 2 **DESCRIBING DATA**

he results of nearly every research investigation are numbers. To make any sense of them and to communicate the results to others, we need ways to simplify, summarize, and present those numbers. Part 2 deals with these topics.

If a picture is worth a thousand words, as popular wisdom has it, then pictures must also be worth thousands of numbers. In fact, when presenting numbers, pictures are sometimes the most effective way to summarize and communicate. Use of visual displays of data is a topic touched on in nearly every chapter of this book, but two of the chapters in this part deal with it extensively. In Chapter 2 we look at ways of summarizing data and presenting them visually, one variable at a time. Chapter 5 returns to the topic of visual display but in the situation where the same individuals are measured in two or more different ways, and we want to illustrate the relationship between the two sets of data.

As effective as illustrations may be, sometimes there's just no substitute for numerical summaries of variables. Chapter 3 presents several summary values whose purpose is to reduce a mass of raw data to a single, easily understood value. Chapter 4 continues with summary values, extending them to developing ways to compare data across different variables using standardized scores and percentile values. Chapter 6 follows the graphical presentation of relationship information with quantitative measures of the correlation between variables. Finally, Chapter 7 uses the concept of correlation to develop a simple procedure for predicting the value of one variable if you have information about another variable.

2 Frequency Distributions and Graphical Data Description

FREQUENCY COUNTING
    Category Data
    Ordinal, Interval, and Ratio Data
PERCENTILE RANKS AND PERCENTILES
    Percentile Rank
    Percentiles
SUMMARY
KEY TERMS
EXERCISES

Here are some scores on the Eysenck Personality Inventory Extroversion (EPIE) scale for each of 84 subjects. At a glance, what can we say about them? What is the range of values? What's an "average" score? Are there two groups of people—introverts and extroverts—or does there appear to be a more or less continuous range of values?

15	14	6	20	14
14	16	15	12	14
14	14	12	11	12
11	14	4	17	13
9	15	19	19	15
16	10	14	15	14
18	15	13	11	17
10	15	10	13	16
11	11	16	20	16
16	14	20	18	18
16	13	6	9	14

19	14	15	16	11
22	15	11	11	15
15	16	13	3	10
9	8	17	13	13
17	20	15	17	12
14	13	8	15	

If you claim that it's very difficult to answer those kinds of questions quickly when confronted by all those numbers, then you've seen the problem involved with looking at raw data. The answers to the questions are there before our eyes, but we can't see them.

Here's an even more difficult question. Following are two groups of scores on the Bartlett Impulsivity Scale (BIS), another personality measure:

Group 1

68	70	74	71	71
53	53	54	55	55
56	56	57	57	57
60	60	89	60	61
63	65	65	67	67
51	52	52	52	53
76	81	83	85	85
89	65			

Group 2

46	49	51	52	23
26	37	37	38	40
34	35	41	42	36
36	37	42	42	42
43	44	44	45	45
52	53	53	46	47
48	48	48	49	53
40	41	27	31	49
49	52	46	33	54

Do these two groups differ, or are they the same? And just what do we mean by "differ"? If we mean, "Do the sets of data differ in number of scores?" then we can obtain the answer by counting. But if we mean, "Do the groups differ in their performance on the BIS?" then it's not easy to answer the question just by looking at the raw numbers. We might have a vague impression that the scores in Group 1 are a little larger, but we don't have a really good way to document that hunch. We could also ask questions like "Does one group tend to be more homogeneous in its scores than the other?" or "Does one group have more large (or small) scores than the other?"

As you can probably guess, the answers to all of these questions are in the data, but we need some special tools to make them stand out from the mass of raw numbers. And that's just what descriptive statistical tools are for—making visible an answer that's already in the data.

FREQUENCY COUNTING

The simplest, but sometimes the most helpful, approach to reducing a mass of values to something more manageable is simple counting. It's just about the only technique we can use with nominal (category) measurement. It's valuable for ordinal, interval, and ratio data as well.

◆ Category Data

John et al. (in preparation) surveyed nearly 700 college and university therapists. Among the questions asked was one about theoretical orientation; the data appeared in Chapter 1, and reappear here in Table 2.1.

This simple tally summarizes the data remarkably well. It's easy to see which categories of therapist are the most common, the least common, and so forth. Because the measurement is nominal, we wouldn't want to take the average of the category numbers—that result would be meaningless. But we can certainly summarize the data by counting, and that summary shows some features that weren't obvious with raw data.

We can convert the raw frequency counts into percentages, because it's often helpful to compare the relative numbers of observations in each category. To determine the percentage, we just divide a frequency by the total number of values and multiply by 100. For example, 179 of the 696 therapists hold a psychodynamic orientation, and so the percentage is

$$\frac{179}{696} * 100 = 25.72$$

If we did the same computation for all categories, we would have the data summary in Table 2.2.

Another arrangement (Table 2.3) brings out yet another aspect of the data. This listing, in descending order by percent, highlights the sizes of the theoretical orientations and shows the relative frequency of their occurrence

TABLE 2.1

Category	Outlook	Number of Therapists
1	Psychodynamic	179
2	Existential/humanistic	137
3	Cognitive	121
4	Behavioral	23
5	Other	236
	Total	696

TABLE 2.2

Category	Outlook	Percentage of Therapists
1	Psychodynamic	25.72
2	Existential/humanistic	19.68
3	Cognitive	17.39
4	Behavioral	3.30
5	Other	33.91
	Total	100.00

TABLE 2.3

Category	Outlook	Percentage of Therapists
5	Other	33.91
1	Psychodynamic	25.72
2	Existential/humanistic	19.68
3	Cognitive	17.39
4	Behavioral	3.30
	Total	100.00

in the data. In all these tables, the category number or numerical "measurement," is really irrelevant to understanding the data.

◆ Ordinal, Interval, and Ratio Data

Where measurement is at least at the ordinal level—that is, where values are measured on an ordinal, interval, or ratio scale—we can be more sophisticated in our counting procedures. The principle is roughly the same, though: Count the number of occurrences of a value or of a group of values.

STEM-AND-LEAF DISPLAYS

A relatively new way of presenting frequency data is the **stem-and-leaf display**. Although stem-and-leaf plots don't often appear in published research reports, they are often found on researchers' desks. They are especially useful in the initial phases of analysis, where you want a quick idea of some of the data's important characteristics.

A stem-and-leaf display is an easily constructed data summary for ordinal, interval, and ratio data. It organizes the data as ordered values, ar-

2	367
3	1345667778
4	0011222234455666678889999
5	12223334

Figure 2.1

ranged in lines across the page, each line beginning with a "stem" value. As an example of a stem-and-leaf display, here are the BIS (Impulsivity) scores for the 45 subjects in Group 2 that we saw at the beginning of the chapter, but now all the scores are represented compactly in the stem-and-leaf display in Figure 2.1.

Each line in the display shows the scores sharing a common first digit. For example, the first line contains the values 23, 26, and 27. The third line represents the scores 40, 40, 41, 41, 42, 42, 42, ..., 49, 49, and so forth. The first digit of each row is the "stem"; the "leaves" are on the right-hand side of the vertical line.[1]

The stem-and-leaf display collapses the data into an easy-to-see form, while still preserving each individual value. From the display, you can easily tell that the original data contain two scores of 36, four 49s, three 52s, and so on. In addition, it shows that the scores tend to cluster in the center of their range. The longest "branch" represents scores in the 40s, and the leaves tell us that most of the digits between 0 and 9 are present in the data. The lowest branch, representing scores in the 50s, shows leaves only in the lower values; higher values predominate on the 30s branch. From Figure 2.1 we can conclude that most of the data fall into the upper 30s to low 50s.

There are several procedures for making the appropriate choice of stems. For example, with three-digit values ranging from 483 to 536, the stems can be as shown in Figure 2.2.

When many values share a single stem, the display may be expanded by using two lines per stem. In this form, the first line holds the leaves 0, 1, ..., 4 and the second the leaves 5, ..., 9. For example, EPIE (introversion/extroversion) data given at the beginning of the chapter appear in Figure 2.3. We can be very flexible in making stem-and-leaf displays. The goal in constructing them is always to display the data clearly, and this normally involves some trial and error. Showing the same data with both single and double stems is often a good idea because one may obscure some feature of the values that the other might highlight.

---

[1] There seems to be no general agreement among textbook writers on the arrangement of the display. Some authors present the values in ascending order going down the page as we show here, while others arrange the values in descending order. This book follows the ascending-order rule. Be sure you know your instructor's preferences before you turn in work to be graded!

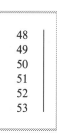

```
48
49
50
51
52
53
```

Figure 2.2

```
0  |  34
0  |  668899
1  |  000011111111222233333334444444444444
1  |  5555555555555666666666677777888999
2  |  00002
2  |
```

Figure 2.3

You might choose to use few stems, in which case the display will be compact but may obscure some features of the data. With more stems, the display will be larger but show more detail. Try several different numbers of stems until the data display reflects the data accurately and compactly. The point is to visualize the character of the data and try to answer a question. In the case of the EPIE data, a display with fewer stems than those shown in Figure 2.3 would make the data so compact as to not be very informative (Figure 2.4).

Note, though, that both displays of the EPIE data answer one of the original questions: There are not two extreme groups of scores, corresponding to introverts and extroverts; rather, most subjects in this research fall into the middle of the range of possible values. Thus, like most traits, introversion/extroversion seems to be distributed across people—most are at neither one extreme nor the other, but fall into the middle range.

FREQUENCY DISTRIBUTIONS

A common data summary is the **frequency distribution**. To use this procedure, we count, and present in a table or a graphic display, the frequency of each data value, or sometimes the range of values.

If there are only a few different values in the data, then a simple table will suffice. Table 2.4 presents the 84 EPIE scores.[2] This arrangement shows

---

[2] Remember that this text uses an ascending-values rule in constructing distributions.

```
0 |  34668899
1 |  000011111111222233333333344444444444445555555555555566666666677777888999
2 |  00002
```

Figure 2.4

EPIE Score	Frequency	Percent	Relative Frequency
3	1	1.19	0.012
4	1	1.19	0.012
5	0	0.00	0.000
6	2	2.38	0.024
7	0	0.00	0.000
8	2	2.38	0.024
9	3	3.57	0.036
10	4	4.76	0.048
11	8	9.52	0.095
12	4	4.76	0.048
13	8	9.52	0.095
14	13	15.50	0.155
15	13	15.50	0.155
16	9	10.70	0.107
17	5	5.95	0.060
18	3	3.57	0.036
19	3	3.57	0.036
20	4	4.76	0.048
21	0	0.00	0.000
22	1	1.19	0.012

TABLE 2.4

the full range of values (3–22) and also illustrates that the values tend to cluster in the middle range; most of the scores fall into the 13–16 range.

As we did with the category data, we can also express the frequencies as a percentage of the total number of observations (84 in this example). These are shown in column 3 of the table.

Sometimes the proportions corresponding to the frequencies are used instead of the percentages. In this context, proportions are usually called **relative frequencies** because they represent the frequency of each value relative to the total number of values present. [For example, the score of 13 was shown by 8 (out of 84) observations, and 8/84 = 0.095.] Column 4 in the table shows the relative frequencies for each data value.

Another form of frequency distribution presents cumulative frequencies. Consider the arrangement of the same data in Table 2.5. (Ignore the

TABLE 2.5			
EPIE Score	Frequency	Cumulative Frequency	Cumulative Percent
3	1	1	1.19
4	1	2	2.38
5	0	2	2.38
6	2	4	4.76
7	0	4	4.76
8	2	6	7.14
9	3	9	10.71
10	4	13	15.47
11	8	21	24.99
12	4	25	29.75
13	8	33	39.27
14	13	46	54.77
15	13	59	70.27
16	9	68	80.97
17	5	73	86.92
18	3	76	90.49
19	3	79	94.06
20	4	83	98.82
21	0	83	98.82
22	1	84	100.01

fourth column for the moment.) The third column shows the cumulative frequency of each score. The **cumulative frequency** shows how many scores are equal to *or less than* each value. For example, using cumulative frequencies it's easy to tell that there are 13 scores of 10 or less, that there are 76 of 18 or less, and so on. If you were one of the 84 people in the data set, then it might be important (and interesting) to know how many people scored at or below you. In these data, if you had received a score of 12, for example, you could see from the table that 25 of the 84 people received a score of 12 or less.

Data are often presented with **cumulative percentages**. For the EPIE data, the cumulative percentage values appear in the fourth column of the table. Using the cumulative percentages, we can clearly see that 70.27% of the students scored 15 or less. Using these values, it is simple to express an individual's standing in a set of data ("You scored higher than 90% of the people who took the test"). This form of information is common in many testing situations. Percentile scores, which we'll come to soon, provide just this kind of information.

SCORE INTERVALS

When we have so many different data values that listing them all becomes impractical or cumbersome (10 to 15 different values or so), we normally group them into intervals of sets of adjacent numbers. The introversion/extroversion data contain values ranging from 3 to 22. Because that represents 20 different test scores, we can group them into intervals. A **score interval** is a group of adjacent scores, like 5–10 or 100–109. We count how many scores fall into each interval. Using the introversion/extroversion data, for example, we might decide to use the intervals from 2 to 3, from 4 to 5, and so forth. That done, counting produces the frequency table shown in Table 2.6.

But what intervals, and how many of them, are appropriate? And how do we decide what values to use to define the intervals? No solution is always best for all data sets, but between 10 and 15 intervals is usually a good choice. With that in mind, we can estimate the size that each interval must be. With the introversion/extroversion data, the scores have values between 3 and 22; this means that the scores are spread across the values between 3 and 22. To determine the intervals, we divide that range of values into a set of intervals. Start by determining how far it is from the lowest to the highest data value (in Chapter 3, we'll call this the *range*). For the introversion/extroversion data, the range is $22 - 3 = 19$. Suppose we want to have about 10 score intervals. Then the range of the scores (19) must be subdivided into 10 intervals. We calculate $19/10 = 1.9$ as a first guess as to how wide each interval must be. Because the data have no decimals, it makes little sense to have a decimal width for the intervals, so we simply round the result to 2, and decide that each interval should cover two score values. This value is called the **interval width**.

Intervals are often defined so the lowest one contains the smallest data value and also has a lower value that is evenly divisible by the interval width. Using the EPIE data, and grouping into intervals of two values, we define the intervals as 2–3, 4–5, and so on, resulting in the frequency distribution in Table 2.6.

TABLE 2.6		
EPIE Score	*Frequency*	*Cumulative Frequency*
2–3	1	1
4–5	1	2
6–7	2	4
8–9	5	9
10–11	12	21
12–13	12	33
14–15	22	58
16–17	14	72
18–19	6	78
20–21	4	83
22–23	1	84

The set of intervals tells us that values of 2 or 3 will be counted into the first interval, 4 and 5 into the second, and so on. For the introversion/extroversion data, these intervals do nicely.

What if we had values such as 75, 132, 45, 85, 104, ..., with the largest and smallest values being 48 and 132? The range is $132 - 45 = 87$. Suppose we want 12 intervals; we would compute the interval width as $87/12 = 7.25$ and round that value to 7. We start the first interval with the smallest number less than 45 that is also divisible by 7, giving 42 as the starting point. This low score value is known as the **lower apparent limit** of the interval and marks the lowest score to be included in the interval. Each interval is to cover seven values, so add 6 to the lower apparent limit to obtain the **upper apparent limit**; the value for the first interval is thus $42 + 6 = 48$. This means that all scores between 42 and 48, inclusive, will be counted in this interval. The next interval is found similarly; begin one step up from the previous upper apparent limit (49), add 6, and the next interval becomes $49 - 55$. The remaining intervals are found in the same way.

Suppose we had decimal values in the data. What should we do with a score of 3.4 if the intervals are 2–3, 4–5, and so forth? To answer that, we continue the discussion of measurement.

MEASUREMENT (AGAIN)

Measurement assigns numerals to objects so that the numerals represent an underlying property of the object measured. In the introversion/extroversion scale, the underlying personality dimension is assumed to be continuous, from very introverted to very extroverted. But the measurement scale assigns only whole numbers between 1 and 25. It's just as if we were measuring with a ruler that had only whole inches, with no fractions allowed. When that's the case, as it is with most psychological scales, we assume that a score of 17 on the scale, for example, really represents an underlying value somewhere between 16.5 and 17.5. That is, the real psychological dimension is continuous but is broken into whole-number chunks, like this:

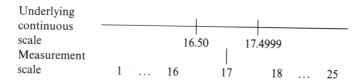

In other words, the measured value is taken to be the midpoint of an interval that extends 0.5 unit on each side of the measured value. The precision of measurement of this example scale is only to the nearest integer, while the underlying scale is continuous.

The same sort of consideration extends to other measurements, of course. If we are measuring reaction time, our timer will have a precision of measurement of perhaps 0.01 sec. Clearly, the underlying dimension of time is continuous, but the timer gives us only values of 5.23, 5.24, or 5.25.

Time, certainly, is a continuous variable that is measured, nevertheless, in individual "chunks" determined by the precision of the timing instrument that we have. Some of the variables that psychologists often use, however, seem to be clearly discrete and not representative of an underlying continuum. The numbers of errors made, or the numbers of problems solved, for example, appear to be discrete variables that don't reflect an underlying continuous variable. If we are *really* interested in just the numbers of errors or problems solved, then the variable is discrete. Usually, though, we're taking those apparently discrete values as measurement of an underlying variable that really may be conceived of as continuous. The number of errors, for example, often appears as a dependent variable in studies where it is presumed to reflect learning. That is, if an animal or a human learns how to perform some task, and if we want evidence of that learning, we can observe a decline in the numbers of errors made on successive trials. Again, our "ruler" uses only whole numbers to measure what may be a continuous latent variable. (We'll ignore a debate among learning theorists concerning the continuous versus incremental nature of the learning process itself, which leaves the whole notion of an underlying continuum up in the air.) A similar argument might be made about many other apparently discrete variables, such as the number of problems solved, which is often used as a measure of an underlying (continuous) skill.

How does all this digression help us? For one thing, it leads to a rule about rounding, and for another it helps to explain the common procedure for dealing with scores that fall exactly on the apparent boundary between intervals.

First, the rounding rule. The results of most computations should be rounded. Computers typically report the computation of an average, for example, to an unreasonably large number of digits. Do we want to use all of those digits? Certainly not; the data themselves have a precision that is determined by the measuring device, and using a large number of digits beyond the original values is meaningless. If we are measuring to the nearest whole integer, as with the introversion/extroversion scores, for example, it makes little sense to have summary values with ten digits after the decimal point. A reasonable rule, then, is to *round to two digits greater precision than are present in the data*. Following that rule, if we computed the average of the introversion/extroversion scores as 13.816735394, we should round the value to 13.82 when we report it.[3]

INTERVALS WITH DECIMALS

Now, to come back to the earlier question—how do we handle the score of 3.4 when the apparent limits of the intervals are 2–3, 4–5, and so on? Because the intervals are probably intended to represent a continuous

---

[3] Many psychologists follow an additional rule when rounding in 0.5 value: Round a 0.5 so that the result is an even number. Following this rule, 33.425663 would round to 33.42, but 33.43565 would round to 33.44. By following this rule consistently, in the long run you will not bias computations either up or down.

underlying variable, we usually assume that the intervals really represent the values

$$1.5-3.5\dots$$

$$3.5-5.5\dots$$

$$5.5-7.5\dots$$

These values are called the **lower** and **upper real** (or *actual*) **limits** of the intervals. Using these values, we can see that the score of 3.4 should be scored into the interval whose apparent limits are 2–3. But what of a score of *exactly* 3.5? Many people regard the upper real limits as ending *just before* the next interval's lower limit, so that the first interval is interpreted as being $1.5 - 3.4999999\dots$. Using this interpretation, then, a score of 3.5 should appear in the next interval because its limits are $3.5 - 5.4999999$.

Note that the actual limits extend 0.5 above and below each interval. This illustrates a rule about constructing the intervals: The actual limits go one-half of a measurement unit above and below. Because the example data are measured to whole-number precision, the intervals are shown as ± 0.5. However, it's awkward to produce tables and illustrations using intervals described with decimals. For this reason, programs usually label intervals with just the midpoints, with the interval understood to extend equal distances on each side of the midpoint.

Following these conventional rules, the introversion/extroversion data would appear as in Table 2.7. In the table, to clarify exactly what they are the upper and lower real limits are shown; normally only the midpoints would be shown.

This summary of the data is compact and easy to comprehend. Like the stem-and-leaf diagram, it also tells us something important that was not

Interval Midpoint	Real Limits	Frequency
2.5	1.5–3.5	1
4.5	3.5–5.5	1
6.5	5.5–7.5	2
8.5	7.5–9.5	5
10.5	9.5–11.5	12
12.5	11.5–13.5	12
14.5	13.5–15.5	26
16.5	15.5–17.5	14
18.5	19.5–21.5	6
20.5	21.5–23.5	4
22.5	23.5–25.5	1

TABLE 2.7

apparent in the raw data—most of the people tested fall into the middle range of the introversion/extroversion scale rather than into either extreme group. The fact that there do not seem to be two distinct groups of people is an important finding (see p. 30), and all we had to do was count the numbers to learn it. As noted, introversion/extroversion seems to be distributed so that most people are at neither one extreme nor the other but tend to fall into the middle range.

As another example using decimal values, consider these data and use 15 intervals:

2.5	3.6	9.2	11.6
5.6	6.1	3.2	8.1
3.2	4.0	5.3	6.8
9.9	2.6	6.8	9.3

The scores range from 2.5 to 11.6. Dividing that range by 15, we calculate the interval width as $(11.6 - 2.5)/15 = 0.607$. Rounding, we use an interval width of 0.6. The first interval can start at 2.40 (it's lower than the lowest value and is divisible by the interval width). Using these values, the intervals become

2.40–2.90

3.00–3.50

3.60–4.10

and so on.

To construct the intervals, we begin with 2.40 and continue, with each interval starting at a point 0.60 above its predecessor; this results in the first column of numbers above. The logic of the upper limit of each interval is as follows. Because the data are measured to 0.1 precision, the actual interval values extend 0.05 (one-half of the measurement unit) below each starting value. Thus, the first two lower limits are actually 2.35 and 2.95 (corresponding to the 2.40 and 3.00 shown). The upper real limit of the first interval coincides with the lower real limit of the second interval (2.95), as shown in Figure 2.5.

The top value for the first interval is one-half measurement unit less than its actual upper limit of 2.95. This leads to 2.90 as the upper limit for the first interval. Once the limits of the first interval are found, all the remaining upper values are determined simply by adding the interval width (0.60) to successive values.

Computer programs have built-in rules to direct forming intervals, usually arriving at around 10 to 15 intervals because those numbers work best for most data. The number of intervals usually is sufficient without being overwhelming. In addition, this is usually enough intervals so that important features of the data won't be obscured, as might happen with too few intervals. But 10 to 15 intervals won't be best for all data, and as with

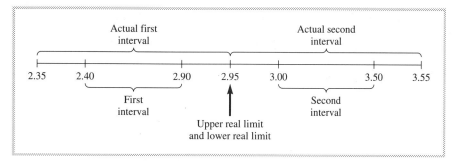

Figure 2.5

stem-and-leaf displays, you should experiment with various numbers of intervals. The ideal presentation will illuminate the important features of the data. You're trying to summarize data, and too much detail, or too many intervals, won't help. Too few intervals won't help, either, because that distribution will mask too much of the data.

A NOTE ON CUMULATIVE DISTRIBUTIONS

When cumulative frequencies, relative frequencies, or percentages are presented, the actual upper limit of each interval is used instead of the interval midpoint. Most computer programs, though, persist in using midpoints. When you use a program's output, be sure you know what's being used as interval labels. If it's midpoints and your frequencies are cumulative, you should relabel the table. The introversion/extroversion data from Table 2.7 would appear as given in Table 2.8 if they were presented using cumulative frequencies.

OUTLIERS

A data value that is far away from the bulk of the values in the data is called an **outlier** because it lies outside the usual values in the data. Outliers are important in data analysis, and for several reasons. Sometimes an extreme value appears as the result of an error—a decimal point out of place, perhaps, or a typing error, or perhaps interchanged digits. Other outliers, though, may be valid data points that simply are unusual. In any event, outliers often have a very heavy impact on descriptive statistics. If the outlier is an error, you want to make sure that it's identified and corrected before it distorts your conclusions.

Computer programs often have built-in rules to identify "potential" outliers. Humans have common "rules of thumb," too. For now, you might want to regard a single score (or two) as outliers if they lie more than two score values or intervals away from their nearest higher or lower neighbor. We will construct more sophisticated rules of thumb using the measures of spread presented in Chapter 3; we'll return to outliers there. Following the simple rule just given, though, the EPIE data in Table 2.8 has no outliers. If

TABLE 2.8

Interval Upper Limit	Cumulative Frequency
3.5	1
5.5	2
7.5	4
9.5	9
11.5	21
13.5	33
15.5	59
17.5	73
19.5	79
21.5	83
23.5	84

the distribution were as shown in Table 2.9, however, the extreme upper score would be an outlier. When you spot an outlier, most often a single value at the high or the low end of the data, you should check it carefully. If it's an erroneous value, correct it.

PRESENTING FREQUENCIES

There are two ways to present frequencies: in tabular form or as an illustration (normally called a *figure*). We'll consider tables first because we've already illustrated them.

TABLES. A **table** is an orderly arrangement of numbers in rows and columns. For frequencies, the table nearly always has either two or three columns and as many rows as there are scores or score intervals. The columns of numbers should be neatly spaced. If values in the table have been rounded, each column should have a consistent number of decimal digits. The numerals in each column should align neatly under their headings. The numerals align on the decimal position even though there are no decimals. There are no vertical rulings dividing the columns.[4]

The most common error in constructing a table isn't a construction error at all, but using a table where one isn't needed. Don't use a table unless you have at least four numbers to present; tables are at their best when you need a compact way of presenting a substantial number of values. However, a table that can't be fit onto a single sheet of paper without maintaining neat spacing and legibility is probably trying to present too much data and can benefit from being subdivided.

---

[4] For some reason, students love to put vertical lines in tables. Do as a graphic designer would do instead—let the "white space" delimit the columns.

TABLE 2.9	
Interval Midpoint	*Frequency*
2.5	1
4.5	1
6.5	2
8.5	5
10.5	12
12.5	12
14.5	26
16.5	14
18.5	6
20.5	4
22.5	1
24.5	0
26.5	0
28.8	1

Another common error is that of transposing the table, that is, having more columns than rows. A table is best built vertically on a page, as shown in Figure 2.6. The point of using a table is to communicate a mass of information. If the reader (the instructor, in the case of most student work) spends too much time trying to decipher a sloppy table, then the illustration isn't doing its job.

GRAPHICS. The other way to present frequency data is graphically, using one of several kinds of illustrations. Line graphs and frequency polygons are the most common in scientific literature; histograms and bar graphs are less common.

A **histogram** is constructed by drawing rectangles whose height represents the frequencies of intervals. For example, the introversion/extroversion frequency data might appear as in Figure 2.7. The figure presents the same data as Table 2.5, but it does so visually. The picture makes it clearer that there is strong tendency for the scores to cluster in the middle range, but also that there is a straggle of individuals with very low scores.

Although tables are best arranged vertically, figures are best kept horizontal. The usual rule is that a figure is best when it's a little wider than it is tall: Two units high for each three units wide is a common rule of thumb. This proportion is illustrated in Figure 2.8. The vertical and horizontal axes should be calibrated so the scale occupies the full length.

Scientific graphics are nearly always drawn in black on white paper; unless your instructor says otherwise, you should follow that rule for all assignments. The axes are labeled with the names of the variables to be shown—frequency and EPIE score, in this case. In a histogram or bar chart,

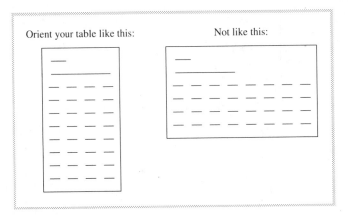

Orient your table like this:

Not like this:

Figure 2.6

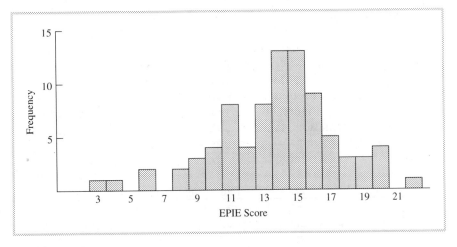

Figure 2.7

a rectangle's height represents the frequency for each midpoint. Note that when frequency data are presented, they should *always* appear on the ordinate or vertical axis.[5]

For continuous variables, most often those measured as interval or ratio, the rectangles are connected, as illustrated in Figure 2.7. When the data represent nominal or ordinal measurements, the rectangles are drawn with space between them, showing graphically that they should not be seen as continuous. A presentation like this is normally called a **bar chart**, to distinguish it from a histogram. The theoretical orientation data would appear in a bar chart as illustrated in Figure 2.9.

[5] The guidelines given here stem from the rules for figures given in the *Publication Manual of the American Psychological Association* (APA, 1983), a standard that many instructors expect in written work. Computer programs violate these rules flagrantly, making "touch up" necessary.

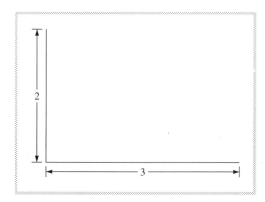

Figure 2.8

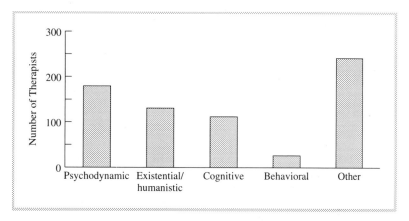

Figure 2.9

Although bar charts are frequently used for category (nominal) and ordinal data, and histograms are used to present data from interval and ratio data, these latter kinds of measurements are more usually illustrated with other representations. In particular, the **frequency polygon**, or **line graph**, is often found in the journals and reports. A polygon is constructed by laying out a set of axes following the same proportions and other rules as for a histogram. The frequency for each score interval is represented by a point, and the points are connected by a straight line. In this format, the EPIE score distribution would appear as in Figure 2.10.

The rules for constructing polygons are similar to those for histograms, at least as far as the axes are concerned. In addition, note that the ends of the polygon are "tied down" to the abscissa or horizontal axis by continuing the line to the baseline at each end.

Box plots, a useful and new variety of graphic presentation, present frequency information as well, but they also show other statistics, and we'll defer their presentation until the next chapter.

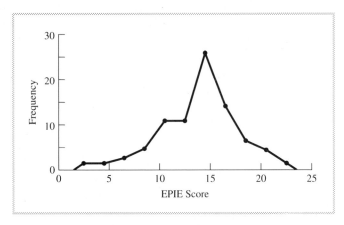

Figure 2.10

Interpreting Frequency Distributions

A great deal of information is available in a frequency distribution. It is usually the first look an investigator gets at data, and often helps to shape the course of data analysis. Of particular importance are the following points:

◆ What is the overall "shape" of the distribution? Is it roughly symmetrical, or does there seem to be a pileup toward one end or the other? Are there bulges or irregularities that make you wonder why so many scores should be in a particular range? Does there seem to be one region of high frequencies or more than one?
◆ Are there obvious outliers in the data that show up as isolated cases at one extreme or the other?
◆ What is the rough middle of the scores?
◆ How spread out are the scores? Do the data appear to be tightly clustered in the center, or do they tend to spread themselves widely over the range?
◆ If two or more sets of data are being compared, what are the similarities and differences in the preceding items?

Referring to Figure 2.10, what might we say about each of these questions? We already noted that the frequency distribution indicates that people tend to cluster in the center of the range of values. This suggests that the introversion/extroversion personality dimension measured does not find two distinct groups of people—introverts and extroverts—but rather that most people tend to be in the middle. There are no obvious outliers, but note that there are comparatively fewer low scores than high. That is, the center seems to be located a little to the right of the center of the scale, indicating that perhaps there are slightly more extroverted people in this group than there are introverted. Finally, we might note that there is some spread in the scores, but that in general most people seem to score between about 10 and 20.

COMPARING THE USE OF TABLES AND FIGURES

Both tables and figures are exceptionally effective ways of communicating information about frequencies. But how do you decide whether a table or a figure is the best way of communicating, and when should you just rely on words alone?

Tables and figures are best when used to communicate a substantial amount of information. Tables should be used for more than four numbers, and they're usually best with many more than that. When there are only a few numbers, they are more easily communicated in sentence format in the text of a report (for example, "The scores ranged from 3 to 22"). Tables are often chosen for their ability to show sets of frequencies or summary statistics side by side for ease of comparison. Figures are useful for showing the shape of a data distribution, but would not normally be used for that purpose unless you were trying to make a point about a distribution's form and a picture seemed easiest.

Both tables and figures are effective ways to communicate. In deciding whether to use either, consider the amount of data you have to communicate and what you want it to say. If you have only a few values, or an unremarkable frequency distribution that you can describe easily, then use words. However, if you have a lot of numbers, perhaps representing several groups, the compact, side-by-side format of a table might be the best way to communicate. If you want to make a point of the shape of the distribution, or if you want to show a trend over time or trials, then a figure may be the choice. In Chapter 15, we discuss how to present and interpret interactions in complicated experimental designs; the figure is the preferred way to show interaction data because it communicates visually what could be difficult to say concisely in words.

In using a computer, you may have a difficulty that is not present with hand computation—too much material. Most computer programs willingly generate pages of tables and figures, all begging to be included in a report. The student's task is often to decide what to *leave out*, rather than what to include. Remember that the job is communication, not trying to flood your reader with a mass of data in the hopes that the "right" answers will be there somewhere. The data are there to give an answer to a particular research question, and it is your responsibility to select only the material that will communicate that answer. Just because you can easily get five different frequency distributions, each done with three different graphic representations, doesn't mean that you must use them all; one will certainly be better than the rest, and you should use only that one.

PERCENTILES AND PERCENTILE RANKS

Suppose you wanted to compare your position in your German class relative to the other students after you have all taken two exams. If your instructor happens to use the same grading scale on both exams, then you may be able to compare one score directly with the other. But if one exam has a possible high grade of 50, and the other a possible top score of 75, then comparing raw test scores might be difficult, and would probably be misleading.

If you happen to receive perfect scores on both exams, and if no one else does, you know exactly how you stand in the class. You can describe your position as being "first in the class," regardless of your actual test scores. Another way to describe your top position is to say that your score is higher than those of 100% of your classmates. You don't have to use actual test scores to describe where you are in class; you can do it all by citing the percentage of scores that are below yours. If you say, "I did better than 75% of the class on the first test," you don't have to worry about whether the test was scored on a 50-point scale, on a 150-point scale, or on any other scale. In the same way, if your score is higher than 75% of the students on the first exam but exceeds 90% on the second, then you know that you have improved relative to your class, regardless of your actual scores.

◆ Percentile Rank

What we have just described is a measure called the percentile rank. The **percentile rank** of a score is the percentage of the distribution below that score. Using such measures of relative standing in a set of data is a common procedure, especially in educational settings.

Suppose there are 15 students in your German class, and that you receive a 33 on a weekly quiz. If you arrange the grades of all the students in order, you might have

The percentile rank of your score of 33 is 40 because it exceeds or is equal to 6/15, or 40%, of the data. If your friend John receives 66 on the same quiz, then his percentile rank is 93 because his 66 exceeds or is equal to 14/15 (93%) of the values in the data.

Only a few computer programs compute the percentile ranks of given data values. But approximate percentile ranks (which are often close enough) may be determined easily from a careful plot of the cumulative distribution. (In fact, complications arise in determining percentile ranks when there are multiple scores close to the percentile point. For that reason, and because we assume that a computer will do most of the work anyway, we're skipping those complexities.) As an example, Table 2.10 gives the distribution of the number of words recalled by 43 subjects when they were asked to repeat a list of 32 words.

By calculating the cumulative percentages and plotting the resulting cumulative distribution, we can determine approximate percentile ranks easily. Table 2.11 gives the necessary figures. Figure 2.11 gives a plot of the cumulative percentages.

To find the approximate percentile rank of a number of words recalled, locate the value on the horizontal line and draw a vertical from it to the cumulative curve. Then move to the left to find the percentile point. The approximate percentile rank for 15 words recalled is shown in Figure 2.11;

TABLE 2.10

Words Recalled (Midpoints)	Frequency
2	0
5	3
8	3
11	4
14	4
17	6
20	8
23	7
26	5
29	2
32	1

TABLE 2.11

Words Recalled (Upper Limits)	Frequency	Cumulative Proportion
3.5	0	0.00
6.5	3	0.07
9.5	3	0.14
12.5	4	0.23
15.5	4	0.32
18.5	6	0.46
21.5	8	0.65
24.5	7	0.81
27.5	5	0.93
30.5	2	0.98
33.5	1	1.00

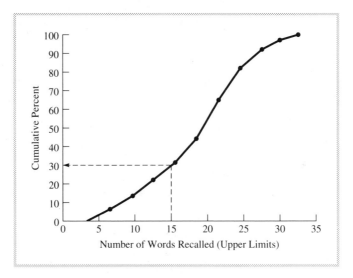

Figure 2.11

the result is about 30, meaning that a recall of 15 words exceeds 30% of the data values. The percentile rank for 26 words recalled is shown in Figure 2.12; here the result is about 90.

Percentile rank is a convenient means for comparing scores in dissimilar distributions because the comparison is on a standard 0–100% scale. It has the additional advantage of being readily understandable by people with no background in statistics or the quantitative treatment of data.

◆ Percentiles

A closely related statistic (indeed, it's the mirror image of the percentile rank) is the **percentile**. A percentile gives the *score* that exceeds a given percentage of the distribution. For example, the score that exceeds 50% of the distribution is called the 50th percentile. A score that is larger than 25% of the distribution is the 25th percentile; that exceeding 85% is the 85th percentile, and so forth. Scores that divide the distribution into four equal-sized segments are called **quartiles**: The 25th percentile is the same as the first quartile, the 50th percentile is the second quartile, and the 75th percentile is the third quartile.

A cumulative frequency plot may be used to locate approximate percentiles. Using the words-recalled data set from Table 2.11, to locate the 75th percentile, for example, begin with the 75% (or 0.75) point on the vertical axis and move to the right until the cumulative frequency line is located. Then drop to the value scale to find the data value of approximately 23, as shown in Figure 2.13.

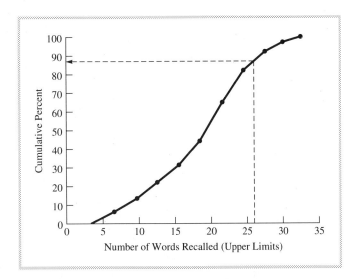

Figure 2.12

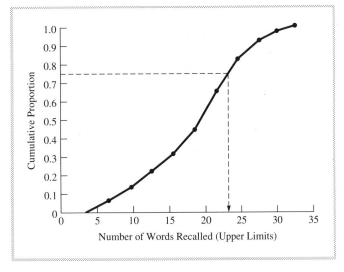

Figure 2.13

The unfortunate similarity of the names *percentile* and *percentile rank* has caused untold confusion among generations of students, but they are really quite different, though related, values. The *percentile rank* is a value between 0 and 100% that shows the standing of a data value relative to the other scores in the distribution. The *percentile*, on the other hand, is a value from the range of the scores themselves; specifically, it is a value that exceeds a specific percentage of the distribution. If you keep the illustration in mind, the percentile is a value from among those on the horizontal axis—that is, it is a score value; the percentile rank is a value on the vertical axis—that is, it is a number between 0 and 100.

Summary

- ◆ *Counting frequencies is a simple and effective way to summarize data.*
- ◆ *A* stem-and-leaf *plot condenses the data into a compact form that preserves all the values in the data.*
- ◆ *The* stem *gives the first digit or digits for all the other numbers on its branch.*
- ◆ *The* leaves *give the last digit in each data value.*
- ◆ *A frequency distribution giving values and their frequencies can be presented either as a table or a figure.*
- ◆ *Ordinal, interval, and ratio data are usually grouped into score intervals so that the range of scores is divided into 10–15 intervals.*
- ◆ *An* outlier *is a value that is far away from the other data.*
- ◆ *Tables present a large number of values and are neatly arranged vertically on the page.*
- ◆ *Figures should be drawn wider than they are tall; 2:3 is a good ratio of height to width.*
- ◆ *The* percentile rank *of a score is the percentage of the distribution below that score.*
- ◆ *A* percentile *gives the score that equals or exceeds a given percentage of the distribution.*
- ◆ *Scores that divide the distribution into four equal segments are called* quartiles.

Key Terms

BAR CHART	OUTLIER
CUMULATIVE FREQUENCIES	PERCENTILE
CUMULATIVE PERCENT	PERCENTILE RANK
FREQUENCY DISTRIBUTION	QUARTILE
FREQUENCY POLYGON	RELATIVE FREQUENCY
HISTOGRAM	SCORE INTERVAL
INTERVAL WIDTH	STEM-AND-LEAF DISPLAY
LINE GRAPH	TABLE
LOWER APPARENT LIMIT	UPPER APPARENT LIMIT
LOWER REAL LIMIT	UPPER REAL LIMIT

1. Here are the class scores for a midterm examination:

61	82	71	87
83	82	92	75
89	67	86	78
76	69	73	62
69	88	81	77
76	75	72	69
86	89	98	71
64	62	75	86

a. Construct a frequency distribution for these values and draw its histogram.

b. Present the same data as a frequency polygon.

c. Using these data, construct the stem-and-leaf display.

d. Use the same data and construct the distributions using 4, 6, 15, and 25 intervals. Which provides the best compromise between showing the nature of the data and too much detail?

2. Use the Eysenck Personality Inventory Extroversion data (EPIE) from the beginning of this chapter to do the following:

a. Construct the frequency distribution. Draw the frequency polygon.

b. Figure 2.3 showed the stem-and-leaf display for the EPIE data using the two lines per stem format. Construct the stem-and-leaf display for the same data using single-line stems. Which display is more informative? Why?

c. Describe the frequency distribution in words, using the suggestions on page 48.

3. The following is a set of 28 reaction times to a tone; the times are given in 100ths of a second (that is, 31 = 0.31 sec):

80	19
82	22
89	28
94	31
21	42
21	53
25	55
18	17
119	22
148	20
149	60
38	72
23	38
26	105

a. Construct the frequency distribution for these data. Show both the frequency polygon and table for the distribution.

b. Present the data as a stem-and-leaf display.

c. Describe the distribution in words.

4. Here are the data giving the number of words recalled in a learning experiment for two groups of subjects—five-year-old children and college students:

CHILDREN	COLLEGE
26	28
21	23
14	25
12	18
29	20
17	24
7	23
28	21
14	16
13	15
8	27
27	21
11	19
20	26
17	24
18	25
6	21
6	25
7	30
16	21
	19
	32
	24
	31
	27
	27
	26
	23
	17
	31

a. Construct the two frequency distributions and plot them as polygons on the same set of axes.

b. Describe the two sets of data in words, paying particular attention to the differences between the two age groups.

5. A study in cognitive psychology presented a group of subjects with a large list of words consisting of equal numbers of verbs, nouns, adverbs, and adjectives. The total number of each kind of word recalled by a group of subjects was:

Verb	153
Noun	178
Adverb	121
Adjective	78

Present the data as a bar graph.

6. Using the data from exercise 2.1, do the following:

a. Find the 25th, 50th, and 75th percentiles.

b. Find the percentile ranks of the following scores: 62, 92, 88, and 71.

7. Use the data from exercise 2.2 and do the following:

a. Construct the cumulative relative frequency distribution.

b. Find the 50th, 40th, 25th, and 90th percentiles.

c. Find the percentile rank for scores of 12, 16, 20, and 19.

8. Use the data from exercise 2.3 and do the following:

a. Construct the cumulative frequency distribution and plot it.

b. Find the 10th, 25th, 40th, 50th, 60th, 75th, and 90th percentiles.

c. Find the percentile ranks for reaction times of 0.40, 1.25, 0.63, and 0.35 sec.

9. Mueller, Haupt, and Grove (1988) presented 71 subjects with a series of nouns (e.g., ankle, candle, garden) in the context of a sentence like "I have a ..." or "Most people have a...." The subject was to answer yes or no to each question. The first kind of sentence they called a *self-reference* sentence because it asked about the person answering, and the

second was called an *other-reference* sentence because it asked about other people. One of the interests the experimenters had was whether people respond faster to self- or to other-reference sentences. The following data are a selection from the actual data and give the total time (in milliseconds—that is, 0.001 sec) that it took for each person to respond to 24 other-reference words and 24 self-reference words.

OTHER REFERENCE	SELF-REFERENCE
2117	1223
2092	1786
1556	1149
663	587
862	959
1034	1195
630	540
1548	1376
1210	872
839	866
1711	1371
1309	922
1005	1211
1005	791
1149	949
1724	1506
1145	963
1459	1284
932	926
1555	1438

a. Construct the frequency distribution for these sets of data and show the frequency polygons and tables.

b. Find the 10th, 25th, 40th, 50th, 60th, 75th, and 90th percentiles for both the self- and the other-reference data.

c. Find the percentile ranks for reaction times of 900, 1100, 1250, and 3000 milliseconds for each set of data.

d. Describe any differences that you see between the self- and the other-reference data. Pay special attention to the overall "shape" of the frequency polygon and differences in the percentile and the percentile rank values.

10. Owens and Tyrrell (1993) recorded errors in

steering (in a driving simulator) as a function of the brightness of the surroundings and the age of the driver. The data below give the average error made by each subject over a test period.

YOUNG SUBJECTS		OLD SUBJECTS	
LIGHT	DARK	LIGHT	DARK
10.75	17.00	22.50	31.50
9.25	9.00	14.75	44.50
7.25	9.00	22.00	45.00
9.50	14.00	16.75	23.00
17.00	18.50	14.50	19.00
15.50	27.50	17.25	34.50
9.50	18.50	15.25	33.50
13.00	14.50	12.75	45.00

a. Combine the light and dark data for the "Young" and "Old" subjects, giving two sets of 16 numbers (16 "Young" scores and 16 "Old" scores). Construct the frequency distribution for "Young" and "Old" as frequency polygons.

b. Find the 10th, 25th, 50th, 60th, and 75th percentiles for young and old subjects.

c. Find the percentile ranks for scores of 10, 15, 20, and 35 for the young and old subjects.

d. Describe any differences that you see between the young and the old drivers. Pay special attention to the overall "shape" of the frequency polygon and the stem-and-leaf display, and to differences in the percentile and the percentile rank values.

11. Jandreau and Bever (1992) presented college students with a set of short essays, typewritten with one of three kinds of spacing around the phrases in each sentence. In the "Normal Space" condition, the material was ordinary typed text. In the "Phrase Spaced" condition, blank space was added at the end of each major phrase in each sentence. In the "Even Space" condition, the spaces between words were all the same length, but the size of that space was determined so that the overall line length was the same as for normal spacing. A small set of multiple-choice questions followed each paragraph. The total number of correct answers was recorded for each subject. The data[6] follow:

SPACING

PHRASE	NORMAL	EVEN
79	85	41
92	56	57
63	60	29
76	62	77
88	58	71
60	33	66
62	83	63
61	88	43
100	68	94
78	65	69
57	55	65
61	67	82
68	55	66
84	62	63
92	68	50
84	59	74
66	96	66
104	47	75
	79	93
	86	62
	47	70
	86	44
	56	
	75	
	65	

a. Construct the frequency distribution for each set of data and present them as frequency polygons and as tables.

b. Find the 1st, 2nd, and 3rd quartiles for each distribution.

c. Find the percentile ranks for scores of 40, 55, and 85 in each distribution.

d. Describe the differences in the three sets of data.

12. Yalch (1991) presented subjects with recordings of several television advertisements. All the advertisements presented a slogan about the product; one-half of the slogans were presented as musical jingles, and one-half were

[6] These data are simulated although their summary values are nearly identical to the original. The group sizes are as in Jandreau and Bever (1992).

not. Among the variables that Yalch investigated was how many of each kind of slogan (Jingle and Nonjingle) were recalled. The following data give the number of slogans correctly paired with the associated product:

JINGLES	NONJINGLES
4	4
3	2
4	2
4	4
3	3
4	2
3	3
4	2
4	4
4	2
4	4
3	2
4	3
4	4
4	1
3	3
4	3
4	2
4	3
3	3

a. Construct the frequency distribution for each set of data and present them as tables.

b. Find the 1st, 2nd, and 3rd quartiles for each distribution.

c. Find the 30th and the 95th percentile for each distribution.

d. Verbally describe the differences in the two sets of data.

3 Describing Data Numerically

Figure 3.1 presents two frequency distributions. These data are from Mueller et al. (1988) (see exercise 2.9). They show the total amount of time taken (in milliseconds—msec—or 1000s of a second) to respond to a set of adjectives and a set of nouns.[1]

What can we say about the differences in the response times for nouns and adjectives on the basis of these frequency distributions? The overall middle of the distribution seems higher for the adjectives; the bulk of the

[1] For ease of comparison, most of the rules for presenting a histogram have been violated in constructing the adjective part of this illustration. In particular, the 2 × 3 ratio normally suggested for the axes was ignored so that the vertical and horizontal scales of both parts of illustration would agree.

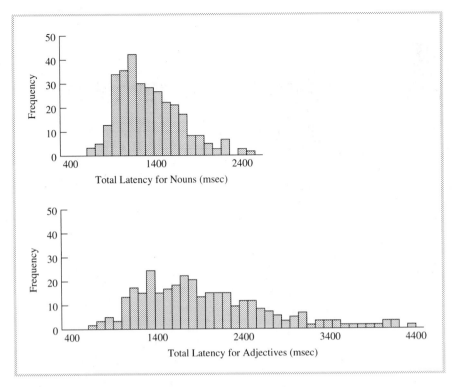

Figure 3.1

latencies is grouped roughly around 1000–2000 msec for the adjectives and 1000–1500 for the nouns, indicating that it takes longer, "on the average," to respond to the adjectives. In addition, the latencies for the adjectives are spread out, while those for the nouns are clustered more tightly. Both distributions show a tendency toward an asymmetric distribution, with the largest pileup toward the left side of the distribution. The effect is much more pronounced for the adjectives, whose graph has a long "tail" extending toward the longer times. From this we may conclude that, in general, the people in the experiment responded quickly, but there were a few instances of longer response times (especially for adjectives), and somewhat fewer fast responses. Finally, we should probably check some of the adjective values because the extreme long right-hand tail suggests the possibility of erroneous outliers in the data.

Those descriptions are easy to make from the frequency distributions. For each set of data, we pointed out three features of the distribution. We described where the rough center of the data was, how spread out the distribution seemed, and the general form of the histogram. But we can be more precise in each of those descriptions. Such precise descriptions are known as descriptive statistics, and address questions about the center, spread, and form of a frequency distribution.

"AVERAGES"

What single value best characterizes a set of data? You were probably in the fifth grade when you learned that the average is calculated by adding all the values and dividing by the number of values added. The result, the "average," was a measure you could use to summarize your performance in school, perhaps, or maybe the number of stamps per country in your collection. At about the same time, you may have learned about another kind of average, the batting averages of baseball players. But those "averages" are computed by dividing the number of hits by the number of times at bat, and so the number is really a proportion. You may have also heard phrases like "the average family income," a statistic that is usually determined by a different computation. And you've undoubtedly heard the phrase "On the average, I like my stat class a lot."

In short, the word **average** is imprecise. We have a sense of what it means, but just the word alone doesn't communicate very well. There are three common measures of center, and we turn to them first.

THE MODE

The **mode** is the score, or the score interval, that occurs most frequently in the data. (Of course, there's always the possibility of more than one mode—when there's a tie in the frequencies—and this is a serious problem with the mode.) When the measurement is nominal, the mode is a very appropriate measure to employ. Consider the category data from Chapter 1, as shown in Figure 3.2.

The most frequent category—that is, the mode—is "Other." Notice that if you were to report only the mode, you wouldn't say anything about any other category. You wouldn't even say whether "Other" is the winner by one person or by 100. Nevertheless, the mode does offer a simple summary of the data, even though there's a lot of information it doesn't communicate.

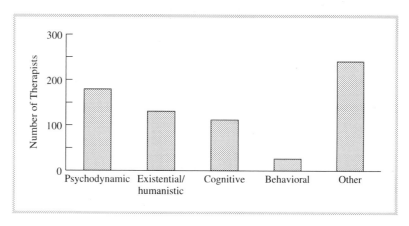

Figure 3.2

When ordinal, interval, or ratio data are counted into intervals for the frequency distribution, the mode is reported as the midpoint of the most frequent interval. Thus, for the introversion/extroversion data shown in Figure 3.3, the mode is 14.5 because it's the midpoint of the most frequent interval.

THE MEDIAN

The **median** is the score at the center of a data distribution in the sense that one-half of the data values are equal to or less than the median, and one-half are greater. Thus, it meets our expectation that an "average" be in the middle of the data, which is not always true of the mode. Because we must at least be able to arrange the data in order from smallest to largest to determine the median, we can't use this statistic for nominal data. But it's very useful for ordinal, interval, and ratio data.

For a few values that are easily ordered, the exact determination of the median is simple, especially when there's an odd number of values, such as

$$17 \quad 23 \quad 45 \quad \underset{\underset{\text{Median}}{\uparrow}}{46} \quad 83 \quad 84 \quad 96$$

Here the median is the center score, with the same number of values above and below it.

For an even number of scores, the median is the midpoint between the two center values, as in

$$23 \quad 45 \quad \underset{\underset{\text{Median} = 64.5}{\uparrow}}{46 \quad 83} \quad 84 \quad 96$$

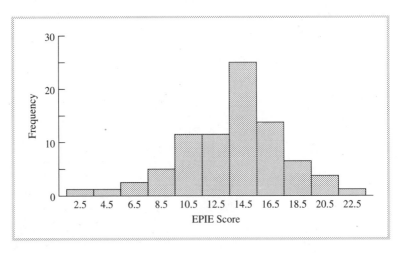

Figure 3.3

The expression $(N + 1)/2$ gives the location of the median in the ordered data. In the first example, there are seven values, so the median is at the $(7 + 1)/2 = 4$th position. In the second illustration, the median is at the $(6 + 1)/2 = 3.5$th position, as illustrated.

Because the median equals or exceeds 50% of the data, you may recognize that it must therefore be the 50th percentile, and that's correct—the median is equal to the 50th percentile.

THE ARITHMETIC MEAN

The **arithmetic mean** is our old friend the "average," with its correct name. The arithmetic mean is nothing but all the scores added up and divided by the number of scores in the data set. You even know the formula:

$$\overline{X} = \frac{\sum X}{N}$$

where N is the number of values in the data. The uppercase Greek letter *sigma*, $\sum$, is used in mathematics to stand for the *summation* or "add-'em-up" operation. We will find the summation operation in several formulas as we proceed, and it always means the same thing—namely "add-'em-up." In the formula, we also used the standard symbol $\overline{X}$ (pronounced "X bar") to stand for the arithmetic mean. (In some books, journals, or computer output, you may encounter the letter M used for the arithmetic mean.)

The mean of the values 17, 23, 45, 46, 83, 84, and 96 is

$$\overline{X} = \frac{\sum X}{N}$$

$$= \frac{17 + 23 + 45 + 46 + 83 + 84 + 96}{7}$$

$$= 56.28$$

◆ Properties of the Measures of Center

Measures of center have two important properties:

1. Adding or subtracting a constant does the same to the measure of the center.
2. Multiplying or dividing by a constant does the same to the measure of the center.

If we take the simple values 4, 6, 7, 8, and 16, with the arithmetic mean of 8.20 and median of 7, and add the value 100 to each data value, we would have the new data set 104, 106, 107, 108, and 116. Clearly, the median of these numbers is 107 and the arithmetic mean is 108.20. In both cases, the new value is the original value plus the constant 100. The rule holds for the addition or subtraction of any value.

In a similar way, if we were to multiply each value by the number 25, for example, then we would have the new data set 100, 150, 175, 200, and 400. The median of these values is 175 (and $175 = 7 * 25$), and the arithmetic mean is 205.0 (which is $8.20 * 25$); the multiplication rule holds as well.

THE EFFECT OF MEASUREMENT SCALE

The mode is the only measure of center that is appropriate to use with nominal (category) data. For nominal data, the values are unordered, and so the idea of a "center" is really meaningless. Nevertheless, the mode is often useful to communicate the most frequent choice. The median is especially useful for ordinal data but sometimes is used with interval and ratio data as well.

The arithmetic mean requires arithmetic operations on intervals between values. For that reason, it is appropriately and meaningfully used with data that have equal intervals—that is, interval and ratio data.

THE MODE

The mode relies on none of the properties of the number system other than the fact that the numbers are different from one another. And even if the data *can* meaningfully be arranged in order, the mode may not be in the "center" of the data at all. To these two problems, we might also add that the mode may not be unique in a set of data. Suppose that a frequency distribution shows a pattern like that in Table 3.1. There are two modes, and very nearly a third. Data sets with multiple modes are common and highlight one reason why the mode is not always useful as a descriptive measure.

THE ARITHMETIC MEAN

The arithmetic mean is the center of a data set in two important ways. First, the sum of the algebraic differences (that is, taking signs into account)

TABLE 3.1	
Midpoint	Frequency
7	2
12	6
17	18
22	13
27	17
32	18
37	6
42	1

between scores and their mean is zero. Second, the sum of the squares of the differences between scores and their mean is less than for any other number (that is, it is a minimum).

We can offer both arithmetic and graphic demonstrations of the first property. Consider the simple data set for a variable (that we call X for convenience) that we used before: 4, 6, 7, 8, 16. The mean of this set is 8.20. If we find the differences $(X - \overline{X})$, they should sum to zero. That is,

X	$X - \overline{X}$
4	−4.2
6	−2.2
7	−1.2
8	−0.2
16	7.8

$$0.0 = \sum(X - \overline{X})$$

The sum, $\sum(X - \overline{X})$, equals zero, meaning that the negative differences have exactly offset the positive; the arithmetic mean is in the center of the distribution in terms of the algebraic differences.

This same property of $\overline{X}$ can be demonstrated visually. Picture a histogram made of a board and bricks, as shown in Figure 3.4. The mean is the

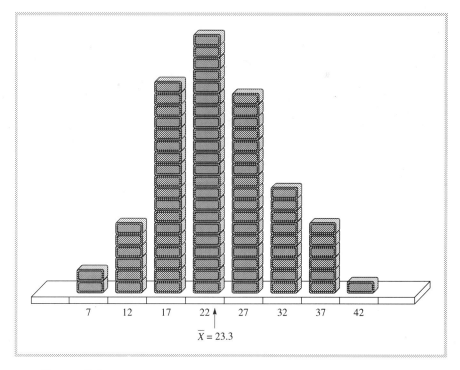

Figure 3.4

point at which the board would balance—that is, where the weights and distances on one side are exactly offset by those on the other. This "center of balance" property is not a property of the median because the median does not take into account distance from the center. To make a point that we return to later in the discussion, relative to the median, the arithmetic mean of the distribution in Figure 3.5 is shifted toward the extreme values on the left. This shift of $\overline{X}$ keeps the histogram "in balance." The median, although it has 50% of the observations on each side of it, is not at the center of balance. If we make a single change in the data set—making the smallest value -5 instead of 1 (Figure 3.6)—we see this easily. The arithmetic mean shifts to the left, compensating for the extremely low value, but the median is unchanged because all we did was substitute one low value for another.

The second property of $\overline{X}$, that $\sum(X - \overline{X})^2 = $ a minimum, means that $\overline{X}$ "best fits" the data in an important mathematical sense. Remember that a measure of the center, such as the arithmetic mean, is a summary value; in some sense, it is a "typical" value in the data. If we were to choose a single value to "represent" all the data, we would like it to come as close to the original values as possible. The quantity $(X - \overline{X})$ is the difference between a score and the mean. You may think of this difference as the amount by which the mean "misses" a value. The mean "fits" the data in the sense that it minimizes the squared "misses." The mean's property of minimizing

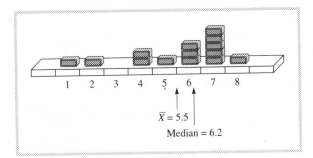

Figure 3.5

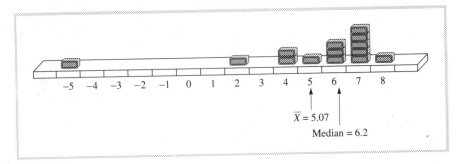

Figure 3.6

squared differences defines the arithmetic mean as the "least-squares" best-fit to the data. Being a **least-squares best-fitting** center gives the arithmetic mean some desirable properties, and relates it closely to some other very powerful statistics, such as the standard deviation and the variance.

THE MEDIAN

The median is a measure of center that is largely uninfluenced by extreme values in the data. It is the center of the data. There are equal numbers of scores above and below the median, a property that it doesn't always share with the arithmetic mean. We might compute the median and then determine the difference between the median and each value in the original data $(X - \text{Mdn})$. The sum of the squares of these "miss" values will probably be greater than for the mean. However, the sum of the *absolute values* of the differences will be smaller for the median than it will be for any other number. That is, the median is the "center" of the data in the sense that it is closest to all the numbers in terms of absolute distance. The arithmetic mean, remember, is the closest in terms of squared differences. Although this feature of the median may not strike you as especially exciting, or even important, it is useful in measuring the spread of the data, a topic that we cover later in the chapter.

CHOOSING A MEASURE

A major consideration in selecting a measure of the center of the data is the scale of measurement. If the measurement is nominal only, then the mode is the only appropriate choice. If it is ordinal, the median is usually the preferred measure of center. If it is interval or ratio, the arithmetic mean is normally preferred.

COMPARING THE MEAN AND THE MEDIAN. Earlier we noted that the arithmetic mean is pulled toward an extreme score in the data if there is one. Although this preserves $\overline{X}$ as a good estimate of the center, it can distort our conclusions. Look at the distribution in Figure 3.7. Which statistic is the better single indicator of the center? Data of this form, with a long tail of low frequencies extending in one direction or the other is called **skewed**, and is often troublesome. A common illustration of the effect of skew on the mean and the median is the distribution of U.S. income. For the year 1987, the arithmetic mean U.S. household income was $32,144, while the median was $25,986 (U.S. Department of Commerce, 1989, p. 442). Which statistic more accurately summarizes the income of most American households? Probably not the mean. It is inflated by a comparatively few extremely high income households; the vast majority of American households have an income less than the mean. For these data, the median is the preferred measure. (Incidentally, when income averages appear in the news, what is being reported is invariably the median.)

There is a corollary to the mean's property of being pulled toward an extreme tail. If the mean and the median have close to the same value, then

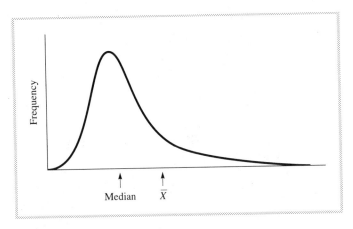

Frequency

Median $\overline{X}$

Figure 3.7

you may conclude that the distribution is symmetrical, a topic we return to later in the chapter.

CHOOSING A MEASURE FOR "SYMMETRIC" DATA. If the mean and the median are about the same for a set of data—that is, if there's no skew—then choose the arithmetic mean as the measure of center. This general recommendation stems from the least-squares property of $\overline{X}$. In addition, because we normally use a statistic like $\overline{X}$ not just to describe a set of data but also to make an inference about a population mean, the least-squares property leads to some powerful inferential statistics.

CHOOSING A MEASURE FOR "UNUSUAL" DATA. A frequency distribution with outliers, or with extreme skewness, is an unusual distribution and often argues against the use of traditional statistical methods. Return briefly to the data on response latencies for nouns and adjectives (Figure 3.1). The means and medians for the two data sets are given in Table 3.2. Note that in each case the mean is higher than the median, having been pulled toward the higher values by the tail of the distribution.

Until recently, a researcher confronted with an unusual distribution typically followed one of four general strategies: (1) Ignore the problem completely. (2) Treat the offending data values (extremely large or small) as errors in coding or data recording and either remove them or edit them into more "normal" values. (3) Drop a few values off both ends of the distribution and apply standard statistical procedures. (4) Use the median as the measure of center. For all cases but the last, standard inferential procedures were available to accompany the arithmetic mean, and so the median was rarely used for statistical inference.

The past decade or so has seen the introduction of numerous new descriptive statistics for unusual distributions, as well as new inferential procedures to accompany them. In addition, with the development of inferential procedures for the median, that measure of center has gained new respect.

TABLE 3.2		
	Nouns	*Adjectives*
Mean	1226.47	1819.43
Median	1159.00	1703.00

In fact, some authorities recommend the median even for nonskewed data; in years past the arithmetic mean was often employed, even for data for which it was inappropriate, simply because few inferential methods existed for use with the median.

Table 3.3 summarizes the recommendations related to choosing a measure of center.

◆ Presenting Measures of Center

Measures of center are frequently presented in sentence form when there are only a few measures to report. For example, we might find this sentence in a paper reporting on sex differences: "The mean running time for males was 38.62 sec, while that for the females was 35.41 sec." For one or two values, the sentence format is a compact and straightforward way to present the values. If there are too many numbers in a sentence, the reader may get confused. For example, the sentence "The mean words recalled on trials 1, 2, 3, 4, 5, and 6 are 7.83, 9.44, 16.22, 18.72, 19.04, and 19.87, respectively" is confusing and doesn't communicate effectively. When several measures of center are presented, an arrangement like that in Table 3.4 makes an effective presentation.

A tabular format makes it easy for the reader to compare adjacent entries. Comparing the mean amounts drunk, for example, is easier to do in this format than it would be if all of the values were presented in sentences.

Sometimes a figure is a good way to present measures of center. Consider data from a learning experiment where the number of words correctly recalled was recorded for each of several trials. The mean numbers of words recalled for a set of six trials are: 7.83, 9.44, 16.22, 18.72, 19.04, and 19.87. There's a large "jump" in the number of words recalled between trials two and three, and a distinct leveling off between trials four and five; those features of the data become more evident if the means are presented in a figure, as in Figure 3.8.

MEASURES OF SPREAD

Suppose you have taken two exams in your chemistry class. After the second exam, you learn that you have scored 62, exactly the same as you did on the

TABLE 3.3 Effect of Measurement Level on Choice of Measure of Center

Level of Measurement	Measure of Center
Nominal	Mode
Ordinal	Median
Interval and ratio	
Symmetric data	Arithmetic mean
Skewed data	Median

TABLE 3.4 Amount Consumed of Four Different Taste Solutions

	Sweet	Salt	Sour	Bitter
Mean	20.35	19.80	8.75	5.55
Median	19.25	19.50	9.00	6.00

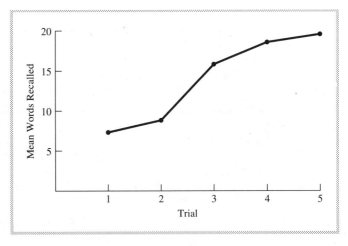

Figure 3.8

first exam, and that the class mean, 52, is also the same for each exam. Because you exceeded the mean by 10 points each time, are you pleased with your consistent performance? Not necessarily—you really need to know more about how you stand relative to the other students.

Suppose that the frequency distributions for the two exams looked like those in Figure 3.9a and b. The second distribution (b) is much more compact, with more of the students' scores falling near the mean. Your score is

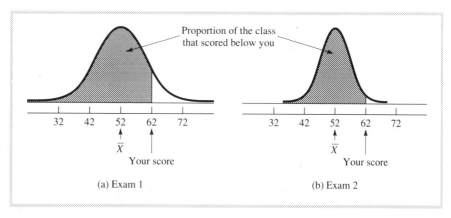

Figure 3.9

10 points above the mean, so on this second exam, more of the distribution is below your score. This means that your score is better than the scores of more students than it was in the first exam. The difference could be expressed by using the percentile ranks of the two scores. On the first exam, your percentile rank is about 85; on the second, it's about 97. Thus, relative to the others in the class, your second exam score is better; it exceeds 97% of the class. The first score exceeds only 85% (still not a bad place to be!). The difference between the two sets of exam scores is not in their center, which is the same for both, but in the extent to which they cluster tightly around that center. This characteristic of data is known as spread or variability.

What if there were a third exam in the class, again with a mean of 52, and that you happen to score 62 once more? But now the exam's grade distribution is that in Figure 3.10. In this distribution, the mean is pulled to the left by a very long tail of infrequent scores, while the bulk of the class scored just about where you did or better. The difference between the distributions of the first and second exams and this one is not one of variability but rather of the shape of the distribution. No longer are the second exam's scores distributed more or less evenly about their mean; instead, they're piled up in the higher values, with a few scores in the low range. Because so many of the students have scores close to yours, your standing relative to the class has changed once again. Now, even though you're still 10 points above the mean, so are a lot of your classmates.

In this section, we deal with the descriptive techniques that summarize information about the spread or variability of a set of data. Several statistics are useful in describing the extent to which the data vary around their center point. Once we've presented that material, we will show how to describe the form of a frequency distribution. Together with a measure of center, a measure of spread and a description of form completely characterize a data distribution. If we're able to summarize those three features of a data set, then there's little left to do with descriptive statistics.

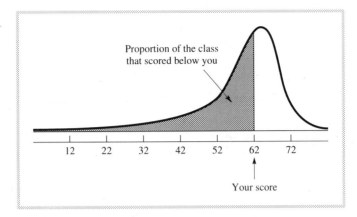

Proportion of the class
that scored below you

12	22	32	42	52	62	72

Your score

Figure 3.10

◆ Sources of Variability

Let's return to the chemistry classroom. Suppose that you and your class-mates differ in your knowledge of the material covered on the exam. You wouldn't be surprised to find that your scores were different, correct? Certainly—it's those differences in knowledge that contribute to the variability in the scores on the exam. Each student in the class may come to the test with a different degree of chemistry knowledge. Because that's probably the case, there must be variability in the exam scores reflecting those differences in knowledge. In fact, a major source of variability in the class's test scores probably comes from individual differences in knowledge of chemistry.

But suppose that you and your roommate, and all the students in the class, actually know the material equally well. If that's the case, then you should all receive the same test score, right? Not necessarily—there are at least three other sources of variation in the scores.

First, the instructor's exam probably is neither perfectly reliable nor perfectly valid. (That's not intended as a criticism of your chemistry instructor, or of any other instructor; it's an acknowledgment that no measuring instrument is perfect.) So even if you and your classmates are really identical in true knowledge, the chances are that your test scores won't be the same. Therefore, there will be some variability in the data due to error in the measurement instrument—the test itself.

A second source of differences among the scores can be called, for lack of any better word, randomness. Perhaps there was a question for which none of you knew the answer and you all guessed. Perhaps the class flipped a coin (mentally, because most instructors take a dim view of flipping actual coins during exams). Your answers were probably different, which resulted in a different total score. Or perhaps you were distracted when the student beside you dropped his pencil and you misread a question. That dropped pencil could have also contributed to the dropper's, and your, lack of attention, and thus influenced both his grade and yours. Or maybe some students glanced out the window and as a result chose an incorrect alternative answer. These occurrences can lead to error that is due neither to validity or reliability nor to individual differences but is best classified as random variability. Such random influences introduce variability into the test. You might argue that randomness is as likely to make your score higher as it is to make it lower, and so should really "balance out" across the class. Your argument is correct, and so the mean of the test shouldn't change much because of random variation, but the test's variability should—and variability is our concern here.

Finally, apart from their knowledge of the material, students vary in their ability to take tests. Some students do better at essay tests, some better at multiple-choice, some better at short-answer questions, and so forth. These differences, along with other individual difference factors (intelligence, writing ability, amount of sleep, etc.) all contribute to variability in the test scores.

So far, then, we have variability in test scores that is due to individual differences in both knowledge and ability, to measurement error, and to randomness. In some situations, there is yet a fourth source of variability. Suppose your chemistry class has two lab sections, and each section uses a different laboratory manual. This could happen if, unknown to the students, the instructor was conducting an experiment on the effect of the lab manual. Maybe he or she established a simple two-condition experiment, with one-half the class using one manual and the remaining half the other. In this case, there's yet another source of variability in the test scores: the effect of the lab manual. Variability here would stem from one manual's producing better learning than the other, even if everyone's knowledge of chemistry (from text and lecture) were actually identical.

Now that we've suggested several possible sources of variation in data —measurement error, randomness, individual differences, and maybe an experimental variable—how shall we measure that variability?

◆ Quantitative Measures of Variability

Quantitative measures of variability or spread can be grouped into two broad categories: those based on distances between certain scores and those based on differences from the center of all the values. In the first category are ranges between various points in a distribution. In the second are the variance and the standard deviation, both of which are based on differences between the scores and their mean.

DISTANCE MEASURES

THE RANGE. The simplest measure of the variability, or **measure of spread**, of a set of data is simply the distance between the smallest and the largest values. This statistic, called the **range**, or the *crude range*, is computed as

$$\text{Range} = \text{Largest value} - \text{Smallest value}$$

The range is a handy statistic that can be obtained without much effort. It offers a simple but effective description of the variability of the values. If the first exam in our chemistry class has a mean of 52 with a range of 59, and the second exam has the same mean with a range of 29, you can tell right away that the class was less variable on the second test. But you will also note that the range uses only two of the scores in the data, and a single outlier in either direction can throw the range off substantially. In the noun and adjective data (Figure 3.1), the effect is quite pronounced. The nouns have a range of 1936; that for the adjectives is 3826. The range in the adjectives may be misleading because it is influenced by the extreme high value in the right-hand tail.

THE INTERQUARTILE RANGE. Because an extreme value can easily distort a range, there are several procedures for producing a range that is "trimmed." For example, assume we find the 25th and 75th percentiles; the difference between them represents "how far" it is across the middle 50% of the data, as shown in Figure 3.11. This range, between the top and the bottom quarters of the data, is called the **interquartile range** and is a common measure of the spread of the data. In the illustration, if the 25th percentile has a value of 40 and the 75th has a value of 60, then the interquartile range is $60 - 40 = 20$. That is, a range of 20 points covers roughly the middle 50% of the distribution.

THE SEMI-INTERQUARTILE RANGE. A value of one-half of the interquartile range is often used as a measure of spread. This statistic is called the **semi-interquartile range**. It is roughly the distance across 25% of the distribution (Figure 3.12). If we take an interval of one semi-interquartile range

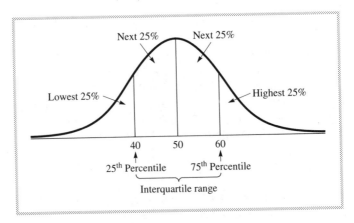

Figure 3.11

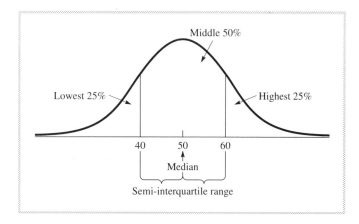

Figure 3.12

on each side of a measure of center, we then have an interval that includes approximately the middle 50% of the data.[2] In the illustration, the semi-interquartile range is $20/2 = 10$. The value can be used easily in simple communication—for example, in the statement "The interval 55 ± 10 contains roughly the middle 50% of the data." In that sentence, the value 50 is some measure of center, such as a median, and the 10 represents a semi-interquartile range.

Range statistics provide a measure of the spread of the values by giving the distance between two points in the data. These statistics are particularly well suited for use as spread measures to accompany the median. The second general variety of spread statistics is based not on distances between two points, but on distances from the center of the data.

CENTER-BASED MEASURES

Several statistics use the center of the data as a point of reference and reflect how data cluster around it. Of these, the variance and the standard deviation are the most widely used and understood; both are based on the arithmetic mean. The median absolute deviation (based on the median) is occasionally found in the literature.

Suppose we take a set of scores and find some measure of center, such as the arithmetic mean. To the extent that the mean is highly typical of the data, we should find that the differences between the data values and their mean (known as *deviations*) are small. This suggests that a measure of spread might use those deviations. For example, with the simple set of numbers 5, 8, 13, 14, and 17, we calculate

---

[2] This is strictly true only for a distribution that is distributed approximately equally around the center.

X	$X - \bar{X}$
5	-6.4
8	-3.4
13	1.6
14	2.6
17	5.6
	$0.0 = \sum(X - \bar{X})$

As pointed out earlier, and as illustrated here, the sum of the differences between scores and their mean is zero. That quantity isn't useful as the basis for a measure of spread, but two related measures are.

THE MEDIAN ABSOLUTE DEVIATION. If we find the median of the absolute deviations from the *median* instead of from the mean, we have a statistic called the **median absolute deviation**. For the example data (whose median = 13), it is computed as

X	$X - \text{Mdn}$	$|X - \text{Mdn}|$
5	-8	8
8	-5	5
13	0	0
14	1	1
17	4	4

The median absolute deviation then is 4.0, which is the median of the values 0, 1, 4, 5, 8.

We pointed out previously that the median is closest to the data in terms of the absolute differences between scores and their center. In other words, the quantity $\sum|X - \text{Mdn}|$ is a minimum. This means that using any number other than the median will result in a larger value for the sum. The median absolute deviation isn't a common measure for psychologists to use, but perhaps it should be. It is a perfectly acceptable statistic to employ when the median is used.

THE VARIANCE. In the same way that $\sum|X - Y|$ is a minimum when Y is the median, so too is $\sum(X - Y)^2$ when Y is the arithmetic mean. In other words, the arithmetic mean is the center of the data in terms of the sum of the squared deviations, meaning that no other possible number can lead to a smaller sum of squared differences. Because that's the case, an average of these squared deviations might be a good measure of the spread around the mean. And in fact the statistic computed as

$$s^2 = \frac{\sum(X - \bar{X})^2}{N - 1}$$

is a very useful statistic called the **variance**. It is simply the arithmetic mean (*almost* the arithmetic mean, actually, because it is computed using $N - 1$ instead of N)[3] of the squared differences.

For the example set of data, the mean is 11.4, and so the variance is computed as

X	$X - \overline{X}$	$(X - \overline{X})^2$
5	-6.4	40.96
8	-3.4	11.56
13	1.6	2.56
14	2.6	6.76
17	5.6	31.36

$$93.20 = \sum(X - \overline{X})^2$$

$$s^2 = \frac{\sum(X - \overline{X})^2}{N - 1} = \frac{93.20}{5 - 1} = 23.3$$

Before we leave it, let's comment just a bit more on the quantity $\sum(X - \overline{X})^2$. This sum of squared deviations about the arithmetic mean is an important value in a number of statistics, and we will encounter it again. It's so useful, in fact, that it's given a special name—sum of squares, or SS for short. When a SS is divided by some other number, typically $N - 1$, or one less than the number of values summed to get the SS itself, it becomes a variance. Variance is the foundation of the most widely used and powerful of the inferential statistics, the analysis of variance. An important part of the development of analysis of variance is examining the sum of squares and dividing it into segments that represent different sources of the variation in the data. For now, though, the important thing to remember is that the sum of squares represents differences between scores and their mean, and thus represents the variation in the data.

THE STANDARD DEVIATION. The variance is the mean of the squared differences between scores and their mean. As useful as it is as a way of describing the spread of data, it is an awkward statistic to use descriptively because it deals with squares of numbers. A much more useful measure of the spread is the square root of the variance, a quantity called the **standard deviation**. For the example data, the standard deviation, s, is

$$s = \sqrt{\frac{\sum(X - \overline{X})^2}{N - 1}} = \sqrt{\frac{93.20}{5 - 1}} = \sqrt{23.3} = 4.83$$

[3] The matter of N versus $N - 1$ is a little complicated; we explore it in Chapter 7. For now, regard the variance as the mean of the squared differences from the mean, and just ignore the fact that the divisor is $N - 1$ and not N.

The sample standard deviation is by far the most commonly used measure of the spread of the data. You won't go far wrong in your understanding of it if you think of it as an average deviation around the arithmetic mean. A larger standard deviation means a more spread out distribution (like that in the first chemistry exam), and a smaller value indicates that the data are more tightly clustered about their mean (as in the second hypothetical chemistry exam). In addition, the standard deviation is a convenient value because it is in the same units as the original data. If we talk of someone who scored, for example, 1 standard deviation below the mean, we know that the score is 4.83 units below the mean in terms of the original data.

Return once more to the noun and adjective data from Figure 3.1. Table 3.5 gives all the measures of spread for the latencies for the two kinds of words. Note that the statistics agree that the adjective data are the more variable. The exception to this is the median absolute deviation, which finds them almost equally variable.

◆ Graphic Presentations of Variability

Although descriptive statistics frequently are presented in tables, there are two common methods of showing spread graphically. Both are coupled with measures of center and are very effective.

BOX PLOTS

A box plot is a relatively new graphic tool, coming into psychology from exploratory data analysis only in the last decade or so. A **box plot** is a compact means of presenting the median, the range, and the interquartile range for multiple groups of data.

As an example, look at Table 3.6, which gives the amount consumed (in milliliters) of each of four taste substances by a group of experimental rats. The median amounts consumed during the test period (in milliliters) and the interquartile ranges for the four test substances also appear in the table.

A box plot shows the interquartile range, the range, and the median in a single illustration, as illustrated in Figure 3.13. The horizontal line in each

TABLE 3.5

	Nouns	Adjectives
Variance	126,572.29	494,265.24
Standard deviation	355.77	703.04
Median absolute deviation	232.50	234.00
Range	1936.00	3820.00
Interquartile range	497.00	896.00
Semi-interquartile range	248.50	448.00

Table 3.6 Amount Consumed of Four Taste Substances (ml)			
	Substance		
	Sweet	Salt	Sour	Bitter
	26.00	30.00	9.00	7.50
	19.00	19.00	8.00	5.00
	23.00	20.00	9.00	5.00
	24.00	19.00	7.50	6.00
	15.00	16.00	9.00	1.00
	20.00	19.50	10.00	6.00
	15.00	22.00	10.50	9.00
	16.00	19.00	8.00	3.00
	18.00	20.00	10.00	6.00
	27.50	13.50	6.50	7.00
Median	19.50	19.75	9.00	6.00
Range	12.50	16.50	4.00	8.00
Interquartile range	8.75	2.25	2.12	2.62

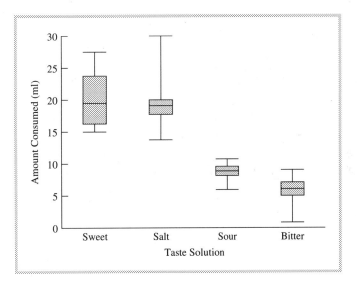

Figure 3.13

vertical rectangle (the "box") shows the median. For example, the medians of both the Sweet and the Salt data appear to be about 19. The vertical extent of the box shows the interquartile range—that is, the middle 50% of the data. Differences in the interquartile range are clearly evident in the plot; note the differences between the boxes for the Sweet and the Salt data. The vertical lines, sometimes called the "whiskers," show the full range of scores in each condition.

The median may appear off-center, depending on the skewness of the data. The Sweet data, for example, has a cluster of scores near and slightly below the median, and the box shows the median as closer to the lower values.

Box plots often are used to show outliers. Outliers appear outside the range indicated by the whiskers. Computer programs normally plot outliers using an asterisk or some other symbol on the plot. The outlier is excluded from the range (that is, it is shown as outside the range, as in Figure 3.14, which shows outliers in both the Salt and the Bitter data).

A common rule for defining outliers in a box plot is to use the length of the box as a ruler (Velleman & Hoaglin, 1981). Any score that is more than 1 1/2 "box-lengths" beyond the box might be an outlier. A score beyond three "box-lengths" should certainly be regarded as an outlier.

Box plots are well suited for comparing conditions or experimental groups. The plots in Figures 3.13 and 3.14 show clearly that the animals consumed the most of the Sweet and the Salt solutions, and that the median amounts consumed of Sour and Bitter were lower, with more Sour consumed than Bitter.

The vertical distances in the box plots make it easy to compare both the ranges and the interquartile ranges for the four sets of data. The most variability in amount consumed was for the Sweet and Salt solutions; the spread of the other two tastes is very similar. Note again that the median is not always in the center of the boxes or of the range.

BARS TO SHOW VARIABILITY

Group or condition data sometimes are presented graphically to show a series of center statistics, often the arithmetic mean. For example, Table

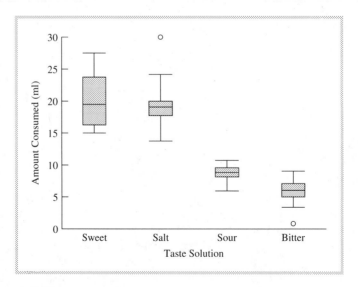

Figure 3.14

3.7 presents some data showing grade point averages from five groups of students. Figure 3.15 presents these same data in a figure, showing their means and standard deviations. The means are plotted along the line and clearly show an increasing trend. The vertical bars show 1 full standard deviation on each side of the arithmetic mean.

The standard deviation bars effectively show the spread of the data around each mean, just as the boxes in the box plots showed the spread and the location of the median. But note a difference: The box plots showed the median and the middle 50%, but the median wasn't necessarily in the center of the box. The off-center median indicated an asymmetric distribution of data about its center. Similar information about the "symmetry" of each

Table 3.7 Mean and Standard Deviations of Grade Point Averages for Five Groups of Students		
Group	*Mean*	*Standard Deviation*
Freshman	1.77	0.85
Sophomore	2.03	0.61
Junior	2.51	0.42
Senior	2.63	0.44
Graduate	3.33	0.14

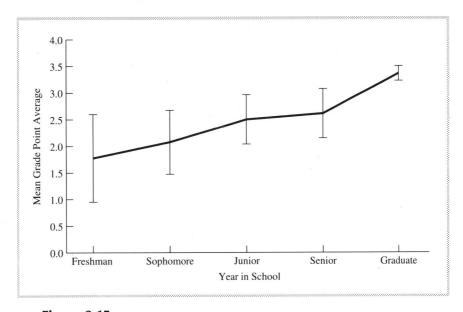

Figure 3.15

distribution is not available in the plot of the arithmetic means and standard deviations.[4]

◆ Tabular Presentations of Variability

Although graphic presentations of variability are important and useful, statistics are often presented in sentence or tabular form. In a research report, for example, you might find the sentence, "The mean number of errors for the subjects was 13.62, with a standard deviation of 3.2." That sentence communicates both the mean and the standard deviation simply and directly. When only a few values, typically a pair or two of measures of center and spread (e.g., mean and standard deviation, or median and interquartile range), are being given, sentences are straightforward ways to communicate. If more than a few values are to be given, a tabular arrangement, like Table 3.7, is often best. A table is valuable when you have a number of values, and also when you want to make it easy to compare adjacent numbers.

Table 3.8 summarizes recommendations on how to present measures of spread or variability.

◆ Choosing a Statistic

As with measures of center, the level of measurement is a consideration in choosing a variability measure. All the statistics that we've introduced rely on differences, either between pairs of data points or around a measure of center. Since differences are not meaningful with nominal measurement, none of the measures are usable for nominal measurement.

If we're measuring on an interval or ratio scale, all the statistics are meaningful and easily interpreted. In interval and ratio measurement, the differences between pairs of values are meaningful, and so both the distance-based and the center-based spread statistics are useful.

If the measurement is ordinal, many psychologists would argue that the distance indices—the various ranges—at least, are appropriate spread statistics. However, there's no universal agreement on that position. The problem is that in ordinal measurement, we cannot assume the equal-interval properties of numbers, and the range statistics all use differences between two points in the distribution. Nevertheless, the semi-interquartile range is often reported for ordinal data and is a reasonable choice, as is the median absolute difference.

---

[4] Figure 3.15 uses a standard deviation above and below the mean for drawing vertical bars; the bar's overall length is thus 2 standard deviations. There are several other ways to draw the vertical bars. Plots are sometimes drawn so the bar extends 1/2 standard deviation above and below the mean; the length of the bar then represents 1 standard deviation. Values other than the standard deviation can also be represented as bars. One such value is the *standard error of the mean*, a value common in inferential statistics. (When that statistic is shown, the vertical lines are often called *error bars*.) Another common use of the bar is to illustrate a confidence interval around the mean, a topic that we explore in Chapter 7. The title of a figure, or its reference in the surrounding text, should always tell you what the vertical bar means. Without explanation, you can't be sure what the vertical bars show.

Table 3.8 Presenting Variability		
	In a Figure	
Box plots	Best for showing data where the median and the interquartile range are to be presented	
	Best used to compare several variables	
Error bars	Used to show standard deviations when several measures of center are presented, often to show a trend	
	In Words	
Sentences	Best used when only a few values are to be presented	
	The measure of spread is usually given in the same sentence as the measure of center	
	In a Table	
Table entries	Best suited for presenting a number of values	
	Especially useful when you want to make it easy to compare adjacent values, or when you have both center and spread statistics	

In general, the best measure of spread is one related to the measure of center. This suggests that we should decide on a descriptive measure for center, and then let that dictate a measure of spread. If the arithmetic mean is used, for example, then the variance or the sample standard deviation is the logical choice for spread. If the median is the center statistic, then the median absolute deviation or the semi-interquartile range is logical. Table 3.9 summarizes the recommendations for a choice of spread measure.

This book often illustrates a variety of statistics for similar purposes because they sometimes appear in computer output, even though they may not be widely known and used. For example, any spread statistic other than the variance or the standard deviation is likely to be unfamiliar to many psychologists.[5] These latter are the "standard" spread statistics in psychology, and many instructors (and journal editors) insist on their use. One reason is simply familiarity—many of the other measures are relatively infrequent in the literature. But, in addition, the variance and the standard deviation have certain mathematical properties that make them very useful. For that reason, they are the measures preferred by most psychologists.

THE EFFECTS OF TRANSFORMATIONS

Earlier we discussed the effects of arithmetic operations, or transformations, on the measures of the center: In short, adding (or subtracting or multiplying or dividing) by a constant has the same effect on all the mea-

---

[5] Indeed, the very terminology of "center" and "spread" are recent additions to the statistical vocabulary; older terms are "central tendency" and "variability."

Table 3.9 Effect of Measurement Level on Choice of Measure of Spread

Level of Measurement	Measure of Spread
Nominal	None
Ordinal	Interquartile range or median absolute deviation
Interval and ratio	
Symmetric data	Variance and/or standard deviation
Skewed data	
Median	Median absolute deviation
Arithmetic mean	Standard deviation

sures of center. For example, if we add 100 to all values, then all measures of center also increase by 100. Or if we multiply each data value by 100, then all measures of center also are multiplied by 100.

For the spread measures, these are the important properties:

1. Adding or subtracting a constant does nothing to any measure of the spread.
2. Multiplying or dividing by a constant multiplies or divides all the measures of the spread—*except* the variance—by the same constant.
3. Multiplying or dividing by a constant multiplies or divides the variance by the square of the constant.

The first property can be described easily: Adding a value does nothing to a set of data except shift it higher on the number scale.

To illustrate the second and third properties, let's use the following data: 7, 9, 9, 9, 9, 10, 11, 12, 12, 14. If we multiply each value by 10, the transformed data values are 70, 90, 90, 90, 90, 100, 110, 120, 120, 140. The range of the original data is 7, and that for the second is 70; thus, the second rule holds for the range (as it would for all the other distance-based measures). The standard deviation of the original data is 2.04; that for the transformed data is 20.4. For the original data, the variance is 2.48 and, for the transformed scores, the variance is 417.78—thus illustrating the second and third rules.

DESCRIBING THE FORM

Not only can distributions differ with respect to the center and their spread, but they can also differ in their shape. For example, there's something clearly different about the two distributions in Figure 3.16, even though they might have the same mean and standard deviation. In part a, there is a large

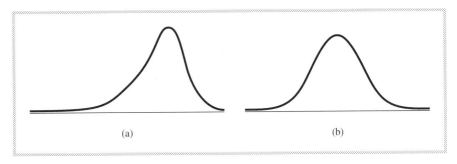

(a)   (b)

Figure 3.16

frequency pileup toward the higher end of the distribution; in part b, the scores are distributed symmetrically around their center. The first distribution (a) has a long tail of less frequent scores extending toward the left end of the number line. If we had the means and the medians of the two distributions, we would find that they would be about equal in part b, while the mean would be less than the median in part a because $\overline{X}$ is pulled toward the long tail.

A distribution may have a long tail—that is, be skewed—with the long tail either toward the low scores or toward the high scores. When the tail is to the left, with the bulk of the scores in the higher end of their range, the distribution is **negatively skewed**, as in Figure 3.16a. If the long tail points toward the higher scores—to the right, as in Figure 3.17—then the distribution is **positively skewed**. (Refer back to Figure 3.1, and note that both of the distributions are positively skewed.) If you have trouble keeping positive and negative straight in your head, visualize the tail as a long arrow pointing toward either the positive or the negative end of the real number line, as illustrated in Figure 3.18.

The use of the words *negative* and *positive* in these descriptions comes from the numerical index frequently employed to quantify skewness. A common skewness measure was developed by the early statistician Pearson, and is thus known as the **Pearson coefficient of skew**. The statistic, which is rarely available in computer programs,[6] is easily computed as

$$\text{Sk}_\text{P} = \frac{3(\overline{X} - \text{Mdn})}{s}$$

This statistic makes use of the difference between the mean and the median in a skewed distribution. In a symmetric distribution, the two centers are equal, so the skewness statistic equals zero. Because the arithmetic mean is pulled in the direction of the skew, the two statistics are unequal unless

---

[6] When a program reports a skewness statistic, it is usually a "third central moment" statistic, similar to a variance but using third powers of differences, such as $\dfrac{\sum(X - \overline{X})^3}{N - 2}$.

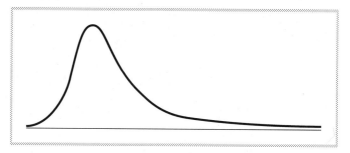

Figure 3.17

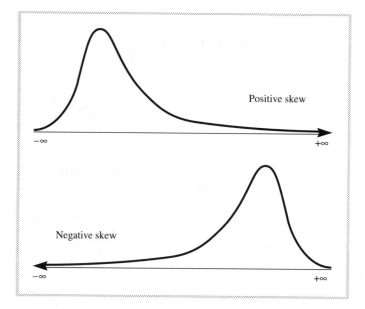

Positive skew

$-\infty$ $+\infty$

Negative skew

$-\infty$ $+\infty$

Figure 3.18

the distribution is symmetric about its center. For a distribution with its long tail to the right, the mean is greater than the median, the difference $(\overline{X} - \text{Mdn})$ is positive, and the value of Sk_P is also positive. If the tail is to the left, the median is greater than the mean, and $(\overline{X} - \text{Mdn})$ and Sk_P are negative. As an example of the skewness statistic, return to the two sets of response latencies for nouns and adjectives illustrated in Figure 3.1. The descriptive statistics are summarized in Tables 3.2 and 3.5. The Pearson skewness statistic for the nouns is

$$Sk_P = \frac{3(\overline{X} - \text{Mdn})}{s} = \frac{3(1266.47 - 1159.00)}{355.77} = 0.91$$

and for the adjectives,

$$\text{Sk}_\text{P} = \frac{3(\overline{X} - \text{Mdn})}{s} = \frac{3(1819.43 - 1703.00)}{703.04} = 0.50$$

The sign of the statistic tells us that the distribution is positively skewed. In addition, the magnitude of Sk_P tells us something about how severe the skew is. Values of Sk_P between -0.5 and 0.5 are usually accepted as showing no real departure from symmetry. A distribution with Sk_P greater than 0.5 in either direction is regarded as skewed. The preceding values thus indicate a moderate positive skew for the nouns and no particular skew for the adjectives.

TRANSFORMATIONS AND FORM

If we were to add a constant to all the values in a set of data, the center would change, but the spread would not, as we've pointed out. In addition, the form of the distribution would be unchanged. We could multiply all values by a constant, and the center and the spread would change; the form would not. In short, a linear transformation changes the center and the spread, but it doesn't change the form of a distribution at all.

Nonlinear transformations, however, do change the shape. Replacing each data value with its square root (a nonlinear operation), for example, changes the center, the spread, and the form. The exercises at the end of the chapter ask you to explore the effect of some other nonlinear operations on form.

When we want to describe a variable, offering a measure of the center, of the spread, and of the form is both necessary and sufficient. That is, a complete description of a data set must address all three elements. In practice, though, only the first two are regularly found in the research literature. The usual practice in reporting results is to describe form only if it is other than symmetric and bell-shaped (that is, other than normal).

Summary

- *Describing a set of data numerically involves a measure of the center, a measure of the spread, and usually a measure (or verbal description) of the form of the distribution.*
- *"Averages" summarize the data by providing a "typical" or "representative" score.*
- *The* mode *is the most frequently occurring score or the midpoint of the most frequently occurring interval.*
- *The* median *is in the center of the data in the sense that it is larger than half of the scores and smaller than half.*
- *The* arithmetic mean *is in the center in the sense that the sum of the squares of the differences between the scores and their mean is a minimum.*

- *The median is the 50th percentile.*
- *The arithmetic mean is the sum of all the scores divided by the number of scores in the data.*
- *Adding or subtracting a constant from the data, or multiplying or dividing by a constant, does the same operation to all the measures of center.*
- *The median is the most appropriate measure of the center when ordinal data are used or when the distribution is skewed.*
- *The arithmetic mean is meaningful only when used with data measured on interval or ratio scales.*
- *Measures of spread describe the extent to which the data values vary among themselves.*
- *Variability in data can come from measurement error, extraneous variables, individual differences, and from independent variables in an experiment.*
- *The range is the difference between the smallest and largest values in the data.*
- *The interquartile range is the difference between the first and third quartiles; it gives the "distance" across the middle 50% of the data.*
- *The semi-interquartile range is one-half of the interquartile range.*
- *The median absolute difference is the median of the absolute values of the differences between scores and their median.*
- *The variance is the mean of the squared differences between scores and their arithmetic mean.*
- *The standard deviation is the square root of the variance; it is convenient to think of it as an "average" difference between scores and their mean.*
- *Measures of center and spread are often presented together—mean with the standard deviation, median with the median absolute deviation, and mode with the range.*
- *Adding or subtracting a constant does not change the spread of the data.*
- *Multiplying or dividing changes the measures of spread.*
- *A distribution with a long tail to the left is* negatively skewed; *one with a long tail to the right is* positively skewed.
- *Linear transformations do not change the form of the frequency distribution, but nonlinear transformations may.*

Key Terms

ARITHMETIC MEAN	MEASURE OF CENTER
AVERAGE	MEASURE OF SPREAD
BOX PLOT	MEDIAN
INTERQUARTILE RANGE	MEDIAN ABSOLUTE DEVIATION
LEAST-SQUARES BEST-FIT	MODE

NEGATIVELY SKEWED
PEARSON COEFFICIENT OF SKEW
POSITIVELY SKEWED
RANGE

SEMI-INTERQUARTILE RANGE
SKEW
STANDARD DEVIATION
VARIANCE

 # EXERCISES

1. Return to the class examination scores in exercise 2.1. Find the mean, median, Pearson skewness, sample variance, and sample standard deviation. Write a short paragraph summarizing the class's performance. (*Hint*: Remember that to describe data, you have to address three aspects of the distribution: form, center, and spread.)

2. Return to exercise 2.2 and use the EPIE introversion/extroversion data from the beginning of Chapter 2. Recall that a question that these data might address is whether or not people fall into two distinct groups along an introversion/extroversion scale. Using the mean, median, variance, and standard deviation, along with the frequency distribution, write a paragraph that reports those statistics and also deals with the question of two groups of people.

3. Find the mean, median, range, interquartile range, Pearson skewness, and standard deviation for the reaction time data in exercise 2.3. Obtain the frequency distribution for the data. Write a paragraph that describes the data.

4. Using the data from exercise 2.4, find the mean, median, standard deviation, and interquartile range for both the Children's and the College Student's data. Describe in words what the differences between the groups seem to be.

5. Following are the data for three groups of students on the Barrett Impulsivity Scale. Find the mean, median, range, interquartile range, median absolute deviation, variance, and standard deviation for each of the three groups. Present the results in a table.

GROUP A	GROUP B	GROUP C
36	46	42
42	49	61
37	52	40
89	60	34
41	43	76
48	44	65
42	50	59
51	48	82
45	55	37
39	59	49
41	47	54
44	53	45

6. Here are the results of a study on learning; the data are the number of errors made on each of six trials. For each trial, find the mean, median, variance, standard deviation, and interquartile range. Present the statistics in a table.

TRIAL

1	2	3	4	5	6
36	21	17	1	2	0
35	1	10	13	0	5
4	23	21	10	5	3
35	5	26	11	3	7
25	5	18	15	4	3
33	2	5	5	5	4
29	22	13	7	0	2
31	11	24	2	4	1
49	14	13	6	6	2
19	36	11	6	1	8
11	26	9	4	5	3
27	27	18	0	4	3

28	25	1	7	7	4
8	13	0	4	7	4
27	17	20	1	2	6
13	4	12	6	6	5
36	26	19	10	7	4
19	14	0	10	2	4
24	14	5	13	0	1
40	11	10	3	2	2
19	18	2	7	1	3
43	16	12	9	4	3

7. The following data give the scores earned by a class of students on four weekly exercise sets. For each exercise set, find the mean, median, sample variance, sample standard deviation, and interquartile range. Present the statistics in a table.

WEEK

1	2	3	4
78	15	54	32
44	42	55	40
20	21	41	23
13	19	49	24
17	19	55	37
36	29	46	35
63	21	58	42
14	31	59	57
70	19	48	48
67	12	48	42
22	19	52	15
71	23	59	62
45	9	50	21
56	24	60	59
49	32	52	56
43	30	57	59
44	36	48	50
19	28	50	14
31	18	45	72
30	21	60	51
65	26	52	46
56	19	49	42
38	37	42	61
44	27	59	48
50	45	43	51
65	20	54	56
39	29	66	38

8. Using the data from exercise 3.5, present the box plots for the three groups of data.

9. Present the data from exercise 3.5 as a plot of the group means with standard deviation bars.

10. Present the medians and interquartile ranges from exercise 3.6 in a box plot.

11. Using the data from exercise 3.7, present the medians and interquartile ranges in a box plot.

12. Using these data, complete the questions that follow:

8	8	8	8	8
9	9	9	10	10
7	7	7	7	8
1	2	3	4	5
5	5	6	6	6
8	8	8	8	8
9	9			

a. Get some descriptive statistics (mean, median, and standard deviation, at least), including the Pearson skewness statistic.

b. Transform the data by changing the signs (that is, multiply each value by -1.0) and get the same measures as in part a. What do you conclude?

c. Transform each value in the original data again, replacing each number by its reciprocal (that is, replace each value by the value of 1/the number). What happens to the skewness measure?

d. Sketch the frequency (as a histogram or a frequency polygon) for the original and each transformed set of data.

13. The following set of data represent reaction times (in seconds), a frequent measure in some fields of psychology. Reaction times are typically positively skewed, and these are no exception.

0.293	0.391	0.195	0.195	0.195
0.293	0.586	0.684	0.586	0.684
0.195	0.195	0.195	0.293	0.195
0.195	0.293	0.391	0.488	0.488
0.391	0.293	0.391	0.488	0.586
0.488	0.391	0.293	0.879	0.782
0.195	0.195	0.097	0.097	0.195
0.293	0.293	0.195	0.195	0.195
0.195	0.097	0.097	0.097	0.097
0.097				

a. Plot the frequency distribution and compute the mean, median, standard deviation, median absolute deviation, and Pearson skewness for the data.

b. Transform the original data so that each number is replaced by its square root. What happens to the form of the distribution and to the skewness measure?

14. For each set of data given, sketch the frequency distribution and the stem-and-leaf diagram, and determine the mean and the median. For each, indicate which measure is probably the best to use, and why.

   a. 3, 4, 2, 1, 5, 2, 3, 4, 3

   b. 19, 8, 8, 8, 8, 5, 10, 14, 10, 6, 7, 2, 11, 9, 11, 14, 9, 12, 10, 9, 11, 7, 12, 7, 6

   c. 13, 3, 7, 3, 3, 3, 4, 5, 8, 4, 6, 7, 4, 5, 6, 10, 6, 4, 5, 4, 2, 5

15. Using the Yalch (1991) data (see exercise 2.13), find the mean, median, standard deviation, and Pearson skewness for Jingle and Nonjingle recall.

16. Use the Jandreau and Bever (1992) data from exercise 2.11.

   a. Find the mean and standard deviation for each of the three phrase spacings. Present the results as a table and as a plot with standard deviation bars.

   b. Find the median, median absolute deviation, and the range for each of the three phrase spacings. Present the results as a box plot.

17. Draw sketches of the distributions for the first chemistry exam (Figure 3.9a). Assume that the first and third quartiles are located at scores of 44 and 60, respectively. Indicate by shading on the sketch the region where the scores are

   a. in the bottom quarter

   b. in the top quarter

   c. in the upper 50%

   d. in the bottom 75%

   e. greater than 60

   f. less than 50

   g. between 52 and 57

   h. between 40 and 65

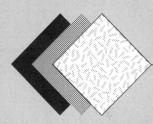

Computational Supplement

MEASURES OF CENTER

For most data sets, direct computation of the arithmetic mean from the raw data is probably best, unless there are a very large number of values. With very large data sets, it may be easier to construct a frequency distribution first, and then compute the mean by using the formula for grouped data:

$$\overline{X} = \frac{\sum fX}{N}$$

where f represents the frequency in an interval and X represents the midpoint of the interval; the summation is over the intervals.[7] For example, here is a distribution from Chapter 2:

INTERVAL MIDPOINT	FREQUENCY
2.5	1
4.5	1
6.5	2
8.5	5
10.5	12
12.5	12
14.5	26
16.5	14
18.5	6
20.5	4
22.5	1

Applying the formula, we have

$$\overline{X} = \frac{\sum fX}{N}$$

$$= \frac{(1)*2.5 + (1)*4.5 + (2)*6.5 + \cdots + (1)*22.5}{84}$$

$$= 13.83$$

[7] All grouped data formulas are actually approximations because the formula "assumes" that all values in a score interval fall exactly at the midpoint, which is highly unlikely. Whenever possible, computations should be done from raw data. Inexpensive pocket calculators offer some statistical functions and calculate from raw data; given care in entering the data, their results are preferable to those from grouped data formulas.

With either grouped or ungrouped data, the median is best calculated from a carefully drawn cumulative frequency plot. Although the result will be only approximately correct, working from the plot eliminates a major source of error and confusion: the presence of duplicate scores near the median. For grouped data, the median is found by drawing the plot *using the upper real limit* of each interval. Because there are 84 scores in the example data, the median will lie between the 42nd and the 43rd. Locate the median as shown by drawing a horizontal line from the point between 42 and 43 on the vertical until it intersects the cumulative curve. Now drop a vertical line to the abscissa, and read the median as approximately 14.3.

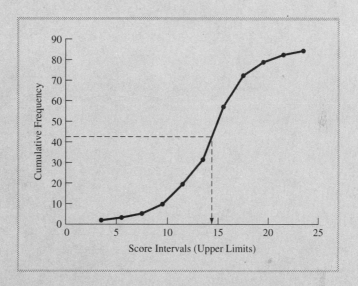

MEASURES OF SPREAD

Except for the variance and the standard deviation, all the computations were illustrated in the text. For the variance, the defining form in the text,

$$s^2 = \frac{\sum(X - \bar{X})^2}{N - 1}$$

can be replaced with a simpler computational formula:

$$s^2 = \frac{\sum X^2 - \frac{(\sum X)^2}{N}}{N - 1}$$

To illustrate the formula, here is the original computation, using the defining formula:

X	$X - \bar{X}$	$(X - \bar{X})^2$
5	-6.4	40.96
8	-3.4	11.56
13	1.6	2.56
14	2.6	6.76
17	5.6	31.36

$$93.20 = \sum (X - \bar{X})^2$$

$$s^2 = \frac{\sum (X - \bar{X})^2}{N - 1} = \frac{93.20}{5 - 1} = 23.3$$

Using the computational equivalent, we need not compute and subtract the mean, so we begin by finding the sum of the values and the sum of the squared values:

X	X^2
5	25
8	64
13	169
14	196
17	289
57	743
$= \sum X$	$= \sum X^2$

Completing the formula,

$$s^2 = \frac{\sum X^2 - \frac{(\sum X)^2}{N}}{N - 1}$$

$$= \frac{743 - \frac{(57)^2}{5}}{5 - 1}$$

$$= 23.3$$

which is the same value as obtained before.

The standard deviation, because it's just the square root of the variance, has the computational formula

$$s = \sqrt{\frac{\sum X^2 - \frac{(\sum X)^2}{N}}{N - 1}}$$

And, for the example,

$$s = \sqrt{23.3}$$

$$= 4.83$$

Calculators frequently offer statistical functions, including the variance and the standard deviation. Some even offer a choice of two formulas for the standard deviation and variance. One formula, as defined in the text, uses $N - 1$ as the divisor. It is normally what you get when you press a calculator key labeled s or s^2. The other form, sometimes called the "population" variance and standard deviation, is computed using N as a divisor; its buttons might be labeled σ or σ^2. You should know which formula your calculator is using. Here's an easy way to find out. Use the simple data set 2, 3, 4, and find the standard deviation using your calculator. If the answer is 0.82, the calculator uses the "N" form; if the answer is 1.00, then it uses the "$N - 1$" formula.

4 Standardized Variables and the Normal Distribution

STANDARDIZING
THE NORMAL DISTRIBUTION
    Using the Normal Distribution
SUMMARY
KEY TERMS
EXERCISES

Susan, a participant in a personality research project with 83 other students, completed both the Eysenck Personality Inventory Extroversion (EPIE) scale and a similar Introversion scale (EPII). She scored 15 on the EPIE and 7 on the EPII. The frequency distributions for 84 subjects on the two variables are presented as histograms in Figures 4.1 and 4.2; Susan's scores are indicated on each. On which scale is Susan more extreme relative to the other research subjects? The means for the two distributions are 13.82 for EPIE and 5.00 for EPII, with standard deviations of 3.60 and 1.56, respectively.

To find which of Susan's scores is more extreme, we need to compare her 7 on the EPII scale with the 15 on the EPIE scale. The measurement scales are quite different and certainly can't be compared directly. From looking at the histograms, we can see that Susan is above the mean for each variable; beyond that, we cannot be more precise.

In Chapter 2 we described how percentile ranks may be used to make comparisons between relative positions in two or more sets of data. Percentile ranks use order information within the data to describe positions. The percentile rank gives the percentage of the distribution below a particular score, without regard to the actual values in the data. Thus, using percentile ranks, we can compare positions in data sets that have different forms, centers, or spreads.

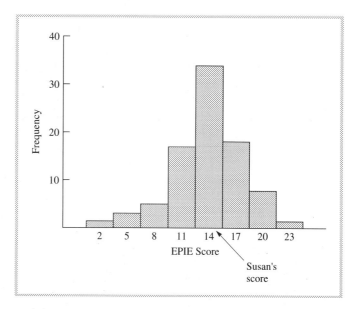

Figure 4.1

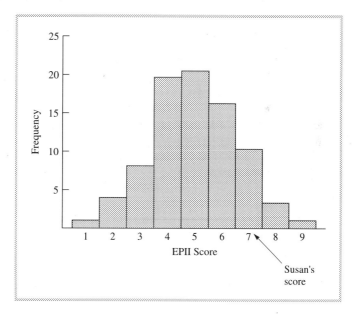

Figure 4.2

Finding percentile ranks is an example of a frequent operation in statistics called a **transformation**. In a transformation, data values are changed by doing some arithmetic operation on them. In Chapter 3 we applied several transformations to values to illustrate that some operations change center or spread, and some do not. Here, we discuss transformations as a means of making comparisons easier. In finding percentile ranks, we transform each score from its raw value into a number that shows the percentage of the data values that fall below it. For example, the distribution of the EPII scores might be summarized as shown in Table 4.1. The percentile rank for each score interval is shown in the table. For Susan's scores, her score of 7 on the EPII equals or exceeds 80 of the 84 scores of the people who completed the personality test, for a percentile rank of about 95. Following a similar computation (not illustrated, but you'll find it in an exercise), her score of 15 on the EPIE exceeds or equals 59 out of the 84 scores, giving her a percentile rank of approximately 70. We can now conclude that Susan is more extreme on the EPII scale, with a percentile rank of 95, than she is on the EPIE, where her percentile rank is 70.

The transformation of scores or score intervals uses only the ordinal position of values within the data set. Thus, it's appropriate for ordinal, interval, and ratio measurements. Notice that finding Susan's percentile ranks uses only a part of the information available in the data. And finding these percentile ranks does not tell us, for example, whether her score on either variable is close to—or far away from—many of the other students' scores. There is no way to show any distance information, and no use at all was made of information about either the center or the spread of the data. All we know is that Susan exceeded a certain percentage of the distribution.

In addition to using the percentile rank transformation, we can use the center and distance information to construct another data transformation that offers a more precise way of comparing scores in different distributions.

TABLE 4.1

EPII Score	Frequency	Cumulative Frequency	Percentile Rank Corresponding to Upper Limit
1	1	1	1.19
2	4	5	5.95
3	8	13	15.48
4	18	31	36.90
5	22	53	63.10
6	17	70	83.33
7	10	80	95.24
8	3	83	98.81
9	1	84	100.00

STANDARDIZING

Suppose we define the transformation operation $X - \overline{X}$. The operation is equivalent to subtracting a constant from every data value, but the constant is the mean. Using the EPII data in Table 4.1, we find that this transformation results in the values in Table 4.2. Now we have a new set of values, each indicating how far the original score is from the mean. Note that the "how far" understanding is in terms of the original measurement values; Susan's score of 7 is 2.0 points above the mean.

The $(X - \overline{X})$ transformation has another feature besides changing the scores to deviations from the mean. Subtracting a constant $(\overline{X}$, in this case) from a set of data subtracts the same constant from each measure of center. In this case, the mean of the transformed data becomes $\overline{X} - \overline{X} = 0.00$. The spread, as measured by the standard deviation, does not change with this additive transformation. Thus, we have the mean and standard deviation of the new variable $X - \overline{X}$, with the values shown at the bottom of the first two columns of Table 4.2.

As the final step in the transformation, divide the $(X - \overline{X})$ scores by their standard deviation. Consider the consequences of that operation. If a score is, for example, exactly 1 standard deviation below the mean in the original data, its transformed score will be -1.0. A score located 1.5 standard deviations above the mean becomes a value of 1.5. In other words, the unit of measurement on the transformed variable becomes the standard deviation, instead of the original score scale. Thus, Susan's score of 7 becomes 0.73; that is, 0.73 standard deviation above the mean of the data.

Putting it all together, we accomplish the transformation by taking the previous transformation $(X - \overline{X})$ and dividing by the standard deviation, using the formula

TABLE 4.2			
EPII Score *(from Table 4.1)*	*Frequency* *(from Table 4.1)*	$X - \overline{X}$	z
1	1	-4	-2.56
2	4	-3	-1.92
3	8	-2	-1.28
4	18	-1	-0.64
5	22	0	0.00
6	17	1	0.64
7	10	2	1.28
8	3	3	1.92
9	1	4	2.56
Mean	5.00		0.00	0.00
Standard deviation	1.56		1.56	1.00

$$z = \frac{X - \overline{X}}{s}$$

The new variable is called z. The z variable, always defined as the original data minus the mean and divided by the standard deviation, is called a **standardized variable** or **z score**. For the example data, $s = 1.56$, and the results of the standardizing transformation for the example data are in the third column of Table 4.2.

Standardizing is a linear transformation of the original data—that is, it relies only on addition/subtraction and multiplication/division. It preserves the distance information in the original data, and thus preserves the meaning in interval and ratio data. In addition, a standardized variable has three important characteristics. First, its mean is always zero. This is so because we subtract $\overline{X}$ from each value; adding or subtracting a constant to each value adds or subtracts the constant from the mean. The mean of the original data was $\overline{X}$, and so the mean of the transformed variable is $\overline{X} - \overline{X} = 0.00$.

Second, the standard deviation of a standardized variable is always 1.0 (and so is the variance because the variance is s^2, and $1.0^2 = 1.0$). This property of standardized scores derives from the operation of multiplying a variable by a constant. Multiplying or dividing by a constant multiplies or divides the standard deviation by the same constant. Thus, because the standard deviation of the unstandardized variable is s, the standard deviation of the variable divided by s will be $s/s = 1.0$. The mean and the standard deviation of the z scores appear in Table 4.2.

The third important property of standardized variables also follows from the effects of linear transformation. A linear transformation does not change the form of the distribution, so the form of a z distribution is unchanged from the form of the original data.

We may summarize the z score, or standardizing, transformation by noting that

$$\overline{z} = 0.0$$

$$s_z = 1.0$$

The form of z is unchanged from the original.

Let's illustrate the use of standardizing by finding the z score for Susan's score of 15 on the EPIE. Because the mean and standard deviation for the EPIE data are 13.82 and 3.60, respectively, the computation is

$$z = \frac{X - \overline{X}}{s}$$

$$= \frac{15.00 - 13.82}{3.60}$$

$$= 0.33$$

meaning that Susan's score of 15 is 0.33 standard deviation above the mean of all the subjects in the research. Her 7 on the EPII scale (see Table 4.2) is 0.73 standard deviation above the mean of that variable. From this we may conclude that Susan scored higher on the EPII scale, because her z score is higher (0.73 standard deviation above the mean, as compared with 0.33 for the EPII).

It's helpful to visualize the standardizing transformation as putting a new measurement scale under the data. The new scale is a linear transformation of the original scale, so the relationships between values are preserved. The original scores are standardized, meaning they are measured in standard deviation units. For the EPII scores, the original and the standardized scales, with Susan's score indicated, appear in Figure 4.3. In this representation, the two means (5.00 and 0.00) are aligned vertically. Looking at the frequency distribution in this way, it's clear that the form of the frequency distribution remains the same, and that the distance information among the data is preserved.

Again, note that standardizing changed only the scale; the form of the distribution remains as it was at the beginning. We made this point earlier, but it is worth repeating here because, as we move into the next section, it's easy to lose track of this rule. When we standardize any variable, the form is unchanged; if the data are skewed, standardizing won't change that fact. However, if the distribution was unimodal and symmetric before standardizing, those properties will remain after standardizing. It's important to remember these facts about form when we consider the normal distribution. Because we don't change the form, standardizing won't produce a normal distribution if it wasn't there to begin with. Some nonlinear transformations

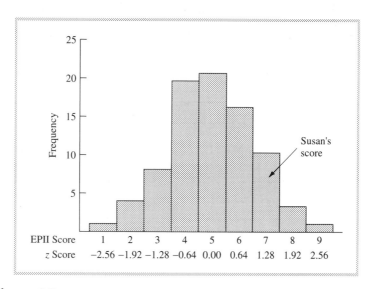

Figure 4.3

can make skewed distributions appear more symmetric because they do change the form. But standardizing alone does not.

COMPARING z SCORES AND PERCENTILE RANKS

Percentile ranks and z scores both may be used to compare the relative position of an individual within a group. How should we decide which to use? There are two major considerations: level of measurement and the audience with whom you want to communicate.

Percentile ranks deal only with the ordinal position. Transforming data to percentile ranks is an operation that relies only on position, and is thus meaningful with ordinal, interval, or ratio measurements. Standardizing is a linear transformation that relies on differences between pairs of values for both its numerator and its denominator. The numerator of the z score formula gives the difference between a score and the mean; the denominator is the standard deviation, which is based on the differences between the data values and their mean. Thus, standardizing is appropriate and meaning-preserving for interval and ratio data, but not for ordinal.

Beyond measurement level, there's another consideration in choosing a statistic that compares the position of an individual across variables: the audience for the data. Percentile ranks are relatively unsophisticated measures that don't take any of the data's distance information into account. But they describe an individual's position in the data by the percent of scores exceeded, and a lay audience can understand that easily.

However, z scores are confusing to people who are unfamiliar with their use. In scientific writing, standardized scores should be no problem, and they have some desirable properties. But try explaining to an irate parent why little Johnny received a negative score on a test!

Standardizing is a fundamental operation in statistics. It is a way of comparing "apples" with "oranges," because you can convert data from two different variables to a standardized common scale. Once they are both on the same numerical scale, comparisons are simplified.

THE NORMAL DISTRIBUTION

In Chapter 3 we used an example of a chemistry class taking an examination. There we argued that a number of factors could lead to variation in the scores, even if everyone in the class had the same "true" knowledge of the subject matter. The scores will tend to cluster around some central value, which is our best guess as to how much the class as a whole "knows" about chemistry. Measures of center are intended to help us locate that central value by summarizing the data with a single value. But it's unrealistic to expect that all the scores in the class would be equal, even if chemistry knowledge were, in fact, identical for all students. The data will contain variability, and we can use a spread statistic to measure that variability. In addition, the scores will form a distribution, and we can describe its form, just as we can describe its center and its spread.

To take another example, suppose you gave one of the personality scales, the Eysenck Personality Index Introversion scale (EPII), for example, to a single individual. Give it again. And again. And again. And again and again, a very large number of times. Now let's make some silly and wildly unrealistic assumptions: Throughout the testing, the individual will not remember taking the test before, will not change in his or her amount of introversion/extroversion, and will not get tired. Finally, assume that all testing conditions remain constant through the testing period. What we will be obtaining is a very large number of EPII scores, all from the same individual, all under identical conditions. Would you expect all of the scores to be equal? No, probably not. Chapter 3 discussed some of the reasons— random error, individual fluctuations in attention, and so forth. There we pointed out that, over a long series of measurements, the random errors might be expected to cancel themselves out (assuming that the test is reliable, of course).

In looking at the distribution of EPII scores, we should find that the scores cluster around some central value, which we might approximate by using the mean or the median. As with trying to estimate how much chemistry knowledge a class has, that center statistic is our best estimate of the individual's "true" score on the EPII scale. All the variation is merely error in measurement.

Distributions of scores in psychological research, whether from a single individual or from a group of individuals, always show variation around a central value. The variation comes from many sources, which are largely independent of each other, and sum to produce an effect on a single individual taking a single test at a single time. For a large number of variables that psychologists normally use in their research, that variation often leads to a distribution with a distinctive form: symmetrical, unimodal, and bell-shaped. And not just any symmetrical, unimodal, and bell-shaped form, but a very specific one known as the **normal distribution**. In fact, many of the variables that psychologists measure follow a normal distribution shape. This fact has led to the development of a number of inferential statistics based on the normal distribution. In addition, a large part of the theory of measurement that underlies most psychological research assumes that a normal distribution is present.

The theory of measurement assumes that the score (like one from the EPII, for example) that we observe is actually a combination of two components: the "true" value and error. We can never "see" the true value (Can you open someone's skull and "see" the amount of introversion inside there? Of course not!), and so the best we can do is to take measurements and assume (hope?) that over repeated measurement, errors will cancel themselves out.

Most of the time, the error part of a measurement may conveniently be assumed to be normally distributed with a mean of 0.00. And, because the mean is the center of the distribution of error, with one side of the distribution exactly balancing the other, error is self-canceling given a large number of measurements. In other words, on the average, the error component will equal zero so that, over a series of measurements, the true value is undistorted by error. In measuring introversion/extroversion with a test like the EPII, then, the observed score from one subject consists of both a "true" representation of the underlying trait of introversion/extroversion, plus measurement error. We can never know the true value, because any individual score may be either too high or too low as a function of measurement error. But if we look at a number of observations, their *mean* can conveniently be taken as an indication of the true value because the errors are expected to average to 0.00.

As a consequence of the error component being normally distributed, the form of the measurement should also be normal. And in fact, a very large number of variables that psychologists use do appear to follow the normal distribution, which makes it an important distribution to understand. In addition, because so many variables are normally distributed, statisticians have devoted a great deal of attention to the distribution and its properties, leading to many useful statistical procedures.

Having said that the normal distribution is important because many variables appear to be normally distributed, we hasten to add that many are not. Psychologists often use reaction time as a dependent variable; reaction times are almost invariably highly positively skewed. The proportion of words recalled from a list of a fixed number of words is also a frequently used variable with a non-normal distribution. In addition, the normal distribution is really a continuous distribution, meaning that variables with only discrete values aren't really appropriate. This is usually not a serious problem because we often can assume that it is our measurement that limits the precision of the data. But more important, we do need to assume interval or ratio measurement in order to employ the normal distribution.

There is a second reason why the normal distribution is important. This is because the possible values of the sample means follow the normal form. To anticipate a point that we will develop in detail in Chapter 7, imagine taking samples of student grade point averages from among all the students at your college or university. The grade points for all the students in the institution constitute a population, and the mean of all the scores is a parameter. Now imagine taking a sample of ten student grade averages and finding the mean of those ten scores. And imagine doing that again and again and again, each time recording the mean of the sample of ten scores. If you took a very large number of samples, and found the mean of each sample, you would find that the means vary among themselves. That is, not all the samples would have the same mean, despite the fact that each sample came from the same population. If you constructed a frequency distribution for all the sample means, you would find that the distribution's form was unimodal, symmetric, and bell-shaped—the normal distribution. The fact that the distribution of means is normal provides the basis for a large group of inferential procedures that we consider in later chapters. For now, though, we explore the normal distribution and learn how to find and use proportions and areas of it.

What is wrong with assuming that a variable is normally distributed when it is not? At the descriptive level, such an assumption has little effect. Descriptive statistics are just that—they describe. The various statistics of center, spread, and form are all descriptive, and, in using them, departures from normality are not serious. When we turn to making inferences in Chapter 8, though, matters get more complicated. There we'll distinguish between inference methods that require that a distribution be normal and those that do not. By and large, the normal distribution–based methods are more powerful (roughly speaking, they have the best chance of drawing a correct inference). Applying a normal-based statistic where the distribution is non-normal, though, may result in an incorrect inference, while using a non-normal statistic would have come to the correct conclusion.

◆ Using the Normal Distribution

The normal distribution is actually a set of distributions that differ from each other in two values, a mean and a variance. Whatever the two values, the distributions will have the same form but somewhat different appearances. For example, Figure 4.4 shows four curves that differ only in s^2 but not in $\overline{X}$. Curves also may be located at different points, depending on their center. Figure 4.5 illustrates three normal curves with the same variance that differ only in $\overline{X}$.

There are an infinite number of normal curves, one for each possible pair of values for $\overline{X}$ and s^2. For now, though, we will worry about only a specific normal distribution, the standardized one.

Because we know it's possible to compare distributions with different means and standard deviations by using standardized scores, the fact that there are many normal distributions is not too important. We can make them all "look alike" by standardizing. An important advantage of standardizing, as we'll see, is that some very tedious computations can be

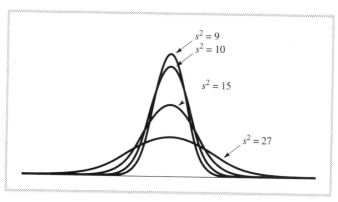

Figure 4.4

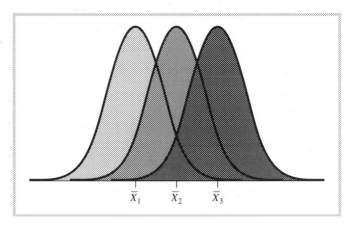

$\overline{X}_1$ $\overline{X}_2$ $\overline{X}_3$

Figure 4.5

avoided, simply by referring to a table that contains important values of a standardized normal distribution. Without the standardizing operation, we would be forced to invoke integral calculus to compute values; mercifully, we can avoid that!

Areas in a frequency polygon or histogram often are used to represent the number of observations, or the proportion of the observations, in that area. For example, Figure 4.6 shows the EPII data from Figure 4.2, with the darker rectangles representing the individuals who scored 6 or 7 on the scale.

Similarly, areas under the normal curve can represent proportions of data in regions of the distribution. For example, the proportion of observations in a normal distribution between 1 and 2 standard deviations above the mean is illustrated in Figure 4.7. Likewise, the proportion between $z = -1.0$ and $z = 1.0$—that is, within a standard deviation either side of the mean—appears in Figure 4.8. The entire number of individuals who took the EPII test is represented by the total area of all the rectangles in the histogram (see Figure 4.6). Likewise, the entire area under the normal curve —theoretically from $-\infty$ to $+\infty$, where $\pm\infty$ are the largest possible negative and positive numbers—is taken as 100%, or the proportion 1.00.

To compute areas under a curve such as the normal, the method of integration from calculus must be applied. Fortunately for us, all the integral computations have been done already and are summarized in tables of the normal curve like the one in Appendix A.

Because any distribution may be standardized to have $\overline{X} = 0$ and $s = 1$, we may present just one table of the areas under the normal curve; we can refer to it to find areas under *any* normal curve, providing we have standardized it first. Appendix A presents areas under a standardized normal distribution, and we won't have to compute a single integral. The ability to standardize, then, lets us use a single table of normal distribution values. If we

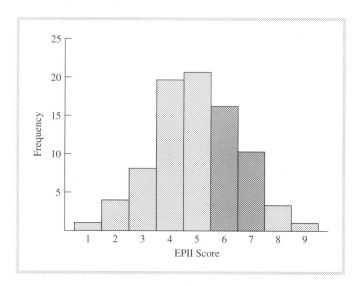

Figure 4.6

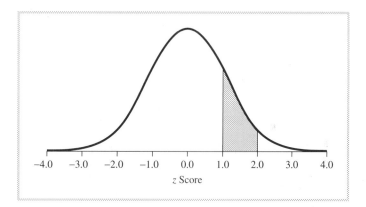

Figure 4.7

couldn't standardize, then we really would have to compute the integral any time we wanted a normal curve area.

To see how to use the table, let's take a few examples. A glance at Appendix A shows that the table is arranged in three columns. The first column lists values of z, beginning with 0.00 and continuing upward in steps of 0.01. The next two columns give, for each value of z, the proportion of the area under the curve between 0.00 and z, or beyond z, as illustrated by the column headings.

Reading down the z column to the value 0.40, for example, you will learn that between the z values of 0.00 and 0.40, there is 0.1554. Therefore, 0.1554, or 15.54%, of the area under the curve lies between a z value of 0.00

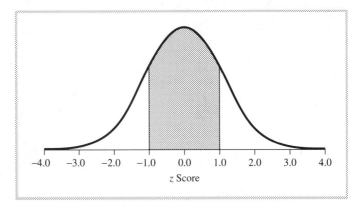

Figure 4.8

and a *z* value of 0.40. The third column gives the proportion of the area that is beyond 0.40—namely, 0.3446 (or 34.46%). Graphically, these areas are illustrated in Figure 4.9.

The normal curve is symmetrical, and so the left-hand side is just like the right; the proportions between 0.00 and −0.40, and the proportion below −0.40 are illustrated in Figure 4.10.

Let's use the standardized normal distribution to find proportions of IQ scores that fall into particular ranges. IQ scores are often regarded as normally distributed, with a mean of 100 and a standard deviation of 15. What proportion of IQ scores are greater than 125? In the distribution of IQ scores, the proportion we want is shown in Figure 4.11.

To use Appendix A, first convert from the IQ scale to the *z* scale. Using the standardizing formula, and the values of 100 and 15 for the mean and standard deviation, we find that

$$z = \frac{X - \overline{X}}{s}$$

$$= \frac{125 - 100}{15}$$

$$= 1.67$$

The distribution, with its original and standardized scales, is shown in Figure 4.11.

In Appendix A, we find that the area under the curve beyond $z = 1.67$ is 0.0475. Thus, 4.75% of the scores in an IQ distribution are beyond 125. In a group of 100 people, than, we should expect to find about five people with IQs of greater than 125. Or, expressing it differently, if we were to randomly select a person and administer an IQ test to him or her, the chances are about 5 out of 100 that the person would have an IQ greater than 125.

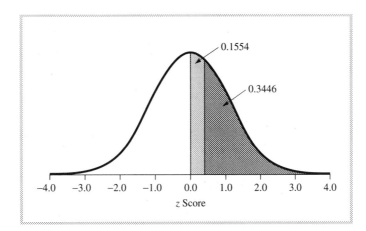

Figure 4.9

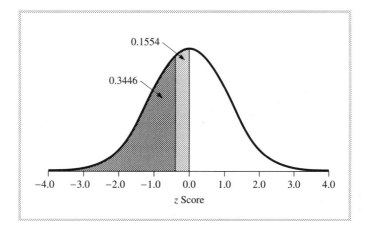

Figure 4.10

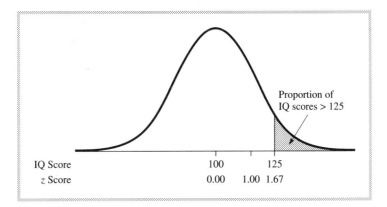

Figure 4.11

What proportion of IQ scores lies between 113 and 123? This is a little more difficult to answer, but if we approach the problem graphically, we can see that we need the area pictured in Figure 4.12. To find the area, we need to find two proportions—that between 100 and 113 and that between 100 and 123. The difference between them will be the region that we need, as illustrated in Figure 4.13. The shaded regions together represent the area between 100 and 123; the darker region represents the area between 100 and 113. The difference between the two—the lighter gray area—is what we need to find.

Computing the z values, we find that

$$z = \frac{X - \overline{X}}{s}$$

$$= \frac{113 - 100}{15}$$

$$= 0.87$$

and

$$z = \frac{X - \overline{X}}{s}$$

$$= \frac{123 - 100}{15}$$

$$= 1.53$$

In Appendix A, we find that the proportions corresponding to the two z scores are 0.43700 for $z = 1.53$, and 0.30786 for $z = 0.87$. The first value corresponds to the total shaded area in Figure 4.13, and the second to the

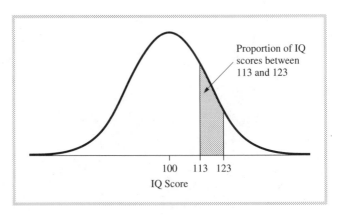

Figure 4.12

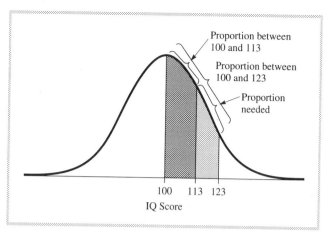

Figure 4.13

darker area only. The difference—the light gray area only—is 0.43700 − 0.30786 = 0.12914, the proportion of IQ scores between 113 and 123.

As another example, what proportion of scores falls within 15 IQ points of the mean of 100? That is, what is the area shown in Figure 4.14? Because the standard deviation of 15 corresponds to ±1.0 on the z scale, we don't even need to compute anything. Proceeding directly to Appendix A, we find that the region between z = 0.0 and z = 1.0 is 0.3413. And because the region between 0 and −1.0 is also 0.3413, the area that we need is then the sum of the two regions, as pictured in Figure 4.15. The proportion of IQ scores between 85 and 115 is thus 0.3413 + 0.3413 = 0.6826. Roughly, then, in any normal distribution, approximately 68% of the data lies within a standard deviation in each direction of the mean.

Next, let's ask what proportion of IQ scores is in the region that is usually classified as "exceptional"—that is, more than 2 standard deviations from the mean in either direction. Graphically, the areas are as shown in Figure 4.16. Because "exceptional" can be either high or low IQ, the regions of interest are in the two tails of the curve. We don't need to calculate z scores; we know we're asking about the ±2.0 points because we defined "exceptional" as 2 or more standard deviations from the mean. So we can proceed directly to Appendix A to find the proportions under the curve more extreme than ±2.00. This time, we look at the third column, because the region that we want is that beyond 2.0.

From the table we learn that 0.0228 of the curve is beyond 2.0. Because we have two tails of interest, the total area is 0.0228 + 0.0228 = 0.0456; just a little under 5% of the IQ distribution is in the exceptional tails.

In Figure 4.16, we point out that 0.0456 is beyond 2 standard deviations from the mean. Thus, 1.0 − 0.0456 = 0.9544 is within 2 standard deviations of the mean. If we want to know the area within 3.0 standard deviations of the mean, Appendix A tells us that 0.9973 (computed as 0.49865 + 0.49865,

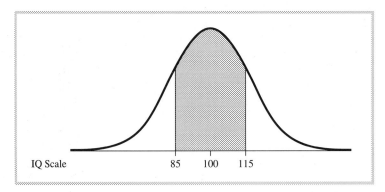

Figure 4.14

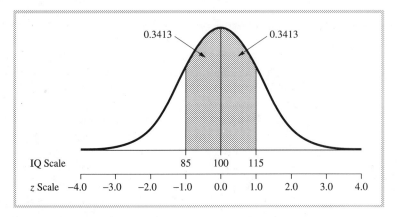

Figure 4.15

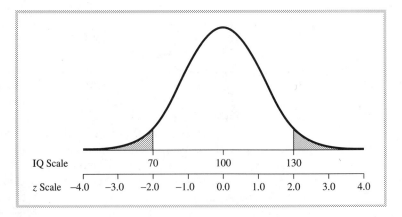

Figure 4.16

the values obtained from the table) lies within 3 standard deviations of the mean. Summarizing, we have the fact that, in a normal distribution, about 68% lies within 1 standard deviation of the center, about 95% with 2 standard deviations, and about 99.7% within 3, as illustrated in Figure 4.17.

Finally, let's take a value just a little under 2.0 and find the area under the curve beyond ±1.96. Figure 4.18 shows the region; it's just slightly larger than that in Figure 4.16. From Appendix A, we learn that 0.025 of the distribution exceeds ±1.96; thus, 5% of a normal distribution exceeds 1.96 standard deviations.

PERCENTILES IN THE NORMAL DISTRIBUTION

With a table of proportions of areas under the normal curve available, it's easy to locate percentile points in the normal distribution. For example, the 25th percentile, that point that exceeds 25% of the distribution, is located

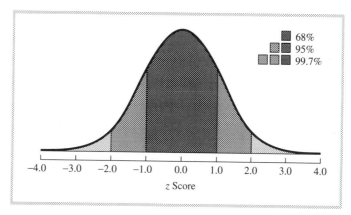

Figure 4.17

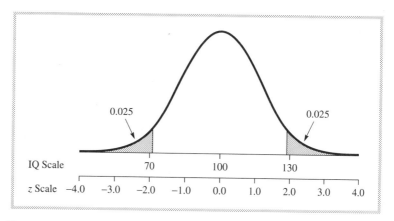

Figure 4.18

along the z scale at the point where the proportion to the left is 0.25, which is shown in Figure 4.19 to be -0.67. Applying the same logic, we find that the z value corresponding to the 10th percentile is -1.280, that for the 20th percentile is -0.840, and so forth, as shown in Figure 4.20. In this figure, each vertical bar under the frequency distribution represents an equal amount of the area, specifically 10% of the total curve.

Finding the percentile rank corresponding to a score in a normal distribution is a straightforward matter of finding the cumulative percentage of the distribution below the score. For example, in a normal distribution with a mean of 125 and a standard deviation of 19, the percentile rank of a score of 132 corresponds to the area below the score (Figure 4.21). To find the area, we first calculate the standardized score corresponding to 132 as

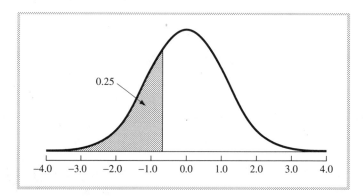

Figure 4.19

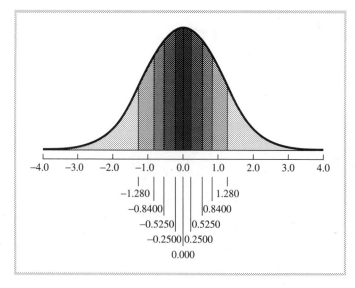

Figure 4.20

$$z = \frac{X - \overline{X}}{s}$$

$$= \frac{132 - 125}{19}$$

$$= 0.37$$

In Appendix A we find that the region between 0.00 and 0.37 is 0.1443. Adding the 0.1443 to the 0.5000 that represents the left half of the curve, we obtain a percentile rank of 64.43% for the score of 132, as illustrated in Figure 4.22.

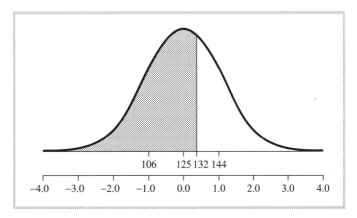

Figure 4.21

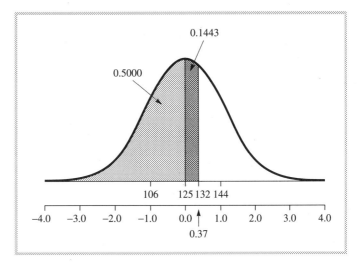

Figure 4.22

For one last example, let's find the percentile rank of the score of 111 in the same distribution. The area that we want is pictured in Figure 4.23.

Computing the z score corresponding to 111, we find

$$z = \frac{X - \overline{X}}{s}$$

$$= \frac{111 - 125}{19}$$

$$= -0.74$$

To find the area to the left of -0.74, we look in Appendix A for the value 0.74 and obtain the area of the curve that is more extreme. Because the curve

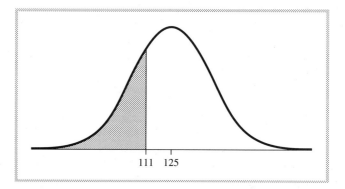

Figure 4.23

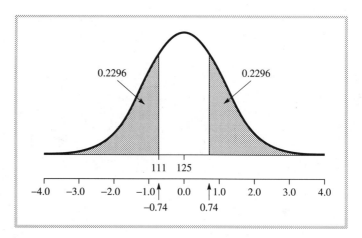

Figure 4.24

is symmetric, the answer is 0.2296, or a percentile rank of nearly 23 (see Figure 4.24).

Summary

♦ *Standardizing a variable uses the formula* $z = \dfrac{X - \bar{X}}{s}$.

♦ *A standardized variable has* $\bar{X} = 0.0$ *and* $s = 1.0$.

♦ *Standardizing puts variables on a common scale, facilitating comparisons across variables.*

♦ *Standardizing does not change the form of a distribution.*

♦ *Variables may also be compared using percentile ranks.*

♦ *In measurement, errors are commonly assumed to be normally distributed, with a mean of 0.00.*

♦ *Many, but by no means all, variables seem to be normally distributed.*

♦ *The distribution of large numbers of means from the same population is normal.*

♦ *Areas under a curve represent proportions of observations.*

♦ *The total area under a curve equals 1.00 or 100% of the observations.*

♦ *In any normal distribution, approximately 68% of the data lies within a standard deviation in each direction of the mean.*

♦ *A little less than 5% of a normal distribution lies beyond* ± 2.0 *standard deviations away from the mean.*

♦ *In a normal distribution, the 50th percentile occurs at a z value of 0.00.*

♦ *In a normal distribution, the 25th and the 75th percentiles occur at z values of* ± 0.67.

Key Terms

NORMAL DISTRIBUTION   TRANSFORMATION
STANDARDIZED VARIABLE   z SCORE

1. You scored 62 on each of two chemistry exams, and the class means for the tests were equal at 52.0. Calculate your z scores on the two exams, assuming that the standard deviations are 8.5 and 3.6, respectively. On which test did you perform better?

2. For the following set of data, compute the mean and the standard deviation, and then do the following operations:

4	6	2	8	7
8	9	8	7	6
5	6	6	5	5
1	4	5	6	9
3	3	4	9	8

   a. Find the z score for each raw data value.

   b. Check your z computations by verifying that the mean and the standard deviation of the z scores are indeed 0 and 1.

3. Use the data from exercise 3.12 for this problem. Apply one more transformation to those data: the z score. Compute all the same descriptive statistics as you did originally. What changes when you do the z score transformation? And what doesn't change?

4. Assume that the distributions for the two chemistry exams (both with means of 52) are normal in form. The standard deviations of the two exams, as given in exercise 4.1, are 8.5 and 3.6. What proportion of the scores on the first exam

   a. is greater than 60?

   b. is less than 50?

   c. is between 52 and 57?

   d. is between 40 and 65?

5. Using the second chemistry exam (mean = 52, standard deviation = 3.6), find the same proportions as in exercise 4.4.

6. Compute your percentile rank on each of the two chemistry exams (remember that you scored 62 on each).

7. A research worker wants to form two extreme groups of subjects with respect to the Barrett Impulsivity Scale (BIS). That is, he wants to

have two specific values for the BIS, so that if someone scores below the lower, that individual would be in the lowest 25% of scores; or if the individual scores above the higher point, then that score would be in the highest 25%. If we assume that BIS is normally distributed, with an overall mean of 50 and a standard deviation of 15, what should the two values be?

8. Using the Yalch (1991) data (see exercise 2.12), find the z scores corresponding to raw scores of 1, 3, and 4 using the Jingle recall data.

9. Repeat exercise 4.8 using the Nonjingle recall data.

10. Use the Jandreau and Bever (1992) data from exercise 2.11. Using the normal-spaced data, find the z scores corresponding to raw scores of 63, 79, 88, and 100.

11. Repeat exercise 4.10, but use the phrase-spaced data.

12. Assume that Jandreau and Bever's (1992) normal-spaced data represent a normal distribution. What proportion of the observations should be in each of the following regions of the distribution?

    a. < 60

    b. > 70

    c. between 66 and 81 inclusive

    d. between 51 and 65 inclusive

    e. > 81

    f. < 51

    g. < 37

    h. > 95

13. Return to Jandreau and Bever's (1992) data, and find what proportion of the observations *actually* occurred in each of the intervals in exercise 4.12.

14. Still using the Jandreau and Bever (1992) normal-spaced data, find the 35th, 60th, and 75th percentiles. Compare those values with the values you would expect with a normal distribution.

15. Use Jandreau and Bever's (1992) phrase-spaced data. Find the proportion of the observations that should be in each of the following regions of the distribution:

a. < 62

b. > 88

c. between 61 and 91

d. > 95

e. < 55

16. Still using the Jandreau and Bever phrase-spaced data, find what proportion of the observations *actually* occurred in each of the intervals in exercise 4.15.

5 Bivariate Descriptive Statistics

Suppose someone asked you to guess an individual's weight, but you were given no other information about the person. Your best strategy would be to guess what you know to be the mean weight of humans (around 150 pounds, for males and females together). [This is your best strategy because the mean, recall, minimizes the quantity $\sum (X - \overline{X})^2$.] This means that $\overline{X}$ is closest to the data points in terms of the squared differences between scores and their mean. But if you were to learn that the individual is a male and is 6'8" tall, you'd probably want to revise your estimate upward, because you know something about the relationship between sex and weight, and between height and weight. Height and weight are positively correlated; people who are score high on one variable (like height) also tend to be high on the other (weight). If you know that fact, you can probably do a better job of predicting one from the other. Your prediction won't be perfect, of course—we all know tall people who weigh less than some short people. But, on the average, we make better predictions if we can use relationship information. However, knowledge of height (or of sex, for that matter) probably wouldn't help you predict a person's grade point average at all because there's no correlation between height (or sex) and GPA.

Our task in this chapter is to develop ways of describing the relationship between two variables. Chapters 1 through 4 presented statistical and graphic ways to describe the center, spread, and form of individual variables. Here we take the next logical step and discuss techniques for showing and describing the relationship between two variables. Chapter 6 discusses how to use information about that relationship to make predictions about values of one variable based on values of the other.

Let's take a second example of data on two variables. When a personality researcher collects data, he or she measures several variables, all at roughly the same time. Each variable, of course, has its own center, spread, and form. But, in addition, each variable has a relationship with every other variable. Hewitt, Flett, and Blankstein (1991) gave several personality tests to groups of college students and to hospitalized psychiatric patients. Among the variables they examined were scales measuring the two personality traits of perfectionism and neuroticism. Because data were collected from the same people for each variable, each person has scores on both the neuroticism and the perfectionism scale. What we are concerned with in this chapter is not the mean, or the median, or the range, or the form of the perfectionism or the neuroticism data. Instead, our interest is in the relationship between the two personality variables.

In particular, we want to be able to ask questions like "Are individuals who score high on the perfectionism scale also likely to score high on the neuroticism scale? Are people who are low on one likely also to be low on the other?" Note that these questions are unrelated to questions about the centers, spreads, and forms of the two variables—they ask specifically about the *relationship*. A related question might be, "If we had someone's score on the perfectionism scale, could we make a prediction or 'educated guess' about his or her value on neuroticism? What confidence would we have in our estimate?" There are two kinds of questions about the *bivariate* (meaning, naturally, two-variable) relationship between the variables. The first question, that of the relationship between variables, is called *correlation*, and is discussed in this chapter. The second question, that of predicting one variable from another, is *regression*, and is presented in Chapter 6.

In our present discussion, we limit ourselves to two variables at a time. At the end of Chapter 6, though, we expand the discussion a little and introduce briefly the idea of multiple correlation and regression. These procedures expand our ability to deal with relationships among variables beyond the bivariate. Chapter 12 discusses multiple correlation and regression in some depth.

TABLE 5.1

Subject	Neuroticism	Perfectionism
1	37	57
2	52	57
3	21	61
4	65	56
5	52	51
6	58	37
7	29	28
8	8	48
9	9	64
10	35	57
11	92	67
12	43	61
13	32	34
14	56	57
15	78	45
16	23	37
17	70	80
18	87	65
19	21	54
20	30	54
21	21	36
22	41	63

REPRESENTING THE RELATIONSHIP GRAPHICALLY

As usual, the techniques for assessing relationship are influenced by the measurement characteristics of the data. When the data on both variables are measured on nominal (category) scales, none of the techniques in this chapter are appropriate. Chapter 11 is devoted entirely to category data, and relationship measures for those appear there. When the measurement is ordinal, interval, or ratio on at least one of the variables, both quantitative and graphic techniques are used; they are discussed here.

◆ Scatterplots

The basic graphic technique for showing the relationship between two interval or ratio variables is the **scatterplot**. A scatterplot illustrates the relationship by plotting the values of one variable against those of the other. Table 5.1 shows a set of data that might have come from the normal subjects in the Hewitt et al. (1991) study.[1]

[1] The data were simulated but show the relationship between variables that was found in the Hewitt et al. (1991) study.

We construct a scatterplot by selecting one variable to place along the vertical axis (neuroticism, for example). We locate the other variable (perfectionism) along the horizontal axis, and label the axes to show the values. Now each subject's pair of scores is plotted as a point on the figure, using the neuroticism value to locate the point vertically and the perfectionism to do so horizontally. For subject 1, for example, we place a point 37 units up and 57 units to the right. Figure 5.1 shows the first four points. We can't continue to show the subject's numbers because the plot would get very cluttered; we just let a single point represent each pair of values. The finished scatterplot for 22 subjects is in Figure 5.2.

When two or more subjects score the same on both variables, computer programs adopt various strategies. One approach is to ignore the duplication, and just use a single point regardless of the number of actual pairs of data values at that location. This is misleading because you can easily overlook the fact that a number of subjects may be located at the same place. Programs most often use a numeral to represent the number of values located there; some use special symbols to stand for the number of values.

◆ Interpreting Scatterplots

The scatterplot is useful in understanding a relationship. For example, in a plot with an up-and-to-the-right pattern, we can tell that high scores on one variable tend to be associated with high scores on the other. All the plots in Figure 5.3, for example, show this relationship to a greater or lesser degree. We say that plots showing this up-and-to-the-right orientation show a posi-

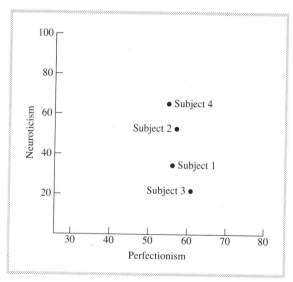

Figure 5.1

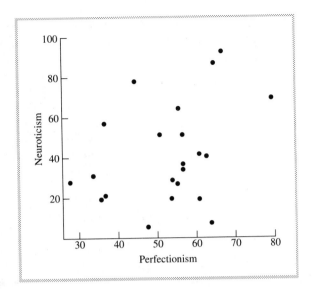

Figure 5.2

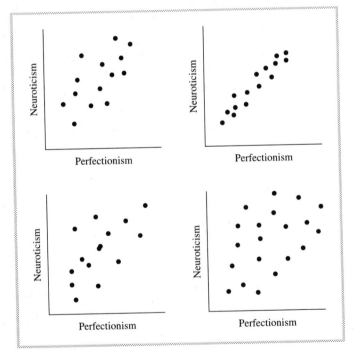

Figure 5.3

tive relationship, or **positive correlation**. In all these plots, individuals with higher neuroticism scores also tend to have higher perfectionism scores. Such people appear in the upper right-hand section of the scatterplots because that area represents the higher values on both variables. The converse is also true: The lower left-hand section of the plot contains those people who scored toward the low end for each variable.

The plots in Figure 5.4 show the opposite of a positive relationship—namely, a negative one, or **negative correlation**. In Figure 5.4, as one variable increases in value, the other decreases, and the pattern of the data points is down-and-to-the-right. Here, a low score on perfectionism, for example, tends to be related to a high score on neuroticism. Scores with that pattern fall in the upper left-hand segment of the plot; opposite scores (high perfectionism coupled with low neuroticism) appear in the lower right-hand segment.

The scatterplot can also tell us about the form of the relationship between the two variables. Variables are sometime related in a linear fashion (**linear relationship**), so the points are distributed more or less evenly about a straight line that you might draw, as in Figure 5.5a.

For some pairs of variables, though, there may be a **nonlinear relationship** —and the scatterplot is a very good, and very simple, way to find out if that is the case. Some variables may be related as illustrated in Figure 5.5b and 5.5c, where a straight line "fits" the data only at the two end points.

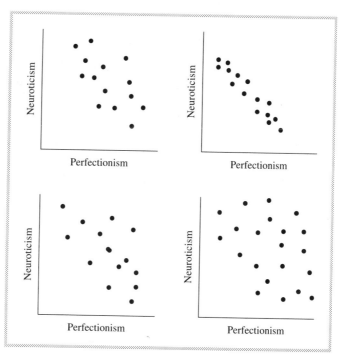

Figure 5.4

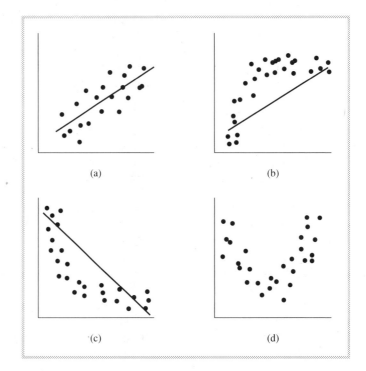

Figure 5.5

Plots like this often occur when one variable has a "ceiling" or a "floor," so that it's impossible to score more than, or less than, some value. For example, if one variable represents the points earned on a 100-point test, values can't exceed 100, and if a number of students were close to that value, a curvilinear relationship might be evident. The same pattern may also show up when one variable represents time. For example, if one variable were the number of items learned on a list and the other was the amount of time spent in study, you might find a relationship like that in Figure 5.5b. Other nonlinear relationships can take the form shown in Figure 5.5d. A plot of this kind can occur when one variable represents some form of "dosage." The classic example is what is called a dose–response curve. Suppose that the vertical axis in Figure 5.5d represented the time it takes an animal to run down a simple alley, and the horizontal the amount of a drug. In low doses, the drug has little effect on running time, but increasing the dosage leads to decreasing values of time; as the dosage continues to increase, however, the running time begins to increase again.

For linearly related variables, the tighter the cluster of the points around the line, the better the fit of the line. Consider the two plots presented in Figure 5.6. Certainly, the data in 5.6a represent a "stronger" relationship between the two variables than that in 5.6b, even though the line that comes the closest to the data points is the same in each plot.

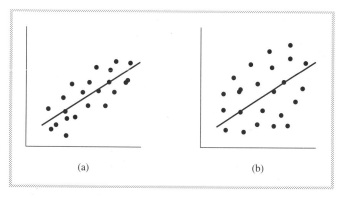

Figure 5.6

If we take the line through the data as a two-dimensional "center" through the scatterplot, then we can think of a "spread" around that "center." In Figure 5.6b, the points are more spread around their center than those in Figure 5.6a. Consider the three scatterplots in Figure 5.7, which illustrate the relationship between the Midterm and a Final exam for a class of students. In all three plots, the data may be approximated by roughly the same line, yet the scatter about the lines differs considerably. Suppose you were given some Midterm values and were asked to predict the corresponding Final exam scores for each by interpolating visually from the illustrations. In which plot—a, b, or c—would you feel the most comfortable? In (a), a low Midterm—for example, 10—is associated with a low range of Final grades, perhaps in the range of about 8 to 18 or so. In (c), however, the same Midterm scores are related to a much larger range of Final exam values, roughly from about 5 to 40. Plot b is intermediate between the two other plots; the lowest Midterm scores here are associated with a Final exam range of perhaps 5 to 25.

REPRESENTING THE RELATIONSHIP NUMERICALLY

There are several statistics for describing the relationship between two variables. These differ primarily in the assumptions they make regarding the measurement characteristics of the variables. This chapter presents statistics for describing the relationship between a nominal variable and an ordinal, interval, or ratio variable; between internal and ratio variables; and a relationship where one or both variables are ordinal. We defer the special case of two nominal variables until Chapter 11.

Measures of relationship are generically called **correlation coefficients**, and have several features in common. In particular, they all use the range 0.0 to 1.0 to describe the relationship between variables, where 0.0 indicates an

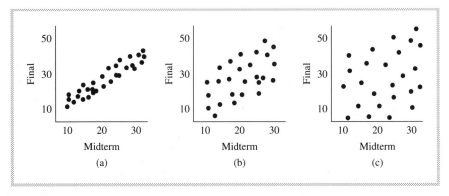

Figure 5.7

absence of relationship and 1.0 indicates an identity relationship. In addition, most correlation coefficients use the sign of the coefficient to indicate the "direction" of the relationship. As we noted earlier, a positive relationship means that high values of one variable go with high values of the other; a negative relationship means that high values of one go with low values of the other. In other words, correlation coefficients range in value between -1.0 and $+1.0$, with the sign indicating the direction and the magnitude of the statistic indicating the strength of the relationship.

◆ Interval and Ratio Data

The correlation coefficient appropriate for describing the relationship between interval and ratio data is an important statistic and we'll develop it carefully. It is closely related to the procedures for making linear predictions, and it also forms the basis for the multiple-variable procedures that we develop in Chapter 13. Specifically, we present the *Pearson product-moment correlation coefficient*, often called **Pearson's r**, or simply r, the universal symbol for the statistic. Pearson's r is probably the most widely used of all correlation coefficients.

Let's take a simple example because it's easiest to work with only a few values. Table 5.2 presents the data on neuroticism and perfectionism of five subjects, selected from Table 5.1. In the data, the first subject scored 65 on the neuroticism scale and 56 on the perfectionism scale; the second scored 92 and 67; and so forth. The means and the standard deviations of the neuroticism and perfectionism variables are given in the table as well. The scatterplot of these variables for these five subjects shows a positive relationship (Figure 5.8). The plot shows that, in general, low scores on neuroticism go with low scores on perfectionism, and the same for the high values. Visually, from the scatterplot, we expect to find a positive correlation.

In Chapter 4 we developed the standardized variable as a way of comparing two different variables on equivalent scales. By converting each vari-

	Neuroticism	Perfectionism
TABLE 5.2		
	65	56
	92	67
	43	61
	32	34
	21	36
Mean	50.60	50.80
Standard deviation	28.29	14.96

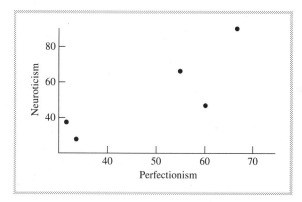

Figure 5.8

able to z scores, we "equated" the spreads by making the standard deviations equal to each other. Standardizing, recall, also makes the means equal to each other. We can apply standardizing here, too. The original data, along with the z values for each variable, are shown in Table 5.3.

By using the z scores, we have scaled the variables so they have the same mean (0.00) and the same standard deviation (1.00). For subject 1, the score on $z_{neuroticism}$ is 0.51, meaning that the score is 0.51 standard deviation above the mean for the variable. The same subject's perfectionism score is 0.35, meaning that the score is 0.35 standard deviation unit above the mean. For subject 3, the neuroticism score is 0.27 unit below the mean, and the perfectionism score is 0.68 unit above. The fourth subject has negative z scores for each variable, meaning that both scores are below their means.

The plot of the two sets of z scores in Figure 5.9 shows that the transformation hasn't changed the form of the relationship at all. Indeed, you shouldn't expect that the form of the relationship—the scatterplot—would change. We simply applied a linear transformation to each variable, and linear transformations do not change the form of a variable's distribution. All that has actually changed is that the scales for the two variables are

TABLE 5.3

Neuroticism	Perfectionism	Neuroticism z Score	Perfectionism z Score	Product
65	56	0.51	0.35	0.177
92	67	1.46	1.08	1.585
43	61	−0.27	0.68	−0.183
32	34	−0.66	−1.12	0.738
21	36	−1.05	−0.99	1.035

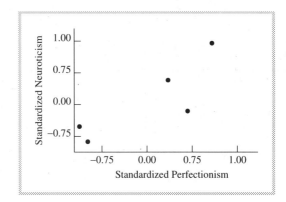

Figure 5.9

different, reflecting the standardized values. As in Figure 5.9, high values (that is, positive z values) are, in general, associated with positive values, and low (negative z) with negative values.

The product column in Table 5.3 gives the products of each pair of z scores. The values are positive where the two z scores have the same sign and negative where they differ. That is, where the neuroticism and the perfectionism scores are both above the mean, or when both are below the mean, the product of the two z values is positive. Conversely, when one score is above the mean and the other below, the product is negative. Figure 5.10 illustrates the situation, with the four quarters of the plot marked to indicate the sign of the product plotted there.

In the example data set, all but one of the products fall into the "positive product" regions, indicating that low scores on neuroticism are associated with low scores on perfectionism; the reverse is true for the high scores. The only exception, subject 3, has the opposite pattern—a low neuroticism score is associated with a high perfectionism score. On balance, though, products tend to be positive, indicating a positive relationship between the two variables, as expected.

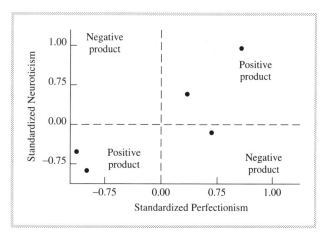

Figure 5.10

The step from the z score products to a measure of relationship is simple. We sum the products, and divide the sum by $N - 1$. As in Chapter 3's discussion of the variance, the result is "almost" the mean of the products of the z scores, but not quite, because the division is by $N - 1$ and not by N. The result of this "almost mean" is the *Pearson product-moment correlation coefficient*, or *Pearson's r*, for short. That is,

$$r = \sum \left(\frac{z_{\text{neuroticism}} z_{\text{perfectionism}}}{N - 1} \right)$$

For the simple example data, the mean of the products is

$$r = \sum \left(\frac{z_{\text{neuroticism}} z_{\text{perfectionism}}}{N - 1} \right)$$

$$= \frac{0.177 + 1.585 - 0.183 + 0.738 + 1.035}{5 - 1}$$

$$= 0.84$$

The value of r can vary between -1.00 and 1.00, regardless of the number of data values, and regardless of the means and standard deviations of the original data. The sign of the coefficient reflects the direction of the relationship. Scatterplots like those shown in Figure 5.3, which have the bulk of their values in the top-right and the bottom-left sections, yield a positive r. Conversely, scatterplots like those in Figure 5.4 lead to negative values of r. If you think about their z scores, all of those figures would have the bulk of their pairs of values in the upper-right and the lower-left sections, which produces a mean product (that is, an r) that is positive. The plots like those in Figure 5.4, with negative correlation coefficients, have most of their points in the upper-left and the lower-right sections.

The size of r is determined by the extent to which the scatterplot is more or less clustered. That is, a plot whose points are more tightly clustered, like those in Figure 5.7a, leads to a higher r value; a plot like 5.7c has a smaller r.

The Pearson product-moment correlation coefficient is important and widely used. As a descriptive statistic, it indicates the strength of the linear relationship between two variables. But just as important, it is closely related to the variance, the most important measure of spread. We proceed now to develop a second definition of the Pearson product-moment correlation coefficient—one that shows these ties to variance.

In Chapter 3 we defined the variance as a measure of spread based on the differences between the values and their mean, specifically the deviations $(X - \overline{X})$. Squaring the differences, summing, and dividing by $N - 1$ gives the variance. We are now ready to define a comparable quantity, called the **covariance**, which is related to the correlation between a pair of variables.

To see the parallel with the variance, rewrite its formula as

$$\text{var}(X) = \frac{\sum(X - \overline{X})^2}{N - 1}$$

$$= \frac{\sum(X - \overline{X})(X - \overline{X})}{N - 1}$$

The numerator of the second expression has exactly the same meaning as that in the first, but the second form emphasizes that the quantities summed are products of deviations between scores and their mean.

Now consider the covariance. The covariance of two variables, X and Y, is defined as

$$\text{cov}(X, Y) = \frac{\sum(X - \overline{X})(Y - \overline{Y})}{N - 1}$$

Note that the numerator is a product of differences between scores and their means, but now it concerns *two* variables. In the variance, of course, the products are actually squares of differences within a single variable. In the covariance, though, the products are formed from a deviation with regard to one variable multiplied by a deviation with regard to the other. In both cases, the sum of products is divided by $N - 1$, the number of subjects less one.

We illustrate the covariance computation using the small set of neuroticism and perfectionism scores from Table 5.2 (see Table 5.4). Using the sum of products in the formula for covariance gives

TABLE 5.4

Neuroticism	Perfectionism	Neuroticism − Mean	Perfectionism − Mean	Product
65	56	14.4	5.2	74.88
92	67	41.4	16.2	670.68
43	61	−7.6	10.2	−77.52
32	34	−18.6	−16.8	312.48
21	36	−29.6	−14.8	438.08
				Sum = 1418.60

$$\text{cov}(X, Y) = \frac{\sum (X - \overline{X})(Y - \overline{Y})}{N - 1}$$

$$= \frac{1418.60}{5 - 1}$$

$$= 354.65$$

The value of the covariance is closely related to the relationship between the two variables. The larger the absolute value of the covariance, the stronger the relationship. This is so because, just as with z scores, data values that are farther from their respective means give large products. That is, if the deviation on one variable is large (that is, the score is far from its mean), and the deviation for the other variable is also far from its mean, their product, too, will be large. If the differences from the means are in the same direction for each variable (above, or below, for each variable), then the products will be positive and contribute highly to the sum. So the covariance is influenced by large deviations from the mean and becomes larger when the data points are farther from their means, just as variance is larger when the data values are more spread out from their mean.

In addition, the sign of the covariance behaves the way we want. As just noted, if a pair of deviations from the X and Y means are in the same direction, indicating that the scores are *both* either above or below their respective means, then their product is positive. However, if one score is above its mean and the other below (that is, the variables may be inversely related), the deviations have different signs and their product is negative. When the products are summed, the sign of the sum indicates whether the relationship is, on balance, positive or negative.

The covariance is not, however, a particularly convenient measure of correlation because its magnitude is heavily dependent on the spread of the variables. Variables with larger ranges have larger deviations to enter into the cross-product computations, making the covariance larger than it would be for a variable with a smaller spread. We can see this effect easily in our example data set if we illustrate by a simple manipulation of the spread. Multiply the neuroticism scores by 10, giving the "new" neuroticism values. The new variable has a mean and a spread increased by a factor of 10 (see Table 5.5). Now calculate the covariance of perfectionism and "new" neuroticism:

$$\text{cov} = \frac{14186.0}{5 - 1} = 3546.5$$

The original covariance was 354.65; now it's 3546.5, exactly ten times as large. We might conclude that multiplying one variable by a constant multiplies the covariance by the same constant. And that's true.

Suppose we multiply the other variable by a constant also. What would happen to the covariance? If you guess that that operation would multiply the covariance by the product of the two constants, you're right.

Now suppose we pick two very special constants and multiply the covariance by their product. The two constants are the reciprocals of the standard deviations of the two original variables. We calculate

$$\text{cov}(X, Y) * \frac{1}{s_X} * \frac{1}{s_Y}$$

Because multiplying by the reciprocal is the same as dividing, the formula becomes

$$r = \frac{\text{cov}(X, Y)}{s_X s_Y}$$

which is a second definition of the Pearson correlation coefficient.

Recall that the standardizing (the z score operation) requires that a difference between a score and the mean be divided by a standard deviation. You might think of this formula for Pearson's r as representing a "standard-

| | "New" | | "New" Neuroticism | Perfectionism | |
Neuroticism	Neuroticism	Perfectionism	Deviation	Deviation	Product
65	650	56	144.0	5.2	748.80
92	920	67	414.0	16.2	6706.80
43	430	61	−76.0	10.2	−775.20
32	320	34	−186.0	−16.8	3124.80
21	210	36	−296.0	−14.8	4380.80
					Sum = 14186.00

TABLE 5.5

izing" operation for the covariance. And in fact, that's very much what it is. The largest absolute magnitude that the covariance can have is the product of the standard deviations of the two variables; dividing that maximum by the product limits the value of Pearson's r to ± 1.0. And that maximum correlation of ± 1.0 can be reached only when the covariance reaches the largest absolute value possible for the data.

For the example data, we have

$$r = \frac{\text{cov}(X, Y)}{s_X s_Y}$$

$$= \frac{354.65}{(28.29)(14.96)}$$

$$= 0.84$$

the same value as calculated earlier.

There are many other formulas for Pearson's r, but this is enough. It is a statistic that ranges between -1.0 and $+1.0$ and provides a good descriptive measure of the linear relationship between variables. Its close tie with variance shows that they are similar statistics, a topic we explore further in later chapters.

INTERPRETING PEARSON'S r

When used with a scatterplot, Pearson's r is a excellent indicator of the relationship between a pair of variables. The coefficient provides a quantitative measure of the extent of the degree to which the variables vary together, while the scatterplot provides a good visual check on the linearity of the relationship. The magnitude of r gives an easy-to-grasp measure of the relationship—the closer to 1.0, the stronger the relationship—and the sign indicates the direction of that relationship.

The ability to interpret correlation coefficients develops through use. Here are a few example scatterplots with correlations. Figure 5.11 shows the plot of perfectionism and neuroticism that we saw earlier. Note that the value of Pearson's r is lower than that computed for the five-score example; this value and the scatterplot are based on the complete set of scores in Table 5.1. Figure 5.12a shows a fairly strong, positive relationship, while Figure 5.12b pictures a negative correlation of roughly the same magnitude, and Figure 5.13 portrays an essentially zero correlation.

To illustrate that the Pearson product-moment correlation coefficient reflects both the relationship and the scatter about the best-fitting straight line through the scatterplot, as discussed previously, consider the pair of plots in Figure 5.14. These two sets of data were carefully constructed so they have the same best-fitting line. Both the r values are high and positive, yet the plots clearly differ in the degree to which the points cluster about the line. The Pearson's r reflects that difference. In Chapter 6 we introduce the

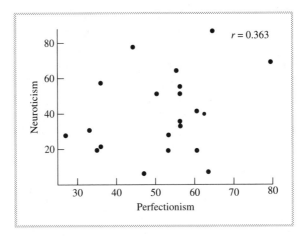

Figure 5.11

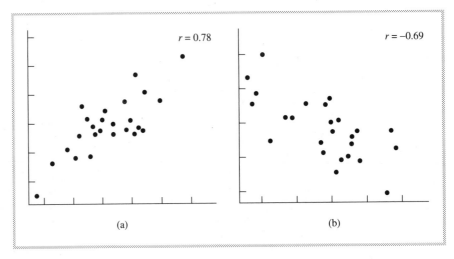

Figure 5.12

measure for variability about the best-fitting line, and see that the value of Pearson's r is directly influenced by that value.

Pearson's r is applicable only to a linear relationship between a pair of variables. Although this seems to be a serious limitation, often it is not. Many variables are actually linearly related, and so the problem goes away. In other cases, replacing the values of one or both variables with, for example, their square roots or logarithms, will solve the problem. We won't explore these options, but you should keep them in mind.

A common constraint on applying Pearson's r is that it requires that both variables be measured on interval or ratio scales. Several alternative correlation measures address this problem, and we turn to them now.

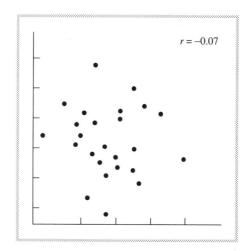

Figure 5.13

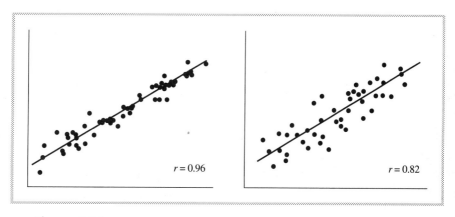

Figure 5.14

◆ Ordinal Data (Spearman's Rho)

When both variables are measured on an ordinal scale, or when one is
ordinal and the other either interval or ratio, the Pearson product-moment
correlation coefficient isn't completely appropriate. Pearson's r is based on
differences between scores and their means, and those differences aren't really meaningful with ordinal measurement. Fortunately, there is a good, and
commonly used, alternative: *Spearman's rank-order correlation*, often called
Spearman's rho, or simply r_s.

Spearman's rho is nothing more than the Pearson product-moment
correlation computed on ranks instead of on raw data values. Converting an
interval or ratio variable to ranks is a simple matter, especially if your
computer program can do it—but even if your program can't, ranking is
easy. Sort the data from smallest to largest value. Then assign the rank 1 to

the smallest, 2 to the next, and so on. If you have sets of tied scores, assign each value the mean rank. Thus, if your data are 5, 7, 12, 15, 15, 18, and 22, the ranks would be

Raw score	5	7	12	15	15	18	22
Rank	1	2	3	4.5	4.5	6	7

Once the data are in ranks for both variables, computation for r_S is simple; just compute Pearson's *r using the ranks*. Although there are numerous computational formulas for r_S, they are invariably more trouble than they're worth. The formula for the r_S found in many older statistics texts is obsolete; it was developed as a computational simplification from the Pearson formula. Because computation is now done by computer, the Spearman formula is no longer needed and we don't even present it.

◆ Other Coefficients for Other Purposes

You may encounter several other "correlation coefficients" in the literature. We summarize them briefly here so they won't be completely foreign.

KENDALL'S TAU. Suppose that, as part of a study in experimental aesthetics, you ask two people to arrange a group of ten paintings in order from most to least attractive. This is an easy task for most people, although they might not be able to tell you exactly how they arrived at their judgments. You could use a Spearman's rank-order correlation to describe the relationship between the two rankings, but a better measure of agreement is given by a different statistic. *Kendall's τ (tau)* is a form of correlation coefficient that is often used to describe the relationship between the rankings or orderings made by two individuals. The tau's value is based on the number of times a painting is ranked the same by each of the two judges.

POINT BISERIAL CORRELATION. Suppose you have a numeric variable, either interval or ratio, and a two-category nominal variable (such as male–female, or single–married, or college graduate–nongraduate) and you want to calculate a measure of relationship between the two. One simple and perfectly reasonable approach is to code the category variables as 0 and 1 (or any two different values) and compute Pearson's *r*. If you do that, the result is a special coefficient known as the *point biserial correlation coefficient*, often symbolized as r_{pb}. The point biserial coefficient is widely used, and is the statistic to employ when one variable is a true two-category (dichotomous) variable.[2] The sign of the coefficient is meaningless because it can be switched by merely reversing the 0–1 variable. The interval or ratio variable should be normally distributed in order to use r_{pb}.

[2] Like the Spearman rank-order correlation, point biserial no longer needs the special computational formulas that appear in older books because it is actually computed as a Pearson *r* between an interval or ratio variable and a 0–1 variable.

BISERIAL CORRELATION. In the examples cited in the preceding section, there were only two categories (male–female, single–married) and no underlying continuous variable. In many cases, though, groups are formed by using an "artificial" dichotomy. You might divide students into two groups by grading them as passing or failing on an exam, for example, using a cutoff point based on a numerical grade. Or you might create two groups of people, calling them introverts and extroverts, by picking some score on the introversion/extroversion scale, and dividing the subjects according to their test value. In either case, the result would be a dichotomy—pass–fail or introvert–extrovert—but one formed by dividing a numeric variable into two categories. In this case, applying the point biserial correlation is inappropriate. The measure to use with one continuous variable and one "artificial" dichotomy is the *biserial correlation coefficient* (r_b), and it is computed differently. We won't develop the coefficient any further here since it's rarely used. Howell (1992, pp. 270–271) discusses the coefficient and gives an example computation.

KENDALL COEFFICIENT OF CONCORDANCE. The *Kendall coefficient of concordance (W)* is not, strictly speaking, a correlation between two variables, but a measure of the agreement among a set of individuals who have ordered the same set of stimuli or objects. It can be thought of as the ratio of the actual variability in the rankings to the maximum variability possible. The statistic W is the ratio

$$W = \frac{\text{Variance in the observed rankings}}{\text{Maximum possible variance in ranks}}$$

Table 5.6 summarizes the measures of relationship presented in this chapter.

◆ Correlation and Causation

The measures described in this chapter—Pearson's r and all the others—are descriptive statistics. Their purpose is to provide a numerical index of the relationship between two variables. Just as the statistics in Chapter 3 describe center and spread, the statistics in this chapter describe a relationship between variables. And that's all! Correlation between two variables says nothing whatever about one of them causing the other. Hewlitt's measures of Neuroticism and Perfectionism say nothing whatever about a cause–effect relationship. The variables simply "go together"—and not very strongly in that particular case. Nothing should be implied about a change in Perfectionism causing a change in Neuroticism.

A check on whether you're confusing correlation and causation is to ask yourself whether it makes any sense to think of one variable as a cause for another. A famous example begins with a correlation between the number of mules in a geographical area and the number of people holding a Ph.D. in the same area. The correlation is negative, meaning areas with

TABLE 5.6 Choosing a Measure of Linear Relationship

If one variable is … \ And the other is …	Nominal	Ordinal	Interval or Ratio
Nominal	See Chapter 10	—	—
Ordinal	Point biserial (Correlate the values and the dichotomous variable.)	Spearman's rho (Correlate the ranks.) Kendall's tau (for rankings) Kendall's coefficient of concordance	Spearman's rho (Correlate the ranks.)
Interval or Ratio	Point biserial (Correlate the values and the dichotomous variable.) Biserial (for artificial dichotomy)	Spearman's rho (Correlate the ranks.)	Pearson's product-moment correlation

more mules have fewer Ph.D.s, and vice versa. But does this imply a causal connection? No—if it did, then bringing more mules into the area would cause Ph.D.s to leave. Or moving a few Ph.D.s out would instantly increase the number of mule births. Both of these are obviously ridiculous conclusions. The two are probably related because both are influenced ("caused," if you will) by factors related to the relative ruralness of the area.

All correlations are not as obviously noncausal as mules and Ph.D.s. Consider the frequently reported negative correlation between the number of hours of television watched per week and grades in school. Does this mean that turning off the television will instantly cause an increase in grades? Probably not, because both TV watching and grades are most likely influenced by a number of underlying factors; motivation, parental pressure, intelligence, and so forth are the easy influences to identify.

Summary

◆ *A* scatterplot *shows the relationship between two variables by plotting them together.*

◆ *Visual inspection of a scatterplot can tell you whether the relationship between variables is linear or not.*

- *A scatterplot reveals whether high values or low values on both variables occur together (a positive relationship) or whether high values on one variable are associated with low values of the other (a negative relationship).*
- *Linear transformations on variables (those involving only add/subtract and multiply/divide operations) do not change the form of the relationship.*
- *Correlation coefficients are measures of the relationship between variables.*
- *Correlation coefficients generally range between −1.0 and +1.0, with the extremes representing very strong relationships.*
- Pearson's r *is the most widely used of all correlation coefficients; it is a measure of the linear relationship between two variables.*
- Pearson's r *is the average product of the z scores on two variables. It is positive if the relationship is high-with-high and low-with-low. Conversely, it is negative if the relationship is high-with-low and low-with-high.*
- *The* covariance *is a measure of relationship that is an average of the products of differences between scores and their means; it is closely related to the variance of a single variable.*
- *The covariance is positive if the relationship is high-with-high and low-with-low, and negative if the relationship is high-with-low and low-with-high.*
- *The covariance is large if variances are large, and small if variances are small.*
- Pearson's r *is a standardized covariance.*
- Spearman's rho *is a commonly used measure of correlation when variables are measured on ordinal scales.*
- Spearman's rho *is a Pearson's r calculated on ranks instead of on raw scores.*
- *There are numerous other coefficients for special purposes.*

Key Terms

CORRELATION COEFFICIENT
COVARIANCE
LINEAR RELATIONSHIP
NEGATIVE CORRELATION
NONLINEAR RELATIONSHIP

PEARSON'S *r*
POSITIVE CORRELATION
SCATTERPLOT
SPEARMAN'S RHO

1. The following table gives the scores for 16 students on two statistics quizzes. Obtain descriptive measures for each quiz and construct a scatterplot showing the relationship between Quizzes 1 and 2.

STUDENT	QUIZ 1	QUIZ 2
1	20	13
2	30	27
3	23	22
4	27	23
5	23	24
6	15	17
7	30	29
8	20	20
9	26	24
10	27	20
11	19	13
12	18	25
13	21	20
14	26	26
15	25	24
16	26	24

2. Here is a set of data giving exercise and final examination scores for 20 students.

EXERCISE	FINAL	EXERCISE	FINAL
2	103	12	121
2	98	12	123
4	109	8	128
3	105	18	123
4	103	7	115
3	111	23	131
13	112	14	133
5	113	17	130
12	116	17	133
10	125	17	136

a. Find the univariate descriptive statistics, including the Pearson skewness statistic, and frequency distributions for each variable.

b. Using the final examination values on the vertical axis, construct the scatterplot.

c. In words, how do you describe the relationship between exercise score and examination score?

3. Here are data from an experiment in learning. The data give the number of errors made on the first trial of the experiment and on the 20th trial.

TRIAL 1	TRIAL 20	TRIAL 1	TRIAL 20
81	9	52	11
19	8	80	10
52	8	6	3
33	6	4	3
33	8	79	11
4	4	23	6
6	7	33	6
33	7	5	4
5	4	9	5
1	2	21	8
2	1	2	1
15	7	13	6
9	5	1	1
13	6	3	2
51	7	14	6
51	10	82	9
2	3	8	7
23	7	2	1
3	2	2	3
6	4	3	3

a. Find the univariate descriptive statistics, including the Pearson skewness statistic, and frequency distributions for each variable.

b. Construct the scatterplot, with Trial 20 on the ordinate.

c. Compute Pearson's r.

d. In words, how do you describe the relationship between Trials 1 and 20?

4. For the data given in exercise 5.1, compute Pearson's r.

5. Compute Pearson's r for the data given in exercise 5.2.

6. Using the same data as for exercise 5.2, convert both variables to ranks and obtain Spearman's rho.

7. Returning to exercise 5.3, replace each score with its square root. Now construct the scatterplot and compute the Pearson product-moment

correlation coefficient for the new (square root) variable. What is the effect of the transformation on the scatterplot and on r?

8. Use the data in Table 5.1 to construct a scatterplot, but with perfectionism on the vertical axis. Describe the relationship between the variables in words. Is it different from what you would have said on the basis of Figure 5.2?

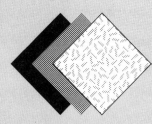

Computational Supplement

◆ **Pearson's *r***

The formula

$$r = \frac{\sum (X - \overline{X})(Y - \overline{Y})}{\sqrt{\sum (X - \overline{X})^2 \sum (Y - \overline{Y})^2}}$$

provides one means of calculating r for any two variables X and Y:

X	Y	$(X - \overline{X})$	$(Y - \overline{Y})$	$(X - X)(Y - Y)$	$(X - \overline{X})^2$	$(Y - \overline{Y})^2$
6	3	1	-3	-3	1	9
9	10	4	4	16	16	16
4	7	-1	1	-1	1	1
2	4	-3	-2	6	9	4
4	6	-1	0	0	1	0
$\overline{X} = 5.0$	$\overline{Y} = 6.0$			18	28	30

$$r = \frac{\sum (X - \overline{X})(Y - \overline{Y})}{\sqrt{\sum (X - \overline{X})^2 \sum (Y - \overline{Y})^2}} = \frac{18}{\sqrt{28 * 30}} = 0.62$$

This computation requires that the two means be computed first and then subtracted from each data value.

Another common formula for Pearson's r, beginning with raw data values so it avoids the need to compute means and subtract, is

$$r = \frac{N\sum XY - (\sum X)(\sum Y)}{\sqrt{[N\sum X^2 - (\sum X)^2][N\sum Y^2 - (\sum Y)^2]}}$$

Although the formula looks cumbersome, it is actually a simple way to make the computation. Return to the raw data and obtain the sums of both X and Y, the sum of squared values of X and Y, and the sum of the products of the X and Y values:

X	Y	X^2	Y^2	XY
6	3	36	9	18
9	10	81	100	90
4	7	16	49	28
2	4	4	16	8
4	6	16	36	24
25	30	153	210	168
↑	↑	↑	↑	↑
$\sum X$	$\sum Y$	$\sum X^2$	$\sum Y^2$	$\sum XY$

The computation is now completed as

$$r = \frac{N\sum XY - (\sum X)(\sum Y)}{\sqrt{[N\sum X^2 - (\sum X)^2][N\sum Y^2 - (\sum Y)^2]}}$$

$$= \frac{5*168 - 25*30}{\sqrt{[5*153 - 25^2][5*210 - 30^2]}}$$

$$= \frac{840 - 750}{\sqrt{140*150}}$$

$$= \frac{90}{144.91}$$

$$= 0.62$$

◆ Spearman's rank-order correlation (r_s)

If you're using a computer for the analysis, finding Spearman's rank-order correlation is a simple matter: Obtain the ranks, and correlate them using the Pearson product-moment correlation coefficient. If you are calculating by hand, however, and have only a few values, the "obsolete" formula given here can be substantially easier. As an example, we use the following simple set of data. The data are the number of trials required for monkeys to learn a simple discrimination between members of two different visual patterns:

	VISUAL PATTERN	
MONKEY	PATTERN A	PATTERN B
1	10	12
2	7	11
3	15	15
4	11	13
5	9	10
6	5	14

The first step in calculating r_s is to convert both sets of data to ranks. For each pattern, we assign 1 to the lowest score, 2 to the next, and so forth, leading to the values shown:

MONKEY	PATTERN A		PATTERN B	
	TRIALS	RANK	TRIALS	RANK
1	10	4	12	3
2	7	2	11	2
3	15	6	15	6
4	11	5	13	4
5	9	3	10	1
6	5	1	14	5

When there are no tied ranks (that is, no duplicate scores in either variable), Spearman's r_S may be calculated as

$$r_S = 1 - \left[\frac{6(\sum D^2)}{N(N^2 - 1)} \right]$$

where D is a difference in the rankings between the two patterns and N is the number of pairs of scores. Adding the differences to the data gives

MONKEY	PATTERN A		PATTERN B		DIFFERENCE
	TRIALS	RANK	TRIALS	RANK	
1	10	4	12	3	1
2	7	2	11	2	0
3	15	6	15	6	0
4	11	5	13	4	1
5	9	3	10	1	2
6	5	1	14	5	-4

Because most of the differences are zero, it's easy to sum the squared differences:

$$\sum D^2 = 1^2 + 0^2 + 0^2 + 1^2 + 2^2 + (-4)^2$$
$$= 22.0$$

so that the value of the coefficient is

$$r_S = 1 - \left[\frac{6(\sum D^2)}{N(N^2 - 1)} \right]$$
$$= 1 - \left[\frac{22.0}{6(6^2 - 1)} \right]$$
$$= 0.37$$

When there are tied ranks, the computation becomes cumbersome. In that case, assign the mean rank for tied scores and then compute the Pearson correlation. That is, if you have two scores tied for positions 6 and 7, for example, assign each score a rank of 6.5.

6 Regression and Linear Prediction

Suppose we have information about two variables. If we knew Jim's neuroticism score, could we predict, or at least make a good guess at, his score on perfectionism? Or, if we knew his score on the SAT, could we make a prediction about, for example, his first-year college grade point? The ability to answer such questions is important for a statistician. There are two reasons for wanting to be able to predict. In some cases, you may really *want* to have predicted values for individuals. If you were a college admissions officer, for example, it would help you considerably if you could estimate how an applicant might actually perform in college. It would be unreasonable to expect a perfectly accurate prediction, of course, but an "educated guess" would be valuable. This is a common application of predicted scores—to provide information that we might otherwise not have. The second reason you might want to predict one variable from another is that working out the details of such a process can tell you something about the relationships between variables.

If there's a relationship between two variables, and if you know the value of one variable, you can do a better job predicting a value on the other one. If you know that you're to guess the weight of a male, you might guess 175 pounds, because that's close to the mean for American males. But suppose you also know that the male whose weight you are to guess is only 4'8" tall. In this case, you'll certainly want to adjust your guess downward. Your adjustment of the "predicted" weight takes advantage of your knowledge of the relationship between height and weight. It's not a perfect relationship— there are, after all, very short people who are also heavy, as there are tall people who are very thin. On the whole, though, there is a strong correlation between weight and height such that taller people tend to weigh more.

LINEAR PREDICTION

Statistical prediction relies on the relationship between variables; the correlation coefficients described in Chapter 5 measure that relationship but don't, by themselves, offer a way to make a prediction. Nevertheless, the fact that two variables are correlated suggests that knowledge of one tells something about the other. If you are asked to guess a person's weight, and are given no additional information, your best guess is the mean weight of humans. But if you also have the individual's height, you can revise your weight estimate appropriately because you know something about the relationship between height and weight. Of course, you can't expect that the prediction will be perfect, but you'll make better predictions if you can use correlational information.

Predicting one variable from another is called **regression**, a term with various meanings. In this context, the word is shorthand for "regression to the mean," a tendency for children to have (or "regress to") a height close to the mean height of their parents. The early statistician, Sir Francis Galton, who did much of the pioneering work leading to the development of correlation techniques, first noted the tendency and published a report on it in about 1885 (see Tankard, 1984). Since his time, the procedures for predicting one variable from another have been termed "regression."

Statistical prediction is done by establishing a simplified statement, or model, of the relationship between two variables. Like all models, a statistical model is an approximation and simplification, one that loses some of the richness and complexity present in the real world. But, in return, a statistical model may let us predict the values of one variable from another.

Although the relationship between two variables might take many different forms, we concentrate on just one: the linear model. A linear model simplifies the relationship between two variables by representing the scatterplot as a straight line, as we suggested in Chapter 5. The straight line has a well-known mathematical representation, and its use is supported by a long tradition of linear modeling in the behavioral sciences.

◆ The Linear Equation

A **linear equation** has the general form

$$Y = bX + a$$

where X and Y are two variables. Y is customarily represented on the ordinate, or vertical, axis of a graph and X on the abscissa. The two constants, b and a, are the **slope** of the line and the Y **intercept**, respectively. The equation

$$Y = 0.67X + 2$$

for example, describes the line shown in Figure 6.1.

The Y intercept (a)—2 in the example—shows where the line crosses the Y axis—that is, the value of Y when X is zero. Changing the value of a shifts the line vertically without changing its slope. With $a = -5$, for example, the line looks like the one in Figure 6.2. The slope of the line (b) gives the rate of climb of the line per unit of X. In the example, the slope of 0.67 means that for every increase of 1.0 in X, the Y value increases 0.67. For instance, suppose that, instead of a slope of 0.67, the slope were 1.5. Then, to construct the line, we'd start by drawing the axes as illustrated in Figure 6.3 and then

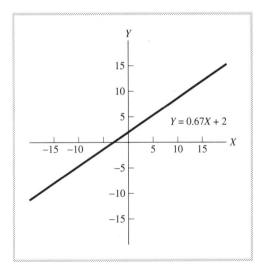

Figure 6.1

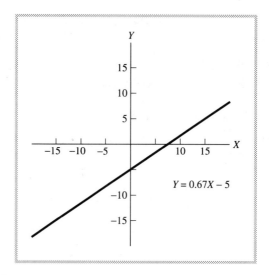

Figure 6.2

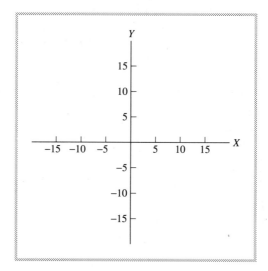

Figure 6.3

calculate the value of Y for any two X values. Suppose we picked $X = 10$. To find the corresponding Y value, we would just substitute 10 into the equation, as

$$Y = 1.5X + 2$$

$$= 1.5(10) + 2 = 17$$

This tells us that when $X = 10$, $Y = 17$; the point ($X = 10$, $Y = 17$) is thus on the line, as is the point corresponding to $X = -15$:

$$Y = 1.5X + 2$$

$$= 1.5(-15) + 2 = -20.5$$

Now, we have determined that when $X = -15$, $Y = -20.5$. Because two points are all that are needed to define a straight line, we can now plot the line by locating the points for the two pairs of X, Y values, and connecting them with a line, as in Figure 6.4. Here the line rises more steeply than the line in the first example (where the slope was 0.67), 1.5 units for every unit of X, but the intercepts are equal ($a = 2.0$), so both lines pass through the Y axis at the same point.

A slope may be negative, or it may be zero. A line with zero slope means that Y does not change for any change in X. For instance, if the slope were zero and the intercept were -7, the line would look like the one in Figure 6.5. A negative slope indicates that for every increase in the value of X, Y decreases in value. A line with a slope of -0.9 and an intercept of 6, for example, appears in Figure 6.6.

We encountered linear functions earlier in talking about the kinds of operations that can be applied to measurements and preserve the meaning in the data. But how are they related to statistical prediction? If we assume that the association between two variables is linear, then the linear equation can serve as the model of the relationship. If we can find an appropriate line—and that means finding the appropriate values of the slope and the

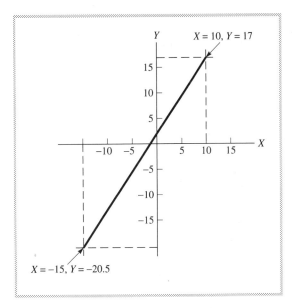

Figure 6.4

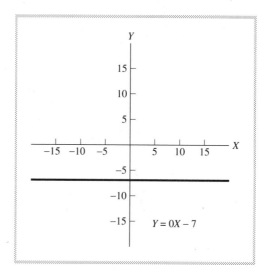

Figure 6.5

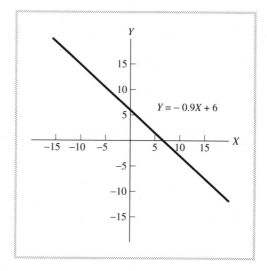

Figure 6.6

intercept—then we can use that equation for prediction. In particular, we'll have a linear equation just like the ones we've been using to describe (or model) the relationship between two variables. For any two variables, X and Y, then, the linear model describing them can be written as

$$\hat{Y} = bX + a$$

where $\hat{Y}$ is the symbol for a predicted Y value.

Having proposed the linear equation as the model for predicting, the next matter is to see how we might find the slope and the intercept, because those two values determine the line.

FITTING THE LINE

The line that we need will pass through the scatterplot, and can serve as a kind of two-dimensional "center" for the data. That is, we want a line that comes close to, and summarizes, the data points, in the same way that our measures of center did. We would like the line to have roughly the same number of data points on each side of it, and to have the points balance around the line. The mean and median serve as the center for a single variable, representing in a single value a score that is "typical" of those in the data. In the same way, the best-fitting line will represent the "typical" position in the two dimensions represented by the pair of variables.

We might define the line that will serve as the model for the relationship between variables in several ways. We'll present just one of them here, using the classic "least-squares" linear logic. The procedure has two goals: (1) to reduce the scatterplot to a single straight line described by a linear equation, and (2) to find the line that comes closest to the data values according to some criterion.

For our example, Table 6.1 presents a data set with two variables, one representing sensation-seeking behavior (SSST) and the other, the Extraversion scale of the Eysenck Personality Inventory (EPIE). The data are real and are from 20 undergraduates.[1] The scatterplot (Figure 6.7) for these data indicates a moderately strong linear relationship (in fact, $r = 0.612$).

To begin to understand the best-fit criterion for a prediction, consider the arithmetic mean. It is the center of each variable in the sense that it minimizes the sum of the squared differences between it and the original scores. Because this sum of squared deviations is a minimum, the arithmetic mean is said to be a **least-squares** measure of the center of the data. In fact, the mean is used so frequently exactly because it is the best-fitting center of the data in this least-squares sense.

The least-squares logic can be applied to fit a line to a scatterplot, making the line the best-fitting center of the data in two dimensions. In this case, the linear equation that describes the line minimizes the squared differences between those given by the line and the actual data points. The mean, recall, fits a set of data best because $\sum (X - \overline{X})^2 = $ a minimum. In regression, the quantity we want to minimize is $\sum (Y - \hat{Y})^2$, where $\hat{Y}$ is a predicted value for the variable Y. Because the actual score is Y and the predicted score is $\hat{Y}$, the difference between them—that is, $(Y - \hat{Y})$—represents an error in prediction.

[1] Data supplied by John B. Campbell.

TABLE 6.1		
Student	SSST	EPIE
1	13	15
2	22	14
3	17	6
4	33	20
5	18	14
6	18	14
7	27	16
8	13	15
9	15	12
10	21	14
11	27	14
12	17	14
13	8	12
14	13	11
15	20	12
16	14	11
17	21	14
18	11	4
19	25	17
20	25	13
Mean	18.90	13.10
Standard deviation	6.32	3.48

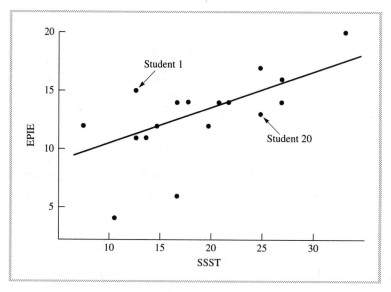

Figure 6.7

Suppose that we find an equation for predicting EPIE from SSST. One possible regression model is shown as the line in Figure 6.7. Now look at the values for the first student in the data, indicated by the marked point in the figure. Student 1 has the actual values of 13 and 15 for SSST and EPIE, respectively. If we use the line as the model of the relationship for student 1 and for any other student who scored a 13 on SSST, we predict a score of about 11 because that's the value of EPIE where the line is directly above 13. Because student 1 has an actual EPIE score of 15, the prediction formula —the line—underestimates the EPIE score by about 4 points, as illustrated in Figure 6.8. In other words, because a higher score on EPIE means more extroverted, we estimate student 1 as less extroverted than the actual score shows. But we should be prepared for such errors. Whenever we use a single line to approximate a relationship, there will be errors. What we mean by a "least-squares center" in a two-dimensional plot is that those errors, which we may symbolize as $(Y - \hat{Y})$, should be as small as possible in terms of the squared prediction errors.

More formally, and more abstractly, we want a formula for the line that will minimize the quantity $\sum (Y - \hat{Y})^2$. If we were all mathematicians, we could use calculus to find the formulas for slope and intercept that would minimize the squared error. But because we don't assume calculus as part of your background, we let someone else worry about the mathematics and merely present the formulas for the best-fitting line.

Remembering that Y represents the variable being predicted and X stands for the variable used to make the prediction, the slope of the best-fitting least-squares line is

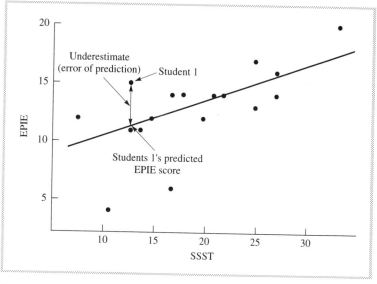

Figure 6.8

$$b = r\frac{s_Y}{s_X}$$

where r is Pearson product-moment correlation coefficient between X and Y. For the example data, where the two standard deviations are $s_X = 6.31 = s_{SSST}$ and $s_Y = 3.48 = s_{EPIE}$ and $r = 0.612$, the slope is

$$b = r\frac{s_Y}{s_X} = r\frac{s_{EPIE}}{s_{SSST}}$$

$$= 0.612\frac{3.48}{6.32}$$

$$= 0.337$$

The formula for the intercept is

$$a = \overline{Y} - b\overline{X}$$

and so, for the example, the intercept is calculated as

$$a = \overline{Y} - b\overline{X}$$

$$= \overline{EPIE} - b\overline{SSST}$$

$$= 13.10 - 0.337 * 18.90$$

$$= 6.73$$

For the first subject in the data, where $X = 13$, the predicted value is found by substituting the values for X, b, and a into the formula:

$$\hat{Y} = 0.337 * X + 6.73$$

$$\widehat{EPIE} = 0.337 * SSST + 6.73$$

$$= 0.337 * 13 + 6.73$$

$$= 11.11$$

The predicted EPIE value, 11.11, is very close to that predicted in Figure 6.8.

As another example, for the 20th subject (where the SSST score is 25), the predicted EPIE score is

$$\hat{Y} = 0.337 * X + 6.73$$

$$\widehat{EPIE} = 0.337 * SSST + 6.73$$

$$= 0.337 * 25 + 6.73$$

$$= 15.16$$

Connecting those two points on the original scatterplot, as shown in Figure

6.8, draws the prediction line defined by the linear model $\hat{Y} = 0.336X +$ 6.750 or, in terms of the actual variables used, $\widehat{EPIE} = 0.336 * SSST + 6.750$. For student 20, the predicted EPIE score is an *overestimate* because the actual score in Table 6.1 is 13.

The full set of actual and predicted EPIE values for the example data appear in Table 6.2. Note that the predicted EPIE values for an SSST of 13 or 25 (or any other SSST value) don't agree precisely with any of the actual values in the data; there is always some error because the relationship between X and Y is modeled by the linear equation, and models rarely agree precisely with reality. What we have accomplished, though, is to present an equation that fits the data according to a criterion that minimizes the squared differences between the predicted and the actual Y values.

RESIDUALS

The differences between actual and predicted values of the Y variable—that is, the values of $(Y - \hat{Y})$—are called **residuals** and are important in several

TABLE 6.2

Student	SSST	EPIE	$\widehat{EPIE}$	$(EPIE - \widehat{EPIE})$	$(EPIE - \widehat{EPIE})^2$
1	13	15	11.11	3.89	15.11
2	22	14	14.14	−0.14	0.02
3	17	6	12.46	−6.46	41.73
4	33	20	17.85	2.15	4.63
5	18	14	12.80	1.20	1.45
6	18	14	12.80	1.20	1.45
7	27	16	15.83	0.17	0.03
8	13	15	11.11	3.89	15.11
9	15	12	11.79	0.21	0.04
10	21	14	13.81	0.19	0.04
11	27	14	15.83	−1.83	3.34
12	17	14	12.46	1.54	2.37
13	8	12	9.43	2.57	6.61
14	13	11	11.11	−0.11	0.01
15	20	12	13.47	−1.47	2.16
16	14	11	11.45	−0.45	0.20
17	21	14	13.81	0.19	0.04
18	11	4	10.44	−6.44	41.47
19	25	17	15.15	1.85	3.41
20	25	13	15.15	−2.15	4.64
Mean	18.90	13.10			
Standard deviation	6.31	3.48			

ways. For now, they can illustrate several features of the linear prediction process. For the example data, the residuals—that is, the (EPIE $-$ $\widehat{\text{EPIE}}$) values—were shown in Table 6.2.

◆ Spread Around the Line[2]

If you have no information about a person's score on a variable, your best strategy—if asked to estimate his or her score—is to use the arithmetic mean. This, of course, means that your error in estimating is minimized because the mean is the least-squares center of the data. The expression "$\sum(X - \overline{X})^2$ = a minimum" formalizes the statement about the best fit. The inner part of the expression, $(X - \overline{X})$, represents the "error" in predicting an X score by using the mean as a "best guess."

If we were to predict the EPIE score for the first subject in the data, assuming that we know only the SSST score and the mean of the EPIE scores, we would use the value 13.10, the mean EPIE score. The difference between the *actual* EPIE score for the first subject (15) and the estimate that we obtain by using the mean is $(15 - 13.10) = 1.9$. Of course, this difference of 1.9 is one of the values symbolized by $(X - \overline{X})$ in the statement "$\sum(X - \overline{X})^2$ = a minimum."

Recall that the variance is defined as approximately the mean of the squared deviations about the mean:

$$s^2 = \frac{\sum(X - \overline{X})^2}{N - 1}$$

In terms of using the mean as an estimate, the variance gives a quantitative measure of how far it "misses" the data, in the least-squares sense.

The point of regression is to predict values, and to do so by using a linear model that, one might hope, will yield a better prediction than using the mean. Using the mean, we use the least-squares center of the data as the "best guess." Applying the same logic to regression, we have a comparable center. This time, though, the "center" is in two dimensions and is represented by the regression equation. In regression, we can still have a measure of variability around the center. But this time, that variability is measured around the two-dimensional center instead of the mean, which is a one-dimensional center. One quantity that serves to measure the variability around the two-dimensional center is

$$s^2_{\text{Error}} = \frac{\sum(Y - \hat{Y})^2}{N - 2}$$

the variance around the best-fitting line. There's a small but important dif-

---

[2] This section presents more advanced material, which your instructor may choose to delete.

ference between this and the variance: The appropriate divisor in this case is $N - 2$, where N is the number of pairs of X, Y scores.

As before, any expression that represents a sum of squared differences —like $\sum(X - \bar{X})^2$ or $\sum(Y - \hat{Y})^2$—is a *sum of squares* (SS). This is often used as part of a measure of variability although, as we shall see, it is sometimes used alone as an index of variation. In this case, it is specifically the sum of the squared differences between the actual values of the Y variables and those predicted by the linear model. The quantities represent the amount of error in the prediction because, with perfect prediction, all the $(Y - \hat{Y})$ values would be zero. For this reason, the quantity $\sum(Y - \hat{Y})^2$ is called the *sum of squares for error* (SS_{Error}). Because the quantity $(Y - \hat{Y})$ is also called a residual, the sum of the squared values—that is, $\sum(Y - \hat{Y})^2$— is often called the **sum of squares for residuals** or $SS_{Residuals}$.

The denominator of the s^2_{Error} formula is the number of pairs of data values, less 2. This number is called a **degrees of freedom** (df) value. (Degrees of freedom is a term from inferential statistics; it will reappear in later chapters.) A variance is sometimes defined as a SS divided by an appropriate df. Using SS and df notation, then, we might write

$$s^2_{Error} = \frac{\sum(Y - \hat{Y})^2}{N - 2} = \frac{SS_{Error}}{df_{Error}}$$

and thereby define "error" variance in regression. The term *error* is used here because the residuals are the errors that result from using the linear model to predict Y values from X.

Using the example data, the computations for $(EPIE - \widehat{EPIE})^2$ leading up to the computations for s^2_{Error} are shown in Table 6.2. The sum of the right-hand column—that is, the values of $(EPIE - \widehat{EPIE})^2$—is 143.86. From that value, we compute s^2_{Error} as

$$s^2_{Error} = \frac{\sum(Y - \hat{Y})^2}{N - 2} = \frac{SS_{Error}}{df_{Error}}$$
$$= \frac{\sum(EPIE - \widehat{EPIE})^2}{N - 2}$$
$$= \frac{143.86}{20 - 2}$$
$$= 7.99$$

In Chapter 3 we learned that the square root of the variance, the standard deviation, is the preferred measure of spread for describing a single variable. In the same way, the square root of the error variance is a much more useful measure of the spread around the prediction line. The regression quantity comparable to the standard deviation,

$$S_{est} = \sqrt{s_{Error}^2} = \sqrt{\frac{\sum(Y - \hat{Y})^2}{N - 2}} = \sqrt{\frac{SS_{Error}}{df_{Error}}}$$

is the known as the **standard error of estimate**. It is nothing more nor less than the standard deviation of the Y scores, but the deviations are taken around the *regression line* instead of the mean. It's a two-dimensional measure of spread, based on a two-dimensional center—the regression line. For the example data,

$$S_{est} = \sqrt{s_{Error}^2} = \sqrt{7.99}$$
$$= 2.83$$

◆ Subdividing Variability[3]

In Chapter 3 we mentioned in passing that variability can often be partitioned into separate segments, each representing a contribution to the overall variation. The ability to subdivide variance is a powerful tool in statistics, and we'll run into it again. In Chapter 3 the discussion also suggested several possible sources of variation in data (measurement error, randomness, individual differences, and experimental variables were mentioned then). In this section we illustrate how to subdivide variance in linear regression. We define two segments of variation—what we call "regression" and "error." The former shows that a part of the variation in a Y (such as EPIE in the example) variable can be connected with X (SSST, for example), so that knowing the correlation between two variables can help to "explain" a part of the variations. The latter term—"error" variation—recognizes that there are sources of variation that we cannot identify clearly.

In Chapters 12 through 15, similar principles of variance partitioning lead to a powerful inferential procedure for differences in means, known appropriately as the *analysis of variance*. In those chapters, the emphasis is on separating variance into components that can be associated with the effect of one or more independent variables and another component that is (again) labeled "error."

Let's go back to the scatterplot of EPIE and SSST and think about an "alternative" linear model, one with the equation

$$\hat{Y} = 0X + \overline{Y}$$

or, in the case of the example,

$$\widehat{EPIE} = 0SSST + \overline{EPIE}$$

This model has zero slope, and the intercept is the mean of the EPIE values.

---

[3] This section presents more advanced material, which your instructor may choose to delete.

Clearly, this model will predict $\overline{\text{EPIE}}$ for any value of SSST. In fact, it's the model implied in the earlier discussion about using the mean and the "best guess" predictor for EPIE. The scatterplot and the line, with two example residuals, appear in Figure 6.9. The residuals in the illustration are, as discussed previously, the differences between the predicted Y values and the actual scores. But because the model predicts the mean for all values, what we're really showing, of course, is the differences $(Y - \overline{Y})$—EPIE $- \overline{\text{EPIE}}$, in the example—and not differences from a predicted value at all. Or are we? One way of looking at these EPIE $- \overline{\text{EPIE}}$ differences is as "errors of prediction," if we were to use the mean as a best guess. In this sense, variance is a measure of the error in prediction—it's an average of the differences between scores and their "predicted" value.

Suppose that a linear model for predicting improves the closeness of the estimate over what we can expect by just using the mean. That is, the least-squares line modeling the X,Y relationship comes closer to the data than does the "line" represented by $\overline{Y}$. In this case, the variability of Y around the regression line should be less than the variability of Y around its mean. Thus, if the least-squares line is a better predictor than is the mean, then s_{est} should be less than s_Y. This will be so to an extent that's directly related to the correlation between the variables. In fact, we can compute the standard error of estimate as

$$s_{\text{est}} = s_Y \sqrt{1 - r^2}\,\sqrt{\frac{N-1}{N-2}}$$

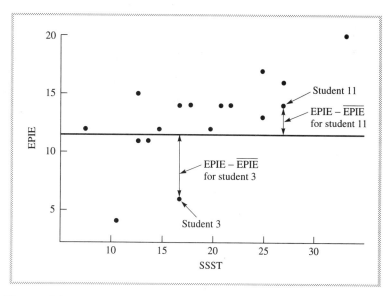

Figure 6.9

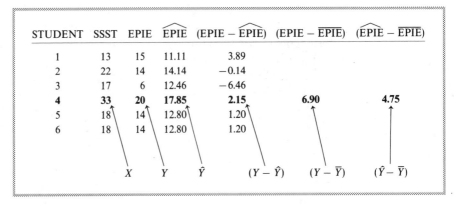

Figure 6.10

where r is the Pearson product-moment correlation coefficient.[4] The formula will result in s_{est} having a smaller value than s_Y as long as r has a value other than 0.0.

In the example, we have

$$s_{est} = s_Y\sqrt{1 - r^2}\sqrt{\frac{N-1}{N-2}}$$

$$= s_{EPIE}\sqrt{1 - r^2}\sqrt{\frac{N-1}{N-2}}$$

$$= 3.48\sqrt{1 - 0.61^2}\sqrt{\frac{20-1}{20-2}}$$

$$= 2.83$$

which is the value obtained previously.

The preceding formula uses the squared Pearson r. In fact, r^2 by itself is an important value. To see why, return to the example data once more and look carefully at just student 4. A segment of Table 6.2, with a few additions showing student 4, appears in Figure 6.10. For student 4, his or her actual EPIE score is 20. The predicted EPIE value is 17.85. Thus, the residual—

[4] Many statistics texts present the formula as

$$s_{est} = s_Y\sqrt{1 - r^2}$$

because the fraction

$$\frac{N-1}{N-2}$$

is very close to 1.0.

showing how far the linear prediction "missed" the actual value—is $(Y - \hat{Y}) = (\text{EPIE} - \widehat{\text{EPIE}}) = 20 - 17.85 = 2.15$.

Return again to show how we might go about predicting if we didn't have a regression formula: We would predict the mean (that is, 13.10) for student 4. This "prediction" also misses the actual value—by $(20 - 13.10) = 6.90$, which is $(Y - \bar{Y})$—that is, $(\text{EPIE} - \overline{\text{EPIE}})$—for subject 4. Both "errors" in prediction are underestimates, but the error in prediction from the regression line is smaller, meaning that the regression estimate came closer to the true value than did the mean. How much closer? If we subtract the two estimates and find $(\widehat{\text{EPIE}} - \overline{\text{EPIE}}) = (\hat{Y} - \bar{Y}) = 17.85 - 13.10 = 4.75$, we see that the regression improved the prediction by a little under 5 points on the EPIE scale. This difference between the two estimation errors is a measure of the refinement in prediction achieved by using the linear model.

As you can easily verify, the error in linear prediction—$(Y - \hat{Y})$ or $(\text{EPIE} - \widehat{\text{EPIE}})$—and the improvement in prediction—$(\widehat{\text{EPIE}} - \overline{\text{EPIE}})$ or $(\hat{Y} - \bar{Y})$—sum to the quantity $(Y - \bar{Y})$, the overall error introduced by simply using the mean. Algebraically,

$$(Y - \bar{Y}) = (\hat{Y} - \bar{Y}) + (Y - \hat{Y})$$

Remember, though, that $(Y - \bar{Y})$ is not just an error measurement. It is also the difference between a score and its mean, and thus is a component of the variance of Y. It is one of the deviations from the mean that are squared and added to form the sum of squares and thus the numerator of the variance. To complete the computation of the numerator of the variance, we would square all of the $(Y - \bar{Y})$ quantities and sum to obtain $\sum(Y - \bar{Y})^2$, which is the **sum of squares for** Y (SS_Y). But what we have accomplished is important. We have partitioned a deviation from the mean into two segments. One segment shows the error in prediction when the regression model is used, and the other the improvement in prediction as compared to the mean.

If we square and sum the left-hand term $(Y - \bar{Y})$, we obtain the sum of squares for the variable being predicted, Y (EPIE in the example). What would happen (algebraically) if we were to square and sum *both* sides of the subdivided $(Y - \bar{Y})$ expression

$$(Y - \bar{Y}) = (\hat{Y} - \bar{Y}) + (Y - \hat{Y})$$

After some algebra that we can safely leave to others, we would have

$$\sum(Y - \bar{Y})^2 = \sum(\hat{Y} - \bar{Y})^2 + \sum(Y - \hat{Y})^2$$

Two of the elements of this expression should already be familiar: the sum of squares for Y (SS_Y) and the sum of squares for error (SS_{Error}). The remaining quantity, $\sum(\hat{Y} - \bar{Y})^2$, is called the *sum of squares for* $\hat{Y}$, or the **sum of squares for regression**. So now the expression can be written as

$$\sum(Y - \overline{Y})^2 = \sum(\hat{Y} - \overline{Y})^2 + \sum(Y - \hat{Y})^2$$

$$SS_Y \qquad = SS_{\hat{Y}} + SS_{Error}$$

Or, using the other name for the sum of squares based on the differences between the predicted Y values and the mean of Y, the expression is

$$SS_Y = SS_{Regression} + SS_{Error}$$

Just what does this tell us? It says that the variability about $\overline{Y}$ (expressed as a sum of squares and not as a variance) can be thought of as having two parts: an error part and a regression part. The error part is based on the amount by which the linear model "misses" the actual values of the Y variable. The other component—the regression component—is the difference between the error part and the overall variation around $\overline{Y}$. Specifically, it is the part of the variability in Y that represents an *improvement* in predictability due to the linear regression. Because the sum of squares for error is generally less than the original sum of squares for Y, the difference represents the reduction in variability that can be attributed to the regression. We can illustrate by returning to the example once more (see Table 6.3). Two columns appear in Table 6.3 that were not in Table 6.2 (page 157). These were illustrated in Figure 6.10 and show the computation of the sum of squares for Y and for regression. With these figures, we can illustrate that the components do sum properly:

$$SS_Y = SS_{Regression} + SS_{Error}$$
$$229.80 = 85.94 + 143.86$$

This illustrates numerically what we said in symbols—the variability around $\overline{Y}$ (expressed as a sum of squares) can be expressed in two parts, an error part and a regression part. The SS_{Error} gives a numerical measure of how far the linear model "misses" the actual values. The other component, the difference between the "error" variation and the total variation, is that part of Y's variability that represents the *improvement* in predictability brought about by the regression model. The sum of squares for error is less than the original sum of squares for Y, and so the difference represents the reduction in variability afforded by the regression.

A ratio of two of the variability components expresses the improvement as a proportion of the total variability in Y:

$$\frac{SS_{Regression}}{SS_Y}$$

This fraction, the ratio of the sum of squares for regression to the total sum of squares for Y, is an informative number. It tells us that a proportion of the

TABLE 6.3

Student	SSST	EPIE	Predicted $\hat{Y}$	Residual $(Y - \hat{Y})$	Residual² $(Y - \hat{Y})^2$	$(Y - \bar{Y})^2$	$(\hat{Y} - \bar{Y})^2$
1	13	15	11.11	3.89	15.11	3.61	3.95
2	22	14	14.14	-0.14	0.02	0.81	1.09
3	17	6	12.46	-6.46	41.73	50.41	0.41
4	33	20	17.85	2.15	4.63	47.61	22.54
5	18	14	12.80	1.20	1.45	0.81	0.09
6	18	14	12.80	1.20	1.45	0.81	0.09
7	27	16	15.83	0.17	0.03	8.41	7.44
8	13	15	11.11	3.89	15.11	3.61	3.95
9	15	12	11.79	0.21	0.04	1.21	1.72
10	21	14	13.81	0.19	0.04	0.81	0.50
11	27	14	15.83	-1.83	3.34	0.81	7.44
12	17	14	12.46	1.54	2.37	0.81	0.41
13	8	12	9.43	2.57	6.61	1.21	13.48
14	13	11	11.11	-0.11	0.01	4.41	3.95
15	20	12	13.47	-1.47	2.16	1.21	0.14
16	14	11	11.45	-0.45	0.20	4.41	2.72
17	21	14	13.81	0.19	0.04	0.81	0.50
18	11	4	10.44	-6.44	41.47	82.81	7.08
19	25	17	15.15	1.84	3.41	15.21	4.22
20	25	13	15.15	-2.15	4.64	0.01	4.22
Sums					143.86	229.80	85.94

$$\sum(Y - \hat{Y})^2 \qquad \sum(Y - \bar{Y})^2 \qquad \sum(\hat{Y} - \bar{Y})^2$$
$$SS_{Error} \qquad\qquad SS_Y \qquad\qquad SS_{Regression}$$

variability in Y can be accounted for if we have knowledge of X and can use the relationship between X and Y in predicting Y values. For the example (see Table 6.3), we have

$$\frac{SS_{Regression}}{SS_Y} = \frac{SS_{Regression}}{SS_{EPIE}} = \frac{85.94}{229.80} = 0.374$$

meaning that 0.374, or roughly 37%, of the variability in EPIE can be explained by, or predicted from, the relationship between SSST and EPIE.

The ratio is also important because it can help us evaluate the strength of the relationship between two variables. If the ratio is very small, the relationship between the variables is weak. If it is large, the relationship is much stronger. This might lead you to conclude that there is a close tie between the value of the Pearson product-moment correlation coefficient and the proportion of variation statistic. And, in fact,

$$r^2 = \frac{SS_{Regression}}{SS_Y}$$

Thus, the square of Pearson's r gives the proportion of the variance of Y that is predictable from X. For this reason, a squared correlation is of considerable importance in understanding the strength of a relationship. A correlation between two variables of, say, 0.61, as in the example, represents a moderate, positive relationship. But a correlation of 0.61 means that the relationship between the two variables can account for only $0.61^2 = 0.37$, or 37%, of the Y variation.

We may see that the relationship holds for the example data by computing the ratio of the two sums of squares,

$$r^2 = \frac{SS_{Regression}}{SS_Y} = \frac{SS_{Regression}}{SS_{EPIE}} = \frac{85.94}{229.80} = 0.37 = 0.61^2 = r^2$$

In Chapter 5 we noted that there was a close relationship among variance, covariance, and correlation. And this presentation illustrates that. A squared Pearson product-moment correlation coefficient gives a proportion of variance, and the same quantity can be computed from a partition of the variability in the variables.

◆ The Idea of Multiple Regression

In this chapter we developed a logic for predicting one variable from another using a linear equation to model the relationship between the two variables. That equation is used to make predictions about one variable from the other. Suppose that, instead of a single X (*predictor* or *independent*) variable, we had two of them and a single Y (*criterion* or *dependent*) variable.[5] We now are in a **multiple regression** situation, instead of a *bivariate* one. In multiple regression there is one dependent (Y) variable but multiple X variables. The X variables are normally called X_1 and X_2. Of course, in any specific research setting, the variables would have more descriptive names. We might, for example, predict EPIE (the Y) from both SSST (X_1) and, perhaps, some other measure of adventuresomeness (X_2).

In bivariate linear regression, a linear model is constructed for predicting Y from X. The same is true in multiple regression, except that the prediction is done from a linear *combination* of the X variables. In bivariate regression, the linear equation defines a line in the two-dimensional region defined

---

[5] Note that the words *independent* and *dependent* are used in a different sense than we used them in Chapter 1. There, an *independent variable* was the one manipulated by the experimenter, while the *dependent variable* was measured. In regression, both variables are normally measured rather than manipulated, but the variable to be predicted (Y) is often called the *criterion* or the *dependent variable*, while the variables that do the predicting (X variables) are called *predictors* or *independent variables*.

by the X and Y variables. In three dimensions, the natural extension of the line is a plane, a two-dimensional surface defined in a three-dimensional space.

Other than computational difficulty (and that can be considerable without a computer[6]), there's no reason why we should be limited to just two predictor (X) variables. We can't draw or even visualize a space of greater than three dimensions (defined by Y, X_1, and X_2), of course, but we can conceive of it, and the appropriate mathematics can provide both a representation and a way to carry out the computations.

Chapter 13 deals with multiple regression in some detail. For now, we want to make three points. First, multiple regression is a straightforward extension of bivariate regression, and the logic of finding a least-squares best-fitting plane in multiple dimensions is the same as it is in fitting a single line. Second, when there are multiple predictor variables, an important use of regression is to find out which are "good" predictors and which are not. In the beginning words of this chapter, we mentioned exploring "relationships between variables" as a major goal of regression. That remark was meant to alert you to the fact that some of the numbers developed here (such as the slope of the regression line, or the use of r^2 as a proportion of variance, or the concept of sums of squares as measures of variability) are important in just such tasks as evaluating predictor variables. Third, the linear model may often be used as a kind of metaphor for research in psychology. We'll address that matter briefly next, and then develop it more fully in Chapter 13.

◆ The Linear Model and Research

Probably every student in an introductory psychology course has seen a formula that looks like

$$\text{Behavior} = f(\text{Stimulus})$$

That simple formula merely expresses the belief that any behavior can be "explained" as a function of the stimulus (or stimuli) that elicit it. In this chapter we introduced a way to express one variable as a function of another. This chapter's model is linear, based on using the best-fitting line to approximate the relationship between a pair of variables. In this model, the f is a linear function. Other models could be used as well; we even implied one of them for the case where we didn't know anything about regression and suggested that the "best" prediction might be accomplished by using $\overline{Y}$. The development of the linear equation was an attempt to improve the accuracy of the model. In both the linear model and the one using the mean, we acknowledged that there would be error in prediction—both $(Y - \overline{Y})$ and $(Y - \hat{Y})$ will be nonzero for most observations. But we also noted that

---

[6] But no one does a multiple regression "by hand" anymore.

often we could achieve better prediction (as measured by a least-squares procedure) by using $\hat{Y}$. In addition, we talked about error in data, as measured by $(Y - \overline{Y})$, as perhaps coming from two sources: regression $(\hat{Y} - \overline{Y})$ and the residuals from regression $(Y - \hat{Y})$.

Implicit in the latter discussion was an assumption that we were talking about a formulation of data analysis as

$$\textbf{Data = Model + Error}$$

That is, the data coming from research can be viewed as due to two sources. One source may be conceptualized as a model of some kind (often linear). The other source is simply error. Thus, we may regard the regression formula resulting in $\hat{Y}$ as a model that explains the data, and $\overline{Y}$ as another model explaining the same data. In either case, we can't expect the model to predict all the values exactly, and there will be error remaining. But all in all, the task of data analysis may be viewed as a search for a model that best accounts for the data in terms of minimizing the errors.

Summary

- Regression *is the logic for predicting one variable from another.*
- *A* linear equation *is often used to model the relationship between two variables.*
- *The best-fitting line can be regarded as a two-dimensional center for the data on two variables.*
- *In a linear equation, the* intercept *gives the value of the vertical axis when the horizontal axis equals 0.0.*
- *The* slope *in a linear equation gives the increase of the vertical axis, in units of the vertical axis, per unit of the horizontal axis.*
- *In a scatterplot, the to-be-predicted variable is plotted vertically.*
- *The* least-squares *criterion is used to define the best-fitting line.*
- *A* residual *is the difference between an actual* Y *value and the predicted value* ($\hat{Y}$) *coming from the regression equation.*
- *The quantity* $\sum (Y - \overline{Y})^2$ (sum of squares for Y) *expresses the variation around the mean of the* Y *variable.*
- *The quantity* $\sum (Y - \hat{Y})^2$ (sum of squares for residuals) *gives the variation around the regression line.*
- *The quantity* $\sum (\hat{Y} - \overline{Y})^2$ (sum of squares for regression) *gives the "improvement" in the predictability due to the linear model.*
- *The* standard error of estimate *is a standard deviation taken around the line.*
- *The square of the Pearson product-moment correlation coefficient* (r^2) *gives the proportion of variability in the* Y *(predicted) variable that can be associated with the predictor* (X) *variable.*

◆ *In* multiple regression, *there is one Y variable and two or more X variables.*

Key Terms

DATA = MODEL + ERROR
DEGREES OF FREEDOM
INTERCEPT
LEAST-SQUARES
LINEAR EQUATION
MULTIPLE REGRESSION
r^2
REGRESSION
RESIDUAL

SLOPE
STANDARD ERROR OF ESTIMATE
$\sum (\hat{Y} - \bar{Y})^2$ (SUM OF SQUARES FOR REGRESSION)
$\sum (Y - \bar{Y})^2$ (SUM OF SQUARES FOR Y)
$\sum (Y - \hat{Y})^2$ (SUM OF SQUARES FOR RESIDUALS)

 EXERCISES

1. Use the data from exercise 5.1 for these exercises.

  a. Find the linear model for predicting Quiz 2 from Quiz 1.

  b. Compute the predicted Quiz 2 values using the model you developed in part a.

  c. Calculate the residuals from the predictions in part b.

  d. Find the sum of squares $[\sum (Y - \hat{Y})^2]$ for the residuals from part c.

  e. Calculate the standard error of estimate for your least-squares model by using the residuals.

  f.[7] Calculate the standard error of estimate using the correlation formula. Does it agree with the value from part e?

2. Use the data from exercise 5.3 for these exercises.

  a. Find the linear model for predicting errors on Trial 20 from errors on Trial 1.

  b. Compute the predicted Trial 20 values using the equation that you developed in part a.

  c. Calculate the residuals from the predictions in part b.

  d. Find the sum of squares $[\sum (Y - \hat{Y})^2]$ for the residuals from part c.

  e. Calculate the standard error of estimate for your model by using the residuals.

  f.[7] Calculate the standard error of estimate for your model by using the correlation formula.

3. Use the data in Table 6.1 to complete these exercises.

  a. Find the linear model for predicting SSST scores from EPIE (that is, predict the "other way," compared to what the text did as an example).

[7] This exercise pertains to an optional section in the text.

b. Compute the predicted SSST values using the equation you developed in part a.

c. Calculate the residuals from the predictions in part b.

d. Find the sum of squares $[\sum(Y - \hat{Y})^2]$ for the residuals from part c.

e. Calculate the standard error of estimate for your model by using the residuals.

f.[8] Calculate the standard error of estimate for your model by using the correlation formula.

g. Plot the residuals from the least-squares model against the predicted values. Will the linear model be acceptable for these data, based on the discussion in this chapter? Why or why not?

4. Use the data from exercise 5.2.

a. Find the linear model to predict the final exam score from the exercise score.

b. Compute the predicted exam scores using the equation you developed in part a.

c. Calculate the residuals from the predictions in part b.

d. Find the sum of squares $[\sum(Y - \hat{Y})^2]$ for the residuals from part c.

e. Calculate the standard error of estimate for your model by using the residuals.

f.[8] Calculate the standard error of estimate for your model by using the correlation formula.

---

[8] This exercise pertains to an optional section in the text.

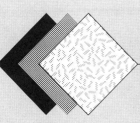

Computational Supplement

◆ Slope and Intercept

A convenient raw data formula for the slope is

$$b = \frac{N\sum XY - (\sum X)(\sum Y)}{N\sum X^2 - (\sum X)^2}$$

The necessary summary values from the raw data presented in Table 6.1 are given in Table 6.4. The calculation is

$$b = \frac{N\sum XY - (\sum X)(\sum Y)}{N\sum X^2 - (\sum X)^2}$$

$$= \frac{20(5207) - 378 * 262}{20(7902) - (378)^2}$$

$$= 0.337$$

The formula for the intercept is

$$a = \overline{Y} - b\overline{X}$$

and so it is calculated as

$$a = \overline{Y} - b\overline{X}$$

$$= 13.10 - 0.337(18.90)$$

$$= 6.73$$

The values $b = 0.336$ and $a = 6.75$ define the least-squares best-fitting linear model for the data as

$$\hat{Y} = 0.337X + 6.73$$

All other computations were presented in the text.

TABLE 6.4

Student	SSST	EPIE	SSST^2	EPIE^2	EPIE * SSST
1	13	15	169	225	195
2	22	14	484	196	308
3	17	6	289	36	102
4	33	20	1089	400	660
5	18	14	324	196	252
6	18	14	324	196	252
7	27	16	729	256	432
8	13	15	169	225	195
9	15	12	225	144	180
10	21	14	441	196	294
11	27	14	729	196	378
12	17	14	289	196	238
13	8	12	64	144	96
14	13	11	169	121	143
15	20	12	400	144	240
16	14	11	196	121	154
17	21	14	441	196	294
18	11	4	121	16	44
19	25	17	625	289	425
20	25	13	625	169	325
Sums	378	262	7902	3662	5207
			$=\sum X^2$	$=\sum Y^2$	$=\sum XY$

PART 3 MAKING INFERENCES

escribing data, as discussed in Part 2, is fine as far as it goes. But it's just a first step because we often want more than just description. The descriptions presented in Part 2 are limited only to the data before us. It's important and interesting to know that the males and females in our research have different means and medians, for example, but similar standard deviations. But we're often not interested in *only* the data from our single research project. Rather, we would like to be able to make an inference beyond our data to, perhaps, males and females in general.

Understanding inferential statistics and drawing inferences from data is the topic of the two chapters in Part 3. In Chapter 7 we explore the probability theory foundation that allows us to make inferences. Then we expand that material to discuss two important kinds of inference—namely, point and interval estimation. Chapter 8 continues to develop the most common of all inference procedures: the hypothesis test. The chapter ends with a consideration of the power of a statistical test (that is, its ability to find an effect if there is one) and how to decide on a sample size that will allow you to have that power.

7 Probability, Sampling Distributions, and Estimation

Suppose you want to know how long it will take for college students in a problem-solving experiment to complete their task. One obvious procedure is to select a few pilot subjects, have them do the task, and record their times. The answer to the question could be given by the arithmetic mean of the times. With the mean in hand, we at least have an estimate of how long it will take the "real" subjects to complete the task once we actually run the experiment.

Using a statistic as a "best-guess" estimate is called **point estimate**; it is an important way to make an inference from a small set of data.

If we computed the standard deviation of the problem-solving times and did a simple additional computation, we could construct an **interval estimate**. An interval estimate gives a slightly different answer to the "how long" question; it provides a range of times in which we expect most people to finish. For example, we might end our pilot study by concluding: "I expect the subjects to complete my task in 22.5 to 26.3 minutes, and I'm 95% confident of that being true."

These examples illustrate two ways to estimate the parameter "mean time to complete the task." The first establishes a point estimate. Point estimates are single values that are used as "best-guess" estimates of parameters. The second gives us interval estimates, which provide a range of values and indicate a probability (often expressed as a percentage) that succeeding samples fall within that range. An interval estimate abandons the precision of the point estimate in return for a statement of confidence that repeated sampling from the same population will produce values in the same range.

There are several forms of statistical inference. We just introduced two: point and interval estimation. This chapter deals with them fully. Chapter 8 examines the most widely used inference procedure: hypothesis testing. A hypothesis test would answer the "how long" question by testing the hypothesis that the mean time to complete the task is some specific value. For example, maybe the task that you will use for problem solving was used by some previous investigator, but the subjects were elementary school students. In the earlier study, the elementary school students took a mean of 15 minutes to complete the task. You might wonder if college students require the same length of time. To answer that question, you might test the hypothesis that the population mean for college students also equals 15 minutes. On the basis of the data from the study, that hypothesis would be either retained or rejected, thereby making an inference. (That is, we could infer either that the mean is 15 minutes for the college students or that it is not.)

POPULATIONS AND SAMPLES

A sample, as defined in Chapter 1, is a small group of observations. For example, a group of ten animals given a particular drug is a **sample** drawn from the large population of animals that might receive the drug. The word *sample* refers to a small group chosen from some larger group that we either did not choose to observe or that were not available to us. But our interest is almost always the population. It is rarely interesting to know what the sample shows, except as it shows us something about the population.

In common parlance, a population is a set of people who make up a well-defined (usually geographically defined) group. So we might speak of the population of the United States, or of the population of Seattle. In inferential statistics, the word has a more precise and limited meaning. Until now, our use of the terms *population* and *sample* have been a little careless.

Statistically, a **population** is a set of data we might observe. Thus, a population might consist of the midterm exam scores of the students in your statistics class; or the IQ scores of all of the third-grade students in the state of Pennsylvania; or the number of trials required to learn a certain list of 20 words by all college students past, present, and future; or the amounts of sucrose consumed by all rats who might ever live. There is little of the usual meaning of *population* here; the populations are sets of *scores*, not people or animals.

Populations vary in size from small and finite (like the test scores in one class) to very large but finite (the IQs of all Pennsylvania third-grade students ...) to infinite in size (introversion/extroversion scores for all students ...). With a very small population, there is little need for inference because we may be able to obtain all the values. The population of IQ scores of all Pennsylvania third-grade students is very large but not infinite; there are a fixed number of third graders in the state on any given day, and so in theory we could obtain all their IQ scores. As a practical matter, though, we could never be able to obtain them all—kids are absent, or sick, or otherwise unavailable during the testing period. So, although the population is real, finite, and, in principle, "knowable," we could never really have all the test scores. If you are an educational researcher, however, it could be very important to have a good estimate of the IQ score of Pennsylvania third graders, and so an inferential procedure is necessary.

A sample is a subset of a population. This definition means that a sample is a set of observations, typically those that we have in hand during a research investigation. In keeping with our preceding discussion, though, remember that a sample is a set of scores taken from a larger population, and not individual animals or third graders. Nothing in the definition of *sample* says anything about whether a sample is representative of the population—a sample is just a subset of a population. In addition, the definition of a sample implies nothing about *how* a sample was selected.

Numerical characteristics of a population, such as a mean, a median, a skewness measure, or a standard deviation, are called **parameters**. Every population has a center, spread, and form. Those values are parameters because they pertain to the population. Usually we can never know the values directly, however much we might like to. The mean IQ score for all Pennsylvania third-grade students, for example, is an actual value. The fact that we cannot know it with absolute certainty makes it no less real. The reason for using inferential statistics is to gain information about a parameter value, or, often, to draw a conclusion about differences in parameters between two or more populations, and to do so from a sample.

Just as there are numerical characteristics of populations, so there are also of samples. A numerical characteristic of a sample is called a **statistic**. Thus, both a population and a sample can have a median, a mean, a standard deviation, and so forth. The population values are *parameters*; the sample's are *statistics*.

Statistical inference makes statements about parameters, and does so from statistics. For example, a population might consist of all the introversion/extroversion scores of all college students—an infinite, unknowable population. Yet the values in that population define something of interest—namely, the personality structure of all college students. In order to draw conclusions about all students, we need to be able to say something about that population. But all we can ever test is a few students—those in our sample. From the sample, we may compute the mean score; from that mean —a sample statistic—we want to make an inference about the corresponding parameter. The procedures of inference thus let us generalize to the population, and also give us an indication of how comfortable we should be in the conclusions that we draw.

Statisticians customarily use Greek letters as symbols for population parameters and Roman letters for statistics. For example, the sample mean, $\overline{X}$, is an estimate of the population mean μ (mu). The sample variance, s^2, estimates the population variance, σ^2 (sigma squared); the sample standard deviation estimates its population value, σ.

A BRIEF INTRODUCTION TO PROBABILITY

Statistical inference is based on the mathematics of probability. Although we need not know much of that field of mathematics for our purposes here, we do need to know a little of its logic and terminology as well as some of its important concepts before we can proceed further into inference.[1]

The term *probability* generally refers to the likelihood that some particular event will occur. Actually, although that is the sense in which we commonly use the word, there is somewhat more to it than that. We often hear weather forecasts that contain the phrase "the probability of precipitation today is...." Just what does that number mean? How did the weather bureau determine it? How should we interpret it?

◆ Relative Frequency as Probability

A useful way of thinking of probability is in terms of a long-run frequency or proportion. If your chemistry instructor has a favorite question (and most instructors do), the chances are she keeps track of how students perform on that item. Suppose that, over the years, the question has been used on many tests, for a total of 300 students. If 180 of those students answered the item correctly, then the proportion or *relative frequency* of students scoring correctly is $180/300 = 0.60$ or 60%. We might also say that the probability of a student answering the item correctly is .60.

The "precipitation probabilities" that weather forecasters report are the same kinds of numbers. They are really relative frequencies and represent the proportion of times that a weather situation similar to the present one has been followed by precipitation. (In fact, weather probabilities are not really probabilities at all but descriptive statistics.)

---

[1] If you want to learn a bit more about probability theory, Lowry (1989) gives a very readable introduction.

The relative frequency interpretation of probability is a useful one. It is not only a convenient and easily understood summary of past data, but it also suggests a reasonable way to predict future occurrences. Our instructor has every reason to expect that, if the same question is used again, then again roughly 60% of the students will answer correctly. In the same way, a weather forecaster's "80% chance of rain" means that on about 80% of the days following such a forecast, there should be rain. Weather forecasts come with no guarantee of accuracy, and neither do probabilities—but at least they provide some guidance in deciding on a wardrobe, or on test questions, or on drawing a conclusion about a parameter.

◆ Some Probability Rules

If a mathematician is asked to define probability formally, he or she would probably say something like "A number between zero and one, inclusive, that attaches to an event, and is assigned in such a way that the sum of all of the probabilities of all the events within a given situation is 1.0." That is not a very satisfying answer to most psychologists, but it is mathematically accurate.

There are two important elements in this definition. First, probabilities are generally expressed as numbers between 0 and 1, though sometimes a percentage figure ("80% chance of rain," for example) is more understandable. The important point here is that the value cannot be negative (though zero is certainly permissible) and cannot exceed 1.0 (or 100%). Second, probabilities must add up to 1.0 (100%) over a certain set of possible occurrences. If you flip a coin, only two things can happen (barring the proverbial "lands on edge"), and if you assign a probability to "heads," the probability assigned to "tails" must be such that the two numbers sum to 1.0. That is, if the probability of "heads" is .5, then the probability of "tails" must also be .5. Or, if past history suggests that the probability of getting a particular chemistry question right is .6, then the probability of "wrong" must be .4.

Notice that the rules and statements about probabilities say nothing at all about the numbers being representative of the likelihood" that some particular event will happen. They also give no guidance about how the probability values should be assigned. The mathematics of probability does not require a likelihood interpretation, and can proceed without any such real-world meaning.

To illustrate and develop some additional probability rules, let's set up an example. Suppose you are a statistics instructor, and you have a file of 125 test questions on descriptive statistics. The questions can be categorized into groups, as shown in Table 7.1.

Now suppose you decide to test your students individually. When a student comes to your office, you reach into a hat and pull out a question at random. What is the probability that the first question you pull out is a z score question? Because there are 125 test items in the hat, and because 10 of these are z score questions, if you are really picking randomly, the proba-

TABLE 7.1

Kind of Question	Number of Questions	Probability
Measures of center	18	.144
Measures of spread	16	.128
Frequency distributions	17	.136
z scores	10	.080
Normal curve areas	9	.072
Scatterplots	12	.096
Correlation	18	.144
Percentiles	15	.120
Percentile ranks	10	.080

bility of drawing a z score question is 10/125, or .080. Likewise, the probability of picking a correlation question is 18/125 or .144.

To the mathematician, each question that you might draw is called an **outcome**. In the example, an outcome is any one of the possible occurrences when one item is drawn from the hat. There are 125 possible outcomes because there are 125 test items and any one of these questions could be drawn.

An **event** is a collection of one or more outcomes. Thus, there are 10 outcomes in the event "z score question," 18 outcomes in the event "correlation question," and so forth.

If all the outcomes are equally likely (the questions are all on the same size index cards, the cards are thoroughly scrambled in the hat, and so forth), we may define the simplest of the probability rules: When the outcomes are equally likely, the probability of an event is

$$\frac{\text{Number of outcomes in the event}}{\text{Total number of outcomes}}$$

The probability of the event "ask a correlation question," then, is

$$\frac{18}{125} = .144$$

If we make a rule that each outcome can be part of only one event (there are no questions that ask about both z scores and correlations, for example), then defining events in this way meets the two requirements that we stated previously: The the events have a probability between 0 and 1, and the probabilities sum to 1.0. (If outcomes can be members of more than one event, the rules are more complicated.)

If the outcome probabilities are not equal, we have to change the rule a bit: When the outcomes are not equally likely, the probability of an event is

Sum of the probabilities of outcomes in the event

Suppose we have a loaded die, with probabilities for each of the six sides of

Number of Spots	Probability
•	.25
••	.10
•••	.10
•• ••	.15
••• •••	.10
••• •••	.30

The probability of the event "even number of spots" is

$$.10 + .15 + .30 = .55$$

because the three outcomes have different probabilities. The probability of "less than 3 spots" is

$$.25 + .10 = .35$$

Let's return to the example of the instructor drawing statistics questions out of a hat. Suppose we want the probability of the event "ask a correlation or a scatterplot question." There are 12 outcomes in "scatterplot" and 18 in "correlation," so the number of outcomes in the event is

$$\frac{12 + 18}{125} = \frac{30}{125} = .240$$

Note that we could also express this as the sum of two separate events. That is, the probability of "correlation or scatterplot question" is

$$\frac{12}{125} + \frac{18}{125} = .240$$

$$= \text{Prob(correlation)} + \text{Prob(scatterplot)}$$

This brings us to the next important probability rule, the *addition rule*: The probability of either of two nonoverlapping events occurring is the sum of their separate probabilities. The addition rule is often called the *or* rule because it deals with the occurrence of either "scatterplot" *or* "correlation."

Suppose we ask two statistics questions, drawing each one randomly. (To keep the example simple, assume that you put the first question back into the hat after you ask it, so that the second pick is from the same 125 questions. Probably we would not really do it that way, of course, but it simplifies the example.) What is the probability, within the two questions, of your asking either a correlation or a regression question? The probability is the sum of the two probabilities, as before.

What if we ask the probability of the event "asking *two* correlation questions"? Now we must introduce the **multiplication rule**: The probability of two independent[2] events occurring jointly is the product of their separate probabilities. (This is sometimes called the *and* rule because it defines the probability that both of two events occur.) For our example, the probability is

$$\text{Prob(correlation)} * \text{Prob(correlation)} = (.144)(.144) = .021$$

In the same way, we can find the probability of asking both a percentile and a percentile rank question. That probability is found by the multiplication rule as

$$\text{Prob(percentile)} * \text{Prob(percentile rank)} = (.120)(.080) = .0096$$

As one more example, the probability of the event "*z* score and correlation" is

$$\text{Prob(}z\text{ scores)} * \text{Prob(correlation)} = (.080)(.144) = .0112$$

The next example requires two events. The first is the event "ask descriptive statistics question." The second event is "ask a normal curve question." The first event is made up of the separate events "center," "spread," "frequency distributions," and "*z* scores," and so its probability is

$$\frac{18}{125} + \frac{16}{125} + \frac{17}{125} + \frac{10}{125} = \frac{61}{125} = .488$$

---

[2] The term *independent* here means that one event has no effect on the probability of the other. That is, the fact that we have drawn and asked a *z* score question, for example, does not change the probability of drawing a correlation question. If the first question is returned to the hat after it is asked, then that requirement is met.

The second event contains the separate events "z scores" and "normal curve areas," and so its probability is

$$\frac{10}{125} + \frac{9}{125} = \frac{19}{125} = .152$$

At first thought, the probability of the event "ask either a descriptive *or* a normal curve question" might appear to be

$$\text{Prob(descriptive question)} + \text{Prob(normal question)} = .488 + .152$$
$$= .640$$

but that is incorrect. To see why, list the separate events that go into the event "ask either a descriptive or a normal curve question," as shown in Table 7.2. There are a total of 70 outcomes in the event, and

$$\frac{70}{125} = .560$$

which is clearly not equal to .640, the value we calculated initially.

What happened? The problem is that we counted one set of questions (z scores) twice because it was included in both events. We might diagram the situation as in Figure 7.1. The numbers of outcomes for each of the events is shown in the figure. Calculating the probability for the "normal curve" event, for example, sums the outcomes in "normal areas" and "z scores." In the same way, calculating the probability for "descriptive" summed the outcomes in "center," "frequency," "spread," and "z scores." Thus, when the probabilities of those two events were added, the ten outcomes in "z scores" were included twice. Correcting this difficulty leads to the complete statement of the **addition rule**: *The probability of either of two events occurring is the sum of their separate probabilities, minus the probability of their joint occurrence.* In this case, we have

TABLE 7.2		
Kind of Question	Number of Questions	Probability
Measures of center	18	.144
Measures of spread	16	.128
Frequency distributions	17	.136
z scores	10	.080
Normal curve areas	9	.072
Total	70	

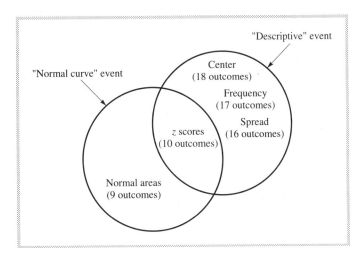

Figure 7.1

Prob(descriptive) + Prob(normal) − Prob(descriptive and normal)

$$= \underbrace{\frac{18}{125} + \frac{16}{125} + \frac{17}{125} + \frac{10}{125}}_{\text{Descriptive}} + \underbrace{\frac{10}{125} + \frac{9}{125}}_{\text{Normal}} - \underset{\substack{\uparrow \\ \text{Descriptive} \\ \text{and Normal}}}{\frac{10}{125}}$$

$$= \frac{70}{125} = .560$$

SAMPLING DISTRIBUTIONS

Suppose you and your classmates write your weights on individual slips of paper. Those values constitute a small population of weights. The mean of the weights, μ, is a parameter because it is a characteristic of a population. Now put all of the slips into a hat and pull out two at random. The values on those two slips are a sample of size $N = 2$ from the population of weights. We could compute the mean for that sample and we would have a statistic. Now return the two weights to the hat, repeat the random sampling, and calculate the mean. If we did that simple sampling and calculating exercise a number of times, we would have a number of sample means, each based on samples of size 2, each drawn from the same population.

Unless everyone in your class weighs exactly the same, the sample means will not all be equal. This is so because, although the population mean weight remains constant, the sample values will not be identical, and

TABLE 7.3

Sample	Mean
(129, 155)	142.0
(149, 120)	134.5
(127, 152)	139.5
(137, 127)	132.0
(162, 154)	158.0
(113, 156)	134.5
(145, 129)	137.0
(145, 147)	146.0
(138, 153)	145.5
(130, 111)	120.5
(129, 163)	146.0
(161, 150)	155.5
(128, 126)	127.0

so there will be a distribution of values of the sample mean. For example, suppose your entire population of weights contained the 30 values

129	149	127	137	162
113	145	145	138	130
129	161	128	155	120
152	127	154	156	129
147	153	111	163	150
126	145	181	102	133

The mean of these weights is 139.9 pounds. Because the entire set of student weights is a population, 139.9 is the population mean μ.

Table 7.3 shows several of the many samples of $N = 2$ that we could obtain from the population, along with the mean of each sample. Though all the means come from scores that were drawn from the same population, the samples are different, and so are their means. In fact, the means of the samples in Table 7.3 have a distribution themselves (Figure 7.2).

Figure 7.2 shows that there is variability among the sample means. Even with the bimodal distribution, the sample means can be seen to cluster around the population mean of 139.9.[3] This is the case even though none of the individual means is equal to μ.

We could have written out *all* possible samples of $N = 2$ (there are 870 such samples), but we will avoid that tedious exercise. If we had, though, we could have found the mean for every sample. Each mean would be an outcome, just as picking a question to ask is an outcome. Because each of the 870 samples (outcomes) is as likely as any other, each possible mean has the probability of $1/870 = .00115$. We could group the sample means into con-

[3] The mean of that set of 13 sample means is 139.85.

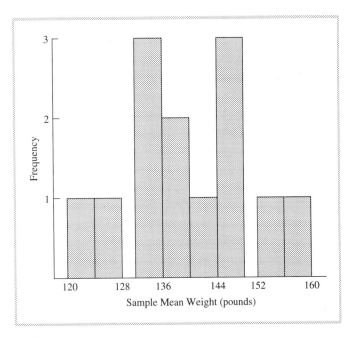

Figure 7.2

venient intervals, each comprising an event (e.g., $\overline{X}$ between 100 and 105, $\overline{X}$ between 105 and 110, and so forth). By summing the probabilities of the means within each event, we could find the probability for each. A plot of the probabilities might look something like Figure 7.3. This distribution gives the probability of each possible mean that we could observe by taking samples of $N = 2$ from the population of 30 student weights. This kind of distribution, because it gives the probabilities of all possible sample statistics from a population, is very important to the logic of inference. Such a distribution—one that gives the probabilities of possible values of a statistic—is called a **sampling distribution**.

A sampling distribution is a formal and abstract way of describing the probability of all the possible values of a statistic, the sample mean in this case. It is usually a theoretical distribution, meaning that we do not actually list all the possible values of the statistic and find their probabilities. If we have some way to know the form, the spread, and the center of all possible sample statistic values, then we can specify probabilities of various events precisely. And that is valuable because the sampling distribution allows us to make inferences.

◆ An Example Sampling Distribution

Suppose you are an instructor and write a short quiz containing four true–false items. Assume for now that your students have not read their assign-

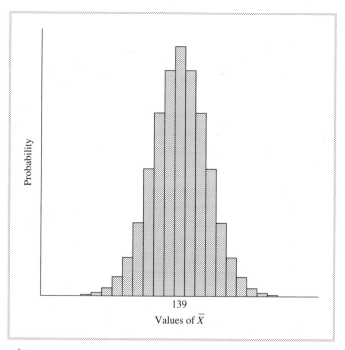

Figure 7.3

ment and will be guessing at each answer. Under these conditions, it is reasonable to assign a probability of .5 to the answer true, and .5 to false. Some specific pattern (for instance, T-T-F-F) will be correct, but it is only one of the possible patterns (like T-T-T-T, or T-F-T-T, or F-F-T-T) that a student might guess.

If we were to write down all the possible patterns of T and F answers in a four-item test, we would discover that there are 16 of them, as shown in Table 7.4. Assuming that the correct pattern of answers is T-T-F-F, we also show the number of correct answers for each possible pattern. If we score a student's paper for the number of items correct, the possible scores are 0, 1, 2, 3, or 4. Only the T-T-F-F pattern represents a correct quiz paper. All the others represent one or more errors. Four patterns represent a single error; six patterns, two errors; and so forth.

The 16 patterns of answers are outcomes in the simple experiment "give a student the quiz." If a student is really guessing, then each of the outcomes is as likely as any other, giving a probability of 1/16 for each. That being the case, we can find the probabilities of several events. For example, the probability of the event "get three correct answers" is 4/16 because 4 of the 16 outcomes (T-T-T-F, T-T-F-T, F-T-F-F, and T-F-F-F) make up the event. We could define a set of events like "get zero right," "get 1 right," and so on, and determine the probability of each. The probabilities of these five possible "events" (test scores, actually) are shown in Table 7.5. What we have just

TABLE 7.4

		Question		
1	2	3	4	Number Correct
T	T	T	T	2
T	T	T	F	3
T	T	F	T	3
T	F	T	T	1
F	T	T	T	1
T	T	F	F	4
T	F	T	F	2
T	F	F	T	2
F	F	T	T	0
F	T	F	T	2
F	T	T	F	2
F	F	F	T	1
F	F	T	F	1
F	T	F	F	3
T	F	F	F	3
F	F	F	F	2

TABLE 7.5

Number of Correct Answers	Number of Ways to Get Them	Probability
0	1	1/16 = .0625
1	4	4/16 = .2500
2	6	6/16 = .3750
3	4	4/16 = .2500
4	1	1/16 = .0625
	16	16/16 = 1.000

done is develop a measurement rule ("Count the number of questions correct") and associate a probability with each possible measurement value (assuming, of course, that the students are actually guessing).

The probability distribution could be represented by a histogram that clearly shows the symmetry of the probabilities (Figure 7.4). This distribution represents the probabilities of a single student's receiving each possible grade, assuming that he or she is guessing. Getting two questions correct is the most likely, and one and three are quite likely as well. But there is a 1/16 probability that the student will guess correctly four times. And it is just as likely that the student will guess all four questions wrong.

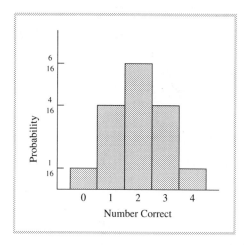

Figure 7.4

In addition to having the unimodal, symmetric form illustrated, the distribution of possible test scores has a center and a spread. Computing the mean and standard deviation is straightforward. Go back to the 16 outcomes in Table 7.4 and compute the mean number of items correct as

$$\mu = (2 + 3 + 3 + \cdots + 1 + 3 + 3 + 2)/16 = 2.0$$

Because we have the entire population of test scores, this value must be a parameter. In words, this parameter tells us that if students are merely guessing on the quiz, then, on average, they should have a score of 2.0 items correct.

But the scores, as noted previously, will not all be 2.0 because there is spread in the distribution. We can also compute the standard deviation of the population by applying a slightly modified[4] formula:

$$\sigma = \sqrt{\frac{\sum (X - \bar{X})^2}{N}}$$

$$= \sqrt{\frac{(2 - 2)^2 + (3 - 2)^2 + \cdots + (3 - 2)^2 + (2 - 2)^2}{16}}$$

$$= 1.0$$

Again, this is a parameter because it is based on all possible values, and we may use the correct Greek letter symbol for the population standard deviation.

Now consider a sample of size $N = 2$ from the class of students taking this four-item quiz. With two students, both could happen to get all four

---

[4] We will come to the reason for this modification soon.

questions right, giving a sample of (4, 4) and a sample mean of 4.0. Or, conceivably, both could miss everything, giving a sample of (0, 0) and $\overline{X} = 0.0$. Any other combination of right and wrong answers is also possible. The possible outcomes for two hypothetical students, John and Fred, appear in Table 7.6. The probabilities in the table are computed by using the multiplication rule. Because John is just guessing, the probability that he gets a 0 is 1/16; the same holds for Fred. The probability that both John and Fred get 0 is the product of the two probabilities. So the probability of getting a sample mean of 0.0 is $1/16 * 1/16$ or $1/256 = .0039$. The same logic can be applied to all the possible values of the sample mean; a few examples are shown in the table.

The only possible values of the mean are $0.0, 0.5, 1.0, 1.5, \ldots, 3.5, 4.0$. We may compute the probability of each by using the multiplication and addition rules. For example, (1, 1), (0, 2), and (2, 0) are the three possible ways of obtaining $\overline{X} = 1.0$. The probability of the (1, 1) outcome is $4/16 * 4/16 = .0625$ (because the probability of each "1" is 4/16). The probability of (0, 2) is $1/16 * 6/16 = .0234$, as is the probability of (2, 0). By summing the probabilities, the probability of obtaining $\overline{X} = 1.0$ is found to be .1093. In a similar way, we can find the probabilities for all the possible mean values (of course, still assuming that the students are guessing). That distribution is given in Table 7.7. Note that we followed the mathematical probability rules requiring each event (each possible value of the sample mean) to be assigned a probability value between 0.0 and 1.0. The rule that the probability values sum to 1.0 is followed as well.

What we just constructed is a distribution that gives the probability of all possible values of the sample mean. This is an important, special kind of distribution called the *sampling distribution of the mean*. It gives the probability for every possible value of a statistic. We just developed the sampling distribution of the mean for samples of $N = 2$. Nothing was required except the application of the addition and multiplication rules and, of course, the assumption that the students taking the quiz were guessing. If we give the

TABLE 7.6			
Some Possible Samples			
John	Fred	Mean Correct	Probability of Sample
0	0	0.0	.0039
0	1	0.5	.0156
0	2	1.0	.0234
⋮			
2	2	2.0	.1406
2	3	2.5	.0937
⋮			
4	4	4.0	.0039

TABLE 7.7

Mean Correct	Probability
0.0	.0039
0.5	.0312
1.0	.1093
1.5	.2186
2.0	.2734
2.5	.2186
3.0	.1093
3.5	.0312
4.0	.0039
	1.0000

quiz to two randomly selected students, then the distribution tells us the probability of obtaining any possible mean score. The mean is most likely to be in the 1.5 to 2.5 range. A mean of 0.0, or of 4.0, for example, is quite unlikely but still possible. A histogram of the sampling distribution (Figure 7.5) shows the values easily. In the illustration, each rectangle shows the probability of a possible $\overline{X}$ value. For example, if the students are guessing, the probability of the event "the mean score is between 1.5 and 2.5, inclusive" is as illustrated in Figure 7.6. We may calculate the probability represented by the darker area by applying the addition rule once more, using the probabilities in Table 7.7:

$$\text{Prob}(1.5) + \text{Prob}(2.0) + \text{Prob}(2.5) = .2186 + .2734 + .2186$$

$$= .7106$$

As another example, the probability that two students scoring a mean of 3.0 or greater if they are guessing is illustrated in Figure 7.7. Computationally, the probability is

$$\text{Prob}(3.0) + \text{Prob}(3.5) + \text{Prob}(4.0) = .1093 + .0312 + .0039$$

$$= .1444$$

Finally, define the event "the mean score is extreme" (where we define 0.0 and 4.0 to be extreme). This is the darker area shown in Figure 7.8. The probability is

$$\text{Prob}(0.0) + \text{Prob}(4.0) = .0039 + .0039$$

$$= .0078$$

We could also define the event "$\overline{X}$ is not extreme" as $\overline{X} = 0.5, 1.0, 1.5,$

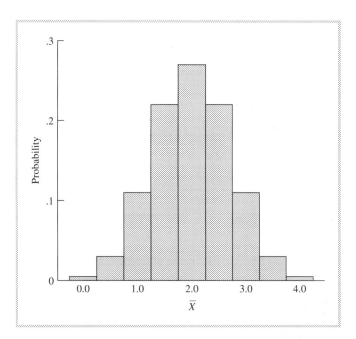

Figure 7.5

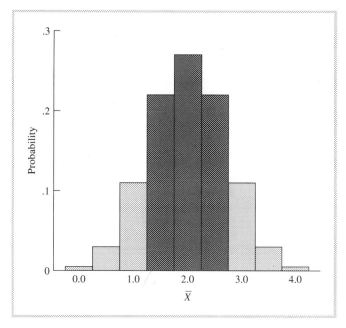

Figure 7.6

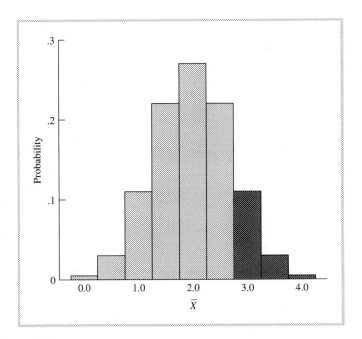

Figure 7.7

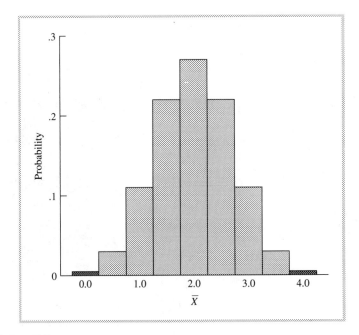

Figure 7.8

2.0, 2.5, 3.0, and 3.5. The probability of this event is illustrated in Figure 7.9. In numbers,

$$\text{Prob}(0.5) + \text{Prob}(1.0) + \text{Prob}(1.5) + \text{Prob}(2.0)$$
$$+ \text{Prob}(2.5) + \text{Prob}(3.0) + \text{Prob}(3.5)$$
$$= .0312 + .1093 + .2186 + .2734 + .2186 + .1093 + .0312$$
$$= .9922$$

We could also calculate the probability of "$\overline{X}$ is not extreme" by noting that it is the complement of "$\overline{X}$ is extreme," and that those two events together account for all of the possible means. That is,

$$\text{Prob}(\overline{X} \text{ is extreme}) + \text{Prob}(\overline{X} \text{ is not extreme}) = 1.0000$$

so that

$$\text{Prob}(\overline{X} \text{ is not extreme}) = 1.0000 - \text{Prob}(\overline{X} \text{ is extreme})$$
$$= 1.0000 - .0078$$
$$= .9922$$

Following procedures similar to those illustrated previously, we could

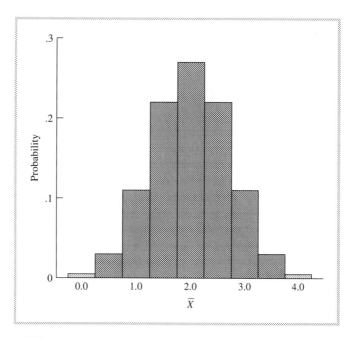

Figure 7.9

compute the mean and the standard deviation of the sampling distribution of $\overline{X}$. If we did, we would find that

$$\mu_{\overline{X}} = 2.0$$

and that

$$\sigma_{\overline{X}} = 0.707$$

Note that the subscript $\overline{X}$ reminds us that these values pertain to the distribution of the mean, and not to the original values. What we have now are the center (the arithmetic mean) and the spread (the standard deviation) of the sampling distribution of $\overline{X}$ for samples of $N = 2$. The fact that the mean of the sampling distribution is equal to the mean of the population is important to our ability to make inferences, and we will return to that property soon.

The other value, the standard deviation of the sampling distribution of the means, needs some special attention. Its value is equal to 0.707 in this case; in general though, it is equal to

$$\sigma_{\overline{X}} = \frac{\sigma}{\sqrt{N}}$$

For $N = 2$,

$$\sigma_{\overline{X}} = \frac{1}{\sqrt{2}} = 0.707$$

This important relationship bears repeating: *The standard deviation of the sampling distribution of the means is equal to the standard deviation of the population divided by the square root of N.* This relationship formalizes an important fact about the mean: As the sample size becomes larger, the variability of the sampling distribution becomes smaller. As a consequence, the sample means cluster tightly around μ, and values far from μ become less likely.

The standard deviation of the sampling distribution of the mean is related to the degree to which a sample mean may differ from the population mean. Clearly, the larger the value of N, the closer $\overline{X}$ is likely to be to μ. Because of this relationship between sample size and the probable error in the sample mean, the standard deviation of the sampling distribution is often called the *standard error of the mean*. Indeed, the standard deviation of the sampling distribution of any statistic is often called the **standard error** of that statistic.

For the arithmetic mean, the mean of the sampling distribution is always equal to the mean of the population. And the standard error of the mean is always equal to

$$\sigma_{\bar{X}} = \frac{\sigma}{\sqrt{N}}$$

For a given sample size, then, we know two of the important features of the sampling distribution of the sample mean: its mean and standard deviation. If we also knew the form of the sampling distribution, then we would be able to use a completely known distribution to make inferences.

Suppose we were to repeat the four-item quiz exercise with samples of size $N = 3$, following the same logic for computing probabilities of events. We would find that the distribution of $\bar{X}$ would become even more "normal looking," with more of the probability concentrated near the center and very little in the extremes. We could also construct the sampling distribution for $\bar{X}$ with $N = 4$, with $N = 5$, and so forth. If we did so, we would discover three things: (1) that the mean of the sampling distribution remains equal to 2.0 regardless of N, (2) that the standard error of the mean continues to be equal to

$$\sigma_{\bar{X}} = \frac{\sigma}{\sqrt{N}}$$

regardless of N, and (3) that the form of the sampling distribution approaches the normal distribution in form. This last characteristic of the sampling distribution of the mean is important and has been formalized in a theorem that serves as an important step in the development of inference logic.

THE CENTRAL LIMIT THEOREM

In a powerful statement known as the **central limit theorem**, mathematicians are able to prove that the form of the sampling distribution of the means of the samples really does become normal as the sample size increases. The only requirements are that the population sampled have a finite mean and variance. Given those conditions, the mean of the sampling distribution of the mean will be equal to μ, and the standard deviation of the sampling distribution will be equal to

$$\sigma_{\bar{X}} = \frac{\sigma}{\sqrt{N}}$$

It is not necessary that the population from which observations are sampled be normal. The central limit theorem applies to the sampling distribution of the mean, regardless of population form.

The central limit theorem provides an important foundation for inference. Because of it, we know the form of the sampling distribution of the mean, at least for sufficiently large samples. If the form of the underlying population is normal, then the sampling distribution of the mean will be normal in form regardless of sample size. For small samples from a normal population, then, we know the form of the sampling distribution of the mean. When the population distribution is not normal, the central limit theorem tells us the form of the sampling distribution, if the sample size is large enough.[5] That is, with a large sample, we may assume that the sampling distribution is normal in form, regardless of the form of the population.

◆ Drawing Samples

Knowing the parameters and form of a sampling distribution lets us determine the probabilities of values of a mean (and other statistics) from randomly drawn samples. The important word here is *randomly*; if the sample is not picked at random, then the probability rules do not necessarily apply. In particular, if the samples are picked in some nonrandom way, we can have no assurance that the central limit theorem will describe the form of the sampling distribution.

In the preceding example, we used a very small sample size. Usually we want to talk about samples larger than $N = 2$. But whatever the sample size, random sampling ensures that the distribution of statistics follows certain known distribution forms, of which the normal is the most important. How do we ensure a random sample? To answer that question, we must first define just what a random sample is.

A sample of size N is a **random sample** if it was chosen from its population in such a way that *every other sample of the same size had the same chance of being selected.*

Notice that the definition of a random sample refers only to the process by which it was selected, and says nothing about its "representativeness." In fact, random sampling guarantees that some samples will be "unrepresentative." The random sampling process merely ensures that any sample is as likely (or unlikely) as any other, so that a statistic based on a random sample—although it may not be "representative" of its parameter—has not been systematically biased in any way.

How do we select random samples? Making up numbers mentally is not a good way to do it because humans are poor random number generators. Taking every fifteenth name in the phone book until you have N names is poor, too, unless you intend to limit your population to those people with telephones (with listed numbers); even then, the sample is random only if you pick your starting name randomly.

One obvious sampling procedure, which follows directly from the definition, would be to write each possible sample on a slip of paper, put them all into a hat (or barrel, or cement mixer, depending on the size of the population), mix them thoroughly, and have a blindfolded assistant pick

---

[5] Many statisticians recommend that samples of 30 or more are "large enough," at least if the population is roughly symmetrical.

one. Obviously, this is impractical for all but the very smallest populations and sample sizes.

Another procedure would be to assign a unique number to each observation in the population, and then draw the numbers out of a hat in handfuls of size N. If the numbers are mixed well, then any handful is as likely as any other, and the sample would be random.

A variant of the handful sampling process is actually the one used most often. Assign a number to each observation in the population, and then obtain a set of N random numbers between 1 and the largest value assigned to a population member. The observations whose numbers have been selected then constitute the random sample. The random numbers can be obtained from a table of random numbers such as Appendix B, though most statistics programs offer the ability to generate samples of numbers in the range 1, 2, ... such that all numbers are equally likely.

PARAMETER ESTIMATES

The ability to specify the sampling distribution of a statistic (most often the mean) and to select a random sample, lets us form probability statements about various outcomes, and thereby make an inference about the population from which a sample came.

There are three common inference procedures: point estimation, interval estimation, and the hypothesis test. We present the first two in the remainder of this chapter, and defer hypothesis testing until Chapter 8.

◆ Point Estimation

When we make a point estimate, we use a statistic whose single value is taken as our "best guess" as to the value of the parameter it is estimating. We all use point estimates regularly in daily life: "When will the mail arrive?" "Around 10:30" or "How late will the instructor be this morning?" "Five minutes." Both of these examples employ point estimates to answer everyday questions. (An answer like "Probably between 10:00 and 11:00" is an interval estimate.) Although we don't understand how humans intuitively combine past evidence to produce such answers, we do it easily, and can make use of point estimate information.

CHARACTERISTICS OF GOOD POINT ESTIMATORS

What makes a good point estimator? For one thing, the estimator should not consistently over- or underestimate its target parameter. That is, although any individual value of the statistic might be either too high or too low, it wouldn't be consistently on one side or the other. Another way of saying the same thing is that we would hope that the mean of a large num-

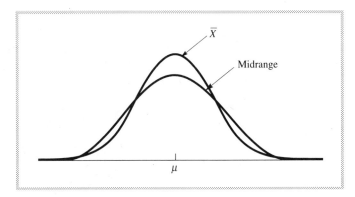

Figure 7.10

ber of the values of the statistic would equal the parameter being estimated. A statistic that is, on the average, neither too high nor too low, is called *unbiased*. An **unbiased statistic** has the mean of its sampling distribution equal to the parameter being estimated. (And, of course, that's just another way of saying that it is neither too high nor too low, on the average.)

Suppose we have two unbiased statistics to estimate the same parameter. In other words, the means of the sampling distributions are equal to each other and to the parameter. Are there still differences between the two estimators? Certainly. For one thing, they might differ in variability. Suppose there are two estimators for μ—for example, $\overline{X}$ and the midrange.[6] The two sampling distributions, based on the same sample size, might look like the curves in Figure 7.10. The statistics have similarly shaped sampling distributions, and both are centered on μ (because they are unbiased). But the distribution for the midrange is more variable. The sampling distribution for $\overline{X}$ is more compact, and thus $\overline{X}$ is likely to be closer than the midrange to μ. The statistic with the smaller variability in its sampling distribution is more **efficient**.

Two other characteristics of good estimators are often cited—namely, *sufficiency* and *consistency*. A **sufficient statistic** uses all the information in the sample to make its estimate. Another way to say the same thing is that a sufficient estimator cannot be improved by adding information from the same sample. The arithmetic mean is sufficient as an estimator; it uses not only all the scores in the data but also their number. A midrange is less sufficient because it omits all but the smallest and the largest data values. The median is also less sufficient than the mean because it uses only the ordinal information in the data and not distance information. Of course, that characteristic can be a benefit in a skewed distribution because the median is less influenced by extreme scores.

---

[6] The midrange, the point halfway between the highest and the lowest scores, is an unbiased estimate of μ in a symmetric population.

A **consistent statistic** is one whose accuracy increases as sample size increases. In other words, taking a larger sample will give greater likelihood that the sample estimate is close to the parameter. All the statistics we will use are consistent. As we note soon, the sample standard deviation is slightly biased as an estimator of σ, but the bias diminishes as the sample size increases. This is the most notable instance of consistency in the statistics that we'll encounter.

ESTIMATION FOR COMMON STATISTICS

The three measures of center discussed in Chapter 3 are adequate as measures of their respective parameters. The decision whether to use the population mean or median as the measure of center, though, isn't usually dictated by the characteristics of the estimator as much as it is by characteristics of measurement and by the data themselves. In a skewed distribution, the median is the better measure, and that's a decision that can be made easily; fortunately, the sample median is an excellent estimator on all counts. Likewise, sample proportions are unbiased, and otherwise good, estimators for their respective parameters.[7]

MEASURES OF SPREAD. Estimating the variance and the standard deviation present special problems because they are often presented in two different forms, a biased and an unbiased form.

In Chapter 3 we defined the variance and sample standard deviation as

$$s^2 = \frac{\sum (X - \overline{X})^2}{N - 1}$$

and

$$s = \sqrt{\frac{\sum (X - \overline{X})^2}{N - 1}}$$

respectively. These definitions are important for understanding the variance as the mean of the squared deviations from the arithmetic mean. And they are also the correct statistics to use as estimates of σ and σ^2. But they are not the values to use if you happen to have a complete population. For a population, in those rare instances when we really have all the values, the parameters σ^2 and σ are defined by formulas where the divisor is N (rather than $N - 1$), making the variance exactly the arithmetic mean of the squared differences between the scores and their mean. Of course, we rarely have complete populations available (except in the examples that statistics book

---

[7] A sample proportion is the arithmetic mean of a sample from a population of 0, 1 values and is thus unbiased. For example, if we're estimating the proportion of males in a population, the sample proportion of males may be computed as (number of males)/N, or by scoring males = 1 and females = 0 and calculating the mean.

authors invent)—but where we do, those formulas are correct. This is why, in the earlier example of a sampling distribution (page 188), we divided by 16 (N) and not 15 ($N - 1$).

The standard deviation of the sampling distribution of the mean is closely related to the standard deviation. Its population value is defined by

$$\sigma_{\overline{X}} = \frac{\sigma}{\sqrt{N}}$$

and the sample estimate may be computed as

$$s_{\overline{X}} = \frac{s}{\sqrt{N}}$$

simply replacing the parameter σ by its estimate.

◆ Interval Estimation

Point estimates use a single sample value to make an estimate of the parameter. An unbiased point estimate, on the average, equals the parameter. But usually we have only a single statistic, and we can never know just how close it is to its parameter. Think about playing darts, where the bull's-eye is the parameter. Unless you are a very good darts player, every throw will not get you a bull's-eye. If you throw a lot of darts and keep track of where you hit each time, you might find that over a lot of throws, your average was a bull's-eye. Nevertheless, each individual throw might be a distance off. That is just like an unbiased point estimator—any individual statistic might not be right on the mark, but "on the average" it will be.[8]

An interval estimate, in contrast to the point estimate, establishes a range of values that should contain the parameter. Instead of a single value, an interval estimate is often presented as a value "plus or minus" some amount. Political polls given in the news media are often interval estimates: "The polls show Jones the leader over Smith by a margin of 32% to 41% plus or minus 3.4%." That is a typical interval estimate. What it means is that Smith's "true" proportion (the parameter) is probably between 28.6% and 35.4%, while that for Jones is most likely between 37.6% and 44.4%. The "probably" indicates that an interval estimate is accompanied by a probability value (not usually reported by the press). The inclusion of a probability with an interval estimate is a second difference between it and the point estimate. A point estimate offers a single value as a "best guess" at the

---

[8] You might also find that you consistently hit too low, or too far to the left, or somewhere else off the mark. Such performance is the equivalent of a biased estimator—off the mark and in a consistent direction.

parameter; an interval estimate establishes a range of values *and* attaches a probability to it.

If a point estimate can be likened to throwing darts, then interval estimation is a little like playing horseshoes. The goal in horseshoes is to throw the U-shaped horseshoe at the target post (called the pin) in the hopes that the U of the horseshoe will "ring" the pin. The parameter is like the pin, and the estimate is the horseshoe. (Actually, the estimate is more like the width across the opening of the horseshoe because the estimate is a distance.) A reasonable horseshoe player may expect to ring the pin in a percentage of tosses that is proportional to the width of the horseshoe—the wider the shoe, the more "ringers."

An interval estimate gives a range of values into which the parameter is "likely" to fall. Just as in horseshoes, the wider the interval, the more likely it is to capture the parameter, as illustrated in Figure 7.11.

The interval is computed by using a point estimate as the starting point and then continuing some distance on either side of it. The distance out from the point estimate is determined by several things, including the probability that we want to have of "capturing" the parameter.

Suppose that the point estimate for μ was 78.2, that we wanted a probability level of .9, and that the distance out from the mean on each side was 1.5. The estimate would then say, in effect, "We have a certainty of 90% that the parameter is within the interval 78.2 $\pm$ 1.5 (or 76.7 to 79.7)." Another way to phrase the estimate that more nearly describes the real meaning is roughly this: "If we repeat the sampling procedure a very large number of times, we would expect that the interval that we compute, which on the basis of the present data is 78.2 $\pm$ 1.5, will enclose the parameter 90% of the time." Or, to continue our horseshoe analogy, "With a horseshoe whose width on this computation is 78.2 $\pm$ 1.5, I expect a ringer 90% of the time."

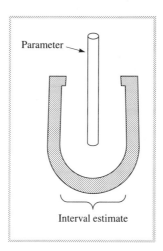

Parameter

Interval estimate

Figure 7.11

An interval estimate is often understood as an expression of how confident you are that the value of the parameter is within the interval. For this reason, interval estimates are frequently called **confidence intervals**.

Determining an interval estimate depends on four factors: a point estimate for the parameter, a measure of spread, a desired probability (confidence level), and an assumption about the form of the population. The population mean is the most common target for an interval estimate, and we present the logic using it. For now, we assume that the form of the population from which the data were sampled is normal.

McGowen and Hart (1992) report a survey of clinical psychologists who were asked a large number of questions about various experiences they had had in their careers. For example, one item was "If faced with a job choice between a job that seems to fit my values and goals in life or one that pays better but is not as important to me, I would choose the valued one" (p. 736). The respondents replied on a scale from 1 (Not true) to 7 (Very true). For the females respondents who answered that question ($N = 81$), the mean rating $\overline{X}$ was 5.8 and s was 1.3.

What is the true mean rating of clinical psychologists on this question? Obviously we can never know for sure, but we can make an inference about it. A confidence interval for μ, the population rating, offers the answer that we seek. As an example, we will find the 95% confidence interval for μ, the true population rating on the question.

First, from the standard deviation given in the results, compute the estimated standard error of the mean as

$$s_{\overline{X}} = \frac{s}{\sqrt{N}} = \frac{1.3}{\sqrt{81}} = 0.14$$

Next, assume that we know something about the sampling distribution of the mean. Because $N = 81$, we can safely assume that the sampling distribution of the mean is normal. If we use the mean of the sample as a point estimate for the value of μ, we have the form (normal), the mean (5.8), and a spread ($s_{\overline{X}} = 0.14$) for the sampling distribution. With these values in hand, the formula for the 95% interval estimate for μ is

$$\overline{X} \pm 1.96(s_{\overline{X}})$$

Applying this formula to the example gives the computation

$$\overline{X} \pm 1.96(s_{\overline{X}}) = 5.8 \pm 1.96(0.14) = 5.8 \pm 0.27$$

Another way of expressing the interval is to say that the 95% confidence interval extends from 5.53 to 6.07. Thus, we can say that we are 95% certain that the true rating of the population of clinical psychologists surveyed is between 5.53 and 6.07. Thus we can infer that the clinicians strongly agree with the statement that they would choose a job that fit their values over one that paid better.

Other interval estimates are determined in the same way, substituting an appropriate value from Appendix A. For example, to find the 99% interval, we would use Appendix A, which tells us that ± 2.58 defines the middle 99% of the normal distribution. Similarly, using ± 1.65 would give the 90% interval because ± 1.65 encloses the middle 90% of the curve.

PRESENTING INTERVAL ESTIMATES

There are several ways to present an interval estimate. Often, a simple sentence format is appropriate. The sentence "The 95% confidence interval for the mean is 5.8 ± 0.27" is direct and to the point. A tabular format is useful if there are several intervals to report. For example, we might see a format like that in Table 7.8.

Finally, confidence intervals are often shown graphically as error bars on a plot. The data from Table 7.8 might appear as in Figure 7.12.

TABLE 7.8				
	Number of Words Recalled		95% Interval	
Age	Mean	SD	Low	High
5	13.62	6.67	11.33	15.91
8	15.74	3.15	13.85	17.63
12	16.22	2.85	14.86	17.58
⋮				

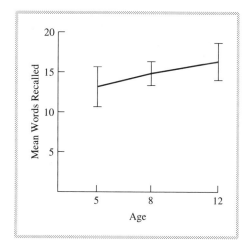

Figure 7.12

Summary

◆ *A* point estimate *is a statistic used to estimate a parameter.*

◆ *An* interval estimate *provides a range of values into which the parameter may fall, and attaches a probability to the parameter's actually being there.*

◆ *A* population *is a set of data that we might observe.*

◆ *A* sample *is a subset of a population.*

◆ *A* parameter *is a numerical characteristic of a population.*

◆ *A* statistic *is a numerical characteristic of a sample.*

◆ *Statistical inference makes statements about parameters on the basis of statistics.*

◆ *We normally use Greek letters as symbols for population parameters and Roman letters for statistics.*

◆ *The word* probability *generally refers to the likelihood that some particular event will occur.*

◆ *We often think of probability as a long-run frequency or proportion.*

◆ *The* addition rule: *The probability of either of two events occurring is the sum of their separate probabilities, minus the probability of their joint occurrence.*

◆ *The* multiplication rule: *The probability of two independent events occurring jointly is the product of their separate probabilities.*

◆ *A* sampling distribution *gives the probabilities of possible values of a statistic.*

◆ *The sampling distribution for* $\overline{X}$ *has a standard deviation equal to* $\sigma_{\overline{X}} = (\sigma/\sqrt{N})$, *which indicates that the variability of the sampling distribution becomes smaller as the sample size increases.*

◆ *The standard deviation of the sampling distribution of any statistic is called the* standard error *of that statistic.*

◆ *The* central limit theorem *tells us that the form of the sampling distribution of the means of the samples becomes normal as the sample size increases.*

◆ *A random sample is a sample chosen from its population in such a way that every other sample of the same size had the same chance of being selected.*

◆ *An* unbiased statistic *is one that is, on the average, neither too high nor too low.*

◆ *If a statistic is unbiased, the mean of its sampling distribution is equal to the parameter being estimated.*

◆ *For two statistics estimating the same parameter, the one with the smaller variability in its sampling distribution is more* efficient.

◆ *The mean and the median are unbiased estimates of their parameters.*

◆ *The variance and the standard deviation, when defined as in Chapter 3, are unbiased estimates of their parameters.*

Key Terms
ADDITION RULE
CENTRAL LIMIT THEOREM
CONFIDENCE INTERVAL
CONSISTENT STATISTIC
EFFICIENT STATISTIC
EVENT
INTERVAL ESTIMATE
μ
MULTIPLICATION RULE
OUTCOME
PARAMETER

POINT ESTIMATE
POPULATION
RANDOM SAMPLE
σ
σ^2
SAMPLE
SAMPLING DISTRIBUTION
STANDARD ERROR
STATISTIC
SUFFICIENT STATISTIC
UNBIASED STATISTIC

 EXERCISES

1. A psychologist interested in taste preferences places five different substances before his experimental animals. If the animals have no taste preferences among the substances, what proportion of the time would you expect each substance to be the first one tasted? Why? Are your numbers probabilities or relative frequencies?

2. In the hypothetical exam described on page 178 and in Table 7.1, find each of the following probabilities (remember that each question is returned to the hat after it is asked):

   a. If one question is asked, what is the probability that it will be either a center or a spread question?

   b. If two questions are asked, what is the probability that both of them are normal curve area questions?

   c. If two questions are asked, what is the probability they are the same question?

   d. Suppose that the instructor makes up a 50-item test by selecting questions at random from his test file. How many of the 50

questions are likely to be from each of the question groups?

3. Continuing from exercise 7.2, define the event "relative location" as the events "z scores," "percentiles," and "percentile ranks."

   a. Find the probability of "relative location."

   b. Find the probability of "relative location" or "normal curve."

   c. Find the probability of "relative location" or "descriptive."

4. Construct a sample population with five values (the weights of five friends, your scores on the last five weekly quizzes, the number of words on each of the last five postcards you've received, or the number of your cousins plus those of four of your friends are all possible examples). Write the population elements on slips of paper.

   a. Find the mean (μ) of the population.

   b. With the population values on separate slips of paper, shuffle them thoroughly. Select a sample of two values randomly from the population. Find the mean and the sample standard deviation for the sample and return the two slips to the population. Shuffle again, and randomly pick two more and find their mean and sample standard deviation. Repeat the process until you have picked 40 samples of size 2. You will now have 40 means and 40 sample standard deviations, one of each from each sample.

c. Construct the frequency distribution of your sample means.

d. Find the mean of your sample means.

e. Describe what the distribution looks like.

f. Keep the sample means and standard deviations for use in a later exercise.

5. Use the random numbers in Appendix B to sample values between 0 and 1. Pick a random starting point in the table, and regard the number as a five-digit decimal (that is, the random number 90214 would be the decimal value 0.90214). Alternatively, use your computer's random number facility to obtain random numbers. In either case, obtain 20 sets of two numbers between 0 and 1. These numbers are 20 samples of size $N = 2$ from a population whose distribution form is rectangular (all values are equally likely). The population has a mean $\mu = 0.5$ and standard deviation $\sigma = 0.289$.

a. Compute the mean for each of your samples of two.

b. Construct the frequency distribution of the sample means.

c. Find the mean and standard deviation of your set of 20 means.

d. What do you conclude about the form of the distribution of means as compared to the form of the population from which the samples were drawn?

e. What do you conclude about the mean of the distribution of means as compared with the mean of the population from which the samples were drawn?

6. Repeat exercise 7.5 with samples of $N = 3$ and $N = 4$.

7. The sampling distribution for the mean of

samples of size $N = 3$ from the four-item quiz example is

MEAN CORRECT	PROBABILITY
0.00	.00024
0.33	.00294
0.67	.01612
1.00	.05372
1.33	.12086
1.67	.19338
2.00	.22264
2.33	.19338
2.67	.12086
3.00	.05372
3.33	.01612
3.67	.00294
4.00	.00024
	1.00000

Using this probability distribution, find the probabilities of the following events (remember the addition and multiplication rules):

a. $\overline{X} \leq 3.0$

b. $1.3 \leq \overline{X} \leq 2.0$

c. $\overline{X} > 2.0$

d. $\overline{X} \geq 2.0$

e. $\overline{X} \leq 1.0$ or ≥ 3.0

f. $\overline{X} < 1.0$ or > 3.0

g. $\overline{X} \leq 0.5$ or ≥ 3.5

h. $0.33 \leq \overline{X} \leq 1.0$ or $3.0 \leq \overline{X} \leq 3.67$

8. If we were to give the four-item exam to a sample of 25 students, what would be μ and $\sigma_{\overline{X}}$ for the sampling distribution of $\overline{X}$?

9. Suppose we give the four-item exam to a sample of 32 students. What would be μ and $\sigma_{\overline{X}}$ for the sampling distribution of $\overline{X}$? What can you say about the form of the sampling distribution? Why?

10. If 30 students take the four-item exam, and are all truly guessing, find the probabilities of each of the following:

a. $1.5 \leq \overline{X} \leq 2.5$

b. $\overline{X} > 3.0$

c. $1.5 \leq \overline{X}$

d. $1.64 \leq \overline{X} \leq 2.36$

e. $\overline{X} < 1.64$ or $\overline{X} > 2.36$

f. $1.82 \leq \overline{X} \leq 2.18$

g. $\overline{X} < 1.82$ or $\overline{X} > 2.18$

11. If you were actually to have 20 random samples of 30 students each who were randomly guessing on a four-item test, of the means of those 20 samples, how many of the 20 would you expect to fall in each of the intervals defined in exercise 7.10?

12. Suppose the instructor who gives our hypothetical four-item quiz awards 10 points for each correct answer. For the sampling distribution of $\overline{X}$ for $N = 2$ scores on the test, what will be μ and $\sigma_{\overline{x}}$ for the distribution of points earned? For $N = 3$? For $N = 30$?

13. For the McGowen and Hart (1992) question (page 202), find the 90% and the 99% confidence intervals.

14. McGowen and Hart (1992) asked the same question of 233 male clinical psychologists. For the males, the mean rating was 5.4 and the standard deviation was 1.4. Find the 90%, 95%, and the 99% confidence intervals for μ.

15. Another of McGowen and Hart's (1992) questions asked how likely it would be for clinicians to ask for a higher salary when offered an attractive job with a salary below expectations. On a scale of 1 (Not likely) to 7 (Highly likely), the 232 responding males yielded a mean rating of 6.1 ($s = 1.1$). For 81 females, the mean was 6.0 ($s = 1.1$). For both males and females, find the 90%, 95%, and the 99% confidence intervals for μ.

8 Hypothesis Testing and Power

Campbell, Tyrrell, and Zingaro (1993) report a study of several personality attributes of people who do white-water canoeing and kayaking. They suspected that such individuals would differ from the norm on dimensions like venturesomeness and sensation seeking. They administered several personality scales to 54 volunteer white-water paddlers and found that the mean score for 34 males on the Zuckerman Thrill and Adventure Seeking scale (TAS) was 7.74 with a standard deviation of 2.08. The mean for unselected ("average") males on this scales is 6.60 with a standard deviation of 2.70. Do the Campbell et al. subjects differ from that norm?

The way to answer the question is to use a **hypothesis test**. Campbell et al. (1993) tested the hypothesis that the population represented by the 34 male scores had a μ of 6.60. By rejecting that hypothesis, they established that there *is* a difference between white-water paddlers and other people.[1]

Of course, Campbell et al. (1993) could also make an interval estimate about the mean of the population represented by their subjects. If the interval included 6.60 for the males, then they might also conclude that, because 6.60 was a "likely" value, their male subjects might be regarded as "normal" in their thrill and adventure seeking. We will return to this equivalence in logic between the hypothesis test and the interval estimate later. First, though, we must explore the hypothesis test thoroughly.

Point and interval estimates, as developed in Chapter 7, are "direct" methods of inference in that they yield values that are statements about probable values of the parameter. The third method of inference, the hypothesis test, uses indirect logic. This chapter develops the logic of the hypothesis test with reference to the normal distribution and explores the kinds of errors that can be made in drawing an inference. Chapter 9 will continue with the hypothesis test, expanding it to those common situations where certain conditions that we use in this chapter do not apply.

A hypothesis test uses the method of **indirect support** to make an inference. It first establishes a hypothesis about a population numeric value or parameter that is *opposite* to the conclusion the investigator wants to draw —that is, if you hope to conclude that there is a difference in two experimental treatments, you define and test the hypothesis that there is *no* difference. Then a computation determines the probability of the data's being correct *on the basis of the hypothesis*. If the probability of the data's being correct is low given the hypothesis, then the hypothesis is "rejected" and its opposite is thereby supported. Rejecting the *opposite* statement gives indirect support to the conclusion the investigator had in mind all along. ("If I reject the hypothesis that there is no difference, then there must be a difference.") It is a cumbersome logic,[2] but it boils down to making two opposing statements about a parameter, testing one of the statements, and—if it is unlikely— supporting its logical opposite.

In all cases in this chapter and the next, the hypothesis test is applicable to what is commonly known as a *one-sample* research design. That is, there is a single group of subjects, and you want to make an inference about a population parameter, often the mean, from it.

---

[1] The results for females were similar.

[2] The cumbersomeness of the logic, along with prima facie incorrectness of many of the hypotheses tested, have led some statisticians to explore other ways of making inference. Primary among the alternatives to hypothesis testing is a method known as Bayesian logic. There is considerable merit to the Bayesian argument, but the methods have not as yet become widely used by psychologists, and for now at least they must remain as a footnote. The interested student might read Hey (1983) for an introduction to Bayesian methods.

TAKING FOUR-ITEM QUIZZES

In Chapter 7 we introduced the concept of the sampling distribution of the mean. To introduce that material, we developed the distribution of the mean score on a four-item true–false test. Taking up that example where we left it, we will develop the logic further to test the assumption (the hypothesis, actually) that the students are guessing. If the guessing hypothesis is true, the population distribution for "number correct on the test" is shown in Figure 8.1. For this population, $\mu = 2.0$ and $\sigma = 1.0$. That is, under the assumption that the students are guessing, the population mean is 2.0; if they are not guessing, then the mean would be something other than 2.0. In either case, though, $\sigma = 1.0$.

Suppose we have a class of 35 students to whom we give the quiz. What do we know about the sampling distribution of the mean? For one thing, we know that if the mean number of items correct is 2.0 (that is, the hypothesis is correct), the mean of the sampling distribution is also 2.0. We know as well that the standard error of the mean (the standard deviation of the sampling distribution) is

$$\sigma_{\bar{X}} = \frac{\sigma}{\sqrt{N}}$$

$$= \frac{1.0}{\sqrt{35}}$$

$$= 0.169$$

And by applying the central limit theorem, we know that the form of the distribution is normal. The sampling distribution of the mean looks like that

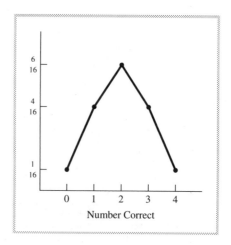

Figure 8.1

shown in Figure 8.2. If the class is guessing at the quiz answers, we would expect to find a mean number of correct answers close to 2.0; if the students are not guessing, then the class's mean should be farther from 2.0.

The next step in hypothesis testing is to define two regions of the sampling distribution—one that is **"likely"** given the hypothesis of a mean of 2.0 (guessing) and one that is **"unlikely."** For now, let us agree that anything so close to 2.0 that it should happen just by chance 95% of the time may be regarded as "likely." Such a likely event will not cause us to doubt the hypothesis of guessing (that is, the hypothesis that $\mu = 2.0$). Results so far from 2.0 as to occur by chance 5% of the time or less will be considered "unlikely" and will cause us to reject the "guessing" hypothesis.

By selecting the 95% region, we are saying that we should define the "likely" and "unlikely" areas of the standardized sampling distribution as shown in Figure 8.3. Computations for the lower and upper bounds of the "likely" region are simple and follow the same general form as those for confidence intervals. Because we know (from Appendix A) that the critical points of the 95% region lie at $z = \pm 1.96$, the bounds are

$$\mu \pm 1.96\sigma_{\overline{X}} = 2.0 \pm 1.96(0.169)$$

$$= 2.0 \pm 0.331$$

$$= 1.669 \text{ and } 2.331$$

And now we come to the crux of the hypothesis test. If we observe a mean between 1.669 and 2.331 (that is, close enough to 2.0 to occur 95% of the time), we conclude that there is no reason to doubt that the class's behavior is anything other than guessing. Conversely, if we observe a sample $\overline{X}$ less than 1.669, or greater than 2.331, we will *reject the hypothesis* that the population mean is 2.0, thus supporting an inference that the class is not guessing.

Suppose, for example, that we give the quiz to the 35 students in the class and find that the mean is 2.86. Because we decided that a mean greater

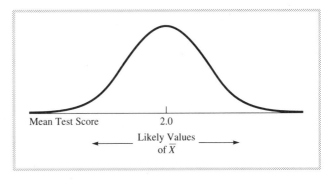

Figure 8.2

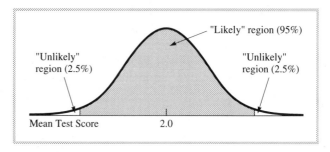

"Likely" region (95%)

"Unlikely" region (2.5%)

"Unlikely" region (2.5%)

Mean Test Score   2.0

Figure 8.3

than 2.331 is unlikely given that the students are guessing, we reject the guessing (that is, $\mu = 2.0$) hypothesis and conclude that the students are not guessing. Notice that our decision makes an inference—the students are not guessing—on the basis of the data. Note also how the first of the two possible conclusions was worded: "… there is no basis for concluding that the student's behavior is anything other than random guessing." We can never really "prove" the hypothesis is true; we can decide either to reject it and conclude that its opposite is true, or we can decide that the evidence does not let us reject the hypothesis of chance behavior.

MORE FORMALLY …

We have just been through the entire logic of the hypothesis test, the third inference method. In particular, we completed the following steps:

Defined a null hypothesis
Defined an alternative hypothesis
Defined the population distribution
Defined the sample size
Specified the sampling distribution of the statistic under the assumption that the null hypothesis was true
Specified a decision rule and inference

Now let's take these one at a time.

NULL HYPOTHESIS.   The **null hypothesis** is the statement of the parameter value that we will test. Normally, it is exactly opposite to what we hope to eventually conclude. In this case, the null hypothesis is that μ is 2.0. Note that the hypothesis is about a specific parameter value and that the value comes directly from the assumption that the students' behavior is random. A value to be tested is normally established in this way—by a logical derivation from some hypothesis. In this example, we want to test the null hypothesis that the students are guessing. By the logic developed earlier, *if* they are guessing, then the sampling distribution will have the properties that we assume. This logical linkage between a verbal statement and a particular parameter value establishes the hypothesis test as a powerful inference method.

The specification of the parameter also implies a statistic to be used as a point estimate. The parameter to be tested is μ, and so we use $\overline{X}$ as the point estimate. Had we been testing a hypothesis about some other parameter—σ^2, for example—then we would of course use an appropriate estimate, such as s^2.

ALTERNATIVE HYPOTHESIS. The **alternative hypothesis** is the logical opposite to the null. In the example, the alternative is that the population mean is not 2.0 (meaning that the class is not behaving randomly). There is an important relationship between the null and the alternative: They must be *mutually exclusive* and *exhaustive*. That is, the two cannot both be true simultaneously (mutually exclusive), and together they must cover all the possibilities (exhaustive). In the example, either $\mu = 2$ or $\mu \neq 2$.

POPULATION DISTRIBUTION. In the example, the population distribution was specified as the probabilities of obtaining the values 0, 1, ... when the students were guessing. By implication, that statement contained the essentials necessary to specify the population—the center, the spread, and the form. In this case, the center is 2.0, $\sigma = 1.0$, and the form is given by the probability distribution. These three elements are necessary for a complete definition of the population to be tested.

SAMPLE SIZE. The sample size is always specified for a hypothesis test. In the example, $N = 35$.

SAMPLING DISTRIBUTION OF THE STATISTIC. The null hypothesis specifies a point estimator. Combined with our knowledge of (or assumptions about) the population distribution and the sample size, it specifies the sampling distribution of the statistic. The sampling distribution, in turn, provides a way to determine the probabilities of all possible values of the sample statistic. For the example, the sampling distribution is assumed to be normal because the sample size is quite large, and the distribution is expected to be reasonably symmetrical (see page 195).

DECISION RULE AND INFERENCE. Specifying a decision rule and making an inference are the final steps in the logic of the hypothesis test. Using the sampling distribution, we decide on a set of possible observations that *supports* the null hypothesis, and a mutually exclusive and exhaustive set that *does not support* it. In our example, we decided that a sample mean between 1.669 and 2.331 supported the null hypothesis and that sample means lower or higher than that range did not. A **decision rule** follows and defines what inference to make given any outcome. In the example, a mean less than 1.669 or greater than 2.331 will lead us to reject the hypothesis that $\mu = 2.0$, and thus conclude that the students probably were not guessing. However, means within the range 1.669–2.331 are likely to occur if the class is behaving randomly. A mean in that range will not contradict the hypothesis of guessing. In either case, we make an inference about the class's behavior. In other words, we are *testing the hypothesis* that the mean number of items correct for the class is 2.00 (implying guessing) against the alternative hypothesis that the mean is not 2.00 (the students are not guessing).

Deciding how much of the area in the sampling distribution to allocate to the "likely" and the "unlikely" regions is a complex matter. Two "traditional" probability values are used to define the "unlikely" area: .01 and .05. These values, called the *significance level* of the test, define the size of the "unlikely" region. For now, either .01 or .05 will suffice. Once one of these is defined, then the decision rule can set the critical points in the sampling distribution.

The logic of the hypothesis test, in sum, sets up two opposing hypotheses: the null and the alternative. A sampling distribution, *constructed under the assumption that the null is true*, establishes the probabilities of the various possible values of the statistic. If we observe a "likely" value (close to the null), then we retain the null hypothesis and infer that we see no evidence to conclude to the contrary. Conversely, if we observe an "unlikely" event, then we reject the null hypothesis, thereby indirectly supporting the alternative.

Earlier we mentioned the notion of indirect support of a hypothesis. The investigator establishes the null as the *opposite* of what he or she really wants to conclude. In our example, the instructor probably wants to conclude that the class is *not* behaving randomly. Our test is thus a test of the hypothesis that there is *no difference* between the behavior of the class and that of students who are randomly guessing. This hypothesis of no difference is what gives the null hypothesis its name. (When we learn, in Chapter 9, about testing for a difference between two experimental conditions, we will see that the usual hypothesis test is that there is no—*null*—difference. If we reject the hypothesis of no difference, then we conclude that there is a difference.)

Note that we could make an error in the inference. Perhaps the class *is* behaving randomly but happens to be lucky. Perfect papers should happen, after all, roughly 1 in every 16 times when the students are guessing. If a number of students have been so lucky, or perhaps if they have just guessed better than their colleagues, we might see an unusual number of good papers. If we see a very low mean number of errors, though, our decision rule leads us to the conclusion that the behavior is nonrandom—and that could be an error.

Actually, there are two kinds of errors, and we explore them fully later in this chapter. The first kind of error—concluding that the null hypothesis is false when it's actually true—is a Type I error. The converse error (accepting the null when it is actually false) is called (what else!) a Type II error. In our example, this kind of error could occur if, for example, a number of students who actually knew the material were distracted during the exam and pulled the class mean down far enough to be so close to 2.0 that our decision rule led us to conclude that the class was guessing.

ONE TAIL OR TWO?

In the example, the "unlikely" region was divided into two pieces, with one-half of the area in each "tail" of the distribution, as shown in Figure 8.4. Dividing the "unlikely" region this way suggests that we regard a deviation from the null hypothesis *in either direction* as evidence that the null hypothesis is incorrect. In other words, there are two ways in which the null hypothesis of $\mu = 2.0$ might be incorrect: $\mu < 2.0$ or $\mu > 2.0$. Either would make us doubt the correctness of the null hypothesis.

A test whose critical region is divided into two segments is known as a *nondirectional*, or **two-tailed**, hypothesis test. In most cases, we recommend a two-tailed testing procedure. Sometimes, though, we might want to use a **one-tailed test**. In this example, perhaps we do not want to consider the possibility that the class does worse than chance, but only that they do better. The alternative hypothesis then would be $\mu > 2.0$, or, in words, the students know the material. In this case, we put all of the "unlikely" area in just the upper tail, as shown in the distribution in Figure 8.5. In Appendix A we can find that the z value of 1.65 defines the one-tailed .05 area, from which we can calculate

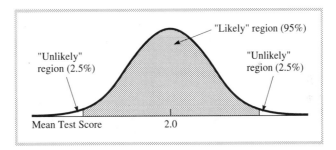

Figure 8.4

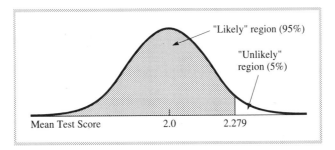

Figure 8.5

$$\mu + 1.65\sigma_{\overline{X}} = 2.0 + 1.65(0.169)$$
$$= 2.0 + 1.65(0.169)$$
$$= 2.0 + 0.279$$
$$= 2.279$$

and our decision rule now becomes one that will reject the null hypothesis if we observe any $\overline{X}$ greater than 2.279 because that value is the critical boundary between the likely and unlikely regions of the distribution.

As compared with the two-tailed test, a one-tailed test requires *less* difference between the null value and the obtained $\overline{X}$ to reject the null. That's a consequence of placing the entire critical region in just one tail. It is easier to reject the null hypothesis with a one-tailed test because the critical point in this test is closer to the null value than it is in a two-tailed test. Critics of one-tailed logic suggest that such a test is sometimes used to obtain a rejection of the null hypothesis when a two-tailed test would not have come to the same conclusion.

A better argument against one-tailed tests is that, at least in our example, you really do want to know whether your class is guessing, and if they are not, you want to know whether they score above 2.0 or below. The argument continues that we should not limit ourselves (with a one-tailed test) to looking at only too-high values but should consider too-low values to be just as suggestive of nonrandomness. A two-tailed test allows us to find effects in *either* direction, where a one-tailed test might not.

Before you conclude from this discussion that you should always use a two-tailed test, you should know there are some situations where a one-tailed test makes perfect sense. Consider an example from industrial quality control, a major employer of statistical methods. You are a quality control statistician for a company that manufactures the breakfast cereal Yummy Crunchies. Federal standards and company policy allow a certain level of "insect fragments" to be present in the Yummy Crunchies sold, and your task is to ensure that each batch of cereal doesn't exceed that standard. There is no penalty for having fewer fragments than the standard, but the production line could be shut down and the company subjected to legal action if the acceptable level is exceeded.

You draw a random sample from each batch of Yummy Crunchies and use it to test the hypothesis that the level of insect fragments is equal to the acceptable level. The hypothesis tested is actually that the level of fragments is at, *or less than*, the acceptable value. You'll also use the significance level of .01 for the test. If we let the acceptable value be 5.0 fragments[3] per box of Yummy Crunchies, then the sampling distribution for the mean number of fragments per box under the null hypothesis would look like that in Figure

---

[3] You may personally think that anything over 0 fragments is unacceptable, but you should know that having 0 fragments is probably impossible, and so standards just like this one have been established. You may feel better, however, knowing that, if the legal standard were actually 5.0, most manufacturers would set a company standard of something less—3.0 or 4.0, perhaps—just to be on the safe side.

8.6. In this situation, any mean value close to 5.0, or any mean value less than 5.0, is likely to occur if the null hypothesis is true and the unlikely critical region is placed entirely in the upper tail. We want to reject the hypothesis that the batch is acceptable (that is, that the level of fragments is 5.0 or less) only if the observed mean is far enough above 5.0 to be very unlikely to have occurred by chance. We could state the two hypotheses as $\mu \leq 5.0$ for the null and $\mu > 5.0$ for the alternative, illustrating that the hypotheses are mutually exclusive and exhaustive.

To continue this example, suppose that Yummy Inc., the parent company of Yummy Crunchies, is installing new equipment that may have an effect on the level of insect fragments in the finished product. You are asked to determine whether the new equipment causes a change in the acceptable fragment level. Because you need to know if there is *any* change in the number of fragments, either more or fewer, you would use a two-tailed test for this analysis.

Most of the applications of one-tailed tests are in situations like that suggested in the example. These are situations in which the theoretical prediction is clearly directional ("Increasing the amount of practice should lead to *increased* learning"). In such cases, *not* using a one-tailed test may lessen our ability to detect the predicted effect. For research purposes, though, such as those discussed throughout this book, we generally recommend nondirectional, or two-tailed, tests.

◆ An Example

A psychologist employed by a school district has been asked to evaluate a class of second-grade students for their performance on a standard test of intelligence. The psychologist administers an IQ test to the 27 children; the scores are given in Table 8.1. She wants to know whether this class differs significantly from the norm for IQ scores (IQ = 100 is the mean for the general population), and the hypothesis test concerning the mean for a single sample will answer the question. We test the hypothesis that $\mu = 100$ against the alternative of $\mu \neq 100$, with the significance level at .05.

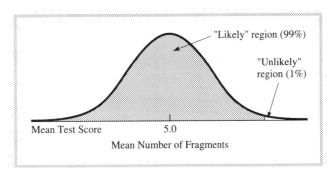

Figure 8.6

TABLE 8.1		
98	114	102
119	90	98
113	101	100
107	110	86
121	101	103
88	104	95
105	128	96
110	102	113
123	127	110

The population standard deviation for IQ scores is 15, and the distribution is normal in form. (Because of the way standard intelligence tests are constructed and scored, working with IQ data is one of the few cases where we can assume we know a parameter value and a population form! Most of the time we do not have this luxury.)

The mean IQ score for the class of 27 children is 106.07. The sampling distribution of the mean for samples of $N = 27$ is normal in form (because the population distribution is normal), with a standard error of

$$\sigma_{\overline{X}} = \frac{\sigma}{\sqrt{N}}$$

$$= \frac{15}{\sqrt{27}}$$

$$= 2.89$$

We will accept the hypothesis of $\mu = 100$ if the sample mean is close enough to that value to happen by chance 95% of the time—that is, so the sampling distribution looks like Figure 8.7.

To find out if the class's mean is within the "likely" region, we refer to the standardized normal distribution in Appendix A. To see where the mean of 106.07 falls in the sampling distribution that's centered around 100, calculate the z value corresponding to the sample $\overline{X}$ of 106.07:

$$z = \frac{\overline{X} - \mu}{\sigma_{\overline{X}}}$$

$$= \frac{106.07 - 100}{2.89}$$

$$= 2.10$$

From Appendix A, we know that z values between -1.96 and $+1.96$ are in

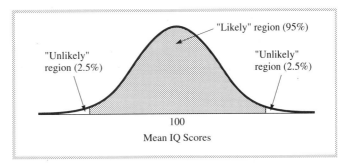

Figure 8.7

the "likely" region, as illustrated in Figure 8.8. The obtained z value[4] is 2.10, which falls outside the central "likely" region and is in the upper "unlikely" tail; thus, we reject the hypothesis that the mean of the population from which this class is drawn is 100. The psychologist then may report that the mean for this class is significantly above the overall population mean of 100.

◆ Another Example

In their reading study, Jandreau and Bever (1992) needed to understand something about their subject's level of ability. They had available each subject's Verbal scale score on the Scholastic Aptitude Test (VSAT). Their 25 subjects had a mean VSAT score of 466.0. Should that value lead Jandreau and Bever to doubt that the mean of the population the subjects represent is 500, which is the norm for "average" subjects?

Because the VSAT has a normal distribution with $\sigma = 100$, we can use that distribution to test the hypothesis. We begin by computing $\sigma_{\overline{X}}$ as

$$\sigma_{\overline{X}} = \frac{\sigma}{\sqrt{N}}$$

$$= \frac{100}{\sqrt{25}}$$

$$= 20.0$$

---

[4] Note how the formula for the z value has changed to adapt it for use with this distribution. It follows the basic form of

$$z = \frac{\text{Value} - \text{Mean}}{\text{Standard deviation}}$$

Because we're referring to the sampling distribution of the mean in this case, the value of interest is an individual $\overline{X}$, the mean of the distribution is μ, and the standard deviation is the standard error of the mean, leading to the formula

$$z = \frac{\overline{X} - \mu}{\sigma_{\overline{X}}}$$

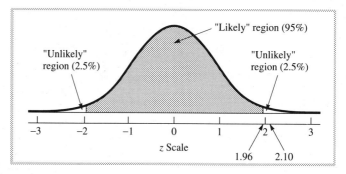

Figure 8.8

Next we calculate the z value as

$$z = \frac{\overline{X} - \mu}{\sigma_{\overline{X}}}$$

$$= \frac{466.0 - 500}{20.0}$$

$$= -1.70$$

If we choose the .05 significance level, a value of $z \geq |1.96|$ is required to reject the hypothesis that the population mean is 500. Because we have a value of -1.70, we do not reject the hypothesis. We can now answer the question: These subjects do not seem to differ from the norm in the VSAT score.

◆ In Sum . . .

We have been through the logic of the hypothesis test three times, showing the logic and the procedure in two different ways. For each example, the process began with a statement of a hypothesis representing a question about a parameter. In the four-item test example, we presented the test in a form that was intended to clarify the logic. From the hypothesized value, we computed the upper and lower critical bounds on the "likely" region and compared the obtained mean to them. Investigators sometimes conduct the test in this way and compute the actual upper and lower critical bounds for the "likely" region, as we did. But more often they follow a procedure like that in the second example.

In the second example, the hypothesis asked a question about the mean of the population represented by a class of students. Data were collected from the class and the mean computed. Using knowledge of the normal distribution, we standardized the obtained $\overline{X}$ to find its location in the sampling distribution. Because the standardized value of the sample mean fell outside the ± 1.96 range in the standardized sampling distribution, we rejected the null hypothesis. That is the usual way of testing the hypothesis; computing the actual upper and lower bounds of the "likely" area is rarely done outside the classroom and statistics texts.

The probabilities used to define the "likely" and "unlikely" regions needs some additional comment. The probability of the "unlikely" region (.05 in the example) is often called the *significance level* of the test and is typically symbolized as α, lowercase Greek alpha). The significance level gives the probability that an unlikely event will occur when the null hypothesis is true. We will have more to say about it later.

PRESENTING HYPOTHESIS TEST RESULTS

Presenting the results of a hypothesis test is usually a simple matter. A sentence format is ideal for simple tests like those illustrated. The sentence contains the conclusion, the name and value of the test statistic, and an indication of the significance level. The American Psychological Association (APA) has a standard form for presenting the results of hypothesis tests. Using this form, the school psychologist might write, "We conclude that the mean IQ for this class differs from 100: $\underline{z} = 2.10$, $\underline{p} < .05$." Notice that the sentence states the conclusion ("... differs from 100"), the test statistic and its value ($\underline{z} = 2.10$), and the significance level ($\underline{p} < .05$). The symbol for the statistic and the letter p are underscored (or printed in italics). The null hypothesis is not stated because it is easily inferred; the critical value (such as 1.96, taken from Appendix A) also does not appear because it, too, is easily obtained by a reader.

◆ Two Sides of a Coin: Hypothesis Tests and Interval Estimates

We can pursue the IQ example further, using the same data to calculate an interval estimate for μ. The formula that we presented in Chapter 7 for the 95% confidence interval was

$$\overline{X} \pm 1.96(s_{\overline{X}})$$

Because we know σ and need not estimate it using s, we can substitute $\sigma_{\overline{X}}$ and calculate the interval as

$$\overline{X} \pm 1.96(\sigma_{\overline{X}})$$

Using the values from earlier, we have

$$106.07 \pm 1.96(2.89) = 100.41 \qquad \text{and} \qquad 111.73$$

Thus, the 95% confidence interval for μ, based on the sample mean of 106.07, is 100.41 to 111.73. Pictorially, the interval is given in Figure 8.9, which shows the interval estimate centered around the sample $\overline{X}$ of 106.07.

When we tested the null hypothesis that $\mu = 100$, we assumed that the sampling distribution of $\overline{X}$ was centered at 100, and the distribution was as presented in Figure 8.10. Note that the null hypothesis value 100 is not included in the 95% interval estimate for μ.

Now consider the same example, but use the 99% interval estimate. For the 99% interval, substitute 2.58 for 1.96 in the formula and calculate:

$$\overline{X} \pm 2.58(\sigma_{\overline{X}}) = 106.07 \pm 2.58(2.89)$$

$$= 98.61 \text{ and } 113.53$$

Pictorially, we have Figure 8.11. In this case, the confidence interval *includes* the null hypothesis value from the hypothesis test.

As the final step in this example, we test the hypothesis that $\mu = 100$ but use the .01 significance level. Compute the z value as before:

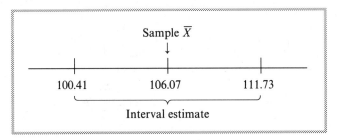

Figure 8.9

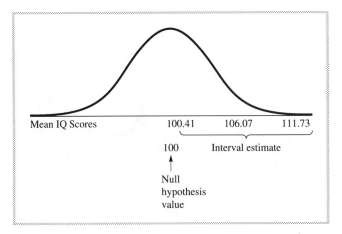

Figure 8.10

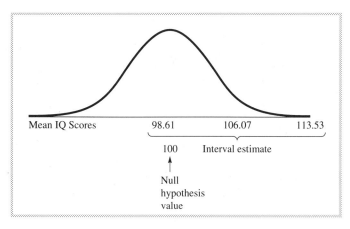

Figure 8.11

$$z = \frac{\overline{X} - \mu}{\sigma_{\overline{X}}}$$

$$= \frac{106.07 - 100}{2.89}$$

$$= 2.10$$

Consulting Appendix A, the critical value is 2.58 (you should have antici-pated that!), and we do not reject the hypothesis that $\mu = 100$. But we al-ready knew as much from the 99% confidence limit. The 99% confidence interval includes the value 100, meaning that 100 is a probable value for μ. Because it is a "likely" value, it should not be rejected in a hypothesis test. And the hypothesis test computation has us conclude that, at the .01 level, we do not reject the null hypothesis of $\mu = 100$.

The point of this illustration is to show that interval estimation and hypothesis testing are two ways of doing the same thing. If the null hypothe-sis value is inside the interval at the chosen confidence level, then the null is not rejected. If the null is outside the interval, then it is rejected. Some investigators prefer this alternate means of conducting the hypothesis test because it provides both the interval estimate and the hypothesis test in one simple and easy-to-understand operation.

ERRORS IN MAKING INFERENCES

Any time we leave the certainty of sample data to make an inference about a parameter, we may come to an incorrect conclusion. Although it would be nice to avoid making any errors, some wrong inferences are more serious than others (e.g., "I should have brought an umbrella" or "I thought the other driver was going to stop.") In statistics, too, some errors are more serious than others, but the situations are usually less clear-cut than weather or driving safety. Before we can intelligently weigh the consequences of errors in inference, we need to see what kinds of wrong inferences we can make.

In the four-item test example, suppose that the class *really was* guessing randomly, and just got lucky. In fact, they got so lucky that, on the average, their mean was 2.85 questions correct. If we follow the rules of the hypothesis test in this case, we reject the null hypothesis that the population mean is 2.0 and support the alternative hypothesis. In other words, we reject the null when it is actually true. We earlier indicated that such an error would be called a Type I error, and now we can formally define a **Type I error** as rejecting a *true* null hypothesis. Of course, we can never know if we make such an error because, to know it, we have to know the value of the population mean, and if we knew that, we would not be making an inference about it. But—and this is important—we *can* know the *probability* of making a Type I error. If the significance level is .05, then 5% of the time, by chance alone, we will observe a sample $\overline{X}$ that is too high or too low; if we do, then we reject the null hypothesis and thus make a Type I error. If the null is true, of course, 95% of the time we will find an $\overline{X}$ "close to" 2.0 and we accept the null, making a correct inference.

If .05 is too large a probability of making a Type I error, we can easily make the value as small as we want—just pick the significance level and find the appropriate critical z from Appendix A. Therefore, we can set the probability of making a Type I error by simply adjusting the "likely" and "unlikely" regions. And this is often done, leading to different "significance" levels, of which .05 and .01 are by far the most common.

A **Type II error** is the converse of a Type I error; it is the error of not rejecting a null hypothesis that is actually false. If, for example, the students in the four-item quiz example are *not* guessing, but we conclude that they are, then we make a Type II error. Figure 8.12 summarizes the situation.

In more general terms, then, if the null hypothesis is not true, to make a correct inference, we should reject it, as Figure 8.13 illustrates. The "actual" state of nature is unknown and is the target of the inference—are the students guessing or not? Of course, because we can never know the true state of nature, we can never know if we have made an inferential error. But we can nevertheless weigh the meaning and importance of the two kinds of errors in a particular situation, and decide to make either or both kinds of error more or less probable.

The significance level of a hypothesis test is *the probability of making a Type I error*. As noted earlier, we often use the Greek letter α to symbolize this probability. Thus, α is the probability that we will reject a null hypothesis that is actually correct. If the null hypothesis is correct, the probability of *not* rejecting the null hypothesis—that is, of being correct—is $1 - \alpha$.

Usually α is set at some small value, with .05 and .01 being the two most frequent, and traditional, choices. These two significance levels indicate, re-

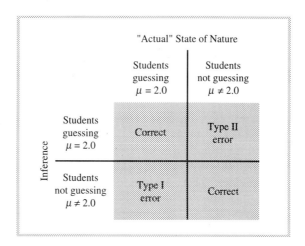

Figure 8.12

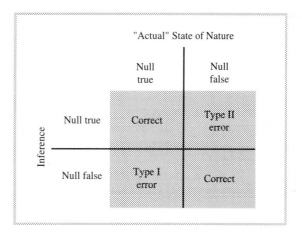

Figure 8.13

spectively, 5 and 1 chances in 100 that a hypothesis test will reject a true null hypothesis. But there is nothing magical or sacred about those two significance levels, and there is sometimes good reason to use a different value.

We may let the symbol β represent the probability of making a Type II error—that of concluding that the null hypothesis is correct when it is actually false. Naturally, if the null is false, then the probability of concluding that it really is false is $1 - \beta$, a quantity known as the **power** of the test. We will return to power shortly, because it is an important concept. First, though, we consider the costs of making the two kinds of error, because the cost of making an error is a factor in deciding on how to approach the matter of Type I and Type II errors.

◆ Relative Costs

It's easy to make a Type I error less likely—just select a smaller α. That's such a simple adjustment that perhaps we should run every test at $\alpha = .01$, or even at $\alpha = .001$. The problem is that, all other things being equal, *if we decrease the probability of a Type I error, we increase the probability of a Type II error*. In other words, Type I and Type II errors are reciprocally related; decreasing the probability of one of them increases the probability of the other.

It is not nearly as easy to change the probability of a Type II error. And, because the two kinds of error are inversely related, opting to reduce the probability of one kind of error increases the probability of the other. Even worse, there is no universal rule to help you decide which is the more important to avoid. A decision on balancing the error probabilities has to be made in each piece of research. To illustrate the considerations involved, let's consider the consequences of the two kinds of error in several situations.

TAKING TESTS

In the four-item test example, a Type I error leads to the erroneous conclusion that the students knew the material when actually they did not and were just guessing. Obviously, we would like to avoid that sort of error if possible; an instructor might conclude wrongly that the students understood the material, and would then offer no additional explanatory materials. That decision would result in the students learning less than they would have if their instructor had correctly inferred that they were guessing.

Concluding that the students did not know the material when they really did would be a Type II error. Perhaps this error is more tolerable, at least in this situation. It might result in the instructor's spending some additional time and effort on the material, at the risk of boring the class. That might be a relatively small price to pay, however. The instructor might opt to reduce the risk of a Type I error, letting the probability of a Type II error increase because the cost associated with the latter seems to be not too bad.

THE CLASS IQ

In the second example, we asked whether a class seems to have been drawn from a population whose mean IQ is 100; that is, is the class normal in intelligence? The errors are summarized in Figure 8.14. In this example, a Type I error would lead the psychologist to conclude that the class's mean IQ is not 100 when it really is (that is, the class is normal in intelligence and the psychologist concludes that it is not). If the class mean was above 100, as in the example, the teacher might assume that she had a brighter-than-normal class, and might present new "enrichment" materials and exercises, push the class faster than usual, and otherwise expect more from the class. A Type II error would result in the psychologist's concluding that the class was normal in intelligence when it actually wasn't. In this latter case, the

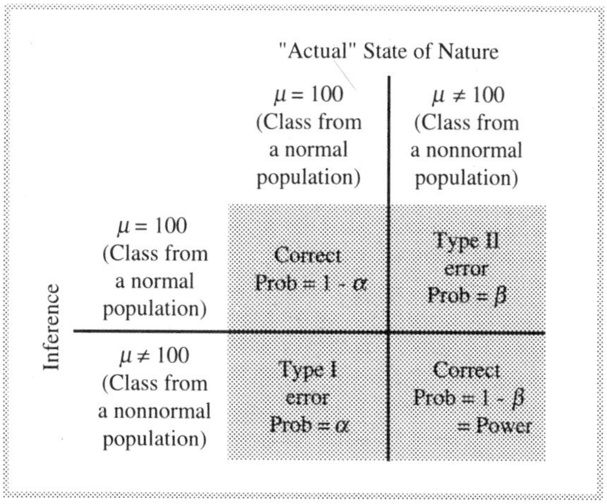

"Actual" State of Nature

	$\mu = 100$ (Class from a normal population)	$\mu \neq 100$ (Class from a nonnormal population)
$\mu = 100$ (Class from a normal population)	Correct Prob $= 1 - \alpha$	Type II error Prob $= \beta$
$\mu \neq 100$ (Class from a nonnormal population)	Type I error Prob $= \alpha$	Correct Prob $= 1 - \beta$ = Power

Inference

Figure 8.14

error would probably result in little change in teaching methods on the teacher's part.

IN ACTIVE RESEARCH

In contrast to the previous two examples, consider an active research project, one dealing with infant perception.

How do you ask questions of very young children and infants? Using words doesn't work, but there is a technique that performs quite well. Research with infants was advanced greatly with the discovery (see Werner & Perlmutter, 1979, for a summary of the research) that infants prefer looking at a novel stimulus. For example, if you let an infant look at a particular picture for a time, and then present that picture along with a different one, the infant will spend more time looking at the new picture than at the old one. This "preference for novelty" has led to the development of powerful techniques in the study of infant cognition.

A preference may be demonstrated by presenting two objects (pictures, patterns, lights, movements, and so forth), one of which is familiar and the other novel. If the novel stimulus is looked at for more than half of the time, then the infant has a preference for it. A hypothesis test can be used to decide whether a group of infants looked at a stimulus for more than half the time. The experiment is simple: Record the proportion of time that infants look at the novel stimulus, and use the data to test the hypothesis of $\mu = 0.5$ (or 50%). The hypothesis and the possible conclusions are diagrammed in Figure 8.15.

Rejecting the hypothesis of $\mu = 50\%$ means concluding that not only can infants detect a difference between the two stimuli, but they prefer one over the other. And that is exactly what the research summarized by Werner and Perlmutter concluded. This was an important finding because it pro-

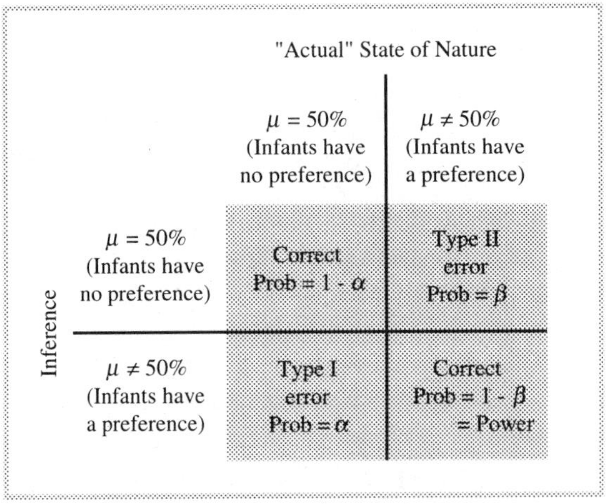

"Actual" State of Nature

	$\mu = 50\%$ (Infants have no preference)	$\mu \neq 50\%$ (Infants have a preference)
$\mu = 50\%$ (Infants have no preference)	Correct Prob = $1 - \alpha$	Type II error Prob = β
$\mu \neq 50\%$ (Infants have a preference)	Type I error Prob = α	Correct Prob = $1 - \beta$ = Power

Inference

Figure 8.15

vides a way for infants to "tell" us that they can detect a difference, without words or training. That result opened a vast new world of infant behavior studies.

What if the first research to find a preference for novelty had made a Type I error? That is, what if the first investigators had reported a preference when there really was none? The most likely result would probably have been a brief flurry of excitement and research activity, most of which would not have found the preference for novelty. As other investigators jumped in to pursue this interesting and important new research area, the first results would not have been replicated, and the whole matter would soon have been dropped as a fruitless endeavor. In other words, a Type I error in an active research area is likely to be self-correcting by failures to replicate.[5] Following that logic, then, in an active research field, Type I errors assume a less bothersome role. We shouldn't increase α too high, but we need not feel compelled to keep it at the traditional very low levels of .05 and .01.

But now consider the effects of a Type II error. What if the investigators had made a Type II error? That is, what if there actually was a preference for novelty, but the research failed to show it? What would be the effect on other research workers? Their likely response would be something like "Well, there's certainly nothing interesting here—it looks like infants can't distinguish between two patterns; at least, they look at them for equal lengths of time." There the matter might die. And a new, important, and exciting research technique might never be developed because of an error in inference. So, to follow this logic to its conclusion, in an active research area it is generally better to avoid a Type II error—such errors often have the effect of closing off new and promising areas.

[5] The argument here is essentially that of Keppel (1973). This highly respected writer on ANOVA has changed his mind somewhat in his latest edition (Keppel, 1991), where, in general, he advocates a power of 0.80—see the following section—and a significance level of .05 or .01.

What have we concluded about Type I and Type II errors? In one example, we decided that the cost of a Type I error was too great, and in another, that the cost of a Type II error was too great. In short, we cannot come to the simple conclusion that just avoiding one or the other will suffice as a rule to live by. We have to consider each situation individually, weighing the consequences of each kind of error in context. And to complicate matters more, all Type II errors are not equal. We can often tolerate some risk of making such an error, depending upon "how false" the null hypothesis must be before you want to reject it.

DEALING WITH ERRORS OF INFERENCE: POWER ANALYSIS

There is one simple way to change the probability of making a Type I error: Change the significance level of the hypothesis test. Just that simple. Changing the probability of making a Type II error, however, is quite a different matter. All things being equal, if we increase the probability of making a Type I error (α), we lower the probability of making a Type II error (β) and increase the power of the test because Power $= 1 - \beta$.

Again, all things being equal, a larger sample size leads to a lower probability of making a Type II error. So why not use a very large sample size for all research? Because it is costly in one way or another. There are more subjects to recruit, pay, feed, or house; there are more data to be processed; there may be a need to hire research assistants; and so forth.

In addition, you might wind up with *too* powerful a test. You want important effects to become visible while trivial ones stay undiscovered. In the classroom IQ example, if the psychologist decides that the class is above average in intelligence, the teacher might use the new "enrichment" materials and exercises. But maybe that would be a mistake. Perhaps the mean IQ for children using the new materials *really is* above 100, but not far enough to warrant introducing the new material. What the teacher wants is a test that is powerful enough to find a meaningful difference. Maybe she would want to introduce the enrichment materials only if she were reasonably certain that the true IQ of her class were, for example, 110 or more. So she wants the test to have the power to detect a 10-point difference; increasing the sample size to locate a difference of less than 10 would mean that the test was overpowered. For example, if the true mean IQ was 101, the null hypothesis that $\mu = 100$ is actually false, and so, failing to reject it would be a Type II error. Increasing the sample size could ensure that the 1-point difference from 100 to 101 would be located. But that 1-point difference is too small to be meaningful, and making the effort to find it is worthless.

Cohen (1977, 1988), among others, developed a straightforward procedure for determining necessary sample size. The method usually is called "power analysis" because of the closely related procedure for determining the power of a completed analysis. We turn first to the problem of determining sample size.

◆ Determining the Sample Size

The probability of a Type II error, and thus the power of a test, is influenced by four things: the significance level (α), the sample size (N), the population variability (usually measured by σ), and the actual difference between the null hypothesis mean (whose values is often symbolized as μ_0) and the true mean (usually denoted μ_1). Any one of these may be computed once the other three are determined. First we deal with N; later we will determine the power of a test given the remainder of the elements.

In a particular piece of research, α is typically set first, thereby establishing the acceptable risk of making a Type I error. An estimate of σ is frequently available from prior research in the same general area. And, for the purpose of determining a sample size, a rough estimate of σ is sufficient. The most difficult decision is often deciding on the size of the effect—the difference between μ_0 and μ_1—to be detected. There are commonly used rules of thumb, but they are not the best way to proceed.

As an example, return to the school psychologist who is interested in making an inference about the mean IQ of a particular class. As before, assume that the psychologist is interested in finding a difference of 10 points or more and that effects of less than 10 are of no interest. With 10 points thus established as the smallest effect size, we proceed.

Effect sizes are most conveniently expressed in standardized form. That is, rather than talking about "a 10-point difference," the size is often called γ (gamma) and is expressed relative to a standard deviation, so we would write

$$\gamma = \frac{|\mu_0 - \mu_1|}{\sigma}$$

For the example, because we can be comfortable using $\sigma = 15$ (the value for most standardized IQ tests), the effect size γ is calculated as

$$\gamma = \frac{|\mu_0 - \mu_1|}{\sigma}$$

$$= \frac{|100 - 110|}{15}$$

$$= 0.667$$

This value expresses the desired minimum effect size as if it were a z score; the 0.667 means that we are interested in finding an effect of 0.667 standard deviation unit or greater from the null hypothesis value.

The next step is to decide on what power we want to have. That is, how likely should it be to locate a difference of γ (0.667 in the example) or greater? For now, assume that we want the power to be 0.80, which is a customary and reasonable value in many instances.

Having decided on the effect size and the power, we next consult Appendix M and determine the value of a statistic named δ (delta) that is necessary for a power of 0.80 and an effect size of 0.667 with $\alpha = .05$. The body of the table gives the power, so we look down the $\alpha = .05$ column until we find 0.80 and find that $\delta = 2.80$.

Finally, the computation

$$N = \left(\frac{\delta}{\gamma}\right)^2$$

gives the desired value for an analysis with one group of subjects as

$$N = \left(\frac{\delta}{\gamma}\right)^2$$
$$= \left(\frac{2.80}{0.667}\right)^2$$
$$= 17.62$$

Because fractional subjects are difficult to achieve, we round the value to the nearest whole number and conclude that 18 subjects are required. This value of N, then, will give a power of 0.80 to finding a difference of 10 points or more from the null hypothesis value of 100. Because there were 27 students in the class, and only 18 were needed to achieve the desired results, the analysis must have been more powerful than necessary; we will compute its actual power below.

◆ Effect Size

In the preceding example, we took the effect size as a given—the psychologist wanted to find an IQ difference of 10 points or more. Where did that value come from? In other words, how large an effect size do we want to be able to detect?

As in many areas of statistics, there is no hard and fast answer to that question. In the example, the psychologist presumably used some criteria to decide that switching curriculum materials would be of little benefit unless the class were 10 points or more above the mean. This kind of personal judgment is not uncommon in situations where direct economic impacts can be assessed. In a school district, switching materials costs real money, and the psychologist simply made the decision that 10 points was the smallest difference to be worthwhile.

In research, neat guidelines are often not available, and setting effect size is difficult. One guideline is sometimes provided by previous research in the same area. Often you can find effects of a certain size, and an investigator wanting to find similar effects can estimate the effect size from that data. In addition, previous research may provide estimates of σ, enabling easy computation of γ.

For areas where previous research, or the investigator's logic, provide no guidance, Cohen (1977) suggested a simple rule of thumb. If you want to find large effects, use $\gamma = 0.80$. To locate medium-sized effects, use $\gamma = 0.50$, and for small effects, $\gamma = 0.20$. Thus, a "large" effect is one where the mean differs from the hypothesized value by nearly a full standard deviation, and a "small" effect is defined as only one-fifth of a standard deviation, a very small difference indeed. (To achieve a power of 0.80, the school psychologist would have to use $n = 196$ to find a "small" difference!) Note that these "small," "medium," and "large" values are intended only as rough rules of thumb; the investigator's judgment or previous research are better sources of guidance.

◆ Finding the Power of a Test

Suppose you want to determine the power of a test for a given effect size, α, and N. This is the reverse of the procedure for finding N, and we can illustrate the process by using the classroom IQ example yet once more. This time, the psychologist has the sample of 27 observations, uses $\alpha = .05$, and wants to know the power of the test at detecting a difference of 10 points or more.

We begin as before by finding the desired effect size by calculating

$$\gamma = \frac{|\mu_0 - \mu_1|}{\sigma}$$

$$= \frac{|100 - 110|}{15}$$

$$= 0.667$$

Next we compute δ as

$$\delta = \gamma \sqrt{N}$$

$$= 0.667 \sqrt{27}$$

$$= 3.46$$

At this point, we find the power directly from Appendix M; look in the column for $\delta = 3.46$ and $\alpha = .05$. There is no entry for that exact value of δ, so we use the closest (3.50) and find that the power of the test is 0.94. This means that if the true mean for the class were 10 points or more away from the null hypothesis value (100), the probability is .94 that we would find the difference. Because the psychologist originally rejected the hypothesis, and the probability of finding the desired magnitude of effect is quite high, we may have considerable confidence in the inference that this class has a mean that is greater than 100.

This brief introduction to power computations will serve as a foundation for additional presentations as we proceed. Similar computations exist for nearly every analysis that we will encounter. We will present them for other tests in the next several chapters. For computations where the presentation would take us too far afield for this book, you are referred to Kraemer and Thiemann (1987).

Of the three methods of inference discussed (point estimation, interval estimation, and hypothesis testing), the last is by far the most widely used. This is so primarily because it generalizes so easily to research situations where more than a single sample is being used to make an inference about a single parameter. So far, we have presented the inference methods in only the simplest of situations—we have a single set of data, and from that sample, we want to make an inference about the population mean. We can make inferences about other parameters, too, and we can also extend the logic to research designs where multiple groups of subjects are treated in different ways. These topics are addressed later in this book. Before we turn to those matters, though, we need to discuss a complication in the single-sample situation; this is considered in Chapter 9.

Summary

- ◆ *A* hypothesis test *uses the method of* indirect support *to make an inference.*
- ◆ *A hypothesis test establishes a hypothesis that is opposite to the conclusion that you probably want to reach and tests it; if the hypothesis is rejected on the basis of the data at hand, then its opposite is supported.*
- ◆ *The* null hypothesis *is the one tested; its opposite is the* alternative hypothesis.
- ◆ *A hypothetical sampling distribution is established assuming that the null is true.*
- ◆ *The null hypothesis is rejected if the outcome is "unlikely" given the assumed sampling distribution.*
- ◆ *A* two-tailed test *will reject a null hypothesis for data that are too extreme in either direction; a* one-tailed test, *conversely, places all of the "unlikely" region in one tail of the sampling distribution.*
- ◆ *A* Type I error *rejects a true null hypothesis.*
- ◆ *A* Type II error *consists of not rejecting a null hypothesis that is actually false.*
- ◆ *The significance level of a hypothesis test is the probability of making a Type I error.*

♦ All else being equal, decreasing the probability of making a Type I error increases the probability of making a Type II error, and vice versa.

♦ In active research, it is usually better to avoid a Type II error.

♦ The power of a hypothesis is the probability of rejecting a null hypothesis that is false.

♦ The probability of a Type II error is influenced by four things: the significance level, the sample size, the population variability, and the actual difference between the null hypothesis mean and the true mean.

♦ Given an effect size, a significance level, and a variability, the sample size to achieve a given power may be calculated.

Key Terms

α

ALTERNATIVE HYPOTHESIS

β

δ

DECISION RULE

γ

HYPOTHESIS TEST

INDIRECT SUPPORT

"LIKELY" AND "UNLIKELY"
    REGIONS

μ_0

μ_1

NULL HYPOTHESIS

ONE-TAILED TEST

POWER

SIGNIFICANCE LEVEL

TWO-TAILED TEST

TYPE I ERROR

TYPE II ERROR

 # EXERCISES

1. Return to the data that you have from exercise 7.5. For each of the 20 samples of size $N = 2$, find:

   a. the 95% confidence interval for μ

   b. the 90% confidence interval for μ

   c. the 60% confidence interval for μ

2. In exercise 8.1a–c, how many of the 20 interval estimates actually contained the true value of μ? (Recall that for the rectangular population sampled, $\mu = 0.5$, and $\sigma = 0.289$.)

3. IQ scores are often regarded as coming from a normal distribution where $\sigma = 15$.

   a. What is the standard error of the mean for samples of size $N = 10$? $N = 15$? $N = 23$? $N = 32$?

   b. If $N = 15$, find the 95% confidence interval (interval estimate) for μ if $\overline{X} = 105$. If $\overline{X} = 97$. If $\overline{X} = 84.6$.

   c. For $N = 23$ and $\overline{X} = 108.6$, find the 70, 90, 95, and 99% interval estimates for μ.

4. Your instructor gave you the following values. You know that he said the data came from a population where σ is 12, but you cannot remember the mean of the population.

Find the 95% and 99% confidence intervals for μ.

66.67
73.96
43.64
42.82
71.81
47.52
75.33
60.41
71.16
65.90

5. Using a computer, generate 20 samples from a normal population with N, μ, and σ of your own choosing. Compute the 60, 75, and 90% confidence intervals for the mean for each of your samples. You should find that about 60%—that is, 12—of your 60% intervals include your known μ, as do about 15 of your 75% intervals, and about 18 of your 90% intervals. Prepare a table that shows both the expected numbers and the actual numbers you obtained.

6. Generate 40 samples of size $N = 10$ from a normal population where $\mu = 20$ and $\sigma = 5$. Find the mean and median of each sample.

   a. Plot both your measures of center as histograms on the same set of axes.

   b. Which measure appears to have the largest spread?

7. Using the samples from exercise 8.6, find the standard deviation of each of your distributions of sample statistics (that is, compute s for the set of 40 means and for the 40 medians). Which of the standard deviations is the smallest?

8. Here is a set of scores on a four-item quiz for a class in statistics. You may assume that these scores come from a population with $\sigma = 1.0$. Using the .01 significance level, test the hypothesis that students are guessing (that is, that $\mu = 2$), and find the 99% confidence interval.

1	2	3	0	0
3	2	1	4	0
0	1	2	2	2
1	1	2	0	3
1	0	3	3	1
0	2			

9. Repeat exercise 8.8 using the .05 significance level and the 95% confidence interval.

10. Repeat exercise 8.8 using the .25 significance level and the 75% confidence interval.

11. Infants were shown a videotape of a person walking, and then shown a side-by-side pair of videotapes of people moving at the same rate of speed as the walker was. The data give the percentage of the time the infants watched the left-hand display.

| 38.48 | 49.04 | 37.23 | 43.89 | 69.34 |
| 53.99 | 40.79 | 49.44 | 54.47 | 47.45 |

   a. What is your null hypothesis?

   b. If you assume that you know that the population from which the scores were taken is normal, with $\sigma = 9.5$, what is your conclusion? (Use $\alpha = .05$.)

   c. What is the power of the test for detecting a difference of 5 points either way from your null hypothesis value?

12. If the investigator using the videotape situation in exercise 8.11 wanted to have a power of 0.80 against an alternative 5 points away from the hypothesis tested, what sample size would be required? How about for a power of 0.90?

13. The scores on a standardized arithmetic achievement test for third-grade children have a population mean of 125 with a standard deviation of 30. Using the data below and a significance level of .05, test the hypothesis that the class represented by these data is typical (that is, has a mean equal to 125).

110	162	124	163	133
100	135	49	100	109
136	166	162	151	191
142	136	74	96	151
87	186	122	100	177
153	97	182		

   a. What are the null and alternative hypotheses?

   b. What is the population standard error of the mean $\sigma_{\bar{x}}$?

   c. What is your conclusion in the hypothesis test?

   d. Find the 90, 95, and 99% confidence intervals for the population mean.

e. In the hypothesis test in part c, what was the power of the test to detect a difference of 5 points from the standard? A 10-point difference?

14. If the teacher in exercise 8.13 wanted to have a power of 0.70 against an alternative 5 points away from the hypothesis tested, how many of the students does he need to use in the computations?

15. Subjects were given a series of word problems. They had 10 trials of 1 minute each. The data below give the mean number of word problems solved by each subject. Using these data, test the hypothesis that the population mean is 5 problems solved. The population standard deviation is 3.0, and the population is normally distributed. Do three hypothesis tests, using the .10, .05, and .01 significance levels.

4.7	3.5	2.4	7.8	6.2
2.7	3.1	7.1	7.5	2.6
3.6	7.3	3.4	4.3	0.1
2.2	0.7	2.4	1.2	0.9
4.3	4.1	5.8	1.9	3.9
8.6	5.3	1.2	5.5	4.8
6.2	2.7	4.9	6.5	0.5

a. What are the null and alternative hypotheses?

b. What is the standard error of the mean?

c. What is your conclusion in each hypothesis test?

d. Find the 90, 95, and 99% confidence intervals for the population mean. Do they agree with the hypothesis tests?

e. Find the power of each hypothesis test against an alternative hypothesis that is 1 point away from μ.

16. The investigator in exercise 8.15 wants to use $\alpha = .10$ and have a power of 0.75 against an alternative 1 point away from the hypothesis tested. What sample size is required? What sample size would be necessary for a power of 0.80 against an alternative 0.5 point away? How about for a power of 0.90 against 1 point away? Or for a power of 0.90 against a .5 difference?

17. Find the power of the test used to determine whether Jandreau and Bever's (1992) subjects scored normally on the VSAT (page 219). A difference of 25 points from the average would be sufficient to cause the investigators to worry about their subjects (that is, $\gamma = 25/100 = 0.25$).

PART 4 **STATISTICS IN RESEARCH**

his final, and longest, part of the book discusses how we apply both descriptive and inferential statistics in actual research. The chapters in Part 4 are organized around a structure of research designs, beginning with the most fundamental single-sample experiment and continuing to fairly complex factorial experimental designs. In Chapter 9, we consider making inferences in a research design with a single group of subjects. Chapter 10 deals with inference in the common situation where there are two experimental conditions. Chapter 11 considers the situation where there are no "measured" variables and where frequency counting is the only reasonable analysis procedure. Chapter 12 presents inference in the common research situation where there is a single independent variable and multiple experimental conditions. Here the analysis of variance (ANOVA)—arguably the most commonly used inference procedure—is developed in detail. Correlation and regression is expanded to include multiple variables in Chapter 13, and the relationship between regression and ANOVA is suggested. Chapter 14 extends ANOVA to the situation where there are multiple measurements on the same individual. Finally, Chapter 15 expands ANOVA to include experiments where there are two independent variables, and suggests how to expand inference into even more complex designs.

9 One-Sample Inference in Research

As part of their study, Jandreau and Bever (1992) had subjects read a passage of text that they believed should take about 80 seconds to read.[1] Because one of their dependent variables was the time taken to read, they might have wanted to ensure that their subjects did not differ from that expectation. For their 25 subjects, they found that the mean was 81.8 seconds. Are their subjects representative of people in general? Clearly, the mean of their subjects is greater than 80 seconds, but could that mean have arisen by chance from people who really take 80 seconds? In other words,

---

[1] Jandreau and Bever do not actually report this test, but the remainder of the example is a correct summary of their results.

are these subjects really representative of people in general (that is, do they need 80 seconds), or are they slightly slower readers?

The answer to all those questions comes as a hypothesis test. Jandreau and Bever could have tested the hypothesis that their data come from a population where $\mu = 80$. If they did not reject that hypothesis, they could have concluded that their students are typical with regard to their reading times, and the research could then have proceeded with some assurance that the students were not abnormal in regard to the reading times. In this chapter we develop the logic for making the hypothesis test in a real research setting.

All inference procedures use some sampling distribution to establish probabilities, but they differ in exactly which distribution they employ. You may have noticed that, until now, the discussion of inference (in both Chapters 7 and 8) has focused largely on the normal distribution. In fact, because of several necessary assumptions, actual research rarely uses the normal distribution as its sampling distribution. To use the normal distribution to make inferences, you must know σ, which we took as known in Chapters 7 and 8, but which, in real research, is hardly ever known. However, if the population distribution of the dependent variable is normal, there is a well-known alternative we can use as the sampling distribution of $\overline{X}$. The first task here is to introduce the distribution and then describe its use.

PARAMETRIC INFERENCES ABOUT CENTER

The most frequent use of the one-sample experiment is in making an inference about the center of a population. And the parameter most often used is the arithmetic mean. Inferences about a population median are much less common, but useful nonetheless.

In making an inference about the population in Chapter 8, we used a familiar formula—namely,

$$z = \frac{\overline{X} - \mu}{\sigma_{\overline{X}}}$$

This formula, remember, was an adaptation of the original standardizing formula from Chapter 4—namely,

$$\frac{\text{Obtained value} - \text{Mean of distribution}}{\text{Standard deviation}}$$

The modification made the formula appropriate to a sampling distribution of the mean where μ is the assumed mean (the null hypothesis value, sometimes symbolized as μ_0), with a standard deviation of $\sigma_{\overline{X}}$.

Now consider the most common situation for making a single-sample inference—testing a hypothesis about μ—when three additional conditions are present: The sample is relatively small, the population of scores sampled is close to normal in form (or at least it is assumed to be), and the population variance σ^2 is not known. Because you already know that we can estimate σ by s, and because you can use s to calculate $s_{\overline{X}}$, you might expect that the standardizing formula would be

$$\frac{\overline{X} - \mu}{s_{\overline{X}}}$$

And you would be correct. But that statistic is not a normally distributed z score, as it was in Chapter 8. This being the case, we introduce a new distribution to allow us to make inferences.

◆ Student's *t* Distribution

When we know that the population distribution of the dependent variable is normal (or are willing to assume that it is), we can be confident that the sampling distribution of $\overline{X}$ is normal, *but only if we know σ*. But we hardly ever know σ because we almost never have knowledge of one parameter while trying to make an inference about another. If σ is unknown, then the sampling distribution of $\overline{X}$ is not normal, even if the population distribution is and even if the sample is large. Without a normal sampling distribution, we cannot use the table in Appendix A, as we did in Chapter 8, to find critical values and probabilities. Because knowing σ is unlikely, we must deal with the common situation where we have a small sample size and must use s to estimate σ.

The problem of finding an appropriate distribution for the common research conditions of unknown σ and small N was explored by a famous statistician named W. S. Gosset during the early years of this century. Gosset studied the problem of small samples while trying to develop interval estimation procedures for μ. He published his research using the pseudonym "Student."[2] Student's distribution, usually called the *t*, or **Student's *t*** distribution, defines the sampling distribution of the statistic

$$t = \frac{\overline{X} - \mu}{s_{\overline{X}}}$$

when the sampled population is normal and σ is unknown. Note that the formula is just like that for the normal distribution

---

[2] William Sealy Gosset (1876–1938) worked as a brewer and statistician at the Guinness Brewery in Dublin nearly all of his adult life. Guinness's policy on research prevented his publishing under his own name except for one publication late in his life. He described the distribution discussed here in a classic paper ("Student," 1908) that also introduced the convention of using Greek and Roman letters for parameters and statistics. For more information on Gosset, see Tankard (1984).

$$z = \frac{\overline{X} - \mu}{\sigma_{\overline{X}}}$$

except that the population standard error of the mean appears in the z formula and its estimate ($s_{\overline{X}}$) in the other. Apart from that, the formula carries out the standardizing operation, subtracting a population mean from a sample value, and dividing by the standard deviation of the sampling distribution. With the sample estimate of the standard error of the mean, though, the distribution follows Student's t and not the normal distribution.

There is but a single standardized normal distribution, but there is a family of t distributions. The Student's t distributions are all symmetrical and unimodal, resembling the normal in form. They differ from the normal in being relatively higher in the tails and lower in the middle.

The t distribution is controlled by a parameter called its *degrees of freedom*, or simply *df*, which must be specified to define the form completely.

DEGREES OF FREEDOM

The term *degrees of freedom* (usually abbreviated **df**) will continue to come up as we move further, and we take this opportunity to elaborate on it briefly.

In general, the number of degrees of freedom of a statistic is the number of data values that are free to vary in the face of some constraint. Write down any five values, say 3, 5, -2, 4, and 8, as an example. Now place a constraint on the problem: The five values must sum to 15. If we begin by writing 3, 5, -2, and 4, we find that we have no "degree of freedom" in picking the last value—it must be 5 in order for the sum to be 15. By placing the constraint on the problem, only four of the five values could be freely chosen. In the first case, we had five degrees of freedom—all five values were free to vary. In the second case, the single constraint reduced the degrees of freedom by one. In general, a statistic will have a number of degrees of freedom that corresponds to the number of data values less the number of constraints.

How does this apply to Student's t? The formula

$$t = \frac{\overline{X} - \mu}{s_{\overline{X}}}$$

involves two statistics: the sample mean and the sample standard error of the mean. And there's a constraint involved in the latter statistic. In order to compute $s_{\overline{X}} = \sqrt{s/N}$, it was necessary to compute s, and its formula,

$$s = \sqrt{\frac{\sum (X - \overline{X})^2}{N - 1}}$$

depends on having the value of $\overline{X}$. The fixed value of the sample mean "costs" a degree of freedom because the mean of the data values (and hence their sum) is already determined.

With N scores going into the mean, there is one constraint placed on the computation of the standard error of the mean, and that leads to the value $N - 1$ as the degrees of freedom for the statistic. The Student's t formula uses $s_{\overline{X}}$ in the denominator, and so the t has $N - 1$ degrees of freedom.

A series of t distributions, superimposed on a normal distribution, is shown in Figure 9.1. Note that, as df increases, the t distributions become more and more normal in form until, at a very large value, the two converge.

Appendix A gives the probability values for a large number of z values for a normal distribution. To construct a similar table for Student's t would require a separate multiple-page table for each value of df. Many computer programs compute the probabilities as needed, and abbreviated tables appear in many books, including this one. Appendix C presents a table of critical values of the t statistic for a number of selected df values. To understand how a table like Appendix C is constructed, consider Figure 9.2, which shows an enlarged segment of three of the curves from Figure 9.1.

Here, the one-tailed .05 critical value is shown for the normal distribution (1.65) in Figure 9.1, along with Student's t curves for df = 2 and df = 10. Because the t curve is higher in the tails than the normal, the .05 critical point is farther away from the center than 1.64, and moves progressively farther out as df decreases. Those values were taken from Appendix C, using the column headed ".05" under the heading "Level of significance for a one-tailed test." That column gives the critical points for a selection of df

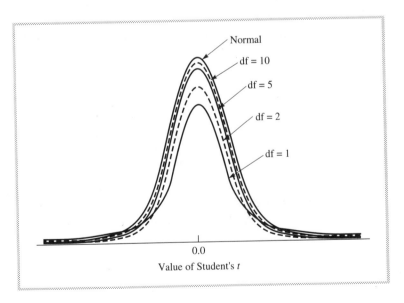

Figure 9.1

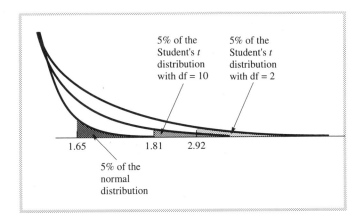

Figure 9.2

values, including the points on the df = 2 and 10 curves that were illustrated in Figure 9.2. Notice that the bottom entry in the table for the column gives the value (1.645) for df = ∞; in other words, at an indefinitely large number of degrees of freedom, the t curve and the normal are identical.

By including only a selected set of significance levels, the t table can be a great deal shorter than that for the normal curve. Appendix C includes the critical points for the two-tailed significance levels of .001, .01, .02, .05, .10, and .20. This selection is usually satisfactory, although larger tables are available. Tables are becoming less necessary because many computer programs compute the exact probability of an obtained t value.

◆ Hypothesis Testing: The One-Sample *t* Test

The hypothesis test using the t distribution proceeds exactly as if we were using the normal distribution except for two things: (1) The standard error of the mean is estimated from

$$s_{\overline{X}} = \frac{s}{\sqrt{N}}$$

instead of from a known σ, and (2) the t distribution in Appendix C is used to find the critical value, instead of Appendix A.

To continue with the example from the beginning of the chapter, Jandreau and Bever had reason to believe that the distribution of reading times should be normally distributed around 80, but had no idea of the variability of the distribution. Because they wanted to test a hypothesis about μ, we must use the t test.

The mean time taken by Jandreau and Bever's 25 subjects to read the passage was 81.8 seconds, and the standard deviation was 20.4 seconds.

Using these values in the formulas presented earlier, we obtain a value of

$$s_{\overline{X}} = \frac{s}{\sqrt{N}}$$

$$= \frac{20.4}{\sqrt{25}}$$

$$= 4.08$$

so that

$$t = \frac{\overline{X} - \mu}{s_{\overline{X}}}$$

$$= \frac{81.8 - 80.0}{4.08}$$

$$= 0.44$$

The degrees of freedom are $N - 1 = 25 - 1 = 24$. Appendix C shows a critical value of 2.064 for significance, $\alpha = .05$, and we conclude that these data do not lead us to reject the hypothesis that the population mean is 80.

PRESENTING STUDENT'S *t* RESULTS

The same sentence format illustrated in Chapter 8 for presenting a hypothesis test is used for Student's t; we need add only the degrees of freedom. For the example, we might write, "We conclude, therefore, that these students have a mean reading time that is not significantly different from the population norm of 80; $\underline{t}(24) = 0.44$, $\underline{p} > .05$." Note that the degrees of freedom are placed in parentheses immediately after the name of the statistic; the remainder of the format is identical to that introduced earlier (see page 221).

◆ ## Interval Estimates Using Student's *t*

Instead of testing a hypothesis about μ, suppose we use the same data to form a confidence interval for μ. We showed earlier that the 95% confidence interval for μ was computed as

$$\overline{X} \pm 1.96\sigma_{\overline{X}}$$

and that for the 99% interval as

$$\overline{X} \pm 2.58\sigma_{\overline{X}}$$

To make similar computations where we estimate σ, we must use $s_{\bar{x}}$. Further, the 1.96 and 2.58 values were taken from the normal curve table, not from the t table. We must make two adjustments, then, to obtain the formula for using Student's t: Substitute $s_{\bar{x}}$ for $\sigma_{\bar{x}}$, and replace the normal curve values with those for the appropriate t distribution. The computations are illustrated in the supplement.

◆ Power Computations for the One-Sample t Test

To compute the required sample size for a given power, you must first find the effect size, γ, as in Chapter 8. To do that, you need some estimate, even a rough one, of σ. With that in hand, the standardized effect size that you wish to detect is computed as

$$\gamma = \frac{|\mu_0 - \mu_1|}{\sigma}$$

Next find the value of δ as

$$\delta = \gamma \sqrt{N}$$

and enter Appendix M to obtain the power, as in Chapter 8. For this example, suppose you estimate σ to be 25, and you would like to be able to detect an effect (that is, a difference between a "true" case and the null hypothesis value) of 8 with $\alpha = .05$. This works out as

$$\gamma = \frac{|\mu_0 - \mu_1|}{\sigma}$$
$$= \frac{8}{25}$$
$$= 0.32$$

leading to

$$\delta = \gamma \sqrt{N}$$
$$= 0.32 \sqrt{25}$$
$$= 1.60$$

Consulting Appendix M, the power of the test is 0.36.

To compute the required number of observations for a given significance level and effect size, the formula for the one-sample t test is

$$N = \left(\frac{\delta}{\gamma}\right)^2$$

The computations are illustrated in the supplement.

NONPARAMETRIC INFERENCES FOR CENTER

Hypothesis tests fall into two general categories: those that assume that the dependent variable is normally distributed and those that do not. Hypothesis tests are called **parametric** if they assume a normal distribution. Inferential statistics that do not have an assumption of normality are called **nonparametric**. The normal-based z and t tests that were presented in this chapter and the preceding one are satisfactory for most single-sample research. But there are times when the distribution is so far from being "normal" in appearance that an alternative might be used. We present the most common parametric and nonparametric hypothesis tests in the following sections.

The measure of center most often used by psychologists is the arithmetic mean; the z and t tests are intended for making an inference about the mean. But the median is also useful in certain circumstances, and sometimes you may need to test a single-sample hypothesis about it. Fortunately, the median has a readily available inferential procedure, one that requires us to use the binomial distribution; we turn our attention there next.

◆ The Binomial Distribution

The binomial is a probability distribution of a variable that is based on the numbers of outcomes in a simple two-outcome experiment. We encountered just such a variable earlier, but we need to be a little more explicit now.

In Chapter 7 we developed an example involving a four-item quiz, under the assumption that students were guessing. We also developed the distribution of the variable "number of questions answered correctly" under the assumption of guessing. We saw that the distribution had the probability distribution shown in Figure 9.3. This is a binomial distribution. Two outcomes underlie the distribution: An individual student gets the question either correct or incorrect. We developed the distribution under the assumption that the student was guessing; that is, the probability of getting an answer correct was equal to the probability of getting it incorrect, and thus both were equal to .5. From that assumption, we developed the probabilities of the events "0 correct," "1 correct," and so forth by using the multiplication and addition rules for probabilities.

In the terminology of probability, each of the outcomes is called the result of a **Bernoulli trial**. In a Bernoulli trial, one of two outcomes occurs. One of the outcomes is usually called a "success" and the other a "failure,"

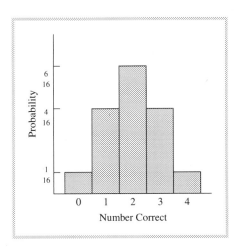

Figure 9.3

although they need have nothing to do with succeeding or failing. In the example, of course, getting the question correct is clearly a "success," while guessing wrong is equally clearly a "failure." But any situation where two outcomes can occur is a Bernoulli trial—for example, flipping a coin is a Bernoulli trial (we could call "heads" a success and "tails" a failure).

In taking the four-item test, there were four Bernoulli trials, each of which could result in a "success" or a "failure." The total number of "successes" could range between 0 and 4. In general, a series of N Bernoulli trials will result in between 0 and N "successes." A specific probability distribution—the **binomial distribution**—gives the probability of each possible number of "successes" in N Bernoulli trials, where there is a probability p of success on each trial. In the four-item quiz, then, there are $N = 4$ Bernoulli trials, each with a probability of success of .5 (if the students are guessing, of course). Thus the test example pictured in Figure 9.3 shows a binomial distribution with $N = 4$ and $p = .5$.

Nothing requires that the probability of a success be .5. Binomial probabilities may be determined readily by following elementary probability rules. For example, suppose we draw a sample of $N = 2$ from an undergraduate class that has 75% women. The probability of choosing two females, calculated by using the multiplication rule, is $.75 * .75 = .5625$. The four possible outcomes, with their probabilities, are shown in Table 9.1.

If we define the variable "number of females in a group of two students," we can easily calculate the binomial probabilities by following the addition rule (see Table 9.2). Figure 9.4 illustrates this distribution as a histogram. The distribution is the binomial with $N = 2$ and $p = .75$.

Appendix G gives the binomial probabilities for a range of values of N and p. For example, looking at the $N = 2$, $p = .75$ entry, you find the values .0625, .3750, and .5625, exactly as just computed. If you check for $N = 4$ and $p = .5$, you find the probabilities we used in Chapter 7 for the four-item test

TABLE 9.1	
Possible Outcome	Probability
F F	.75 * .75 = .5625
F M	.75 * .25 = .1875
M F	.25 * .75 = .1875
M M	.25 * .25 = .0625

TABLE 9.2	
Number of Females	Probability
0	.0625
1	.1875 + .1875 = .3750
2	.5625

example. In both cases, we calculated the probabilities by applying the multiplication and addition rules; all we would have had to do was look in Appendix G.

The binomial is a useful distribution for finding probabilities of events, where the events are counts of the number of occurrences of something to which you can assign a probability *p* of happening. The distribution is surprisingly versatile because a large number of events can be categorized into "success" and "failure." Male–female, alive–dead, pass–fail, complete–incomplete, introvert–nonintrovert, and so on are all Bernoulli events that could serve as the foundation for a binomial distribution.

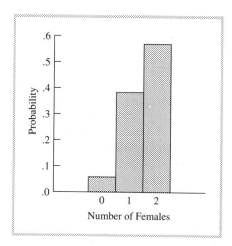

Figure 9.4

For any binomial distribution, the population mean μ is equal to Np. Thus, for the four-item test, when students are guessing, $\mu = Np = 4 * .5 = 2.0$, which we already knew. For the number of females in the preceding example, the population mean number of females is $Np = 2 * .75 = 1.50$.

The population variance of a binomial variable is

$$\sigma^2 = Np(1 - p)$$

so that for the four-item quiz, we have

$$\sigma^2 = Np(1 - p)$$
$$= 4(.5)(.5)$$
$$= 1.0$$

while for the number of females distribution, it is

$$\sigma = Np(1 - p)$$
$$= 2(.75)(.25)$$
$$= .375$$

The form of the binomial varies with p. When $p = .5$, the binomial is symmetric; for any other value, it is skewed, with a mode at approximately[3] the value of the mean.

The binomial distribution leads easily to a hypothesis test for the population median, which is why we introduced it here.

◆ Inferences About the Median

We could consider both hypothesis testing and interval estimation for the median, but in fact interval estimates are rarely used. Calculating them is not difficult, but doing so leads to probability computations that are unnecessarily complex for our purposes given that inferences about medians are so infrequently made.

A simple and exact hypothesis test for the median comes from the binomial distribution. If the population median is, for example, 150, then about 50% of a sample should be above 150 and the remainder below. Another way to say the same thing is that, if the null is true, then the probability of a score falling above the population median is .50. To test the hypothesis of Mdn = 150, simply count the number of data values above 150. Then you can determine the probability of obtaining a value that is larger by consulting the binomial probabilities in Appendix G.

Let's look at an example. The following data were obtained from a

---

[3] "Approximately" because in some cases the binominal has two adjacent modes.

study in which 15 laboratory-maintained birds built nests. The nesting material provided was different from that used by the same birds in the wild, and the investigator wanted to know if the size of the nests was different. The 15 nests were weighed. In the wild, this species builds nests weighing about 150 grams. Does this group differ from the norm? The weights for these 15 birds were:

70	190	145	172	173
168	161	155	141	178
121	163	92	24	158

Because the distribution is severely skewed (see Figure 9.5), the median is the appropriate measure of center. For the sample, the median is 158 grams. We want to test the hypothesis that the population median is 150 grams, using $\alpha = .05$. Of the set of 15 nest weights, 9 are above the population median of 150 (155, 158, 161, 163, 168, 172, 173, 178, and 190). Note that we count above the *population* median—the null hypothesis value—and not above the *sample* median. Because the median is the midpoint of the population, there are as many scores above it as below it. In other words, if we were to pick a value at random from a population whose median was 150, we would be as likely to observe a larger score as a smaller one. Using probability terms, then, the probability of a value greater than 150 is equal to the probability of a value less than 150, or .5 for each event.

With a sample of size $N = 15$ from the population with a median of 150, how likely is it that we would observe 7 or fewer nests weighing more than 150 grams? The probabilities are given by the binomial distribution and can be found in Appendix G. In Appendix G, use the entry for $N = 15$ and the $p = .50$ column. This column gives the probability of getting 0, 1, 2, …, 15

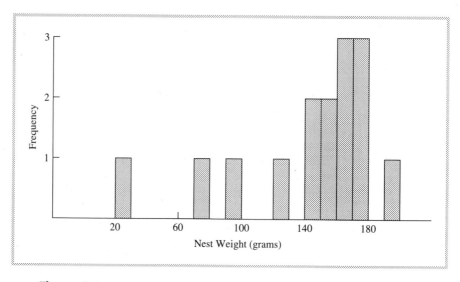

Figure 9.5

scores above the median, assuming that the null hypothesis (median = 150) is true. The distribution appears as in Figure 9.6.

What is the probability of observing 9 or more scores greater than 150, if the null is true? It is the probability of exactly 9 scores, plus the probability of exactly 10 scores, plus the probability of exactly 11 scores, and so on. (We're applying the addition rule again.) For this set of data, the values are .1527 + .0916 + .0417 + .0139 + .0032 + .0005 + .0000 = .3036 (see Figure 9.6). Because this probability is considerably greater than the chosen significance level of .05, the conclusion is that we have observed a "likely" event given that the true median is 150. In short, the data do not lead us to reject the null hypothesis that this flock of captive birds builds nests that differ in weight from the norm for the species in the wild.

Appendix G supplies binomial probabilities for $N = 0, 1, \ldots, 15, 20, 25,$ and 30. For other values of N, the supplement illustrates a normal distribution approximation to the binomial that is perfectly satisfactory.

◆ Inferences About Relationship

Chapter 5 introduced several measures of relationship. Two of them, the Spearman rank order coefficient (rho) for data measured on ordinal scales, and the Pearson product-moment coefficient for interval and ratio measurement, are by far the most common. In this section, we present inference procedures appropriate to these two statistics.

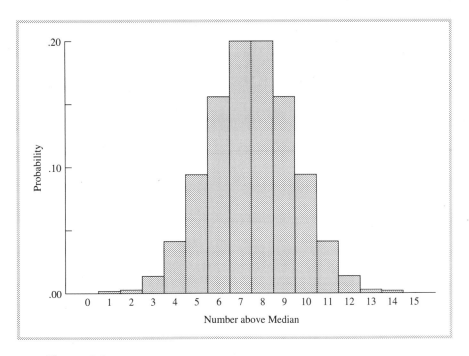

Figure 9.6

◆ Hypothesis Tests for *r* and Slope

A common hypothesis is that the population correlation coefficient, usually called ρ, equals 0.00.[4] The test is typically conducted using a formula yielding a value of Student's *t*. The result is referred to a standard *t* table with df = $N - 2$, where N is the number of *pairs* of scores. Example computations, including a test for a nonzero null hypothesis value, are shown in the supplement. As a practical matter, when N is relatively small, it is easier to test the hypothesis that $\rho = 0$ by using a table of critical values of *r*, such as the one in Appendix K.

As an example, suppose that 20 students in a statistics class show a correlation between the first and second exams of 0.62. Using $\alpha = .05$, does that value cause us to reject the hypothesis that the population correlation is 0.00? We use a two-tailed test because we want to know if the correlation is different for 0.00 in *either* direction. Entering Appendix K with df = $N - 2 = 20 - 2 = 18$, and with two-tailed $\alpha = .05$, we find a critical value of 0.444. Because the obtained correlation (0.62) exceeds that value, we reject the hypothesis that the population correlation is 0.00.

In Chapter 6 we developed the regression equation for predicting the Y given information on X. The equation was

$$\hat{Y} = bX + a$$

The slope coefficient *b*, which is also called the regression coefficient, is a statistic that estimates a population parameter β. In some circumstances, we may want to test the hypothesis that $\beta = 0$ in the population. This hypothesis is identical to saying that there is no predictability from X to Y.

In the two-variable situation, with a single X predicting Y, the test of the hypothesis that $\rho = 0.00$ is identical to a test of the hypothesis that $\beta = 0.00$ so we need not pursue the matter further here. We bring it up only to note that, in multiple regression, where there are two or more X variables, it makes sense to be able to test the hypothesis of predictability for each X separately. Indeed, such tests are available and are valuable in a multivariate situation.

◆ Hypothesis Tests for Spearman's Rho

We rarely need to use any inference for Spearman's rho other than a test of the null hypothesis that the population value is zero. There are two procedures for doing so, however, depending on sample size. The test for small samples ($N \leq 10$) is simple and requires only a table, while the second is identical to a test for ρ.

---

[4] Bayesian statisticians (see footnote, page 209), among others, regard this as a particularly silly hypothesis to test because most variables are related to most others, at least to some small degree. Nevertheless, it is a common hypothesis, offered by nearly every computer program, and so we include it.

TABLE 9.3 Single-Condition Hypothesis Testing Summary	
Inferences About Center	
Data Condition	*Use*
With data that may be assumed to come from a normal population	Student's t to test for a value of μ or a t-based interval estimate
With data that probably do not come from a normal population	Binomial test for the population median
Inferences About Relationship	
Data are interval or ratio scales and roughly linearly related	Appendix K to test the hypothesis that $\rho = 0$ or The r-to-z transformation t formula for ρ other than 0 from the computational supplement
Data are ranks	Student's t formula to test the hypothesis that $r_s = 0$ in the population

For small samples, Appendix E gives the values of Spearman's rho that are significant at the .01 and the .05 levels for several sample sizes. The table is used by simply finding the entry for the sample size and significance level desired; if the obtained correlation exceeds the tabled value, reject the hypothesis of no association.

For larger samples, the test is conducted exactly as if testing a hypothesis about Pearson's r because the Spearman is nothing but a Pearson computed on ranks.

Table 9.3 summarizes the hypothesis testing and interval estimation procedures presented in this chapter.

Summary

- *To use the normal distribution as a sampling distribution for the mean, you must know σ, even if the population distribution is known.*
- *Student's t describes the sampling distribution for $\overline{X}$ when σ is unknown and must be estimated from the data.*
- *A parametric statistical test assumes that the underlying distribution is normal in form.*
- *A nonparametric test does not assume a normal distribution.*
- *The form of the t distribution depends on its df.*
- *To make interval estimates for μ using Student's t, replace $\sigma_{\overline{x}}$ with*

$s_{\bar{x}}$, *and obtain a value from the t table instead of from the normal table.*

◆ *A* Bernoulli trial *is an event with a single two-choice outcome.*
◆ *The* binomial distribution *gives the probability of a number of "successes" in a series of Bernoulli trials.*
◆ *Testing a hypothesis about a median may be done by counting the number of scores greater than the assumed population median and referring to the binomial distribution.*
◆ *A common hypothesis about a correlation coefficient is that the population value equals zero.*

Key Terms

BERNOULLI TRIAL	NONPARAMETRIC TEST
BINOMIAL DISTRIBUTION	PARAMETRIC TEST
DEGREES OF FREEDOM (df)	STUDENT'S *t*

EXERCISES

1. The following data represent Reading Achievement Test scores from a group of first-grade children. The national norm (that is, μ) on this test is 200. Using the 5% significance level, do these children differ from the norm?

177	206	221	195	232
222	196	205	231	213
189	195	222	204	209

2. Using the data in exercise 9.1, find the 80, 90, 95, and 99% confidence intervals for μ.

3. Write a summary paragraph to presents the results from exercises 9.1 and 9.2.

4. It's possible to buy "maze-bright" and "maze-dull" rats. Such animals have been highly selected for generations, and the "maze-bright" animals can be counted upon to learn a ten-element T-maze quickly, perhaps in about five trials. A new shipment of rats has just arrived in the lab, and the label has been misplaced: The rats might be normal animals, or they might be maze-bright. From the 40 animals in the shipment, a sample of 10 was selected and taught the maze to a criterion of one error-free trial. The following are the number of trials to reach that criterion for each animal. Based on the data and using $\alpha = .05$, do you conclude that these are normal animals, or are they maze-bright?

| 5 | 9 | 4 | 8 | 12 |
| 7 | 10 | 7 | 9 | 4 |

5. In exercise 9.4, the significance level was set at .05, meaning that there was a 5% chance we could conclude that the animals were not maze-bright when in fact they actually were. Because it is important to the experimenter who will use the remaining 30 rats to know whether they are maze-bright or not, the experimenter suggests that a 5% chance of making a Type I error is too high. Conduct the analysis again, using $\alpha = .01$. What is your conclusion this time?

6. On a standard test of impulsiveness, a score of 50 is regarded as neutral. For the following set of data, determine whether the students who supplied the scores are neutral in impulsiveness. (Use $\alpha = .05$.)

66	45	55	64	75
44	63	61	59	52
55	49	57	55	58
57	65			

7. The weight of 90-day-old rats is typically about 125 grams. For the following data, test the hypothesis that the median weight is 125. (Use $\alpha = .10$.)

90	98	132	103	106
116	112	128		

8. For the following data, test the hypothesis that the population median is 75, using $\alpha = .05$:

63	66	59	33	87
31	83	67	68	81
88	88	61	68	82
58	85	49	76	96
79	85	48	83	83
95	90	85		

9. Here's another set of data, this representing scores on an extroversion scale:

14	7	11	10	19
12	14	11	15	17

Write a paragraph, with supporting statistics and hypothesis tests, that communicates the answer to the question: Do these data seem to represent a population whose population mean score is 10 (use $\alpha = .01$)?

10. Is the Spearman rank-order correlation 0.63 significantly different from zero for $N = 8$, using $\alpha = .05$?

11. Is the Spearman rank-order correlation 0.85 significantly different from zero for $N = 5$?

The next seven questions are based on the following set of data obtained from students in an individual differences class.

12. Using the Personality Scale data, compute the rank-order order correlation between V and I. Is it significant at $\alpha = .05$?

13. Again using the Personality Scale data, compute the rank-order correlation between EPIE and SSST. Is it significant at $\alpha = .02$?

PERSONALITY SCALE

Student	EPIE	SSST	BIS	V	I	TAS	ES
1	15	13	36	3	2	2	10
2	14	22	42	13	3	9	17
3	6	17	37	11	4	9	14
4	20	33	89	14	16	10	26
5	14	18	41	9	9	6	13
6	14	18	48	14	2	9	15
7	16	27	42	12	6	7	19
8	15	13	61	6	12	2	7
9	12	15	40	11	2	9	11
10	14	21	34	9	8	4	14
11	14	27	76	13	13	8	20
12	14	17	65	9	6	7	13
13	12	8	59	3	10	4	6
14	11	13	31	5	8	6	9
15	12	20	49	5	6	5	16
16	11	14	52	4	6	0	8
17	14	21	60	14	13	10	16
18	4	11	43	5	4	5	5
19	17	25	44	14	7	9	21
20	13	25	85	15	12	10	18

The personality test scales are:

EPIE   Extroversion scale from the Eysenck Personality Index (EPI)

SSST   Total score on Zuckerman's Sensation-Seeking Scale, Version 5 (SSS-V)

BIS   Total score on the Barratt Impulsivity Scale

V   Venturesomeness scale on the Eysenck & Eysenck Impulsiveness-Venturesomeness-Empathy questionnaire (IVE)

I   Impulsiveness on the IVE

TAS   Thrill and Adventure Seeking subscale of the SSS-V

ES   Experience Seeking subscale of the SSS-V

14. Both SSST and V appear to measure similar personality traits. Obtain the correlation between them and determine whether it is significantly different from zero at the .10 level.

15. What is the correlation between BIS and I? Is it significantly different from 0.5 at the .05 level?

16. Some theorists suggest that, because of differences in their internal states of arousal, persons with low scores on the EPIE scale (often called introverts) tend to avoid external sources of additional stimulation, while those with high scores (extroverts) tend to seek external stimulation. Obtain the correlation between EPIE and TAS and test it for signifi-

cant difference from zero at .05. What do you conclude?

17. The same theorists suggest a relationship between EPIE and ES. Using those variables, do the same computations you did in exercise 9.16. Are your conclusions the same or different?

18. Compute the correlation between TAS and ES. Is it significantly different from zero using $\alpha = .01$? From 0.6 (also using .01)?

19. Here is a set of data from Tyrrell, Stauffer, and Snowman (1991). The values are the percent of the time that infants looked at one of two different stimulus patterns.

60.00	83.33	83.67	74.03	76.42
82.42	69.49	77.17	61.90	76.55
70.47	75.20	66.39	87.16	74.78
59.02	87.60	80.77	62.42	42.20
76.42	82.42	74.03	70.91	

a. Find the 0.90, 0.95, and 0.99 confidence intervals for μ.

b. If the infants have no preference for one stimulus over the other, then they should look at each for the same amount of time. Based on the confidence intervals you found in part a, does that seem to be the case for these infants? How did you arrive at that conclusion?

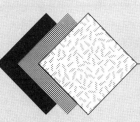

Computational Supplement

◆ The One-Sample *t* Test

The following data are scores for a group of college students on the Sociability scale of the Eysenck Personality Index. The norm for Sociability scores in the college population is 6.0; does this sample seem to come from that population?

9	10	7	8	10
7	8	4	10	7
4	7	7	6	8
11	10	10	8	9

For these data, $\overline{X} = 8.00$ and $s = 1.947$ so that

$$s_{\overline{X}} = \frac{s}{\sqrt{N}}$$

$$= \frac{1.947}{\sqrt{20}}$$

$$= 0.435$$

We are willing to assume that the population distribution is normal and so we use Student's *t* to test the null hypothesis that $\mu = 6.0$:

$$t = \frac{\overline{X} - \mu}{s_{\overline{X}}}$$

$$= \frac{8.0 - 6.0}{0.435}$$

$$= 4.598$$

Is the value of *t* sufficiently far away from 0.0 to reject the null hypothesis that the population mean of Sociability scores is 6.0? Consulting Appendix C and using the column for a two-tailed test at .05 and the row for df = 19 (because df = $N - 1 = 20 - 1 = 19$), we find that the critical *t* value is 2.093. Graphically, the situation is as pictured in Figure 9.7. As the illustration shows, the obtained *t* exceeds the critical value of 2.093. Thus we reject the null hypoth-

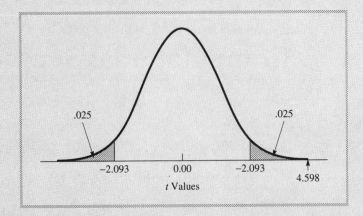

Figure 9.7

esis that the population mean is 6.0, and conclude its opposite: that the population mean is not 6.0.

◆ Interval Estimates with Student's *t*

Instead of testing a hypothesis about μ, we could use the preceding data to form a confidence interval for μ. We learned in Chapter 7 that the 95% confidence interval for μ could be computed as

$$\overline{X} \pm 1.96(\sigma_{\overline{X}})$$

and the 99% interval as

$$\overline{X} \pm 2.58(\sigma_{\overline{X}})$$

To make this computation where we don't know σ and must use s as an estimate, we need to use the t distribution instead of the normal. But the 1.96 and the 2.58 values in the formulas are from the normal distribution, and so we must replace them with values from the t. There are thus two changes to make in the formulas: Substitute $s_{\overline{X}}$ for $\sigma_{\overline{X}}$, and replace the normal curve values with those for the appropriate t distribution. As a formula, we thus write

$$\overline{X} \pm t_{1-\alpha,\,\mathrm{df}} s_{\overline{X}}$$

where $t_{1-\alpha,\,\mathrm{df}}$ indicates the critical value for a test at the significance level α (taken from Appendix C) and df $= N - 1$. For example, to compute the 95% confidence interval from the preceding data, we obtain the critical t value of 2.093 from Appendix C and use the value of $s_{\overline{X}}$ of 0.435, so that the interval is

$$\overline{X} \pm t_{1-\alpha,\,\mathrm{df}} s_{\overline{X}}$$
$$8.0 \pm 2.093 * 0.435 = 8.0 \pm 0.910$$
$$= 7.09 \quad \text{and} \quad 8.91$$

To calculate the 99% confidence interval, we would substitute the t value of 2.861 from Appendix C for the 2.093, giving 6.755 and 9.245 for the upper and lower bounds of the interval.

◆ Inferences About the Median

For a large-sample test of a hypothesis about the median, we follow the same logic as illustrated in the text, but instead of using the binomial distribution directly, we use the normal distribution to approximate it. When $p = .5$, as is the case in tests about the median, the binomial is symmetric around its center. With a large enough N, the distribution is approximately normal. Because the binomial has a standard deviation of

$$\sigma = \sqrt{Np(1 - p)}$$

and a mean $\mu = Np$, we can employ the usual standardizing formula to convert the observed number of values greater than the null hypothesis median to a z score, and then refer to Appendix A to determine the probability.

John et al. (in preparation) asked a sample of clinicians how often they had been asked to write a letter of recommendation for a former client or supervisee. The clinicians responded on a scale of 1–5, where 1 indicated a very rare event, and 5 meant that such a request occurred regularly. The median response from the clinicians was 2.0. Because a total of 322 clinicians responded to the question, we can use the large-sample method to test the hypothesis that the population median is 3.0. First we compute the mean and the standard deviation as

$$\mu = Np$$
$$= 322 * .5$$
$$= 161.0$$

and

$$\sigma = \sqrt{Np(1 - p)}$$
$$= \sqrt{322 * .5 * (1 - .5)}$$
$$= 8.97$$

Next we return to the original data and find that 76 of the clinicians responded with a value greater than 3.0. Using the standardizing formula, we find that

$$Z = \frac{\text{Number above median} - \mu}{\sigma}$$
$$= \frac{76 - 161}{8.97}$$
$$= -9.48$$

Because, at $\alpha = .05$ a z of ± 1.96 represents a significant departure from chance, we reject the null hypothesis that the median response is 3.0 and conclude that clinicians are asked to write recommendations much less often than the "occasionally" suggested by a rating of 3.0.

◆ Inferences About Correlations

TESTING THE HYPOTHESIS THAT $\rho = 0$

Suppose we have some data on impulsivity, the tendency of an individual to give in to sudden urges. There are several measures of impulsivity, and you would expect that the two measures of impulsivity might correlate. For a sample of 84 college students, an investigator found a correlation of $r = 0.425$ between two different impulsivity measures. The value is not high, but does it differ from zero, using a significance level of .01? This question may be answered with the hypothesis test, or we may simply look in Appendix K. There we find that a Pearson r of 0.256 or greater is significantly different from zero for $N = 80$ and $\alpha = .01$. In this example, we reject the hypothesis that $\rho = 0$. (If the necessary df is not listed in the table, choose the next lower entry, which gives a *higher* critical value.)

For degrees of freedom exceeding the table entries, the formula

$$t = \frac{r\sqrt{N-2}}{\sqrt{1-r^2}}$$

may be used. The formula yields a value that is distributed approximately as Student's t.

If we apply the formula to the preceding example, we get:

$$t = \frac{r\sqrt{N-2}}{\sqrt{1-r^2}}$$

$$= \frac{0.425\sqrt{84-2}}{\sqrt{1-0.425^2}}$$

$$= 4.25$$

Referring to Appendix C, we see that the table does not have an entry for $df = N - 2 = 82$, so we use the next smaller value, df(70), and find that the critical value for a two-tailed test at $\alpha = .05$ is 1.994. The hypothesis that $\rho = 0$ is rejected: Although the correlation between the two impulsivity measures is small, it *is* significantly greater than zero.

TESTING OTHER VALUES OF ρ

Hypothesis testing becomes more complicated if we want to test a hypothesis other than $\rho = 0$. Few computer programs even offer the option. To test a hypothesis about a nonzero population value, we must know something about the sampling distribution of the product-moment correlation coefficient. When $\rho = 0$ and when N is large enough (greater than 50 or so in this case), the form of the sampling distribution can be regarded as being normal with

$$\sigma_r = \frac{1}{\sqrt{N}}$$

But when $\rho \neq 0$, the distribution of r is markedly skewed, becoming more so as the absolute value of r approaches 1.0. As r approaches $+1.0$, the distribution becomes negatively skewed; as it approaches -1.0, the skew is positive. Fortunately, the great early statistician R. A. Fisher (about whom we'll hear more later) developed a formula that transforms r into a z value that is normally distributed when N is greater than about 10. That formula, known appropriately as *Fisher's r-to-z transformation*, was used to compute the values in Appendix L, which gives the transformed values of a large number of r values. To test a hypothesis about ρ, we use the sampling distribution for the transformed r; it is normal in form, centered around the transformed null hypothesis value, and has a standard deviation of

$$\sigma_r = \sqrt{\frac{1}{N-3}}$$

To test a hypothesis, we form the test statistic

$$z = \frac{z_\rho - \mu_r}{\sigma_r}$$

which may be referred to an ordinary normal curve table like Appendix A.

As an example, let's take yet more impulsivity data. For two particular measures, previous research suggests that the correlation between them is likely to be about 0.60. For 84 students, $r = 0.51$. Do these individuals differ from the assumed population, where $\rho = 0.6$?

To answer the question, use the r-to-z transformation table in Appendix L to convert the obtained and the null hypothesis values of r and ρ into z, obtaining the values $z_\rho = 0.5627$ and $\mu_r = 0.6931$.

We compute the standard deviation of the sampling distribution as

$$\sigma_r = \sqrt{\frac{1}{N-3}} = \sqrt{\frac{1}{84-3}} = 0.111$$

Finally, we calculate the z score for the transformed values:

$$\frac{z_\rho - \mu_r}{\sigma_r} = \frac{0.5627 - 0.6931}{0.111} = -1.175$$

Because a z must be 1.96 or greater to reject the null hypothesis at the .05 level, we conclude that this group of subjects does not differ from the norm where $\rho = 0.60$.

Note that there is no reasonable way to test the hypothesis that $\rho = 1.0$ or that $\rho = -1.0$, as students sometimes want to do. The reason why we cannot make those tests is that we must assume that the null is true in order to construct the sampling distribution. But if it were true, then all the points in the scatterplot would be on a single straight line, and there could be no variability around that line. Because that's the case, *any* deviation from the single-line scatterplot would result in an automatic rejection of the hypothesis at *any* significance level.

10 Hypothesis Testing in Experiments with Two Conditions

Several different substances taste sweet to humans. For example, we consider both saccharin and sucrose as "sweet"—at least as long as the concentration of saccharin is not too strong. Do these substances taste "sweet" to other animals as well? Other animals are often used in psychological research because they are convenient for various reasons. For example, because the rat has nutritional needs that are almost identical to those of humans, it is often used in research on nutritional deficits that would be difficult (or unethical) to do using humans. Do saccharin and sucrose both taste sweet to rats? Another way to ask that question is to ask whether, if given a choice, rats will consume equal amounts of the two substances.

Note that we are suggesting an experimental design with two conditions: Offer sucrose and offer saccharin. Such a design is often regarded as the prototype of "real" research. And for good reason. When you can simplify a research question to two distinct conditions, and when you find a difference (or a lack of difference), the results are clear and unambiguous. No other research design offers such a clear interpretation of its results. Indeed, most of the more complicated designs that we introduce later provide only a "first look" at overall results, and leave it to two-condition comparisons to clarify the results.

Despite the esteem in which the **two-condition experiment** is held, however, few such experiments actually appear in the literature; most investigators design more complex experiments, typically with several independent variables. Conducting multivariable research is economical of time and allows exploration of interactions among variables. Because variables in psychology rarely operate independently of one another, particular combinations sometimes have unexpected consequences. Limiting research to single independent-variable designs like the two-condition experiment makes finding such interactions impossible. Nevertheless, the two-condition experiment remains the prototype of "good" research, and we analyze it in this chapter.

INFERENTIAL TECHNIQUES FOR CENTERS

The logic of inference for the two-condition experiment follows the same steps that we first presented in Chapters 7, 8, and 9. We begin with a null hypothesis about a parameter (or parameters) for one or more populations. We then develop the sampling distribution of some statistic under the assumption that the null hypothesis is true. Once that has been done, we define a decision rule, and finally draw a conclusion about difference in the two conditions.

Hypothesis tests and interval estimates, as in the single-condition experiment, fall into two general classes, depending on whether they assume that some underlying distribution is normal or not. We begin our presentation with procedures that assume a normal distribution, and then present those that do not assume normality.

The most common inference to be made in the two-condition design concerns the difference between the centers of the two experimental conditions. Let's return to the question of whether rats consume more sucrose or saccharin, when given the choice between them. How might we get an answer to the question? Here's one way. We could equip some cages with two drinking tubes. In one tube we put plain water, and in the other tube we place water containing either sucrose or saccharin. Now we randomly assign animals to the cages, and over a fixed period of time measure how much of the two sweet solutions the animals consume. Suppose that over a 24-hour period the animals given a choice between water and sucrose consumed a mean of 58.5 milliliters of the sucrose solution, while those given a choice between saccharin and water consumed 55.8 milliliters. From the values, it seems that sucrose is slightly preferred over saccharin. But is the difference real, or did we just happen to get the observed differences by chance? Or, to put it differently, if we repeated the experiment, perhaps using different animals, how confident are we that we would see roughly the same results? What if there were *really* no difference between the two groups of animals, and we just saw a chance variation? Then we would have no confidence in a conclusion about a taste preference because the next time, the results could just as easily go the other way.

What we need is a way to make a statement about the probability of the obtained results. And, most often, that confidence statement will take the form of a hypothesis test. Suppose for the moment that there was really no difference, overall, in the consumption of sucrose and saccharin. Would you expect that *every* pair of groups of animals would show *exactly* the same consumption? No, of course not. They might be close, and sometimes the sucrose group would drink more, and sometimes the saccharin group would drink more. But in the long run, there wouldn't be any difference.

A hypothesis test is a way to make a statement about the likelihood of observing a difference in consumption when there really is no difference. Typically, a null hypothesis is established that suggests no difference between the means of the populations represented by the two groups. If that hypothesis is true, then we expect most of the means from the two groups to have close to the same mean consumption; the difference in the means of the two groups should be close to zero. With a few simple assumptions, we can construct the sampling distribution of differences in means and then employ the logic developed in Chapters 7, 8, and 9 to test the hypothesis.

There's a second way to approach the question. Note that we have two separate groups of rats in the experiment. We might just have more "sucrose lovers" in the sucrose group; this alone could lead to a difference in mean consumption. To avoid this possibility, we might form a single group of animals and use the group twice, once to test consumption of sucrose, and once to measure consumption of saccharin. (We would have to be careful to give some animals sucrose first, and others saccharin first; if we didn't do that, then we might not be able to tell whether they preferred sucrose or simply preferred the first substance we gave them.)

What we just suggested is a second form of the two-condition experiment. As first proposed, the two experimental conditions (sucrose and saccharin) were represented by two separate experimental groups. In Chapter 1, this kind of experimental design was labeled the *between-groups* design, because a comparison of the sucrose and the saccharin conditions is a comparison *between* two different groups of subjects. The second way to conduct the experiment corresponds to Chapter 1's *within-groups* design. In a within-groups design, the two experimental conditions are given to the same subjects; thus, comparing sucrose and saccharin consumption is a comparison *within* the same group of subjects.

The within-groups design eliminates the possibility of differences between the groups of animals having an effect on the results. (That is, because there's only one group of animals, the sucrose lovers won't all be together in a separate group.)

◆ Parametric Tests for Independent Groups (Between-Groups Design)

The two forms of the two-condition experiment have two slightly different hypothesis tests. Both use the Student's t distribution, and both test the hypothesis that there is no difference between the two conditions. However, there are differences in the distributions from which the data are sampled, and in the sampling distribution used for the hypothesis test. We begin with the test for the between-groups experimental design. In this design, there is no connection between the subjects that receive the two treatments, and the analysis is often called an **independent-groups** analysis.

THE DISTRIBUTIONS

The sucrose consumption scores of the rats in the sucrose group may be thought of as a random sample drawn from the population "sucrose consumption of all rats that might ever live." This population of sucrose consumption values has a mean that we might label μ_{Sucrose}. In the same way, the saccharin consumption data from the other group can be regarded as a random sample from the population "saccharin consumption of all rats that might ever live." We may symbolize this population mean as $\mu_{\text{Saccharin}}$. The answer to the question "Do rats differ in their saccharin and sucrose consumption?" is obtained from a test of the hypothesis that μ_{Sucrose} is equal to $\mu_{\text{Saccharin}}$. Or, to state the null hypothesis more exactly, $\mu_{\text{Sucrose}} - \mu_{\text{Saccharin}} = 0.0$.

So far, we have taken only the first steps in the underlying logic of the hypothesis test by noting that there are two conceptual populations, one corresponding to each of the two experimental conditions. The experiment is conducted by drawing two random samples from the two populations and obtaining two sets of data, one collected under each of the two experimental conditions. We might assume that each sample is the same size, but we do not need to make that assumption. We can have a sample of size n_{Sucrose} from the first population, and of size $n_{\text{Saccharin}}$ from the second. The mean of each sample is a point estimate of the mean of its population.

We could use each sample mean to test a hypothesis or make an interval estimate about its own population mean. There are two population distributions and two separate sampling distributions. Of the latter, one is based on samples of size n_{Sucrose}, and the other on samples of size $n_{\text{Saccharin}}$. See Figure 10.1. If you look at just one side or the other, we have a single-sample design, just like those in Chapters 7, 8, and 9. The sampling distribution for the means each have a form, a center, and a spread. Because we are keeping it simple and considering only the normal population case now, each sampling distribution is normal and its center is equal to the center of its population. The spreads of the two sampling distributions, $\sigma_{\overline{X}_{\text{Sucrose}}}$ and $\sigma_{\overline{X}_{\text{Saccharin}}}$, may be estimated from the two-sample standard deviations, just as in Chapter 9. So far, aside from the presence of two populations and sampling distributions, nothing is different here.

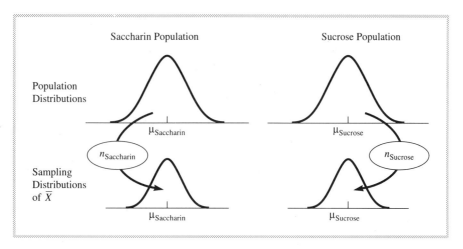

Figure 10.1

But there is something different. We're not interested in the values of $\mu_{Sucrose}$ and $\mu_{Saccharin}$ themselves but specifically in the difference between them—namely, $\mu_{Sucrose} - \mu_{Saccharin}$. In particular, for the present example, we're interested in testing the hypothesis that $\mu_{Sucrose} - \mu_{Saccharin} = 0.0$ To make that test, we must define a different sampling distribution, one based on the differences between pairs of means, one mean taken randomly from each population. In other words, we must add another level to our conceptual diagram of the distributions, as shown in Figure 10.2. This is a new sampling distribution. It consists of differences in means, one mean drawn randomly from each population. Like any sampling distribution, this one has a form, a center, and a spread. The form of the distribution is normal because its parent distributions are both normal, and the center is $\mu_{Saccharin} - \mu_{Sucrose}$. If the null hypothesis is correct, the center is zero. The spread of the sampling distribution of mean differences between means is a function of the two sample sizes and the spreads of the two original populations.

THE EQUAL VARIANCES CASE

If the variances of the two populations, $\sigma^2_{Saccharin}$ and $\sigma^2_{Sucrose}$, are equal, then the standard deviation of the sampling distribution of the mean differences may be estimated by a statistic that combines, or "pools," the two-sample variances to make an estimate of the standard error of both populations. This computation results in the **pooled variance estimate**, and the resulting test a "pooled t test." The pooled formula is appropriate only when the population variances are equal (or nearly so). This statistic is often symbolized as $s_{\bar{X}_1 - \bar{X}_2}$ and called the *standard error of the difference*. It is an unbiased estimate of the standard deviation of the sampling distribution of the differences in means.

As we introduced it in Chapter 4 and restated in Chapters 8 and 9, the

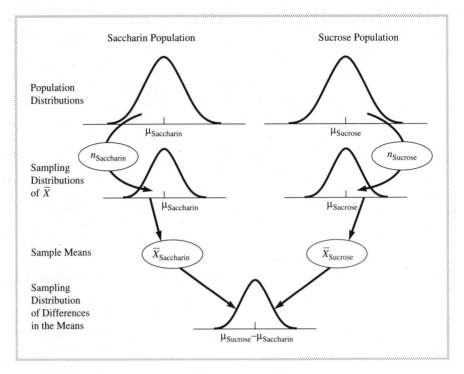

Figure 10.2

formula for standardizing is

$$\frac{\text{Obtained value} - \text{Mean of distribution}}{\text{Standard deviation}}$$

We saw this formula most recently as adapted to Student's t for a one-sample experiment, as

$$t = \frac{\overline{X} - \mu}{s_{\overline{X}}}$$

in Chapter 9.

We make one more adaptation of the same formula, this time to make it applicable to the distribution of mean differences. The statistic

$$t = \frac{(\overline{X}_1 - \overline{X}_2) - (\mu_1 - \mu_2)}{s_{\overline{X}_1 - \overline{X}_2}}$$

is distributed as Student's t with df $= n_1 + n_2 - 2$, and used to test the two-sample hypothesis. As in the single-sample test, the right-hand part of the numerator gives a null hypothesis value. In most cases, the null hypothesis is that the two population means are identical, but that need not be the case. We could test a hypothesis about any value for the difference of μ values. Because the null hypothesis value is usually 0.0, you will sometimes see the formula written as

$$t = \frac{(\overline{X}_1 - \overline{X}_2)}{s_{\overline{X}_1 - \overline{X}_2}}$$

but we continue to use the full formula as a reminder that we are doing the same standardizing operation—namely,

$$\frac{\text{Obtained value} - \text{Mean of distribution}}{\text{Standard deviation}}$$

as introduced in Chapter 4.

The degrees of freedom for the t are calculated as $\text{df} = n_1 + n_2 - 2 = 10 + 10 - 2 = 18$.

In order to obtain the value of $s_{\overline{X}_1 - \overline{X}_2}$, we combine the two-sample variances to estimate the value of the standard error of the difference between the means. When the groups are equal in size, as they are in the example, the formula is simple:

$$s_{\overline{X}_1 - \overline{X}_2} = \sqrt{\frac{s_1^2}{n_1} + \frac{s_2^2}{n_2}}$$

When the samples are unequally sized, the formula is a bit more complicated; it appears in the computational supplement.

As an example, the data in Table 10.1 give sucrose and saccharin con-

TABLE 10.1		
	Sucrose	*Saccharin*
	2.5	26
	2	19
	5	23
	1	24
	7	15
	4	20
	4	15
	5	16
	1	18
	9	27.5
Mean	4.05	20.35
St. Dev.	2.59	4.56
Variance	6.69	20.78

sumption (in milliliters drunk in a 15-min test period) by two groups of rats. We will use the .05 significance level for the test. Clearly, the means are different, and in the direction that suggests that the aversion to the taste transferred from saccharin to sucrose, but are we confident in our conclusion that the two conditions differ? The question is whether the mean difference of −16.30 is sufficiently far from the hypothesized value of 0.0 to reject the hypothesis of no difference. If it is, then we may reject the hypothesis of no difference and support the conclusion that there is a difference, thus providing an affirmative answer to the question about the equivalence in preference of the two tastes.

For the data in Table 10.1, the value of the standard error of the difference is

$$s_{\overline{X}_1 - \overline{X}_2} = \sqrt{\frac{s_1^2}{n_1} + \frac{s_2^2}{n_2}}$$

$$= \sqrt{\frac{2.59^2}{10} + \frac{4.56^2}{10}}$$

$$= \sqrt{2.75}$$

$$= 1.66$$

Using this value in the expression for Student's t, we obtain

$$t = \frac{(\overline{X}_1 - \overline{X}_2) - (\mu_1 - \mu_2)}{s_{\overline{X}_1 - \overline{X}_2}}$$

$$= \frac{(4.05 - 20.35) - 0}{1.66}$$

$$= -9.82$$

This t, recall, has df = 18. According to Appendix C, the critical value with df = 18 and α = .05 is 2.101. Because the obtained value of −9.82 exceeds the critical value, we reject the hypothesis of no difference at the .05 level. We conclude that the rats drink more saccharin.

THE UNEQUAL VARIANCES CASE

When the variances are not equal,[1] we make two adjustments in the computations. First, instead of using the preceding formula to estimate the standard error of the difference, we use a formula based on separate variances estimated from the two groups. Second, we make an adjustment in the df. This computation often results in a fractional value that is normally

[1] You might suspect unequal variances if one variance is three or more times as large as the other. The business of testing for equal variances is complicated, and we leave it to others (e.g., Howell, 1992); when in doubt, use the unequal variances t test.

rounded to the nearest integer. The actual computations are shown in the supplement.

INTERVAL ESTIMATES FOR $\mu_1 - \mu_2$

Some computer programs offer a confidence interval for the difference between two population means. The logic of the procedure follows directly from that developed in Chapter 7 except that it deals with the distribution of $\overline{X}_1 - \overline{X}_2$ and not to a single $\overline{X}$.

◆ Parametric Tests for Within-Subjects (Repeated Measures) Data

The **repeated measures**, or *within-subjects, design* is very common in psychology, and is exceptionally powerful. The power comes about because the design eliminates much of the between-group variability by using the same subjects in both experimental conditions. This controls against many of the extraneous variables that sometimes complicate the analysis of between-groups data. Using a within-groups design eliminates the need to make sure that the groups are identical with regard to sex distribution, age of subjects, prior experience, and so forth. The fact that the same subjects appear under both experimental conditions means that the two sets of data are most likely correlated with each other, and so this design is often called the **correlated groups** or the *dependent groups* experimental design.

As an example, the data in Table 10.2 come from an experiment where an infant was shown a videotape of a person either walking or jogging. After a short interval, the infant was shown two moving stimuli, one at the same

TABLE 10.2			
Infant	Familiar Stimulus	Unfamiliar Stimulus	Difference
1	38.48	66.67	−28.19
2	49.04	73.96	−24.92
3	37.23	43.64	−6.41
4	43.89	42.82	1.07
5	69.34	71.81	−2.47
6	53.99	47.52	6.47
7	40.79	75.33	−34.54
8	49.44	60.41	−10.97
9	54.47	71.16	−16.69
10	47.45	65.90	−18.45
Mean	48.412	61.922	−13.51
St. Dev.	9.489	12.715	13.39

walking or jogging speed just seen (a "familiar" stimulus) and one at a different speed (a "novel" stimulus). The dependent variable is "time spent looking at each second stimulus" and was measured in seconds. The question is whether the infants can distinguish between the two speeds of movement; if they can, then they should look longer at the unfamiliar pattern. If they cannot, the times should be the same for the two patterns. The data look like those for a correlation analysis because there are two scores for each infant. We could, of course, calculate a correlation coefficient between the two sets of scores, but that does not address the question of whether they look at the familiar and the unfamiliar stimuli for equal lengths of time.

A reasonable null hypothesis is that there is no difference; that is, the infants look at the unfamiliar pattern as much as they look at the familiar one. If this hypothesis is correct, the data from each infant on the two stimuli should be close to the same—the difference in the time spent looking at the two patterns should be about zero for each infant. In fact, if we were to subtract the two values for each child, we would have data that reflect the *difference* in looking time for the two stimuli. Table 10.2 presents those differences.

If there is no difference between the looking times, the difference scores are a sample from a population whose mean is 0.0. The hypothesis that the population mean difference score is 0.0 is conducted as an ordinary one-sample hypothesis test, exactly like those in Chapters 8 and 9, testing the hypothesis that the mean difference is 0.0. We might use the symbol μ_{diff} (thus making it clear that we are talking about the differences between the pairs of scores), and state the hypothesis as $\mu_{\text{diff}} = 0.0$.

To illustrate the computation, we might modify the t formula from Chapter 9 to specify the differences:

$$t = \frac{\overline{X}_{\text{diff}} - \mu_{\text{diff}}}{s_{\overline{X}_{\text{diff}}}}$$

With the hypothesis that $\mu = 0.0$, we can proceed to calculate the standard error of the mean as

$$s_{\overline{X}_{\text{diff}}} = \frac{s_{\text{diff}}}{\sqrt{n}} = \frac{13.387}{\sqrt{10}} = 4.23$$

so that

$$t = -\frac{13.51 - 0}{4.23}$$

$$= -3.194$$

This statistic is distributed as Student's t, with df $= n - 1$. If we choose to use $\alpha = .05$, Appendix C shows that the critical value for t with df $= 10 - 1 = 9$ is 2.262; we reject the null hypothesis that the infants look at the two speeds of motion for equal lengths of time. Returning to the original means, it's clear they spend longer watching the unfamiliar pattern of lights.

◆ Power Computations for the Two-Sample *t* Test

INDEPENDENT GROUPS (BETWEEN-SUBJECTS) ANALYSES

To determine the sample size needed for a given power, a straightforward extension from the single-sample experiment works well. First decide how large a difference between the population means you want to detect. For the two-sample case with equal variances, the effect size is calculated as you expect:

$$\gamma = \frac{|\mu_1 - \mu_2|}{\sigma}$$

That is, the effect is expressed relative to the population standard deviation. In the formula, σ refers to the variance of each of the two populations and is normally based on past research. Once the effect size is available, δ can be found in Appendix M, as before. Finally, the formula

$$n = 2\left(\frac{\delta}{\gamma}\right)^2$$

provides n for each sample. As an example, suppose you wanted a power of 0.90 in the study of taste preferences in rats, with the ability to detect a difference of 5 milliliters in consumption between the groups (see Table 10.1), while using a significance level of .02. Based on previous research, you estimate that σ is about 3.5. The effect size is calculated as

$$\gamma = \frac{|\mu_1 - \mu_2|}{\sigma}$$

$$= \frac{5}{3.5}$$

$$= 1.43$$

In Appendix M, we obtain $\delta = 3.60$, so that

$$n = 2\left(\frac{\delta}{\gamma}\right)^2$$

$$= 2\left(\frac{3.60}{1.43}\right)^2$$

$$= 12.68$$

Thus, a sample size of 13 will be sufficient.

Determining the power of an already completed analysis is easy if the sample sizes are equal, but a little more complicated if they are not. In both cases, you need to find δ from the effect size and the sample sizes following the formula

$$\delta = \gamma \sqrt{\frac{n}{2}}$$

given earlier. In the equal group size case, you just calculate δ and refer to Appendix M to find the power. But if there are unequal group sizes, you have to calculate an "average" group size to use for n in the formula. The usual suggestion is not to use an arithmetic mean of the group sizes, but instead to use a special kind of mean, specifically the harmonic mean, which is calculated as

$$\tilde{n} = \frac{2n_1 n_2}{n_1 + n_2}$$

where n_1 and n_2 are the two sample sizes.

In the taste preference example, where there were ten subjects in each sample and $\alpha = .02$, using the effect size from earlier (1.43),

$$\delta = \gamma \sqrt{\frac{n}{2}}$$

$$= 1.43 \sqrt{\frac{10}{2}}$$

$$= 3.20$$

so the power from Appendix M is 0.81. Note that this is the *actual* power of the test as conducted. We saw earlier that to achieve a power of 0.90, a sample of size 13 per group would have been necessary.

The modification to the procedure for unequal group sizes is illustrated in the supplement.

REPEATED MEASURES (WITHIN-SUBJECTS) ANALYSES

The procedures for calculating the power of the t test for within-subjects or repeated measures data are similar to those for a single-sample t test, with two exceptions. First, n refers to the number of *pairs* of scores instead of the number of individual scores. But more importantly, there is an additional step in the computations. Because the data for the test are actually differences between two scores, we need an estimate of the standard deviation of the population distribution of those differences.

As usual, the critical effect size is

$$\gamma = \frac{|\mu_1 - \mu_2|}{\sigma}$$

but the denominator refers to the population of *differences* in scores, which we can call σ_{diff}. To compute this, we use the estimated population correlation coefficient between the scores and incorporate it into the formula as

$$\sigma_{diff} = \sigma\sqrt{2(1 - \rho^2)}$$

where σ is the population standard deviation of both sets of scores. (That is, the variances of the two populations are assumed to be equal, and σ is the best estimate of that standard deviation on the basis of previous research.) Thus the effect size is determined as

$$\gamma = \frac{|\mu_1 - \mu_2|}{\sigma_{diff}}$$

Once σ_{diff} is available, the computations proceed as for a single-sample test.

In the event that you don't have a convenient value for the standard error of the difference from previous research, or must estimate it from published statistics, you may use the formula

$$\sigma_{diff} = \sqrt{\frac{s_1^2}{n} + \frac{s_2^2}{n} - 2r\left(\frac{s_1}{n}\frac{s_2}{n}\right)}$$

In the formula, s_1 and s_2 are the standard deviations of the two conditions, n is the sample size, and r is the correlation between the two data sets.

◆ Nonparametric Tests for Center

In many cases, especially with small samples, there is concern about the normality of the underlying distributions, and a nonparametric alternative to the t test is needed. The supplement illustrates two common nonparametric procedures for making inferences about differences between experimental conditions without normal distribution assumptions. Both tests are due to Wilcoxon, one for matched pairs and the other for two independent groups. We describe the tests briefly here along with some others, and illustrate their computations in the supplement.

TESTS FOR WITHIN-SUBJECTS (OR MATCHED-PAIRS) DESIGNS

Two tests are widely used for testing the equality of centers for two sets of data from repeated measures or from matched pairs of individuals. The tests actually are sensitive to *any* differences in the distributions represented by the groups. So although they are widely used and regarded as tests of equality of *center* (often conceptualized as the median), they reject a hypothesis of equality if the groups are substantially different in spread or in form, even if the medians are actually equal. You must be careful; the hypothesis is not just that *centers* are equal.

The most widely known test is the **Wilcoxon test for matched groups**, and it is illustrated in the supplement. You may also see a procedure called the *sign test* in the literature. It, too, tests the equality of two related sets of data.

TESTS FOR TWO INDEPENDENT GROUPS

When the two conditions are represented by two independent groups, there are even more procedures for testing a hypothesis of equality. The Mann-Whitney U test is frequently cited, as is another test developed by Wilcoxon (similar to the one just presented): the **Wilcoxon test for independent groups**. The Wilcoxon and the Mann-Whitney are identical in logic, and in fact the critical value of one can be easily converted to the other. We present the Wilcoxon version of the test in the supplement. Among other tests that might be found in the literature or in the offerings of computer programs are the median test, the Kolmogorov-Smirnov test, and the Siegel-Tukey test.

POWER AND THE TWO WILCOXON TESTS

Siegel and Castellan (1988) report that the power of the Wilcoxon is about 95% that of the comparable t test. Thus, to determine the power of a Wilcoxon test, find the power of the equivalent t test and multiply it by 0.95. In finding a sample size, increase the value obtained from the n computation by about 5%. If the assumptions that underlie the t are violated (such as equal variances and normal distributions), though, the nonparametric tests can actually be *more* powerful than the t.

INFERENCE FOR CORRELATION

All of the tests so far in this chapter address one question: Do the two conditions differ in center? Questions about equality of center are by far the most common research question asked. Such questions occur in both the two-condition experiment that we're discussing here, and in more complicated designs as well. But the two-condition experimental design is not limited to asking about centers. Although less commonly done, the design can also ask about spread, form, or correlation. Here we present only a test for the difference in two correlations.

In Chapter 9 we presented a test of whether a Pearson product-moment correlation coefficient differs significantly from zero. Now we expand that question to the two-condition design and ask whether two Pearson's r values are different from each other.

For example, some high school students invest time and money taking courses that prepare them to take the Scholastic Aptitude Test (SAT), a test that is required for admission to many colleges. Although there seems little doubt that such courses increase the score on the SAT, questions remain. The SAT is used as a screening tool by colleges because it tends to predict (using regression methods like those in Chapter 6) academic success, often as measured by college grades. Suppose, completely hypothetically, that the correlation between the SAT total score and the freshman year grade point average (GPA) for a large university is .5 for students who have not taken an SAT training course. (As discussed in Chapter 6, that means that about 25% of the variance in freshman GPA can be predicted from SAT scores.) If we looked at students who have taken SAT training courses, we would expect to see a higher mean SAT total, but what of the correlation? Perhaps the SAT course succeeds in raising students' ability to *take the test,* but not in their academic ability; in that case, we would expect to see a *weaker* relationship between SAT and freshman GPA because scores on the SAT were artificially inflated by the training program.

Suppose that a large university offers free SAT training to a random selection of high school seniors and not to others. The university could then compute the correlations between SAT and GPA for the two groups of students. (Of course, some students in the nontraining group might have taken a similar course at their own expense; they could be excluded from the analysis.) Suppose further that for the SAT-training students ($n = 36$) $r = 0.41$, while for ($n = 42$) nontrained students $r = 0.53$. Do these correlations differ? Following the procedure illustrated in the supplement, we obtain the value $z = 0.651$. Since the z value required for significance at the .05 level is 1.96, we may conclude that there is no difference in the relationship between SAT total score and freshman GPA caused by taking the SAT training course.

MATCHED GROUPS When the correlations to be tested result from a matched group or a within-subjects design, the situation is considerably more complicated than for independent groups. Howell (1992, pp. 253–254) gives a procedure and an example, but only in the case where there are a total of three correlations and you want to know if two of them are different. To pursue the matter further would take us too far afield for this book.

SUMMARY OF TECHNIQUES

This chapter has presented a number of procedures for testing hypotheses that arise in experiments with two conditions. Table 10.3 summarizes the tests that we've discussed.

TABLE 10.3	Summary of Two-Condition Tests	
	Inferences About Center	
	Independent Variable Is Manipulated	
	Between Subjects	*Within Subjects*
Parametric (normal distribution) test	Student's *t* for independent groups	Student's *t* for matched groups
Nonparametric test	Wilcoxon test for independent groups	Wilcoxon test for matched pairs
	Inferences About Correlation	
	z test with transformed *r* values	No test

Summary

◆ The logic of the t test for two independent groups is similar to that for one group, except that the sampling distribution is of differences in means.

◆ The statistic used to estimate the standard deviation of the sampling distribution on mean differences is different depending on whether the population variances are equal.

◆ A test of the difference between means for two matched groups is done using the differences in pairs of scores.

◆ Two tests developed by Wilcoxon, one for matched groups and one for independent groups, are frequently used.

◆ We may also test for equality of two correlations.

Key Terms

CORRELATED GROUPS
INDEPENDENT GROUPS
POOLED VARIANCE
    ESTIMATE
REPEATED MEASURES DESIGN

TWO-CONDITION
    EXPERIMENT
WILCOXON TEST FOR
    INDEPENDENT GROUPS
WILCOXON TEST FOR
    MATCHED GROUPS

1. Subjects in a verbal learning study learned two equally difficult sets of words to a criterion of one complete trial through the list without error. In one condition, the subjects were tested with a vocal of the song "Tomorrow" from the musical *Annie* as background music; in the other condition, the song and its loudness were the same, but the music was an instrumental arrangement. The dependent variable was number of trials to criterion. Conditions were counterbalanced so that half the subjects had the instrumental condition first and half had the vocal first. Data for the experiment follow.

SUBJECT	VOCAL	INSTRUMENTAL
1	18	13
2	13	9
3	22	17
4	9	13
5	10	10
6	18	14
7	16	21
8	18	11
9	8	5
10	19	13
11	22	16
12	16	11
13	25	19
14	20	15
15	9	7

a. Conduct the appropriate t test to see if the difference between the two experimental conditions is statistically significant. (Use $\alpha = .05$.)

b. Conduct the appropriate Wilcoxon test on the same data. (Use $\alpha = .05$.) Do the results agree with those of part a?

2. Two groups of chickens were raised from hatching either singly or in a group of five hatch-mates. At the age of six weeks, all subjects were placed in a small cage with a same-aged, group-reared chicken (in the case of group-reared subjects, the test chicken was from a different group). The dependent variable was amount of grain consumed (in grams) during a 30-min test period.

GROUP-REARED	INDIVIDUALLY REARED
35	9
27	16
29	13
9	13
37	26
25	11
28	5
26	
45	
19	

a. Conduct the appropriate t test to see if the difference between the two experimental conditions is statistically significant. (Use $\alpha = .01$.)

b. Conduct the appropriate distribution-free test on the same data. (Use $\alpha = .01$.) Do the results agree with those of part a?

3. Here are some animal taste preferences, giving the consumption of a dilute solution of hydrochloric acid (sour taste). The data give amount consumed in milliliters in a 15-min test period.

SOUR	WATER
7	9
14	8
9	9
12	7.5
9	9
9	10
12	10.5
10	8
9	10
11	6.5

a. Conduct the appropriate t test to see if the difference between the two experimental conditions is statistically significant. (Use $\alpha = .10$.)

b. Conduct the appropriate distribution-free test on the same data. (Use $\alpha = .10$.) Do the results agree with those of part a?

4. Following is a set of "looking time" data for each of two patterns:

FAMILIAR	UNFAMILIAR
55.87	60.85
53.76	65.33
54.90	54.66
48.33	59.45
34.76	54.55
56.99	47.10
68.91	71.13
61.84	56.61
67.33	44.73
42.41	56.73
68.21	46.93

a. Conduct the appropriate t test to see if the difference between the two experimental conditions is statistically significant. (Use $\alpha = .05$.)

b. Conduct the appropriate distribution-free test on the same data. (Use $\alpha = .05$.) Do the results agree with those of part a?

5. The correlation between the amount of sucrose consumed and the amount of quinine consumed by ten animals is -0.096 for an aversion-conditioned group and 0.409 for ten control animals. Do the correlations differ using $\alpha = .10$?

6. The correlation between the amount of salt consumed and the amount of quinine consumed by the same animals in exercise 10.5 is -0.559 for the aversion group and 0.430 for the control animals. There are still ten animals in each condition. Do the correlations differ using $\alpha = .10$?

7. McGowen and Hart (1992) report the results of a survey of clinical psychologists. The survey collected data on a number of aspects of career experiences. Of particular interest were differences between male and female therapists. In one question, the respondents were asked whether they would refuse a job if accepting it would jeopardize an important relationship with another person. The ratings were on a 1–7 scale, where 1 = "not likely" and 7 = "very likely." Using a t test and the given data,[2] complete the following.

[2] The data are simulated, but the means and standard deviations are similar to those of McGowen and Hart. The group sizes are proportional to the original (many more males) but are smaller.

a. Do males and females differ in their ratings (use $\alpha = .05$)?

b. Write your conclusion in words, using the appropriate form for reporting a significance test.

WOMEN	MEN	
6	5	6
5	5	5
5	5	5
6	6	6
5	5	5
6	5	7
5	6	4
5	6	5
6	6	4
6	6	5
5	4	5
6	6	5
5	5	5
6	5	5
6	5	5
5	5	6
6	6	6
6	5	5
6	5	5
6	6	6
7	6	4
5	5	5
	5	6
	5	5
	6	6
	3	4
	5	5
	5	5
	5	6
	6	5
	5	5
	6	6
	6	5
	4	4
	4	6
	6	5
	5	5
	5	5
	5	6
	5	5
	5	6
	5	5
	6	
	5	

8. In another question, McGowen and Hart (1992) asked whether their respondents would ask for a specific salary when they received a job offer at less than their expectations. The response scale was the same as in exercise 10.7, and the data[3] follow.

a. Do males and females differ in their ratings (use $\alpha = .05$)?

b. Write your conclusion in words, using the appropriate form for reporting a significance test.

WOMEN	MEN	
7	7	5
4	7	7
5	6	6
6	4	7
5	7	4
6	7	4
4	7	5
5	6	7
7	7	7
6	6	7
6	6	7
7	5	6
6	7	7
6	6	5
7	6	7
7	7	6
7	6	7
7	6	7
7	7	6
7	6	3
6	6	6
4	7	4
	5	7
	6	7
	5	5
	6	6
	7	6
	6	6
	6	7
	7	7
	5	5
	6	7
	5	4
	6	6
	6	6
	5	6
	4	5
	5	5
	6	
	6	

9. Here are some data taken from an instructor's grade book.

STUDENT	REPORT 1	REPORT 2	MIDTERM EXAM	FINAL EXAM
1	96	64	63	77
2	85	56	76	75
3	87	59	79	68
4	57	34	73	52
5	66	31	93	97
6	71	45	74	81
7	50	22	66	51
8	63	31	58	47
9	52	42	74	64
10	98	71	60	42
11	70	43	50	38
12	47	29	61	52
13	92	52	72	59
14	40	24	72	38
15	87	73	62	45
16	93	71	65	61
17	53	37	80	73
18	96	68	82	73
19	64	42	72	89
20	73	41	60	55
21	60	49	42	45
22	77	52	67	46
23	61	41	70	74
24	56	44	83	97
25	92	62	68	68
26	88	54	51	33
27	54	42	41	28

a. Using $\alpha = .01$, is there a significant difference between Report 1 and Report 2? Using $\alpha = .05$?

b. Using $\alpha = .01$, is there a significant difference between the midterm and the final exams? Using $\alpha = .05$?

c. Compute the correlation between Reports 1 and 2. Is it significantly different from zero using $\alpha = .05$?

d. Compute the correlation between the midterm and the final. Is it significantly different from zero using $\alpha = .05$?

e. Last year, the correlation between Reports 1 and 2 was 0.86 in a class of 32 students. Does this year's class differ from last year's in its correlation? Use $\alpha = .05$.

f. Last year, the correlation between the midterm and the final was 0.62. Does this year's class differ from last year's in its correlation? Use $\alpha = .05$.

---

[3] Again, simulated but with means and standard deviations similar to those of McGowen and Hart.

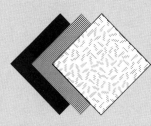

Computational Supplement

◆ Test for Means of Two Independent Samples

EQUAL VARIANCES

The formulas for this test when the sample sizes are equal are given in the text. To illustrate the case of unequal group sizes, we use the simple data in Table 10.4. The formula for $s_{\bar{X}_1 - \bar{X}_2}$ with unequal sample sizes follows, with the computation:

$$
\begin{aligned}
s_{\bar{X}_1 - \bar{X}_2} &= \sqrt{\frac{(n_1 - 1)s_1^2 + (n_2 - 1)s_2^2}{n_1 + n_2 - 2}\left(\frac{1}{n_1} + \frac{1}{n_2}\right)} \\
&= \sqrt{\frac{(6 - 1)1.47^2 + (8 - 1)1.96^2}{6 + 8 - 2}\left(\frac{1}{6} + \frac{1}{8}\right)} \\
&= 0.96
\end{aligned}
$$

The Student's t value is calculated as

$$
\begin{aligned}
t &= \frac{(\bar{X}_1 - \bar{X}_2) - (\mu_1 - \mu_2)}{s_{\bar{X}_1 - \bar{X}_2}} \\
&= \frac{(7.17 - 4.88) - 0}{0.96} \\
&= 2.38
\end{aligned}
$$

With $\alpha = .05$, and with df $= 10 + 10 - 2 = 18$, the critical value of t from Appendix C is 2.101. Because the computed value of t exceeds the critical value, we reject the null hypothesis of no difference between the two population means.

THE UNEQUAL VARIANCE CASE

When the population variances are not equal, we make two adjustments in the computations. First, use this formula to calculate the standard error of the difference:

$$
\begin{aligned}
s_{\bar{X}_1 - \bar{X}_2} &= \sqrt{\frac{s_1^2}{n_1} + \frac{s_2^2}{n_2}} \\
&= \sqrt{s_{\bar{X}_1}^2 + s_{\bar{X}_2}^2}
\end{aligned}
$$

TABLE 10.4	Example Data	
	8	5
	9	6
	8	3
	7	4
	5	5
	6	4
		3
		9
n	6	8
Mean	7.17	4.88
St. Dev.	1.47	1.96

The hypotheis test proceeds as illustrated through the t formula. But then compute df as follows (Welch, 1947):

$$df = \left[\frac{\left(\frac{s_1^2}{n_1} + \frac{s_2^2}{n_2} \right)^2}{\frac{\left(\frac{s_1^2}{n_1} \right)^2}{n_1 + 1} + \frac{\left(\frac{s_2^2}{n_2} \right)^2}{n_2 + 1}} \right] - 2$$

This computation will probably result in a fractional value that should be rounded to the nearest integer.

As an example of the computations for the unequal variance case, consider these data:

	CONDITION 1	CONDITION 2
	2	1
	3	7
	3	15
	4	13
	3	6
		8
Mean	3.00	8.33
St. Dev.	0.71	5.05
Variance	0.50	25.47

Clearly, these data show a substantial difference in variance. If we were to compute the pooled estimate of the standard deviation of the sampling distribution and complete the t computation, we would have $t = -2.323$ with 9 df. The critical value of t for df = 9 and $\alpha = .05$ is 2.262, and so we would reject the null hypothesis that the two sets of data come from populations with equal means.

However, if we follow the computations for unequal variances, as we should, we have

$$s_{\overline{X}_1 - \overline{X}_2} = \sqrt{\frac{s_1^2}{n_1} + \frac{s_2^2}{n_2}}$$

$$= \sqrt{\frac{0.50}{5} + \frac{25.47}{6}}$$

$$= 2.08$$

so that

$$t = \frac{(\overline{X}_1 - \overline{X}_2) - (\mu_1 - \mu_2)}{s_{\overline{X}_1 - \overline{X}_2}}$$

$$= \frac{(3.0 - 8.33) - 0}{2.08}$$

$$= -2.562$$

The Student's t value is only slightly different from that obtained using the pooled estimate of $s_{\overline{X}_1 - \overline{X}_2}$, though the df is quite different:

$$df = \left[\frac{\left[\frac{s_1^2}{n_1} + \frac{s_2^2}{n_2} \right]^2}{\frac{\left[\frac{s_1^2}{n_1} \right]^2}{n_1 + 1} + \frac{\left[\frac{s_2^2}{n_2} \right]^2}{n_2 + 1}} \right] - 2$$

$$= \left[\frac{\left[\frac{0.50}{5} + \frac{25.47}{6} \right]^2}{\frac{\left[\frac{0.50}{5} \right]^2}{5 + 1} + \frac{\left[\frac{25.47}{6} \right]^2}{6 + 1}} \right] - 2$$

$$= 7.329 - 2$$

$$\simeq 5$$

With df = 5, the critical value of t at $\alpha = .05$ is 2.571, so that we do not reject the null hypothesis, an opposite conclusion from that drawn earlier with the same data.

The example data were constructed specifically to show different conclusions from the two forms of the t test to illustrate that they can differ. In fact, the two procedures often come to the same conclusion. To be on the safe side, though, you may wish to use the unequal sample size computations routinely.

◆ Power Computations for the Independent Groups t with Unequal n's

To illustrate these computations, we use the data from Table 10.4. We begin by calculating the harmonic mean sample size as

$$\tilde{n} = \frac{2n_1 n_2}{n_1 + n_2}$$

$$= \frac{2(6)8}{6 + 8}$$

$$= 6.88$$

Once this value is in hand, the rest of the computation follows from that illustrated in the text. Assume that the test was conducted at $\alpha = .05$ and we want to know the power against a difference of 2.0. Guessing σ to be about 1.70, we calculate the effect size as

$$\delta = \gamma \sqrt{\frac{\tilde{n}}{2}}$$

$$= 1.18 \sqrt{\frac{6.88}{2}}$$

$$= 2.19$$

Thus

$$\delta = \gamma \sqrt{\frac{\tilde{n}}{2}}$$

$$= 1.43 \sqrt{\frac{6.88}{2}}$$

$$= 2.65$$

so that the power from Appendix M is about 0.60.

◆ **Power Computations for the Repeated Measures** *t*

Table 10.5 presents some very simple data from an instructor's grade book that illustrates the computations. Suppose that the hypothesis of no difference between exam 1 and exam 2 had been tested at $\alpha = .05$. What was the power of the test to detect a difference of 1.0 between the two exams? To answer that question, first calculate the population standard deviation of the difference. From past years, the instructor expects the standard deviation of the differences in scores to be close to 1.00 (this particular class has a value of 2.88). In addition, the correlation between the two exams is typically about 0.40. With these values we start by calculating

$$\sigma_{\text{diff}} = \sigma \sqrt{2(1 - \rho^2)}$$

$$= 1.00 \sqrt{2(1 - 0.40^2)}$$

$$= 1.09$$

TABLE 10.5

Subject	Exam 1	Exam 2	Difference
1	8	3	5
2	12	9	3
3	7	6	1
4	10	12	−2
5	4	6	−2
6	8	5	3
Mean	8.17	6.83	1.33
St. Dev.	2.71	3.19	2.88

From this, we compute

$$\gamma = \frac{|\mu_1 - \mu_2|}{\sigma_{\text{Diff}}}$$

$$= \frac{1.0}{1.296}$$

$$= 0.77$$

and

$$\delta = \gamma \sqrt{n}$$

$$= 0.77 \sqrt{6}$$

$$= 1.89$$

From Appendix M, we find that the power of the test was about 0.48 at $\alpha = .05$ with the six students in the class. This means that the instructor has a little less than an even chance of detecting a difference of 1.0 point on the exams.

What size class would make it possible to detect a one-point difference on the exams with a power of 0.75? To answer that, we determine the required n for this situation. We have the necessary σ_{diff} from the previous computation, and proceed to find δ in Appendix M. There, because we wish the power to be 0.75 and $\alpha = .05$, δ must be about 2.60.

Now we apply the formula for n from Chapter 9,

$$n = \left(\frac{\delta}{\gamma}\right)^2$$

$$= \left(\frac{2.60}{0.77}\right)^2$$

$$= 11.40$$

and conclude that the instructor needs at least five more students in the class to have a power of 0.75.

◆ The Wilcoxon Test for Matched Groups

We illustrate the computations for the Wilcoxon test for matched groups with the infant "looking time" data in Table 10.2. Normally, we do not use two different tests on the same data; we are doing it in this case to compare the two analyses. You should decide whether to use parametric or nonparametric tests on the basis of measurement level or the form of the distributions, and then do either one or the other analysis, but not both.

Here are the data again, showing the time spent looking at familiar and unfamiliar patterns. The differences between the pairs of values for each infant are also shown:

INFANT	FAMILIAR	UNFAMILIAR	DIFFERENCE
1	38.48	66.67	−28.19
2	49.04	73.96	−24.92
3	37.23	43.64	−6.41
4	43.89	42.82	1.07
5	69.34	71.81	−2.47
6	53.99	47.52	6.47
7	40.79	75.33	−34.54
8	49.44	60.41	−10.97
9	54.47	71.16	−16.69
10	47.45	65.90	−18.45

The Wilcoxon test uses the differences, and the null hypothesis is that the differences are from a symmetric population centered around zero, as they would be if the two sets of scores actually came from the same population.

The first step in the analysis is to arrange the differences in order from smallest to largest, *disregarding their sign*, so that the absolute values are ranked:

INFANT	ABSOLUTE DIFFERENCE	RANK	SIGNED RANK
4	1.07	1	+1
5	2.47	2	−2
3	6.41	3	−3
6	6.47	4	+4
8	10.97	5	−5
9	16.69	6	−6
10	18.45	7	−7
2	24.92	8	−8
1	28.19	9	−9
7	34.54	10	−10

Now attach the ranks $(1, 2, \ldots)$ to the sorted scores and mark with a + the ranks that were formerly positive and with a − those that were negative, as shown in the right-most column. Now sum to two sets of values, those with the + and those with the, −—giving two sets of rank sums:

$$\text{Sum}(+) = 1 + 4 = 5$$

$$\text{Sum}(-) = 2 + 3 + 5 + \cdots + 10 = 50$$

The test statistic, often called T, is the *smaller* of the two values—in this case, 5. To determine whether the obtained value leads to a conclusion of a significant difference, consult Appendix H. That table gives critical values for several significance levels and for a small set of values of n (the number of pairs of scores). In contrast to nearly every other table of critical values, tables of T typically show lower-tail values, so that *if the obtained value* is *less than* the tabled value, then *we have a significant difference* between the two conditions. In our example, the critical value for T at $\alpha = .05$ and for $n = 10$ from Appendix H is 8. The calculated value is 5. Because 5 is less than 8, we conclude that the distributions of looking times from the walking and the jogging patterns most likely come from two different populations. In other words, there is a significant difference between the two speeds. (That is the same conclusion we reached using the t test.) When reporting the results of the test, we might write "We conclude that the infants do not look at the two stimuli for equal time. They spend more time watching the novel pattern; Wilcoxon $T = 5$, $p < .05$."

When the number of pairs is fairly large, greater than 25 or so, we use a normal curve approximation for the Wilcoxon test. The T statistic has the two parameters

$$\mu_T = \frac{n(n + 1)}{4}$$

$$\sigma_T = \sqrt{\frac{n(n + 1)(2n + 1)}{24}}$$

Given those two values, the statistic

$$z = \frac{T - \mu_T}{\sigma_T}$$

is approximately normally distributed. For example, suppose we have a set of $n = 36$ pairs of values with a computed value of T equal to 515. We calculate

$$\mu_T = \frac{36(36 + 1)}{4} = 333$$

$$\sigma_T = \sqrt{\frac{36(36 + 1)(2 * 36 + 1)}{24}}$$

$$= 63.65$$

and then

$$z = \frac{515 - 333}{63.65}$$

$$= 2.86$$

If we use a .01 significance level, the critical value in the normal distribution is 2.58, and we reject the hypothesis that the two sets of scores are the same.

Tied scores in the Wilcoxon test for matched pairs need special attention. There are two kinds of ties, zeros and nonzeros. A zero difference occurs when the subject's (or pair's) scores are the same in both conditions. Discard any pairs of data that have a zero difference, reducing n by 1 for each pair discarded. For nonzero ties, assign each the mean rank. For example, in this set of data,

DIFFERENCE	RANK
0.0	
−2.9	1
3.6	2
4.1	3.5
−4.1	3.5
5.4	5
−8.2	6.5
−8.2	6.5

we drop the 0.0 difference, leaving $n = 7$ pairs of scores. The two largest values, −8.2, are tied for the highest rank, namely positions 6 and 7 in the list. They are assigned the mean of the ranks that they occupy: 6.5. Also, because the differences are ranked without regard to sign, the differences 4.1 and −4.1 are also tied, and assigned the mean rank of 3.5. From this point, the analysis proceeds as before.

THE WILCOXON TEST FOR INDEPENDENT GROUPS

There are two forms of the Wilcoxon test for independent groups depending on the sample sizes. If both samples are less than 10, then use the small sample method; if the groups are larger than 10, a normal curve approximation is applicable.

The small sample test uses the following data set. The dependent variable is the number of errors made in a problem-solving task, and the independent variable is the sex of the subject:

	MALES	FEMALES
	53	58
	76	66
	69	68
	72	71
	70	78
	52	47
	50	56
	61	
	67	
Mean	63.33	63.43
St. Dev.	9.64	10.42
Variance	92.93	108.58

The first step is to rank all the values from smallest to largest, keeping track of the group membership:

RANK	ERRORS	SEX
1	47	Female
2	50	Male
3	52	Male
4	53	Male
5	56	Female
6	58	Female
7	61	Male
8	66	Female
9	67	Male
10	68	Female
11	69	Male
12	70	Male
13	71	Female
14	72	Male
15	76	Male
16	78	Female

Now find the sum of the ranks, which we'll call R, for the smallest group (females in the example):

$$R = 1 + 5 + \cdots + 16 = 59$$

Appendix I gives a table of the largest value of R that would be significant at the level shown. In other words, if R is *less than or equal to* the tabled value, the difference is significant. The table is entered by using the two group sizes. Select the subtable for the smallest group size (7 in the example), and use the row for the larger sample (9). In the example, the critical value with $\alpha = .05$ is 43. Because the obtained value is 59, we do not reject the null hypothesis that the number of errors made by males and females is equal.

Appendix I gives one-tailed values. To complete the test, we should compute a second sum of ranks for the other tail, and look that up as well. The second sum is calculated as

$$R' = n_1(n_1 + n_2 + 1) - R$$

For the example, the value is

$$R' = n_1(n_1 + n_2 + 1) - R$$
$$= 7 * (7 + 9 + 1) - 59$$
$$= 60$$

That value is also greater than the critical value, and there is no significant difference.

Of course, we just tested for significance in two one-tailed tests at $\alpha = .05$, and so we have really done a two-tailed test at $.05 + .05 = .10$. To have the probability at .05 overall, we would have needed to use the .025 critical value. In Appendix I, that value is 40, and there is still no significant difference between the two groups of individuals.

In reporting the results of this analysis, we might write "There is no difference between males and females; Wilcoxon $R = 59, 60, p \geq .05$."

The table for the Wilcoxon test in Appendix I includes values only up to $n = 10$ for the smallest sample size. When the samples are too large for the table, we can use a normal distribution approximate test. Consider the following data from an experiment with two conditions:

	CONDITION 1	CONDITION 2
	2	1
	5	7
	3	15
	4	13
	4	6
	3	8
	8	6
	6	12
	10	2
	7	3
		14
Mean	5.20	7.91
St. Dev.	2.53	4.95
Variance	6.40	24.49

The first step is to rank the combined data from smallest to largest, keeping track of which condition is which:

SCORE	RANK	CONDITION
1	1	2
2	2.5	1
2	2.5	2
3	5	1
3	5	1
3	5	2
4	7.5	1
4	7.5	1
5	9	1
6	11	1
6	11	2
6	11	2
7	13.5	1
7	13.5	2
8	15.5	1
8	15.5	2
10	17	1
12	18	2
13	19	2
14	20	2
15	21	2

For Condition 1 (the smaller group), $R = 93.5$.

The sum of the ranks for the smaller group is distributed approximately normally with

$$\mu_R = \frac{n_1(n_1 + n_2 + 1)}{2}$$

and

$$\sigma_R = \sqrt{\frac{n_1 n_2(n_1 + n_2 + 1)}{12}}$$

so that

$$z_R = \frac{R - \dfrac{n_1(n_1 + n_2 + 1)}{2}}{\sqrt{\dfrac{n_1 n_2(n_1 + n_2 + 1)}{12}}}$$

may be referred to the z table in Appendix A. For our example, we have

$$z_R = \frac{R - \dfrac{n_1(n_1 + n_2 + 1)}{2}}{\sqrt{\dfrac{n_1 n_2(n_1 + n_2 + 1)}{12}}}$$

$$= \frac{93.5 - \dfrac{10(10 + 11 + 1)}{2}}{\sqrt{\dfrac{10 * 11(10 + 11 + 1)}{12}}}$$

$$= \frac{93.5 - 110}{\sqrt{201.67}}$$

$$= \frac{-16.5}{14.20}$$

$$= -1.16$$

Because we require a value of 1.96 or greater in absolute value to reject a hypothesis of no difference between the two conditions at the .05 level, we conclude that there is no evidence to suggest that the two conditions differ.

Like the Wilcoxon test for matched pairs, this test requires some additional computations when there are ties (as there are in this case). In particular, the denominator (that is, σ_R) changes to

$$\sigma_R = \sqrt{\frac{n_1 n_2}{12}\left[(n_1 + n_2 + 1) - \frac{\sum t(t^2 - 1)}{(n_1 + n_2)(n_1 + n_2 - 1)}\right]}$$

where t is the number of scores in a tied group, and the summation is over all the groups of ties. In the example,

SCORE	RANK	CONDITION	
1	1	2	
2	2.5	1	$t = 2$
2	2.5	2	
3	5	1	
3	5	1	$t = 3$
3	5	2	
4	7.5	1	$t = 2$
4	7.5	1	
5	9	1	
6	11	1	
6	11	2	$t = 3$
6	11	2	
7	13.5	1	$t = 2$
7	13.5	2	
8	15.5	1	$t = 2$
8	15.5	2	
10	17	1	
12	18	2	
13	19	2	
14	20	2	
15	21	2	

There are six sets of tied scores, four of them containing two values and two with three values. The computation thus becomes

$$\sigma_R = \sqrt{\frac{n_1 n_2}{12}\left[(n_1 + n_2 + 1) - \frac{\sum t(t^2 - 1)}{(n_1 + n_2)(n_1 + n_2 - 1)}\right]}$$

$$= \sqrt{\frac{10(11)}{12}\left[(10 + 11 + 1) - \frac{2(2^2 - 1) + 3(3^2 - 1) + \cdots + 2(2^2 - 1)}{(10 + 11)(10 + 11 - 1)}\right]}$$

$$= 14.14$$

Using this value, the z computation, as corrected for ties, becomes

$$z_R = \frac{R - \dfrac{n_1(n_1 + n_2 + 1)}{2}}{\sqrt{\dfrac{n_1 n_2}{12}\left[(n_1 + n_2 + 1) - \dfrac{\sum t(t^2 - 1)}{(n_1 + n_2)(n_1 + n_2 - 1)}\right]}}$$

$$= \frac{93.5 - \dfrac{10(10 + 11 + 1)}{2}}{14.14}$$

$$= \frac{93.5 - 110}{14.14}$$

$$= \frac{-16.5}{14.14}$$

$$= -1.17$$

which scarcely differs from the original answer; there is still no significant difference between the two conditions.

◆ Significance Test for Two Independent Correlations

For two independent groups, the statistic

$$z = \frac{z_{r_1} - z_{r_2}}{\sqrt{\dfrac{1}{n_1 - 3} + \dfrac{1}{n_2 - 3}}}$$

where z_{r_1} and z_{r_2} are the Fisher's r-to-z transformed values of the two correlation coefficients, is a normally distributed variable that tests the hypothesis that the two population correlation coefficients (ρ_1 and ρ_2) are equal.

To illustrate, use the example correlations from page 277. For the SAT-training students ($n = 36$) $r = 0.41$, while for nontrained students ($n = 42$) $r = 0.53$. Computing the two r-to-z transformations, the values are 0.436 for the training group and 0.590 for the nontraining group. Substituting in the formula for z gives

$$z = \frac{z_{r_1} - z_{r_2}}{\sqrt{\dfrac{1}{n_1 - 3} + \dfrac{1}{n_2 - 3}}}$$

$$= \frac{0.436 - 0.590}{\sqrt{\dfrac{1}{36 - 3} + \dfrac{1}{42 - 3}}}$$

$$= -0.651$$

Because the z value required for significance at the .05 level is 1.96, we may conclude that taking the SAT training course causes no difference in the correlation between SAT total score and freshman GPA.

11 Dealing with Category and Frequency Data

In all the analyses discussed so far, the research question has been one of center or, occasionally, of correlation. Sometimes, though, the research question concerns frequency, and the statistics introduced so far aren't appropriate. Frequency questions may arise from the distribution of a numeric variable, but more often they appear when the data represent a nominal (category) variable. We might, for example, ask how many dogs, cats, mice, and rats were seen in a sample neighborhood. Or we might want to know how many people fall into each of ten different occupational groups. Or we might be interested in how males and females intend to vote on certain ballot issues. In these examples, the measurement is category or nominal. One set of categories might include the items dog, cat, mouse, and rat. Another might be a set of categories representing occupations: teacher, lawyer, mechanic, artist, and so on. Data of this sort are common in many social science disciplines, psychology included.

In this chapter we present inferential procedures for frequency data. We have few descriptive statistics, although we do introduce two "correlation-like" statistics for category data. Traditional descriptive statistics—measures of center or spread—are irrelevant with category data, and frequency counting is the most common procedure for summarizing data.

Two general kinds of questions arise with frequency data. In some cases, the data address one nominal variable at a time and pertain to a unidimensional question like "Are the proportions of people in the 'Agree' and 'Disagree' categories the same or different?" or "Is this set of frequencies different from the one suggested by theory?" In other cases, the data are two dimensional: "Is there an association between sex and voting intentions?" or "Are freshmen, sophomores, juniors, and seniors equally likely to live in apartments?"

INFERENCE WITH A SINGLE CATEGORY VARIABLE

Suppose we ask a sample of 45 senior psychology majors about their post-graduation plans. We give the students five choices of response and obtain the data in Table 11.1 (Ignore the "No preference" column for now.) This is a descriptive summary of the 45 students' responses. We could present this table in a report; we could convert the data to percentages, or we could use a histogram to illustrate the results. The purpose of a display of the data is to show how the 45 students answered the question. And if our interest is in merely describing what these 45 seniors plan, we can stop with just these descriptive results.

But we want to ask if these data show a "real" preference, or if the unequal frequencies are merely chance fluctuations. To ask the question differently, how confident are we that if we were to repeat our survey with 45 different students we would obtain something similar to this pattern? In short, are these frequencies really different from each other, or are the underlying population frequencies really equal and we just got this distribution by

TABLE 11.1

Choice	Frequency	"No Preference" Frequency
Grad school	13	9
Professional school	7	9
Family business	5	9
Other job	15	9
Undecided	5	9
Total	45	45

chance? If the students *really* have no preference (and that's a null hypothesis that we can test), then they should choose response categories at random. If they did choose at random, then we should find roughly the same number of responses in each category. Because there are 45 students in the survey and five choices, then we would expect $45/5 = 9$ observations in each category. Those "expected" frequencies are shown in the "No preference" frequency column in Table 11.1. The null hypothesis is that the students have no preference; the equal frequencies are what we would expect to find under that hypothesis. If the students do have preferences, then their frequencies will depart from the "No preference" values.

◆ The Chi-Square Test for Fit

To let us answer the question about preference, we need a way to test the null hypothesis that the population distribution has the numbers shown in the null hypothesis column (the "No preference" column). For that, we turn to a new sampling distribution—namely, the distribution of the chi-square (χ^2) statistic.

Like Student's t, χ^2 is a family of different distributions, depending on the degrees of freedom (df). Again similar to the t, the df for χ^2 is often the number of items summed, less 1. Examples of several χ^2 distributions are shown in Figure 11.1. The value of χ^2 must be zero or greater, and the curves are positively skewed, becoming less so as df increases. We can use an approximation to the chi-square distribution to test the agreement between two columns of frequencies. As a later example will illustrate, this test is very

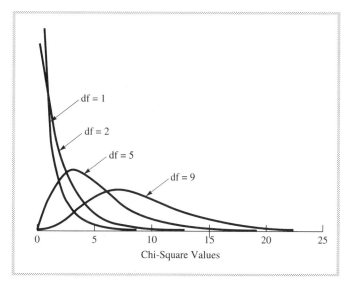

Figure 11.1

general and can be applied to any two sets of hypothetical and observed frequencies.

The test statistic is

$$\chi^2 = \sum \frac{(f_o - f_e)^2}{f_e}$$

where f_o and f_e are observed and expected frequencies, respectively, and the summation is taken over all pairs of observed and expected frequencies. The number of degrees of freedom for the χ^2 value is the number of categories (pairs of frequencies), minus 1. Notice the numerator of the formula. It shows that the differences between the observed and expected frequencies are to be squared, divided, and summed. The net effect is that, the greater the degree of disagreement between the observed and the expected values, the larger will be the value of the χ^2 itself.

Although the chi-square distribution correctly applies only to a continuous variable, the preceding χ^2 formula (properly called a **Pearson chi-square**) is a reasonable approximation under the right conditions. Many texts present this formula as the *only* chi-square formula, which it is not; we label it appropriately as the Pearson approximation.

The conditions for using the chi-square distribution are: (1) the categories must be mutually exclusive (in the example, this means that students are not permitted to select two or more alternatives); (2) the observations must be independent (that is, student A's response cannot influence that of student B); and (3) the expected frequencies must be large enough (usually five or so) to allow the approximation to the continuous chi-square distribution to be reasonably accurate.

For the data in Table 11.1, the computation for χ^2 proceeds as

$$\chi^2 = \sum \frac{(f_o - f_e)^2}{f_e}$$

$$= \frac{(13 - 9)^2}{9} + \frac{(7 - 9)^2}{9} + \frac{(5 - 9)^2}{9} + \frac{(15 - 9)^2}{9} + \frac{(5 - 9)^2}{9}$$

$$= \frac{88}{9} = 9.78$$

The statistic has $5 - 1 = 4$ df. In Appendix D we find that the critical value at $\alpha = .05$ with df $= 4$ is 9.49. In other words, the sampling distribution is as shown in Figure 11.2. To reject the null hypothesis that the two sets of frequencies come from the same population, the obtained χ^2 must exceed 9.49. Because it does, we conclude that our seniors are not responding randomly when asked about their postgraduation plans. In other words, we reject the hypothesis that the frequencies of the categories are equal.

The next logical question concerns just what the differences between the obtained and the theoretical frequencies actually tell us. In this regard, it's

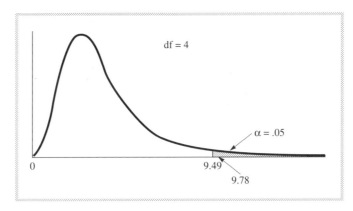

Figure 11.2

often helpful to look at the residuals from the analysis. The residual is defined as

$$\frac{(f_o - f_e)}{\sqrt{f_e}}$$

For our example, the residuals are given in Table 11.2. The residuals show how much each of the obtained frequencies differs from the expected. The larger values indicate where the greatest discrepancies between the two sets of frequencies lie. The residuals directly reflect a contribution to the test statistic and are thus good to use for interpretive purposes. For the example data, the largest difference is in the "Other job" category, while the smallest is for "Professional school." This means that the "most different" category is "Other job," because it contributes heavily to the χ^2 value.

Employing residuals to interpret chi-square computations is a useful procedure, and one too often overlooked by students. Students often stop an analysis with a statement like "These frequencies differ significantly from those expected by chance" without any further interpretation. Looking at the residuals can help a great deal in understanding the data, and should be done routinely.

ANOTHER EXAMPLE

Nothing says that the null hypothesis must specify equal frequencies in all categories. In some cases, like that in the previous section, the question of preference is appropriately addressed by testing a "no preference" hypothesis. Other times, though, the question might be whether the data fit with a set of frequencies derived from some other null hypothesis. For example, hair color in rats is thought to be controlled by two genes operating in classic dominant-recessive fashion. If that's the case, then the mating of pairs of black and "yellow" rats should yield offspring in roughly the proportions given in Table 11.3. Those expected frequencies come from the understand-

TABLE 11.2

Choice	Observed	Expected	Residual
Grad school	13	9	1.33
Professional school	7	9	−0.67
Family business	5	9	−1.33
Other job	15	9	2.00
Undecided	5	9	−1.33

TABLE 11.3

Color	Expected Number
Gray	9
Black	3
Yellow	3
Cream	1
Total	16

ing of how genes combine to control certain features; if the genetic laws operate as expected, then the resulting body features should follow roughly those proportions.

Suppose we have a group of 74 rats, all the offspring of black-yellow matings, with the color frequencies shown in Table 11.4. Does this distribution of colors represent a significant departure from the expected frequencies? In other words, is some genetic process other than the classic dominant-recessive pattern operating here? First, calculate the expected frequencies. To find the expected frequencies, note that (from Table 11.3) $9/16 = 0.56$ of the animals should be gray. Because there are 74 animals in our group, then, we would expect $0.56 * 74 = 41$ gray rats. Applying the same logic to black and to yellow animals, we would expect $3/16 * 74 = 14$ each of black and of yellow rats. And we would expect $1/16 * 74 = 5$ cream-colored rats. Completing the calculations yields the frequencies in Table 11.5.

Following the computations, we obtain

$$\chi^2 = \sum \frac{(f_o - f_e)^2}{f_e}$$

$$= \frac{(47 - 41)^2}{41} + \frac{(9 - 14)^2}{14} + \frac{(12 - 14)^2}{41} + \frac{(6 - 5)^2}{5}$$

$$= 3.01$$

With df $= 4 - 1 = 3$, Appendix D shows a critical χ^2 value of 7.815 at $\alpha =$

TABLE 11.4

Color	Observed Number
Gray	47
Black	9
Yellow	12
Cream	6
Total	74

TABLE 11.5

	Observed	Expected
Gray	47	41
Black	9	14
Yellow	12	14
Cream	6	5

.05; thus we do not reject the hypothesis that this distribution is identical to that suggested by genetic theory. For these data, then, because the obtained frequencies fit with those indicated by theory, we may conclude that hair color in rats seems to be controlled by the classic dominant-regressive gene operation.

PRESENTING CHI-SQUARE RESULTS

The APA style for presenting the results of a hypothesis test is to use a chi-square statistic, with one addition: Inside the parentheses, with the degrees of freedom, give the value of N as well. Thus, for the preceding example, we would write "The distribution of coat color does not differ from that expected under classical genetic theory, $\chi^2(3, N = 74) = 3.01, p > .05$."

◆ Fitting a Distribution Form

Inferences about the form of a distribution are unusual, but sometimes questions of form are important in research. In addition, tests of form can help determine whether a normal distribution–based procedure should be used. Several different tests may be used to test hypotheses about form. We illustrate here one that uses the Pearson chi-square procedure.[1]

---

[1] When the variable being counted is at least ordinal, the Kolmogorov-Smirnov one-sample test is appropriate; see Siegel and Castellan (1988).

Because the Pearson chi-square can help assess the fit between two sets of frequencies, it can be used to test whether a frequency distribution differs from a normal distribution (or from any other form, for that matter). All we need is to find the expected frequencies for intervals under a normal distribution, and compare them with the obtained frequencies using the Pearson chi-square. There is also a minor modification in the df value to illustrate when we reach that point.

Let's illustrate the process by using data from 84 subjects on the sociability subscale of the Eysenck Personality Inventory (call the variable EPIS for short). The frequency distribution of EPIS is illustrated in Figure 11.3. The Pearson skewness is -0.56, while the mean and median are 7.69 and 8.0, respectively. The standard deviation is 2.3. The expected frequencies are those that we would find if the form of the distribution were normal, with $\mu = 7.69$ and $\sigma = 2.3$. We leave the actual computations to the supplement and just show here the expected frequencies, superimposed on the histogram, in Figure 11.4.

Having found the expected frequencies under the null hypothesis (that the distribution has a normal form), the computations are carried out by using the Pearson chi-square test. Following the computations illustrated in the supplement, we conclude that the frequencies of the EPIS scores do not differ from those expected under a normal distribution: $\chi^2(9, N = 84) = 14.38, p > .05$.

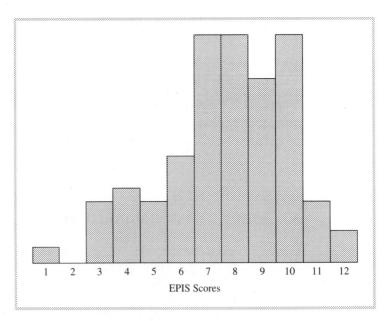

Figure 11.3

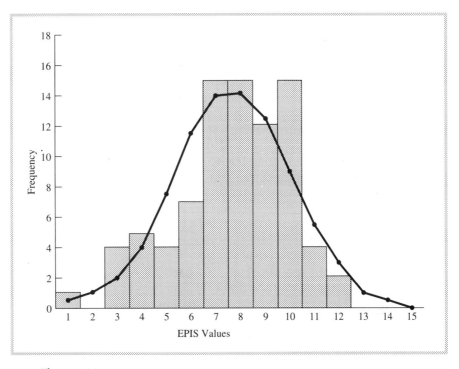

Figure 11.4

BINOMIAL TESTS FOR PROPORTIONS

It's a very short step from thinking about tests of frequencies to tests of proportions. Suppose we have a variable with only two categories: pass–fail, male–female, oppose–support, or something similar. We could test hypotheses about the frequencies in such a case using the Pearson chi-square, establishing the expected frequencies in each of the two categories. But there are easier alternatives that are at least as accurate.

Asking whether a hypothetical sample distribution of eight males and five females differs from an expected distribution of 50/50 is equivalent to asking whether the proportion of males in the sample group differs from 0.5; for this reason, categorical inferences in the two-category case are usually called tests of proportions, or **binomial tests**. When we have a sample of 15 or less, Appendix G may be used to obtain a precise test of a hypothesis about a proportion.

As an example of a test about proportions, suppose that we're developing a set of multiple-choice test items to accompany a textbook. A question has four alternatives, only one of which is correct. If the students are guessing at the answer, then 25% of them should get the answer correct by chance. Suppose we have a sample of 15 students, and 8 of them got the correct answer. Are the students guessing?

You'll recall from Chapter 9 that Appendix G gives binomial probabilities. In particular, it gives the probabilities of the numbers of "successes" in N Bernoulli trials when the probability of a success on each trial is p. Giving a four-choice question to 15 students under the null hypothesis of guessing is the same as flipping a coin whose probability of "heads" is .25 a total of 15 times. It's also the same as a series of 15 Bernoulli trials with $p = .25$. In Appendix G we find the probabilities of each of the possible numbers of students getting the item correct when guessing (that is, with a .25 probability of being correct), as shown in Table 11.6.

Under the null hypothesis that $p = .25$, what's the probability of 8 or more students getting the question right? It's $.0131 + .0034 + .0007 + \cdots$, which equals .0173. If we had chosen $\alpha = .05$, we would reject the hypothesis that the students are guessing because the probability of 8 or more correct answers by chance is less than .05. Note that we use 8 *or more*, since we're really interested not in exactly 8 correct but in the probability that the students will do that well *or better*.

In a large-sample situation, we may use the normal curve approximation to the binomial distribution introduced in Chapter 9. There we pointed out that the binomial distribution can be approximated by a normal distribution with

$$\mu = Np$$
$$\sigma = \sqrt{Np(1 - p)}$$

TABLE 11.6

Number	Probability
0	.0134
1	.0668
2	.1559
3	.2252
4	.2252
5	.1651
6	.0917
7	.0393
8	.0131
9	.0034
10	.0007
11	.0001
12	.0000
13	.0000
14	.0000
15	.0000

Suppose that instead of 15 students we have 46, and find that 19 have the correct answer. In this case, we calculate

$$\mu = Np \qquad \sigma = \sqrt{Np(1 - p)}$$
$$= 46 * .25 \qquad = \sqrt{46 * .25 * .75}$$
$$= 11.5 \qquad = 2.94$$

Then, using the standardizing formula,

$$z = \frac{X - \overline{X}}{s}$$
$$= \frac{19 - 11.5}{2.94}$$
$$= 2.55$$

With $\alpha = .05$, we reject the hypothesis that $p = .25$ because the obtained value of 2.55 exceeds the critical z value of 1.96. We conclude, therefore, that the students are not guessing on this test item.

INFERENCE WITH TWO CATEGORY VARIABLES

Suppose we ask members of the freshman, sophomore, and junior classes in a psychology department whether they agree with the proposed addition of a course required for majors. The data are given in Table 11.7. Here we have frequency data, certainly, but with two-category variables[2] instead of one. We could easily investigate either of the two variables separately and ask, for example, whether the proportion of "yeses" is different from 50% for freshmen, or for sophomores, or for juniors. We could also ask whether the distribution of "no" choices, for example, differs across the three classes. But what we really are interested in knowing is whether the classes feel the same way about the question of adding a required course. The frequencies suggest

TABLE 11.7		
Class	Yes	No
Freshman	1	11
Sophomores	8	4
Juniors	11	3

[2] If you're being really strict, year in school is ordinal; that's unimportant for the example.

otherwise, but can we test a hypothesis that will give us some confidence in our judgment? The answer, naturally, is yes, which brings us to the most common application of the Pearson chi-square: the test for association or contingency.

◆ Testing for Contingency

The **contingency test** investigates the null hypothesis that there is no relationship or dependency between the "row" variable ("class" in our example) and the "column" variable ("opinion on adding a required course"). If there is no association between the two—if the three classes have the same opinion—then student opinion is not contingent upon the class of the student, which gives the procedure the name "contingency test."

As with a single-variable Pearson chi-square, we look at the difference between obtained and expected frequencies in that table. If there is no contingency or relationship, then the proportion of freshmen who answer "yes" should represent the same proportion of freshmen as of sophomores and juniors.

Look at the row and column totals for the example data in Table 11.8. In a frequency table, each individual frequency is often called a "cell." To illustrate the logic of finding expected frequencies, we obtain them for two freshmen cells, under the null hypothesis that there is no contingency. If there's no association (or contingency) between opinion and year in school, the 12 freshmen should divide themselves between "yes" and "no" in the same proportions as the total "yes"/"no" vote for all classes combined. Of the 38 students, 20 answered "yes"; in each of the three classes, then, 20/38 of the students should say "yes." To calculate the expected number of freshmen saying "yes," then, we have

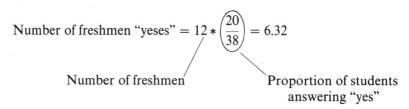

$$\text{Number of freshmen "yeses"} = 12 * \left(\frac{20}{38}\right) = 6.32$$

Number of freshmen

Proportion of students answering "yes"

Class	Yes	No	Total
TABLE 11.8			
Freshman	1	11	12
Sophomores	8	4	12
Juniors	11	3	14
Total	20	18	38

By changing the form of the equation a little, we can write

$$\text{Number of freshmen ``yeses''} = \frac{12 * 20}{38} = 6.32$$

The same logic holds for freshmen answering "no," so that

$$\text{Number of freshman ``nos''} = 12 * \frac{18}{38} = \frac{12 * 18}{38} = 5.68$$

because 18 of the 38 total responses are "no."

The computational supplement at the end of the chapter shows how to generalize the logic to all cells in the frequency table. The full matrix of expected frequencies, derived from this generalized procedure, is given in Table 11.9.

Once we have the expected frequencies for each cell, we calculate the χ^2 statistic as the sum of the fraction $(f_o - f_e)^2/f_e$ over all cells:

$$\chi^2 = \sum\sum \frac{(f_o - f_e)^2}{f_e}$$

where the $\sum\sum$ merely means to sum over both the rows and the columns of the table. The supplement shows the calculation of the χ^2 value.

The degrees of freedom for the Pearson chi-square for contingency are

$$df = (\text{Number of rows} - 1)(\text{Number of columns} - 1)$$

For this example,

$$df = (\text{Number of rows} - 1)(\text{Number of columns} - 1)$$
$$= (3 - 1)(2 - 1) = 2$$

From Appendix D we determine that the critical value for χ^2 with $df = 2$ at $\alpha = .05$ is 5.992. Because the obtained value of 14.18 (see the supplement) exceeds that value, we reject the hypothesis that there is no association

TABLE 11.9

Class	Yes	No
Freshman	6.32	5.68
Sophomore	6.32	5.68
Junior	7.37	6.63

between year in school and the students' opinions about the additional course. The hypothesis that we support is that there is a relationship between year and opinion; the next task is to understand that relationship.

RESIDUALS ANALYSIS

Let's look at the residuals from the analysis. We define the residual in the same way as before, namely

$$\frac{(f_o - f_e)}{\sqrt{f_e}}.$$

The residuals for our data are presented in Table 11.10. The residuals highlight what was visible in the raw data—specifically that the differences are primarily between freshmen and juniors and that they respond in opposite ways. The freshmen are opposed to adding another course while the juniors generally favor it. The sophomores are less divided, but tend to vote like the juniors, as can be seen from the signs of the residuals.

In a table with two category variables, we may estimate the standard deviation of each residual, making it possible to compute a z score for each. The procedure is illustrated in the supplement, and leads to the standardized residuals shown in Table 11.11. If N is reasonably large, we may regard the standardized residuals as coming from a standardized normal distribution. In the normal distribution, any z value of 1.96 or greater is significantly different from the mean with $\alpha = 0.05$; thus freshmen answering "no" shows a significantly large residual. Looking at the overall pattern of the standardized residuals, it's clear that there are substantial differences between the opinions of the freshmen and the juniors, with the freshmen being in general quite opposed to the new course requirement.

TABLE 11.10

Class	Yes	No
Freshman	−2.12	2.23
Sophomores	0.67	−0.70
Juniors	1.34	−1.41

TABLE 11.11

Class	Yes	No
Freshman	−1.76	1.96
Sophomore	0.56	−0.62
Junior	1.16	−1.29

◆ "Correlation" with Category Data

Several statistics have been developed to index the relationship between two category variables on a 0–1 scale like that of correlation coefficients. (Please note that these are *not* correlation coefficients in anything but name and 0–1 scale. Beyond that they have nothing in common with the statistics discussed in Chapter 5.) The most common of these "correlation-like coefficients" is the **contingency coefficient**, defined as

$$C = \sqrt{\frac{\chi^2}{\chi^2 + N}}$$

where χ^2 is the value obtained from a contingency analysis and N is the number of observations. For the class opinion example, then,

$$C = \sqrt{\frac{\chi^2}{\chi^2 + N}}$$
$$= \sqrt{\frac{14.18}{14.18 + 38}}$$
$$= 0.52$$

This value may be interpreted as a correlation coefficient with a value of 0.52, indicating a modest degree of relationship between class in school and opinion. Although the contingency coefficient is a common measure of the association, it's not an especially good one because it doesn't behave quite the way you'd like a correlation coefficient to behave. A serious problem with C is that it can never obtain a value of 1.0, even with perfect agreement. Even worse, the maximum value of C is a function of the number of observations: The larger N, the smaller the largest possible value of C.

Some of the problems with the contingency coefficient are addressed by **Cramer's Φ (phi**; Cramer, 1946). The Φ coefficient is defined as

$$\Phi = \sqrt{\frac{\chi^2}{N(k - 1)}}$$

Here, χ^2 and N have the same meanings they had for the contingency coefficient, and k is the *smaller* of the number of rows or columns. For our example, there are three rows and two columns, so $k = 2$. The value of Φ for the example is thus

$$\Phi = \sqrt{\frac{\chi^2}{N(k - 1)}}$$
$$= \sqrt{\frac{14.18}{38 * (2 - 1)}}$$
$$= .61$$

This value is slightly higher than was the contingency coefficient on the same data.

The Φ coefficient solves the problem that plagues the contingency coefficient because it has 1.0 as an upper limit regardless of the sample size. But neither Φ nor C offers another feature that helps in the interpretation of the Pearson product-moment correlation coefficient—that the square of the coefficient give a proportion of variance explained by the relationship. A measure proposed by Light and Margolin (1971; see also Berenson, Levine, & Goldstein, 1983) does offer such an interpretation.

OTHER SOURCES OF EXPECTED FREQUENCIES

Until now, the discussion assumed that you were testing for some association between the row and the column category variables. The computations for the expected frequencies establish a null hypothesis of no contingency between row and column. There's no reason to use the Pearson chi-square *only* to test for association. Any set of frequencies can be used, as they could in the single-variable instance.

◆ More Than Two Category Variables

The procedures we have described so far are limited to two separate tasks: fitting frequency data to one set of expected frequencies (that is, to a single category variable), or assessing the contingency between two category variables. But frequently we have more than two variables—often many more than two. Can we extend the notion of contingency analysis to multivariate data? The answer is yes, but not nearly as simply as you might hope. We can't just construct a three-dimensional frequency table, generalize an expected frequency procedure, and begin. Instead, we must rely on a much more complicated process, known as log-linear modeling. We do not explore this process here because it would take us too far afield. For a short introduction see Berenson, Levine, and Goldstein (1983, pp. 488–498). For an advanced treatment, see Fienberg (1980). Marascuilo and Serlin (1988) present a nice single-chapter introduction, as does Howell (1992).

Summary

◆ *The* Pearson chi-square, χ^2, *statistic may be used to test the "fit" between sets of obtained and expected frequencies when data are just counts of the number of occurrences of discrete events.*

◆ *In order to use the chi-square distribution to approximate the sampling distribution of the Pearson chi-square statistic, be sure that (1) the categories are mutually exclusive, (2) the observations are independent, and (3) the expected frequencies are greater than or equal to 5.*

- *Exploring the residuals from a Pearson chi-square analysis is usually a good way to understand the data.*
- *The Pearson chi-square may be used to test whether the form of a frequency distribution differs from the normal.*
- *When there are just two possible responses, the binomial distribution may be used to test* (binomial test) *a hypothesis about a proportion.*
- *If there are two category variables, the Pearson chi-square may be used to determine whether a significant contingency* (contingency test) *exists between them.*
- *The* contingency coefficient *and Cramer's* Φ *are correlation-like measures for two category variables.*

Key Terms

BINOMIAL TEST
CONTINGENCY COEFFICIENT
CONTINGENCY TEST

CRAMER'S Φ (PHI)
PEARSON CHI-SQUARE
χ^2

 EXERCISES

1. The psychology department described early in the chapter has always been viewed as highly preprofessional, with many more of its students planning to attend graduate or professional school than planning to go on to other future endeavors. This suggests that perhaps the null hypothesis distribution of equal frequencies that we tested earlier might not have been appropriate. Use the following data (and $\alpha = .01$) to test the revised hypothesis:

CHOICE	FREQUENCY	"CHANCE" FREQUENCY
Grad school	13	14
Professional school	7	13
Family business	5	6
Other job	15	6
Undecided	5	6
Total	45	45

State your conclusions verbally. (You might want to look at residuals.)

2. A count of students in a computers in psychology class showed that 7 of 11 students were female. Does that proportion differ significantly (with $\alpha = .05$) from 50%?

3. A count of students in an abnormal psychology class showed that 32 of 48 students were male. Does that proportion differ significantly (with $\alpha = .05$) from 50%?

4. A table of random numbers, like that in Appendix B, should not favor any digit over any other. That is, if you count the number of 0s, 1s, and so forth, they should all occur an equal number of times. Take a random sample of 100 values from Appendix B, and count the number of times each digit occurs. Test whether your sample differs from what would

be expected if the table really contained random values. Use $\alpha = .05$.

5. (*Optional*) This problem investigates the behavior of the random number generator in your statistics program. Generate a sample of 100 values from a rectangular distribution in the range 0.0–1.0. If your random number generator is performing correctly, 10% of the values should be in the range 0.0–0.1, 10% in the 0.1–0.2 range, and so forth. Use $\alpha = .05$ to determine if your distribution follows the expected pattern. Try this with at least five different samples of size 100.

6. Exercise 11.1 used the survey of senior psychology majors' postgraduation plans. The following data give the frequencies for the same 45 seniors, but also the choices made by a group of juniors. Is there a relationship between class and choice? If so, describe it verbally. (Use $\alpha = .01$.)

CHOICE	SENIORS	JUNIORS
Grad school	13	20
Professional school	7	7
Family business	5	6
Other job	15	3
Undecided	5	23

7. Compute C and Φ for the data in exercise 11.6

8. Following are data for a number of birds, categorized as to species (A, B, or C) and whether they build nests low or high (L, H) above the ground. Compute the chi-square for association, and also C and Φ. Is there an association between species and nest location? (Use $\alpha = .05$.) Describe it verbally.

	NEST LOCATION	
	LOW	HIGH
Species A	10	3
Species B	12	14
Species C	5	18

9. The following data[3] give the frequencies for a colony of nine monkeys engaging in five different classes of behavior. The large, open, housing room contains a number of items, arranged roughly in "levels." Level 1 includes

[3] These data were provided by Roger Thompson and Melissa Painter.

the floor and several low objects on it. Level 2 includes platforms attached to the wall, poles, and a rubber tire suspended from the poles. Level 3 contains several platforms, a swing, and two metal boxes. Level 4 is the wire mesh ceiling.

a. Using chi-square and $\alpha = .01$, determine if there is a contingency between the behaviors and the levels in the housing room.

b. Compute the standardized residuals and use them to interpret the relationship between activity and level.

	LEVEL			
ACTIVITY	1	2	3	4
Sit	170	516	1355	3
Eat	26	109	531	9
Groom	42	100	407	0
Locomotion	202	351	660	137
Rest	9	177	488	1

10. An environmental psychologist was studying traffic flow through a large hotel lobby containing the usual array of furniture, potted plants, and open space. Disregarding new arrivals, who go directly from the door to the registration desk, most people entering the hotel head for either the elevators or the dining room, both located directly at the other end of the lobby from the main door. People moving from the entrance to the elevator/dining room follow one of three pathways: straight across (which means dodging furniture, plants, and maybe people, but is a shorter distance than the other paths), left (an open pathway, but frequently crowded with people at the registration desk), or right (again, a largely open pathway, but with a few desks and plants that must be dodged). The data below give the frequencies of people using the pathways during an 8-hour day during a convention. Are the people choosing their pathway randomly?

	FREQUENCY
Straight across	1252
Left	1026
Right	921

11. As a second part of the study described in exercise 11.10, two different furniture arrangements were used. The arrangement used in ex-

ercise 11.10 is called "Original." The new arrangements are called "New 1" and "New 2." The frequencies are at the right. Are there differences in the patterns of pathway use in the three arrangements? Describe them, and report C and Φ as well.

	ORIGINAL	NEW 1	NEW 2
Straight across	1252	751	998
Left	1026	572	1432
Right	921	1024	667

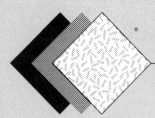

Computational Supplement

◆ Residuals in the Pearson Chi-Square

The formula for residuals was given in the text; here we show another use for them.

Squaring and summing the residuals yields the χ^2 value. For that reason, it makes a handy computational check. For the data in Table 11.2,

$$\chi^2 = 1.33^2 + (-0.67)^2 + (-1.33)^2 + 2.00^2 + (-1.33)^2$$
$$= 9.76$$

Within rounding, that's the same value as the original chi-square.

◆ Using the Pearson Chi-Square for Fitting a Distribution Form

We illustrate this computation using the data from Figure 11.3. To calculate the expected frequencies, use $\overline{X}$ and s as point estimates of μ and σ. If the population is normally distributed with $\mu = 7.69$ and $\sigma = 2.3$, then we can find the proportion of the normal curve that should appear in each of the score intervals, as in Chapter 4. For an EPIS score of 2.0, for example, we assume that 2.0 is the midpoint of an interval that extends from 1.5 to 2.5, that 3.0 is the midpoint of the 2.5 to 3.5 interval, and so on. Because 1.0 is the lowest value of EPIS, assume that it represents all values below 1.5, and that the score intervals are as illustrated in Table 11.12. Converting the interval limits into z scores using $\overline{X} = 7.69$ and $s = 2.3$, we obtain (from Appendix A) the proportions of the normal curve. For the interval 1.5 to 2.5, for example, compute two z scores, as

$$z = \frac{1.5 - 7.69}{2.3}$$
$$= -2.69$$

for the lower limit of 1.5 and

$$z = \frac{2.5 - 7.69}{2.3}$$
$$= -2.26$$

TABLE 11.12

EPIS Score	Score Interval	
1		Below 1.5
2	1.5	2.5
3	2.5	3.5
4	3.5	4.5
5	4.5	5.5
6	5.5	6.5
7	6.5	7.5
8	7.5	8.5
9	8.5	9.5
10	9.5	10.5
11	10.5	11.5
12	Above 11.5	

for the upper (2.5). From Appendix A, we find the proportion of the curve between those two points; this is shown in Figure 11.5. The proportion is 0.0083. This means that, of 84 subjects, $0.0083 * 84 = 0.70$ are expected to have a score of 2.0. Following the same procedure for each of the EPIS scores, we obtain the following expected frequencies, listed together in Table 11.13 with the z intervals, their probabilities, and the obtained frequencies from the histogram.

The χ^2 formula leads to

$$\chi^2 = \sum \frac{(f_o - f_e)^2}{f_e}$$

$$= \frac{(1 - 0.30)^2}{0.30} + \frac{(0 - 0.70)^2}{0.70} + \cdots + \frac{(2 - 4.07)^2}{4.07}$$

$$= 14.38$$

If this were an ordinary χ^2 computation, we would compute $N - 1$ df and proceed to the χ^2 table to test for the significance of the statistic. But here's where the difference lies in this distribution-fitting application. From the df that we would have if this were an ordinary test, we must subtract *1 df for each separate parameter that we estimated*. In this case, we estimated both μ and σ so we could compute the z scores, and the df are thus

$$df = N - 1 - 2$$

$$= 12 - 1 - 2$$

$$= 9$$

In Appendix D, we find that the critical value for χ^2 with $\propto = .05$ and df $= 9$ is 16.919; we may thus conclude that there is no evidence to indicate that the EPIS data do not come from a normal distribution.

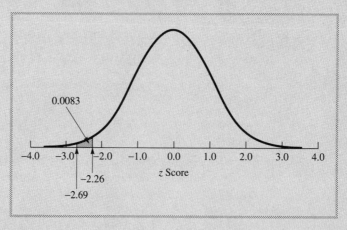

Figure 11.5

TABLE 11.13				
EPIS Score	Range of z	Probability of Interval	Obtained Frequency	Expected Frequency
1	≤ -2.69	0.0036	1	0.30
2	-2.69 -2.26	0.0083	0	0.70
3	-2.26 -1.82	0.0225	4	1.89
4	-1.82 -1.39	0.0479	5	4.02
5	-1.39 -0.95	0.0888	4	7.46
6	-0.95 -0.52	0.1304	7	11.54
7	-0.52 -0.08	0.1666	15	13.99
8	-0.08 0.35	0.1687	15	14.17
9	0.35 0.79	0.1484	12	12.47
10	0.79 1.22	0.1036	15	8.70
11	1.22 1.66	0.0627	4	5.27
12	≥ 1.66	0.0485	2	4.07
			84	84.00

◆ Chi-Square Test for Contingency

We can generalize the logic for computing expected frequencies to all rows and columns, and summarize the rule: The expected frequency for each cell may be calculated as the product of the row and column sums divided by the total number of observations. As a formula,

$$f_e = \frac{R * C}{N}$$

where R and C are row and column sums corresponding to the cell being calculated. Thus the computation for juniors answering "no" would be

CLASS	YES	NO	TOTAL
Freshman			12
Sophomores			12
Juniors		$\dfrac{14*18}{38} = 6.63$	14
Total	20	18	38

or, using the formula,

$$f(e) = \frac{R * C}{N}$$

$$= \frac{14 * 18}{38}$$

$$= 6.63$$

For our example, the value is

$$\chi^2 = \sum\sum \frac{(f_o - f_e)^2}{f_e}$$

$$= \frac{(1 - 6.32)^2}{6.32} + \frac{(11 - 5.68)^2}{5.68} + \cdots + \frac{(3 - 6.63)^2}{6.63}$$

$$= 14.18$$

The formula for the standard deviation of a residual is

$$sd_{resid} = \sqrt{\frac{N - R}{N - C}}$$

where R and C are the row and column totals for the cell whose residual is being computed. For the "freshman–yes" cell, we would have

$$sd_{resid} = \sqrt{\frac{N - R}{N - C}}$$

$$= \sqrt{\frac{38 - 12}{38 - 20}}$$

$$= 1.20$$

The standardized residual for any cell is computed as

$$z_{resid} = \frac{residual}{sd_{resid}}$$

$$= \frac{\frac{(f_o - f_e)}{\sqrt{f_e}}}{\sqrt{\frac{N - R}{N - C}}}$$

A computationally simpler form is given by

$$z_{\text{resid}} = \frac{(f_o - f_e)}{\sqrt{f_e}} \sqrt{\frac{N - C}{N - R}}$$

For the "freshman–yes" cell, the standardized residual is

$$z_{\text{resid}} = \frac{(f_o - f_e)}{\sqrt{f_e}} \sqrt{\frac{N - C}{N - R}}$$
$$= \frac{(1 - 6.32)}{\sqrt{6.32}} \sqrt{\frac{38 - 20}{38 - 12}}$$
$$= -1.76$$

Applying the formula to all of the cells results in the full table of standardized residuals presented in Table 11.11.

◆ The 2 × 2 Contingency Table

When there are only two categories in both the row and the column categories, the χ^2 computation simplifies a great deal. If we let the letters a, b, c, and d stand for the frequencies in the table as

$$\begin{array}{c|c} a & b \\ \hline c & d \end{array}$$

then we may compute the chi-square value as

$$\chi^2 = \frac{N(|ad - bc| - N/2)^2}{(a + b)(c + d)(a + c)(b + d)}$$

As an example, suppose we count the number of males and females in two campus organizations, the camera club and the marching band, with these results:

	CAMERA	BAND	GRAND TOTAL
Male	11	54	65
Female	19	34	53
Grand Total	30	88	118

Using the formula, we find that the chi-square value is

$$\chi^2 = \frac{N(|ad - bc| - N/2)^2}{(a + b)(c + d)(a + c)(b + d)}$$

$$= \frac{118(|(11 * 34) - (54 * 19)| - 118/2)^2}{(11 + 54)(19 + 34)(11 + 19)(54 + 34)}$$

$$= 4.56$$

If we choose $\alpha = .05$, the critical value for chi-square with df $= (2 - 1)(2 - 1) = 1$ is 3.84, and we reject the hypothesis that there is no relationship between sex and choice of these two extracurricular activities. By inspection of the data, it appears that women are more likely to join the camera club, while men join the marching band more often.

12 More Than Two Between-Subjects Conditions

Suppose we select three groups of subjects on the basis of their scores on an introversion/extroversion scale, choosing one group from each extreme of the personality scale (introverts and extroverts) and a third group of subjects from the center (ambiverts). Now, we administer a scale designed to measure sensation seeking. Some theories suggest there should be differences in the three groups of subjects, with extroverts scoring high on sensation seeking, introverts low, and ambiverts somewhere in the middle. Thus the research question to be answered is "Are there differences among the groups of subjects in their sensation-seeking scores? If there are differences, which group or groups score higher? Which lower?"

In this research, introversion/extroversion is the independent variable. Establishing three introversion/extroversion groups defines three "degrees" or "amounts" of the independent variable. The independent variable now has more than two conditions, so Student's *t* from Chapter 10 is not applicable as a hypothesis test. Here, the overall hypothesis test, the one that addresses the first question ("Are there differences ...?"), is known as the **analysis of variance (ANOVA)**. In this chapter, we develop its logic fully. Then we show how to approach the follow-up ("If there are ...") questions that are always present when you decide there are differences.

Because of the multiple-condition, single independent variable nature of this experimental design, it is called a one-variable, single-factor, or one-way design. It is one of the most commonly used experimental designs in psychology.

Chapter 1 introduced the idea of manipulating an independent variable either as a between-subjects variable or as a within-subjects variable. The current example, of course, could only be a between-subjects experiment. (How could you, for example, have someone be an ambivert for one testing session and an introvert the next time?) But you can easily conceive of an independent variable where the manipulation might be within subjects. Suppose you were looking at a problem-solving task; you could have four different problems, and it would be perfectly reasonable to have each subject solve all of them. The within-subjects manipulation is advantageous because of its economy (fewer subjects are needed) and because of its power (which comes mainly from the control of extraneous variation achieved by eliminating the differences between subjects).

In the two-condition experiment (Chapter 10), the hypothesis test differed depending on whether the design used a between- or a within-subjects manipulation of the independent variable. It should come as no surprise, then, to learn that the analysis of variance also changes depending on the way the independent variable is manipulated. This chapter presents analyses for only the between-subjects design. Analyses for the repeated measures design are presented in Chapter 14.

For Student's *t*, we assumed that the dependent variable was measured on an interval or a ratio scale and that its distribution was normal. Those same assumptions apply to ANOVA. In addition, Chapter 10 demonstrated that there are complications in Student's *t* depending on whether the population variances are equal or not. In ANOVA, however, there are no alternative ways to do the computations—we must assume that the variances of all the population distributions are equal and that the populations are normal. When these assumptions don't hold, there are nonparametric tests we can apply; we discuss one of them after developing parametric procedures.

◆ An Overview of the Logic

The t test is used to answer a question about the equality of two population means. The null hypothesis, as pointed out in Chapter 10, is that two population means are equal ($\mu_1 = \mu_2$) or, stating it differently, that $\mu_1 - \mu_2 = 0.0$. Rejecting the hypothesis means concluding that there is a difference in the two means. Thus the t is a way to test a hypothesis about *center*, and so is ANOVA. One common way to state the null hypothesis is that $\mu_1 = \mu_2 = \mu_3 = \cdots$ for as many populations (and thus experimental conditions) as are present in the research.

A simple form of the formula for the two-sample test in Chapter 10 was

$$t = \frac{(\overline{X}_1 - \overline{X}_2)}{s_{\overline{X}_1 - \overline{X}_2}}$$

This formula is a variant of the basic standardizing formula first presented in Chapter 4, and directs that we divide the difference between the two means by a measure of variability. (The variability, recall, is based on the standard deviations of the two groups of experimental data, and thus reflects variation within each set of data.) If the ratio of the difference of the means to the variability is "large enough" that it is unlikely to happen by chance, we conclude that there is a difference between the two populations.

Another way to look at the t is to note that the numerator is a measure of the variation *between* two experimental treatments, while the denominator represents variation *within* the two groups. That variability can be due to several causes, but is most simply thought of as "error" variation. The basic ratio is thus between *variability due to experimental treatment* (the difference in the two means) and *variability due to error*.

The same distinction between two sources of variability forms the entire basis of analysis of variance. Indeed, the very name of the technique implies an analysis that identifies some of the total variation as due to error and some to differences caused by the independent variable. The null hypothesis in ANOVA is that there is *no* variation due to the independent variable and that only error variation is present. Rejecting the hypothesis means, obviously, that variation is also caused by the independent variable.

The fundamental formula for the hypothesis test in ANOVA is

$$\frac{\text{Error variation} + \text{Independent variable variation}}{\text{Error variation}}$$

making the verbal statement explicit. If the null hypothesis about no variation due to the independent variable is true, then the ratio should be about 1.0; if it's false, the ratio should be greater than 1.0. Our first task in this chapter is to develop the logic that can lead to estimates of the two components of variability.

INTRODUCTION TO THE ANALYSIS OF VARIANCE

In a two-condition experiment, there are two conceptual populations, and the experimental groups are regarded as samples from them. The same is true in a multiple-condition experiment. Each set of data is regarded as a sample from a population that might be observed under a particular experimental treatment. The overall null hypothesis in the analysis of variance is that there is no difference among the means of the populations. If it seems strange that we test hypotheses about *means* by using the analysis of *variance*, we'll clear up that mystery soon. For now, though, let's remind ourselves what a variance really is.

Variance is a measure of the variability or spread among values. Each population has a variance σ^2, and we defined a statistic to estimate it as

$$s^2 = \frac{\sum (X - \overline{X})^2}{N - 1}$$

The numerator part of the formula, recall, is a sum of the squared differences between the scores and their mean. We call such a term a **sum of squares**, or simply *SS*. The denominator is the number of items summed in the numerator, minus 1, and is a **degrees of freedom (df)** value. As a whole, then, a variance estimate is made up of a SS divided by its df, and represents an average of the squared differences between the scores and their mean.

Variance measures the variability in the data. What causes that variability? In previous discussions, we listed three major sources:

♦ Error in measurement
♦ Error in control
♦ Individual variability

That is, imperfections in measuring instruments, uncontrolled extraneous variables, and individual differences in subject variables all contribute to variability. In the analysis of variance, these three sources of variability are collectively called error variance. Although the goal of careful experimentation is to minimize these sources of variation, they can never be completely eliminated.

In earlier discussions, we also mentioned another source of variance, though we didn't explore it at the time:

♦ Effects of the independent variable

If we combine all the data in an experiment, then some of the variability we find may be due to differences among the experimental conditions. That is, if we have three different experimental conditions (for example, defined by three levels of introversion/extroversion), and if those conditions differ among themselves, then in the combined data, some of the variability among scores (in sensation-seeking scores in the example)—that is, some of the variance—must be related to differences among the levels of introversion/extroversion. However, if the levels of introversion/extroversion are identical in their effects on sensation seeking, then the differences among experimental conditions don't contribute to the variance.

Here's a set of scores on a scale designed to measure sensation-seeking behavior:

10	12	15
7	10	11
11	11	14
9	11	10
8	11	12
11	13	13
10	12	13
10	12	12
9	11	13

The histogram of these data, shown in Figure 12.1, shows the variability. This distribution has a mean and a standard deviation of $\overline{X} = 11.15$, $s = 1.79$, with $s^2 = 3.21$. The distribution is approximately symmetric and is not particularly interesting. Except, of course, that there's something special about it—it really represents the *combined* distribution of three separate groups of data for a three-condition experiment. Table 12.1 shows the same data, labeled as to their introversion/extroversion group.

The sensation-seeking scores for each of the three separate introversion/extroversion groups has its own mean, standard deviation, and form. The statistics were shown in Table 12.1, and the histograms are presented in Figure 12.2. Presenting the data this way shows that each group has

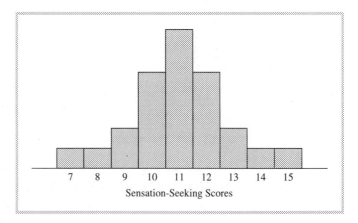

Figure 12.1

TABLE 12.1

	Introverts	Ambiverts	Extroverts
	10	12	15
	7	10	11
	11	11	14
	9	11	10
	8	11	12
	11	13	13
	10	12	13
	10	12	12
	9	11	13
Mean	9.44	11.44	12.56
Std. Dev.	1.33	0.88	1.51

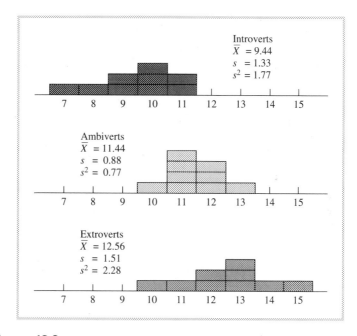

Figure 12.2

its own spread and center, which are illustrated with each distribution. In each of the three conditions, the standard deviation is based on a quantity $\sum(X - \overline{X})^2$, as always, but notice that the mean is different for each set of data. In fact, each of those three means is different from what we know to be the mean of all the data together ($\overline{X} = 11.15$). In addition, the variability of the overall distribution ($s = 1.79$, so $s^2 = 3.21$) is greater than that for any individual group of scores.

We can combine all groups into a single histogram again, keeping the groups identified, and showing the center and spread of the entire set of data across experimental conditions. See Figure 12.3. In the figure, the separate identities of the three groups are maintained, yet the overall picture of the combined data is evident as well. The picture makes it clear that, although each group is clustered reasonably close to its individual center, the spread of the combined data is somewhat greater. It is this latter variability—that of all of the sensation-seeking scores—that ANOVA analyzes.

From Figure 12.1, it should be clear that all the sensation-seeking scores depicted in the histogram are not equal. And from Figure 12.2, it should be just as obvious that even within each group of data, the sensation scores are not all equal. From Figure 12.3, it should be clear that *some* of the variability pictured in the overall data is due to the fact that, as a group, the introverts score lower than the extroverts, and that the ambiverts are somewhat different from both of the other groups. There's overlap between the groups, certainly, but the illustration suggests that it might be possible to divide the overall variability in the data into two pieces, one reflecting the apparent differences among the three experimental groups.

◆ Partitioning Variance

The total variability in the data is based, as usual, on the differences between each score and the mean of all the scores, so the quantity $(X - \overline{X})$, where $\overline{X}$ is the mean of all the scores, forms the basis of what we can think of as the *total variability* in the data. That is, if we were to compute

$$s^2 = \frac{\sum (X - \overline{X})^2}{N - 1}$$

summing the differences between all the scores in all the experimental conditions and the overall mean, we would have the total variance $s^2 = 3.21$.

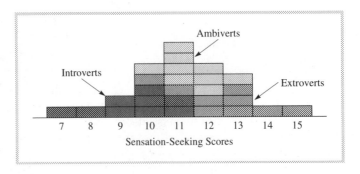

Figure 12.3

At this point, we need to introduce a little more terminology to develop a general notation for the analysis of variance. Let's let a stand for the number of experimental conditions, so that the experimental conditions can be called Condition 1, Condition 2, and so on, through Condition a. Because this is a between-subjects design, there are a groups of subjects. When we want to talk about a particular group or condition without explicitly naming it, we'll refer to it as group j. The subscript j, then, refers to any one of these experimental conditions. In this example, when $j = 1$, we're talking about the introvert group; when $j = 2$, we mean the ambivert group; and when $j = 3$, we mean the extroverts.

We use the letter n to represent the number of observations in an experimental group (for this chapter, we'll keep matters simple and assume that the groups are equal in size). The formula for variance uses the value of na in place of N (there are n scores in each group and there are a groups, so that $N = na$) to indicate the total number of values summed. The rewritten variance formula now is

$$s^2 = \frac{\sum(X - \overline{X})^2}{na - 1}$$

In a two-condition experiment we used subscripts on the means (e.g., $\overline{X}_1$ and $\overline{X}_2$) to indicate which condition the mean represented; we can continue that notation here. Thus $\overline{X}_1$ is the mean of the first experimental condition, $\overline{X}_2$ is that for the second, and so on, with $\overline{X}_j$ being the mean for the jth condition and (naturally) $\overline{X}_a$ indicating the mean of the last (the ath) condition.

Because we have a symbol for the mean of each condition, we need a separate symbol for the overall mean. We call it the **grand mean** and use the symbol **GM** to indicate it. It is calculated, of course, as the sum of all of the scores (the *grand total* or GT) divided by the number of scores, or

$$GM = \frac{\text{Total of all scores}}{na} = \frac{GT}{na}$$

Making one final modification to the formula for variance, we use GM to stand for the mean of all the data, giving the total variance formula

$$s^2 = \frac{\sum(X - GM)^2}{na - 1}$$

Computations for the example data appear in Table 12.2.

The discussion thus far has focused on the total variation, the variation around the mean of all the scores in all the conditions. But we also showed that each condition has its own mean and its own variance. The variance for an individual group of scores is based on the difference between a score and the mean of its group, $(X - \overline{X}_j)$. The differences, notice, are *within* each

TABLE 12.2

	Introverts	Ambiverts	Extroverts
	10	12	15
	7	10	11
	11	11	14
	9	11	10
	8	11	12
	11	13	13
	10	12	13
	10	12	12
	9	11	13
$\overline{X}_j$	9.44	11.44	12.56

$$na = 9(3) = 27$$
$$GT = 85 + 103 + 113 = 301$$
$$GM = \frac{301}{27} = 11.15$$

$$s^2 = \frac{\sum (X - GM)^2}{na - 1}$$
$$= \frac{\sum (X - 11.15)^2}{27}$$
$$= 3.21$$

group of data. Using them we can calculate s_j^2, the variance for each individual experimental condition. We might also calculate the standard deviation for each of the groups as

$$s_j = \sqrt{\frac{\sum (X - \overline{X}_j)^2}{n - 1}}$$

where the subscript indicates the group. Note again that the formula uses differences within each group to compute that group's variance and standard deviation.

In the example data, no two of the three group means were equal. And the grand mean was different from all of them. As a consequence, the difference between any group mean and the grand mean—that is, $(\overline{X}_j - GM)$—is nonzero in each group of data.

The formula for the overall variance, recall, was

$$s^2 = \frac{\sum (X - GM)^2}{na - 1}$$

In the numerator is the expression $(X - GM)$, the difference between an individual score and the overall mean. This is a *different* quantity from the $(X - \overline{X}_j)$; the latter quantity is a difference between a score and its group mean.

In the preceding few paragraphs, we discussed three sets of differences:

- $(X - GM)$ Differences between individual scores and the overall mean
- $(X - \overline{X}_j)$ Differences between individual scores and their group mean
- $(\overline{X}_j - GM)$ Differences between group means and the overall mean

These three differences are an important step in the process of analyzing the total variance into two separate segments.

Let's continue now to the next step in developing the analysis of variance, one where we consider a possible way of looking at the score of a single subject in one of the experimental conditions in the experiment. Don't forget those three differences—they'll reappear very soon.

◆ The Model of a Score

Now let's consider one particular score—for example, the third score in the extrovert group (which has the value 14)—see Figure 12.4. The score for this subject is located above the grand mean (11.15); in computing the overall variance, this subject contributed its difference from the grand mean: $(X - GM) = (14 - 11.15) = 2.85$. In computing the variance within the extrovert group, though, the same individual contributes a dissimilar amount: $(\overline{X} - \overline{X}_3) = 14 - 12.56 = 1.44$.

The difference between the score of 14 and the GM of 11.15 is, we saw, $(14 - 11.15) = 2.85$. Of that, 1.44 is the difference between the score of 14 and its group mean $(14 - 12.56)$, and the remainder is the difference between the group mean and the grand mean, as illustrated in Figure 12.5. We represent the same equivalences schematically in Figure 12.6.

The point of this detailed analysis of a single score in relation to two

INTROVERTS	AMBIVERTS	EXTROVERTS	
10	12	15	
7	10	11	
11	11	(14)	
9	11	10	
8	11	12	Third
11	13	13	extrovert
10	12	13	subject
10	12	12	
9	11	13	

Figure 12.4

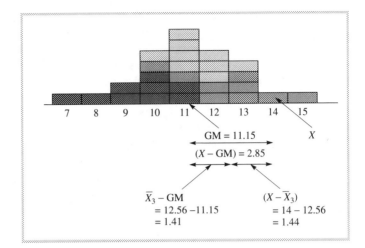

Figure 12.5

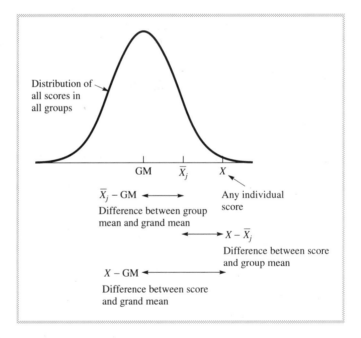

Figure 12.6

means is to show that differences between a score and the overall mean $(X - GM)$ can be expressed as two additive components, one expressing the deviation of the score from its group mean $(X - \overline{X}_j)$, and the other the deviation of the group mean from the overall mean $(\overline{X}_j - GM)$. For the third extrovert, we have

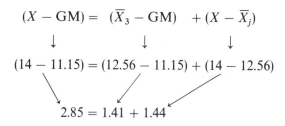

$$(X - \text{GM}) = (\overline{X}_3 - \text{GM}) + (X - \overline{X}_j)$$

$$(14 - 11.15) = (12.56 - 11.15) + (14 - 12.56)$$

$$2.85 = 1.41 + 1.44$$

More generally, in symbols, we have

$$(X - \text{GM}) = (\overline{X}_j - \text{GM}) + (X - \overline{X}_j)$$

This expression represents the difference between any individual score (X) and the mean of all the scores as a sum of two separate values. One of those values gives a measure of how different a score is from its group ($X - \overline{X}_j$). Because all the subjects in a group are treated exactly the same (in the example, they have roughly equal introversion/extroversion scores), the differences within each group represent error. The second value—the difference between group mean and grand mean ($\overline{X}_j - \text{GM}$)—is a measure of how different the group is from the other groups. This difference is due to the effect of the independent variable. Clearly, if an independent variable (such as introversion/extroversion score) has an effect, that effect should be seen as the experimental condition's being different from the overall mean, and the quantity ($\overline{X}_j - \text{GM}$) is an estimate of that effect. However, if an experimental treatment has no effect, the group mean should not differ from the other means.

So far, we have been dealing with statistics based on the data in the a different treatment groups. Because statistics are used to estimate parameters, we can define the parameter equivalents of the various statistics. The statistic GM, the grand mean of all scores in all groups, is an unbiased estimate of the population parameter μ, the mean of the population of all sensation-seeking scores that might ever be observed in this particular experiment. A group mean $\overline{X}_j$ estimates μ_j, the mean of the population of all possible observations under the jth experimental treatment. In this case, it's the mean sensation-seeking scores of all introverts (or ambiverts or extroverts). The difference between the GM and $\overline{X}_j$, again, is a measure of the effect of a particular experimental treatment or, in this case, of one's particular introversion/extroversion score.

The difference between the overall population mean μ and the mean of a population μ_j is called a **treatment effect**. A treatment effect is represented by the symbol $\boldsymbol{\alpha_j}$, so we can write the expression

$$\alpha_j = \mu_j - \mu$$

as a definition of the parameter α_j. In words,

Treament effect = Mean of the jth population − Overall mean

Earlier we said that the null hypothesis in ANOVA states that all the populations have the same mean μ. Another way of saying the same thing is that treatment effects equal zero—that is, that no experimental treatment has any effect. Written a little more formally, the null hypothesis is that $\alpha_j = 0.0$ for all values of j.

In ANOVA, any differences between individual (X) scores and the mean of the population of all subjects treated in the same way (μ_j) are regarded as error. The differences between scores and their treatment mean—that is, $X - \mu_j$—therefore, represent error. The source of the error is unimportant in ANOVA—individual differences between subjects, measurement error, or the influence of extraneous variables are all regarded the same.

As we did for statistics, we can express parameter relationships; these are shown in Figure 12.7. We now have three quantities expressing differences between various components of the population mean and the individual score value—namely,

$$(X - \mu) = (\mu_j - \mu) + (X - \mu_j)$$

The expression says that it's possible to express the difference between a score and the mean of all scores as a sum of two separate items. The quantity $(X - \mu)$, remember, is estimated in data by $(X - \text{GM})$, and that quantity in turn is an essential part of the overall variance formula

$$s^2 = \frac{\sum (X - \text{GM})^2}{na - 1}$$

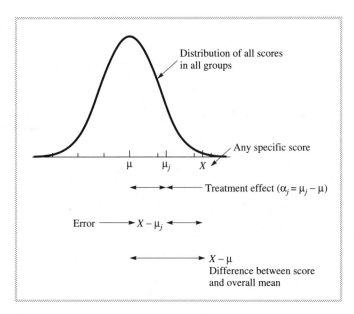

Figure 12.7

This suggests that it's possible to subdivide the numerator of the variance into separate segments—one due to error and one to the experimental treatment. How do we turn all of this into a procedure for making an inference about differences among experimental treatments? The next step is to explore sums of squares in detail.

SUMS OF SQUARES

We began our development of the analysis of variance by expanding the familiar formula for variance into

$$s^2 = \frac{\sum (X - GM)^2}{na - 1}$$

The numerator of the variance—the sum of squares or $\sum (X - GM)^2$—involves deviations between the grand mean and the individual scores $(X - GM)$. Earlier, we developed the expression

$$(X - GM) = (\overline{X}_j - GM) + (X - \overline{X}_j)$$

for that difference. Substituting the right-hand half of the preceding expression into the definition of the sum of squares gives

$$\sum (X - GM)^2 = \sum [(\overline{X}_j - GM) + (X - \overline{X}_j)]^2$$

Applying a little intermediate algebra on the right side (which we mercifully omit), the result is this expression for sums of squares:

$$\underbrace{\sum (X - GM)^2}_{\substack{\text{Differences of scores} \\ \text{from the grand mean}}} = \underbrace{n \sum (\overline{X}_j - GM)^2}_{\substack{\text{Differences between condition} \\ \text{means and the grand mean}}} + \underbrace{\sum (X - \overline{X}_j)^2}_{\substack{\text{Differences of scores} \\ \text{from their condition mean}}}$$

These three quantities are all sums of squares, or SSs, and they represent variation of three different kinds. The first, based on variations around the grand mean, is usually called the *total sum of squares*, or SS_{Total}:

$$SS_{Total} = \sum (X - GM)^2$$

It is the numerator of the formula for the overall variance and represents the total variation present among all data values.

The second component of the expression represents variation of the group means about the overall mean:

$$SS_{\text{Between}} = n \sum (\overline{X}_j - GM)^2$$

and is called the *sum of squares between groups*, or simply SS_{Between}. This quantity represents a portion of the overall variance. In particular, it is that part of the overall variation that represents differences between the experimental treatments.

The last term in the expression represents variance within experimental conditions:

$$SS_{\text{Within}} = \sum (X - \overline{X}_j)^2$$

It is called the *sum of squares within groups*, or SS_{Within}, and represents a measure of error.

Putting them all together, we have

$$\underbrace{\sum (X - GM)^2}_{SS_{\text{Total}}} = \underbrace{n \sum (\overline{X}_j - GM)^2}_{SS_{\text{Between}}} + \underbrace{\sum (X - \overline{X}_j)^2}_{SS_{\text{Within}}}$$

Symbolically,

$$SS_{\text{Total}} = SS_{\text{Between}} + SS_{\text{Within}}$$

The total sum of squares represents all the variation in the data. What we have just accomplished is to divide it into two separate, and additive, components. One component represents variation within each group and thus is a measure of error. The other component measures variation between the experimental conditions and thus represents treatment effects:

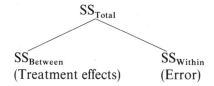

If you recall that our goal is to test the hypothesis of no treatment effect by forming the ratio

$$\frac{\text{Error variation} + \text{Independent variable variation}}{\text{Error variation}}$$

you can see that we have accomplished a lot. The total variation, as measured by a sum of squares, has been broken into two segments—one representing error and the other representing treatment effects.

To take the next step, remember that a variance consists of two parts: a sum of squares and a degrees of freedom. Now we proceed to partition the df as we did the sums of squares.

DEGREES OF FREEDOM

The total number of degrees of freedom in the analysis is, as usual, $N - 1$. In this case, we replace N by na because there are n subjects in each of a groups. Thus we have $df_{Total} = na - 1$.

For $df_{Between}$, we follow the familiar rule and use the number of values summed minus 1, yielding $df_{Between} = a - 1$.

Finally, for df_{Within}, note that we have a groups, each with n observations, giving $n - 1$ degrees of freedom for each group. Combining those two facts gives $df_{Within} = a(n - 1) = na - a$.

We have now completed the separation of the total degrees of freedom into two segments as

$$df_{Total} = df_{Between} + df_{Within}$$

It's easy to see that the equation is correct:

$$df_{Total} = \underbrace{a - 1}_{df_{Between}} + \underbrace{na - a}_{df_{Within}} = \underbrace{na - 1}_{df_{Total}}$$

FORMING VARIANCE ESTIMATES

Any sum of squares divided by its degrees of freedom yields an estimate of a variance. Let's first look at the variance estimates in the analysis of variance, and then define the parameters they estimate. Once we take the last step, it'll be clear how to test a hypothesis about equality of means.

During the early twentieth century, when most of today's statistics were being developed, the mean of the squared differences about the arithmetic mean was universally called a **mean square (MS)**. That practice continues in the analysis of variance. We know, of course, that dividing a sum of squares by its df gives an estimate of a variance. But the practice of calling these variances by their earlier name—mean square—continues. Thus, dividing the sum of squares between by its degrees of freedom gives the mean square between groups:

$$\frac{SS_{Between}}{df_{Between}} = MS_{Between}$$

$$= \text{"Variance" between groups}$$

Likewise, dividing the sum of squares within by its degrees of freedom gives a mean square:

$$\frac{SS_{Within}}{df_{Within}} = MS_{Within}$$

$$= \text{"Variance" within groups}$$

There is no point in computing the mean square based on the total sum of squares and its df. That would give the overall variance of all the data, but that is not useful as a descriptive statistic. (The standard deviation of each individual group is much more important.) Moreover, it's not independent of the other two mean squares.

With two mean squares (variances) defined, we now come to the question of just what parameter(s) they estimate. In the case of the MS_{Within}, it's easy: MS_{Within} is an unbiased estimate of σ_e^2, the error variance. Recall that ANOVA regards all variation (*except* that due to the independent variable) as error. MS_{Within} provides an unbiased estimate of that error variance.

If MS_{Within} estimates σ_e^2, then what does $MS_{Between}$ estimate? It estimates the quantity

$$\sigma_e^2 + \frac{n \sum \alpha_j^2}{a - 1}$$

Look at the two estimation formulas carefully. Both of the two mean squares estimate error variance. In the case of MS_{Within}, *only* error variance is estimated. But $MS_{Between}$ *also* estimates a quantity based on the treatment effects, α_j. Thus we have two mean squares. One of them estimates error, and the other estimates error *plus* the effects of the experimental treatment (independent variable effects).

Now remember that the null hypothesis is that all the treatment effects are zero. If the null hypothesis is true, the right-hand part of the latter formula will equal zero, and *both* MS_{Within} and $MS_{Between}$ will be estimates of the same quantity—namely, error variance. But if the null hypothesis is false—that is, at least one of the treatment effects is nonzero—then $MS_{Between}$ will include a nonzero second component, and so should be larger than MS_{Within}.

THE *F* RATIO

We have but one step left: construct the ratio

$$\frac{\text{Error variation} + \text{Independent variable variation}}{\text{Error variation}}$$

which we described early in this chapter. In terms of the mean squares, the ratio becomes

$$\frac{MS_{Between}}{MS_{Within}}$$

In terms of parameters, this is

$$F = \frac{\sigma_e^2 + \dfrac{n \sum \alpha_j^2}{a - 1}}{\sigma_e^2}$$

The ratio of the two variances is called the **F ratio** and is used to test the hypothesis of no treatment effects.

If the null hypothesis of no treatment effects is true (that is, all population means are equal and thus all $\alpha_j = 0.0$), then the second term in the numerator equals zero, and the numerator and the denominator of the ratio are independent estimates of the same parameter (see Figure 12.8). In the first case (Figure 12.8a), the ratio should have a value of approximately 1.0. If the hypothesis is false, however (Figure 12.8b), then the treatment effects would be nonzero, and the numerator would exceed the denominator, giving the ratio a value greater than 1.0. The sampling distribution of the F ratio is well known and may be used for testing a hypothesis.

◆ Testing the Null Hypothesis

There are two ways of expressing the null hypothesis that we want to test. The most straightforward expression is

$$\mu_1 = \mu_2 = \cdots = \mu_j = \cdots = \mu_a = \mu$$

This is the direct extension of the two-sample Student's t test to the multiple-condition design (although we usually expressed the $\mu_1 = \mu_2$ hypothesis as $\mu_1 = \mu_2 = 0.0$). A more useful expression when it comes to understanding the F ratio, though, is

$$\alpha_j = 0.0 \qquad \text{for all } j = 1, 2, \ldots, a$$

as we have noted several times previously. This expression declares that all treatment effects are 0.0. Because MS_{Between} estimates the parameter

$$\sigma_e^2 + \frac{n \sum \alpha_j^2}{a - 1}$$

when the null hypothesis is true, the entire right-hand term is 0.0, and the F

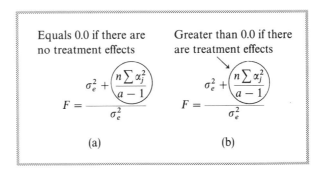

Figure 12.8

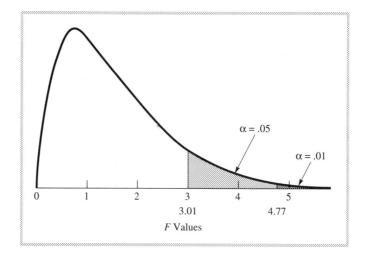

Figure 12.9

ratio consists of two statistics that independently estimate σ_e^2:

$$F = \frac{\sigma_e^2}{\sigma_e^2}$$

Thus, when the null hypothesis is true, the value of F should be about 1.0,[1] while it should be greater than 1.0 when the null hypothesis is false and there are between-conditions differences.

Note that the values of α_j are squared. This means that any difference between μ and μ_j, whether it is greater or less than zero, makes the mean square increase when treatment effects are nonzero. Thus the value of the F ratio should be greater than 1.0 regardless of whether the treatment effects are positive or negative. The implication of this is that the F ratio tests a hypothesis that is sensitive to *any* differences from μ, making ANOVA the equivalent of a two-tailed or nondirectional t test.

When the null hypothesis is true, the sampling distribution for F is controlled by two df parameters, one for the numerator of the ratio and one for the denominator. The distribution is asymmetric and positively skewed, as illustrated in Figure 12.9, which happens to be the F distribution with numerator df = 4 and denominator df = 16. The values of the ratio must necessarily be positive because both the numerator and the denominator are sums of squared values. When the null hypothesis is true, most of the values of F cluster around 1.0. When the null hypothesis is false, though, the ratio tends to be larger than 1.0, so the critical region of the curve is in the right-hand tail.

---

[1] Actually, this statement is a considerable oversimplification, but it's convenient to think of the distribution in this way and won't lead you astray in using the distribution and making inferences.

Appendix F gives the critical values for the F distribution for a large number of sets of df values and for several significance points. With df $= 4$ for the numerator and 16 for the denominator, two critical points given in Appendix F are 3.01 and 4.77 for $\alpha = .05$ and $\alpha = .01$, respectively (see Figure 12.9). With 4 and 16 degrees of freedom, any obtained F ratio of 3.01 or larger represents a significant difference among the group means at the .05 level, while at the .01 level, a difference of 4.77 or more will result in rejecting the null hypothesis.

Just what does it mean to reject a null hypothesis in ANOVA? It means that we reject the hypothesis that all the treatment population means are equal. By rejecting the null, we support the alternative hypothesis, which merely states that all the means are not equal (or, alternatively, that not all the treatment effects are zero). But that is not a very satisfying conclusion because the means can be unequal in a number of ways. Consider, for example, the introversion/extroversion study. If we conclude that the three groups are not all alike in their sensation-seeking scores, where are we left? It could be that the extrovert and the ambivert groups are alike, but different from the introverts. Or maybe ambivert and introvert groups are alike, but different from extroverts. Or perhaps the introverts and the extroverts are the same, but different from those in the ambivert group. Or maybe all three are different from each other. There's no way to tell from the overall hypothesis test.

In a three-condition experiment, the null hypothesis can be incorrect in any of four possible ways, as we just suggested:

$$\mu_1 = \mu_2 \neq \mu_3$$

$$\mu_1 \neq \mu_2 = \mu_3$$

$$\mu_1 = \mu_3 \neq \mu_2$$

$$\mu_1 \neq \mu_2 \neq \mu_3$$

If there are four conditions in the design, the situation becomes more complex because the null hypothesis can be incorrect in any of 14 different ways. And more conditions lead to even more possibilities.

It's clear, then, that the hypothesis test provides only an overall indication about the null hypothesis. For this reason, the hypothesis test just presented is called an *omnibus* test; it gives only a general indication about the equality of conditions. The second step in the analysis uses a variety of techniques, often called *post hoc*, or *follow-up*, tests, which we discuss in the next section. Of course, if we conclude that there are no differences among conditions, then the analysis is completed and there's no need to pursue the data further.

PRESENTING ANOVA RESULTS

ANOVA results are often presented as illustrated in Table 12.9, in the computational supplement, which summarizes an analysis for the three introversion/extroversion groups. A table like that contains a great deal of information and can be condensed into a simple sentence format. Using the values from Table 12.9, we might write "We conclude that there is a significant difference among the sensation-seeking scores of the three groups: $F(2, 24, MS_E = 1.61) = 13.89$, $p < .05$." The sentence format follows the same pattern we have seen for other significance tests, but includes the MS_{Error}. This format is much more compact than a table and conveys the same information.[2] For more complicated analyses, such as those in Chapters 14 and 15, where multiple F ratios are presented, a tabular presentation is normal.

POWER AND SAMPLE SIZE IN ANOVA

The principles of choosing a sample size to achieve a given power that applied to the two-sample t test in Chapter 10 apply equally here. There are a couple of differences to consider, though. First, recall that the formula in Chapter 10 yields the sample size for each *group* of subjects. Because there are multiple groups in an ANOVA design, the total number of subjects required for the full design may increase rapidly. Second, because the power computations are modeled on the two-group t test, you should define the effect size in terms of differences in pairs of population means, and *not* in terms of the α_j effects defined previously. In ANOVA, α_j reflects the difference between the mean of population j and the mean of all the population means (μ). The effect size used to calculate the sample size, though, should be based on the smallest difference between two means that you want to detect. Finally, the estimate of σ used in the calculation of γ should be the best estimate of σ_{Error} that you can obtain. In some cases, that will be an estimate based on a standard deviation from previous studies. In other cases, though, a previous analysis of variance may be available. In that case, you should use $\sqrt{MS_{Error}}$ from that analysis as your estimate of σ_{Error}.

AFTER THE ANALYSIS

As indicated earlier, the acceptance or rejection of the overall null hypothesis is just one part of the data analysis for a multiple-group design. If we reject the hypothesis that all experimental conditions have identical means, our next task is to locate where the differences actually are. However, if the overall analysis shows no significant differences, we accept the null hypothesis that no differences exist among the conditions and do no additional testing, but simply present the summary statistics and ANOVA results.

[2] In fact, you can reconstruct the entire table from the values given in the sentence.

Analyses that are conducted after, or in addition to, the overall F test, are often grouped into two categories, though the distinctions are sometime blurred. The most frequently reported tests are those that are classified as *post hoc*, meaning that they are specifically intended for use *after* an overall test has concluded that a significant difference exists somewhere among the experimental groups. Most of these tests are designed to ask whether members of pairs of experimental conditions differ from each other, just as a two-sample t test would do. Other tests allow more complicated questions to be addressed ("Does the control condition differ from the mean of the others?" for example). The other category of test is often called *planned*, because such tests can be specified *before* the overall analysis is completed. Planned tests are sometimes just called comparisons or contrasts, but the distinction is unclear because comparisons can be carried out either before or after the main analysis. We begin our discussion with planned tests.

◆ Comparisons[3]

The two-condition experiment provides the clearest results in an experimental design—when two conditions are pitted against each other, a significant (or insignificant) result is unambiguous. The two-condition design also provides us with an example of the meaning of the phrase "a comparison."

The two-sample t test (for a between-groups design) has the formula

$$t = \frac{(\overline{X}_1 - \overline{X}_2) - (\mu_1 - \mu_2)}{s_{\overline{X}_1 - \overline{X}_2}}$$

Because the usual null hypothesis is that $\mu_1 - \mu_2 = 0$, the second term is often dropped, leaving

$$t = \frac{(\overline{X}_1 - \overline{X}_2)}{s_{\overline{X}_1 - \overline{X}_2}}$$

The numerator is the difference between the two sample means. It is also called a *comparison* between the two means. Because the two sample means are estimates of parameters, the numerator is also an estimate of $\mu_1 - \mu_2$, the difference between the population means.

If the ANOVA null hypothesis is correct, the difference between any two pairs of means should be zero, as should the difference between any combinations of means. For example, the arithmetic mean of any two population means should be equal to the mean of a third population. The expression

---

[3] This section, and several others later that make use of this material, presents a somewhat advanced topic and may be omitted, depending on the instructor's wishes.

$$\frac{\mu_1 + \mu_2}{2} - \mu_3 = 0$$

states that the average of the first two population means should be equal to the mean of the third (if the null hypothesis is true).

In the preceding examples—that is, in the expressions $(\mu_1 - \mu_2) = 0$ and

$$\frac{\mu_1 + \mu_2}{2} - \mu_3 = 0$$

there was a subtraction, with the elements on one "side" compared to those on the other. Further, the value of each comparison is zero when the null hypothesis is true. This is an important characteristic of a comparison: It represents a difference between two sets of population means, and is expected to equal zero under the null hypothesis.

We ordinarily talk about comparisons of sample means and not population means, so comparisons are written using statistics. But because sample values are usually regarded as point estimates, our conclusions will be about parameters, as always in statistical inference. Regardless of whether the discussion is explicitly about parameters or statistics, however, comparisons involve subtractions, and the null hypothesis value of a comparison is always zero.

Suppose we want to compare two personality groups (introverts and ambiverts) with extroverts. We can write

$$\frac{\mu_{\text{Introvert}} + \mu_{\text{Ambivert}}}{2} - \mu_{\text{Extrovert}}$$

to represent the population comparison. Normally, sample means would be used, so the comparison would be calculated as

$$\frac{\overline{X}_{\text{Introvert}} + \overline{X}_{\text{Ambivert}}}{2} - \overline{X}_{\text{Extrovert}}$$

We can also write

$$\tfrac{1}{2}\overline{X}_{\text{Introvert}} + \tfrac{1}{2}\overline{X}_{\text{Ambivert}} - \overline{X}_{\text{Extrovert}}$$

with exactly the same meaning. This change in notation accomplishes an important step because we can now define a comparison as a sum of the products of means and appropriate coefficients, or

$$C = \sum c_j \overline{X}_j$$

where C stands for the value of a comparison and c is a coefficient. In the example, the coefficient values are $1/2$, $1/2$, and -1. A comparison of this form is often called a *linear contrast*, or a *linear comparison* among the means, because the formula represents an ordinary linear equation.

The values of the coefficients are arbitrary, but they must sum to zero. For computational simplicity, whole numbers are usually suggested, so the previous comparison can be written as $1, 1, -2$. Coefficients should not all be zero because such a comparison would be meaningless. But whatever their values, a comparison is always between all the positively signed means and all those with the opposite sign.

Any experimental condition that is not part of a comparison has a coefficient of zero, so the coefficients $0, 1, -1$ indicate a comparison between the ambivert and extrovert means; the introverts are ignored. Many of the interesting comparisons involve pairs of means, while others, such as perhaps the difference between all drug conditions and a single placebo, involve more than two means.

TESTING HYPOTHESES ABOUT COMPARISONS

The major reason for calculating comparisons is to allow you to test hypotheses about them. Each comparison embodies a question: "Are the sets of means represented by the positive and the negative signs equal?" A comparison with the coefficients $1, 0, -1$ asks whether the introverts and the extroverts are equal in their sensation-seeking scores. Likewise, the comparison $1, 1, -2$ asks if the introverts and the ambiverts jointly are different from the extroverts.

We may calculate a sum of squares for each comparison as follows. First, find the value of the comparison using the formula

$$C = \sum c_j \overline{X}_j$$

Now the sum of squares is

$$\text{SS}_{\text{A comparison}} = \frac{nC^2}{\sum c_j^2}$$

The degrees of freedom for a comparison is 1, so the mean square is simply the sum of squares divided by 1. Finally, to test the hypothesis that the comparison equals 0 in the population, form the F ratio by dividing the mean square for the comparison by the mean square from the overall analysis:

$$F = \frac{\text{MS}_{\text{A comparison}}}{\text{MS}_{\text{Error}}}$$

The comparison is significant if the F exceeds the critical value in Appendix F with the numerator df $= 1$ and the denominator df $= \text{df}_{\text{Error}}$.

Tests conducted with comparisons are sometimes referred to as *planned comparisons* because they are often of such importance that they can be defined even before looking at any results, and conducted regardless of the significance of the overall F. Consider the case where several concentrations of a drug are being compared, along with a control condition. An important comparison might ask whether *any* amount of the drug is different from none. If there were four amounts of the drug, and a fifth condition formed a no-drug control, a comparison with the coefficients 1, 1, 1, 1, -4 would compare the mean of all the drug conditions with the control. In effect, it compares just the two conditions "drug" and "nondrug," just as a two-sample t test would. A question like this might be *so* important that it would be analyzed *first*, perhaps even before the overall analysis.

INDEPENDENT (ORTHOGONAL) COMPARISONS

In the literature, you are likely to see "orthogonal" or "independent comparisons" mentioned. We define them here so they will be familiar, and also so we can use them later.

A pair of comparisons, C_I and C_II, is *independent*, or *orthogonal*, if the sum of the products of their coefficients equals zero. Consider this pair, from an experiment with four conditions:

$$C_\mathrm{I} = (1 * \overline{X}_1) - (2 * \overline{X}_2) + (1 * \overline{X}_3) + (0 * \overline{X}_4)$$
$$C_\mathrm{II} = (1 * \overline{X}_1) + (1 * \overline{X}_2) + (1 * \overline{X}_3) - (3 * \overline{X}_4)$$

Just writing the coefficients, we would have

$$C_\mathrm{I}:\ 1 \quad -2 \quad 1 \quad\ \ 0$$
$$C_\mathrm{II}:\ 1 \quad\ \ 1 \quad 1 \quad -3$$

The first set of coefficients defines a comparison between groups 1 and 3 versus group 2 (comparison I). The second compares the mean of groups 1, 2, and 3 with the mean of group 4. To check for independence of the two comparisons, form the products of pairs of values:

$$C_\mathrm{I}:\ 1 \qquad -2 \qquad 1 \qquad 0$$
$$\diagdown 1 \qquad \diagdown -2 \qquad \diagdown 1 \qquad \diagdown 0$$
$$C_\mathrm{II}:\ 1 \qquad 1 \qquad 1 \qquad -3$$

and then calculate the sum of the products

$$1 - 2 + 1 + 0 = 0$$

Because the sum is zero, the two comparisons are independent, or orthogonal.

But consider this pair of comparisons:

$$C_{II}: 1 \quad 1 \quad 1 \quad -3$$
$$C_{III}: 0 \quad 1 \quad 1 \quad -2$$

This is a comparison between groups 1–3 versus group 4 (comparison II), and between groups 2–3 and group 4 (comparison III). Checking for independence, the products are

$$
\begin{array}{ccccc}
C_{II}: 1 & 1 & 1 & -3 \\
 & 0 & 1 & 1 & 6 \\
C_{III}: 0 & 1 & 1 & -2 \\
\end{array}
$$

and the sum is

$$0 + 1 + 1 + 6 = 8 \neq 0$$

and so this pair is not orthogonal.

Orthogonality, or independence, is related to the extent to which a pair of comparisons tests overlapping hypotheses. In the latter pair, the hypotheses are nearly identical, both testing the relationship between group 4 and several others. Only the first group is included in one comparison and not the other; much the same information is involved in both comparisons. Comparisons I and II, however, are quite separate from one another.

◆ Post Hoc Tests

A look into either the research literature or computer program instructions will reveal numerous[4] tests used after a significant overall F. Nearly all post hoc tests address the fundamental problem that using the same data repeatedly, as you must do to compare groups, increases the probability of making a Type I[5] error. Simply stated, the probabilities of making a Type I error summate; if you conduct four tests at the .05 level, your *overall* probability of making a Type I error is roughly $4(.05) \approx .20$. All post hoc tests are designed to investigate differences among population means, but they differ in how they deal with the probability of making Type I or Type II errors. We return to this discussion in more detail later in the chapter.

We cannot present all the tests. Instead, we focus here on two procedures that are useful in comparing pairs of experimental conditions. The computational supplement illustrates three other pairs-of-groups tests and also shows how to adapt one of those procedures to investigate more com-

[4] Wilcox (1987) reviews nearly 20 such tests.

[5] If you don't remember this error, you should review Chapter 8 carefully.

plicated comparisons. If you're using a computer for ANOVA and its follow-ups, your program may offer numerous choices. A summary table at the end of the chapter will help you sort out the options.

THE FISHER LEAST-SIGNIFICANT-DIFFERENCE (LSD) TEST

Because each group in an ANOVA experiment is separate, using a Student's t test (from Chapter 10) might seem to be a simple and effective way to test for a difference between groups. This is sometimes done, but it is not really appropriate. A better way to do the same test is to use all the data in all the groups to measure error variation, leading to the formula

$$t_{LSD} = \frac{\overline{X}_j - \overline{X}_k}{\sqrt{\dfrac{2MS_{Within}}{n}}}$$

where $\overline{X}_j$ and $\overline{X}_k$ are the means of the two groups, and MS_{Within} is the within-groups, or error, mean square from the overall analysis. The statistic follows Student's t distribution with df $= a(n-1)$. If the value of t_{LSD} exceeds the critical value in Appendix C at the chosen significance level, then you may conclude that groups j and k are significantly different. The LSD is nothing but a t test with a different denominator, and its repeated use for multiple pairs of groups leads to an increase in the probability of making a Type I error.

BONFERRONI ADJUSTMENTS AND THE DUNN TEST

Suppose you want to use the Fisher LSD test to follow up on a significant overall F. Because the overall Type I error probability is roughly the significance level for each test times the number of tests, it may have occurred to you that there is a simple way to set an overall rate. If you want to conduct five tests and keep your *total* Type I probability at .05, just conduct each test at $\alpha = .01$; with five tests, you have $\alpha_{Overall} = 5(.01) \approx .05$. You can easily make this adjustment; just use the .01 level for each test. Such a modification is often called a **Bonferroni adjustment** because it relies on an inequality postulated by Bonferroni.[6]

The only real difficulty with using the Bonferroni procedure is that tables of the appropriate critical values are often unavailable. The previous example was easy, but suppose you wanted to conduct four tests while keeping $\alpha_{Overall}$ at .05. Each test would have to be conducted at the $.05/4 = .0125$ level; tables with $\alpha = .0125$ are *very* hard to find. This difficulty was eliminated by Dunn (1961), who presented a set of tables that allows the Bonferroni adjustment to be made easily. Howell (1992) presents similar tables. The Bonferroni/Dunn procedure offers an easy way to adjust for multiple comparisons, as long as there are only a few of them. With a sub-

---

[6] The Bonferroni inequality states that the probability of one or more events occurring cannot be greater than the sum of the individual probabilities of the events.

stantial number of comparisons, the Bonferroni adjustment makes the individual error probability very small. As a consequence, there is a considerable loss of power for each comparison, making a Type II error quite likely.

Many computer programs make it easy to use a Bonferroni adjustment because they report the actual probability associated with a test. Summing the probabilities over all the analyses gives the overall probability of Type I error.

◆ Choosing a Comparison Procedure

With so many possible comparison procedures, how should we decide which we should use? There are almost as many answers to that question as there are authors who address it. In every case, though, the answer invariably hinges on the trade-offs between Type I and Type II errors. We make some recommendations here, and suggest sources for additional reading.

TYPES OF ERRORS

Until this chapter, experimental designs asked only a single question and thus had only a single null hypothesis. In designs with a single null hypothesis, picking a significance level defines the probability of rejecting the null hypothesis when it's true (Type I error). In multiple-condition designs, though, there are several hypothesis tests, and so establishing the probability of a Type I error becomes more complicated.

In a single-hypothesis design, the probability of making a Type I error is whatever we choose as the value for α. When we make a number of tests in a single experiment, though, we must consider Type I error in two ways: the probability of making a Type I error *on each individual hypothesis test*, or of making a Type I error *somewhere in all the tests*. Suppose we have the three-condition introversion/extroversion experiment. And suppose the overall F test (with $\alpha = .05$) concluded that there was a difference in sensation seeking among the three groups. So far, the probability of making a Type I error is .05. Now suppose we conduct a follow-up test at the .05 level, looking for a difference between the introverts and the extroverts. The probability of making a Type I error in *that test alone* is .05. Now we carry out yet another test, perhaps between the introverts and the ambivert subjects, and again use the .05 level. We made three hypothesis tests, *each at the .05 level*. On each test, then, the probability of making a Type I error is .05. But what is the probability that we made a Type I error *somewhere* in the analysis of the full experiment? As suggested earlier, it's roughly .15, or .05 for each of the three tests.

What we just illustrated is the difference between thinking about Type I errors on a *per-comparison* (PC), or *individual*, basis and on an *experiment-wise* (EW), or *overall*, basis. In an experiment with a single hypothesis test, the two probabilities are the same; when there is more than one test in the same experiment, the probability of erroneously rejecting a true increases.

So far, we have identified two approaches to regarding Type I error—on a PC basis (**PC error rate** or α_{PC}) or on an EW basis (**EW error rate** or α_{EW}). There is yet another basis for error rates—the family-wise (FW) error rate (α_{FW}). For now, we can regard the EW and FW rates as the same. In Chapter 15, though, we present the factorial experimental design. In that design, there are at least three overall tests that are independent of one another, and it makes sense to think of families of tests, each family centered around an overall F ratio. We discuss family-wise error rates at that time.

Controlling Errors

Deciding on the comparison technique depends in large part on the method chosen to control the error rate. Probably the most important aim of most research is to find differences among experimental conditions if they exist (that is, avoiding a Type II error). For this reason, we recommend choosing a minimum effect size and using that to select a sample size before beginning the data collection. At the same time, most people would agree that the probability of making a Type I error should be kept from increasing without bound. All the careful sample size selection and effect size determination can go out the window if the follow-up analyses allow Type I error probability to compound needlessly.

◆ General Recommendations

A good general procedure to keep the EW error rate reasonable and, at the same time, allow sufficient power in the comparisons is as follows. First, follow the procedures discussed earlier for deciding on an effect size, select a significance level for the overall test, and choose a sample size accordingly. Then, if the overall analysis indicates a significant difference among the conditions, proceed with follow-up tests. If there are no more than $a - 1$ specific group differences of interest, conduct Fisher LSD tests and make no adjustment for multiple tests. If there are more than $a - 1$ tests, make a Bonferroni adjustment to the significance level, either directly in the Fisher test or by using the Dunn procedure.[7] To keep a tight control on Type I errors, however, use one of the common follow-up tests, such as those illustrated in the computational supplement or those offered in common statistics programs. Among the tests frequently offered, the Tukey (HSD) test is probably the best when you want to control EW errors and make numerous tests of differences between means.[8] Because of its extreme loss of power,

---

[7] Keppel (1982) recommends that the EW error rate used as the basis for the Bonferroni adjustment should be the one that would result from applying $a - 1$ comparisons—namely, $(a - 1) * \alpha_{PC}$. Thus, if you had an experiment with four conditions and $\alpha = .05$ and you wanted to do five comparisons, then each comparison would be done with $\alpha_{PC} = [(4 - 1) * .05]/5 = .03$.

[8] The Dunnett C is a better choice because it is less affected by unequal variances and differing group sizes, but it is rarely offered in ANOVA programs.

Test	Comments
Scheffé test*	Very conservative and consequently has limited power
	Can accommodate complex comparisons (other than only pairs of means)
	Protects EW error rate at α for all possible comparisons
Tukey (HSD) test*	Protects EW error rate at α for all paired comparisons
	More powerful than the Scheffé test
Fisher's LSD test*	Most powerful test available
	Offers no protection against increasing Type I error unless used with a Bonferroni adjustment
	Can accommodate complex comparisons (other than only pairs of means)
Dunn test	Quite powerful; perhaps too much so
	Does not fully protect α_{EW}
Dunnett test for comparing groups with a single control	Powerful special-purpose test
	Protects α_{EW}
Duncan test	Quite powerful; perhaps too much so
	Does not fully protect α_{EW}
Newman–Keuls test	Quite powerful
	Does not fully protect α_{EW} with a large number of groups
Dunnett C test*	Powerful test
	Especially recommended with unequal group sizes and/or unequal group variances
	New test; rarely found in computer programs
Dunnett T_3 test	Powerful test
	Especially recommended with unequal group sizes and/or unequal group variances
	New test; rarely found in computer programs
	Requires a special table of critical values
Games–Howell test	Powerful test
	Especially recommended with unequal group sizes and/or unequal group variances
	New test; rarely found in computer programs

*Illustrated in the computational supplement.

avoid the often-cited Scheffé test unless you want to be *very* certain of avoiding a Type I error.

Howell (1992) has an extensive and readable discussion of the considerations in choosing a follow-up procedure. Keppel (1973, 1982, 1991) is another noted authority.[9] These texts contain numerous references to the

---

[9] Between these two editions of his text, Keppel changed his mind; you should read both versions.

TABLE 12.4

	Drug A	Experimental Condition Placebo	Drug B	Drug C
Mean	7.62	9.75	10.38	12.50
Placebo	2.13			
Drug B	2.76	0.63		
Drug C	4.88*	2.75	2.12	

*$p < .05$, Tukey test.

TABLE 12.5

Drug A	Placebo	Drug B	Drug C
7.62	9.75	10.38	12.50

Means of the four conditions; groups sharing a common underline do not differ (Tukey test, $p < .05$).

ongoing debate concerning comparison procedures. A recent literature review is reported by Wilcox (1987).

Table 12.3 summarizes numerous comparison procedures found in the research literature and in ANOVA computer programs.[10]

◆ Presenting Comparison Results

Several different techniques are used in the literature for showing tests of pairs of means. A table of mean differences with the significant differences marked serves very well. See Table 12.4 for a hypothetical example using three drugs and a placebo.

A table could show significant differences that are at different levels—a single * might mean .05 and a double ** indicate .01, for example. The table has the added advantage of including the individual means.

An underlining scheme is sometimes used to show pairwise differences. Table 12.5 illustrates this method, presenting the same results as in Table 12.4.

DISTRIBUTION-FREE "ANALYSIS OF VARIANCE"

The analysis of variance assumes that the underlying distribution of the dependent variable is normal in form for all populations, and that all popu-

[10] A convenient source for information on these tests is Wilcox (1987).

lations have equal variances. With equal group sizes, violating those assumptions usually is not a problem, and the probabilities of Types I and II error are largely unchanged. However, when there are small sample sizes, or when there are substantial differences in variance, or when there are severe departures from the normal distribution, a distribution-free test is sometimes applied. The most common alternative to the overall analysis of variance is the Kruskal–Wallace test. It is offered by some computer programs, and it's illustrated in the computational supplement.

A FINAL COMMENT

This chapter has presented the conceptual foundation of the analysis of variance. The design where the analysis of variance is applied involves multiple experimental groups, each receiving a distinct treatment. The analysis provides a test of the hypothesis that all the populations represented by the groups have equal means. Rejecting the hypothesis that all experimental conditions have equal means leads to conducting follow-up tests to determine where the differences lie.

Summary

◆ *The null hypothesis for* analysis of variance *is that there is no difference among the means of the populations.*

◆ *The variance in experimental data comes from four sources: measurement error, control error, individual differences, and the independent variable.*

◆ *A* treatment effect *is the difference between a population mean and the overall mean.*

◆ *Differences within each group represent error.*

◆ *Dividing a sum of squares by its* degrees of freedom *gives a variance estimate; variance estimates are called* mean squares *in the analysis of variance.*

◆ *If the null hypothesis is true, then the mean square for within groups and between groups should be roughly equal, and their ratio should be about 1.0. If the null hypothesis is false, the ratio should tend to be greater than 1.0.*

◆ *In a multiple-group experiment, there are multiple-hypothesis tests, and you can think about the probability of a Type I error for each test, and for the entire experiment.*

◆ *The probability of making a Type I error somewhere in the analysis (that is, "experiment-wise," or EW) is roughly the probability of making an error on any single test, times the number of tests made.*

◆ *Numerous follow-up tests are designed to guard against an increase in the EW probability of making a Type I error.*

Key Terms

α_{EW}

α_{PC}

ANALYSIS OF VARIANCE (ANOVA)

BONFERRONI ADJUSTMENT

DEGREES OF FREEDOM (df)

EW ERROR RATE

F RATIO

GRAND MEAN (GM)

MEAN SQUARE (MS)

PC ERROR RATE

SUM OF SQUARES (SS)

TREATMENT EFFECT (α_j)

 # EXERCISES

1. The following data are from an experiment with three age groups of animals. The dependent variable is the number of trials required to reach a criterion of one error-free run through a maze. Calculate property. descriptive statistics, carry out the overall analysis of variance, and present the results properly. Follow up a significant F with Tukey follow-up tests and include them in the results presentation. Use $\alpha = .05$.

90 DAYS	120 DAYS	150 DAYS
25	7	1
26	15	7
33	37	27
55	24	4
19	3	3
33	2	25
6	7	19
41	23	9
18	17	29
31	15	15
18	11	28
6	14	19
24	9	13
23	1	14

2. Following is a set of data from an experiment on pain reduction. The data give the degree of pain relief (higher value means more relief) 30 minutes after taking one of three different drugs or a placebo pill. Calculate appropriate descriptive statistics and carry out the overall analysis of variance. Follow up a significant F with Dunnett C tests. Use $\alpha = .05$.

DRUG CONDITION

A	B	C	PLACEBO
5	13	15	10
7	12	11	8
11	12	13	5
10	8	10	9
10	7	10	6
6	8	16	13
4	12	14	11
8	11	11	16

3. The following data give the time, in minutes, that it took students to complete four different lengths of tests. The tests consisted of either 10, 15, 20, or 25 four-choice multiple-choice items. Conduct the analysis of variance, a Tukey follow-up test, and obtain the appropriate descriptive statistics. Use $\alpha = .01$. Report the results properly.

NUMBER OF TEST ITEMS

10	15	20	25
13	17	18	16
10	5	17	21
13	13	10	28
5	14	23	22
6	11	24	24
6	12	17	12
2	3	10	9

12	16	27	18
17	18	21	18
12	8	24	9
12	14	23	15
2	7	8	15
17	13	14	10
3	16	1	7
7	14	8	30
1	18	10	14

61	88	43
100	68	94
78	65	69
57	55	65
61	67	82
68	55	66
84	62	63
92	68	50
84	59	74
66	96	66
104	47	75

4. Here are data from an experiment similar to that reported by Jandreau and Bever (1992). Subjects were asked to read a passage in one of three different formats and then to answer questions about what they had read. A passage could be printed with normal spacing (ordinary typewriter spacing), *phrase spacing* (each phrase in each sentence was surrounded by extra space so it "stood out" more clearly), or *even spacing* (the total amount of space on each line was the same as that for phrase spacing, but it was distributed evenly along the line). Each subject read several different passages, all in the same printing format. The data give the total number of questions correct over the several passages. Conduct the analysis of variance, a Dunnett C follow-up test, and obtain the appropriate descriptive statistics. Use $\alpha = .05$. Report the results properly.

SPACING

PHRASE	NORMAL	EVEN
79	85	41
92	56	57
63	60	29
76	62	77
88	58	71
60	33	66
62	83	63

5. Repeat the analysis of the data in exercise 12.1, but use the Kruskal–Wallis test (see computational supplement). What do you conclude this time?

6. Repeat the analysis of the data in exercise 12.2, but use the Kruskal–Wallis test. What do you conclude this time?

7. Repeat the analysis of the data in exercise 12.4, but use the Kruskal–Wallis test. What do you conclude this time?

8. (*Optional—computer use required.*) Use your program's random number generator to obtain three sets of $n = 12$ values from a normal population where $\mu = 10$ and $\sigma = 4$. Conduct the analysis of variance using those three groups. Write down the F value. Repeat the process 24 or more times, recording the F value for each analysis. Now find the frequency distribution and the mean of the set of F values. You should have a distribution that is positively skewed, with a mean F of approximately 1.0. Because each F was computed with the null hypothesis actually true, your distribution is an approximation of the sampling distribution of the F statistic with df = 2, 33. If you combine your data with those of your fellow students, you'll have an even better approximation of the F distribution.

Computational Supplement

◆ Overall Analysis

The formulas given earlier are definitions; they show what each sum of squares actually represents. To develop the hand computational methods, we need more notational detail.

Many ANOVA computations are done with condition (group) totals instead of with means. For each individual group of scores in the experiment, designate their sum as T, and use a subscript to distinguish among them. The sum for the first experimental condition, then, will be T_1, while that for the second is T_2. In general, T_j is the sum of the scores in an unspecified group, and the total for the last condition is T_a. The sum of all the scores in all the conditions is called the grand total, symbolized as GT. The grand total is easily calculated as the sum of the group totals—that is,

$$GT = \sum_j T_j.$$

The notation is summarized in Table 12.6.

Until now, we kept the notation simple by not attaching subscripts to individual data values. And we will be able to keep it simple for the most part, but now we need a way to distinguish an individual score. To do that, we use a simple scheme of attaching two subscripts to the X. Any score in any experimental group can be symbolized by X_{ij}, where the values of the two subscripts tell us which subject (the first subscript: i) and which group (j: the second subscript). Thus the first score in the first group is symbolized as $X_{1,1}$. In the example data in Table 12.1, $X_{1,1} = 10$, while $X_{3,2} = 11$ (the third score in the second group), and $X_{9,3} = 13$ (the ninth score in the third group). Figure 12.10 illustrates this notational scheme.

If we want to symbolize summing all the scores in all groups, the simple notation of $\sum X$ will suffice for most purposes. To be really complete, however, the summation should be a double one, indicating that we add within each set of scores (that is, over the i subscript) and also across all the sets of scores (over the j subscript). That is, if we write

$$\sum_j \sum_i X_{ij}$$

the symbols instruct us to sum first across the i subscript (subjects within each condition) and then to sum those sums across the j subscript, as illustrated in Figure 12.11.

As illustrated, the first set of summations are down the columns, first for

TABLE 12.6

	Experimental Conditions					
	1	*2*	…	*j*	…	*a*
n Subjects per condition	X	X	…	X	…	X
	X	X	…	X	…	X
	⋮	⋮		⋮		⋮
	X	X	…	X	…	X
Group totals ⟶	T_1	T_2	…	T_j	…	T_a
Group means ⟶	$\overline{X}_1$	$\overline{X}_2$	…	$\overline{X}_j$	…	$\overline{X}_a$

$$N = na \qquad \overline{X}_j = \frac{T_j}{n}$$

$$\text{GT} = \sum_j T_j \qquad \text{GM} = \frac{\text{GT}}{na}$$

	CONDITION 1	CONDITION 2	CONDITION 3	
$X_{1,1}$	**(10)**	12	15	$X_{3,3}$
	7	10	11	
	11	**(11)**	**(14)**	
	9	11	10	
	8	11	12	
$X_{3,2}$	11	13	13	$X_{9,3}$
	10	12	13	
	10	12	12	
	9	11	**(13)**	

Figure 12.10

$j = 1$, then for $j = 2$, and finally for $j = 3$. Once that is done, then the summation is across the j subscript, resulting in the grand total.

To symbolize the summation, within each group and then across groups, of the squared deviations of the individual scores for the grand mean we write

$$\sum_j \sum_i (X_{ij} - \text{GM})^2$$

This formula for the sum of the squared deviations around the grand mean still says, "Find the differences, square 'em, and then add 'em all up," just as does $\sum(X - \overline{X})^2$, but now it says it much more explicitly.

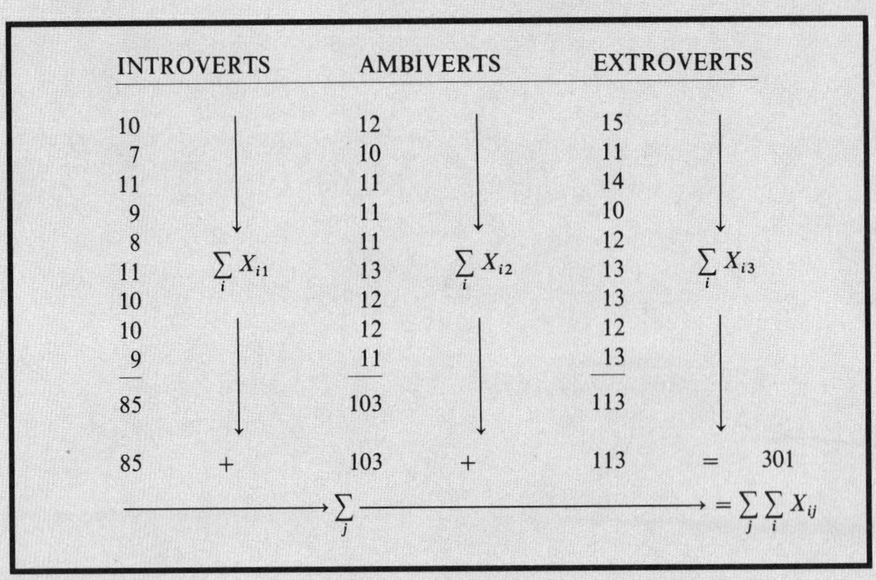

	INTROVERTS		AMBIVERTS		EXTROVERTS	
	10		12		15	
	7		10		11	
	11		11		14	
	9		11		10	
	8		11		12	
	11	$\sum_i X_{i1}$	13	$\sum_i X_{i2}$	13	$\sum_i X_{i3}$
	10		12		13	
	10		12		12	
	9		11		13	
	85		103		113	
	85	+	103	+	113	= 301

$$\longrightarrow \sum_j \longrightarrow = \sum_j \sum_i X_{ij}$$

Figure 12.11

With the notation scheme developed, Table 12.7 gives the definitions of the three sums of squares and their computational equivalents.

As an example of these computations, we use the data from Table 12.1, which gives the sensation-seeking scores for three groups of individuals: introverts, ambiverts, and extroverts. Table 12.8 repeats the data and gives some important summary values. Proceeding to the analysis of variance, we'll use a .05 significance level. The first step in the analysis is computing the sum of the scores (T_j) in each experimental group as well as the sum of the squared scores ($\sum X^2$) for each. These values are shown in the table.

Begin the computations with the total sum of squares. Following the computational formula from Table 12.7,

$$SS_{Total} = \sum_j \sum_i X_{ij}^2 - \frac{GT^2}{na}$$

we can first calculate the grand total as

$$GT = \sum_j T_j = 85 + 103 + 113 = 301$$

Next, we sum the squared scores across all conditions and then subtract the squared grand total divided by the total number of observations. That is,

$$SS_{Total} = \sum_j \sum_i X_{ij}^2 - \frac{GT^2}{na}$$

$$= (817 + 1185 + 1437) - \frac{301^2}{9 * 3}$$

TABLE 12.7

Quantity	Definition	Computations
SS_{Total}	$\sum(X - GM)^2$	$\sum_j \sum_i X_{ij}^2 - \dfrac{GT^2}{na}$
$SS_{Between}$	$n\sum(\overline{X}_j - GM)^2$	$\dfrac{\sum_j T^2}{n} - \dfrac{GT^2}{na}$
SS_{Within}	$\sum(X - \overline{X}_j)^2$	$\sum_j \sum_i X_{ij}^2 - \dfrac{\sum_j T^2}{n}$

TABLE 12.8

	Introverts	Ambiverts	Extroverts
	10	12	15
	7	10	11
	11	11	14
	9	11	10
	8	11	12
	11	13	13
	10	12	13
	10	12	12
	9	11	13
Mean	9.44	11.44	12.56
Std. dev.	1.33	0.88	1.51
Sums (T_j)	85	103	113
Sum of squared values ($\sum X^2$)	817	1185	1437

$$= 3439 - 3355.59$$

$$= 83.41$$

For the sum of squares between groups, we have

$$SS_{Between} = \frac{\sum_j T^2}{n} - \frac{GT^2}{na}$$

$$= \frac{85^2 + 103^2 + 113^2}{9} - \frac{301^2}{9 * 3}$$

$$= 3400.33 - 3355.59$$

$$= 44.74$$

Finally, for the within-groups sum of squares,

$$SS_{\text{Within}} = \sum_j \sum_i X_{ij}^2 - \frac{\sum_j T^2}{n}$$

$$= (817 + 1185 + 1437) - \frac{85^2 + 103^2 + 113^2}{9}$$

$$= 3439 - 3400.33$$

$$= 38.67$$

As a computational check (always a good idea), make sure that the component sums of squares add up to the total sum of squares:

$$SS_{\text{Total}} = SS_{\text{Between}} + SS_{\text{Within}}$$

$$83.41 = 44.74 + 38.67$$

Following the formulas presented in the text, next find the degrees of freedom for each sum of squares as

$$df_{\text{Total}} = na - 1 = 9 * 3 - 1 = 26$$

$$df_{\text{Between}} = a - 1 = 3 - 1 = 2$$

$$df_{\text{Within}} = a(n - 1) = na - a = 9 * 3 - 3 = 24$$

A convenient way to keep your computations neat is to construct a summary table like that in Table 12.9.

Following the usual ANOVA custom, we have identified the sources of variation in the table with descriptive terms. The source of the between-groups sum of squares is the independent variable in the experiment (the degree of introversion/extroversion) and that for within groups is error. The sum of squares and the degrees of freedom are entered in the appropriate columns.

The variance estimates (the mean squares) are computed by dividing the SS_{Between} and SS_{Within} by their degrees of freedom, and the results are placed in the summary table. Note that the mean square for "Total" is not computed. Although we know that that value is the total variance of all subjects in all conditions, it is not a meaningful number in this analysis. The MS_{Total} does not

TABLE 12.9

Summary Table

Source	SS	df	MS	F
I/E group	44.74	2	22.37	13.89
Error	38.67	24	1.61	
Total	83.41	26		

equal the sum of the two mean squares above it, and so calculating it cannot serve as a computational check; the value is never reported in a summary table.

Finally, we calculate the F ratio as

$$F = \frac{MS_{Between}}{MS_{Within}}$$

$$= \frac{22.37}{1.61}$$

$$= 13.89$$

and the summary table is complete.

The next task is to determine whether the F value is large enough to make us reject the hypothesis that the three introversion/extroversion groups represent populations with equal means. With $\alpha = .05$, consult Appendix F with $df = 2$ for the numerator and $df = 24$ for the denominator. The tabled critical value is 3.40 if we picture the sampling distribution of F as shown in the figure. From the tabled value and the illustration, we can easily determine that there is a significant difference among the groups because the obtained F value of 13.89 greatly exceeds the critical value of 3.40.

Most computer programs eliminate the need for a table like Appendix F by providing an exact probability for the obtained F value. For our example, the program might give the probability value .0038. This means that, if the null hypothesis were actually true, then we would observe an F value this, or more, extreme, with a probability of .0038. Because .0038 is less than the chosen significance level, we reject the null hypothesis.

Our conclusion, whether we reach it by an exact probability or by consulting a table, is to reject the hypothesis that all conditions have the same population mean. By drawing that conclusion, we make the inference that at least one of the treatment effects is nonzero. That is, at least one of the three introversion/extroversion groups is different from the others.

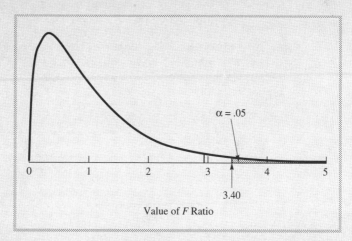

Figure 12.12

♦ Follow-up Tests

THE TUKEY TEST. The noted statistician John Tukey developed several techniques for conducting post hoc tests. The one we present here is sometimes called the *Tukey A* test, or sometimes the *Tukey honestly significant difference* (*HSD*) test. The test is widely used, and is appropriate for exploring differences in pairs of means after a significant overall F.

The Tukey procedure establishes a value for the smallest possible significant difference between two condition means; any mean difference greater than that amount is significant. The Tukey critical mean difference is calculated as

$$D = \frac{q(\alpha, \text{df}, a)\sqrt{\text{MS}_{\text{Within}}}}{\sqrt{n}}$$

where $q(\alpha, \text{df}, a)$ is a Studentized range value from Appendix J. Appendix J is entered using the number of degrees of freedom for within groups and the number of groups, a.

The Tukey test is usually carried out by constructing a matrix containing the differences between all pairs of means. We frequently construct this matrix by first writing the conditions as column headers, in order of increasing mean value. We next list the experimental conditions vertically at the left, and then enter the differences between the row and column means. For the complete example data, the means and differences appear in Table 12.10. The critical difference for the Tukey test is calculated as

$$D = \frac{q(\alpha, \text{df}, a)\sqrt{\text{MS}_{\text{Within}}}}{\sqrt{n}} = \frac{3.53\sqrt{1.61}}{\sqrt{9}} = 1.49$$

We next compare the mean differences to the critical value and write the significant differences in the matrix. In the example, two of the differences in pairs of means exceeds the Tukey critical value. We conclude therefore that, according to the Tukey test, there are significant differences between introverts and both the ambiverts and the extroverts.

THE DUNNETT C TEST. The Dunnett C test is a new addition to the set of follow-up tests, and is highly recommended for general use. It is particularly good when the populations seem to have unequal variances, and/or when the group sizes happen to be unequal.

TABLE 12.10			
	Introversion/Extroversion Group		
	Introvert	*Ambivert*	*Extrovert*
Mean	9.44	11.44	12.56
Ambivert	2.00		
Extrovert	3.12	1.12	

To calculate the critical value for the Dunnett C, we use the formula

$$D = 0.71 \left(q_{(\alpha, n-1, a)} \sqrt{\frac{s_i^2 + s_j^2}{n}} \right)$$

where q is taken from the Studentized range table in Appendix J, as with the Tukey test, and s_i^2 and s_j^2 are the variances of the two groups. Because each group has a different standard deviation, a different D must be calculated for each pair of mean differences. For the introverts compared with the ambiverts, for example, the value is

$$D = 0.71 \left(q_{(a, n-1, a)} \sqrt{\frac{s_i^2 + s_j^2}{n}} \right)$$

$$= 0.71 \left(4.04 \sqrt{\frac{1.33^2 + 0.88^2}{n}} \right)$$

$$= 1.52$$

using the standard deviations from Table 12.8. This value leads to the conclusion that these two groups differ, the same conclusion reached by the Tukey computations.

Following the same procedure, the critical difference for the ambiverts and the extroverts is 1.67, and that for comparing the introverts and the extroverts is 1.92. In this case, we come to exactly the same conclusion using the Dunnett C as we did with the Tukey.

THE SCHEFFÉ TEST. The Scheffé test, which is offered by nearly every computer program, is extremely conservative and is not recommended unless you want to guard in the most stringent way possible against making a Type I error. It is included here because it is one of the very few post hoc tests that can be expanded to deal with more complicated comparisons; we'll do that later.

The critical difference between means for the Scheffé is given by the formula

$$D = \sqrt{(a - 1)F} \sqrt{\frac{2MS_{\text{Error}}}{n}}$$

where F is the critical value of F that was used in the overall analysis and MS_{Error} is the within-groups mean square from the overall analysis.

For the example, we calculate the critical value as

$$D = \sqrt{(a - 1)F} \sqrt{\frac{2MS_{\text{Error}}}{n}}$$

$$= \sqrt{(3 - 1) * 3.40} \sqrt{\frac{2 * 1.61}{9}}$$

$$= 1.56.$$

Comparing the critical value to the differences in Table 12.10, we see that the difference between introverts and extroverts and that between introverts and ambiverts is significant according to the Scheffé test.

COMPLEX COMPARISONS[11]

We defined a comparison among condition means as

$$C = \sum c_j \overline{X}_j$$

and the sum of squares for a comparison as

$$SS_{A \text{ comparison}} = \frac{nC^2}{\sum c_j^2}$$

where C is the value of the comparison and the c's are the coefficients in the comparison equation. The value has 1 df and may be used to test the null hypothesis that the population value of the comparison,

$$\sum c_j \mu_j$$

is equal to zero.

Because the sum of squares has 1 df, its mean square is computed easily by dividing by the df:

$$MS_{A \text{ comparison}} = \frac{SS_{A \text{ comparison}}}{1}$$

The F ratio to test the hypothesis uses the MS_{Within} as the denominator:

$$F = \frac{MS_{A \text{ comparison}}}{MS_{\text{Within}}}$$

The ratio has df $= 1$, df_{Within}.

As an example of the computation, we use $\alpha = .05$ and ask if the mean of the extroverts is equal to the average of the means of the introverts and the ambiverts. That is, does

$$\frac{\mu_{\text{Introvert}} + \mu_{\text{Ambivert}}}{2} - \mu_{\text{Extrovert}} = 0.0$$

We can use coefficients 1, 1, and -2. Using the means from Table 12.8, we find that the comparison value is

$$\sum c_j \overline{X}_j = (1)9.44 + (1)11.44 - (2)12.56 = -4.24$$

We compute the sum of squares for the comparison as

---

[11] This section presents a somewhat advanced topic and may be omitted, depending on the instructor's wishes. In particular, this section describes how to test hypotheses defined by comparisons that may involve more than two experimental conditions.

$$SS_{A \text{ comparison}} = \frac{nC^2}{\sum c_j^2} = \frac{(9) * (-4.24)^2}{1^2 + 1^2 + (-2)^2} = 26.97$$

and its mean square as

$$MS_{A \text{ comparison}} = \frac{SS_{A \text{ comparison}}}{1} = \frac{26.97}{1} = 26.97$$

And finally, the F ratio for the comparison is

$$F = \frac{MS_{A \text{ comparison}}}{MS_{\text{Within}}}$$

$$= \frac{26.97}{1.61}$$

$$= 16.75$$

The critical F at $\alpha = .05$ with df = 1, 24 is 4.26, and the comparison is clearly significant. We conclude that there is a difference between the extroverts and the mean of the introverts and the ambiverts.

THE SCHEFFÉ TEST FOR COMPLEX COMPARISONS

In the Scheffé test, a comparison among means is defined and the F ratio computed as given in the preceding section. Then the critical value of F is calculated as

$$F_{\text{crit}} = (a - 1)F_{(df_{\text{Between}}, df_{\text{Within}})}$$

where $F_{(df_{\text{Between}}, df_{\text{Within}})}$ is the critical value used to establish the significance of the *overall* F ratio. In the example, to use the Scheffé instead of the ordinary F (that is, to guard against making a Type I error when doing follow-up tests), we use the F from before and compare it to the critical value calculated by the formula, giving

$$F_{\text{crit}} = (a - 1)F_{(df_{\text{Between}}, df_{\text{Within}})}$$

$$= (3 - 1) * 3.40 = 6.80$$

Because the F value calculated previously is 16.75, the comparison is significant. [But note the difference in the critical value. The ordinary F (with df = 1, 24) was 4.26, while the Scheffé method leads to a higher value of 6.80.]

◆ Unequal Group Sizes

Research in psychology normally begins with equal group sizes, but often ends with unequal sizes. Most often, subject loss is accidental—a subject forgets the appointment, the equipment fails, the experimenter makes a mistake, or an animal dies. Such subject loss, as long as it's not related to the manipulation of the independent variable, is of no serious consequence, but does add a computational complication. When subject loss affects the experimental conditions randomly and is unrelated to the independent variable, many investigators use an analysis of variance procedure known as the "unweighted means" computation. That computation makes only a slight adjustment to the computational formulas. The unweighted means procedure is falling into disfavor, however, as computers take over the computations. It provides a convenient way to simplify computations when the arithmetic is done by hand, but with computers, it is no longer necessary. Nevertheless, in this section, we present unweighted means, along with weighted means, procedures as two different ways to accommodate unequal group sizes. Either may be used, though in general we prefer the weighted means procedure. This latter can be easily done by a computer using a multiple regression program; we present that method in the next chapter.

Previously, we used n to indicate the number of subjects in each group; with unequal group sizes, we'll let n_j designate the number of scores in group j. This means that the total number of observations is $N = \sum n_j$, instead of na. The total number of degrees of freedom is the total number of subjects minus 1, as always, but we use the notation

$$\sum n_j - 1$$

We turn first to the weighted means analysis.

WEIGHTED MEANS ANALYSIS

The adjustment of the equal-group-size formulas to those for weighted means is simple. In the computational formula for the between-groups sum of squares, which was originally

$$SS_{\text{Between}} = \frac{\sum\limits_{j} T^2}{n} - \frac{GT^2}{na}$$

we divide by each group size *before* summing, and the formula for weighted means becomes

$$SS_{\text{Between}} = \sum_{j} \left(\frac{T_j^2}{n_j} \right) - \frac{GT^2}{\sum n_j}$$

There's another simple adjustment as well—wherever the quantity na appeared in the previous formulas, we substitute $\sum n_j$ because it now represents the total number of observations.

The formula for SS_{Within} originally was

$$SS_{\text{Within}} = \sum_{j} \sum_{i} X_{ij}^2 - \frac{\sum\limits_{j} T^2}{n}$$

Its adjusted version for weighted means is

$$SS_{\text{Within}} = \sum_{j} \sum_{i} X_{ij}^2 - \sum_{j} \left(\frac{T_j^2}{n_j} \right)$$

The SS_{Total} formula follows from the same adjustments:

$$SS_{Total} = \sum_j \sum_i X_{ij}^2 - \frac{GT^2}{\sum n_j}$$

As an example of the computations, consider three drug conditions and a placebo. The raw data and the first sums are shown in Table 12.11. Beginning the analysis, we have

$$GT = 36 + 64 + 63 + 70 = 233$$

and so

$$SS_{Between} = \sum_j \left(\frac{T_j^2}{n_j} \right) - \frac{GT^2}{\sum n_j}$$

$$= \frac{36^2}{5} + \frac{64^2}{6} + \frac{63^2}{5} + \frac{70^2}{7} - \frac{233^2}{5 + 6 + 5 + 7}$$

$$= 2435.67 - 2360.39$$

$$= 75.28$$

For the within-groups sum of squares, the value is

$$SS_{Within} = \sum_j \sum_i X_{ij}^2 - \sum_j \left(\frac{T_j^2}{n_j} \right)$$

$$= 298 + 706 + 823 + 788 - \frac{36^2}{5} + \frac{64^2}{6} + \frac{63^2}{5} + \frac{70^2}{7}$$

$$= 2615 - 2435.67$$

$$= 179.33$$

TABLE 12.11

		Drug Condition		
	A	B	C	Placebo
	5	13	15	10
	11	12	11	5
	10	8	10	9
	6	8	16	6
	4	12	11	13
		11		11
				16
$\overline{X}_j$	7.20	10.67	12.60	10.00
Std. dev.	3.11	2.16	2.70	3.83
n_j	5	6	5	7
T_j	36	64	63	70
$\sum X^2$	298	706	823	788

Finally, the total sum of squares is

$$SS_{Total} = \sum_j \sum_i X_{ij}^2 - \frac{GT^2}{\sum n_j}$$

$$= 298 + 706 + 823 + 788 - \frac{233^2}{5 + 6 + 5 + 7}$$

$$= 2615 - 2360.39$$

$$= 254.61$$

The degrees of freedom are calculated using the same logic as previously. For $df_{Between}$, the value is one less than the number of groups of scores summed; that is, $a - 1$. For the example, $df_{Between} = 4 - 1 = 3$. The df_{Within} follows the same rule as well: There are $n_j - 1$ degrees of freedom for each group, or $df_{Within} = \sum n_j - a$. For the example, the value is $5 + 6 + 5 + 7 - 4 = 19$.

The summary table for the analysis is completed as in Table 12.12. With $df = 3, 19$ and with $\alpha = .05$, the critical F from Appendix F is 3.13 and thus we do not reject the null hypothesis that the four drug conditions have identical means.

UNWEIGHTED MEANS ANALYSIS

When unequal sample sizes result randomly, then we can apply unweighted means analysis, a commonly used procedure until computers made it unnecessary. In the unweighted means procedure, a simple adjustment is made to the group totals T_j, and the analysis continues as if it were an equal-size procedure. The modification to the group sums consists of multiplying each group mean by the harmonic mean of the group sizes to give a value that we'll symbolize T_j^*. In symbols,

$$T_j^* = \overline{X}_j * \tilde{n}$$

where the harmonic mean of the group sizes is defined as

$$\tilde{n} = \frac{a}{\sum_j \frac{1}{n_j}}$$

With these definitions done, the between-groups sum of squares is com-

TABLE 12.12

Source	SS	df	MS	F
Drugs	75.28	3	25.09	2.66
Error	179.33	19	9.44	
Total	254.61	22		

puted with the formula

$$SS_{Between} = \frac{\sum_j T_j^{*2}}{\tilde{n}} - \frac{\left(\sum_j T_j^*\right)^2}{\tilde{n}a}$$

which is the original formula, modified to use T_j^* instead of the actual group sums T_j.

The sum of squares for within groups is computed as it was in the weighted means calculation—namely,

$$SS_{Within} = \sum_j \sum_i X_{ij}^2 - \sum_j \left[\frac{T_j^2}{n_j}\right]$$

Note that this formula uses the *actual* group total and size.

As an example of the computations for unweighted means, we'll use the same data as we used for the weighted means in Table 12.11. First, we calculate the harmonic mean of the group sizes:

$$\tilde{n} = \frac{a}{\sum_j \frac{1}{n_j}}$$

$$= \frac{4}{\frac{1}{5} + \frac{1}{6} + \frac{1}{5} + \frac{1}{7}}$$

$$= 5.64$$

Continuing, we calculate the modified group sums T_j^*:

$$T_j^* = \overline{X}_j * \tilde{n}$$
$$T_1^* = \overline{X}_1 * \tilde{n} = 7.20 * 5.64 = 40.61$$
$$T_2^* = \overline{X}_2 * \tilde{n} = 10.67 * 5.64 = 60.18$$
$$T_3^* = \overline{X}_3 * \tilde{n} = 12.60 * 5.64 = 71.06$$
$$T_4^* = \overline{X}_4 * \tilde{n} = 10.00 * 5.64 = 56.40$$

Now we can use the formula for the between-groups sum of squares:

$$SS_{Between} = \frac{\sum_j T_j^{*2}}{\tilde{n}} - \frac{\left(\sum_j T_j^*\right)^2}{\tilde{n}a}$$

$$= \frac{40.61^2 + 60.18^2 + 71.06^2 + 56.40^2}{5.64}$$

$$- \frac{(40.61 + 60.18 + 71.06 + 56.40)^2}{5.64 * 4}$$

$$= \frac{13501.29}{5.64} - \frac{228.25^2}{22.56}$$

$$= 2393.84 - 2309.31$$

$$= 84.53$$

SS_{Within} can be calculated, as before, as

$$SS_{Within} = \sum_j \sum_i X_{ij}^2 - \sum_j \left(\frac{T_j^2}{n_j} \right)$$

$$= 298 + 706 + 823 + 788 - \frac{36^2}{5} + \frac{64^2}{6} + \frac{63^2}{5} + \frac{70^2}{7}$$

$$= 2615 - 2435.67$$

$$= 179.33$$

The degrees of freedom for $SS_{Between}$ are, as expected, $a - 1$. For SS_{Within}, the df are $\sum n_j - a$. The summary table is given in Table 12.13. In these computations, the sums of squares for between and within do not sum to SS_{Total} and are not computed or shown in the summary table.

Consulting Appendix F, we find that the critical value of F at .05 is 3.13. (Because the df were the same as in the weighted means analysis, the critical value is the same as well.) And again we do not reject the hypothesis that the drug conditions differ.

◆ The Kruskal–Wallis Test for Independent Groups

The Kruskal–Wallis test is a distribution-free alternative to the between-groups analysis of variance. It is computed by ranking all the data in all the conditions, keeping track of group membership. (This process is identical to that for the Wilcoxon two-sample test from Chapter 10.) Then a sum of the ranks is calculated for each experimental condition, and the sums are entered into the test statistic:

$$H = \frac{12}{N(N + 1)} \sum \frac{R_j^2}{n_j} - 3(N + 1)$$

where R_j is the sum of the ranks in a group, n_j is the group size, and N is the total number of observations in all groups. The null hypothesis tested by the

TABLE 12.13				
Source	SS	df	MS	F
Drugs	84.53	3	28.18	2.98
Error	179.33	19	9.44	

Kruskal–Wallis test is that the population distributions represented by the groups sampled are identical. The test is especially sensitive to differences in center, and so it is appropriate as a parallel to the analysis of variance.

As an example, suppose subjects are asked to solve ten arithmetic problems under one of three different conditions: quiet room, rock music, and "elevator" music. The data, in terms of the number of problems solved within a 5-min test period, might be those illustrated in Table 12.14. Box plots (see the figure) of the

TABLE 12.14		
Rock	Quiet	"Elevator"
5	6	3
5	5	4
7	4	4
6	6	4
3	6	2
5	8	3
7	7	4
7	7	2
1	5	
2	6	
2		
3		

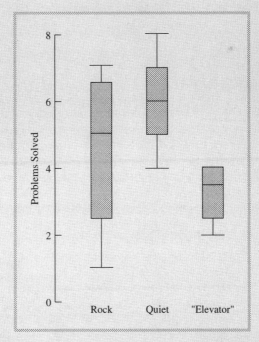

Figure 12.13

groups show differences in variability as well as in center, and so the Kruskal–Wallis test seems appropriate for the overall analysis.

The analysis begins by combining all the data and assigning ranks to each value; the scores and the ranks assigned to them are in Table 12.15. The data are next summarized by groups and the sums of ranks are calculated, as illustrated in Table 12.16. Entering the sums of the ranks and the group sizes, we compute the Kruskal–Wallis statistic as

$$H = \frac{12}{N(N+1)} \sum \frac{R_j^2}{n_j} - 3(N+1)$$

$$= \frac{12}{30(30+1)} \left(\frac{177^2}{12} + \frac{218^2}{10} + \frac{70^2}{8} \right) - 3(30+1)$$

TABLE 12.15

Rank	Problems Solved	Music Group
1	1	Rock
3.5	2	"Elevator"
3.5	2	"Elevator"
3.5	2	Rock
3.5	2	Rock
7.5	3	"Elevator"
7.5	3	"Elevator"
7.5	3	Rock
7.5	3	Rock
12	4	"Elevator"
12	4	"Elevator"
12	4	"Elevator"
12	4	"Elevator"
12	4	Quiet
17	5	Quiet
17	5	Quiet
17	5	Rock
17	5	Rock
17	5	Rock
22	6	Quiet
22	6	Quiet
22	6	Quiet
22	6	Quiet
22	6	Rock
27	7	Quiet
27	7	Quiet
27	7	Rock
27	7	Rock
27	7	Rock
30	8	Quiet

TABLE 12.16

	Rock		Quiet		"Elevator"	
	Score	Rank	Score	Rank	Score	Rank
	5	17	6	22	3	7.5
	5	17	5	17	4	12
	7	27	4	12	4	12
	6	22	6	22	4	12
	3	7.5	6	22	2	3.5
	5	17	8	30	3	7.5
	7	27	7	27	4	12
	7	27	7	27	2	3.5
	1	1	5	17		
	2	3.5	6	22		
	2	3.5				
	3	7.5				
Sum of ranks		177.0		218		70.0

$$= 0.0129(7975.65) - 93$$

$$= 9.89$$

The Kruskal–Wallis H value is distributed as χ^2 with df $= a - 1$. From Appendix D, we find that the critical value for df $= 3 - 1 = 2$ at the .05 significance level is 5.99; we thus reject the null hypothesis that the population distributions represented by the three experimental groups are identical.

A follow-up procedure for comparing any pair of experimental groups is given by Siegel and Castellan (1988, pp. 213–215).

Multiple Regression and Correlation

Much research in psychology is conducted using the classic model of an experiment and the analysis of variance. Analysis of variance, though, is far from being the sole statistical approach in common use. In this chapter, we develop an important alternative—multiple regression, an extension of the bivariate descriptive methods discussed in Chapter 6. Actually, this chapter demonstrates that the two techniques are fundamentally identical, though they have different histories, superficially different computations, and typically are used to address different kinds of research questions.

 The analysis of variance is most commonly employed in experimental situations where independent variables are manipulated, extraneous variables controlled, and causal inferences made. In short, the questions addressed by analysis of variance are: "If I change the level of background noise, is there a change in performance?" or "Is there a difference in sensation seeking among the groups defined on the basis of introversion/extroversion?" or "Does the spacing of phrases in a paragraph lead to differences in retention?"

Multiple regression, conversely, is widely applied outside the laboratory, where variables are not controlled and manipulated, but simply measured. The questions asked by multiple regression concern the relationships among variables and the ability to predict values on a variable from the relationships. Typical questions for multiple regression include: "What are the predicted scores for academic achievement, given that I have scores on IQ, reading, and mathematics aptitude tests?" or "Given that I have scores on several aptitude and academic achievement tests, what's my best prediction of how this job applicant will actually perform on the job?" or even further, "Which variables are the best to use if I want to predict on-the-job performance?" or "If I have scores on a battery of personality scales, can I predict an individual's anxiety level when embarking on a risky activity?"

ELEMENTS OF MULTIPLE REGRESSION

Chapter 6 developed the logic for predicting one variable from another by using a linear equation to model the relationship between the two variables. The equation that defined the line was then used for making predictions about one variable. For example, the linear relationship in the scatterplot in Figure 13.1 has the equation

$$\hat{Y} = 0.68X + 0.99$$

Chapter 6 presented the formulas for the slope (0.68) and the intercept (0.99). Those two values define the line that fits the data best in terms of minimizing the squared differences between actual Y and the predicted ($\hat{Y}$) values. Specifically, they are formulas for the slope and the intercept defined so that they minimize the quantity $\sum(Y - \hat{Y})^2$. The resulting line comes as close to the Y values as possible in terms of minimizing the squared errors of prediction.

Suppose that, instead of a single X variable, we had two of them, but still with a single Y variable. Now we have **multiple regression**, instead of **bivariate regression**. In multiple regression there is one Y (*criterion*, or *dependent*) variable but multiple X (*predictor*, or *independent*) variables.[1] The

---

[1] Note the use of the terms *independent variable* and *dependent variable* in a different sense than before. In regression, the variable to be predicted (Y) is often called the *dependent variable* (or sometimes the criterion variable), while the variables that do the predicting (X variables) are called *predictors* or *independent variables*.

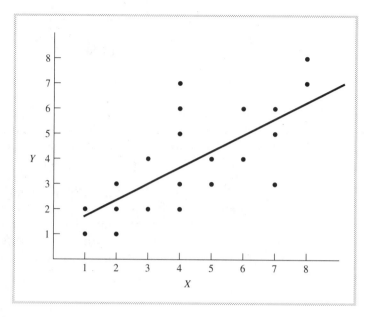

Figure 13.1

predictor variables, the variables whose values are used for prediction, are normally called X_1, X_2, and so forth. In any given situation, of course, Y and the Xs will have more descriptive names (e.g., final exam score, Quiz 1, Quiz 2, midterm exam, etc.)

Suppose an instructor gives a 10-point quiz, a 40-point exam, and a 50-point final. For two students, the grades might look something like

	QUIZ	EXAM	FINAL
John	7	25	71
Sue	6	16	7
⋮			

We can represent a relationship among three variables, quiz, exam, and final (or, more generally, Y, X_1, and X_2), in a three-dimensional plot, such as that illustrated in Figure 13.2. In the illustration, the points are in a three-dimensional space defined by two X variables (quiz and exam) and a single Y (the final exam). As with two dimensions, each point represents a score of a single subject. For example, John's scores are $X_1 = 7$, $X_2 = 25$, and $Y = 71$, and are shown in the figure.

In two dimensions, the model of the relationship between two variables was the line. If we were to model this relationship in three dimensions, the natural extension of the line into two dimensions is a plane, so a best-fitting plane might be as pictured in Figure 13.3. The equation for this particular plane is

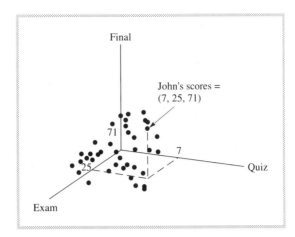

Figure 13.2

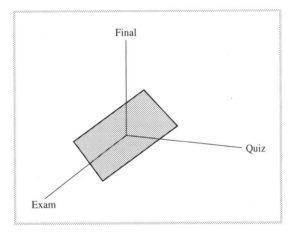

Figure 13.3

$$\widehat{\text{Final}} = 3.53 \text{ Quiz} + 1.71 \text{ Exam} - 12.08$$

In the equation, there are two "slopes" (one for each of the two predictor variables) and an intercept. The equation is linear, but in three dimensions. For any pair of X values (quiz and exam scores), the equation gives the *predicted value* on the Y (final) axis. For example, for John's scores of 7 and 25, the $\hat{Y}$ (or predicted final) is computed as

$$\begin{aligned}
\widehat{\text{Final}} &= 3.53 \text{ Quiz} + 1.71 \text{ Exam} - 12.08 \\
&= 3.53 * 7 + 1.71 * 25 - 12.08 \\
&= 55.38
\end{aligned}$$

There's no reason, other than computational difficulty (and that can be considerable), why we need to limit ourselves to only two Xs and one Y. In principle, there can be any number of X variables combined to predict a single Y. We cannot easily draw a picture of a space greater than three dimensions, of course, but we can conceive of it. And the appropriate mathematics provide both a representation and a way to carry out the computations.

The mathematics of fitting a multidimensional plane so that it minimizes $\sum(Y - \hat{Y})^2$ is difficult, and the computations are cumbersome and tedious. But if there's a computer nearby to do the arithmetic, there is little problem. (And, in fact, no one ever does a multiple regression "by hand" anymore.) Nearly every statistical program can compute the regression coefficients (slopes) and the constant (the intercept). Here we omit both the computational formulas (they're best expressed using matrix algebra) and the computations themselves. Instead, we look only at some defining formulas and typical program output.

The general form of the linear equation for predicting Y from any number of Xs is

$$\hat{Y} = b_1 X_1 + b_2 X_2 + \cdots + b_k X_k + a$$

where k is the number of X (predictor) variables. Note that the form of the equation is similar to the one-X version, but now each X has its own b, or slope. The equation describes a plane in $k + 1$–dimensional space, just as the simple equation

$$\hat{Y} = bX + a$$

describes a line in two-dimensional space. In multiple regression, each variable (X) has a separate slope, and the intercept has the same interpretation it does in the simplest model. The slope for each variable has the same meaning as in the bivariate equation: It defines the increase in Y per unit increase in X. In the example, X_1 (the quiz) has a slope of 3.53, indicating that for every increase of 1.0 in quiz score, Y increases by 3.53. The slope for X_2 (the exam) is 1.71, meaning that a unit increase in exam score will increase Y by 1.71.[2] As in simple regression, the slope coefficients are normally called **regression coefficients**; the intercept may be called a *constant* in some computer programs.

◆ An Example

As a simple example, let's expand on the class records illustration. Suppose that during the term an instructor records grades on two exams, two pro-

---

[2] These two sentences represent a considerable simplification. They are true *only* if there is no correlation between the quiz and the exam, which, of course, is not likely to be true. That is, if the quiz score increased by 1, *and there was no associated change in exam*, then Y would increase by 3.53. But because quiz and exam are probably correlated, a change in quiz will be associated with a change in *both* exam *and* Y; consequently, the impact of a unit change in quiz will not have exactly a 3.53 impact on Y.

jects, and a score based on all laboratory exercises. At the end of the term, the instructor assigns a final grade based on a combination of the recorded grades.

The grades for the 26 students in the most recent class appear in Table 13.1. (For simplicity, assume that the letter grades are recorded by their numerical values: $A = 4.0$, $A- = 3.7$, $B+ = 3.3$, $B = 3.0$, ..., $D- = 0.7$, $F = 0.0$). The relationships among the grades may be summarized by the Pearson product-moment intercorrelation matrix in Table 13.2. Each entry in the table gives the product-moment correlation between the row and the column variables. For example, the correlation between the two exams is 0.677, while that between the final grade and lab exercise total is 0.194. Note also that the correlation of each variable with itself (1.00, of course) is given on the diagonal of the matrix of coefficients.

TABLE 13.1						
Student	Exam 1	Exam 2	Lab Total	Project 1	Project 2	Final Grade
Amy C.	2.3	3.0	3.7	2.0	2.0	2.3
Barbara L.	1.7	2.0	3.7	3.0	3.3	2.7
Carol V.	4.0	3.7	3.0	3.3	3.0	3.7
Caroline V.	4.0	3.7	3.0	2.3	1.3	3.0
Cheryl L.	2.0	2.7	2.3	2.3	2.0	2.3
Chuck L.	4.0	3.0	3.3	2.7	2.3	3.0
Dan B.	4.0	3.0	2.0	2.7	2.3	3.0
Dave P.	3.0	2.7	2.0	3.3	3.3	3.0
Dick S.	3.3	3.3	4.0	3.7	3.7	3.3
Don J.	3.7	3.3	3.7	2.3	1.3	2.7
Fred G.	3.7	3.0	3.3	3.0	2.0	3.0
Gary P.	3.0	2.7	3.7	3.3	2.3	3.0
Jean B.	2.0	2.0	1.3	2.0	2.7	2.0
Jennifer K.	3.0	2.7	2.3	3.0	2.0	2.7
John M.	4.0	3.3	3.0	3.7	3.3	3.7
Kathy S.	3.3	3.3	4.0	3.3	3.3	3.3
Lisa M.	2.7	3.7	2.3	3.0	3.7	3.0
Mary Anne J.	3.3	2.7	3.0	3.0	4.0	3.3
Mike S.	4.0	3.0	2.0	3.7	2.3	3.0
Phyllis A.	1.7	2.7	4.0	3.0	2.7	2.7
Roger B.	3.3	3.0	3.7	3.3	3.0	3.3
Sandy E.	3.7	3.3	3.3	4.0	3.3	3.7
Sherri G.	4.0	3.0	2.7	3.3	3.7	3.3
Susan R.	2.7	3.0	4.0	3.0	4.0	3.3
Tammy A.	1.7	2.0	3.7	2.0	2.0	2.0
Tony S.	3.0	3.3	3.3.	2.3	1.3	2.7
Mean	3.12	2.96	3.09	2.94	2.70	2.96
Standard Dev.	0.80	0.47	0.76	0.57	0.83	0.46

TABLE 13.2

	Exam 1	Exam 2	Lab	Project 1	Project 2	Grade
Exam 1	1.000					
Exam 2	0.677	1.000				
Lab	−0.121	0.122	1.000			
Project 1	0.453	0.313	0.098	1.000		
Project 2	−0.009	−0.000	0.057	0.611	1.000	
Grade	0.710	0.637	0.194	0.823	0.542	1.000

OVERALL ANALYSIS

If we submit the raw data to a computer program for multiple regression, and identify the final grade as the variable whose value is to be predicted, we might receive something similar to the output in Table 13.3.[3] A great deal of information is presented in the table, and we consider it in detail as we develop the logic and use of multiple regression.

The regression results in Table 13.3 are in three groups: a table of values for each predictor variable at the top, an ANOVA summary table at the bottom, and two lines dealing with the multiple R statistic in the middle. The first two columns of the top section give the slopes and the intercept (labeled as the coefficient for the constant) for the variables in the multiple regression equation. Using those values, we write the prediction equation as

$$\hat{Y} = 0.24743 * \text{Exam 1} + 0.21606 * \text{Exam 2} + 0.10149 * \text{Labs}$$
$$+ 0.28263 * \text{Project 1} + 0.18174 * \text{Project 2} - 0.08598$$

To find the predicted value for any student, we need only substitute the values for each variable into the equation. For example, to predict Amy C.'s final grade, we use her scores from the original data, and complete the computation as

$$\hat{Y} = 0.24743 * 2.3 + 0.21606 * 3.0 + 0.10149 * 3.7$$
$$\overset{\uparrow}{\text{Exam 1}} \qquad \overset{\uparrow}{\text{Exam 2}} \qquad \overset{\uparrow}{\text{Labs}}$$
$$+ 0.28263 * 2.0 + 0.18174 * 2.0 - 0.08598$$
$$\overset{\uparrow}{\text{Project 1}} \qquad \overset{\uparrow}{\text{Project 2}}$$
$$= 2.436$$

Because Amy's actual final grade was 2.3, the formula overestimated the

---

[3] This particular output was created by Minitab, a widely available statistics program. Although your computer may not format its output exactly this way, you should be able to find nearly everything discussed here in your own output.

TABLE 13.3

Variable	Coefficient	St. Dev.	t-ratio
Exam 1	0.24743	0.05289	4.68
Exam 2	0.21606	0.07910	2.73
Labs	0.10149	0.03684	2.76
Project 1	0.28263	0.07300	3.87
Project 2	0.18174	0.04376	4.15
Constant	−0.08598		

Multiple R = 0.967   s = 0.1313
Multiple R squared = 93.6%   Adjusted R-square = 92.0%

Analysis of Variance

Source	df	SS	MS	F
Regression	5	5.0568	1.0114	58.67
Error	20	0.3447	0.0172	
Total	25	5.4015		

grade by 0.136. This overestimate is the quantity $Y - \hat{Y}$, and is the difference between the actual Y score and that predicted by the linear model. From Chapter 6 you should recall that this difference is known as a residual and is a measure of the error in prediction.

◆ Predicted and Residual Values

With the computer, obtaining the **predicted values** and the **residual values** for each subject is simple because many programs offer a regression operation option . The actual final grades (which, for simplicity, we'll call Y here), the predicted final grades, and the residuals corresponding to the values in Table 13.1 appear in Table 13.4.

SUBDIVIDING THE VARIANCE[4]

In this section, we show that the difference between a score and the mean $(Y - \bar{Y})$ can be expressed as a sum of two things: the difference between the score and its predicted value, and the difference between the predicted value and the score. We touched on this concept in Chapter 6, but the presentation here is more detailed because this subdivision is important for several purposes in this chapter. As you read, note how closely this development parallels the exposition of the components of variability in Chapter 12.

---

[4] This section presents more advanced material that the instructor may choose to omit.

TABLE 13.4

Student	Actual Total (Y)	Predicted Total ($\hat{Y}$)	Residual ($Y - \hat{Y}$)
Amy C.	2.3	2.436	−0.136
Barbara L.	2.7	2.590	0.110
Carol V.	3.7	3.486	0.214
Caroline V.	3.0	2.894	0.106
Cheryl L.	2.3	2.239	0.061
Chuck L.	3.0	3.068	−0.068
Dan B.	3.0	2.936	0.064
Dave P.	3.0	2.975	0.025
Dick S.	3.3	3.568	−0.268
Don J.	2.7	2.804	−0.104
Fred G.	3.0	3.024	−0.024
Gary P.	3.0	2.966	0.034
Jean B.	2.0	2.029	−0.029
Jennifer K.	2.7	2.684	0.016
John M.	3.7	3.567	0.133
Kathy S.	3.3	3.382	−0.082
Lisa M.	3.0	3.135	−0.135
Mary Anne J.	3.3	3.193	0.107
Mike S.	3.0	3.219	−0.219
Phyllis A.	2.7	2.662	0.037
Roger B.	3.3	3.232	0.068
Sandy E.	3.7	3.608	0.092
Sherri G.	3.3	3.431	−0.131
Susan R.	3.3	3.211	0.089
Tammy A.	2.0	2.071	−0.071
Tony S.	2.7	2.590	0.109
Mean	2.96		

Chapter 12 began with a consideration of the variability of a variable around its mean as measured by the variance:

$$s^2 = \frac{\sum (X - \overline{X})^2}{N - 1}$$

In presenting the analysis of variance, we illustrated how this overall variability could be partitioned into two segments: one representing differences between scores and their group means, and the other differences between group means and the overall mean. Similarly, in this section, we show how it's possible to subdivide the variability around the mean differently, but again into two segments. In this case, one segment will measure error in prediction and the other will measure the "improvement" in prediction achieved by using regression to predict values. But it will be the *same* variability as before—just divided up differently.

In Chapter 6, and again above, we defined a residual or error in prediction as $(Y - \hat{Y})$, the difference between a score (Y) and the value predicted by the linear model $(\hat{Y})$. Squaring and summing that value over all the subjects in the data can lead to a measure similar to variance:

$$s^2_{\text{Error}} = \frac{\sum (Y - \hat{Y})^2}{N - 2}$$

This formula expresses a "variance" of a different kind. It represents variance around the *regression line* rather than around the arithmetic mean of the data. The numerator of the formula represents the sum of the squared residuals—the differences between the actual Y values and those predicted by the linear model; it is called the **sum of squares for error** (SS_{Error}). The denominator represents the number of degrees of freedom associated with the error sum of squares, and again we have the expression

$$s^2_{\text{Error}} = \frac{\sum (Y - \hat{Y})^2}{N - 2} = \frac{SS_{\text{Error}}}{df_{\text{Error}}}$$

as in Chapter 6, where this quantity was first introduced. This "variance" around the regression plane extends to the multivariate case—the $(Y - \hat{Y})$ values continue to represent "error" because they are deviations from a plane defined by the linear equation. And, of course, the squared and summed deviations are still a sum of squares.

However, we do need to make a slight change in the degrees of freedom to make the formula applicable to the multivariate case. The full formula is

$$df_{\text{Error}} = N - k - 1$$

where k is the number of predictor (X) variables. Note that this formula applies in the bivariate case where there is but a single predictor variable too, giving

$$df_{\text{Error}} = N - k - 1$$
$$= N - 1 - 1$$
$$= N - 2$$

illustrating that the $N - 2$ value in Chapter 6 was a special case of the more general formula.

The sum of squares for error appears, with its degrees of freedom, in the analysis of variance summary table that is often a part of the output of a multiple regression program: The value is 0.3447 in Table 13.3.

The square root of that variance,

$$s_{\text{Est}} = \sqrt{s^2(\text{Error})} = \sqrt{\frac{SS_{\text{Error}}}{df_{\text{Error}}}}$$

STUDENT	ACTUAL TOTAL (Y)	PREDICTED TOTAL $(\hat{Y})$	RESIDUAL $(Y - \hat{Y})$	$(Y - \bar{Y})$	$(\hat{Y} - \bar{Y})$
Amy C.	2.3	2.436	−0.136		
Barbara L.	2.7	2.590	0.110		
Carol V.	**3.7**	**3.486**	**0.214**	**0.740**	**0.526**
Caroline V.	3.0	2.894	0.106		

Figure 13.4

is the **standard error of estimate**. For the example data,

$$s_{est} = \sqrt{\frac{SS_{Error}}{df_{Error}}}$$

$$= \sqrt{\frac{0.3447}{20}}$$

$$= \sqrt{0.0172}$$

$$= 0.1313$$

This value, likewise, appears in the output (Table 13.3), where it is labeled s.

Chapter 6 presented an example of subdividing the difference between a score and the mean into two segments (see Figure 6.11). Following the same format, Figure 13.4 presents a similar illustration, this time showing the first several students listed in Table 13.4, with Carol V. highlighted. Look first at the quantity $(Y - \bar{Y})$, which for Carol is 0.740. This quantity indicates how far Carol's score is from the mean of all the students. When squared and combined with similar quantities from all the other students, the result is the total **sum of squares for** Y, $\sum(Y - \bar{Y})^2 = SS_Y$, a measure of the variation in the variable. Dividing by $N - 1$ gives the overall variance:

$$s_Y^2 = \frac{\sum(Y - \bar{Y})^2}{N - 1} = \frac{SS_Y}{df_Y}$$

Suppose you're asked to predict a student's Y score. One way to make an "educated guess" would be to use the arithmetic mean of all the Y scores as your prediction. As pointed out in Chapter 6, the arithmetic mean is in the center of the data according to a least-squares criterion.[5] As such, it represents the "best guess" you can make about an unknown value. In this context, $(Y - \bar{Y})$ indicates how far each "prediction" (the mean) misses the mark (the actual score). For Carol's data in Figure 13.4, the actual score is

[5] Chapter 3 indicated that $\sum(X - \bar{X})^2$ equals a minimum, meaning that any value other than the arithmetic mean will produce a larger sum of squares. This, in turn, means that the mean is in the center of the data by that criterion.

3.7. Because the mean $\overline{Y}$ is 2.96, the amount by which the mean misses her actual score is the difference $(Y - \overline{Y}) = 3.7 - 2.96 = 0.74$.

If you have some knowledge about Y's relationship to other variables, you may be able to construct a regression model as an alternative way to predict a score. In Chapter 6, we constructed a two-variable model by using least-squares logic, such as defining the mean as the center. For regression, though, the model is one that minimizes the squared residuals.[6] In the regression context, the residual $(Y - \hat{Y})$ shows how far the regression-predicted value $(\hat{Y})$ misses the actual (Y) value. For Carol, the value is $(Y - \hat{Y}) = 3.7 - 3.486 = 0.214$. Because using the mean as an estimate produced an error of 0.74, Carol's regression-predicted value is closer to the actual score.

How much closer to Carol's actual score was $\hat{Y}$ as compared with $\overline{Y}$? If we subtract the two "errors" in prediction, the difference is $0.74 - 0.214 = 0.526$. By predicting Carol's score using the regression formula, we came 0.526 closer to her true value than if we had used the arithmetic mean. This value, appearing in the last column of Figure 13.4, represents the "improvement" in prediction achieved by using the regression model. The column is headed $(\hat{Y} - \overline{Y})$ because

$$(\hat{Y} - \overline{Y}) = (Y - \overline{Y}) - (Y - \hat{Y})$$

The final result of all this is to obtain the final expression for the breakdown of the difference between a score and the mean into the sum of two components. One component is the measure of "improvement" just obtained, $(\hat{Y} - \overline{Y})$, and the other is the error remaining—namely, $(Y - \hat{Y})$. In symbols,

$$(Y - \overline{Y}) = (\hat{Y} - \overline{Y}) + (Y - \hat{Y})$$

This expression provides the basis for developing three separate sums of squares. To develop these, we remember that $(Y - \overline{Y})$ provides the basis for the total sum of squares—$\sum(Y - \overline{Y})^2$. Substituting the above expression into the definition of the total sum of squares, and skipping the algebra, we obtain the expression

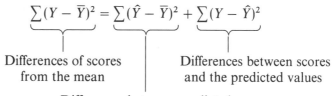

$$\sum(Y - \overline{Y})^2 = \sum(\hat{Y} - \overline{Y})^2 + \sum(Y - \hat{Y})^2$$

Differences of scores   Differences between scores
from the mean   and the predicted values

Differences between predicted
scores and the mean

which was defined earlier as

[6] That is, where $\sum(Y - \hat{Y})^2 = A$ minimum.

$$SS_Y = SS_{Regression} + SS_{Error}$$

These sums of squares indicate a partition of Y's total variability $[\sum(Y - \bar{Y})^2 = SS_{Total}]$ into two segments. The error part $[\sum(Y - \hat{Y})^2 = SS_Y]$ is a measure of how far the linear model is from the actual data. The other quantity $[\sum(\hat{Y} - \bar{Y})^2 = SS_{Regression}]$ measures the differences between the predicted values and the mean of the Y values. This represents an "improvement" in prediction as compared to using the arithmetic mean to predict Y. In effect, the **sum of squares for regression** ($SS_{Regression}$) is a measure of how "good" the regression is, because a large value means that the model predicted a score far away from the mean (and thus probably closer to the actual value).

The lower part of Table 13.3 gives the three sums of squares for the example class data; virtually every computer program presents this information, and in virtually the same way. Note that this presentation parallels exactly the way that ANOVA results are normally presented (see Table 12.9).

The F ratio in Table 13.3 (**F ratio for regression**) allows a test of the hypothesis that the regression is "significant." We might place several meanings on that test for "significance"; for now, we just conclude that the F informs us that we can do a significantly better job of predicting by using the regression model than we could if we predicted by using only $\bar{Y}$. That is, the "improvement" over predicting using the mean is significantly greater than zero.

MULTIPLE CORRELATION

The earlier presentation of regression in Chapter 6 also introduced the ratio of two parts of the variability in Y—namely,

$$\frac{SS_{Regression}}{SS_Y}$$

As before, this ratio represents the proportion of the total variation in Y that can be accounted for by the regression. For the example, we have

$$\frac{5.0568}{5.4015} = 0.9362$$

meaning that 0.9362 of the variation in Y, the final scores in the class, can be predicted by knowledge of the predictor variables. This same value, expressed as a percentage, appears in the computer results as well, labeled "Multiple R squared"; see Table 13.3. From Chapter 6 you may recall that this proportion of the variation in the Y variable that can be accounted for by the regression is also the square of the Pearson product-moment correlation coefficient, r. This relationship holds in multiple regression as well, so the value 0.9362 is the square of a correlation coefficient. In fact, it's a *multiple* correlation.

A **multiple correlation** is the correlation between Y and *the entire set of X variables*. The actual correlation is the value that appears just above the "R squared" entry in Table 13.3. It's labeled, appropriately, "Multiple R." But how can you correlate one variable with many? To answer that, suppose we compute the Pearson product-moment correlation coefficient between the *predicted* and the *actual* scores. That correlation (the value for the example is $r = 0.967$) gives the linear relationship between the actual Y scores and the values predicted by the best-fitting linear combination of the X values. Because that predicted value is the best possible linear function relating the Xs, it "captures" all the information about the relationships between the Xs. Thus the correlation is between the Y variable and a function that combines all the information in the set of X variables. This correlation between a single variable and a function of a set of other variables, then, *is* the multiple correlation. It is normally given the symbol R, and its value is reported by multiple regression programs, usually along with its square. The square is actually the more useful value because it gives the proportion of Y's variability "explained" by the relationship with the Xs.

The multiple R is a sample statistic and describes the relationships among the variables in the data. Like some other descriptive statistics, it is biased as an estimator for its corresponding population value. For that reason, many statistics programs also report an **adjusted R** or an "Adjusted R^2." Such a statistic serves as an unbiased estimate of the population multiple correlation.

As one final point, the F ratio in the ANOVA summary table can be used as a test of the null hypothesis that the population multiple correlation is equal to zero. In the example, then, we not only have a strong correlation between the component scores and final grades ($R = 0.9592$) but evidence in Table 13.3 that the correlation is significantly different from zero: $F(5, 20) = 58.67$, $p < .001$.

We have now introduced enough of the detail of multiple regression that we can turn to a very important use of multiple regression—namely, evaluating the variables that are to serve as predictors.

EVALUATING PREDICTOR VARIABLES

The multiple correlation coefficient is a useful descriptive statistic, but its usefulness is rarely the reason for using multiple regression. A far more important and frequent use of multiple regression is to evaluate the contributions of the predictor variables in the regression. This activity is important when the goal is to actually predict scores. A graduate school admissions committee, for example, might want to predict how well applicants will succeed in their program, using only the information available when a student applies for admission. Here the goal is prediction, but which variables are the best predictors? Does the admissions committee really need all the test scores and grades they are currently receiving, for example?

In the example we have been pursuing, all the X variables are important contributors to the final grade. That should not be surprising because the final grade—the Y variable—was the sum of the individual scores. But most research situations do not present such a clear set of relationships, and how variables work together is an important question—and one for which multiple regression is well suited. The topic of evaluating the predictor variables is complex, and a thorough presentation of all the methods and logic easily requires a separate book. We content ourselves here with an overview of the methods, and leave advanced presentations to more specialized texts.[7]

Let's take another example to develop the procedures for evaluating predictor variables. A university graduate program is evaluating its selection criteria. In particular, members of the graduate faculty are puzzled that some of the information it uses in choosing among the applicants seems to be unrelated to future performance, while other data seem to be quite good in predicting the future performance of graduate students. They would like to stop collecting information that isn't helpful, and would like to be able to predict who will be successful in their program.

The department has records on 32 current graduate students that it can use in evaluating the factors that predict success. When they apply to the program, students submit scores on the Graduate Record Examination (GRE) Verbal and Quantitative tests. In addition, the faculty has data on undergraduate grade point averages (GPAs), both overall and in the applicant's major. They also rate the applicants' letters of recommendation (rating is on a 1–10 scale, where 10 represents a very strong letter). The faculty argues that first-year graduate GPA for their students is a good measure of success; students who do well in their first year normally continue, and those who do poorly usually leave the program, voluntarily or otherwise. Thus the faculty decided to use the student's grade point average after one year as the criterion variable in a regression analysis.

The data[8] for a few of the 32 students, along with means and standard deviations, are shown in Table 13.5; the full data set appears in the exercises (see Table 13.15). The correlations among the variables (based on all 32 students) are shown in Table 13.6.

Based on these data, the multiple regression results for predicting first-year graduate GPA from the five variables are shown in Table 13.7.[9] The results show, among other things, a significant F value. This means that

<hr>

[7] Kerlinger and Pedhazur (1973) is very good, as are Marascuilo and Levin (1983) and Tabachnick and Fidell (1989).

[8] Although these data are artificial, you may be sure that many graduate programs have data exactly like these, and are interested in the same questions we are exploring here.

[9] This particular output was created by The Data Desk®, a statistics program for the Apple Macintosh®. Although your computer may not format its output exactly this way, you should be able to find in your own output nearly everything discussed here.

TABLE 13.5

Student	GPA in Major	GPA Overall	Letters of Recommendation	GRE Verbal	GRE Quantitative	Graduate GPA
1	3.22	2.64	10	701	692	4.00
2	3.43	2.94	7	606	638	3.87
3	3.25	2.61	4	552	590	4.00
4	2.88	2.30	9	423	415	2.91
5	2.96	2.16	6	431	572	3.68
$\vdots$						
$\bar{X}$	3.08	2.73	5.47	551.44	585.22	3.32
SD	0.62	0.53	2.58	111.12	89.32	0.77

TABLE 13.6

	GPA Major	Overall	Letters	Verbal	Quantitative	GPA Graduate
GPA Major	1.000					
Overall	0.438	1.000				
Letters	0.354	−0.029	1.000			
Verbal	0.370	0.501	−0.213	1.000		
Quantitative	0.387	0.196	0.402	0.126	1.000	
GPA Graduate	0.577	0.301	0.601	−0.017	0.650	1.000

TABLE 13.7

Dependent variable is: GPA Grad
$R^2 = 68.0\%$ R^2(adjusted) = 61.9%
s = 0.4744 with 32 − 6 = 26 degrees of freedom

Source	Sum of Squares	df	Mean Square	F-ratio
Regression	12.4504	5	2.490	11.1
Residual	5.85236	26	0.225091	

Variable	Coefficient	s.e. of Coeff	t-ratio
Constant	−0.319188	0.6948	−0.459
GPA maj	0.388877	0.1806	2.15
GPA over	0.298475	0.1952	1.53
Letter	0.085695	0.0409	2.10
GRE-V	−0.001562	0.0010	−1.62
GRE-Q	0.003452	0.0011	3.15

predicting a graduate GPA using the five predictor variables is significantly better than just using the mean of all graduate GPA scores.

With this overview of the setting, we now present two ways to evaluate the predictor variables. The first method uses information from the regression to evaluate the contribution of each predictor in defining the dependent variable (graduate school grade point). The second method builds the prediction equation in steps, with each step adding one more predictor until no more significant predictors remain to be used.

◆ Comparing and Testing Regression Coefficients

Any variable whose regression coefficient equals zero makes no contribution to the prediction. Thus, you might think, looking at the coefficients in Table 13.7, that the two GRE scores contribute little to the equation. But you're being misled; the regression coefficient values are highly influenced by each variable's mean and standard deviation. The mean for the GRE Verbal test, for example, is 551.44 with a standard deviation of over 100. But the mean for the variable being predicted (graduate GPA) is only 3.32 ($s = 0.77$). Thus, even if GRE Verbal was a *perfect* predictor of graduate GPA (that is, if we could write

$$\text{Grad GPA} = b * \text{GRE Verbal} + a$$

and have perfect prediction), the value of b would have to be very small to convert a variable with a mean of over 500 into one whose mean is a little over 3.0. So, although the magnitude of a regression coefficient might seem like a good candidate for evaluating the importance of a predictor variable, it really is not.

If all the variables were standardized before the regression values were computed, then you might think you could compare the regression coefficients directly. This would be a good argument; because standardized variables have equal means and standard deviations, their regression coefficients are not contaminated by differences in mean and standard deviation. Although it's unfortunately not quite that simple, we should explore the analysis briefly anyway because many programs present both sets of coefficients. The regression values from an analysis of the Table 13.1 data, but with each variable converted to z scores, are shown in Table 13.8.

Note that the intercept value is 0.0; with standardized variables it always will be, indicating that the regression plane passes through the zero point on the Y axis. Because the predicted values are similar to z scores (they are the best estimates of the *standardized Y* values but are not in themselves z scores), the regression plane should pass through the zero point because the mean of the predicted scores is zero.

Many authors and computer programs refer to these regression coefficients from standardized variables as β values, to distinguish them from the b's obtained when raw data are used, and we continue that tradition. Unfor-

TABLE 13.8

Standardized Variable	Beta Coefficient	Semipartial Correlation	Standard Deviation	t Test
GPA in Major	0.312	0.239	0.145	2.15
GPA Overall	0.207	0.170	0.136	1.52
Letters	0.287	0.232	0.137	2.09
GRE Verbal	−0.226	−0.179	0.140	−1.61
GRE Quantitative	0.401	0.349	0.127	3.16
Constant	0.000			

tunately, for purposes of comparing predictor variables, the βs are not much better than the b values because they depend not only on each variable's relationship with Y but also on their relationships with other variables in the model. Just looking at the β values in Table 13.8, it would be easy to conclude that the GRE quantitative test is the best predictor because its β is largest, and that the undergraduate major GPA is the next best predictor. Unfortunately, that conclusion could be incorrect or at least misleading because there are four other variables in the model and their presence distorts the predictive value of the βs.[10]

If neither the b's nor the βs allow us to compare the predictor variables, what can we use? Two values reported by many programs are quite useful. One is a t or F statistic, which every program reports for each variable, and the other is a statistic called the **semipartial correlation**. We won't explore either in detail because doing so would take us farther afield than necessary, but we can explain them briefly.

A semipartial correlation (sometimes called a *part* correlation) is a Pearson product-moment correlation coefficient between the Y variable (graduate GPA, for example) and a single predictor (like GPA in the undergraduate major) *with the effects of all other variables removed*. That is, it is just the correlation we might want—a look at the relationship between two variables with all other variables eliminated. Some programs routinely present this information, and it is included in Table 13.8. From it, we may conclude that GPA in the major accounts for about $0.239^2 = 5.7\%$ of the variability in graduate GPA *by itself*, while the GRE Verbal test supplies, *in the absence of the other variables*, only $-0.179^2 = 3.2\%$.

Table 13.8 presents the semipartial correlations as r, but programs sometimes report the values as r^2, making them interpretable as a proportion of the variance in Y that can be predicted by each of the other variables, with the effects of all other variables removed. Whether you find the semipartial or the squared semipartial in your output, however, the largest absolute value corresponds to the best predictor variable, the next largest to the next best, and so on. Thus, using the semipartials, we can rank the predictors in terms of their ability to predict.

[10] The problem is the same as that discussed in the footnote on page 376.

Are there any variables in the regression whose contribution to prediction is nil? Or at least so negligible that the variable could be eliminated with no adverse effect on prediction? One way of addressing these questions is to test a hypothesis that the actual population value of a regression coefficient is 0.0. That test is provided automatically by many programs; the necessary values appear in the "Standard Deviation" and "t Test" columns in Table 13.8. Each t tests the null hypothesis that the population regression coefficient is equal to zero. The t values are computed by dividing the difference between each regression coefficient and the null hypothesis value (0.0) by an estimate of its variability, leading to the familiar formula

$$t = \frac{b - 0.0}{s_b}$$

(The variability is labeled "Standard Deviation" in the table, but more correctly is analogous to a standard error.) The statistic is distributed as Student's t, with degrees of freedom equal to the residual df in the analysis of variance summary table. In the illustration (see Table 13.8), df $= 26$; at $\alpha =$ .05, the critical t value is 2.056, so the regression coefficients for GPA in the major, letters of recommendation, and GRE Quantitative test are the only significant predictors.

The magnitude of the t provides the second common means of selecting the best predictors in a regression model. The larger the absolute value of the t, the better the predictor. Some programs report an F instead of t, but no matter. Since $F = t^2$ in this instance, the larger the F, the better the predictor.

Before turning to the other major procedure for evaluating predictor variables, let's summarize what the graduate faculty has learned so far. The evaluative statistics—semipartials and the significance tests—suggest that only three predictors seem to be needed. GRE Quantitative score seems to be the best single predictor, followed by undergraduate GPA in the major and letters of recommendation. These three variables have the largest semipartial correlations with graduate GPA, and have the largest t values. Not only that, their b values are significantly different from 0.0, as determined by the t tests. Overall GPA and the GRE Verbal test seem to contribute little if anything to predicting first-year graduate GPA; their regression coefficients are not significantly different from 0.0 according to the t values.

◆ Stepwise Regression

Another approach to testing for significant predictor variables is to build up a linear regression model "stepwise," adding a single variable at a time until additional variables do not increase the "goodness" of the prediction. Many computer programs provide an automated stepwise procedure, usually offering several options relating to how to choose the next variable to be entered into the model.

Stepwise regression is a straightforward procedure that can be carried out with any program capable of multiple regression. The best way to explain the procedure is, as usual, by example. We may begin with any single predictor variable.[11] Let's start with GPA in the major. Now carry out the regression computations, using only GPA in the major to predict graduate GPA. The $R^2 = 0.333$ for this single-predictor model. Now select a second variable, say letters of recommendation. Conduct the regression again, using both GPA in the major and letters. For this two-predictor model, $R^2 = 0.513$, an increase of 0.180 in the proportion of the variance accounted for by the linear model.

Is 0.180 a significant R^2 **increase**? In other words, does the model with those two variables predict significantly better than did the first model? To answer that question, we compute an F to test the hypothesis that the change in R^2 is zero:

$$F_{\text{Change}} = \frac{(R^2_{\text{Larger}} - R^2_{\text{Smaller}})/(k_1 - k_2)}{(1 - R^2_{\text{Larger}})/(N - k_1 - 1)}$$

where k_1 is the number of predictor variables for the larger R^2 and k_2 is that for the smaller. For the example,

$$F_{\text{Change}} = \frac{(R^2_{\text{Larger}} - R^2_{\text{Smaller}})/(k_1 - k_2)}{(1 - R^2_{\text{Larger}})/(N - k_1 - 1)}$$

$$= \frac{(0.513 - 0.333)/(2 - 1)}{(1 - 0.513)/(32 - 2 - 1)}$$

$$= 10.719$$

This ratio has df $= (k_1 - k_2)$ and $(N - k_1 - 1)$ or, for this case, df $= 1, 29$. At $\alpha = .05$, the critical F value is 4.18, and we conclude that the two-variable model with major GPA and letters is significantly better at predicting graduate GPA than is the single-variable model using only major GPA.

To continue the example for another step, add overall GPA to the model. Now $R^2 = 0.521$, and the F ratio for the change becomes

$$F_{\text{Change}} = \frac{(R^2_{\text{Larger}} - R^2_{\text{Smaller}})/(k_1 - k_2)}{(1 - R^2_{\text{Larger}})/(N - k_1 - 1)}$$

$$= \frac{(0.536 - 0.513)/(3 - 2)}{(1 - 0.536)/(32 - 3 - 1)}$$

$$= 0.694$$

[11] The choice of starting variable, and the order of entry of subsequent variables, has a major influence on the solution. For that reason, many statisticians view stepwise regression with considerable, and justified, skepticism. Some authors find a stepwise analysis acceptable only if the entire goal of the project is to find a prediction model, while others find it useful in evaluating predictors as well.

With an F less than 1.0, the change is obviously not significant, and so we would discard overall GPA as a predictor. The process could continue in this stepwise fashion, adding and/or discarding predictors until we were comfortable that we had the best prediction model we could construct from the available data.

A stepwise procedure for evaluating predictor variables is a powerful method for exploring and testing the variables. But it's not without its problems. The order in which variables are entered has a powerful effect on the final result. This is so because the predictors are usually correlated among themselves. When they are, adding a variable that might be a good predictor by itself may have little or no effect, leading to the erroneous conclusion that it is a poor predictor. That can happen when some combination of variables already in the equation predicts very well. For example, suppose we had already included letters and GRE Quantitative in the model. When we add major GPA, we might find no increase in predictive ability. This could easily happen because letters and GRE Quantitative already do a good job of predicting. Adding variables in a different order may stop this from happening, but may also result in a different final model—this is always a puzzling finding, but it's one of the risks of using the stepwise procedure. Another real risk, especially in using an automated stepwise procedure in a statistics program, is placing too much faith in the particular order in which variables are added to the model. Computer output can easily lead you to conclude that some *particular* ordering is "the truth." Because programs use various criteria for selecting the first variable and for adding subsequent variables, the odds are that it's not.

The logic of stepwise regression can be applied in two other ways, often called **backwards regression** and *setwise regression*. In backwards regression, an initial model is formed using all the predictor variables. Then variables are *removed* one at a time until a significant reduction in R^2 occurs. The final model is the one before the significant drop in R^2. In setwise regression, variables are added, or removed, in groups, or sets, to test their effect on the regression.

USING RESIDUALS AS DIAGNOSTIC TOOLS

The differences between the actual Y values and those predicted by the regression model (that is, the residuals, $Y - \hat{Y}$) are useful numbers. They measure the error in the prediction, and as such can help us to understand how well a regression accounts for the relationships among the variables. A large error in prediction (that is, a large residual) means that the regression model did not fit that data point well. Perhaps that subject is unusual because a data value is erroneous (perhaps the data were entered incorrectly, or the raw data were coded wrong). Or maybe the subject is simply unusual, though correct. In either case, a subject with a very large residual probably

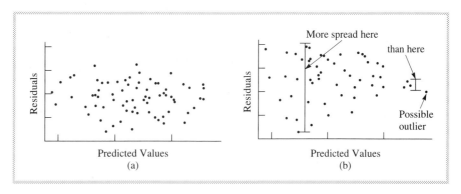

Figure 13.5

has a substantial effect on the regression solution, and should be checked for accuracy.

Residuals, or functions closely related to them, are often used diagnostically to locate erroneous or highly influential data values. Multiple regression is extremely sensitive to outliers—so much so that a great deal of effort is often spent to ensure that the data are "clean" before the final analyses are undertaken. Multiple regression is also quite sensitive to violations in its assumption of linear relationships among variables. Again, residuals can help to identify violations in those assumptions.

As Chapter 6 pointed out, there should be no correlation between residuals and predicted values. The scatterplot should show an equal distribution of residuals across all values of $\hat{Y}$; see, for example, the scatterplot in Figure 13.5a. Figure 13.5b, however, shows several potential problems. There is a possible outlier as well as a strong suggestion of unequal spread over the range of the predicted values.

Looking at the raw residual values with a histogram or a box plot often reveals the large errors of prediction. But the actual residual values themselves usually are not the best numbers to use. Regression programs often report several functions of residuals and other values that are more helpful. One of those values is the **standardized residual**. One definition of the standardized residual is[12]

$$z_{\text{Resid}} = \frac{Y - \hat{Y}}{s_{\text{Est}}},$$

which looks very much like the standardizing formula from Chapter 4. Standardized residuals may be regarded as normally distributed z scores. That being the case, any standardized residual with a value greater than ± 1.96 should occur by chance less than 5% of the time. Following a standard rule for hypothesis testing, we can regard any standardized residual exceeding

---

[12] This formula is due to Howell (1992).

± 1.96 to be "unlikely," probably an outlier, and thus warranting a closer look.

Another kind of standardized residual is given by some programs. This statistic, the **Studentized residual**, is similar to the standardized residual except that it is computed in such a way as to follow Students's t instead of the normal distribution.[13] A Studentized residual follows t with df $= N - k - 1$, so that a residual greater than the tabled critical value for that df at a chosen α is a significant outlier.

The standardized and the Studentized residuals both identify outliers with respect to the predicted variable. Many multiple regression programs identify outliers of another kind. These statistics include "leverage" values, Cook's distances, and Mahalanobis' distances. These three statistics measure the "importance" that each observation has in determining the regression model. Observations with large values on these statistics are highly influential, meaning that the model would change considerably if they were removed from the analysis. Such influential observations are probably unusual in some way, and their data should be checked for accuracy. As rough rules of thumb in dealing with these values, you may use the following. If a leverage value is greater than roughly $2k/N$, then that case is exceptionally influential. A Cook's distance of greater than 1.0 also indicates an outlier. A Mahalanobis' distance requires a special table to evaluate; Stevens (1984) includes such a table.

Henderson and Velleman (1981) present an interesting and thorough guide to conducting regression analyses by interactive computer. They discuss both interpreting regression and locating outliers. They also incorporate several techniques from exploratory data analysis. Their paper is worth several hours of careful study.

ANALYSIS OF VARIANCE USING MULTIPLE REGRESSION

Until now, we have presented multiple regression as if it were useful primarily in situations where the research is correlational in nature. In fact, it can be employed much more widely than that. Indeed, it is actually the "parent" of all the parametric procedures discussed so far. To illustrate the point, we will use multiple regression to conduct an analysis of variance. There are three reasons for doing so in this book. First, much of the current writing in statistics builds on a linear model as the general paradigm for research, and regards data analysis as primarily the search for an appropriate model of the data. Multiple regression is a fairly direct look at the linear model. Second, it is often of some interest to students to learn that, as disparate as regression and ANOVA seem, they are fundamentally identical. And third, conducting "analysis of variance" using a regression model is a simple and computationally correct way to handle the problem of unequal group sizes.

[13] There are at least two varieties of Studentized residuals, called internally and externally Studentized, but we won't pursue the distinction.

◆ Equal-Sized Groups

The analysis of variance example shown in Chapter 12 compared the sensation-seeking scores of subjects who had been placed into one of three groups depending on their introversion/extroversion score. The example used the data in Table 13.9. The summary table showed a significant difference among the three conditions; see Table 13.10.

To show how these data can produce the same summary table from regression, combine all the data into a single variable, and define two new variables, as shown in Table 13.11 (the horizontal lines indicate the original groups). The new variables, $D1$ and $D2$, are called **dummy variables** and serve to distinguish the groups from one another. Note that each group of data has a unique pattern of values on the dummy variables. The introvert group has the pattern 0, 1 on the dummy variables, the ambiverts are coded as 1, 0, and the extroverts are characterized by 1, 1. (The dummy variable values are 0 and 1, but any two unique values can be used.)

The three groups require two dummy variables to differentiate among them; four groups would require three dummies. In general, $a - 1$ dummy

TABLE 13.9

	Introverts	Ambiverts	Extroverts
	10	12	15
	7	10	11
	11	11	14
	9	11	10
	8	11	12
	11	13	13
	10	12	13
	10	12	12
	9	11	13
Mean	9.44	11.44	12.56
Std. dev.	1.33	0.88	1.51

TABLE 13.10

Summary Table				
Source	SS	df	MS	F
I/E group	44.74	2	22.37	13.89
Error	38.67	24	1.61	
Total	83.41	26		

TABLE 13.11

	Sensation-Seeking Score	D1	D2
Introverts	10	0	1
	7	0	1
	11	0	1
	9	0	1
	8	0	1
	11	0	1
	10	0	1
	10	0	1
	9	0	1
Ambiverts	12	1	0
	10	1	0
	11	1	0
	11	1	0
	11	1	0
	13	1	0
	12	1	0
	12	1	0
	11	1	0
Extroverts	15	1	1
	11	1	1
	14	1	1
	10	1	1
	12	1	1
	13	1	1
	13	1	1
	12	1	1
	13	1	1

variables are required to distinguish among a groups. (And a groups have $a - 1$ degrees of freedom, not coincidentally.)

Now take the three variables, the data and the two dummies, and use them in a multiple regression, with the dummy variables as the predictors and the data as the criterion. The results are in Table 13.12.[14]

In the ANOVA summary, the values are precisely the same as those in Table 13.10, showing that analysis of variance and multiple regression are really two ways of doing the same computations.

Of course, there are other values in the regression output that were not available from the ANOVA. For example, a brief look at the regression formula for predicting the dependent variable (sensation-seeking scores) from the dummy variables is very informative. The prediction formula, using the values from Table 13.12, is

[14] These results obtained from The Data Desk®.

TABLE 13.12

$R^2 = 53.6\%$ $R^2(\text{adjusted}) = 49.8\%$
$s = 1.269$ with $27 - 3 = 24$ degrees of freedom

Source	SS	df	MS	F-ratio
Regression	44.74	2	22.37	13.89
Residual	38.67	24	1.61	

Variable	Coefficient	s.e. of Coeff	t-ratio
Constant	8.33	0.73	11.40
D1	3.11	0.60	5.20
D2	1.11	0.60	1.86

$$\hat{Y} = 3.11(D1) + 1.11(D2) + 8.33$$

Applying the formula for the three groups of people, we have

For all introverts: $\hat{Y} = 3.11(0) + 1.11(1) + 8.33 = 9.44$
For all ambiverts: $\hat{Y} = 3.11(1) + 1.11(0) + 8.33 = 11.44$
For all extroverts: $\hat{Y} = 3.11(1) + 1.11(1) + 8.33 = 12.55.$

Comparing these values with the group means in Table 13.9 reveals that the predicted values are equal to the three group means in the original analysis. In other words, predicting the scores from the regression equation yields three different values, one for each distinct pattern of dummy values. Those predicted values are the best-fitting estimates of the dependent variable, and correspond to group means. We know that the regression equation predicts the least-squares best-fitting value for each subject, and that value turns out to be the mean of the group the subject is in. But that should not be surprising because we know from Chapter 3 that the least-squares best measure of center of any group of data is the group's arithmetic mean.

Even more information can be found in the regression results. The regression coefficients (b's) for the two dummy variables are equal to the differences between pairs of means.[15] For $D1$, the regression coefficient's value (3.11) is equal (within rounding) to the difference between the means of the introverts (9.44) and the extroverts (12.56). And for $D2$, the difference between the means for the ambiverts (11.44) and the extroverts (12.56) is again equal (within rounding) to the regression coefficient (1.11).

And there's more. The t value for each of the dummy variables is similar

---

[15] This is so because of the specific values chosen for the dummy variables. Other patterns of dummy values would result in regression coefficients with different values and with different interpretations.

to the Student's t^{16} that would be obtained if you tested for a difference between introverts and extroverts ($D1$), and between ambiverts and extroverts ($D2$). The t values have df = 24, the number of degrees of freedom for the residual in the summary table. In short, the tests of the regression coefficients may be used to test hypotheses about differences in groups of subjects. That makes sense if you remember that the t values are for testing the null hypothesis that the regression coefficient has a value of 0.0; that's precisely the hypothesis about the difference in group means that's tested in a two-sample t test. The test is not identical to the ordinary two-sample t (Chapter 10) because the "error term" in regression includes both variability information and degrees of freedom from the third groups of subjects.

◆ Unequal Group Sizes

Until now, we have assumed that analysis of variance is done only with equal-sized groups of subjects, one group under each experimental condition. In the real world of research, though, unequal group sizes are the norm. How does that fact change the analysis? Considerably, as it turns out. For one thing, the various tests that might be made become nonindependent, which in turn has unpredictable effects on the probabilities and Type I and II errors. The discussion of exactly why the analysis changes would take us far afield, and we will not pursue it further. For our purposes, suffice it to say that equal group sizes are to be hoped for, and if they turn out to be unequal, the analysis should be done through multiple regression. (Or, for the single-independent-variable designs discussed thus far, by using the weighted means procedure illustrated in the computational supplement in Chapter 12.)

With unequal group sizes in ANOVA, the computations are set up exactly as they were in the demonstration with equal groups, and the regression analysis proceeds as illustrated. The resulting summary table from the regression serves as the ANOVA table. The balance of the regression output, including the R value and the regression coefficients and their tests, is normally omitted. Of course, with unequal group sizes, follow-up test computations change too. We illustrate those changes in the computational supplement.

Any analysis of variance computation (including the factorial and repeated measures designs to be discussed in the next two chapters) can be done through multiple regression, given the proper dummy variable coding and several analyses. We will not show the dummy variable coding for these repeated measures in this book. Howell (1992) gives a good elementary overview, and Keppel and Zedeck (1989) present full details. An optional section in Chapter 15 shows the treatment of the factorial design via multiple regression.

---

[16] Actually, it is similar to the t that would be obtained from the Fisher Least-Significant-Difference (LSD) Test described in Chapter 12.

THE GENERAL LINEAR MODEL

The numerical equivalence of multiple regression and the analysis of variance suggests that, at a fundamental level, they are really the same thing. They are. They represent two different ways of conceptualizing the variability in data, yet they arrive at the same final values. And that fact illustrates a fundamental truth about nearly all the statistics we have presented: They all derive from a common statistical model, called the **general linear model**. This model forms the basis for nearly all the inferential (and descriptive) methods presented in this book.

Chapter 6 presented the expression

$$\text{Data} = \text{Model} + \text{Error}$$

In words, the data that we observe in research can be thought of as coming from two sources: an underlying hypothetical "model" and error. Much of what we are doing in data analysis can be conceived as a search for the correct "model." In the simplest case, the "model" is some elementary statistic like an arithmetic mean. If we look at only a single group of values, collected in a situation where no extraneous or experimental variables are known to be present, we might say that each individual's score (the "data") can be written as

$$\text{Data} = \text{Arithmetic Mean} + \text{Error}$$

This simple expression indicates that, except for error, everyone has the same score, and that the arithmetic mean is the best estimate (model) of that value. This conceptualization is the foundation of descriptive statistics, and we can think of this expression as perhaps the simplest "model" for much data.

A slightly more complex expression might be

$$\text{Data} = \text{Mean} + \text{Independent Variable} + \text{Error}$$

This expression allows for the possibility of something other than error influencing an individual's score. It is very similar to one from Chapter 12:

$$X_{ij} = \mu + \alpha_j + \varepsilon$$

In this fundamental expression from analysis of variance, an individual score is conceptualized as the sum of a population mean (μ), a treatment effect (α), and error (ε). This form of the expression leads to the analysis of variance as a way of asking whether the model

$$\text{Data} = \text{Mean} + \text{Independent Variable} + \text{Error}$$

represents a significant improvement over the simpler form—namely,

$$\text{Data} = \text{Arithmetic Mean} + \text{Error}$$

In other words, the research question might be which model provides better agreement with the actual data. ANOVA, in this context, can be seen as a technique for comparing two models of data, one containing an independent variable and one without it.

Another possible model might be

$$\text{Data} = bX + a + \text{Error}$$

Here, the "model" is a linear equation representing a relationship with a second variable and a constant. A model like this leads to conceiving of the research in a regression setting. A comparison of this model to the simpler

$$\text{Data} = \text{Arithmetic Mean} + \text{Error}$$

leads to a test for the significance of the regression because, if the regression is not significant, the correlational model will not fit the data any better than will the arithmetic mean alone.

From the previous formulation, it's but a short step to

$$\text{Data} = b_1 X_1 + b_2 X_2 + \cdots + a + \text{Error}$$

where a full general expression from multiple regression constitutes the "model." In this case, X can represent measured variables, leading to a multiple regression conceptualization of the research, or they can be "dummy" variables representing combinations of experimental treatments, which suggests an ANOVA experimental design. In either case, the fundamental form of the expression remains the same. A hypothesis test in either becomes a test of whether the more complex model, be it ANOVA or regression, "fits" better than does a simple one that postulates only an overall population mean.

Judd and McClelland (1989) have written an interesting text, more advanced than this one, that approaches data analysis for psychologists in a fashion that is consistent with the discussion in this section. They view all analysis as a search for a model, and present a statistic ("PRE"—the proportional reduction in error) that is used in all designs, whether simple t tests or complex analysis of variance in factorial experimental designs. For the adventurous student, their text would be an interesting sequel to this book.

◆ Comparisons, Hypotheses, and Dummy Variables[17]

Tables 13.6 and 13.7 contain Student's t values for each predictor variable. Those t values were used earlier to test whether each predictor variable was

[17] This section offers an advanced treatment of orthogonal comparisons and dummy variables; your instructor may elect to have you omit it.

TABLE 13.13

$R^2 = 53.6\%$ $R^2(\text{adjusted}) = 49.8\%$
$s = 1.269$ with $27 - 3 = 24$ degrees of freedom

Source	Sum of Squares	df	Mean Square	F-ratio
Regression	44.7407	2	22.37	13.9
Residual	38.6667	24	1.61111	

Variable	Coefficient	s.e. of Coeff	t-ratio
Constant	11.1481	0.2443	45.6
Comp1	−0.703704	0.1727	−4.07
Comp2	−1.00000	0.2992	−3.34

significant. But when using multiple regression for analysis of variance, the dummy variables are the "predictors." Because the t values (or the logically equivalent F values) are readily available in every computer program, can we use them to test for specific hypotheses? Certainly, and this gives us a very powerful analytic tool.

Return to the three introversion/extroversion groups and define two orthogonal comparisons among the groups, as we did in Chapter 12, using the coefficients 1, 1, −2 for the first and 1, −1, 0 for the second. The first comparison is between the combined introvert and ambivert groups and the extroverts, and the second is between the introverts and the ambiverts. Now we use the values in the two comparisons to define the two dummy variables. That is,

All introverts:	1	1
All ambiverts:	1	−1
All extroverts:	−2	0

The regression results using these values appear in Table 13.13.[18]

First note that the overall analysis summary table is identical (within rounding) to that in Table 13.12. Again, using dummy variable coding has reproduced the original analysis of variance. But now look at the t values for the two comparisons. Comparison 1, recall, compares the combined introverts and ambiverts with the extroverts. In Chapter 12, we conducted this same comparison by computing the SS for the comparison and then finding the F ratio. With df = 1, 24, $F = 16.75$. Because $F = t^2$, we can obtain the same value by squaring the value from the regression computation: $t^2 = -4.07^2 = 16.58$; this is very nearly identical to the F obtained earlier. With df = 24, this t is significant, meaning that there is a significant difference between the combined introverts and ambiverts and the extroverts, the same

---

[18] These results obtained from The Data Desk®.

conclusion reached in Chapter 12. The Student's t value for the second comparison likewise converts easily to the F from Chapter 12: $t^2 = -3.34^2 = 11.16$, which is nearly identical to the value obtained in Chapter 12.

What we have just demonstrated is that the language of comparisons can be applied in the regression approach to analysis of variance. Any set of $a - 1$ orthogonal comparisons can be used to define dummy variables for a regression. The significance of each "predictor variable" (that is, comparison) is tested in the process of the regression analysis with the same results as obtained in the earlier analysis of variance computations.

Summary

◆ *In* multiple regression, *the prediction is done from a linear combination of the set of the X variables.*

◆ *A multiple regression equation with two predictors has two "slopes," one for each of the two predictor variables, and an intercept.*

◆ *Slope coefficients in the multiple regression equation are normally called* regression coefficients.

◆ *The intercept in the multiple regression equation is frequently called the* constant.

◆ *As in bivariate regression, the difference between an actual Y value and the predicted Y (that is, $\hat{Y}$) is called a* residual.

◆ *The standard error of estimate is analogous to the standard deviation, except that it is based on deviations around the regression plane instead of around the mean.*

◆ *The F ratio allows a test of the hypothesis that the regression is "significant."*

◆ *The ratio $\dfrac{SS_{Regression}}{SS_Y}$ represents the proportion of the total variation in Y that can be accounted for by the regression.*

◆ *The ratio $\dfrac{SS_{Regression}}{SS_Y}$ also gives the square of the multiple correlation between Y and all the X variables.*

◆ *The adjusted R is an unbiased estimate of the population multiple correlation.*

◆ *The Pearson product-moment correlation coefficient between the predicted and the actual scores is the multiple correlation coefficient.*

◆ *Multiple regression is often used to evaluate the relative contributions of the predictor variables.*

◆ *The raw regression coefficient, b, is influenced by the size of the mean and the standard deviation of its variable.*

◆ *Regression coefficients for standardized variables are usually called βs.*

◆ *The semipartial correlation gives the correlation between the predicted variable and a predictor, with the influence of the other variables eliminated.*

◆ *To determine if a predictor is significant, we may test a hypothesis that the population value of the regression coefficient is 0.0.*

◆ *A multiple regression can be constructed stepwise, with a new variable added to the equation at each step.*

◆ *In* stepwise regression, *the order in which variables are entered into the equation has a powerful effect on the final result.*

◆ *Residuals are often used for diagnostic purposes to reveal problems in the data.*

◆ *Multiple regression computations are very sensitive to outliers.*

◆ Standardized *and* studentized residuals *identify outliers with respect to the predicted variable.*

◆ *"Leverage," Cook's distances, and Mahalanobis' distances measure the importance of each observation in determining the regression.*

◆ Dummy variables *are used to indicate group membership.*

◆ *ANOVA may be conducted in regression by using dummy variables to predict the dependent variable.*

◆ *In an ANOVA done with regression, the regression coefficients have meaning in terms of group means, and the tests for significance of the coefficients may be used to test hypotheses about mean differences.*

◆ *The general linear model is the "parent" of all the parametric procedures discussed in this book.*

Key Terms

ADJUSTED R	R^2 INCREASE
b	REGRESSION COEFFICIENT
β	RESIDUAL VALUE
BACKWARDS REGRESSION	SEMIPARTIAL CORRELATION
BIVARIATE REGRESSION	SS_{Error} (SUM OF SQUARES FOR ERROR)
DUMMY VARIABLE	
F RATIO FOR REGRESSION	$SS_{Regression}$ (SUM OF SQUARES FOR REGRESSION)
F_{Change}	
GENERAL LINEAR MODEL	SS_Y (SUM OF SQUARES FOR Y)
MULTIPLE CORRELATION	STANDARD ERROR OF ESTIMATE
MULTIPLE REGRESSION	STANDARDIZED RESIDUAL
PREDICTED VALUE	STEPWISE REGRESSION
PREDICTOR VARIABLES	STUDENTIZED RESIDUAL

EXERCISES

1. Table 13.14 gives data on several personality variables for a group of students. The personality test scales are:

EPIE — Extroversion scale from the Eysenck Personality Inventory (EPI)

SSST — Total score on Zuckerman's Sensation Seeking Scale, Version 5 (SSS-V)

BIS — Total score on the Barratt Impulsivity Scales

V — Venturesomeness scale on the Eysenck & Eysenck Impulsiveness-Venturesomeness-Empathy questionnaire (IVE)

I — Impulsiveness on the IVE

TAS — Thrill and Adventure Seeking subscale of the SSS-V

ES — Experience Seeking subscale of the SSS-V

Carry out the overall multiple regression, using EPIE as the variable to be predicted.

a. Compute the *b* values for each variable.

b. Find the predicted scores for each subject.

c. Compute the residuals and the standardized residuals.

2. Use the example graduate school data (Table 13.15) and conduct a multiple regression, predicting graduate GPA.

a. Compute the *b* values for each variable.

b. Find the predicted scores for each subject.

TABLE 13.14

| | | | *Personality Scale* | | | | |
Student	EPIE	SSST	BIS	V	I	TAS	ES
1	15	13	36	3	2	2	10
2	14	22	42	13	3	9	17
3	6	17	37	11	4	9	14
4	20	33	89	14	16	10	26
5	14	18	41	9	9	6	13
6	14	18	48	14	2	9	15
7	16	27	42	12	6	7	19
8	15	13	61	6	12	2	7
9	12	15	40	11	2	9	11
10	14	21	34	9	8	4	14
11	14	27	76	13	13	8	20
12	14	17	65	9	6	7	13
13	12	8	59	3	10	4	6
14	11	13	31	5	8	6	9
15	12	20	49	5	6	5	16
16	11	14	52	4	6	0	8
17	14	21	60	14	13	10	16
18	4	11	43	5	4	5	5
19	17	25	44	14	7	9	21
20	13	25	85	15	12	10	18

TABLE 13.15

Student	GPA in Major	GPA Overall	Letters of Rec.	GRE Verbal	GRE Quant.	Graduate GPA
1	3.22	2.64	10	701	692	4.00
2	3.43	2.94	7	606	638	3.87
3	3.25	2.61	4	552	590	4.00
4	2.88	2.30	9	423	415	2.91
5	2.96	2.16	6	431	572	3.68
6	3.21	2.69	9	462	625	4.00
7	3.70	2.64	6	574	607	3.29
8	3.62	3.14	3	714	411	2.06
9	2.62	3.03	5	579	525	2.85
10	2.78	2.11	8	487	477	2.00
11	4.00	4.00	4	617	629	4.00
12	3.83	2.92	8	720	814	4.00
13	3.24	2.37	4	462	500	3.00
14	2.86	2.44	2	583	428	2.71
15	3.09	2.25	1	551	637	3.04
16	2.42	2.29	6	514	589	3.35
17	3.57	2.96	9	582	708	3.80
18	3.43	2.28	7	418	688	4.00
19	3.04	3.94	5	534	649	4.00
20	3.28	2.37	8	524	650	4.00
21	3.70	2.59	8	400	593	4.00
22	2.38	2.13	6	462	505	3.36
23	2.58	2.43	2	630	587	2.58
24	3.46	2.36	5	526	591	4.00
25	3.20	3.15	7	603	670	4.00
26	1.34	2.77	4	394	534	2.55
27	2.39	2.28	1	483	576	1.14
28	3.95	3.25	7	661	630	4.00
29	3.38	3.48	7	414	609	4.00
30	1.92	2.45	2	563	497	2.33
31	2.09	2.39	3	575	587	2.74
32	3.63	3.94	2	901	504	2.94
$\overline{X}$	3.08	2.73	5.47	551.44	585.22	3.32
SD	0.62	0.53	2.58	111.12	89.32	0.77

  c. Compute the residuals and the standardized residuals.

3. Using the graduate school data, carry out a stepwise analysis, adding variables in at least three different orders of entry. Summarize the results by writing a recommendation to the graduate faculty about which variables they should continue to use in screening applicants.

4. Based on the graduate school data in Table 13.15, student 27 is a possible outlier on the GRE Verbal test.

  a. Look at the standardized residuals and a plot of predicted by residual to confirm that this might be an outlier.

  b. Remove student 27 from the data and repeat the analysis from exercise 13.2.

TABLE 13.16

	Spacing	
Phrase	Normal	Even
79	85	41
92	56	57
63	60	29
76	62	77
88	58	71
60	33	66
62	83	63
61	88	43
100	68	94
78	65	69
57	55	65
61	67	82
68	55	66
84	62	63
92	68	50
84	59	74
66	96	66
104	47	75
	79	93
	86	62
	47	70
	86	44
	56	
	75	
	65	

TABLE 13.17

	Drug Condition		
A	B	C	Placebo
5	13	15	13
7	11	11	16
11	12	13	5
8	8	10	11
10	7	10	6
6	8	16	
4		14	
		11	

c. Write a paragraph summarizing the differences in results when student 27 is removed.

5. Use the data from exercise 12.1.

   a. Repeat the analysis of variance by using multiple regression.

   b. Compute the predicted values for each of the three age groups, and be sure they agree with the group means.

6. Exercise 12.4 presents a set of data similar to that of Jandreau and Bever (1992). Table 13.16 gives another set, this time using the actual group sizes reported by Jandreau and Bever. Conduct the overall analysis of variance using the regression method. Use $\alpha = .05$.

7. Table 13.17 gives data similar to those in exercise 12.2, except that there are unequal group sizes. Conduct the overall analysis of variance using the regression method. Use $\alpha = .05$.

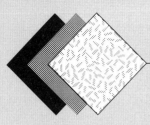

Computational Supplement

The overall computations for multiple regression are assumed to be carried out by computer, and there are few additional computations required in this section. The few auxiliary computations, such as the test for a significant change in R^2, were illustrated earlier in the chapter. All that really remains is to show how to set up dummy variables and show some ANOVA follow-up tests for unequal group sizes.

◆ Defining Dummy Variables

The essential rules in setting up dummy variables are (1) that there be $a - 1$ dummy variables and (2) that each group have a distinct pattern of values on the dummies. Beyond those rules, little else is required.[19] The main problem is keeping the coding simple and consistent. Here is a common set of rules and some of the coding that results.

- ◆ For a experimental groups, you will need $a - 1$ dummy scores for each subject.
- ◆ For the ath group, enter -1 for every dummy.
- ◆ For groups 1 to $a - 1$, enter 1 as the value for the dummy corresponding to that group (that is, group 1 has 1 on dummy 1, group 2 has 1 on dummy 2, etc.).
- ◆ Enter zeros everywhere else. For example, for $a = 3$, 4, and 5, the rules give the patterns shown in Table 13.18.

◆ Two-Group Follow-Up Tests with Unequal Group Sizes

THE TUKEY-KRAMER TEST. The *Tukey honestly significant difference (HSD)* test from Chapter 12 is easily modified for unequal group sizes, following the suggestion of Kramer (1956).

As before, the Tukey-Kramer procedure establishes a value for the smallest possible significant difference between two condition means; any mean difference greater than that amount is significant. The Tukey-Kramer critical mean difference is

---

[19] In fact, different patterns in dummies can be used to embody different specific hypothesis tests, but we will not explore that matter further. Cohen (1968) gives an exceptionally clear exposition of some of these matters. For a more detailed treatment, see Darlington (1990).

TABLE 13.18

		Dummy Variable			
a	Group	D1	D2	D3	D4
3	1	1	0		
	2	0	1		
	3	−1	−1		
4	1	1	0	0	
	2	0	1	0	
	3	0	0	1	
	4	−1	−1	−1	
5	1	1	0	0	0
	2	0	1	0	0
	3	0	0	1	0
	4	0	0	0	1
	5	−1	−1	−1	−1

$$D = q_{(\alpha,\,\mathrm{df},\,a)} \sqrt{\frac{\mathrm{MS}_{\mathrm{Error}}\left(\dfrac{1}{n_i} + \dfrac{1}{n_j}\right)}{2}}$$

where $q(\alpha, \mathrm{df}, a)$ is a Studentized range value from Appendix J, and n_i and n_j are the two group sizes. Appendix J is entered using the number of degrees of freedom for error and the number of groups, a. Note that this will result in a *different* critical difference for every set of different group sizes.

The Tukey-Kramer test is usually carried out by constructing a matrix containing the differences between all pairs of means, as was the Tukey test in Chapter 12.

As an example, suppose that in a study with $a = 5$ groups, the two groups being compared have sizes 10 and 12, that $\mathrm{MS}_{\mathrm{Error}}$ is 4.68 with df = 16, and that $\alpha = .05$.

The critical difference for the Tukey-Kramer test is calculated as

$$D = q_{(\alpha,\,\mathrm{df},\,a)} \sqrt{\frac{\mathrm{MS}_{\mathrm{Error}}\left(\dfrac{1}{n_i} + \dfrac{1}{n_j}\right)}{2}}$$

$$= 4.33 \sqrt{\frac{4.68\left(\dfrac{1}{10} + \dfrac{1}{12}\right)}{2}}$$

$$= 2.84$$

The mean difference between two groups with sizes 10 and 12 would be compared to the critical value and, if they exceed 2.84, we conclude that they are significantly different.

THE DUNNETT C TEST. The Dunnett C test is highly recommended when group sizes are unequal, and especially so when group variances are different. To calculate the critical value for the Dunnett C, use the formula

$$D = 0.71 \left[\frac{\dfrac{q_{(\alpha, n_i - 1, a)} s_i^2}{n_i} + \dfrac{q_{(\alpha, n_j - 1, a)} s_j^2}{n_j}}{\sqrt{\dfrac{s_i^2}{n_i} + \dfrac{s_j^2}{n_j}}} \right]$$

where q is taken from the Studentized range table in Appendix J, as with the Tukey-Kramer test, s_i^2 and s_j^2 are the variances of the two groups, and n_i and n_j are the two group sizes. Because each group has a different standard deviation, a different size, and therefore a different Studentized range value, a different D is calculated for each pair of mean differences. As an example, take the values used in the Tukey-Kramer illustration and suppose that the two variances were 6.55 and 14.59. The critical value is then calculated as

$$D = 0.71 \left[\frac{\dfrac{q_{(\alpha, n_i - 1, a)} s_i^2}{n_i} + \dfrac{q_{(\alpha, n_j - 1, a)} s_j^2}{n_j}}{\sqrt{\dfrac{s_i^2}{n_i} + \dfrac{s_j^2}{n_j}}} \right]$$

$$= 0.71 \left[\frac{\dfrac{4.76 * 6.55}{10} + \dfrac{4.57 * 14.59}{12}}{\sqrt{\dfrac{6.55}{10} + \dfrac{14.59}{12}}} \right]$$

$$= 4.50$$

If the two groups differ by 4.50 or more, then we conclude by the Dunnett C that they are significantly different.

THE SCHEFFÉ TEST. Again, we caution that the Scheffé test, offered by nearly every computer program, is extremely conservative and is not recommended for general use. The formula for the critical difference between means for the Scheffé test is given by the formula

$$D = \sqrt{(a - 1) F_{(\alpha, a-1, N-a)} \text{MS}_{\text{Error}} \left(\frac{1}{n_i} + \frac{1}{n_j} \right)}$$

where F is a value of F taken from Appendix F with df $= a - 1$ and $N - a$, N is the total number of subjects in the entire experiment, and MS_{Error} is the within-groups mean square from the overall analysis.

Using the same example, and assuming there are 58 subjects in the entire experiment, we calculate the critical value as follows. From Appendix F, we need the value for $\alpha = .05$, with $(5 - 1) = 4$ and $(58 - 5) = 53$ df; the value is 2.61 (following the rule of picking the next lower number of df when the desired value is not in the table). Recalling that the two group sizes are 10 and 12, and that MS_{Error} is 4.68, the computation is

$$D = \sqrt{(a-1)F_{(\alpha, a-1, N-a)}MS_{Error}\left(\frac{1}{n_i} + \frac{1}{n_j}\right)}$$

$$= \sqrt{(5-1)*2.61*4.68\left(\frac{1}{10} + \frac{1}{12}\right)}$$

$$= 2.99$$

FISHER'S LSD TEST. Fisher's LSD test is easily conducted as a Student's t, as in Chapter 12. The formula is

$$t_{LSD} = \frac{\overline{X}_i - \overline{X}_j}{\sqrt{MS_{Error}\left(\frac{1}{n_i} + \frac{1}{n_j}\right)}}$$

The degrees of freedom for the test are $N - a$.

More consistently with the presentation here, the critical difference for the Fisher LSD may be calculated as

$$D = \sqrt{F_{(\alpha, 1, N-a)}}\sqrt{MS_{Error}\left(\frac{1}{n_i} + \frac{1}{n_j}\right)}$$

In the example that we have been following, the critical difference between means is

$$D = \sqrt{F_{(\alpha, 1, N-a)}}\sqrt{MS_{Error}\left(\frac{1}{n_i} + \frac{1}{n_j}\right)}$$

$$= \sqrt{4.08}\sqrt{4.68\left(\frac{1}{10} + \frac{1}{12}\right)}$$

$$= 1.87$$

so that two groups of sizes 10 and 12 whose means differ by 1.87 or more are significantly different.

14 Experiments with More Than Two Within-Subjects Conditions

Analyzing the Variance
Follow-Up Analyses
Power and the Within-Subjects Design
A DISTRIBUTION-FREE ALTERNATIVE TO ANOVA
SUMMARY
KEY TERMS
EXERCISES
◆ *COMPUTATIONAL SUPPLEMENT*

Chapter 12 presented the first look at the multiple condition, or ANOVA, experimental design. In that design, the independent variable is manipulated between subjects so that each condition in the design contains a different group of subjects. In that between-subjects design, variation in the data can come from only two sources: the independent variable (if it has any effect) and the subjects. If the independent variable has any effects, those effects will make the experimental conditions different from one another. That being the case, the scores from the different experimental conditions will be different from each other and thus will contribute to the overall variability in the data. The remainder of the variability in the data—that is, variability other than that due to the independent variable—must be due to the subjects. Because subjects differ among themselves independently of the independent variable, individual differences are a part of the variability among subjects, as are measurement error, random variation, and the other sources of variability discussed earlier.

We can reduce between-groups variability by making the groups more homogeneous. Two common techniques for reducing subject variability are matching subjects or using the same subject in multiple conditions. Chapter 1 described the differences between the between- and the within-subjects experimental designs. In Chapter 10 we saw the within-subjects logic applied to the two-condition experiment, and noted its increase in power. The logic holds in multiple-condition experiments; if we can use the same subject in multiple conditions, we can reduce the error variation and thus make the effect of the independent variable stand out more clearly. Chapter 12 showed how we may separate the overall variability into two components, one part showing the effects of the independent variable and the other part the error variability. That partition of variability led directly to a test of the hypothesis that *only* error variability was present. This chapter shows how the variability in the data is again subdivided into separate components, but this time also removing between-subjects variability, thereby letting the effects of an independent variable stand out more clearly.

A Short-Term Memory Experiment

Here is a classic experiment concerning the properties of visual short-term (often called iconic) memory.[1] The experiment presents subjects with an array of 12 letters on a computer screen. A typical array might look like this:

$$
\begin{array}{cccc}
A & X & H & G \\
O & B+W & K \\
V & I & M & R
\end{array}
$$

Subjects were instructed to fixate on the $+$ in the center of the screen, and the matrix of letters flashed for a short time (200 msec). Then the subjects were asked to recall as many letters as possible from one of the three rows. The subject was told which row to recall by either a visual presentation of a number beside the row to be recalled, or by an auditory cue—a high tone meant the top row, a low tone the bottom row, and an intermediate tone signaled the center row.[2] The presentation was repeated multiple times, and each subject has three scores: the mean total number of letters recalled from row 1, from row 2, and from row 3 over a series of trials. In other words, the experiment has three different conditions—the subject is to recall from the top, middle, or bottom row—and each subject appears in each condition the same number of times. The raw data, along with means and standard deviations, are given in Table 14.1. The box plot of the data (Figure 14.1) shows substantial differences in the means.

---

[1] This experiment is very similar to a classic investigation in cognition conducted by Sperling (1960). These data were collected in a cognitive psychology course laboratory.

[2] A fundamental question in the actual experiment was whether memory is coded visually or auditorially; if visual, then recall should be better with a visual cue, and vice versa for auditory storage. For this chapter, though, we look only at recall differences among the three rows of the stimulus display.

TABLE 14.1

Subject	Recall from		
	Row 1	Row 2	Row 3
1	14.7	13.8	12.9
2	13.5	50.1	16.8
3	39.9	58.2	27.0
4	23.4	46.5	18.3
5	27.9	46.5	32.1
6	26.4	51.6	26.1
7	27.3	44.1	17.4
8	36.3	49.8	36.6
9	23.4	43.4	17.1
10	30.9	33.6	13.5
11	9.9	43.8	12.0
Mean	24.87	43.76	20.89
Standard deviation	9.34	11.67	8.27

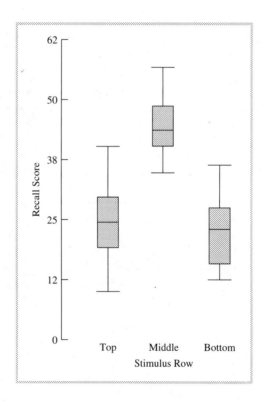

Figure 14.1

◆ Analyzing the Variance

In Chapter 12's development of the analysis of variance in the between-subjects (or nonrepeated measurements) design, we broke down total variation, as represented by the total sum of squares, into a between-conditions part and a within-conditions part:

$$\underbrace{\sum (X - GM)^2}_{SS_{Total}} = \underbrace{n\sum (\bar{X}_j - GM)^2}_{SS_{Between}} + \underbrace{\sum (X - \bar{X}_j)^2}_{SS_{Within}}$$

In that analysis, the "within" part of the variation was based on the differences between subjects and the mean of the group that each subject was in. Those differences represent error; when divided by its df, the "within" part estimates σ_e^2, the error variance. The "between" part of the variation is based on the differences between the means of the experimental conditions and the grand mean. The $SS_{Between}$ contains the differences between the experimental conditions *and also* differences between the groups of subjects. When divided by its df, the "between" part estimates a combination of error variance and treatment effects:

$$\sigma_e^2 + \frac{n\sum \alpha_j^2}{a - 1}$$

Because different subjects receive the different treatments, variation between the experimental conditions is completely confounded with variation between the groups of subjects. That is, all the between-subjects variation is included in the between-conditions component. The **repeated measures design** allows us to separate the two, removing the **between-subjects variation** from the **between-experimental-conditions variation**.

The total variation present in the experiment, expressed as a sum of squares (SS_{Total}), just as in the between-subjects analysis in Chapter 12, is

$$SS_{Total} = \sum (X - GM)^2$$

where GM is still the grand mean. In Chapter 12, we partitioned this total variation (SS_{Total}) into two components, $SS_{Between}$ and SS_{Within}. In the within-subjects design, we follow a similar logic, but in two separate steps. First, we partition the overall variation into two segments, one representing variation *between subjects* and the other the variation *within subjects*. Because each subject in the repeated measures experiment participates in every condition, variation due to differences between the treatments becomes a part of the within-subjects variation. Therefore the second step partitions the within-subjects variation into two segments—*between conditions* and *error*.

A subject's mean, which we can symbolize as $\bar{S}$, across all conditions is a point estimate of that individual's overall performance in the task. The difference between a subject's mean and the grand mean $(\bar{S} - GM)$ is that part of the variation around the grand mean that can be attributed to a subject difference. Summing across all the n subjects and multiplying by the number of conditions gives a sum of squares:

$$SS_{\text{Between subjects}} = a\sum(\bar{S} - GM)^2$$

This sum of squares is that portion of the total variation that is due to the differences between the subjects and the grand mean. Because subjects differ from one another, those differences contribute to the total variation present, and this sum of squares provides a measure of that variation.

The difference between an individual subject's score and his or her *own* mean in all the conditions in the experiment $(X - \bar{S})$ gives an indication of the variation *within a subject*. Squaring that quantity and summing across all subjects and conditions gives a sum of squares for within subjects:

$$SS_{\text{Within subjects}} = \sum(X - \bar{S})^2$$

These two sums of squares together add up to the total variation in the experiment

$$\sum(X - GM)^2 = a\sum(\bar{S} - GM)^2 + \sum(X - \bar{S})^2$$

or

$$SS_{\text{Total}} = SS_{\text{Between subjects}} + SS_{\text{Within subjects}}$$

and we have completed the first step of the analysis. Pictorially, what we have just done is

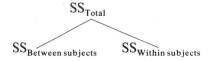

Because all subjects receive all the experimental conditions, differences among experimental conditions must be included in the within-subjects variation. The second step of the analysis partitions that sum of squares into two parts.

The variability due to the different conditions in the experiment can be assessed as the differences between condition means and the grand mean, $(\bar{X} - GM)$. Squaring and summing across the a experimental conditions and multiplying by the numbers of subjects, we have

$$SS_{\text{Conditions}} = n\sum(\bar{X} - GM)^2$$

This is the part of the overall variation that is due to differences between the conditions, just as it was in the between-subjects analysis.

We have not mentioned error variation yet, and it assumed an important role in Chapter 12. In the between-subjects design, error variation was based on the differences between an individual score and the mean of the particular group the score was in. In the present analysis, though, the logic of the error estimate is somewhat more complicated. The estimate for error is that part of the variation that's "left over" after the effects of conditions and subjects have been removed:

$$(X - GM) - (\bar{S} - GM) - (\bar{X} - GM)$$

Squaring and summing this complicated expression over subjects and experimental conditions gives the remaining sum of squares:

$$SS_{Error} = \sum [(X - GM) - (\bar{S} - GM) - (\bar{X} - GM)]^2$$

The SS_{Error} and the $SS_{Conditions}$ sum to the $SS_{Within\,subjects}$, so we can write

$$SS_{Within\,subjects} = SS_{Conditions} + SS_{Error}$$

and we have completed the second step in the analysis of variance. Finally, combining the two steps, we have completed the division of SS_{Total}:

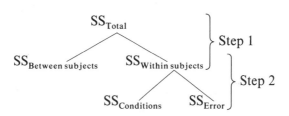

The full expression for the partition is

$$\sum (X - GM)^2 = a\sum (\bar{S} - GM)^2 + n\sum (\bar{X} - GM)^2$$
$$+ \sum [(X - GM) - (\bar{S} - GM) - (\bar{X} - GM)]^2$$

Or, most simply,

$$SS_{Total} = SS_{Between\,subjects} + SS_{Conditions} + SS_{Error}$$

The degrees of freedom for subjects, conditions, and total are determined by following the usual rule—the number of elements summed, minus 1—so that

$$df_{Total} = na - 1$$
$$df_{Between\,subjects} = n - 1$$
$$df_{Conditions} = a - 1$$

TABLE 14.2

Source	SS	df	MS	F
Subjects	2000.13	10	200.01	
Stimulus row	3284.90	2	1642.45	35.77
Error	918.49	20	45.92	
Total	6203.52	32		

The degrees of freedom for error is

$$df_{Error} = (n-1)(a-1)$$

Putting the sums of squares together with their degrees of freedom yields estimates for several variance components, and leads to an F ratio testing the null hypothesis of no difference among the means of the treatment populations. The summary table for the analysis of the data in Table 14.1 is shown in Table 14.2. With 2 and 20 degrees of freedom[3] and $\alpha = .01$, the critical value for F is 5.85, so we clearly may reject the hypothesis that the row where the letters were presented has no effect on the recall. Note that there is no F given for "subjects." In most cases, we are not interested in testing the between-subjects variation for significance (everyone will agree that subjects differ); this entry represents the variation in the data that was "removed" by the repeated measures analysis.

COMPARING A BETWEEN AND A WITHIN ANALYSIS[4]

In Table 14.1, there are three sets of scores, one from each of the three rows in the stimulus display. Just for now, let's ignore the fact that the scores come from a within-subjects design and treat the three sets of values as if they came from three separate groups. That is, we will analyze the data *inappropriately*, just to make a point. If we do that, the means and standard deviations of each set of values don't change. But if we conduct the analysis of variance, we obtain the summary values in Table 14.3. Note first that the *totals* for the sums of squares and degrees of freedom are exactly the same

[3] Repeated measures ANOVA is especially sensitive to certain violations in its assumptions. For that reason, some computer programs report a value called the Huynh-Feldt, or Epsilon, correction. If it is available in your output, the df values should be adjusted by multiplying them by the correction. The new values are used to find the critical value in Appendix F. For this example, the correction factor is 0.80, and so the degrees of freedom are corrected to

$$df_{Between\,subjects} = Correction * (n-1) = 0.80(3-1) \cong 2$$

$$df_{Error} = Correction * (n-1)(a-1) = 0.80(11-1)(3-1) = 16$$

The critical value from Appendix F is now 6.23; we still reject the hypothesis. Note that the df value is rounded to the nearest integer. Wilcox (1987, pp. 234–236) summarizes the logic and the computations for the correction.

[4] This section presents a somewhat advanced topic and may be omitted, depending on the instructor's wishes.

Source	SS	df	MS	F
TABLE 14.3				
Stimulus row	3284.90	2	1642.45	16.88
Error	2918.62	30	97.29	
Total	6203.52	32		

as those in Table 14.2. They should be because the data are identical. The three sets of 11 scores each give $df_{Total} = 33 - 1 = 32$, and the 33 data values are the same as before and thus have the same variability, so SS_{Total} is also exactly the same. What is very different is the error variation. In Table 14.3, the error sum of squares is *much* larger. Larger, in fact, by 2000.13—*exactly* the amount of the $SS_{Subjects}$ in Table 14.2. The numbers thus bear out the partition of the within-subjects variation. In the (inappropriate) between-subjects analysis in Table 14.3, the error sum of squares contains *both* the error variablity and the between-subjects variability. This results in an error mean square of 97.29. When the data are appropriately analyzed (Table 14.2), the variation between subjects is removed, resulting in an error mean square of 45.92, nearly one-half its previous value. Because the mean square for the effect of stimulus row remains unchanged in the two analyses at 1642.45, the *F* ratio in Table 14.2 is much larger. The ratio is significant in either case but might not alway be so.

Recall from Chapter 12 that the *F* is really

$$\frac{\text{Error variation} + \text{Independent variable variation}}{\text{Error variation}}$$

and it's apparent that the smaller the "error term," the more likely we are to reject the hypothesis of no treatment effects. Because the goal of research is to reject the null hypothesis whenever appropriate and thus uncover effects of an experimental treatment, an experimental design that reduces the error term is more likely to find an effect if it's there. In short, the repeated measures design, with its reduction in the error term due to eliminating between-subject variability, has more power.

◆ Follow-Up Analyses

From the means in Table 14.1 and the box plot in Figure 14.1, it is clear that the middle row leads to far better recall than do either the top or the bottom rows. Although the differences are obvious, we need to support the "eyeball" conclusions with follow-up analyses, as we did for the between-subjects design. Computer programs offer various choices for follow-up tests after a significant overall *F*. The best course of action is to ignore them and just conduct repeated measures *t* tests between the conditions, perhaps with a

Bonferroni adjustment to the significance level. The computational supplement shows a straightforward example computation.

The major difference between follow-up tests in the between- and the within-subjects designs is the statistic used to estimate error variance. In the between-subjects design, the within-groups mean square was used as the "error term" in both the overall analysis and in the follow-up tests. That statistic was appropriate there because it offers the most stable estimate of the overall error variance available. In the within-subjects design, though, each subject appears in all conditions, and thus contributes to SS_{Error} multiple times. If each subject responded to every experimental condition in exactly the same way, the overall MS_{Error} would again provide the best available estimate of σ_e^2, just as it did before. However, subjects typically respond differently to the conditions of the experiment. In that case, then, as Keppel (1982, pp. 393–398) emphasizes, the appropriate "error term" may not be the overall estimate of σ_e^2, but rather an estimate based on only those conditions involved in a particular comparison. For example, to compare the top and the middle stimulus rows in the data, we would base the error estimate on just those two conditions. Computer programs sometimes offer a choice of whether to use the "overall" error term or an error term based just on the data for the specific comparison; opt for the latter. If you're doing the analysis by hand, the repeated measure t accomplishes exactly the same thing.

Beyond the choice of an error term, deciding how to conduct follow-up tests is based on decisions regarding Type I and Type II errors. The considerations here are exactly the same as those in Chapter 12.

◆ Power and the Within-Subjects Design

The within-subjects design considered in this chapter is similar to the two-condition within-subjects design discussed in Chapter 12. And the determination of power and sample size is similar. To find a sample size, first determine the size of the smallest difference between two conditions that you consider important and decide on the power you want to detect that difference. Then refer to the procedures illustrated in Chapter 12 for the repeated measure t test.

A DISTRIBUTION-FREE ALTERNATIVE TO ANOVA

Several tests might be employed in cases where the group sizes are fairly small and when the distribution seems to be nonnormal. These are also especially appropriate when the measurement of the dependent variable is ordinal, because the analysis of variance assumes interval or ratio measurement. Only the most frequently used test is illustrated in the computational supplement, the **Friedman Test for Correlated Groups**. It is offered by some computer programs.

Summary
◆ *The* repeated measures design *offers an effective way to reduce between-conditions variability and thus increase power.*

◆ *In an independent groups design,* between-subjects variation *is confounded with* between-experimental-conditions *variation.*

◆ *The repeated measures design removes the between-subjects variation from the between-experimental-conditions variation.*

◆ *The total variation can be partitioned into between subjects and within subjects; the latter can be partitioned into between conditions and error.*

◆ *The difference between a subject's mean and the grand mean is that part of the variation around the grand mean that represents subject difference.*

◆ *The* Friedman Test for Correlated Groups *is a nonparametric alternative to within-subjects ANOVA.*

Key Terms

BETWEEN-EXPERIMENTAL- CONDITIONS VARIATION	REPEATED MEASURES DESIGN
BETWEEN-SUBJECTS VARIATION	$SS_{\text{Between subjects}}$
FRIEDMAN TEST FOR CORRELATED GROUPS	$SS_{\text{Conditions}}$
	$SS_{\text{Within subjects}}$
	$\bar{S}$

EXERCISES

1. The following data give the number of words recalled correctly on Trials 3, 5, 7, and 9 of a learning experiment. Use the analysis of variance to test for differences among the trials of the experiment. Follow up appropriately, keeping the EW error rate below 0.10. Present the results appropriately.

TRIAL 3	TRIAL 5	TRIAL 7	TRIAL 9
4	10	12	14
10	16	20	19
9	11	13	15
9	7	13	16
8	6	14	17
5	6	9	13
5	18	18	11
6	7	9	14
10	11	20	20
3	4	10	13
7	15	20	20
5	9	11	19

2. Students were asked to take multiple choice tests under three different conditions of crowding. In one condition, the subjects worked alone at a table. In another, each subject was at a table with three other individuals, who were all working at the same task. In the third condition, there were seven other people at the table. The presentation order was counterbalanced and each subject participated in all three conditions. The dependent variable was the number of items correct out of a total of 50 questions. Does crowding have an effect on the number correct? Follow up the overall analysis appropriately, keeping the EW error rate below 0.10. Present the results appropriately.

SUBJECT	ALONE	THREE OTHERS	SEVEN OTHERS
1	31	13	26
2	49	34	24
3	33	21	23
4	34	35	33
5	37	19	20
6	29	25	21
7	29	16	26
8	30	43	20
9	17	21	22
10	29	23	12
11	41	30	16
12	50	10	29
13	32	28	16
14	44	18	27
15	30	18	25

3. Nasby and Yando (1988) asked children to recall a series of words. There were 24 adjectives to be recalled. Of the words, 6 had been previously categorized as "Highly positive" words, 6 as "Slightly positive," 6 more as "Slightly negative," and 6 as "Highly negative." The following data[5] give the total number of words that each of 12 children recalled from each of the four word groups. Does the positiveness or negativeness of the word have an effect on the number recalled? Follow up the overall analysis, and present the results appropriately. Use $\alpha_{EW} = .05$.

CHILD	HIGHLY POSITIVE	SLIGHTLY POSITIVE	SLIGHTLY NEGATIVE	HIGHLY NEGATIVE
1	2	3	2	2
2	3	2	2	4
3	2	2	2	3
4	2	1	1	1
5	3	3	2	3
6	3	2	1	2
7	2	1	1	1
8	1	1	2	2
9	3	1	1	3
10	4	2	1	2
11	2	2	1	3
12	2	1	2	2

[5] These data are simulated to resemble those of Nasby and Yando (1988), in that the means approximate the overall means from their Experiment 1.

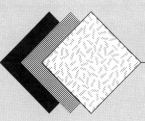

Computational Supplement

◆ Computations for the Overall Analysis

Naturally, the defining formulas aren't the ones best suited for computations. The more convenient computational formulas are in Table 14.4. As a first step in the analysis, Table 14.5 gives the raw data from Table 14.1, with the sums for each row and column, and the sum of squared values for each row and column.

We begin the analysis of variance by computing the total sum of squares:

$$SS_{Total} = \sum X^2 - \frac{GT^2}{na}$$

$$= 35592.34 - \frac{984.8^2}{11 * 3}$$

$$= 35592.34 - 29388.82$$

$$= 6203.52$$

Then, for the sum of squares between subjects,

$$SS_{Between\ subjects} = \frac{\sum S^2}{a} - \frac{GT^2}{na}$$

$$= \frac{41.4^2 + 80.4^2 + \cdots + 65.7^2}{3} - \frac{984.8^2}{11 * 3}$$

$$= 31388.95 - 29388.82$$

$$= 2000.13$$

and

$$SS_{Conditions} = \frac{\sum T^2}{n} - \frac{GT^2}{na}$$

$$= \frac{273.6^2 + 481.4^2 + 229.8^2}{11} - \frac{984.8^2}{11 * 3}$$

$$= 32673.72 - 29388.82$$

$$= 3284.90$$

Finally, the error sum of squares is calculated as

423

TABLE 14.4

Quantity	Definition	Computations
SS_{Total}	$\sum\sum(X - GM)^2$	$\sum\sum X^2 - \dfrac{GT^2}{na}$
$SS_{Between\ subjects}$	$a\sum(\bar{S} - GM)^2$	$\dfrac{\sum S^2}{a} - \dfrac{GT^2}{na}$
$SS_{Conditions}$	$n\sum(\bar{X} - GM)^2$	$\dfrac{\sum T^2}{n} - \dfrac{GT^2}{na}$
SS_{Error}	$\sum\sum[(X - GM) - (\bar{S} - GM)$ $- (\bar{X} - GM)]^2$	$\sum\sum X^2 - \dfrac{\sum S^2}{a}$ $- \dfrac{\sum T_j^2}{n} + \dfrac{GT^2}{na}$

TABLE 14.5

	Recall from Stimulus Row				
Subject	1	2	3	S	$\sum X^2$
1	14.7	13.8	12.9	41.4	572.94
2	13.5	50.1	16.8	80.4	2974.50
3	39.9	58.2	27.0	125.1	5708.25
4	23.4	46.5	18.3	88.2	3044.70
5	27.9	46.5	32.1	106.5	3971.07
6	26.4	51.6	26.1	104.1	4040.73
7	27.3	44.1	17.4	88.8	2992.86
8	36.3	49.8	36.6	122.7	5137.29
9	23.4	43.4	17.1	83.9	2723.53
10	30.9	33.6	13.5	78.0	2266.02
11	9.9	43.8	12.0	65.7	2160.45
T	273.6	481.4	229.8	984.8	
$\sum X$	7676.64	22430.56	5485.14		35592.34

$$SS_{Error} = \sum X^2 - \frac{\sum S^2}{a} - \frac{\sum T^2}{n} + \frac{GT^2}{na}$$

$$= 35592.34 - \frac{41.4^2 + 80.4^2 + \cdots + 65.7^2}{3}$$

$$- \frac{273.6^2 + 481.4^2 + 229.8^2}{11} + \frac{984.8^2}{11*3}$$

$$= 35592.34 - 31388.95 - 32673.72 + 29388.82$$

$$= 918.49$$

Entering the figures in a summary table (see Table 14.2), we can verify that the three component sums of squares add up to SS_{Total}.

Using the definitions for degrees of freedom given earlier, we complete the summary table as shown in Table 14.2. With 2 and 20 degrees of freedom and $\alpha = .01$, the critical value for F is 5.85, and so we reject the hypothesis that the row where the letters were presented has no effect on the recall.

◆ Follow-Up Tests

For most purposes, simple t tests for repeated measures are sufficient. Adjustments for multiple comparisons using the Bonferroni procedure are easy to make. As an example, let's compare the recall from the bottom row with that from the top row. (From what we already know of the data from Table 14.1 and Figure 14.1, we expect that the comparison will not be significant.)

Begin by extracting the data from the two rows, as shown in Table 14.6. The test is conducted as a single-sample Student's t test of the hypothesis that the population mean of the difference is zero. The computations are straightforward and follow the procedure given in Chapter 9. The null hypothesis is that, in the population, the top and the bottom rows lead to equal recall. The mean of the differences is 3.98, and their standard deviation is 7.03. Applying the single-sample t from Chapter 9, we have

$$s_{\overline{X}} = \frac{s}{\sqrt{N}} = \frac{7.03}{\sqrt{11}}$$
$$= 2.12$$

so that

$$t = \frac{\overline{X} - \mu}{\hat{s}_{\overline{X}}}$$

TABLE 14.6			
	Recall from		
Subject	*Row 1*	*Row 3*	*Difference*
1	14.7	12.9	1.80
2	13.5	16.8	−3.30
3	39.9	27.0	12.90
4	23.4	18.3	5.10
5	27.9	32.1	−4.20
6	26.4	26.1	0.30
7	27.3	17.4	9.90
8	36.3	36.6	−0.30
9	23.4	17.1	6.30
10	30.9	13.5	17.40
11	9.9	12.0	−2.10

$$= \frac{3.98 - 0.0}{2.12}$$

$$= 1.88$$

We can conclude that recall from the top row and recall from the bottom row do not differ significantly; $t(10) = 1.88$, $p > .05$.

Note that this computation uses only the data in the two conditions, and thus bases the error term on only the data in the two conditions being compared, as recommended in the text.

Conducting repeated t tests on the same set of data results in the tests being nonindependent of each other. Nonindependent tests, in turn, cause the EW probability of a Type I error to increase. If you are uncomfortable with the EW error rate that results from repeated analyses, a Bonferroni adjustment is easy to make; simply divide the EW probability that you want by the number of tests to be made, and use that as the significance level for each test.

◆ The Friedman Test for Correlated Groups

The distribution-free analog to the within-groups analysis of variance is the Friedman Test for Correlated Groups. This may also be used in designs where matched sets of subjects are assigned to the different conditions. The null hypothesis in the Friedman test is that the data in all conditions come from the same population. You may also think of the null hypothesis as being that all population medians are equal.

The test statistic for the Friedman is computed using the formula

$$\chi_F^2 = \frac{12}{na(a + 1)} \sum R^2 - 3n(a + 1)$$

where R is the sum of ranks for an experimental condition, a is the number of experimental conditions, and n is the number of subjects. In this test, ranking is done *within* each subject, as will become clear shortly, and the ranks are summed across subjects to give the R value for each condition.

Suppose that a group of 18 subjects is asked to rate each of five fragrances according to their perceived pleasantness, with a rating of 10 representing a pleasant odor and 1 representing a noxious odor. There would be five ratings for each subject, one for each odor. The data, with their associated ranks shown in parentheses, are given in Table 14.7. (For now, ignore the values in parentheses.) For Subject 1, odor A was given a 5, odor B a 7, odor C a 2, and so on.

The first step in the analysis is to rank each subject's data. The ranking is within each subject. For subject 1, for example, the ratings of the odors are

		ODOR			
SUBJECT	A	B	C	D	E
1	5	7	2	4	3

The lowest rated odor—that is, the one with the smallest value (2)—is assigned rank 1, the next higher rating (3) is given the rank 2, and so forth through the

TABLE 14.7

Subject	Odor				
	A	*B*	*C*	*D*	*E*
1	5 (4)	7 (5)	2 (1)	4 (3)	3 (2)
2	5 (4)	9 (5)	4 (3)	2 (1)	3 (2)
3	9 (4)	10 (5)	3 (2)	7 (3)	2 (1)
4	2 (2.5)	7 (5)	1 (1)	2 (2.5)	4 (4)
5	6 (4)	7 (5)	1 (1)	4 (2.5)	4 (2.5)
6	6 (4)	8 (5)	4 (2)	5 (3)	3 (1)
7	4 (4)	8 (5)	2 (1)	3 (2.5)	3 (2.5)
8	2 (1)	5 (4.5)	4 (3)	3 (2)	5 (4.5)
9	2 (1)	7 (4.5)	4 (3)	7 (4.5)	3 (2)
10	2 (1.5)	2 (1.5)	3 (3.5)	3 (3.5)	4 (5)
11	5 (4)	8 (5)	3 (2)	3 (2)	3 (2)
12	5 (3.5)	9 (5)	4 (1.5)	5 (3.5)	4 (1.5)
13	2 (1.5)	9 (5)	2 (1.5)	4 (4)	3 (3)
14	8 (4.5)	8 (4.5)	1 (1)	6 (3)	2 (2)
15	1 (1)	4 (2.5)	4 (2.5)	9 (5)	5 (4)
16	4 (2.5)	10 (5)	2 (1)	8 (4)	4 (2.5)
17	4 (2.5)	6 (5)	2 (1)	5 (4)	4 (2.5)
18	10 (5)	6 (3.5)	4 (1)	6 (3.5)	5 (2)
$\sum R_j$	54.5	81.0	32.0	56.5	46.0

largest value (7), which receives the rank of 5, as shown in parentheses:

| 1 | 5 (4) | 7 (5) | 2 (1) | 4 (3) | 3 (2) |

When there are ties, the ratings receive the mean rank of the tied values. Here is an example for subject 4:

| 4 | 2 (2.5) | 7 (5) | 1 (1) | 2 (2.5) | 4 (4) |

where both odors A and D were rated 2. The two 2s are tied for ranks 2 and 3, so each receives the mean rank of 2.5.

After the subjects' ranks are computed, they are summed for each condition (odor, in this case), as shown. The sums are entered into the formula, giving

$$\chi_F^2 = \frac{12}{na(a+1)} \sum R_j^2 - 3n(a+1)$$

$$= \frac{12}{18 * 5 * (5+1)} (54.5^2 + 81.0^2 + 32.0^2 + 56.5^2 + 46.0^2) - 3 * 18 * (5+1)$$

$$= 0.0222 \, (15863.5) - 324$$

$$= 28.17$$

The Friedman χ^2_F is distributed as χ^2 with df $= a - 1$; consulting Appendix D, we find that the critical value at the .05 level is 9.49, and we may thus reject the hypothesis that the five odors are identical in pleasantness.

A follow-up procedure for comparing pairs of experimental conditions is given by Siegel and Castellan (1988, pp. 180–183).

15 ANOVA in Factorial Experiments

In this chapter we introduce and illustrate the factorial experimental design. In a **factorial design**, there are two independent variables (or often more, but we won't go that far). In such a design, it's possible to look at each variable separately, as we might do in a design with a single independent variable. But it's also possible to study how the two variables may work together to influence behavior. As an example, we will look at an experiment that combines a physiological independent variable with a personality variable.

Transmission of nerve impulses involves substances known as neurotransmitters. A particular neurotransmitter called dopamine is active in many neurological events, and a substance related to it, L-dopa, is often used in research. In its research use, L-dopa is often found to speed mental processes. At the same time, substances that act opposite to a neurotransmitter should interfere with neural transmission. For example, the drug haloperidol is an antagonist to L-dopa, and should show an opposite effect.

Assume we are interested in the effects of L-dopa and haloperidol and want to test them is an experiment, along with a placebo control condition where subjects are given no drug. Chapter 12 presented a multiple-condition experimental design that would allow us to ask about the effects of the drugs. In fact, the independent variable (the drugs: L-dopa, haloperidol, and placebo) could be manipulated across different subjects (Chapter 12) or within the same subject (Chapter 14). In either case, though, the one-way experimental design could address questions like "Are there differences among the drugs in the effect on reaction time?" or "Does haloperidol differ from L-dopa?" or perhaps "Does L-dopa differ from the placebo in its effect on reaction time?" In the following example, the question deals with performance on a complex decision-making task. If L-dopa speeds or enhances neural events, we expect better performance with it, especially if compared to an antagonist like haloperidol.

The three columns in Table 15.1 present a set of data[1] from an experiment on these three drugs. Each column gives the change in performance on a decision task. The task was given before and after drug administration. A negative value means the subject's performance *improved*—that is, got faster —after the drug administration. A total of 24 subjects received each different drug condition; the means and standard deviations for each drug appear at the bottom of the table. A quick look at the means suggests there is probably no difference between the L-dopa and the placebo conditions, while haloperidol leads to substantially larger values, indicating a deterioration in performance.

But there is more to the experiment than just the three drug conditions. Subjects were pretested on a scale that measured their susceptibility to boredom, a trait often closely linked to introversion/extroversion. Each group of 24 drug treatment subjects contains 12 high-boredom-susceptible subjects and 12 low-boredom-susceptible subjects, as shown in Table 15.1. The high- and low-boredom-susceptibility groups make up a second independent variable. If we had *only* those two conditions, a two-sample *t* test would answer the question of whether the boredom groups differ in their performance on the decision task.

However, the two independent variables are combined in the experiment. The columns represent an independent variable with three conditions (drug). The upper and lower parts of the table represent a two-condition independent variable with high- and low-boredom-susceptible subjects. All together, there are six groups of subjects in the experiment: high boredom

---

[1] These data are fictional, but the values are similar to those of Netter and Rammsayer (1991); this example is modeled after their experiment.

TABLE 15.1

	Drug Condition		
	L-dopa	Placebo	Haloperidol
Low Boredom Susceptibility			
	−0.77	1.42	7.13
	−1.09	−0.22	7.66
	−2.55	−2.32	8.04
	1.46	0.38	7.28
	−0.60	−3.33	9.29
	−2.82	2.14	10.03
	−2.09	−5.35	9.31
	1.51	−2.00	11.05
	−4.79	1.55	6.50
	−2.50	0.04	4.31
	−2.70	−0.96	6.85
	−4.47	−3.28	8.48
High Boredom Susceptibility			
	−2.40	1.52	2.91
	−1.71	0.34	3.70
	1.27	0.58	0.98
	1.76	0.67	−0.37
	1.56	0.83	3.82
	−1.52	1.55	1.31
	1.65	1.97	−0.43
	4.07	4.93	−1.43
	3.28	3.78	4.19
	4.03	1.99	0.35
	4.02	−2.56	0.40
	2.30	3.07	2.29
Mean Standard Deviation			
	−0.13	0.28	4.74
	2.70	2.44	3.78

L-dopa, low boredom L-dopa, high boredom placebo, low boredom placebo, high boredom haloperidol, and low boredom haloperidol.

The mean decision task performance of the boredom-susceptibility groups in each of the three drug conditions is presented in Table 15.2. The means of the three drug conditions are also presented. These means are obtained by disregarding the boredom condition and simply finding the mean of each column in Table 15.1. In addition, the means of the high- and the low-boredom-susceptibility groups are shown, averaged across the three drugs. With the data in this form, we can see that the three drugs have quite different effects on reaction time performance for the two boredom groups. For example, the three drugs seem to have very little effect on the performance of the high-boredom subjects—the three means are very simi-

TABLE 15.2

	Drug Condition			Mean Improvement by Boredom Groups
	L-dopa	Placebo	Haloperidol	
Low Boredom Susceptibility	−1.78	−0.99	7.99	1.74
High Boredom Susceptibility	1.52	1.56	1.48	1.52
Mean Performance by Drug Condition	−0.13	0.28	4.74	1.63

lar—but the pattern is quite different for the low-boredom group, where performance decreases markedly under haloperidol.

Independent variables in a factorial design are chosen because of a particular interest in their interaction. In the drug-by-boredom example, we might have reason to believe that the drugs will have different effects on the two kinds of individuals. Of course, we could look at either drug or boredom separately, but if we did, we would not learn anything about how the variables work together, or interact, to influence reaction time. This ability to study the interaction of two variables is the bonus in the factorial. We can still look at the effect of both independent variables alone ("Do the two boredom groups differ?" "Do the three drugs differ?"), but only the factorial lets us also study the two variables together.

Each independent variable can be manipulated as either a between-subjects or a within-subjects variable. In the factorial design, this can lead to several combinations of between- and within-subjects designs. In the drug–boredom example, we've suggested that there are six independent groups of subjects, where each group has a particular boredom and drug. But we could easily have just two groups of subjects (low and high boredom susceptibility) and use each subject under all three drug conditions.[2] In this case, the boredom is a between-subjects variable, while drug is a within-subjects variable.

A personality variable like boredom susceptibility cannot be manipulated within subjects, but you can easily imagine an experiment with a variable that is. Age might be such an example, and you might have an experiment where each subject receives only a single drug (making drug a between-subjects variable), but receives it over a lifetime, with testing done at two ages. Under this plan, the age variable is within subjects. Or both variables could be manipulated within subjects, with every subject receiving

[2] In fact, Netter and Rammsayer (1991) did the experiment in just that way; each subject received all drugs, in a counterbalanced order, with sufficient time between administrations for all drug effects to dissipate.

each drug at each age. The latter plan uses only a single group of subjects.[3] Within-subjects factorial experiments, like mixed designs, are very common in psychology. Because the inferential statistics for the factorial—the analysis of variance—is different for between- and within-subjects single-factor experiments, you might expect a difference in factorial designs too, and you're correct. This text covers only the simplest design—both variables between subjects.

◆ Descriptive Analysis of a Factorial Experiment

Let's return to the drug and boredom example. The design has two drugs and a placebo as one independent variable. The second independent variable is a personality trait: high and low boredom susceptibility. The dependent variable is the change in performance on a choice reaction time task. Before we even begin to develop the inferential statistics for the factorial, let's look at the results descriptively. The place to begin is with the means in Table 15.2. Table 15.3 repeats those mean performance changes for the 12 subjects in each of the six experimental conditions and adds their standard deviations. For example, the mean performance change for the low-boredom subjects given L-dopa is -1.78 with a standard deviation of 1.99. The table also gives, in the rightmost column, the means and standard deviations for each boredom group averaged over the three drugs. As an example, the mean of the 36 low subjects, averaged by combining all the drug groups, is 1.74, with a standard deviation of 4.91.

TABLE 15.3				
	Drug Condition			
	L-dopa	*Placebo*	*Haloperidol*	*Boredom Mean*
Low Boredom Susceptibility				
	−1.78	−0.99	7.99	1.74
	1.99	2.30	1.80	4.91
High Boredom Susceptibility				
	1.52	1.56	1.48	1.52
	2.30	1.90	1.88	1.97
Drug Mean				
	−0.13	0.28	4.74	1.63
	2.70	2.44	3.78	3.72

Means for all subjects in the boredom groups

Means for all high-boredom subjects

[3] Clearly, using age as a within-subjects variable requires either a great deal of patience on the part of the experimenter, or subjects with short life spans!

The means for the three drug groups, averaged across boredom group, appear in the last row. The mean of all the subjects receiving haloperidol is 4.74, as was also illustrated in Table 15.2.

The grand mean and standard deviation, based on all 72 subjects, are shown in the lower right-hand corner of Table 15.3. Over all the subjects in all boredom groups and drug conditions, then, the mean performance change is 1.63, with a standard deviation of 3.72.

From the means on the right-hand side, it seems that the two personality groups differ little in their change in performance before and after the drug (a mean of 1.74 for the low-boredom subjects compared with 1.52 for the high-boredom group). The analysis of variance will let us conclude whether those differences are significant, but for now we are looking only at the descriptive statistics.

Looking only at the bottom row, we might conclude that haloperidol produces the greatest performance decrement, since its overall mean is highest. But look at the two individual group means for haloperidol. Although the low-boredom subjects were certainly affected by the haloperidol, the high-boredom subjects show no such effect. Clearly, there is something going on here that is not evident from the overall means of drug and personality groups.

Comparing the performance changes for the personality groups shows differences between the drugs. For the low-boredom-susceptibility subjects, there is slight improvement (negative scores) for L-dopa and for the placebo, but a large performance decrement with haloperidol. The high-boredom-susceptibility subjects, conversely, show a pattern of very slight performance decrease regardless of the drug. The differences in the responses of the two groups can be seen clearly if we graph the mean performance change scores for the two sets of boredom-susceptibility data separately as in Figure 15.1. A plot like this, called an **interaction plot**, places one independent variable across the abscissa, and uses separate lines on the graph to show the other; the values plotted are the means of the individual groups. Seen this way, it's clear that the two personality groups react very differently to the drugs. The high-boredom subjects seem virtually unaffected by the drugs. The low-boredom group, however, reacts strongly to the haloperidol.

The plot also makes it easy to see that two of the drug–boredom combinations are more successful at the task, but that the same personality group also shows the worst performance; see Figure 15.2. The figure also makes it visually clear that the high-boredom-susceptibility subjects are unaffected by the drugs.

What we are illustrating here is the **interaction** between the two independent variables boredom susceptibility and drug. We would never have learned about the personality differences in drug response if we had not been able to study the way the two variables act in different combinations. Nothing in the overall drug means suggested a personality difference in the drug response.

When two variables interact, the effect of one variable changes with a change in the other. In the example, for L-dopa and for the placebo, the

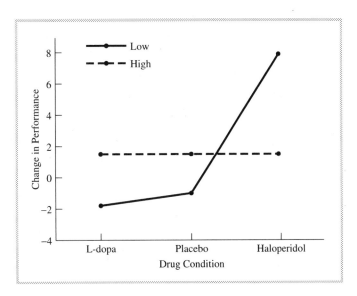

Figure 15.1

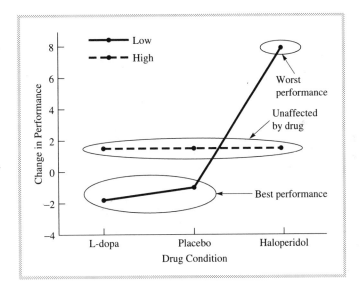

Figure 15.2

effect of the personality variable is that low-boredom subjects perform better. However, when we look at personality with regard to haloperidol, the effect changes. In particular, as we move from L-dopa and placebo to haloperidol, the effect of the personality variable reverses; where formerly (under L-dopa and placebo) low-boredom subjects performed best, they perform exactly the opposite under haloperidol.

What if the plot of the means had been as shown in Figure 15.3? Here the lines are flat and parallel, indicating there is no change due to the drug conditions. There *is* an effect of personality group: Low-boredom subjects perform better than high-boredom subjects, and that's uniformly true for *all* drug conditions. Because there are no differences among the drugs, only differences between personality types, there is no interaction is this illustration; the effect of personality is the same for all drug conditions, including the placebo. This pattern of the means shows only a **main effect**, the effect of one variable alone. Specifically, this illustration shows a main effect for boredom susceptibility, but no effect for drug, and no interaction.

Contrast Figure 15.3 with Figure 15.4. There is virtually no difference between the two personality groups, but the drugs differ in their effects. This pattern shows a main effect for the drug variable because there certainly are effects of that variable. But there is no effect for boredom because the high- and the low-boredom-susceptibility subjects are exactly the same under all three drug conditions. And there's no interaction, either—high and low are the same relative to each other under each drug.

It's possible to have a pattern that shows main effects of both boredom group and drug, but with no interaction, as illustrated in Figure 15.5. Here there are effects of both boredom and drug: High is consistently above low, but the lines are not flat, indicating a drug effect. But the boredom groups do not change relative to each other under different drug conditions—the lines are parallel—so there is no interaction.

We might also have a pattern like the one illustrated in Figure 15.6, which shows both an interaction and a main effect for boredom. The groups are different in their relationship across the drugs; the relationship between

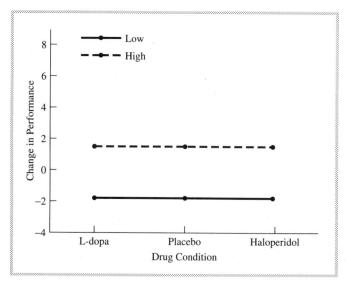

Figure 15.3

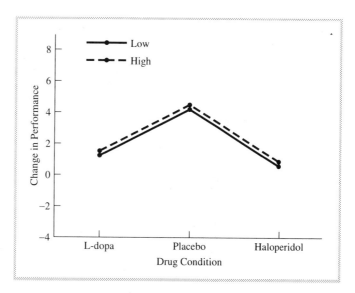

Figure 15.4

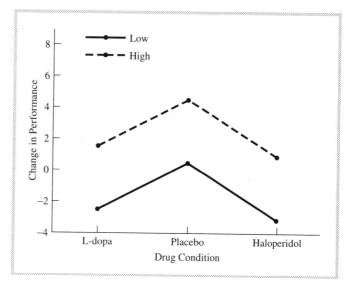

Figure 15.5

the boredom groups changes as a function of the drug. A main effect, though, looks at the average across the conditions of the other variable. In this case, the mean performance change, averaged across the drug conditions, is higher for high boredom than it is for low, despite the fact that they're the same in the haloperidol condition.

Other interaction patterns are also possible. Several are sketched in Figure 15.7. In each case, there is an interaction between boredom suscepti-

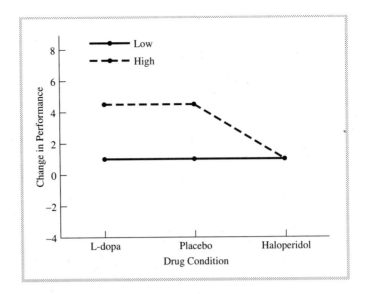

Figure 15.6

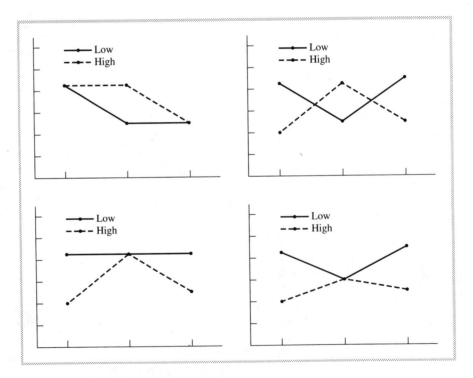

Figure 15.7

bility and drug, as indicated by the nonparallel lines. Parallel lines, like those in Figures 15.4 and 15.5, indicate that the boredom groups are affected in the same way by the drugs. Although they may differ between the kinds of subjects (the lines are not atop each other, as in Figure 15.4), the pattern remains the same across the drugs. While lines are not parallel, though, it means that not all subjects are reacting in the same way to all the treatment combinations.

We've discussed two components to interpreting factorial results. There are the two independent variables separately—these are the two main effects. And there is also the interaction. It should come as no surprise to learn, then, that there are three hypothesis tests in the analysis of variance, one for the main effect of each independent variable and a third for the interaction. The three tests are independent of one another, meaning there can be an effect of either one, both, or neither independent variable. And the interaction can occur whether or not either main effect is significant.

INFERENCE IN THE TWO-FACTOR, BETWEEN-SUBJECTS DESIGN

The total variation present in the entire experiment—in all experimental groups—forms the basis of the analysis. By partitioning it properly, we can estimate the portion contributed by each independent variable, by the interaction of the two independent variables, and by error. Finally, three overall null hypotheses are tested, one for each independent variable and the third for interaction.

◆ Null Hypotheses

In single-factor analysis of variance (Chapter 12), we tested the null hypothesis that all treatment effects were zero—that is,

$$\alpha_j = 0, \quad j = 1, 2, \ldots, k$$

In the factorial experiment, we identify three separate and independent hypotheses:

$$\alpha_i = 0, \quad i = 1, 2, \ldots, a$$
$$\beta_j = 0, \quad j = 1, 2, \ldots, b$$
$$\gamma_{ij} = 0, \quad i = 1, 2, \ldots, a, \quad j = 1, 2, \ldots, b$$

where α, β, and γ are the effects of the A variable (drug, in the example), the B variable (boredom susceptibility), and their interaction. In words, the three hypotheses are: There are no effects of independent variable A (all drugs are equal), there are no effects of the independent variable B (boredom group has no effect), and there are no interaction effects (the boredom groups react identically to all drugs). If these null hypotheses are true, all α_i equal 0, all β_j equal 0, and all $\gamma_{ij} = 0$ as well. The three null hypotheses are independent of one another, and they are tested individually.

◆ Partitioning the Total Variation

In analyzing the variance in the factorial experiment, we follow the same plan as in Chapters 12 and 14. First we consider the difference between a single score and the overall mean, and then partition that difference into separate components. Next we look at sums of squares arising from the partition, and finally we convert the sums of squares into mean squares and use them to test the three hypotheses.

Before we can introduce the comparable expression for the factorial experiment, we have to develop the symbolic notation of the design and a simple notation system for talking about means. Schematically, we may represent the two-factor experiment as illustrated in Figure 15.8. The letters A and B here stand for the two independent variables; in any particular experiment, obviously, they represent real variables, like drug and boredom susceptibility in the example. In the single-factor experiment, the letter a

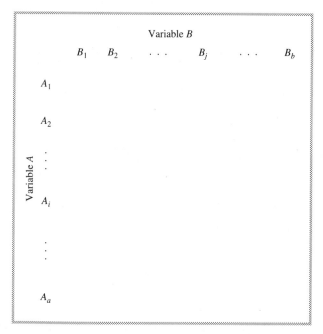

Figure 15.8

stood for the number of experimental treatments. The same scheme can work with two variables; independent variable A has a treatments or levels, and variable B has b conditions. In our example, $a = 3$ and $b = 2$ because A is drug and B is boredom susceptibility, as in Figure 15.9. The figure also shows the first three data values for each experimental group, taken from Table 15.1.

When we need to distinguish between specific rows and columns in the design, the letter i will stand for a row, and j for a column. Thus, writing A_1 means the L-dopa condition and A_3 means haloperidol. A_i indicates any row; i can take on any value between 1 and a. Likewise, B_1 means low boredom susceptibility, and B_j indicates any column. A specific treatment combination, then, is designated by its row and a column number: row 3 and column 2 in the example is the condition "haloperidol, high boredom susceptibility." We might refer to that same set of data as group $AB_{3,2}$.

Because this is a completely between-subjects design, each combination of treatments represents a single group of subjects. Each group is of the same size, n (for now, anyway), and represents a set of scores from individuals treated the same way with regard to the independent variables. The mean for an individual group can be designated by using appropriate subscripts. For example, the mean of all scores in the "haloperidol, high-boredom-susceptibility" group (that is, group $AB_{3,2}$) is $\overline{X}_{3,2}$. Naturally, it is calculated by summing the n scores in the group and dividing by n. This mean is an

		Boredom Group (Independent Variable B)	
		Low B_1	High B_2
Drug (Independent Variable A)	L-dopa A_1	-0.77 -1.09 -2.55 . .	-2.40 -1.71 1.27 . .
	Placebo A_2	1.42 -0.22 -2.32 . .	1.52 0.34 0.58 . .
	Haloperidol A_3	7.13 7.66 8.04 . .	2.91 3.70 0.98 . .

Figure 15.9

estimate of the population mean for all individuals under the "haloperidol, high-boredom-susceptibility" experimental conditions.

We can also calculate the means for all the subjects who receive each row treatment (drug). For example, the mean of all subjects given treatment A_1 (L-dopa) is the sum of all the subjects (in all the boredom conditions) who receive L-dopa, divided by the number of subjects summed. Because there are n subjects per group, and there are b groups who all receive the same L-dopa treatment, a total of bn subjects are given L-dopa. Their mean is calculated as

$$\overline{X}_{A_1} = \frac{\text{Sum of all L-dopa subjects}}{nb}$$

This mean, naturally, estimates μ_{A_1} (the mean of the population of all individuals who might receive L-dopa), *regardless* of their boredom susceptibility score. In a similar way, we could find the mean of all the subjects receiving the placebo ($\overline{X}_{A_2}$) and the mean of all subjects who received haloperidol ($\overline{X}_{A_3}$).

Looking at the columns in Figure 15.9, we could find the mean of all the low-boredom subjects by summing all the scores in the first column. There are three groups of subjects (in three drug conditions), so the mean of the first column is based on an scores and is computed as

$$\overline{X}_{B_1} = \frac{\text{Sum of all low-boredom subjects}}{na}$$

The mean of all the scores in all rows and columns can be computed by summing all the scores in all the groups. Because there are n subjects in each group, and there are ab groups, the total number of subjects is abn. Thus we compute the grand mean of all subjects in all conditions as

$$GM = \frac{\text{Sum of all subjects in all groups}}{abn}$$

Figure 15.10 gives all the means and their symbolic notation, both the group means and the row and column means, for the example. (The values, of course, are the same as those shown in Tables 15.2 and 15.3.)

With symbols developed for the overall mean (GM) and for row, column, and individual group means, we can now proceed to partition the variation present in the data.

SUMS OF SQUARES

The total variation present in the data (that is the variation of all subjects in all combinations of boredom susceptibility and drug) is the sum of the squared differences between the data values and the overall mean. The overall variance, as always, is

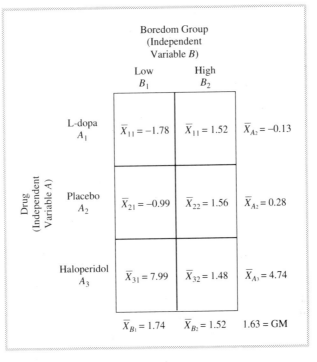

Figure 15.10

$$s^2 = \frac{\sum(X - \overline{X})^2}{N - 1}$$

Rewritten into notation appropriate for the two-factor design, the overall variance expression is

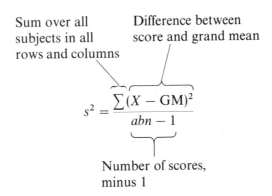

Consider only the numerator of the variance, the total sum of squares $\sum(X - \text{GM})^2$. Inside the parentheses is nothing but the difference between an individual score in some specific group of data and the grand mean.

That value can be expressed as differences between the score and the group means:

$$(X - GM) = (\overline{X}_{A_i} - GM) + (\overline{X}_{B_j} - GM)$$
$$+ (\overline{X}_{ij} - \overline{X}_{A_i} - \overline{X}_{B_j} + GM) + (X - \overline{X}_{ij})$$

This complicated formula says that the difference between a score in the ijth group and the grand mean can be expressed as the sum of a number of other differences. The first term on the right is the difference between the row mean and the grand mean. The second term is the difference between a column mean and the grand mean. And the third term shows the differences between the individual group mean $\overline{X}_{ij}$ and row and column means. The final term is the difference between a single score and the mean of its group $(\overline{X}_{ij})$.

If we substitute this expression into the expression for the total sum of squares $\sum(X - GM)^2$, and complete some very tedious algebra, we arrive at the division of the sum of squares shown in Figure 15.11. The total variation in the data (SS_{Total}) on the left-hand side of Figure 15.11 has been partitioned into four distinct parts. The first term sums the differences between the A_i means and the overall mean; we call this quantity the sum of squares for the A variable, or simply SS_A. Likewise, the second term deals with the B_j means, and so it is the sum of squares for B, or SS_B. The third term is the sum of squares for interaction ($SS_{Interaction}$, or simply SS_{AB}). The final component sums the differences within each group; it is thus the SS_{Within} or simply SS_{Error}. In short, we have

$$SS_{Total} = SS_A + SS_B + SS_{AB} + SS_{Error}$$

With this expression, we have analyzed the numerator of the variance (SS_{Total}) into four separate parts. Now we turn to the mean squares and their parameter expressions.

$$\sum(X - GM)^2 = nb\sum(\overline{X}_{A_i} - GM)^2 + na\sum(\overline{X}_{B_j} - GM)^2$$

$$\underbrace{\qquad}_{SS_{Total}} \qquad \underbrace{\qquad}_{SS_A} \qquad \underbrace{\qquad}_{SS_B}$$

$$+ n\sum(\overline{X} - \overline{X}_{A_i} - \overline{X}_{B_j} + GM)^2 + \sum(X - \overline{X}_{ij})^2$$

$$\underbrace{\qquad}_{SS_{Interaction}} \qquad \underbrace{\qquad}_{SS_{Within\ (Error)}}$$

Figure 15.11

Mean Squares

Just as we subdivided the total sum of squares into four segments, we can also partition the degrees of freedom into corresponding parts. This is done as follows:

$$df_A = a - 1$$

$$df_B = b - 1$$

$$df_{AB} = (a - 1)(b - 1)$$

$$df_{Error} = ab(n - 1)$$

$$df_{Total} = abn - 1$$

We now form variance estimates in the usual way—by dividing a sum of squares by its degrees of freedom. This yields the four statistics shown, along with the parameters they estimate. See Table 15.4. Each mean square in Table 15.4 estimates the error variance σ_e^2. In addition, three of the mean squares estimate a single additional parameter. In each case, that additional parameter contains exactly one of the three hypothesized effects: the effect of the A independent variable, the effect of the B independent variable, and the effect of the interaction. In each case, when a null hypothesis is true, the term for that hypothesis equals zero. For example, if there are no effects of A, then all values of α_i equal zero; the entire second term of the MS_A parameter equals zero as well.

Forming F Ratios

By this time, the general rule for forming an F ratio should be apparent. An F ratio for any hypothesis is constructed by finding two statistics whose parameter value differs only by a single term, and that term is one that

---

TABLE 15.4

Mean Square	Parameter Estimated
$MS_A = \dfrac{SS_A}{df_A}$	$\sigma_e^2 + \dfrac{bn \sum \alpha_i^2}{a - 1}$
$MS_B = \dfrac{SS_B}{df_B}$	$\sigma_e^2 + \dfrac{an \sum \beta_i}{b - 1}$
$MS_{AB} = \dfrac{SS_{AB}}{df_{AB}}$	$\sigma_e^2 + \dfrac{n \sum \gamma_{ij}^2}{(a - 1)(b - 1)}$
$MS_{Error} = \dfrac{SS_{Error}}{df_{Error}}$	σ_e^2

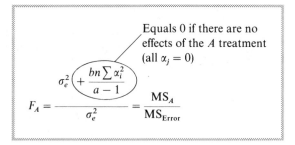

Figure 15.12

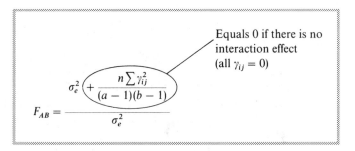

Figure 15.13

should be zero if the null hypothesis is true. For example, the F for testing the A independent variable is shown in terms of parameters in Figure 15.12, while that for interaction is illustrated in Figure 15.13. The F for testing the effect of the B independent variable is constructed in the same manner—namely, $F = \dfrac{MS_B}{MS_{Error}}$.

Applying the rules for F ratios and following the procedures in the computational supplement or on a computer, using the data in Table 15.1, leads to the analysis of variance summary table in Table 15.5. The F for boredom susceptibility is made up of $MS_{Boredom}$ divided by MS_{Error}. The numerator of the ratio has df = 1, while the denominator has df = 66. Consulting Appendix F, we find that the critical F value at the .05 level is 4.00[4] and conclude that there is no overall effect of boredom susceptibility. Using df = 2, 66, the critical F from Appendix F is 3.15, and we conclude that there is a significant effect for drug, and that the interaction is also significant. (At this point, you might want to review the discussion of Figures 15.1 and 15.2.)

---

[4] Because df = 66 is not listed, we use the next smaller entry, this time df = 60.

TABLE 15.5

Source	SS	df	MS	F
Boredom susceptibility	0.865	1	0.865	0.209
Drug	349.405	2	174.702	42.131
Interaction	358.754	2	179.377	43.258
Error	273.678	66	4.147	
Total	982.702	71		

FOLLOW-UP ANALYSES

The three hypothesis tests—for variables A, B, and for their interaction—lead to three conclusions. Each independent variable may or may not have a significant effect by itself, and there may or may not be an interaction. As with the single-factor experiment, finding an overall effect is merely the first step in the analysis. Next we may need to explore further with various follow-up tests. Exactly how to proceed, though, depends on whether or not the interaction is significant.

◆ Follow Up: Interaction Not Significant

Establishing that there is no interaction between two independent variables means that each variable can be explored individually, and that conclusions about one variable will hold regardless of the value of the other variable. The actual follow-up analysis simplifies to the logical equivalent of two independent one-way analyses, one for each independent variable, but with two very important changes.

The follow-up analysis for each variable in the factorial follows the procedures illustrated in Chapter 12 for the single-factor experiment, with two differences. First, MS_{Error} from the full factorial analysis is the error term used for all follow-up comparisons, and in any post hoc tests. Second, the value of n changes; it is always the number of values entering into the means that are being compared. For example, if our interaction had been nonsignificant in the example, and we wished to compare the drug conditions, we would have had to remember that the three drug means are based not on $n = 12$, but rather on $2 * 12 = 24$, because each drug mean is taken across the two boredom conditions. Apart from those adjustments, all follow-up analyses of the main effects proceed exactly as in a single-factor experiment.

In a factorial design, we can distinguish between experiment-wise (EW) and family-wise (FW) error rates. The EW error rate refers, as it did in Chapter 12, to the probability of making a Type I error *somewhere* during the entire analysis. The FW error rate refers to the probability of making a

Type I error somewhere within a *family* of analyses. A family is the set of the follow-ups of one (or more) of the three overall effects tested. Thus, follow-up tests of a nonsignificant interaction are in two families: those pursuing the *A* main effect and those pursuing the *B* main effect. In a one-way analysis, there is only a single "family" of effects—namely, the effect of the single independent variable. In a factorial, though, we might have three families of analyses—for the two main effects and for the interaction.

In psychology, the recommended procedure is to control Type I error on a FW basis. We discuss error rates again later in this chapter, but for now we recommend establishing an error rate for the *A* and the *B* main effect families of tests, and proceeding with the follow-up analyses as if you were carrying out two unrelated single-factor experiments (using MS_{Error} from the overall analysis, of course). The EW error rate, naturally, is the sum of the FW rates.

◆ Follow Up: Interaction Significant

When the interaction is significant, there are two general strategies. The first is exactly comparable to the single-factor analysis in its logic; it uses a single level of one independent variable, and then conducts an analysis of variance on the other independent variable. The second analysis, analogous to follow-up comparisons in the one-way design, looks at differences within a single level of an independent variable. We'll follow Keppel's (1982) terminology, and designate the first analysis a **simple effects** analysis, and the second, **simple comparisons**.

SIMPLE EFFECTS AND SIMPLE COMPARISONS

A simple effect is conceptually a one-way analysis, but it is conducted at a single level of the other independent variable. In the drug–boredom susceptibility example, we might conduct the equivalent of one single-factor analysis of variance using just the high-boredom subjects, and another using only the low-boredom subjects. Each analysis would contain three drug conditions, and a significant result would mean that at least one comparison among the drug groups is significant. That analysis would be followed by simple comparisons, which are the equivalent of post hoc tests.

Two simple effect analyses are illustrated in Figure 15.14. In one analysis, we ask whether there are significant differences among the three drugs for the high-boredom subjects, and in a second analysis, whether there are significant drug effects for the low-boredom subjects. From looking at the plot, we might guess there is a significant difference among the drugs for the low subjects, but not for the high. The analysis treats the low and the high subjects in Table 15.1 as data from two separate experiments, and proceeds with two separate one-way analyses.[5] If either F ratio is significant, then appropriate follow-up analyses are carried out, following the logic in Chap-

[5] Except that the MS_{Error} from the overall analysis is used whenever an error term is required.

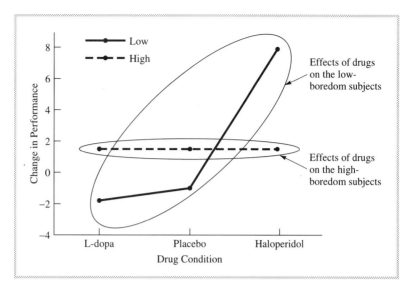

Figure 15.14

ter 12. These follow-up analyses are called *simple comparisons* because they involve only a single level of one of the independent variables.

In the example (see Figure 15.14), the simple effect of drug on the high-boredom subjects is most likely nonsignificant because the means are nearly identical. The simple effect of drug on the low-boredom subjects, however, is probably significant. The simple comparison analyses, then, will be carried out using only the low-boredom data. Using any of the follow-up procedures from Chapter 12, we could determine which of the three pairs of means (L-dopa–placebo, L-dopa–haloperidol, placebo–haloperidol) differ for the low-boredom subjects.

There is another way of looking at the data in Figure 15.14, and that is illustrated in Figure 15.15. Here, the simple effect analyses are conducted the "other way around" by looking for differences between the high- and low-boredom subjects for each drug individually. This analysis uses the data from Table 15.1, and treats each column as a separate analysis.

In the example data, the simple effects analyses would ask about the pairs of means shown in Figure 15.15. If any analysis indicated a significant difference, there would be no need for simple comparisons because only two groups are involved.

Table 15.6 summarizes the follow-up procedures.

ERROR CONTROL IN FACTORIAL DESIGNS

Chapter 12 discussed control of Type I and Type II errors extensively, and we will not review the arguments here. Although they still hold, current

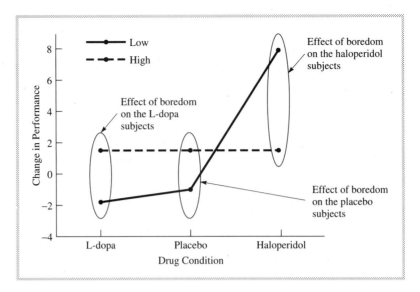

Figure 15.15

practice in psychological research is to do little to deal with error rates in the factorial design (Keppel, 1982). Just why this should be the case is unclear, but the literature contains very few references to Scheffé or Tukey or indeed any other procedures in factorials.

　　When adjustments are made, they're made on a FW basis, with the two main effects and the interaction as the families. When the interaction is not significant, it's easy to treat the two independent variables separately and control Type I error family-wise within each of the two one-way analyses that result. But how to best proceed in following up a significant interaction is unclear. The active research literature seems to suggest ignoring the problem of the compounding Type I error. If you are not comfortable with that, the reasonable approach is to decide on a basis for controlling error and apply Bonferroni adjustments within those limits. For example, in following up the drug example, we might decide to let the drug variable constitute one "family" and the combined boredom and interaction another. Suppose we want to hold Type I error at about .05 for each of the three original hypothesis families (boredom, drug, and interaction). Combining boredom and interaction as a single family allows a .10 FW error rate (.05 each for the drug and the boredom/interaction effects) for simple effects analyses. Now conduct the three simple effects tests at a Bonferroni-adjusted PC rate of $0.10/3 = 0.033$. We might then follow any significant simple effects with simple comparisons, using an uncorrected .05 level for each. If you're particularly concerned with Type I error, make a Tukey or even a Scheffé adjustment to the critical F value for the simple comparisons, as illustrated in Chapter 12.

POWER AND SAMPLE SIZE COMPUTATIONS IN THE FACTORIAL EXPERIMENT

The advice and procedures for the factorial are similar to those suggested in Chapter 12 for the one-way analysis. This means that the considerations here are identical to those discussed in Chapter 10 for the two-condition experiment. The difference is, of course, that you now have to contend with two independent variables and their interaction.

For determining sample size, begin with the interaction. Consider the meaning of each cell in the experimental design, and decide how large a difference between conditions you want to be able to detect. Computation of effect size is based on the smallest difference in individual cell means you want to be able to detect. Once that is decided, the computation proceeds as it did in Chapter 10, and the resulting n applies to all the groups in the design.

PRESENTING THE RESULTS OF A FACTORIAL EXPERIMENT

Presenting the results of a factorial experiment normally follows a standard outline. First, descriptive statistics are shown, usually as tables of means and standard deviations. If the interaction is significant, the plot also appears. Then the overall analysis of variance summary table is shown, with accompanying verbal statements about the data. Finally, follow-up tests are presented, again with accompanying verbal materials. When the interaction is not significant, follow-up results look very much like the results of one-way analyses and normally present pairwise tests on the main effect means. If the interaction is significant, simple effects tests often appear as standard summary tables. Pairwise simple effects tests are normally described verbally (e.g., "The mean of the high-boredom, placebo subjects differed from that of the low-boredom, placebo subjects (Dunnet C test, $p < .05$), but there were no other significant differences.")

FACTORIAL ANOVA VIA REGRESSION[6]

Factorial ANOVA may be conducted using a multiple regression approach, just as was a single-factor analysis of variance. It is cumbersome because it requires multiple analyses to construct the summary table, but the results are identical. As a benefit, though, we are sometimes able to include specific comparisons as part of the analysis.

In the factorial, there are two independent variables and an interaction to be specified using dummy variables.[7] The following general rules can be used to construct the set of dummy variables:

- ◆ For a levels of A, you will need $a - 1$ dummy scores for each subject.
- ◆ For b levels of B, you will need $b - 1$ dummy scores for each subject.
- ◆ For interaction, you will need $(a - 1)(b - 1)$ dummy variables.
- ◆ For the A dummy variables, follow the rules for one-way analysis: (1) For the ath group, assign -1 to all dummy variables , (2) assign a 1 to dummy 1 for the first A condition, 1 to the second dummy for the second A group, and so forth, and (3) enter zeros everywhere else.
- ◆ For B dummy variables, follow the same rules as for the A dummies.
- ◆ The interaction dummies are the products of all pairs of A and B dummies.

As an example, we will use the boredom susceptibility and drug example (Table 15.1). In this example, $a = 2$ and $b = 3$. There are six distinct groups of subjects, as listed in Table 15.7. The first dummy variable, labeled A in the table, distinguishes between the high- and low-boredom-susceptibility groups. The second and third dummies, B_1 and B_2, code the three drug conditions. The values were determined by following the rules just given.

---

[6] This section presents an advanced treatment of the topic and may be omitted if the instructor so desires.

[7] The presentation here focuses on "overall" analyses parallel to the overall analysis with three null hypotheses presented for equal group sizes. In fact, the dummy variables may be used to embody quite specific tests ("Do L-dopa and placebo (considered together) differ from haloperidol?"), as illustrated in Chapter 13. Although this topic takes us too far afield for this text, Judd and McClelland (1989) consider the situation fully.

TABLE 15.7

Group	A	B_1	B_2	AB_1	AB_2
Low boredom, L-dopa	1	1	0	1	0
Low boredom, placebo	1	0	1	0	1
Low boredom, haloperidol	1	−1	−1	−1	−1
High boredom, L-dopa	−1	1	0	−1	0
High boredom, placebo	−1	0	1	0	−1
High boredom, haloperidol	−1	−1	−1	1	1

The bth condition (haloperidol) was assigned -1 on each dummy. Then groups 1 and 2 (L-dopa and placebo) were given values of 1 on B_1 and B_2, respectively, with zeros elsewhere. The two interaction dummy variables (AB_1 and AB_2) were calculated as the products of A and B dummies. AB_1 is the product of the values in the A and the B_1 dummy variables, while AB_2 is the product of A and B_2.

The dummy variables are created, and each subject is given the pattern corresponding to the condition. All L-dopa, low-boredom subjects, for example, receive the values 1, 1, 0, 1, and 0, and high-boredom, placebo subjects receive -1, 0, 1, 0, and -1. The data look like the extract shown in Table 15.8.

A multiple regression with all the dummy variables produces Table 15.9. The summary table is for the total regression model, with the data values being "predicted" from the dummy variables for A (boredom susceptibility), B (drug), and AB (interaction). Note that the regression is significant ($F = 34.20$) and that it accounts for 72.2% of the variability (R^2, expressed as a percentage of the variability in the dependent variable). The total variability, shown as a sum of squares, is 982.701. The $SS_{Regression}$ contains the effects of A, B, and AB (that is, boredom susceptibility, drug, and interaction), and $SS_{Residual}$ is the "error" component in the analysis.

To construct the full ANOVA table, we must conduct several "reduced model" regressions and subtract to find the sums of squares for boredom, drug, and interaction. For example, suppose we carry out the regression with only A, B_1, and B_2 as predictors. The result of that analysis is shown in Table 15.10.

First note that the total sum of squares is identical to that obtained previously ($350.269 + 632.432 = 982.701$), indicating that the total amount of variability has not changed. But now the $SS_{Regression}$ contains only the boredom and drug effects, but *not* the interaction. The difference between the two $SS_{Regression}$ values must, therefore, be the sum of squares for interaction; we can obtain that value by subtraction: $SS_{Interaction} = SS_{Regression}$ (full model) $- SS_{Regression}$ (A and B only) $= 709.023 - 350.269 = 358.754$.

The sums of squares for boredom susceptibility and drug can be obtained similarly. For boredom susceptibility, calculate the regression using only the drug and interaction dummy variables (B_1, B_2, AB_1, and AB_2). To

TABLE 15.8

Data value	A	B_1	B_2	AB_1	AB_2	
⋮						
1.51	1	1	0	1	0	
−4.79	1	1	0	1	0	
−2.50	1	1	0	1	0	Low-boredom,
−2.70	1	1	0	1	0	L-dopa subjects
−4.47	1	1	0	1	0	
1.42	1	0	1	0	1	
−0.22	1	0	1	0	1	
−2.32	1	0	1	0	1	
⋮						Low-boredom,
						placebo subjects
0.04	1	0	1	0	1	
−0.96	1	0	1	0	1	
−3.28	1	0	1	0	1	
7.13	1	−1	−1	−1	−1	
7.66	1	−1	−1	−1	−1	
8.04	1	−1	−1	−1	−1	Low-boredom,
7.28	1	−1	−1	−1	−1	haloperidol subjects
9.29	1	−1	−1	−1	−1	
10.03	1	−1	−1	−1	−1	
⋮						etc.

TABLE 15.9

Source	SS	df	MS	F
Regression	709.023	5	141.8046	34.20
Residual	273.678	66	4.1466	
Total	982.701	71		

Variable	Coefficient	SE	t
Intercept	1.62903	0.2400	6.79
A	0.109583	0.2400	0.46
B_1	−1.75819	0.3394	−5.18
B_2	−1.34819	0.3394	−3.97
AB_1	−1.76458	0.3394	−5.20
AB_2	−1.38458	0.3394	−4.08

$$R^2 = 0.722$$

TABLE 15.10

Source	SS	df	MS	F
Regression	350.269	3	116.7563	12.55
Residual	632.432	68	9.3005	
Total	982.701	71		

$$R^2 = 0.356$$

calculate the sum of squares for drug, calculate the regression using only boredom (A) and interaction (AB_1 and AB_2). The final summary, with the reconstructed sums of squares, is in Table 15.11, along with the degrees of freedom, mean squares, and F ratios. Comparing this table with Table 15.5 shows the values to be identical.

Before leaving this discussion of how to conduct a factorial analysis of variance using multiple regression, it is instructive to look at the correlations among the dummy variables; they are shown in Table 15.12. The pattern of correlations shows that A (boredom susceptibility) is uncorrelated with both B (drug) and AB (interaction). In addition, both B variables are uncorrelated with both interaction variables, and the interaction dummies are uncorrelated with A and both Bs. But note that with the sets of dummy variables for an effect, there is a correlation. This means that the effects (A, B, and AB, or boredom, drug, and interaction, respectively) are uncorrelated with (or **orthogonal** to) each other. It is important to keep that pattern in mind as we move to considering the case of unequal group sizes.

UNEQUAL GROUP SIZES[8]

We turn now to the case of unequal group sizes. In Chapter 12, we pointed out that there are two general ways to carry out the computations for analysis of variance when there are unequal group sizes. In that chapter, we recommended trying to have equal sizes. Then in Chapter 13, we introduced multiple regression and showed how to do analysis of variance computations with unequal group sizes by using regression. That is the preferred means of calculation. In the preceding section, we showed how to set up dummy variables to use regression in factorial experimental designs.

To illustrate the analysis with unequal group sizes, consider the following data from a hypothetical[9] study of the visibility of three different coating

---

[8] This section presents an advanced treatment of the topic and may be omitted if the instructor so desires.

[9] Although the study is hypothetical, the "new" paint is a real product. The data values are based on actual visibility studies, and have approximately the values they would have if this experiment were really done.

TABLE 15.11

Source	SS	df	MS	F
Boredom susceptibility	0.865	1	0.865	0.209
Drug	349.405	2	174.702	42.131
Interaction	358.754	2	179.377	43.258
Error	273.678	66	4.147	
Total	982.702	71		

TABLE 15.12

	A	B_1	B_2	AB_1	AB_2
A	1.000				
B_1	0.000	1.000			
B_2	0.000	0.500	1.000		
AB_1	0.000	0.000	0.000	1.000	
AB_2	0.000	0.000	0.000	0.500	1.000

materials for highway signs: normal paint, "reflective" paint, and a new paint called "retroflective." Subjects viewed the signs under either daylight or night conditions (with simulated automobile headlights). The dependent variable was the distance (in meters) at which a word on the sign could be read. The data are given in Table 15.13.

The means of the six conditions, along with the main effect and grand means, are shown in Table 15.14. The plot of the means in Figure 15.16 suggests a strong interaction.

The analysis proceeds using the rules for defining dummy variables described earlier. There are six separate groups to be defined:

Day, ordinary paint
Day, reflective paint
Day, retroflective paint
Night, ordinary paint
Night, reflective paint
Night, retroflective paint

In this case, note, there are unequal numbers of subjects for each experimental group, and so there will be unequal numbers of each pattern of dummy values. This fact has an important implication, which we will illustrate later.

The summary for the analysis (Table 15.15) shows a significant regression ($p < .01$).

TABLE 15.13

	Paint Type		
	Ordinary	Reflective	Retroflective
Day			
	126	121	114
	116	93	119
	79	123	111
	96	105	104
		109	
Night			
	68	52	99
	41	70	104
	32	59	115
	65	94	97
	69	85	118
	58		108

TABLE 15.14

	Paint Type			
	Ordinary	Reflective	Retroflective	
Day	104.25	110.20	112.00	108.92
Night	55.50	72.00	106.83	78.47
	75.00	91.10	108.90	91.67

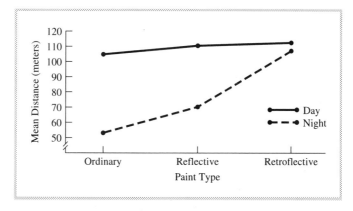

Figure 15.16

TABLE 15.15

Source	SS	df	MS	F
Regression	15166.8	5	3033.4	15.1
Residual	4821.9	24	200.9	
Total	19988.7	29		

To obtain the values for the sums of squares[10] for day/night, paint, and interaction, we carry out three additional regressions, each one omitting one of the three sources of variation. Subtracting the $SS_{Regression}$ for each reduced analysis from the $SS_{Regression}$ for the total analysis in Table 15.15 yields the SS for that effect. For example, including only the A, B_1, and B_2 dummy variables eliminates the interaction effect. In that analysis, the $SS_{Regression} = 12679.6$, so that

$$SS_{Interaction} = SS_{Regression \, (full \, model)} - SS_{Regression \, (A, B \, only)}$$

$$= 15166.8 - 12679.6$$

$$= 2487.2$$

Similarly,

$$SS_{Day/night} = SS_{Regression \, (full \, model)} - SS_{Regression \, (B, AB \, only)}$$

$$= 15166.8 - 8286.7$$

$$= 6880.1$$

and

$$SS_{Paint} = SS_{Regression \, (full \, model)} - SS_{Regression \, (A, AB \, only)}$$

$$= 15166.8 - 10895.1$$

$$= 4271.7$$

Entering the above values into a summary table, finding the degrees of freedom, and completing the computations leads to the summary in Table 15.16. The "error term" is the $SS_{Residual}$ from the full regression. With a significance level of .01, both main effects and their interaction are significant.

Note that the total sum of squares is not given in Table 15.16. This is because the sums of squares do not add to the SS_{Total} in this analysis. Ex-

---

[10] The procedure illustrated here corresponds to the "Type I sums of squares" as defined by Overall and Spiegel (1969). See Howell (1992) for additional details.

TABLE 15.16

Source	SS	df	MS	F
Day/Night	6880.1	1	6880.1	34.25
Paint	4271.7	2	2135.8	10.63
Interaction	2487.2	2	1243.6	6.19
Error	4821.9	24	200.9	

TABLE 15.17

	A	B_1	B_2	AB_1	AB_2
A	1.000				
B_1	0.000	1.000			
B_2	0.082	0.500	1.000		
AB_1	. 0.000	−0.200	−0.100	1.000	
AB_2	. 0.011	−0.100	−0.100	0.502	1.000

plaining just why this is the case would take us far afield, but it is related to the fact that with unequal group sizes, the dummy variables are correlated. As Table 15.12 demonstrated, with equal group sizes, the correlations between the sets of dummy variables representing the effects of the two independent variables and their interaction were zero, meaning that the sources of variation were independent or orthogonal. For an unequal groups design, on the other hand, the correlations are nonzero, as shown in Table 15.17 for the preceding analysis.

The nonzero correlations between the sets of dummy variables means that the sources of variation (the independent variables and their interaction) are not independent (nonorthogonal). An experimental design in which the sources of variation are not independent is called a **nonorthogonal design**. This nonorthogonality is the reason why unequal-sized groups give so much difficulty in the analysis of variance, why we recommend the use of the regression model for computations, and why the component sums of squares are nonadditive.

Summary

◆ A factorial design *combines two independent variables so that all levels of one are paired with all levels of the other.*

◆ *A factorial design lets you test hypotheses about each independent variable alone and about their interaction.*

- *When two variables interact, the effect of one variable changes at different levels of the other variable.*
- *The effect of one variable alone is known as its* main effect.
- *The total variation in a factorial design is partitioned into four components: the* A *variable, the* B *variable, interaction, and error.*
- F *ratios are always formed so that their value should be greater than 1.0 if the null hypothesis being tested is false.*
- *When the* interaction *is not significant, the follow-up tests are conducted by following the logic of two separate analyses, one for each independent variable.*
- *When the interaction is significant, both* simple effects *and* simple comparisons *are used as follow-up tests.*
- *A simple effect analysis is similar to a one-way analysis of variance that is conducted using a single level of one independent variable.*
- *Simple comparisons are just like follow-up analyses in a one-way design except that they deal with one row or one column of a factorial design.*
- *The best way to handle unequal group sizes in a factorial design is to use a multiple regression analysis.*
- [11] *Multiple regression computes the analysis of variance by using dummy variables to code the levels of each independent variable and the interaction.*
- [11] *If there are equal group sizes, the dummy variables representing the main effects and the interaction are uncorrelated; unequal group sizes lead to correlated (nonorthogonal) effects.*

Key Terms

FACTORIAL DESIGN	[11]NONORTHOGONAL
INTERACTION	DESIGN
INTERACTION PLOT	[11]ORTHOGONAL DUMMY
MAIN EFFECT	VARIABLES
	SIMPLE COMPARISON
	SIMPLE EFFECT

[11] This item occurs in an optional section.

1. Tonic immobility (TI), often called death-feigning, is a common response among some birds to threatening situations. In this hypothetical study, two different species of birds—chickens and quail—were subjected to one of four different stimulus conditions just before an experimental manipulation that typically induces TI. The stimuli were presented for 60 seconds, following which the experimenter grasped the bird firmly and held it on its side until it stopped struggling. At that point, a timer was started that stopped when the bird regained its feet. The data give duration of TI (in seconds). The stimulus conditions were (1) silence (control condition), (2) sound of species-specific "distress call," (3) sound of species-specific feeding/contented call, and (4) visual appearance of a stuffed hawk. Carry out the overall analysis and construct the summary table for the analysis.

STIMULUS CONDITION

	SILENCE	DISTRESS CALL	COMFORT CALL	HAWK
Chickens	30	55	20	50
	26	65	32	43
	39	33	28	65
	31	49	18	39
	28	59	25	52
Quail	40	45	30	70
	35	50	24	72
	47	48	32	53
	38	30	30	68
	42	42	27	74

2. Conduct the simple effects analysis for the data in exercise 15.1, looking at the effect of species for each stimulus condition.

3. Based on what you have done in exercises 15.1 and 15.2, write a complete results presentation.

4. Here are the results of a study of kindergarten, second-grade, and fourth-grade boys and girls on a vocabulary test. The scores are assumed to be standardized; that is, each group is compared with a set of norms for children their own age. (Because children's vocabularies normally increase with age, using raw scores would result in a main effect solely due to that. Using standard scores eliminates that problem.) Conduct the analysis of variance, along with any appropriate follow-up procedures.

	KINDERGARTEN	GRADE 2	GRADE 4
Boys	60	63	55
	55	68	64
	66	72	48
	56	58	57
Girls	60	45	55
	58	54	53
	66	55	48
	52	50	59

5. Conduct the simple effects analysis for the data in exercise 15.4, looking at the effect of gender for each age.

6. Based on what you have done in exercises 15.4 and 15.5, write a complete results presentation.

7. Use the data in Table 15.1 and conduct a full analysis, including simple effects both ways. Write the full results presentation.

8. Following are data from an experiment where animals were trained to avoid a sweet taste (aversion conditioning). After conditioning, the animals were given a choice of two solutions, plain water and one of four different flavored waters. The amount of the flavored water drunk (in milliliters) in a 30-min test is presented in the data. Carry out the overall analysis of variance.

	SWEET	SALT	SOUR	BITTER
Aversion	2.5	24.0	7.0	7.0
	2.0	23.0	14.0	14.0
	5.0	11.0	9.0	10.0
	1.0	12.0	12.0	11.0
	7.0	21.5	9.0	8.5
	4.0	30.0	9.0	5.0
	4.0	24.5	12.0	4.5
	5.0	17.0	10.0	11.0
	1.0	16.0	9.0	9.0
	9.0	18.0	11.0	10.0
Control	26.0	30.0	9.0	7.5
	19.0	19.0	8.0	5.0
	23.0	20.0	9.0	5.0

24.0	19.0	7.5	6.0
15.0	16.0	9.0	1.0
20.0	19.5	10.0	6.0
15.0	22.0	10.5	9.0
16.0	19.0	8.0	3.0
18.0	20.0	10.0	6.0
27.5	13.5	6.5	7.0

9. Plot the interaction from the data in exercise 15.8. Carry out the simple effects analysis, looking at the effect of aversion conditioning on each taste. Write the results presentation.

10. Following are data from an experiment on pain reduction. There were three groups of subjects (young, middle, and old), and four different drugs (call them A, B, C, and placebo). Carry out the overall analysis of the data.

	AGE OF SUBJECT		
	YOUNG	MIDDLE	OLD
Drug A	11	9	10
	8	12	9
	6	10	9
	8	11	15
	11	13	10
	6	9	11
	10	11	13
	9	8	13
	5	8	13
	6	14	14
Drug B	14	5	9
	10	5	8
	10	10	7
	12	8	9
	12	5	8
	13	9	7
	11	9	7
	11	8	8
	10	6	7
	10	7	7
Drug C	14	9	7
	13	7	6
	11	10	6
	15	8	6
	13	4	5
	13	14	6
	15	10	8
	12	13	7
	15	10	7
	18	8	6
Placebo	9	12	8
	8	16	11
	9	10	6
	12	16	10
	13	14	8
	8	12	8
	10	12	9
	6	9	12
	8	11	14
	13	13	11

11. Using the data from exercise 15.10, plot the interaction of age and drug.

12. Carry out the appropriate follow-up tests for the data in exercise 15.10. This will involve both simple effects and simple comparisons. Use $\alpha = .01$.

13. Write the complete results presentation for the analysis in exercises 15.10–15.12.

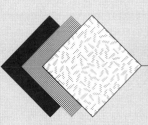

Computational Supplement

This chapter presents computations for the factorial design with two independent variables. As in the single-factor experiment, the computations for the analyses differ depending on whether or not there are equal group sizes. We take the simplest case first.

◆ Overall Analysis (Equal Group Sizes)

The first analysis tests three overall hypotheses: that there is no effect of the two independent variables alone (specifically, that $\alpha_i = 0.0$ and that $\beta_j = 0.0$), and that there is no interaction (that is, that $\gamma_{ij} = 0.0$). Once these hypotheses are tested, the analysis proceeds to follow-up tests.

As an example, we use the boredom susceptibility–drug experiment. The raw data for the 2-by-3 factorial appear in Table 15.1. We begin the analysis by finding the total T_{ij} and the sum of the squared values $(\sum X_{ij}^2)$ in each experimental condition. The totals for the each A row (T_{A_i}) and for each B column (T_{B_j}), along with the grand total, are shown in Table 15.18.

From the totals, we proceed to the sums of squares. The most convenient computational formulas are presented in Table 15.19.

Beginning with SS_A (high/low boredom susceptibility), we have

$$SS_A = \frac{\sum T_{A_j}^2}{bn} - \frac{GT^2}{abn}$$

$$= \frac{62.59^2 + 54.70^2}{3 * 12} - \frac{117.29^2}{2 * 3 * 12}$$

$$= 191.93 - 191.07$$

$$= 0.86$$

For SS_B (drug), the computations are

$$SS_B = \frac{\sum T_{B_i}^2}{an} - \frac{GT^2}{abn}$$

$$= \frac{-3.10^2 + 6.74^2 + 113.65^2}{2 * 12} - \frac{117.29^2}{2 * 3 * 12}$$

$$= 540.47 - 191.07$$

$$= 349.40$$

TABLE 15.18

		B Drug condition			
		B_1 L-dopa	B_2 Placebo	B_3 Haloperidol	
A Boredom Susceptibility	A_1 Low	−21.41 81.84	−11.93 69.97	95.93 802.50	$T_{A_1} = 62.59$
	A_2 High	18.31 85.88	18.67 68.72	17.72 64.88	$T_{A_2} = 54.70$
		T_{B_1} −3.10	T_{B_2} 6.74	T_{B_3} 113.65	GT = 117.29

TABLE 15.19

Quantity	Definition	Computations
SS_{Total}	$\sum (X - GM)^2$	$\sum X^2 - \dfrac{GT^2}{abn}$
SS_A	$nb \sum (\overline{X}_{A_i} - GM)^2$	$\dfrac{\sum T_{A_i}^2}{nb} - \dfrac{GT^2}{abn}$
SS_B	$na \sum (\overline{X}_{B_j} - GM)^2$	$\dfrac{\sum T_{B_j}^2}{na} - \dfrac{GT^2}{abn}$
SS_{AB}	$n \sum (\overline{X}_{ij} - \overline{X}_{A_i} - \overline{X}_{B_j} + GM)^2$	$\dfrac{\sum T_{ij}^2}{n} - \dfrac{\sum T_{B_j}^2}{na} - \dfrac{\sum T_{A_i}^2}{nb} + \dfrac{GT^2}{abn}$
SS_{Error}	$\sum (X - \overline{X}_{ij})^2$	$\sum X^2 - \dfrac{\sum_i \sum_j T_{ij}^2}{n}$

Computing SS_{AB}, we have

$$
\begin{aligned}
SS_{AB} &= \frac{\sum\sum T_{ij}^2}{n} - \frac{\sum T_{A_i}^2}{bn} - \frac{\sum T_{B_j}^2}{an} + \frac{GT^2}{abn} \\[2mm]
&= \frac{-21.41^2 + -11.93^2 + 95.93^2 + 18.31^2 + 18.67^2 + 17.72^2}{12} \\[2mm]
&\quad - \frac{62.59^2 + 54.70^2}{3 * 12} - \frac{-3.10^2 + 6.74^2 + 113.65^2}{2 * 12} + \frac{117.29^2}{2 * 3 * 12} \\[2mm]
&= 900.09 - 191.93 - 540.47 + 191.07 \\[2mm]
&= 358.76
\end{aligned}
$$

For SS_{Error}, the calculations are

$$SS_{Error} = \sum X^2 - \frac{\sum \sum T_{ij}^2}{n}$$

$$= 81.84 + 69.97 + 802.50 + 85.88 + 68.72 + 64.88$$

$$- \frac{-21.41^2 + -11.93^2 + 95.93^2 + 18.31^2 + 18.67^2 + 17.72^2}{12}$$

$$= 1173.79 - 900.09$$

$$= 273.70$$

Finally, we may compute the total sum of squares as

$$SS_{Total} = \sum X^2 - \frac{GT^2}{abn}$$

$$= 81.84 + 69.97 + 802.50 + 85.88 + 68.72 + 64.88 - \frac{117.29^2}{2*3*12}$$

$$= 1173.79 - 191.07$$

$$= 982.72$$

The summary table for the analysis, using the degrees of freedom formulas from before (see page 445), is in Table 15.20. The significance values are shown; there is no difference between the two boredom groups, while both the drug effect and the interaction are significant.

We looked at these data carefully early in this chapter as an example of an interaction. Figure 15.1 illustrates that interaction. The next logical step is to look at the simple effects of boredom susceptibility for each drug condition.

◆ Simple Effects

The simple effects can be visualized easily as parts of the interaction plot. Figure 15.17 shows the interaction, with some simple effects marked. The simple effects illustrated are, of course, the effects of boredom susceptibility for each drug. To investigate the effects of the drugs on high- and low-boredom individuals is to look at the interaction "the other way," as illustrated in Figure 15.18.

TABLE 15.20

Summary Table

Source	SS	df	MS	F	
Boredom	0.86	1	0.86	0.21	$p > .05$
Drug	349.40	2	174.70	42.10	$p < .01$
Interaction	358.76	2	179.38	43.22	$p < .01$
Error	273.70	66	4.15		
Total	982.66	71			

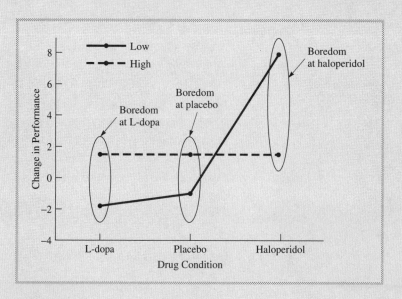

Figure 15.17

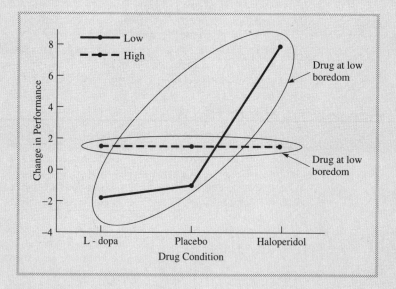

Figure 15.18

Simple effects computations proceed from a table of group sums (*not* group means), such as the one in Table 15.21. (This table is identical to Table 15.18, except that the sums of squared values are omitted for clarity.)

The first step in testing for the simple effect is to form the sum of squares for the effect of interest. In general terms,

TABLE 15.21

		B Drug condition		
Boredom Susceptibility *A*		B_1 L-dopa	B_2 Placebo	B_3 Haloperidol
	A_1 Low	−21.41	−11.93	95.93	$T_{A_1} = 62.59$
	A_2 High	18.31	18.67	17.72	$T_{A_2} = 54.70$
		T_{B_1} −3.10	T_{B_2} 6.74	T_{B_3} 113.65	GT = 117.29

$$SS_{B \text{ at } A_i} = \frac{\sum T_{ij}^2}{n} - \frac{T_{A_i}^2}{bn}$$

or, for the other independent variable,

$$SS_{A \text{ at } B_j} = \frac{\sum T_{ij}^2}{n} - \frac{T_{B_j}^2}{an}$$

Specifically for L-dopa, as an example, we have

$$SS_{\text{Boredom at L-dopa}} = \frac{\sum T_{1j}^2}{n} - \frac{T_{B_1}^2}{an}$$

The formula is much simpler in practice than it is in symbols. It instructs us to square the group sums (the T_{1j} values), sum the results, and then divide by the group size. From that value, subtract the squared total of all L-dopa scores (T_{B1}) divided by *an*. Using the values from Table 15.21, we have

$$SS_{\text{Boredom at L-dopa}} = \frac{\sum T_{1j}^2}{n} - \frac{T_{B_1}^2}{an}$$

$$= \frac{-21.42^2 + 18.31^2}{12} - \frac{-3.10^2}{2 * 12}$$

$$= 65.74$$

This sum of squares has df = $a - 1$ (as usual, the number of elements summed, minus 1), so that the mean square is

$$MS_{\text{Boredom at L-dopa}} = \frac{SS_{\text{Boredom at L-dopa}}}{df_{\text{Boredom at L-dopa}}}$$

$$= \frac{65.74}{1} = 65.74$$

Finally, we compute an F, using the MS_{Error} from the overall analysis:

$$F = \frac{\text{MS}_{\text{Boredom at L-dopa}}}{\text{MS}_{\text{Error}}} = \frac{65.74}{4.15} = 15.84$$

With df $= 1, 66,$[12] the critical value for F at $\alpha = .01$ is $4.00,$[13] we may reject the null hypothesis that the two boredom-susceptibility groups have identical population means under L-dopa.

We continue the analysis and compute the simple effects of age under each of the remaining drug conditions. The sum of squares for boredom at placebo is calculated as

$$\text{SS}_{\text{Boredom at placebo}} = \frac{\sum T_{2j}^2}{n} - \frac{T_{A_2}^2}{an}$$

$$= \frac{-11.93^2 + 18.67^2}{12} - \frac{6.74^2}{2 * 12}$$

$$= 39.02$$

while that for boredom at haloperidol is

$$\text{SS}_{\text{Boredom at haloperidol}} = \frac{\sum T_{3j}^2}{n} - \frac{T_{A_3}^2}{an}$$

$$= \frac{95.93^2 + 17.72^2}{12} - \frac{113.65^2}{2 * 12}$$

$$= 254.87$$

We can summarize all the computations in a table and compute the F ratios easily, as shown in Table 15.22.

In the summary table, the entries for boredom and for interaction from the overall analysis have been replaced by the simple effects values. The sum of the set of sums of squares is identical to the SS_{Total} from the original analysis. That is not a coincidence; the simple effects analysis has merely partitioned the variability differently, so that the variation that was previously partitioned into drugs and interaction has been redistributed into the four simple effects sums of squares. To be explicit about this relationship,

$$\sum \text{SS}_{B \text{ at } A_i} = \text{SS}_B + \text{SS}_{\text{Interaction}}$$

This relationship will always hold, within rounding, and serves as a check on the accuracy of the computations.

The simple effects analyses so far have examined the effects of boredom at

---

[12] As before, we use the closest lower df entry, which is for df $= 1, 60$.

[13] Note that the error term is taken from the overall analysis, and so this analysis is not quite the same as if we had done a one-way analysis or a t test using *only* the drug A data. Conceptually it's the same, but the overall error term provides a better estimate of σ_{Error}^2. This analysis assumes that the variances of all experimental groups are equal. If there is evidence that they are not, then an ordinary one-way analysis (or a t test) should be run using only the L-dopa data.

TABLE 15.22

Source	SS	df	MS	F
Drug	349.35	2	174.68	42.09
Boredom at L-dopa	65.74	1	65.74	15.84
Boredom at Placebo	39.02	1	39.02	10.40
Boredom at Haloperidol	254.87	1	254.87	61.41
Error	273.70	66	4.15	
Total	982.68	71		

each level of drug. The same procedure is equally applicable "the other way"—that is, looking at the effects of drug at each boredom level, as illustrated in Figure 15.19. The formulas for the analysis are

$$SS_{A \text{ at } B_j} = \frac{\sum T_{ij}^2}{n} - \frac{T_{B_j}^2}{an}$$

$$df = a - 1$$

$$\sum SS_{A \text{ at } B_j} = SS_A + SS_{\text{Interaction}}$$

As an example, here are the computations for drug at low boredom; the sums are taken from Table 15.21. The sum of squares is computed as

$$SS_{\text{Drug at low}} = \frac{\sum T_{ij}^2}{n} - \frac{T_{B_j}^2}{an}$$

$$= \frac{-21.42^2 + -11.93^2 + 95.93^2}{12} - \frac{62.59^2}{3 * 12}$$

$$= 708.12$$

This sum of squares has df $= a - 1 = 3 - 1 = 2$, so that the mean square is

$$MS_{\text{Drug at low}} = \frac{SS_{\text{Drug at Low}}}{df_{\text{Drug at Low}}}$$

$$= \frac{708.12}{2}$$

$$= 354.06$$

The F is calculated as before, as

$$F = \frac{MS_{\text{Drug at low}}}{MS_{\text{Error}}} = \frac{354.06}{4.15} = 85.32$$

We may conclude from this F that there are significant differences among the three drugs for low-boredom-susceptible subjects. Just exactly what the differences are not completely clear, and we must continue to another analysis.

SIMPLE COMPARISONS

When a simple effects analysis involves only two conditions, such as the illustration in Figure 15.18, then no additional analyses are needed. The simple effects analysis is sufficient (either the two boredom conditions differ for each drug or they do not). However, if there are more than two conditions and the simple effect shows a significant difference, as in the preceding analysis, then the effect should be pursued further. At this point, we are left with the same dilemma as in a one-way design—there is a difference, but the overall test does not pinpoint it. In the single-factor design, we followed an overall test with comparisons and post hoc tests; the same procedures are applicable in the factorial design, with only slight modification. Because these comparisons follow a simple effects analysis, we call them *simple comparisons*.

Simple comparisons are conducted by removing a single row or column from the table of means and applying the comparison, just as if it were the results for a one-way design. The only difference in the procedure comes in the choice of the "error term": The MS_{Error} from the overall analysis is used. To illustrate, let us pursue the simple effect of drug at low boredom, using the Tukey test. Of course, any other follow-up procedure from Chapter 12 could be used as easily. The simple effect of drug for the low-boredom-susceptible subjects is significant, as we concluded earlier, and we continue with the Tukey test.

As in Chapter 12, the Tukey procedure establishes a value for the smallest possible significant difference between two condition means; any mean difference greater than that amount is significant. The Tukey critical mean difference is calculated as before as

$$D = \frac{q_{(\alpha, df, a)}\sqrt{MS_{Within}}}{\sqrt{n}}$$

where $q_{(\alpha, df, a)}$ is a Studentized range value from Appendix J. Appendix J is entered using the number of degrees of freedom for error and the number of groups being compared.

The Tukey test is carried out on a matrix giving the differences between all pairs of means. This table of mean differences is constructed by listing the conditions in order of increasing mean value, as shown in Table 15.23.

Using a .05 significance level, the critical difference for the Tukey test is calculated as

TABLE 15.23

	Drug Group		
	L-dopa	Placebo	Haloperidol
Mean	−1.78	−0.99	7.99
Placebo	−0.79		
Haloperidol	−9.77	−8.98	

$$D = \frac{q_{(\alpha, \text{df}, a)} \sqrt{\text{MS}_{\text{Error}}}}{\sqrt{n}} = \frac{3.40 \sqrt{4.15}}{\sqrt{12}} = 2.00$$

The mean differences are now compared to the critical value and the significant differences marked in the matrix. In the example, two of the differences in pairs of means exceed the Tukey critical value in absolute value. We conclude therefore that, according to the Tukey test, there are significant differences between haloperidol and both the L-dopa and the placebo condition for low-boredom-susceptible subjects. For these subjects, though, the L-dopa and the placebo conditions do not differ.

To complete the analysis, of course, the next step would be to conduct the simple effects analysis looking for differences in the drug conditions for high-boredom-susceptible subjects. (See Figure 15.18; visually, it appears there will be no significant differences because the line is essentially flat.) If there were a significant simple effect, then it, too, would be followed up by using a post hoc procedure, using only the high-boredom subject's data.

OTHER COMPARISONS CONDUCTED AS SIMPLE COMPARISONS[14]

Using individual coefficients permits us to test any comparison, just as it did in a single-factor analysis of variance. As an example, let's look at the comparison of the placebo with the mean of the L-dopa and the haloperidol low-boredom subjects, using coefficients of $-1, 2, -1$. Following the formula from Chapter 12 for the sum of squares for a comparison, we have

$$\begin{aligned} \text{SS}_{\text{A comparison}} &= \frac{nC^2}{\sum c_j^2} \\ &= \frac{12[(-1)(-1.78) + 2(-0.99) + (-1)(7.99)]^2}{(-1)^2 + 2^2 + (-1)^2} \\ &= 134.15 \end{aligned}$$

This sum of squares has df = 1, so its mean square has the same value. Thus we form the F for testing the hypothesis that the comparison has a value of zero as

$$F = \frac{\text{MS}_{\text{A comparison}}}{\text{MS}_{\text{Error}}} = \frac{134.15}{4.15} = 32.32$$

If we adopt a significance level of .05, the critical F for df = 1, 66 is 4.00, and we may reject the hypothesis that the placebo condition differs significantly from the mean of the two drug conditions. The next step would be to explore further and probably ask about a difference between L-dopa and haloperidol for these low-boredom subjects.

Simple comparisons offer a highly versatile way to explore a significant interaction in detail. They allow comparisons within a level of an independent variable, and are ideally suited for following a significant simple effect. Together,

---

[14] This section presents an advanced treatment of the topic and may be omitted if the instructor so desires.

simple effects analysis and simple comparisons are the most frequently used procedures in a factorial design. There are other procedures; Keppel (1982) and others describe them fully.

◆ Unequal Group Sizes (The Harmonic Means Procedure)[15]

We turn now to the case of unequal group sizes using hand computation. In general, it is best to use multiple regression for unequal group sizes, and all of the necessary computations were illustrated previously. If, however, you must do these computations by hand, this section illustrates the simplified, approximate solution known as the "unweighted means" or the "harmonic means" solution.

OVERALL ANALYSIS

The harmonic means analysis is carried out by multiplying each group mean by the harmonic mean of all the group sizes $\tilde{n}$, where $\tilde{n}$ is defined as

$$\tilde{n} = \frac{ab}{\sum \frac{1}{n_{ij}}}$$

where n_{ij} is the number of observations in an experimental condition. Each group mean, $\overline{X}_{ij}$, is multiplied by $\tilde{n}$ to give a new group "total," T_{ij}^*. That sum is then used in all further calculations.

To illustrate the unweighted means analysis, consider the data[16] given in Table 15.13 from a study of the visibility of three different coating materials for highway signs: normal paint, "reflective" paint, and a new paint called "retro-flective." Subjects viewed the signs under either daylight or night conditions (with simulated automobile headlights). The dependent variable was the distance (in meters) at which a word on the sign could be read. The group means and sample sizes are given in Table 15.24. The plot of the means is shown in Figure 15.19.

We begin by calculating the harmonic mean sample size as

$$\tilde{n} = \frac{ab}{\sum_i \sum_j \frac{1}{n_{ij}}}$$

$$= \frac{2 * 3}{\frac{1}{4} + \frac{1}{5} + \frac{1}{4} + \frac{1}{6} + \frac{1}{5} + \frac{1}{6}}$$

$$= 4.86$$

[15] This section illustrates a less-preferred method for dealing with unequal group sizes. It may be bypassed on advice from your instructor.

[16] These data were used in the optional section describing the analysis using multiple regression; see pp 455–459.

TABLE 15.24

	Paint Type			
	Ordinary	Reflective	Retroflective	
Day	104.25 4	110.20 5	112.00 4	108.92
Night	55.50 6	72.00 5	106.83 6	78.47
	75.00	91.10	108.90	91.67

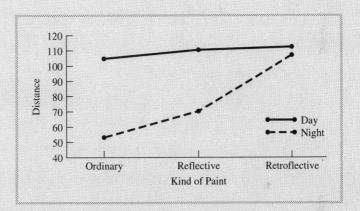

Figure 15.19

The next computation is to obtain the T^* for each condition as

$$T_{ij}^* = \overline{X}_{ij} * \tilde{n}$$

so that

$$T_{1,1}^* = \overline{X}_{1,1} * \tilde{n}$$
$$= 104.25 * 4.86 = 506.66$$

Completing the computations, the T^* values are

$$T_{1,2}^* = \overline{X}_{1,2} * \tilde{n}$$
$$= 110.20 * 4.86 = 535.57$$

$$T_{1,3}^* = \overline{X}_{1,3} * \tilde{n}$$
$$= 112.00 * 4.86 = 544.32$$

$$T_{2,1}^* = \overline{X}_{2,1} * \tilde{n}$$
$$= 55.50 * 4.86 = 269.73$$

$$T_{2,2}^* = \overline{X}_{2,2} * \tilde{n}$$
$$= 72.00 * 4.86 = 349.92$$

$$T_{2,3}^* = \overline{X}_{1,1} * \tilde{n}$$
$$= 106.83 * 4.86 = 519.19$$

Table 15.25 summarizes the values thus far.

To calculate SS_A, we need to make a slight modification in the formula for equal group sizes to reflect the use of $\tilde{n}$ and the T_{ij}^* values:

$$SS_A = \frac{\sum T_{A_i}^{*2}}{b\tilde{n}} - \frac{GT^{*2}}{ab\tilde{n}}$$
$$= \frac{1586.55^2 + 1138.84^2}{3 * 4.86} - \frac{2725.39^2}{2 * 3 * 4.86}$$
$$= 261597.90 - 254723.96$$
$$= 6873.94$$

A corresponding change is made in SS_B:

$$SS_B = \frac{\sum T_{B_j}^{*2}}{a\tilde{n}} - \frac{GT^{*2}}{ab\tilde{n}}$$
$$= \frac{776.39^2 + 885.49^2 + 1063.51^2}{2 * 4.86} - \frac{2725.39^2}{2 * 3 * 4.86}$$
$$= 259046.04 - 254723.96$$
$$= 4322.08$$

TABLE 15.25

	Ordinary	Reflective	Retroflective		
Day	506.66	535.57	544.32	1586.55	$T_{A_1}^*$
Night	269.73	349.92	519.19	1138.84	$T_{A_2}^*$
	776.39 $T_{B_1}^*$	885.49 $T_{B_2}^*$	1063.51 $T_{B_3}^*$	2725.39	GT*

The pattern repeats for the interaction sum of squares:

$$SS_{AB} = \frac{\sum T_{ij}^{*2}}{\tilde{n}} - \frac{\sum T_{A_i}^{*2}}{b\tilde{n}} - \frac{\sum T_{B_j}^{*2}}{a\tilde{n}} + \frac{GT^{*2}}{ab\tilde{n}}$$

$$= \frac{506.66^2 + \cdots + 519.19^2}{4.86} - \frac{1586.55^2 + 1138.84^2}{3*4.86}$$

$$- \frac{776.39^2 + 885.49^2 + 1063.51^2}{2*4.86} + \frac{2725.39^2}{2*3*4.86}$$

$$= 268432.18 - 261597.90 - 259046.04 + 254723.96$$

$$= 2512.20$$

In the single-factor analysis for unequal group sizes, we used the formula

$$SS_{\text{Within}} = \sum X^2 - \sum \left(\frac{T_j^2}{n_j} \right)$$

for the SS_{Error} term. Note that the T^* and the $\tilde{n}$ values are not used; instead we employ the actual group totals and sizes. The formula is easily modified for the two-factor experiment:

$$SS_{\text{Within}} = \sum X^2 - \sum \left(\frac{T_{ij}^2}{n_{ij}} \right)$$

The logic of the formula is exactly the same. The value is the sum of the squared raw scores, and the sum of all of the squared group sums divided by the group sizes. Again, note that computations use actual group totals and sizes—T^* and $\tilde{n}$ are not used. Employing the formula, we have

$$SS_{\text{Within}} = \sum X^2 - \sum \left(\frac{T_{ij}^2}{n_{ij}} \right)$$

$$= 126^2 + 116^2 + \cdots + 118^2 + 108^2 - \left(\frac{417^2}{4} + \frac{551^2}{5} + \cdots + \frac{641^2}{6} \right)$$

$$= 272072 - 267250.12$$

$$= 4821.88$$

With the sum of squares completed (we do not compute SS_{Total} in unweighted means analysis), we proceed to the degrees of freedom:

$$df_A = a - 1$$
$$df_B = b - 1$$
$$df_{AB} = (a - 1)(b - 1)$$
$$df_{\text{Error}} = \sum m_{ij} - ab$$

The only change here is in the degrees of freedom for error—we must sum the group sizes. Now we can complete the analysis with the summary table (see Table 15.26).

TABLE 15.26

Source	SS	df	MS	F	
		Summary Table			
Light	6873.94	1	6873.94	34.21	$p < .01$
Paint	4322.08	2	2161.04	10.76	$p < .01$
Interaction	2512.20	2	1256.10	6.25	$p < .01$
Error	4821.88	24	200.91		

SIMPLE EFFECT ANALYSES IN HARMONIC MEANS ANALYSIS

Follow-up analyses for the unequal groups factorial design using harmonic means analysis parallel those for equal group sizes. For simple effects, we have the modified formulas

$$SS_{A \text{ at } B_j} = \frac{\sum T_{ij}^{*2}}{\tilde{n}} - \frac{T_{A_i}^{*2}}{a\tilde{n}}$$

and

$$SS_{B \text{ at } A_i} = \frac{\sum T_{ij}^{*2}}{\tilde{n}} - \frac{T_{A_i}^{*2}}{b\tilde{n}}$$

Let's illustrate the procedure by examining the simple main effect of day–night lighting at the reflective paint condition (see Figure 15.19).

Returning to Table 15.25 for the T^* values, we find that the sum of squares for the effect of day–night at the reflective paint is

$$SS_{A \text{ at } B_2} = \frac{\sum T_{i2}^{*2}}{\tilde{n}} - \frac{T_{A_2}^{*2}}{a\tilde{n}}$$

$$= \frac{535.57^2 + 349.92^2}{4.86} - \frac{885.49^2}{2 * 4.86}$$

$$= 3545.88$$

The degrees of freedom for the sum of squares, as usual, equals the number of items summed minus 1, so that the df here is $2 - 1 = 1$. The mean square is thus

$$MS_{A \text{ at } B_2} = \frac{3545.88}{1} = 3545.88$$

Using the MS_{Within} from the overall analysis, we have

$$F = \frac{MS_{A \text{ at } B_2}}{MS_{\text{Within}}} = \frac{3545.88}{200.91} = 17.65$$

With df = 1, 24, the difference is significant. We can thus conclude that the reflective paint leads to word recognition at a significantly greater distance in daylight than in darkness.

SIMPLE COMPARISONS WITH UNEQUAL GROUP SIZES

A follow-up analysis of a simple effect is a simple comparison. As an example, we will look at the simple comparison between the reflective and the retroflective paints in the dark. We will use the Dunnett C procedure because it is especially appropriate with unequal group sizes, but any of the other tests described in Chapter 12 might also be appropriate.

For the Dunnett C, we find the critical value for the difference between the means of the two groups of interest. In this case, we have $\overline{X}_{\text{Retroflective}} - \overline{X}_{\text{Reflective}} = 106.83 - 72.00 = 34.83$. The critical value is computed using the formula

$$D = 0.71 \left[\frac{\dfrac{q_{(\alpha, n_i - 1, a)} s_i^2}{n_i} + \dfrac{q_{(\alpha, n_j - 1, a)} s_j^2}{n_j}}{\sqrt{\dfrac{s_i^2}{n_i} + \dfrac{s_j^2}{n_j}}} \right]$$

where n_i is a group size and s_i^2 is a group variance. Note that a separate Studentized range (q) value is required for each n_i.

Returning to Table 15.13 for the raw data, we find that for the reflective paint at night, $n_i = 5$ and $s_i^2 = 306.50$, while for the retroflective paint, $n_i = 6$ and $s_i^2 = 71.77$. Using $\alpha = .05$, the Studentized range values are 5.04 and 4.60. (Note that the table in Appendix J is headed "df error," and we used the group sizes minus 1 instead of the df_{Error} from the overall analysis.) With these values, we can calculate the critical difference between the two group means as

$$D = 0.71 \left[\frac{\dfrac{q_{(\alpha, n_i - 1, a)} s_i^2}{n_i} + \dfrac{q_{(\alpha, n_j - 1, a)} s_j^2}{n_j}}{\sqrt{\dfrac{s_i^2}{n_i} + \dfrac{s_j^2}{n_j}}} \right]$$

$$= 0.71 \left[\frac{\dfrac{5.04 * 306.50}{5} + \dfrac{4.60 * 71.77}{6}}{\sqrt{\dfrac{306.50}{5} + \dfrac{71.77}{6}}} \right]$$

$$= 30.19$$

Because the actual difference between the means for the two paints is 34.83 and is greater than that required by the Dunnett C critical value, there is a significant difference between the conditions. We therefore conclude that the retroflective paint leads to word recognition at a significantly greater distance than does reflective paint. (And you may be interested to know that results like these have led some U.S. states to adopt retroflective paint for their highway signs.)

References

AMERICAN PSYCHOLOGICAL ASSOCIATION. (1981). Ethical principles of psychologists. *American Psychologist, 36,* 633–638.

AMERICAN PSYCHOLOGICAL ASSOCIATION. (1983). *Publication manual of the American Psychological Association* (3rd ed.). Washington, DC: Author.

BERENSON, M.L., LEVINE, D.M., & GOLDSTEIN, M. (1983). *Intermediate statistical methods and applications: A computer package approach.* Englewood Cliffs, NJ: Prentice-Hall.

BORYS, D.S., & POPE, K.S. (1989). Dual relationships between therapist and client: A national study of psychologists, psychiatrists, and social workers. *Professional Psychology: Research and Practice, 20,* 283–293.

CAMPBELL, J.B., TYRRELL, D.J., & ZINGARO, M. (1993). Sensation seeking among whitewater canoe and kayak paddlers. *Personality and Individual Differences, 14,* 489–491.

COHEN, J. (1968). Multiple regression as a general data-analytic system. *Psychological Bulletin, 70,* 426–443.

COHEN, J. (1977). *Statistical power analysis for behavioral sciences.* New York: Academic Press.

COHEN, J. (1988). *Statistical power analysis* (2nd ed.). Hillsdale, NJ: Erlbaum.

CRAMER, H. (1946). *Mathematical methods of statistics.* Princeton, NY: Princeton University Press.

DARLINGTON, R.B. (1990). *Regression and linear models.* New York: McGraw-Hill.

DUNN, O.J. (1961). Multiple comparisons among means. *Journal of the American Statistical Association, 56,* 52–64.

FIENBERG, S. (1980). *The analysis of cross classified categorical data.* Cambridge, MA: MIT Press.

HENDERSON, H.V., & VELLEMAN, P.F. (1981). Building multiple regression models interactively. *Biometrics, 37,* 391–411.

HEWITT, P.L., FLETT, G.L., & BLANKSTEIN, K.R. (1991). *Personality and individual differences, 12,* 273–279.

HEY, J.D. (1983). *Data in doubt.* London: Martin Robertson.

HOLLANDER, M., & WOLFE, D.A. (1973). *Nonparametric statistical methods.* New York: Wiley.

HOWELL, D.C. (1992). *Statistical methods for psychology* (3rd ed.). Boston: PWS-Kent.

JANDREAU, S., & BEVER, T. (1992). Phrase-spaced formats improve comprehension in average readers. *Journal of Applied Psychology, 17,* 143–146.

JOHN, K., FORBES, K., & LEHMAN, R.S. (in preparation). Dual relationships on campus.

JUDD, C.M., & MCCLELLAND, G.H. (1989). *Data analysis: A model-comparison approach.* New York: Harcourt Brace Jovanovich.

KEPPEL, G. (1973). *Design and analysis: A researcher's handbook.* Englewood Cliffs, NJ: Prentice-Hall.

KEPPEL, G. (1982). *Design and analysis: A researcher's handbook* (2nd ed.). Englewood Cliffs, NJ: Prentice-Hall.

KEPPEL, G. (1991). *Design and analysis: A researcher's handbook* (3rd ed.). Englewood Cliffs, NJ: Prentice-Hall.

KEPPEL, G., & ZEDECK, S. (1989). *Data analysis for research design: Analysis of variance and multiple regression/correlation approaches.* New York: Freeman.

KERLINGER, F.N. (1986). *Foundations of behavioral research* (3rd edition). New York: Holt, Rinehart and Winston.

KERLINGER, F.N., & PEDHAZUR, E.J. (1973). *Multiple regression in behavioral research.* New York: Holt, Rinehart and Winston.

KRAEMER, H.C., & THIEMANN, S. (1987). *How many subjects: Statistical power analysis in research.* Newbury Park, CA: Sage Publications.

KRAMER, C. (1956). Extension of the multiple range test to group means of unequal number of replications. *Biometrics, 12,* 307–310.

LEHMAN, R.S. (1991). *Statistics and research design in the behavioral sciences.* Pacific Grove, CA: Brooks/Cole.

LIGHT, R.J., & MARGOLIN, B.H. (1971). An analysis of variance for categorical data. *Journal of the American Statistical Association, 66,* 534–544.

LORD, F.M. (1953). On the statistical treatment of football numbers. *American Psychologist, 8,* 750–751.

LOWRY, R. (1989). *The architecture of chance: An introduction to the logic and arithmetic of chance.* New York: Oxford University Press.

MARASCUILO, L.A., & LEVIN, J.R. (1983). *Multivariate statistics in the social sciences: A researcher's guide.* Pacific Grove, CA: Brooks/Cole.

MARASCUILO, L.A., & SERLIN, R.C. (1988). *Statistical methods for the social and behavioral sciences.* New York: Freeman.

MCGOWEN, K.R., & HART, L.E. (1992). Exploring the contribution of gender identity to differences in career experiences. *Psychological Reports, 70,* 723–737.

MUELLER, J.H., HAUPT, S.G., & GROVE, T.R. (1988). Personal relevance of traits and things. *Bulletin of the Psychonomic Society, 26,* 445–448.

NASBY, W., & YANDO, R. (1988). Selective encoding and retrieval of affectively valent information: Two cognitive consequences of children's mood states. *Journal of Personality and Social Psychology, 43,* 1244–1253.

NETTER, P., & RAMMSAYER, T. (1991). Reactivity to dopaminergic drugs and aggression related personality traits. *Personality and Individual Differences, 12,* 1009–1017.

OVERALL, J.E., & SPIEGEL, D.K. (1969). Concerning least squares analysis of experimental data. *Psychological Bulletin, 72,* 311–322.

OWENS, D.A., & TYRRELL, R.A. (1993). Visual guidance of young and older drivers in challenging conditions. *Investigative Ophthalmology and Visual Science, 34,* 1418.

PEDHAZUR, E.J. (1982). *Multiple regression in behavioral research: Explanation and prediction* (2nd ed.). New York: Holt, Rinehart and Winston.

SIEGEL, S., & CASTELLAN, N.J. (1988) *Nonparametric statistics for the behavioral sciences* (2nd ed.). New York: McGraw-Hill.

SPERLING, G. (1960). The information available in brief visual presentations. *Psychological Monographs, 74* (Whole no. 11).

STEVENS, J.P. (1984). Outliers and influential data points in regression analysis. *Psychological Bulletin, 95,* 334–344.

STEVENS, S. (1951). Mathematics, measurement, and psychophysics. In. S. Stevens (Ed.), *Handbook of experimental psychology.* New York: Wiley.

STILSON, D.W. (1966). *Probability and statistics in psychological research and theory.* San Francisco: Holden-Day.

STINE, W.W. (1989). Meaningful inference: The role of measurement in statistics. *Psychological Bulletin, 103,* 147–155.

"STUDENT" (W.S. GOSSET). (1908). The probable error of a mean. *Biometrika, 6,* 1125.

TABACHNICK, B.G., & FIDELL, L.S. (1989). *Using multivariate statistics* (2nd ed.). New York: Harper & Row.

TANKARD, J.W., JR. (1984). *The statistical pioneers.* Cambridge, MA: Schenkman.

TYRRELL, D.J., STAUFFER, L.B., & SNOWMAN, L.G. (1991). Perception of abstract identity/difference relationships by infants. *Infant Behavior and Development, 14,* 125–129.

UNITED STATES DEPARTMENT OF COMMERCE. (1989). *Statistical abstract of the United States 1989* (109th edition). Washington, DC: United States Government Printing Office.

VELLEMAN, P.F., & HOAGLIN, D.C. (1981). *Applications, basics and computing of exploratory data analysis.* Boston: Duxbury.

VELLEMAN, P.F., & WILKINSON, L. (1993). Nominal, ordinal, interval, and ratio typologies are misleading. *The American Statistician, 47,* 65–72.

WELCH, B.L. (1947). The generalization of Student's problem when several different population variances are involved. *Biometrika, 34,* 28–35.

WERNER, J.S., & PERLMUTTER, M. (1979). Development of visual memory in infants. In H.W. Reese and L.P. Lipsitt (Eds.), *Advances in child development and behavior,* Vol. 14 (pp. 2–56). New York: Academic Press.

WILCOX, R.R. (1987). *New statistical procedures for the social sciences: Modern solutions to basic problems.* Hillsdale, NJ: Erlbaum.

YALCH, R.F. (1991). Memory in the jingle jungle: Music as a mnemonic device in communicating advertising slogans. *Journal of Applied Psychology, 76,* 268–275.

APPENDIX A AREAS UNDER THE NORMAL DISTRIBUTION

Z	Area between mean and Z	Area beyond Z	Z	Area between mean and Z	Area beyond Z
0.00	0.00000	0.50000	0.43	0.16641	0.33359
0.01	0.00400	0.49600	0.44	0.17003	0.32997
0.02	0.00798	0.49202			
0.03	0.01198	0.48802	0.45	0.17366	0.32634
0.04	0.01595	0.48405	0.46	0.17724	0.32276
			0.47	0.18083	0.31917
0.05	0.01995	0.48005	0.48	0.18439	0.31561
0.06	0.02392	0.47608	0.49	0.18794	0.31206
0.07	0.02791	0.47209			
0.08	0.03188	0.46812	0.50	0.19146	0.30854
0.09	0.03587	0.46413	0.51	0.19498	0.30502
			0.52	0.19847	0.30153
0.10	0.03983	0.46017	0.53	0.20195	0.29805
0.11	0.04381	0.45619	0.54	0.20540	0.29460
0.12	0.04776	0.45224			
0.13	0.05173	0.44827	0.55	0.20885	0.29115
0.14	0.05567	0.44433	0.56	0.21226	0.28774
			0.57	0.21567	0.28433
0.15	0.05963	0.44037	0.58	0.21904	0.28096
0.16	0.06356	0.43644	0.59	0.22242	0.27758
0.17	0.06751	0.43249			
0.18	0.07142	0.42858	0.60	0.22575	0.27425
0.19	0.07536	0.42464	0.61	0.22908	0.27092
			0.62	0.23237	0.26763
0.20	0.07926	0.42074	0.63	0.23566	0.26434
0.21	0.08318	0.41682	0.64	0.23891	0.26109
0.22	0.08706	0.41294			
0.23	0.09096	0.40904	0.65	0.24216	0.25784
0.24	0.09483	0.40517	0.66	0.24537	0.25463
			0.67	0.24858	0.25142
0.25	0.09872	0.40128	0.68	0.25175	0.24825
0.26	0.10257	0.39743	0.69	0.25491	0.24509
0.27	0.10643	0.39357			
0.28	0.11026	0.38974	0.70	0.25804	0.24196
0.29	0.11410	0.38590	0.71	0.26116	0.23884
			0.72	0.26424	0.23576
0.30	0.11791	0.38209	0.73	0.26732	0.23268
0.31	0.12173	0.37827	0.74	0.27035	0.22965
0.32	0.12552	0.37448			
0.33	0.12931	0.37069	0.75	0.27338	0.22662
0.34	0.13307	0.36693	0.76	0.27637	0.22363
			0.77	0.27936	0.22064
0.35	0.13684	0.36316	0.78	0.28230	0.21770
0.36	0.14058	0.35942	0.79	0.28525	0.21475
0.37	0.14432	0.35568			
0.38	0.14803	0.35197	0.80	0.28814	0.21186
0.39	0.15174	0.34826	0.81	0.29104	0.20896
			0.82	0.29389	0.20611
0.40	0.15542	0.34458	0.83	0.29674	0.20326
0.41	0.15911	0.34089	0.84	0.29955	0.20045
0.42	0.16276	0.33724			

SOURCE: Entries in this table were computed by the author.

Z	Area between mean and Z	Area beyond Z	Z	Area between mean and Z	Area beyond Z
0.85	0.30235	0.19765	1.34	0.40988	0.09012
0.86	0.30511	0.19489	1.35	0.41150	0.08850
0.87	0.30786	0.19214	1.36	0.41309	0.08691
0.88	0.31057	0.18943	1.37	0.41467	0.08533
0.89	0.31328	0.18672	1.38	0.41621	0.08379
			1.39	0.41775	0.08225
0.90	0.31594	0.18406			
0.91	0.31860	0.18140	1.40	0.41924	0.08076
0.92	0.32121	0.17879	1.41	0.42074	0.07926
0.93	0.32383	0.17617	1.42	0.42220	0.07780
0.94	0.32639	0.17361	1.43	0.42365	0.07635
			1.44	0.42507	0.07493
0.95	0.32895	0.17105			
0.96	0.33147	0.16853	1.45	0.42648	0.07352
0.97	0.33399	0.16601	1.46	0.42785	0.07215
0.98	0.33646	0.16354	1.47	0.42923	0.07077
0.99	0.33892	0.16108	1.48	0.43056	0.06944
			1.49	0.43190	0.06810
1.00	0.34134	0.15866			
1.01	0.34376	0.15624	1.50	0.43319	0.06681
1.02	0.34614	0.15386	1.51	0.43449	0.06551
1.03	0.34851	0.15149	1.52	0.43574	0.06426
1.04	0.35083	0.14917	1.53	0.43700	0.06300
			1.54	0.43822	0.06178
1.05	0.35315	0.14685			
1.06	0.35543	0.14457	1.55	0.43944	0.06056
1.07	0.35770	0.14230	1.56	0.44062	0.05938
1.08	0.35993	0.14007	1.57	0.44180	0.05820
1.09	0.36215	0.13785	1.58	0.44295	0.05705
			1.59	0.44409	0.05591
1.10	0.36433	0.13567			
1.11	0.36651	0.13349	1.60	0.44520	0.05480
1.12	0.36864	0.13136	1.61	0.44631	0.05369
1.13	0.37077	0.12923	1.62	0.44738	0.05262
1.14	0.37286	0.12714	1.63	0.44846	0.05154
			1.64	0.44950	0.05050
1.15	0.37494	0.12506			
1.16	0.37698	0.12302	1.65	0.45054	0.04946
1.17	0.37901	0.12099	1.66	0.45154	0.04846
1.18	0.38100	0.11900	1.67	0.45255	0.04745
1.19	0.38299	0.11701	1.68	0.45352	0.04648
			1.69	0.45450	0.04550
1.20	0.38493	0.11507			
1.21	0.38687	0.11313	1.70	0.45543	0.04457
1.22	0.38877	0.11123	1.71	0.45638	0.04362
1.23	0.39066	0.10934	1.72	0.45728	0.04272
1.24	0.39251	0.10749	1.73	0.45820	0.04180
			1.74	0.45907	0.04093
1.25	0.39436	0.10564			
1.26	0.39617	0.10383	1.75	0.45995	0.04005
1.27	0.39797	0.10203	1.76	0.46080	0.03920
1.28	0.39973	0.10027	1.77	0.46165	0.03835
1.29	0.40149	0.09851	1.78	0.46246	0.03754
			1.79	0.46328	0.03672
1.30	0.40320	0.09680			
1.31	0.40491	0.09509	1.80	0.46407	0.03593
1.32	0.40658	0.09342	1.81	0.46486	0.03514
1.33	0.40825	0.09175			

Z	Area between mean and Z	Area beyond Z	Z	Area between mean and Z	Area beyond Z
1.82	0.46562	0.03438	2.30	0.48928	0.01072
1.83	0.46639	0.03361	2.31	0.48957	0.01043
1.84	0.46712	0.03288	2.32	0.48983	0.01017
1.85	0.46785	0.03215	2.33	0.49011	0.00989
1.86	0.46856	0.03144	2.34	0.49036	0.00964
1.87	0.46927	0.03073	2.35	0.49062	0.00938
1.88	0.46995	0.03005	2.36	0.49086	0.00914
1.89	0.47063	0.02937	2.37	0.49112	0.00888
1.90	0.47128	0.02872	2.38	0.49134	0.00866
1.91	0.47194	0.02806	2.39	0.49159	0.00841
1.92	0.47257	0.02743	2.40	0.49180	0.00820
1.93	0.47321	0.02679	2.41	0.49203	0.00797
1.94	0.47381	0.02619	2.42	0.49224	0.00776
1.95	0.47442	0.02558	2.43	0.49246	0.00754
1.96	0.47500	0.02500	2.44	0.49266	0.00734
1.97	0.47559	0.02441	2.45	0.49287	0.00713
1.98	0.47615	0.02385	2.46	0.49305	0.00695
1.99	0.47672	0.02328	2.47	0.49325	0.00675
2.00	0.47725	0.02275	2.48	0.49343	0.00657
2.01	0.47780	0.02220	2.49	0.49362	0.00638
2.02	0.47831	0.02169	2.50	0.49379	0.00621
2.03	0.47883	0.02117	2.51	0.49397	0.00603
2.04	0.47932	0.02068	2.52	0.49413	0.00587
2.05	0.47983	0.02017	2.53	0.49431	0.00569
2.06	0.48030	0.01970	2.54	0.49446	0.00554
2.07	0.48078	0.01922	2.55	0.49462	0.00538
2.08	0.48124	0.01876	2.56	0.49477	0.00523
2.09	0.48170	0.01830	2.57	0.49493	0.00507
2.10	0.48214	0.01786	2.58	0.49506	0.00494
2.11	0.48258	0.01742	2.59	0.49521	0.00479
2.12	0.48300	0.01700	2.60	0.49534	0.00466
2.13	0.48342	0.01658	2.61	0.49548	0.00452
2.14	0.48382	0.01618	2.62	0.49560	0.00440
2.15	0.48423	0.01577	2.63	0.49574	0.00426
2.16	0.48461	0.01539	2.64	0.49585	0.00415
2.17	0.48501	0.01499	2.65	0.49599	0.00401
2.18	0.48537	0.01463	2.66	0.49609	0.00391
2.19	0.48575	0.01425	2.67	0.49622	0.00378
2.20	0.48610	0.01390	2.68	0.49632	0.00368
2.21	0.48646	0.01354	2.69	0.49644	0.00356
2.22	0.48679	0.01321	2.70	0.49653	0.00347
2.23	0.48714	0.01286	2.71	0.49665	0.00335
2.24	0.48745	0.01255	2.72	0.49674	0.00326
2.25	0.48779	0.01221	2.73	0.49684	0.00316
2.26	0.48809	0.01191	2.74	0.49693	0.00307
2.27	0.48841	0.01159	2.75	0.49703	0.00297
2.28	0.48870	0.01130	2.76	0.49711	0.00289
2.29	0.48900	0.01100	2.77	0.49721	0.00279

Z	Area between mean and Z	Area beyond Z	Z	Area between mean and Z	Area beyond Z
2.78	0.49728	0.00272	3.00	0.49865	0.00135
2.79	0.49738	0.00262	3.02	0.49874	0.00126
2.80	0.49744	0.00256	3.04	0.49882	0.00118
2.81	0.49753	0.00247	3.06	0.49889	0.00111
2.82	0.49760	0.00240	3.08	0.49896	0.00104
2.83	0.49768	0.00232			
2.84	0.49774	0.00226	3.10	0.49903	0.00097
			3.12	0.49910	0.00090
2.85	0.49782	0.00218	3.14	0.49916	0.00084
2.86	0.49788	0.00212	3.16	0.49921	0.00079
2.87	0.49796	0.00204	3.18	0.49926	0.00074
2.88	0.49801	0.00199	3.20	0.49931	0.00069
2.89	0.49808	0.00192	3.25	0.49943	0.00057
2.90	0.49813	0.00187	3.30	0.49952	0.00048
2.91	0.49820	0.00180	3.35	0.49961	0.00039
2.92	0.49825	0.00175	3.40	0.49966	0.00034
2.93	0.49832	0.00168			
2.94	0.49836	0.00164	3.45	0.49973	0.00027
			3.50	0.49977	0.00023
2.95	0.49842	0.00158	3.60	0.49984	0.00016
2.96	0.49846	0.00154	3.70	0.49989	0.00011
2.97	0.49852	0.00148	3.80	0.49993	0.00007
2.98	0.49856	0.00144			
2.99	0.49862	0.00138	3.90	0.49995	0.00005
			4.00	0.49997	0.00003

	1	2	3	4	5	6	7	8	9	10
1	39614	74819	23303	87516	18981	42314	89531	07870	12536	41222
2	02541	85748	56140	72328	54780	21638	30219	04220	69476	45002
3	87434	15686	74598	54299	92089	30832	30118	18505	67564	75455
4	69937	72720	06396	45725	93951	14151	03069	64938	81282	92018
5	30217	90732	03477	69920	05899	64950	96540	41121	73559	47139
6	74643	92005	05388	42797	34732	31463	27872	58056	98703	85255
7	17723	79504	30484	09868	38245	29772	19579	09007	79314	71295
8	09395	89991	28279	51552	18198	47560	09070	06643	68828	87934
9	21973	26112	67133	39727	85483	49720	28341	64165	90276	26897
10	85933	70911	43491	53764	43614	54764	63356	47404	78254	60403
11	42238	49831	20973	03463	40351	16448	58791	13781	68649	30077
12	11679	22530	97439	79312	50730	50080	59519	66892	71575	68744
13	58854	35870	07032	91644	63494	00611	26018	45269	14037	81753
14	21489	69392	25387	52044	48854	21681	56769	56484	56748	46908
15	06469	62608	95975	95649	95550	22440	05049	16259	06264	42268
16	38751	02296	73270	13029	86045	75368	19512	56590	98819	22963
17	44689	16095	95770	86491	51064	24154	44686	91832	09545	65321
18	38733	27628	56475	64890	14744	30022	70836	08636	42319	36704
19	91265	37053	27298	16684	75518	86499	33758	63366	40964	31788
20	12341	31819	18943	69025	18575	55021	86764	30701	35862	30606
21	02772	52994	83438	66689	77898	57471	51105	25160	21380	98977
22	83632	79155	07501	94003	33840	64639	49638	20189	01406	37403
23	60273	69879	05014	66353	82444	04590	01591	52172	11244	48747
24	72043	56215	15075	80363	69817	95706	53583	68622	64000	71738
25	62198	76663	33956	06407	46018	65251	55897	86686	72765	49192
26	44391	91384	10573	61162	97936	58620	28613	33529	15322	99018
27	81137	70046	51476	70815	99604	35304	45699	35201	35014	99538
28	88919	01999	59446	45609	48651	31870	21733	66319	46648	90205
29	28016	75902	55462	20746	70013	21517	46756	12227	12172	63905
30	32688	50818	09219	69417	67210	92271	22840	40948	74473	27807
31	21085	99986	90579	05026	84208	29442	78843	47748	56599	82832
32	20428	52337	29526	05211	99377	10956	26259	16837	83248	02443
33	16377	63587	18741	77267	60596	36977	74605	20893	19462	61136
34	43752	18312	70650	78635	04359	35347	66054	42705	31321	25522
35	74595	21172	56672	02362	24411	66963	68042	65596	46193	86219
36	78700	35203	59012	87472	90460	29115	60164	99859	37950	29774
37	37686	43145	48745	45825	70982	38692	24111	18725	19787	52035
38	62836	37190	64406	55495	38545	79690	65020	85005	63094	73190
39	28237	43483	72763	35049	46008	73602	71899	41478	79980	13053
40	17896	78913	34611	45389	87031	59593	89049	74395	58014	81329
41	61395	89603	15298	68711	36087	35310	03766	12297	96362	96068
42	13860	41531	99262	75077	59394	34074	63052	56053	26579	60969
43	99201	77070	30502	89537	64812	49188	97991	97408	69927	83253
44	50815	81403	80027	73638	20195	60928	95619	98857	99743	06373
45	12553	07045	19554	66426	91173	37564	45736	98952	29124	50288

SOURCE: Entries in this table were computed by the author.

	1	2	3	4	5	6	7	8	9	10
46	08202	76964	86354	04138	68315	45098	29781	00994	86391	76668
47	78681	49348	69232	49665	88576	31435	45445	45114	86855	30974
48	21523	02344	41744	91052	48033	55259	20070	35304	50175	89839
49	37052	10834	24631	22659	58800	96513	76076	72730	06103	58816
50	62268	63136	85899	35687	04210	75126	39473	89465	65075	29856
51	38277	46021	96899	69062	81152	18475	65337	98823	70185	15787
52	68620	46563	17963	40057	24590	22575	38124	45939	88238	11588
53	27711	75053	21842	41145	13065	40777	93404	51071	97728	13453
54	51428	98976	65864	79424	48966	20822	17848	11282	22393	46946
55	87111	40920	04568	85241	73261	17863	62151	11495	19426	04623
56	31457	69197	14278	52489	20250	04312	72765	55459	93634	08114
57	11275	57354	99108	67783	20867	57633	36529	79894	67442	78749
58	24738	81623	43339	62377	31994	36636	24127	79170	57644	43142
59	26063	90696	52743	10239	79951	29431	68850	06024	84278	17774
60	86890	70786	17291	39544	84737	26281	36076	26550	69395	56119
61	73325	46838	18946	92976	43299	66005	57006	80058	74934	49419
62	68557	22870	35913	30957	51765	10392	84551	00596	83520	71631
63	16866	67316	34663	48594	65436	75575	51737	33602	35529	58560
64	41298	17974	48171	13238	35468	58663	55432	25165	73844	52543
65	46178	44975	25344	31026	29358	49777	90658	80651	01983	02169
66	25930	87929	80510	15778	85107	58678	01983	97126	00564	61244
67	02526	32123	10916	34572	56443	48753	26536	33219	69122	74163
68	80622	16039	42225	14679	88050	62365	14988	27681	78312	31629
69	51091	87347	61458	08651	84822	64159	33320	59188	12526	42756
70	32032	13964	68743	50019	61049	87889	87827	71689	81379	45268
71	00484	82620	41074	13235	10252	13118	58967	39269	83221	40147
72	05746	52643	34139	09318	39429	54018	33098	85708	60355	75997
73	90147	64441	05184	41040	75236	14018	96502	70565	41085	18877
74	17112	86434	91901	81315	16663	75722	90165	38789	74615	19435
75	98138	35097	09900	58316	44812	25627	07634	94965	73637	12743
76	73340	00030	16175	79663	96139	09620	06533	85526	76017	92204
77	62739	84532	19307	38191	03080	73877	72350	80278	40811	35350
78	93650	63688	02908	80620	91836	45855	66053	31548	63180	17397
79	84818	18939	30581	59102	66185	28215	28117	62472	63920	82709
80	07087	27776	18856	08117	44135	72470	51614	23486	84133	95086
81	69759	29092	43043	52467	06441	85442	49094	77087	96653	59989
82	77457	31420	04997	97650	48963	93232	61394	76641	21065	07790
83	35642	68168	99463	53054	70143	98368	01507	24563	58748	93819
84	19616	74320	18093	14482	53798	80896	08118	48166	60022	97799
85	08824	87697	01286	55376	77956	27591	98054	17596	40841	21085
86	98876	87868	79050	76638	84380	17690	61811	70118	56245	09904
87	97436	44511	65629	71628	84806	07059	51058	67597	99117	52987
88	15029	29791	99460	26758	21267	84526	57465	85288	35734	69944
89	47481	35745	80478	97125	93401	18676	45882	28755	31805	78987
90	57727	63038	23891	60592	04956	00819	66778	54903	32145	21366
91	59052	74855	74779	34359	62203	19150	94757	37866	08921	34590
92	31759	26526	36958	87795	56661	93495	40992	05477	12394	50493
93	13408	10419	47588	91004	71438	14162	15913	10582	53356	30935
94	40784	60942	35067	17352	35933	22404	54003	85497	91733	37114
95	25578	27194	01185	59301	22981	17753	80426	85534	52412	65731
96	67281	90510	24773	20692	45928	81741	07638	34250	00151	12611
97	75156	28476	85861	62232	06904	28497	98585	31225	88651	63209

	1	2	3	4	5	6	7	8	9	10
98	00886	22699	53246	58311	95808	54463	04665	37068	72314	23986
99	93941	16409	78208	07727	10916	27584	29695	56751	80052	19454
100	87662	58023	67325	24651	18807	33435	88961	07716	09155	37966
101	87406	41154	03732	79059	60241	48157	77044	77070	28044	44254
102	42504	56673	10818	70240	54765	70672	95660	99951	46891	42404
103	75291	55474	38747	61821	65945	70604	28728	65794	87930	89340
104	36299	20993	99257	28539	04857	30763	53472	71252	95633	34483
105	84597	57437	16084	90543	44311	02420	92687	07700	52520	23447
106	01339	77912	98217	10354	13171	74500	90741	94559	86479	33587
107	84989	02220	32025	46312	60161	69590	67297	54002	77403	99503
108	49861	06783	45287	94178	50448	75576	53502	70408	03920	25679
109	20478	38323	96404	14624	43440	47789	62906	30155	82719	13838
110	25084	77112	46461	19607	88120	48998	39298	68961	94980	21665
111	99683	13728	46550	95970	42861	62645	64706	98971	15590	39086
112	88576	30968	62474	79066	35947	62261	91816	52373	85427	06401
113	87947	50767	13082	08535	50007	47251	79627	47161	90388	29648
114	97363	25452	91936	29043	54051	57839	66414	79440	04298	39566
115	07026	25551	62334	06898	68193	49025	04204	12642	86638	94295
116	94855	98806	94977	95905	05111	21859	99540	13116	34542	63316
117	54471	84019	78520	71743	15765	57428	22745	00065	61402	58077
118	95598	95449	30163	53934	15973	94787	29088	94468	92550	62199
119	79508	72698	93936	75445	67148	88316	72824	31091	70792	71189
120	69344	49406	45440	87520	55163	82209	00015	75305	94560	04186
121	40533	96074	72805	46226	06984	19928	36835	85262	80041	09725
122	32773	90316	22391	23971	42671	97667	10877	53548	16961	01869
123	84652	88429	89859	33272	94329	32874	78670	39467	34944	12929
124	06242	28165	30158	04448	08559	85133	12497	54417	57171	04664
125	31100	58358	56923	62643	47467	99735	20279	85524	59862	30169
126	19164	37522	32866	06495	10800	90370	45175	87631	52395	00920
127	62020	24007	98973	37366	94360	34991	70207	33776	44159	14853
128	99251	74203	71903	88835	73058	30061	54450	76256	36346	78890
129	04925	95455	94235	04948	21374	38608	00057	88482	04851	66123
130	16018	42290	56522	24473	70916	96268	70235	00728	74961	15370
131	77381	86478	27238	30733	53391	78252	43413	84165	12623	99856
132	16003	92042	66817	36298	03878	09742	05626	77638	11872	18914
133	79728	37849	45869	03904	68625	89163	96263	23888	25640	34053
134	62114	46023	17421	20212	27285	91385	15777	68808	88835	78987
135	54511	83298	99598	76251	88026	25910	89371	41611	86307	45995
136	39020	38705	44814	39677	97245	70233	82746	76238	58675	76171
137	00746	47633	33976	06011	63868	74571	85602	21805	73681	43811
138	96320	83130	41974	48664	59590	55024	12837	96231	10198	83482
139	03776	05966	21234	66527	83292	31998	74478	72815	46140	66065
140	53693	45801	35060	50247	04379	33108	83377	70812	69079	49249
141	04186	36371	25790	07918	89173	94202	81339	56386	97721	45273
142	52483	58626	93586	31781	50513	18920	43677	74414	42727	46413
143	49922	08374	68933	16398	69784	73560	57482	59586	21831	24220
144	88842	42747	41742	78893	31387	81376	21615	05030	20766	72671
145	24924	07377	73544	02921	13514	51621	99312	68729	08790	48673
146	38697	67357	41388	93283	56187	39093	60747	19652	24476	02488
147	65492	25507	31924	52593	40211	39907	54692	53553	68653	62542
148	46981	25733	51790	52181	99713	11791	22826	00439	37716	31124
149	92419	75268	32477	83407	67761	08239	38105	58212	27761	71403
150	78531	83192	50803	58800	02666	10611	33547	88029	59575	15901

	1	2	3	4	5	6	7	8	9	10
151	87437	42161	88427	69610	62154	35744	68137	01001	52384	89931
152	35364	36300	28277	31799	25887	58083	62152	23623	23866	12418
153	78507	38711	04464	64415	44923	10182	26411	04577	79555	36987
154	74289	16564	00908	48107	81211	98003	14101	16451	86728	83127
155	19576	85966	99421	35398	66511	30070	46573	23475	69632	79835
156	83888	86715	58167	86628	98900	19323	01825	51833	77123	53643
157	52558	94886	04931	54523	00624	55637	34924	15361	87079	25507
158	30848	82175	66593	35466	37781	69025	23122	04826	20732	30385
159	34973	97296	74459	88391	10128	94123	06391	92267	75463	48468
160	27611	93970	06005	98616	28890	54076	11271	22845	90072	24261
161	92969	71154	26181	52033	39471	66386	98334	59917	68143	53807
162	65164	02318	89278	28928	25601	58202	31328	02889	00448	25801
163	13595	38529	16446	38407	22204	93038	48948	44041	51749	55322
164	45369	95706	53339	71707	58546	08168	45724	78256	79998	88561
165	87521	71220	75032	11141	39703	45972	18256	20494	94619	82744
166	57989	34739	98175	06613	75091	98872	48501	49961	95042	31934
167	52398	29427	28754	16681	51950	27962	40229	19272	92997	49047
168	17324	65519	92394	25938	62611	28707	58305	41235	98394	57274
169	11889	86230	95333	95371	64746	92052	69767	04007	81467	09769
170	63788	85653	25664	67469	39180	08755	05926	28259	54662	58646
171	92840	09580	15761	16788	98042	97741	38720	98341	36444	39095
172	82305	44880	93304	64691	56025	51409	14584	58225	49723	52991
173	49955	38728	69481	01323	17723	83157	11448	60597	51916	90819
174	58358	56847	19975	00370	58842	16104	83533	07008	56022	18152
175	92320	05584	63857	63593	76564	63939	69237	04346	09895	07589
176	62279	72652	44480	67863	09559	05803	17639	61096	47394	78575
177	11550	56073	14387	20361	95577	88556	30101	52452	57955	05884
178	12211	46742	79984	46120	65738	34460	54416	45960	02082	75050
179	89384	68977	51273	79285	80139	69109	43032	41572	99802	86265
180	29882	01181	29545	88598	46398	02495	28403	74115	13013	29574
181	75420	24581	34180	02933	28180	84180	55863	55840	32788	33225
182	31330	21475	29404	04200	77341	95351	65166	19097	76598	92505
183	12884	57531	42825	13240	53387	41705	06960	84919	15835	41466
184	64343	40221	34644	67312	97550	60273	69171	51882	59601	68260
185	05635	72277	57640	05453	81853	02426	48333	07194	82639	24739
186	84420	19310	66969	33379	46081	83319	00109	94211	67572	47230
187	71780	77359	64586	23169	65061	93813	66523	46301	51425	66324
188	95712	12537	51767	32514	45629	52188	67692	26389	90531	32632
189	04069	86663	47975	84019	75108	57378	30548	37394	75405	76086
190	69785	86331	79153	87718	02453	14194	23406	95085	51354	72282
191	11077	13740	64078	36461	07998	74833	65394	56414	70730	61476
192	84178	34007	09641	14986	06694	64621	68345	42105	39839	87089
193	28128	74988	84266	07257	92892	14904	96410	70228	30322	14319
194	55526	47006	75447	94935	78536	25446	29456	16446	39872	06648
195	16145	81233	16323	37456	85440	35355	47389	37981	40452	07443
196	27166	27857	04848	33880	57246	38181	05127	77578	21639	47405
197	92173	59159	21696	01258	80090	93765	91472	67657	82374	17086
198	27633	14604	56124	18439	14520	26787	02600	56703	02522	99362
199	59354	46227	21428	66633	26728	22227	21993	15473	86893	04117
200	60591	87491	71349	47470	24207	61775	21366	58257	72358	49467

APPENDIX C CRITICAL VALUES FOR THE STUDENT'S *t* DISTRIBUTION

Two tails One tail df	0.200 0.100	0.100 0.050	0.05 0.025	0.02 0.010	0.01 0.005	0.001 0.002
1	3.078	6.314	12.706	31.821	63.657	127.322
2	1.886	2.920	4.303	6.965	9.925	14.089
3	1.638	2.353	3.182	4.541	5.841	7.453
4	1.533	2.132	2.776	3.747	4.604	5.598
5	1.476	2.015	2.571	3.365	4.032	4.773
6	1.440	1.943	2.447	3.143	3.707	4.317
7	1.415	1.895	2.365	2.998	3.499	4.029
8	1.397	1.860	2.306	2.896	3.355	3.833
9	1.383	1.833	2.262	2.821	3.250	3.690
10	1.372	1.812	2.228	2.764	3.169	3.581
11	1.363	1.796	2.201	2.718	3.106	3.497
12	1.356	1.782	2.179	2.681	3.055	3.428
13	1.350	1.771	2.160	2.650	3.012	3.372
14	1.345	1.761	2.145	2.625	2.977	3.326
15	1.341	1.753	2.131	2.602	2.947	3.286
16	1.337	1.746	2.120	2.583	2.921	3.252
17	1.333	1.740	2.110	2.567	2.898	3.222
18	1.330	1.734	2.101	2.552	2.878	3.197
19	1.328	1.729	2.093	2.539	2.861	3.174
20	1.325	1.725	2.086	2.528	2.845	3.153
21	1.323	1.721	2.080	2.518	2.831	3.135
22	1.321	1.717	2.074	2.508	2.819	3.119
23	1.319	1.714	2.069	2.500	2.807	3.104
24	1.318	1.711	2.064	2.492	2.797	3.091
25	1.316	1.708	2.060	2.485	2.787	3.078
26	1.315	1.706	2.056	2.479	2.779	3.067
27	1.314	1.703	2.052	2.473	2.771	3.057
28	1.313	1.701	2.048	2.467	2.763	3.047
29	1.311	1.699	2.045	2.462	2.756	3.038
30	1.310	1.697	2.042	2.457	2.750	3.030
32	1.309	1.694	2.037	2.449	2.738	3.015
34	1.307	1.691	2.032	2.441	2.728	3.002
36	1.306	1.688	2.028	2.435	2.719	2.990
38	1.304	1.686	2.024	2.429	2.712	2.980
40	1.303	1.684	2.021	2.423	2.704	2.971
42	1.302	1.682	2.018	2.418	2.698	2.963
44	1.301	1.680	2.015	2.414	2.692	2.956
46	1.300	1.679	2.013	2.410	2.687	2.949
48	1.299	1.677	2.011	2.407	2.682	2.943
50	1.299	1.676	2.009	2.403	2.678	2.937
55	1.297	1.673	2.004	2.396	2.668	2.925
60	1.296	1.671	2.000	2.390	2.660	2.915
65	1.295	1.669	1.997	2.385	2.654	2.906
70	1.294	1.667	1.994	2.381	2.648	2.899
100	1.290	1.660	1.984	2.364	2.626	2.871

SOURCE: Entries in this table were computed by the author.

df	Lower tail values					Upper tail values				
	0.005	0.010	0.025	0.050	0.100	0.100	0.050	0.025	0.010	0.005
1	0.0000393	0.0001570	0.000982	0.003930	0.016	2.706	3.841	5.024	6.635	7.879
2	0.010	0.020	0.051	0.103	0.211	4.605	5.992	7.378	9.210	10.597
3	0.072	0.115	0.216	0.352	0.584	6.251	7.815	9.348	11.345	12.838
4	0.207	0.297	0.484	0.711	1.064	7.779	9.488	11.143	13.277	14.860
5	0.412	0.554	0.831	1.146	1.610	9.236	11.071	12.833	15.086	16.750
6	0.676	0.872	1.237	1.635	2.204	10.645	12.592	14.449	16.812	18.548
7	0.989	1.239	1.690	2.167	2.833	12.017	14.067	16.013	18.475	20.278
8	1.344	1.647	2.180	2.733	3.490	13.362	15.507	17.535	20.090	21.955
9	1.735	2.088	2.700	3.325	4.168	14.684	16.919	19.023	21.666	23.589
10	2.156	2.558	3.247	3.940	4.865	15.987	18.307	20.483	23.209	25.188
11	2.603	3.054	3.816	4.575	5.578	17.275	19.675	21.920	24.725	26.757
12	3.074	3.571	4.404	5.226	6.304	18.549	21.026	23.337	26.217	28.300
13	3.565	4.107	5.009	5.892	7.042	19.812	22.362	24.736	27.688	29.819
14	4.075	4.660	5.629	6.571	7.790	21.064	23.685	26.119	29.141	31.319
15	4.601	5.229	6.262	7.261	8.547	22.307	24.996	27.488	30.578	32.801
16	5.142	5.812	6.908	7.962	9.312	23.542	26.296	28.845	32.000	34.267
17	5.697	6.408	7.564	8.672	10.085	24.769	27.587	30.191	33.409	35.718
18	6.265	7.015	8.231	9.391	10.865	25.989	28.869	31.526	34.805	37.156
19	6.844	7.633	8.907	10.117	11.651	27.204	30.144	32.852	36.191	38.582
20	7.434	8.260	9.591	10.851	12.443	28.412	31.410	34.170	37.566	39.997
21	8.034	8.897	10.283	11.591	13.240	29.615	32.671	35.479	38.932	41.401
22	8.643	9.543	10.982	12.338	14.042	30.813	33.925	36.781	40.290	42.796
23	9.260	10.196	11.689	13.091	14.848	32.007	35.172	38.076	41.638	44.181
24	9.886	10.856	12.401	13.848	15.659	33.196	36.415	39.364	42.980	45.559
25	10.520	11.524	13.120	14.611	16.473	34.382	37.653	40.647	44.314	46.929
26	11.160	12.198	13.844	15.379	17.292	35.563	38.885	41.923	45.642	48.290
27	11.808	12.879	14.573	16.151	18.114	36.741	40.113	43.195	46.963	49.645
28	12.461	13.565	15.308	16.928	18.939	37.916	41.337	44.461	48.278	50.994
29	13.121	14.257	16.047	17.708	19.768	39.088	42.557	45.722	49.588	52.336
30	13.787	14.954	16.791	18.493	20.599	40.256	43.773	46.979	50.892	53.672
40	20.707	22.164	24.433	26.509	29.051	51.805	55.759	59.342	63.691	66.767
50	27.991	29.707	32.357	34.764	37.689	63.167	67.505	71.420	76.154	79.490
60	35.535	37.485	40.482	43.188	46.459	74.397	79.082	83.298	88.381	91.955
70	43.275	45.442	48.758	51.739	55.329	85.527	90.531	95.023	100.424	104.213

SOURCE: Entries in this table were computed by the author.

APPENDIX E CRITICAL VALUES FOR THE SPEARMAN RANK-ORDER CORRELATION

Two tails	0.20	0.10	0.05	0.02	0.01	0.005	0.002	0.001
One tail	0.10	0.05	0.025	0.01	0.005	0.0025	0.001	0.0005
N								
4	1.000	1.000						
5	0.800	0.900	1.000	1.000				
6	0.657	0.829	0.886	0.943	1.000	1.000		
7	0.571	0.714	0.786	0.893	0.929	0.964	1.000	1.000
8	0.524	0.643	0.738	0.833	0.881	0.905	0.952	0.976
9	0.483	0.600	0.700	0.783	0.833	0.867	0.917	0.933
10	0.455	0.564	0.648	0.745	0.794	0.830	0.879	0.903
11	0.427	0.536	0.618	0.709	0.755	0.800	0.845	0.879
12	0.406	0.503	0.587	0.671	0.727	0.776	0.825	0.860
13	0.385	0.484	0.560	0.648	0.703	0.747	0.802	0.835
14	0.367	0.464	0.538	0.622	0.675	0.723	0.774	0.811
15	0.354	0.443	0.521	0.604	0.654	0.700	0.754	0.786
16	0.341	0.429	0.503	0.582	0.635	0.679	0.732	0.765
17	0.328	0.414	0.485	0.566	0.615	0.662	0.713	0.748
18	0.317	0.401	0.472	0.550	0.600	0.643	0.695	0.728
19	0.309	0.391	0.460	0.535	0.584	0.628	0.677	0.712
20	0.299	0.380	0.447	0.520	0.570	0.612	0.662	0.696
21	0.292	0.370	0.435	0.508	0.556	0.599	0.648	0.681
22	0.284	0.361	0.425	0.496	0.544	0.586	0.634	0.667
23	0.278	0.353	0.415	0.486	0.532	0.573	0.622	0.654
24	0.271	0.344	0.406	0.476	0.521	0.562	0.610	0.642
25	0.265	0.337	0.398	0.466	0.511	0.551	0.598	0.630
26	0.259	0.331	0.390	0.457	0.501	0.542	0.587	0.619
27	0.255	0.324	0.382	0.448	0.491	0.531	0.577	0.608
28	0.250	0.317	0.375	0.440	0.483	0.522	0.567	0.598
29	0.245	0.312	0.368	0.433	0.475	0.513	0.558	0.589
30	0.240	0.306	0.362	0.425	0.467	0.504	0.549	0.580
31	0.236	0.301	0.356	0.418	0.459	0.496	0.541	0.571
32	0.232	0.296	0.350	0.412	0.452	0.489	0.533	0.563
33	0.229	0.291	0.345	0.405	0.446	0.482	0.525	0.554
34	0.225	0.287	0.340	0.399	0.439	0.475	0.517	0.547
35	0.222	0.283	0.335	0.394	0.433	0.468	0.510	0.539
36	0.219	0.279	0.330	0.388	0.427	0.462	0.504	0.523
37	0.216	0.275	0.325	0.383	0.421	0.456	0.497	0.526
38	0.212	0.271	0.321	0.378	0.415	0.450	0.491	0.519
39	0.210	0.267	0.317	0.373	0.410	0.444	0.485	0.513
40	0.207	0.264	0.313	0.368	0.405	0.439	0.479	0.507
41	0.204	0.261	0.309	0.364	0.400	0.433	0.473	0.501
42	0.202	0.257	0.305	0.359	0.395	0.428	0.468	0.495
43	0.199	0.254	0.301	0.355	0.392	0.423	0.463	0.490
44	0.197	0.251	0.298	0.351	0.386	0.419	0.458	0.484
45	0.194	0.248	0.294	0.347	0.382	0.414	0.453	0.479

SOURCE: The values in this table were obtained from Zar, J. H. (1972). Significance testing of the Spearman rank correlation coefficient. *Journal of the American Statistical Association, 67*, 578–580. Used by permission of the publisher.

Two tails	0.20	0.10	0.05	0.02	0.01	0.005	0.002	0.001
One tail	0.10	0.05	0.025	0.01	0.005	0.0025	0.001	0.0005
N								
46	0.192	0.246	0.291	0.343	0.378	0.410	0.448	0.474
47	0.190	0.243	0.288	0.340	0.374	0.405	0.443	0.469
48	0.188	0.240	0.285	0.336	0.370	0.401	0.439	0.465
49	0.186	0.238	0.282	0.333	0.366	0.397	0.434	0.460
50	0.184	0.235	0.279	0.329	0.363	0.393	0.430	0.456
52	0.180	0.231	0.274	0.323	0.356	0.386	0.422	0.447
54	0.177	0.226	0.268	0.317	0.349	0.379	0.414	0.439
56	0.174	0.222	0.264	0.311	0.343	0.372	0.407	0.432
58	0.171	0.218	0.259	0.306	0.337	0.366	0.400	0.424
60	0.168	0.214	0.255	0.300	0.331	0.360	0.394	0.418
62	0.165	0.211	0.250	0.296	0.326	0.354	0.388	0.411
64	0.162	0.207	0.246	0.291	0.321	0.348	0.382	0.405
66	0.160	0.204	0.243	0.287	0.316	0.343	0.376	0.399
68	0.157	0.201	0.239	0.282	0.311	0.338	0.370	0.393
70	0.155	0.198	0.235	0.278	0.307	0.333	0.365	0.388
72	0.153	0.195	0.232	0.274	0.303	0.329	0.360	0.382
74	0.151	0.193	0.229	0.271	0.299	0.324	0.355	0.377
76	0.149	0.190	0.226	0.267	0.295	0.320	0.351	0.372
78	0.147	0.188	0.223	0.264	0.291	0.316	0.346	0.368
80	0.145	0.185	0.220	0.260	0.287	0.312	0.342	0.363
82	0.143	0.183	0.217	0.257	0.284	0.308	0.338	0.359
84	0.141	0.181	0.215	0.254	0.280	0.305	0.334	0.355
86	0.139	0.179	0.212	0.251	0.277	0.301	0.330	0.351
88	0.138	0.176	0.210	0.248	0.274	0.298	0.327	0.347
90	0.136	0.174	0.207	0.245	0.271	0.294	0.323	0.343
92	0.135	0.173	0.205	0.243	0.268	0.291	0.319	0.339
94	0.133	0.171	0.203	0.240	0.265	0.288	0.316	0.336
96	0.132	0.169	0.201	0.238	0.262	0.285	0.313	0.332
98	0.130	0.167	0.199	0.235	0.260	0.282	0.310	0.329
100	0.129	0.165	0.197	0.233	0.257	0.279	0.307	0.326

APPENDIX F CRITICAL VALUES
OF THE *F* DISTRIBUTION

Denom. df	α	\multicolumn{10}{c}{Numerator Degrees of Freedom}
		1	2	3	4	5	6	7	8	9	10
1	0.25	5.828	7.500	8.200	8.581	8.820	8.983	9.102	9.192	9.263	9.320
	0.1	39.862	49.500	53.593	55.833	57.240	58.204	58.906	59.439	59.857	60.195
	0.05	161.448	199.500	215.707	224.583	230.161	233.985	236.768	238.882	240.543	241.881
	0.025	647.790	799.501	864.163	899.583	921.847	937.110	948.216	956.654	963.282	968.625
	0.01	4052.17	4999.50	5403.35	5624.57	5763.64	5859.00	5928.33	5981.05	6022.45	6055.82
	0	4052.92	5000.09	5403.89	5625.10	5764.16	5859.48	5928.85	5981.56	6022.96	6056.34
2	0.25	2.571	3.000	3.153	3.232	3.280	3.312	3.335	3.353	3.366	3.377
	0.1	8.526	9.000	9.162	9.243	9.293	9.326	9.349	9.367	9.381	9.392
	0.05	18.513	19.000	19.164	19.247	19.296	19.329	19.353	19.371	19.385	19.396
	0.025	38.506	39.000	39.166	39.248	39.298	39.331	39.355	39.373	39.386	39.397
	0.01	98.503	99.000	99.166	99.249	99.299	99.333	99.356	99.374	99.388	99.399
	0.001	998.544	999.013	999.179	999.263	999.313	999.346	999.370	999.388	999.402	999.413
3	0.25	2.024	2.280	2.356	2.390	2.409	2.422	2.430	2.436	2.441	2.445
	0.1	5.538	5.462	5.391	5.343	5.309	5.285	5.266	5.252	5.240	5.231
	0.05	10.128	9.552	9.277	9.117	9.013	8.941	8.887	8.845	8.812	8.786
	0.025	17.444	16.044	15.439	15.101	14.885	14.735	14.624	14.540	14.473	14.419
	0.01	34.116	30.817	29.458	28.710	28.237	27.911	27.672	27.489	27.345	27.229
	0.001	167.031	148.504	141.110	137.102	134.581	132.849	131.587	130.620	129.862	129.248
4	0.25	1.807	2.000	2.047	2.064	2.072	2.077	2.079	2.080	2.081	2.082
	0.1	4.545	4.325	4.191	4.107	4.051	4.010	3.979	3.955	3.936	3.920
	0.05	7.709	6.944	6.591	6.388	6.256	6.163	6.094	6.041	5.999	5.964
	0.025	12.218	10.649	9.979	9.605	9.365	9.197	9.074	8.980	8.905	8.844
	0.01	21.198	18.000	16.694	15.977	15.522	15.207	14.976	14.799	14.659	14.546
	0.001	74.138	61.246	56.178	53.436	51.712	50.526	49.658	48.997	48.475	48.053
5	0.25	1.692	1.853	1.884	1.893	1.895	1.894	1.894	1.892	1.891	1.890
	0.1	4.060	3.780	3.619	3.520	3.453	3.405	3.368	3.339	3.316	3.297
	0.05	6.608	5.786	5.409	5.192	5.050	4.950	4.876	4.818	4.772	4.735
	0.025	10.007	8.434	7.764	7.388	7.146	6.978	6.853	6.757	6.681	6.619
	0.01	16.258	13.274	12.060	11.392	10.967	10.672	10.456	10.289	10.158	10.051
	0.001	47.181	37.123	33.203	31.085	29.753	28.835	28.163	27.650	27.245	26.917
6	0.25	1.692	1.853	1.884	1.893	1.895	1.894	1.894	1.892	1.891	1.890
	0.1	4.060	3.780	3.619	3.520	3.453	3.405	3.368	3.339	3.316	3.297
	0.05	6.608	5.786	5.409	5.192	5.050	4.950	4.876	4.818	4.772	4.735
	0.025	10.007	8.434	7.764	7.388	7.146	6.978	6.853	6.757	6.681	6.619
	0.01	16.258	13.274	12.060	11.392	10.967	10.672	10.456	10.289	10.158	10.051
	0.001	47.181	37.123	33.203	31.085	29.753	28.835	28.163	27.650	27.245	26.917
7	0.25	1.573	1.701	1.717	1.716	1.711	1.706	1.701	1.697	1.693	1.690
	0.1	3.589	3.257	3.074	2.961	2.883	2.827	2.785	2.752	2.725	2.703
	0.05	5.591	4.737	4.347	4.120	3.972	3.866	3.787	3.726	3.677	3.637
	0.025	8.073	6.542	5.890	5.523	5.285	5.119	4.995	4.899	4.823	4.761
	0.01	12.246	9.547	8.451	7.847	7.461	7.191	6.993	6.840	6.719	6.620
	0.001	29.245	21.689	18.772	17.198	16.206	15.521	15,019	14.634	14.330	14.083
8	0.25	1.538	1.657	1.668	1.664	1.658	1.651	1.645	1.640	1.635	1.631
	0.1	3.458	3.113	2.924	2.806	2.726	2.668	2.624	2.589	2.561	2.538
	0.05	5.318	4.459	4.066	3.838	3.687	3.581	3.500	3.438	3.388	3.347
	0.025	7.571	6.059	5.416	5.053	4.817	4.652	4.529	4.433	4.357	4.295
	0.01	11.259	8.649	7.591	7.006	6.632	6.371	6.178	6.029	5.911	5.814
	0.001	25.415	18.494	15.830	14.392	13.485	12.858	12.398	12.046	11.767	11.540
9	0.25	1.512	1.624	1.632	1.625	1.617	1.609	1.602	1.596	1.591	1.586
	0.1	3.360	3.006	2.813	2.693	2.611	2.551	2.505	2.469	2.440	2.416
	0.05	5.117	4.256	3.863	3.633	3.482	3.374	3.293	3.230	3.179	3.137
	0.025	7.209	5.715	5.078	4.718	4.484	4.320	4.197	4.102	4.026	3.964
	0.01	10.562	8.022	6.992	6.422	6.057	5.802	5.613	5.467	5.351	5.257
	0.001	22.857	16.387	13.902	12.560	11.714	11.128	10.698	10.368	10.107	9.894
10	0.25	1.491	1.598	1.603	1.595	1.585	1.576	1.569	1.562	1.556	1.551
	0.1	3.285	2.924	2.728	2.605	2.522	2.461	2.414	2.377	2.347	2.323
	0.05	4.965	4.103	3.708	3.478	3.326	3.217	3.135	3.072	3.020	2.978
	0.025	6.937	5.456	4.826	4.468	4.236	4.072	3.950	3.855	3.779	3.717
	0.01	10.044	7.559	6.552	5.994	5.636	5.386	5.200	5.057	4.942	4.849
	0.001	21.040	14.905	12.553	11.283	10.481	9.926	9.517	9.204	8.956	8.754

SOURCE: Entries in this table were computed by the author.

12	14	16	18	20	25	30	40	50	60	∞
9.406	9.468	9.515	9.552	9.581	9.634	9.670	9.714	9.741	9.759	9.850
60.705	61.072	61.350	61.566	61.740	62.054	62.265	62.528	62.688	62.793	63.300
243.905	245.363	246.462	247.322	248.012	249.258	250.093	251.141	251.773	252.191	254.000
976.705	982.524	986.913	990.344	993.099	998.076	1001.410	1005.59	1008.11	1009.78	1077.10
6106.29	6142.64	6170.06	6191.49	6209.00	6239.79	6260.62	6286.74	6302.49	6312.93	6728.36
6106.81	6143.16	6170.58	6192.01	6209.22	6240.31	6261.14	6287.25	6303.01	6313.46	6727.87
3.393	3.405	3.414	3.421	3.426	3.436	3.443	3.451	3.456	3.459	3.573
9.408	9.420	9.429	9.435	9.441	9.451	9.458	9.466	9.471	9.475	9.747
19.412	19.424	19.433	19.440	19.446	19.456	19.462	19.470	19.475	19.478	19.969
39.414	39.425	39.435	39.442	39.448	39.458	39.465	39.473	39.478	39.481	40.504
99.416	99.428	99.436	99.443	99.449	99.458	99.464	99.471	99.479	99.482	102.018
999.430	999.442	999.450	999.457	999.463	999.472	999.479	999.486	999.493	999.490	1024.788
2.450	2.454	2.456	2.459	2.460	2.463	2.465	2.467	2.469	2.470	2.517
5.216	5.205	5.196	5.190	5.185	5.175	5.168	5.160	5.155	5.151	5.218
8.745	8.715	8.692	8.675	8.660	8.634	8.617	8.594	8.581	8.572	8.655
14.337	14.277	14.232	14.196	14.167	14.116	14.081	14.037	14.010	13.992	14.092
27.052	26.924	26.827	26.751	26.690	26.579	26.505	26.411	26.355	26.317	26.490
128.318	127.648	127.137	126.739	126.420	125.839	125.451	124.960	124.665	124.468	125.170
2.083	2.083	2.083	2.083	2.083	2.083	2.082	2.082	2.082	2.082	2.105
3.896	3.878	3.864	3.853	3.844	3.828	3.817	3.804	3.795	3.790	3.797
5.912	5.873	5.844	5.821	5.803	5.769	5.746	5.717	5.699	5.688	5.682
8.751	8.684	8.633	8.593	8.560	8.501	8.461	8.411	8.381	8.360	8.327
14.374	14.249	14.153	14.080	14.020	13.911	13.838	13.745	13.690	13.652	13.590
47.412	46.948	46.597	46.322	46.101	45.699	45.429	45.089	44.884	44.746	44.433
1.888	1.886	1.884	1.883	1.882	1.880	1.878	1.876	1.875	1.874	1.885
3.268	3.247	3.230	3.217	3.207	3.187	3.174	3.157	3.147	3.140	3.127
4.678	4.636	4.604	4.579	4.558	4.521	4.496	4.464	4.444	4.431	4.392
6.525	6.456	6.403	6.362	6.329	6.268	6.227	6.175	6.144	6.123	6.048
9.888	9.770	9.680	9.610	9.553	9.449	9.379	9.291	9.238	9.202	9.066
26.418	26.057	25.783	25.568	25.395	25.080	24.869	24.602	24.441	24.333	23.916
1.888	1.886	1.884	1.883	1.882	1.880	1.878	1.876	1.875	1.874	1.885
3.268	3.247	3.230	3.217	3.207	3.187	3.174	3.157	3.147	3.140	3.127
4.678	4.636	4.604	4.579	4.558	4.521	4.496	4.464	4.444	4.431	4.392
6.525	6.456	6.403	6.362	6.329	6.268	6.227	6.175	6.144	6.123	6.048
9.888	9.770	9.680	9.610	9.553	9.449	9.379	9.291	9.238	9.202	9.066
26.418	26.057	25.783	25.568	25.395	25.080	24.869	24.602	24.441	24.333	23.916
1.684	1.680	1.676	1.674	1.671	1.667	1.663	1.659	1.657	1.655	1.650
2.668	2.643	2.623	2.607	2.595	2.571	2.555	2.535	2.523	2.514	2.477
3.575	3.529	3.494	3.467	3.445	3.404	3.376	3.340	3.319	3.304	3.236
4.666	4.596	4.543	4.501	4.467	4.405	4.362	4.309	4.276	4.254	4.150
6.469	6.359	6.275	6.209	6.155	6.058	5.992	5.908	5.858	5.824	5.663
13.707	13.434	13.227	13.063	12.932	12.692	12.530	12.326	12.202	12.119	11.719
1.624	1.619	1.615	1.612	1.609	1.603	1.600	1.595	1.591	1.589	1.580
2.502	2.475	2.455	2.438	2.425	2.400	2.383	2.361	2.348	2.339	2.294
3.284	3.237	3.202	3.173	3.150	3.108	3.079	3.043	3.020	3.005	2.930
4.200	4.130	4.076	4.034	3.999	3.937	3.894	3.840	3.807	3.784	3.674
5.667	5.559	5.477	5.412	5.359	5.263	5.198	5.116	5.065	5.032	4.862
11.195	10.943	10.752	10.601	10.480	10.258	10.109	9.919	9.804	9.727	9.337
1.579	1.573	1.568	1.564	1.561	1.555	1.551	1.545	1.541	1.539	1.525
2.379	2.351	2.330	2.312	2.298	2.272	2.255	2.232	2.218	2.208	2.159
3.073	3.025	2.989	2.960	2.936	2.893	2.864	2.826	2.803	2.787	2.706
3.868	3.798	3.744	3.701	3.667	3.604	3.560	3.505	3.472	3.449	3.332
5.111	5.005	4.924	4.860	4.808	4.713	4.649	4.567	4.517	4.483	4.310
9.570	9.334	9.154	9.012	8.898	8.689	8.548	8.369	8.260	8.187	7.812
1.543	1.537	1.531	1.527	1.523	1.517	1.512	1.506	1.502	1.499	1.499
2.284	2.255	2.233	2.215	2.201	2.174	2.155	2.132	2.117	2.107	2.073
2.913	2.865	2.828	2.798	2.774	2.730	2.700	2.661	2.637	2.621	2.557
3.621	3.550	3.496	3.453	3.419	3.355	3.311	3.255	3.221	3.198	3.101
4.706	4.601	4.520	4.457	4.405	4.311	4.247	4.165	4.115	4.082	3.936
8.445	8.220	8.048	7.913	7.804	7.604	7.469	7.297	7.193	7.122	6.801

Denom. df	α	1	2	3	4	5	6	7	8	9	10

Numerator Degrees of Freedom

Denom. df	α	1	2	3	4	5	6	7	8	9	10
11	0.25	1.475	1.577	1.580	1.570	1.560	1.550	1.542	1.535	1.528	1.523
	0.1	3.225	2.860	2.660	2.536	2.451	2.389	2.342	2.304	2.274	2.248
	0.05	4.844	3.982	3.587	3.357	3.204	3.095	3.012	2.948	2.896	2.854
	0.025	6.724	5.256	4.630	4.275	4.044	3.881	3.759	3.664	3.588	3.526
	0.01	9.646	7.206	6.217	5.668	5.316	5.069	4.886	4.744	4.632	4.539
	0.001	19.687	13.812	11.561	10.346	9.578	9.047	8.655	8.355	8.116	7.922
12	0.25	1.461	1.560	1.561	1.550	1.539	1.529	1.520	1.512	1.505	1.500
	0.1	3.177	2.807	2.606	2.480	2.394	2.331	2.283	2.245	2.214	2.188
	0.05	4.747	3.885	3.490	3.259	3.106	2.996	2.913	2.849	2.796	2.753
	0.025	6.554	5.096	4.474	4.121	3.891	3.728	3.607	3.512	3.436	3.374
	0.01	9.330	6.927	5.953	5.412	5.064	4.821	4.640	4.499	4.388	4.296
	0.001	18.643	12.974	10.804	9.633	8.892	8.379	8.001	7.710	7.480	7.292
13	0.25	1.450	1.545	1.545	1.534	1.521	1.511	1.501	1.493	1.486	1.480
	0.1	3.136	2.763	2.560	2.434	2.347	2.283	2.234	2.195	2.164	2.138
	0.05	4.667	3.806	3.411	3.179	3.025	2.915	2.832	2.767	2.714	2.671
	0.025	6.414	4.965	4.347	3.996	3.767	3.604	3.483	3.388	3.312	3.250
	0.01	9.074	6.701	5.739	5.205	4.862	4.620	4.441	4.302	4.191	4.100
	0.001	17.816	12.313	10.209	9.073	8.354	7.856	7.489	7.206	6.982	6.799
14	0.25	1.440	1.533	1.532	1.519	1.507	1.495	1.485	1.477	1.470	1.463
	0.1	3.102	2.726	2.522	2.395	2.307	2.243	2.193	2.154	2.122	2.095
	0.05	4.600	3.739	3.344	3.112	2.958	2.848	2.764	2.699	2.646	2.602
	0.025	6.298	4.857	4.242	3.892	3.663	3.501	3.380	3.285	3.209	3.147
	0.01	8.862	6.515	5.564	5.035	4.695	4.456	4.278	4.140	4.030	3.939
	0.001	17.143	11.779	9.729	8.622	7.922	7.436	7.077	6.802	6.583	6.404
15	0.25	1.432	1.523	1.520	1.507	1.494	1.482	1.472	1.463	1.456	1.449
	0.1	3.073	2.695	2.490	2.361	2.273	2.208	2.158	2.119	2.086	2.059
	0.05	4.543	3.682	3.287	3.056	2.901	2.790	2.707	2.641	2.588	2.544
	0.025	6.200	4.765	4.153	3.804	3.576	3.415	3.293	3.199	3.123	3.060
	0.01	8.683	6.359	5.417	4.893	4.556	4.318	4.142	4.004	3.895	3.805
	0.001	16.587	11.339	9.335	8.253	7.567	7.092	6.741	6.471	6.256	6.081
16	0.25	1.425	1.514	1.510	1.497	1.483	1.471	1.460	1.451	1.443	1.437
	0.1	3.048	2.668	2.462	2.333	2.244	2.178	2.128	2.088	2.055	2.028
	0.05	4.494	3.634	3.239	3.007	2.852	2.741	2.657	2.591	2.538	2.494
	0.025	6.115	4.687	4.077	3.729	3.502	3.341	3.219	3.125	3.049	2.986
	0.01	8.531	6.226	5.292	4.773	4.437	4.202	4.026	3.890	3.780	3.691
	0.001	16.120	10.971	9.006	7.944	7.272	6.805	6.460	6.195	5.984	5.812
17	0.25	1.419	1.506	1.502	1.487	1.473	1.460	1.450	1.441	1.433	1.426
	0.1	3.026	2.645	2.437	2.308	2.218	2.152	2.102	2.061	2.028	2.001
	0.05	4.451	3.592	3.197	2.965	2.810	2.699	2.614	2.548	2.494	2.450
	0.025	6.042	4.619	4.011	3.665	3.438	3.277	3.156	3.061	2.985	2.922
	0.01	8.400	6.112	5.185	4.669	4.336	4.102	3.927	3.791	3.682	3.593
	0.001	15.722	10.658	8.727	7.683	7.022	6.563	6.223	5.962	5.754	5.584
18	0.25	1.408	1.493	1.487	1.472	1.457	1.444	1.432	1.423	1.414	1.407
	0.1	2.990	2.606	2.397	2.266	2.176	2.109	2.058	2.017	1.984	1.956
	0.05	4.381	3.522	3.127	2.895	2.740	2.628	2.544	2.477	2.423	2.378
	0.025	5.922	4.508	3.903	3.559	3.333	3.172	3.051	2.956	2.880	2.817
	0.01	8.185	5.926	5.010	4.500	4.171	3.939	3.765	3.631	3.523	3.434
	0.001	15.081	10.157	8.280	7.265	6.623	6.175	5.845	5.590	5.388	5.222
19	0.25	1.408	1.493	1.487	1.472	1.457	1.444	1.432	1.423	1.414	1.407
	0.1	2.990	2.606	2.397	2.266	2.176	2.109	2.058	2.017	1.984	1.956
	0.05	4.381	3.522	3.127	2.895	2.740	2.628	2.544	2.477	2.423	2.378
	0.025	5.922	4.508	3.903	3.559	3.333	3.172	3.051	2.956	2.880	2.817
	0.01	8.185	5.926	5.010	4.500	4.171	3.939	3.765	3.631	3.523	3.434
	0.001	15.081	10.157	8.280	7.265	6.623	6.175	5.845	5.590	5.388	5.222
20	0.25	1.404	1.487	1.481	1.465	1.450	1.437	1.425	1.415	1.407	1.399
	0.1	2.975	2.589	2.380	2.249	2.158	2.091	2.040	1.999	1.965	1.937
	0.05	4.351	3.493	3.098	2.866	2.711	2.599	2.514	2.447	2.393	2.348
	0.025	5.872	4.461	3.859	3.515	3.289	3.128	3.007	2.913	2.837	2.774
	0.01	8.096	5.849	4.938	4.431	4.103	3.871	3.699	3.564	3.457	3.368
	0.001	14.819	9.953	8.098	7.096	6.461	6.019	5.692	5.440	5.239	5.075
22	0.25	1.396	1.477	1.470	1.454	1.438	1.424	1.413	1.402	1.394	1.386
	0.1	2.949	2.561	2.351	2.219	2.128	2.061	2.008	1.967	1.933	1.904
	0.05	4.301	3.443	3.049	2.817	2.661	2.549	2.464	2.397	2.342	2.297
	0.025	5.786	4.383	3.783	3.440	3.215	3.055	2.934	2.839	2.763	2.700
	0.01	7.945	5.719	4.817	4.313	3.988	3.758	3.587	3.453	3.346	3.258
	0.001	14.380	9.612	7.796	6.814	6.191	5.758	5.438	5.190	4.993	4.832

Numerator Degrees of Freedom

12	14	16	18	20	25	30	40	50	60	∞
1.514	1.507	1.501	1.497	1.493	1.486	1.481	1.474	1.469	1.466	1.462
2.209	2.179	2.156	2.138	2.123	2.095	2.076	2.052	2.036	2.026	1.986
2.788	2.739	2.701	2.671	2.646	2.601	2.570	2.531	2.507	2.490	2.419
3.430	3.359	3.304	3.261	3.226	3.162	3.118	3.061	3.027	3.004	2.898
4.397	4.293	4.213	4.150	4.099	4.005	3.941	3.860	3.810	3.776	3.623
7.626	7.409	7.244	7.113	7.008	6.815	6.684	6.518	6.417	6.348	6.027
1.490	1.483	1.477	1.472	1.468	1.460	1.454	1.447	1.443	1.439	1.432
2.147	2.117	2.094	2.075	2.060	2.031	2.011	1.986	1.970	1.960	1.914
2.687	2.637	2.599	2.568	2.544	2.498	2.466	2.426	2.401	2.384	2.308
3.277	3.206	3.152	3.108	3.073	3.008	2.963	2.906	2.871	2.848	2.738
4.155	4.052	3.972	3.909	3.858	3.765	3.701	3.619	3.569	3.536	3.374
7.005	6.794	6.634	6.507	6.405	6.217	6.090	5.928	5.829	5.762	5.440
1.470	1.462	1.456	1.451	1.447	1.438	1.432	1.425	1.420	1.416	1.405
2.097	2.066	2.042	2.023	2.007	1.978	1.958	1.931	1.915	1.904	1.853
2.604	2.554	2.515	2.484	2.459	2.412	2.380	2.339	2.314	2.297	2.214
3.153	3.082	3.027	2.983	2.948	2.882	2.837	2.780	2.744	2.720	2.605
3.960	3.857	3.778	3.716	3.665	3.571	3.507	3.425	3.375	3.341	3.175
6.519	6.314	6.158	6.034	5.934	5.751	5.626	5.467	5.370	5.305	4.981
1.453	1.445	1.438	1.433	1.428	1.420	1.414	1.405	1.400	1.397	1.383
2.054	2.022	1.998	1.979	1.962	1.933	1.912	1.885	1.869	1.857	1.803
2.534	2.484	2.445	2.413	2.388	2.341	2.308	2.266	2.241	2.223	2.137
3.050	2.979	2.923	2.879	2.844	2.778	2.732	2.674	2.638	2.614	2.493
3.800	3.698	3.619	3.556	3.505	3.412	3.348	3.266	3.215	3.181	3.011
6.130	5.930	5.776	5.655	5.557	5.377	5.254	5.098	5.002	4.938	4.614
1.438	1.430	1.423	1.417	1.413	1.404	1.397	1.389	1.383	1.380	1.362
2.017	1.985	1.961	1.941	1.924	1.894	1.873	1.845	1.828	1.817	1.758
2.475	2.424	2.385	2.353	2.328	2.280	2.247	2.204	2.178	2.160	2.069
2.963	2.891	2.836	2.792	2.756	2.689	2.644	2.585	2.549	2.524	2.399
3.666	3.564	3.485	3.423	3.372	3.278	3.214	3.132	3.081	3.047	2.873
5.812	5.615	5.464	5.345	5.248	5.071	4.950	4.796	4.702	4.638	4.312
1.426	1.417	1.410	1.404	1.399	1.390	1.383	1.374	1.369	1.365	1.345
1.985	1.953	1.928	1.908	1.891	1.860	1.839	1.811	1.793	1.782	1.720
2.425	2.373	2.333	2.302	2.276	2.227	2.194	2.151	2.124	2.106	2.011
2.889	2.817	2.761	2.717	2.681	2.614	2.568	2.509	2.472	2.447	2.318
3.553	3.451	3.372	3.310	3.259	3.165	3.101	3.018	2.967	2.933	2.755
5.547	5.353	5.205	5.087	4.992	4.817	4.697	4.545	4.451	4.388	4.062
1.414	1.405	1.398	1.392	1.387	1.377	1.370	1.361	1.355	1.351	1.329
1.958	1.925	1.900	1.879	1.862	1.831	1.809	1.781	1.763	1.751	1.686
2.381	2.329	2.289	2.257	2.230	2.181	2.148	2.104	2.077	2.058	1.960
2.825	2.753	2.697	2.652	2.616	2.548	2.502	2.442	2.405	2.380	2.247
3.455	3.353	3.275	3.212	3.162	3.068	3.003	2.920	2.869	2.835	2.653
5.324	5.132	4.986	4.869	4.775	4.602	4.484	4.332	4.239	4.177	3.850
1.395	1.386	1.378	1.372	1.367	1.356	1.349	1.339	1.333	1.329	1.313
1.912	1.878	1.852	1.831	1.814	1.782	1.759	1.730	1.711	1.699	1.639
2.308	2.256	2.215	2.182	2.156	2.106	2.071	2.026	1.999	1.980	1.887
2.720	2.647	2.591	2.546	2.509	2.441	2.394	2.333	2.295	2.270	2.142
3.297	3.195	3.117	3.054	3.003	2.909	2.844	2.761	2.709	2.674	2.499
4.967	4.780	4.636	4.522	4.430	4.259	4.143	3.994	3.902	3.840	3.526
1.395	1.386	1.378	1.372	1.367	1.356	1.349	1.339	1.333	1.329	1.313
1.912	1.878	1.852	1.831	1.814	1.782	1.759	1.730	1.711	1.699	1.639
2.308	2.256	2.215	2.182	2.156	2.106	2.071	2.026	1.999	1.980	1.887
2.720	2.647	2.591	2.546	2.509	2.441	2.394	2.333	2.295	2.270	2.142
3.297	3.195	3.117	3.054	3.003	2.909	2.844	2.761	2.709	2.674	2.499
4.967	4.780	4.636	4.522	4.430	4.259	4.143	3.994	3.902	3.840	3.526
1.387	1.378	1.370	1.363	1.358	1.348	1.340	1.330	1.324	1.319	1.301
1.892	1.859	1.833	1.811	1.794	1.761	1.738	1.708	1.690	1.677	1.614
2.278	2.225	2.184	2.151	2.124	2.074	2.039	1.994	1.966	1.946	1.850
2.676	2.603	2.547	2.501	2.464	2.396	2.349	2.287	2.249	2.223	2.093
3.231	3.130	3.051	2.989	2.938	2.843	2.778	2.695	2.643	2.608	2.429
4.823	4.637	4.495	4.382	4.290	4.121	4.005	3.856	3.765	3.703	3.388
1.374	1.364	1.355	1.349	1.343	1.332	1.324	1.314	1.307	1.303	1.280
1.859	1.825	1.798	1.777	1.759	1.726	1.702	1.671	1.652	1.639	1.571
2.226	2.173	2.131	2.098	2.071	2.020	1.984	1.938	1.909	1.889	1.787
2.602	2.528	2.472	2.426	2.389	2.320	2.272	2.210	2.171	2.145	2.008
3.121	3.019	2.941	2.879	2.827	2.733	2.667	2.583	2.531	2.495	2.310
4.583	4.401	4.260	4.149	4.058	3.891	3.776	3.629	3.538	3.476	3.156

Denom. df	α	\multicolumn{10}{c}{Numerator Degrees of Freedom}
		1	2	3	4	5	6	7	8	9	10
24	0.25	1.390	1.470	1.462	1.445	1.428	1.414	1.402	1.392	1.383	1.375
	0.1	2.927	2.538	2.327	2.195	2.103	2.035	1.983	1.941	1.906	1.877
	0.05	4.260	3.403	3.009	2.776	2.621	2.508	2.423	2.355	2.300	2.255
	0.025	5.717	4.319	3.721	3.379	3.155	2.995	2.874	2.779	2.703	2.640
	0.01	7.823	5.614	4.718	4.218	3.895	3.667	3.496	3.363	3.256	3.168
	0.001	14.028	9.339	7.554	6.589	5.977	5.550	5.235	4.991	4.797	4.638
26	0.25	1.385	1.463	1.454	1.437	1.420	1.406	1.393	1.383	1.374	1.366
	0.1	2.909	2.519	2.307	2.174	2.082	2.014	1.961	1.919	1.884	1.855
	0.05	4.225	3.369	2.975	2.743	2.587	2.474	2.388	2.321	2.265	2.220
	0.025	5.659	4.265	3.670	3.329	3.105	2.945	2.824	2.729	2.653	2.590
	0.01	7.721	5.526	4.637	4.140	3.818	3.591	3.421	3.288	3.182	3.094
	0.001	13.739	9.116	7.357	6.406	5.802	5.381	5.070	4.829	4.637	4.480
28	0.25	1.380	1.457	1.448	1.430	1.413	1.399	1.386	1.375	1.366	1.358
	0.1	2.894	2.503	2.291	2.157	2.064	1.996	1.943	1.900	1.865	1.836
	0.05	4.196	3.340	2.947	2.714	2.558	2.445	2.359	2.291	2.236	2.190
	0.025	5.610	4.221	3.626	3.286	3.063	2.903	2.782	2.687	2.611	2.547
	0.01	7.636	5.453	4.568	4.074	3.754	3.528	3.358	3.226	3.120	3.032
	0.001	13.498	8.931	7.193	6.253	5.657	5.241	4.933	4.695	4.505	4.349
30	0.25	1.376	1.452	1.443	1.424	1.407	1.392	1.380	1.369	1.359	1.351
	0.1	2.881	2.489	2.276	2.142	2.049	1.980	1.927	1.884	1.849	1.819
	0.05	4.171	3.316	2.922	2.690	2.534	2.421	2.334	2.266	2.211	2.165
	0.025	5.568	4.182	3.589	3.250	3.026	2.867	2.746	2.651	2.575	2.511
	0.01	7.562	5.390	4.510	4.018	3.699	3.473	3.305	3.173	3.067	2.979
	0.001	13.293	8.773	7.054	6.125	5.534	5.122	4.817	4.581	4.393	4.239
35	0.25	1.368	1.443	1.432	1.413	1.395	1.380	1.367	1.355	1.345	1.337
	0.1	2.855	2.461	2.247	2.113	2.019	1.950	1.896	1.852	1.817	1.787
	0.05	4.121	3.267	2.874	2.641	2.485	2.372	2.285	2.217	2.161	2.114
	0.025	5.485	4.106	3.517	3.179	2.956	2.796	2.676	2.581	2.504	2.440
	0.01	7.419	5.268	4.396	3.908	3.592	3.368	3.200	3.069	2.963	2.876
	0.001	12.896	8.470	6.787	5.876	5.298	4.894	4.595	4.363	4.178	4.027
40	0.25	1.363	1.435	1.424	1.404	1.386	1.371	1.357	1.345	1.335	1.327
	0.1	2.835	2.440	2.226	2.091	1.997	1.927	1.873	1.829	1.793	1.763
	0.05	4.085	3.232	2.839	2.606	2.449	2.336	2.249	2.180	2.124	2.077
	0.025	5.424	4.051	3.463	3.126	2.904	2.744	2.624	2.529	2.452	2.388
	0.01	7.314	5.179	4.313	3.828	3.514	3.291	3.124	2.993	2.888	2.801
	0.001	12.609	8.251	6.595	5.698	5.128	4.731	4.436	4.207	4.024	3.874
50	0.25	1.355	1.425	1.413	1.393	1.374	1.358	1.344	1.332	1.321	1.312
	0.1	2.809	2.412	2.197	2.061	1.966	1.895	1.840	1.796	1.760	1.729
	0.05	4.034	3.183	2.790	2.557	2.400	2.286	2.199	2.130	2.073	2.026
	0.025	5.340	3.975	3.390	3.054	2.833	2.674	2.553	2.458	2.381	2.317
	0.01	7.171	5.057	4.199	3.720	3.408	3.186	3.020	2.890	2.785	2.698
	0.001	12.222	7.956	6.336	5.459	4.901	4.512	4.222	3.998	3.818	3.671
60	0.25	1.349	1.419	1.405	1.385	1.366	1.349	1.335	1.323	1.312	1.303
	0.1	2.791	2.393	2.177	2.041	1.946	1.875	1.819	1.775	1.738	1.707
	0.05	4.001	3.150	2.758	2.525	2.368	2.254	2.167	2.097	2.040	1.993
	0.025	5.286	3.925	3.343	3.008	2.786	2.627	2.507	2.412	2.334	2.270
	0.01	7.077	4.977	4.126	3.649	3.339	3.119	2.953	2.823	2.718	2.632
	0.001	11.973	7.768	6.171	5.307	4.757	4.372	4.086	3.865	3.687	3.541
70	0.25	1.346	1.414	1.400	1.379	1.360	1.343	1.329	1.316	1.305	1.296
	0.1	2.779	2.380	2.164	2.027	1.931	1.860	1.804	1.760	1.723	1.691
	0.05	3.978	3.128	2.736	2.503	2.346	2.231	2.143	2.074	2.017	1.969
	0.025	5.247	3.890	3.309	2.975	2.754	2.595	2.474	2.379	2.302	2.237
	0.01	7.011	4.922	4.074	3.600	3.291	3.071	2.906	2.777	2.672	2.585
	0.001	11.799	7.637	6.057	5.201	4.656	4.275	3.992	3.773	3.596	3.452
100	0.25	1.339	1.406	1.391	1.369	1.349	1.332	1.317	1.304	1.293	1.283
	0.1	2.756	2.356	2.139	2.002	1.906	1.834	1.778	1.732	1.695	1.663
	0.05	3.936	3.087	2.696	2.463	2.305	2.191	2.103	2.032	1.975	1.927
	0.025	5.179	3.828	3.250	2.917	2.696	2.537	2.417	2.321	2.244	2.179
	0.01	6.895	4.824	3.984	3.513	3.206	2.988	2.823	2.694	2.590	2.503
	0.001	11.495	7.408	5.857	5.017	4.482	4.107	3.829	3.612	3.439	3.296

Numerator Degrees of Freedom

12	14	16	18	20	25	30	40	50	60	∞
1.362	1.352	1.343	1.337	1.331	1.319	1.311	1.300	1.293	1.289	1.262
1.832	1.797	1.770	1.748	1.730	1.696	1.672	1.641	1.621	1.607	1.534
2.183	2.130	2.088	2.054	2.027	1.975	1.939	1.892	1.863	1.842	1.735
2.541	2.468	2.411	2.365	2.327	2.257	2.209	2.146	2.107	2.080	1.937
3.032	2.930	2.852	2.789	2.738	2.643	2.577	2.492	2.440	2.403	2.212
4.393	4.212	4.074	3.963	3.873	3.707	3.593	3.447	3.356	3.295	2.971
1.352	1.342	1.333	1.326	1.320	1.309	1.300	1.289	1.282	1.277	1.256
1.809	1.774	1.747	1.724	1.706	1.671	1.647	1.615	1.594	1.581	1.512
2.148	2.094	2.052	2.018	1.990	1.938	1.901	1.853	1.823	1.803	1.698
2.491	2.417	2.360	2.314	2.276	2.205	2.157	2.093	2.053	2.026	1.886
2.958	2.857	2.778	2.715	2.664	2.569	2.503	2.417	2.364	2.327	2.140
4.238	4.059	3.921	3.812	3.723	3.558	3.445	3.299	3.208	3.147	2.829
1.344	1.333	1.325	1.317	1.311	1.299	1.291	1.279	1.271	1.266	1.242
1.790	1.754	1.726	1.704	1.685	1.650	1.625	1.592	1.572	1.558	1.484
2.118	2.064	2.021	1.987	1.959	1.906	1.869	1.820	1.790	1.769	1.660
2.448	2.374	2.317	2.270	2.232	2.161	2.112	2.048	2.007	1.980	1.835
2.896	2.795	2.716	2.653	2.602	2.506	2.440	2.354	2.300	2.263	2.070
4.109	3.932	3.795	3.687	3.598	3.434	3.321	3.176	3.085	3.024	2.701
1.337	1.326	1.317	1.310	1.303	1.291	1.282	1.270	1.263	1.257	1.229
1.773	1.737	1.709	1.686	1.667	1.632	1.606	1.573	1.552	1.538	1.460
2.092	2.037	1.995	1.960	1.932	1.878	1.841	1.792	1.761	1.740	1.626
2.412	2.338	2.280	2.233	2.195	2.124	2.074	2.009	1.968	1.940	1.790
2.843	2.742	2.663	2.600	2.549	2.453	2.386	2.299	2.245	2.208	2.010
4.001	3.825	3.689	3.581	3.493	3.330	3.217	3.072	2.981	2.920	2.593
1.323	1.311	1.302	1.294	1.288	1.275	1.266	1.253	1.245	1.239	1.211
1.739	1.703	1.674	1.651	1.632	1.595	1.569	1.535	1.513	1.497	1.417
2.041	1.986	1.942	1.907	1.878	1.824	1.786	1.735	1.703	1.681	1.563
2.341	2.266	2.207	2.160	2.122	2.049	1.999	1.932	1.890	1.861	1.707
2.740	2.639	2.560	2.497	2.445	2.348	2.281	2.193	2.137	2.099	1.896
3.792	3.618	3.484	3.378	3.290	3.128	3.016	2.871	2.781	2.719	2.389
1.312	1.300	1.291	1.283	1.276	1.263	1.253	1.240	1.231	1.225	1.190
1.715	1.678	1.649	1.625	1.605	1.568	1.541	1.506	1.483	1.467	1.378
2.003	1.948	1.904	1.868	1.839	1.783	1.744	1.693	1.660	1.637	1.510
2.288	2.213	2.154	2.107	2.068	1.994	1.943	1.875	1.832	1.803	1.639
2.665	2.563	2.484	2.421	2.369	2.271	2.203	2.114	2.058	2.019	1.806
3.642	3.471	3.338	3.232	3.145	2.984	2.872	2.727	2.636	2.574	2.234
1.297	1.285	1.275	1.266	1.259	1.245	1.235	1.221	1.212	1.205	1.164
1.680	1.643	1.613	1.588	1.568	1.529	1.502	1.465	1.441	1.424	1.327
1.952	1.895	1.850	1.814	1.784	1.727	1.687	1.634	1.599	1.576	1.438
2.216	2.140	2.081	2.033	1.993	1.919	1.866	1.796	1.752	1.721	1.545
2.562	2.461	2.382	2.318	2.265	2.167	2.098	2.007	1.949	1.909	1.683
3.443	3.273	3.142	3.037	2.951	2.790	2.679	2.533	2.441	2.378	2.027
1.287	1.274	1.264	1.255	1.248	1.234	1.223	1.208	1.198	1.191	1.151
1.657	1.619	1.589	1.564	1.543	1.504	1.476	1.437	1.413	1.395	1.295
1.917	1.860	1.815	1.778	1.748	1.690	1.649	1.594	1.559	1.534	1.393
2.169	2.093	2.033	1.985	1.944	1.869	1.815	1.744	1.699	1.667	1.485
2.496	2.394	2.315	2.251	2.198	2.098	2.028	1.936	1.877	1.836	1.604
3.315	3.147	3.017	2.912	2.827	2.667	2.555	2.409	2.316	2.252	1.894
1.280	1.267	1.257	1.248	1.240	1.225	1.214	1.199	1.189	1.181	1.137
1.641	1.603	1.572	1.547	1.526	1.486	1.457	1.418	1.392	1.374	1.267
1.893	1.836	1.790	1.753	1.722	1.664	1.622	1.566	1.530	1.505	1.355
2.136	2.059	1.999	1.950	1.910	1.833	1.779	1.707	1.660	1.628	1.438
2.450	2.348	2.268	2.204	2.150	2.050	1.980	1.886	1.826	1.785	1.542
3.227	3.060	2.930	2.826	2.741	2.581	2.469	2.322	2.229	2.164	1.795
1.267	1.254	1.243	1.234	1.226	1.210	1.198	1.182	1.171	1.163	1.112
1.612	1.573	1.542	1.516	1.494	1.453	1.423	1.382	1.355	1.336	1.216
1.850	1.792	1.746	1.708	1.676	1.616	1.573	1.515	1.477	1.450	1.285
2.077	2.000	1.939	1.890	1.849	1.770	1.715	1.640	1.592	1.558	1.349
2.368	2.265	2.185	2.120	2.067	1.965	1.893	1.797	1.735	1.692	1.429
3.074	2.908	2.780	2.676	2.591	2.431	2.319	2.170	2.076	2.009	1.617

APPENDIX G BINOMIAL PROBABILITIES

Entries are the probabilities of x "successes" in N trials, where p gives the probability of a "success" on each trial. For $p > 0.50$, use $(1 - p)$ entry.

N	x	\multicolumn{11}{c}{Probability p}
		0.01	0.05	0.10	0.15	0.20	0.25	0.30	0.33	0.40	0.45	0.50
2	0	0.9801	0.9025	0.8100	0.7225	0.6400	0.5625	0.4900	0.4444	0.3600	0.3025	0.2500
	1	0.0198	0.0950	0.1800	0.2550	0.3200	0.3750	0.4200	0.4444	0.4800	0.4950	0.5000
	2	0.0001	0.0025	0.0100	0.0225	0.0400	0.0625	0.0900	0.1111	0.1600	0.2025	0.2500
3	0	0.9703	0.8574	0.7290	0.6141	0.5120	0.4219	0.3430	0.2963	0.2160	0.1664	0.1250
	1	0.0294	0.1354	0.2430	0.3251	0.3840	0.4219	0.4410	0.4444	0.4320	0.4084	0.3750
	2	0.0003	0.0071	0.0270	0.0574	0.0960	0.1406	0.1890	0.2222	0.2880	0.3341	0.3750
	3	0.0000	0.0001	0.0010	0.0034	0.0080	0.0156	0.0270	0.0370	0.0640	0.0911	0.1250
4	0	0.9606	0.8145	0.6561	0.5220	0.4096	0.3164	0.2401	0.1975	0.1296	0.0915	0.0625
	1	0.0388	0.1715	0.2916	0.3685	0.4096	0.4219	0.4116	0.3951	0.3456	0.2995	0.2500
	2	0.0006	0.0135	0.0486	0.0975	0.1536	0.2109	0.2646	0.2963	0.3456	0.3675	0.3750
	3	0.0000	0.0005	0.0036	0.0115	0.0256	0.0469	0.0756	0.0988	0.1536	0.2005	0.2500
	4	0.0000	0.0000	0.0001	0.0005	0.0016	0.0039	0.0081	0.0123	0.0256	0.0410	0.0625
5	0	0.9510	0.7738	0.5905	0.4437	0.3277	0.2373	0.1681	0.1317	0.0778	0.0503	0.0313
	1	0.0480	0.2036	0.3281	0.3915	0.4096	0.3955	0.3602	0.3292	0.2592	0.2059	0.1563
	2	0.0010	0.0214	0.0729	0.1382	0.2048	0.2637	0.3087	0.3292	0.3456	0.3369	0.3125
	3	0.0000	0.0011	0.0081	0.0244	0.0512	0.0879	0.1323	0.1646	0.2304	0.2757	0.3125
	4	0.0000	0.0000	0.0005	0.0022	0.0064	0.0146	0.0284	0.0412	0.0768	0.1128	0.1563
	5	0.0000	0.0000	0.0000	0.0001	0.0003	0.0010	0.0024	0.0041	0.0102	0.0185	0.0313
6	0	0.9415	0.7351	0.5314	0.3771	0.2621	0.1780	0.1176	0.0878	0.0467	0.0277	0.0156
	1	0.0571	0.2321	0.3543	0.3993	0.3932	0.3560	0.3025	0.2634	0.1866	0.1359	0.0938
	2	0.0014	0.0305	0.0984	0.1762	0.2458	0.2966	0.3241	0.3292	0.3110	0.2780	0.2344
	3	0.0000	0.0021	0.0146	0.0415	0.0819	0.1318	0.1852	0.2195	0.2765	0.3032	0.3125
	4	0.0000	0.0001	0.0012	0.0055	0.0154	0.0330	0.0595	0.0823	0.1382	0.1861	0.2344
	5	0.0000	0.0000	0.0001	0.0004	0.0015	0.0044	0.0102	0.0165	0.0369	0.0609	0.0938
	6	0.0000	0.0000	0.0000	0.0000	0.0001	0.0002	0.0007	0.0014	0.0041	0.0083	0.0156
7	0	0.9321	0.6983	0.4783	0.3206	0.2097	0.1335	0.0824	0.0585	0.0280	0.0152	0.0078
	1	0.0659	0.2573	0.3720	0.3960	0.3670	0.3115	0.2471	0.2048	0.1306	0.0872	0.0547
	2	0.0020	0.0406	0.1240	0.2097	0.2753	0.3115	0.3177	0.3073	0.2613	0.2140	0.1641
	3	0.0000	0.0036	0.0230	0.0617	0.1147	0.1730	0.2269	0.2561	0.2903	0.2918	0.2734
	4	0.0000	0.0002	0.0026	0.0109	0.0287	0.0577	0.0972	0.1280	0.1935	0.2388	0.2734
	5	0.0000	0.0000	0.0002	0.0012	0.0043	0.0115	0.0250	0.0384	0.0774	0.1172	0.1641
	6	0.0000	0.0000	0.0000	0.0001	0.0004	0.0013	0.0036	0.0064	0.0172	0.0320	0.0547
	7	0.0000	0.0000	0.0000	0.0000	0.0000	0.0001	0.0002	0.0005	0.0016	0.0037	0.0078
8	0	0.9227	0.6634	0.4305	0.2725	0.1678	0.1001	0.0576	0.0390	0.0168	0.0084	0.0039
	1	0.0746	0.2793	0.3826	0.3847	0.3355	0.2670	0.1977	0.1561	0.0896	0.0548	0.0313
	2	0.0026	0.0515	0.1488	0.2376	0.2936	0.3115	0.2965	0.2731	0.2090	0.1569	0.1094
	3	0.0001	0.0054	0.0331	0.0839	0.1468	0.2076	0.2541	0.2731	0.2787	0.2568	0.2188
	4	0.0000	0.0004	0.0046	0.0185	0.0459	0.0865	0.1361	0.1707	0.2322	0.2627	0.2734
	5	0.0000	0.0000	0.0004	0.0026	0.0092	0.0231	0.0467	0.0683	0.1239	0.1719	0.2188
	6	0.0000	0.0000	0.0000	0.0002	0.0011	0.0038	0.0100	0.0171	0.0413	0.0703	0.1094
	7	0.0000	0.0000	0.0000	0.0000	0.0001	0.0004	0.0012	0.0024	0.0079	0.0164	0.0313
	8	0.0000	0.0000	0.0000	0.0000	0.0000	0.0000	0.0001	0.0002	0.0007	0.0017	0.0039
9	0	0.9135	0.6302	0.3874	0.2316	0.1342	0.0751	0.0404	0.0260	0.0101	0.0046	0.0020
	1	0.0830	0.2985	0.3874	0.3679	0.3020	0.2253	0.1556	0.1171	0.0605	0.0339	0.0176
	2	0.0034	0.0629	0.1722	0.2597	0.3020	0.3003	0.2668	0.2341	0.1612	0.1110	0.0703
	3	0.0001	0.0077	0.0446	0.1069	0.1762	0.2336	0.2668	0.2731	0.2508	0.2119	0.1641

SOURCE: The values in this table were computed by the author.

N	x						Probability p					
		0.01	0.05	0.10	0.15	0.20	0.25	0.30	0.33	0.40	0.45	0.50
	4	0.0000	0.0006	0.0074	0.0283	0.0661	0.1168	0.1715	0.2048	0.2508	0.2600	0.2461
	5	0.0000	0.0000	0.0008	0.0050	0.0165	0.0389	0.0735	0.1024	0.1672	0.2128	0.2461
	6	0.0000	0.0000	0.0001	0.0006	0.0028	0.0087	0.0210	0.0341	0.0743	0.1160	0.1641
	7	0.0000	0.0000	0.0000	0.0000	0.0003	0.0012	0.0039	0.0073	0.0212	0.0407	0.0703
	8	0.0000	0.0000	0.0000	0.0000	0.0000	0.0001	0.0004	0.0009	0.0035	0.0083	0.0176
	9	0.0000	0.0000	0.0000	0.0000	0.0000	0.0000	0.0000	0.0001	0.0003	0.0008	0.0020
10	0	0.9044	0.5987	0.3487	0.1969	0.1074	0.0563	0.0282	0.0173	0.0060	0.0025	0.0010
	1	0.0914	0.3151	0.3874	0.3474	0.2684	0.1877	0.1211	0.0867	0.0403	0.0207	0.0098
	2	0.0042	0.0746	0.1937	0.2759	0.3020	0.2816	0.2335	0.1951	0.1209	0.0763	0.0439
	3	0.0001	0.0105	0.0574	0.1298	0.2013	0.2503	0.2668	0.2601	0.2150	0.1665	0.1172
	4	0.0000	0.0010	0.0112	0.0401	0.0881	0.1460	0.2001	0.2276	0.2508	0.2384	0.2051
	5	0.0000	0.0001	0.0015	0.0085	0.0264	0.0584	0.1029	0.1366	0.2007	0.2340	0.2461
	6	0.0000	0.0000	0.0001	0.0012	0.0055	0.0162	0.0368	0.0569	0.1115	0.1596	0.2051
	7	0.0000	0.0000	0.0000	0.0001	0.0008	0.0031	0.0090	0.0163	0.0425	0.0746	0.1172
	8	0.0000	0.0000	0.0000	0.0000	0.0001	0.0004	0.0014	0.0030	0.0106	0.0229	0.0439
	9	0.0000	0.0000	0.0000	0.0000	0.0000	0.0000	0.0001	0.0003	0.0016	0.0042	0.0098
	10	0.0000	0.0000	0.0000	0.0000	0.0000	0.0000	0.0000	0.0000	0.0001	0.0003	0.0010
11	0	0.8953	0.5688	0.3138	0.1673	0.0859	0.0422	0.0198	0.0116	0.0036	0.0014	0.0005
	1	0.0995	0.3293	0.3835	0.3248	0.2362	0.1549	0.0932	0.0636	0.0266	0.0125	0.0054
	2	0.0050	0.0867	0.2131	0.2866	0.2953	0.2581	0.1998	0.1590	0.0887	0.0513	0.0269
	3	0.0002	0.0137	0.0710	0.1517	0.2215	0.2581	0.2568	0.2384	0.1774	0.1259	0.0806
	4	0.0000	0.0014	0.0158	0.0536	0.1107	0.1721	0.2201	0.2384	0.2365	0.2060	0.1611
	5	0.0000	0.0001	0.0025	0.0132	0.0388	0.0803	0.1321	0.1669	0.2207	0.2360	0.2256
	6	0.0000	0.0000	0.0003	0.0023	0.0097	0.0268	0.0566	0.0835	0.1471	0.1931	0.2256
	7	0.0000	0.0000	0.0000	0.0003	0.0017	0.0064	0.0173	0.0298	0.0701	0.1128	0.1611
	8	0.0000	0.0000	0.0000	0.0000	0.0002	0.0011	0.0037	0.0075	0.0234	0.0462	0.0806
	9	0.0000	0.0000	0.0000	0.0000	0.0001	0.0001	0.0005	0.0012	0.0052	0.0126	0.0269
	10	0.0000	0.0000	0.0000	0.0000	0.0000	0.0000	0.0000	0.0001	0.0007	0.0021	0.0054
	11	0.0000	0.0000	0.0000	0.0000	0.0000	0.0000	0.0000	0.0000	0.0000	0.0002	0.0005
12	0	0.8864	0.5404	0.2824	0.1422	0.0687	0.0317	0.0138	0.0077	0.0022	0.0008	0.0002
	1	0.1074	0.3413	0.3766	0.3012	0.2062	0.1267	0.0712	0.0462	0.0174	0.0075	0.0029
	2	0.0060	0.0988	0.2301	0.2924	0.2835	0.2323	0.1678	0.1272	0.0639	0.0339	0.0161
	3	0.0002	0.0173	0.0852	0.1720	0.2362	0.2581	0.2397	0.2120	0.1419	0.0923	0.0537
	4	0.0000	0.0021	0.0213	0.0683	0.1329	0.1936	0.2311	0.2384	0.2128	0.1700	0.1208
	5	0.0000	0.0002	0.0038	0.0193	0.0532	0.1032	0.1585	0.1908	0.2270	0.2225	0.1934
	6	0.0000	0.0000	0.0005	0.0040	0.0155	0.0401	0.0792	0.1113	0.1766	0.2124	0.2256
	7	0.0000	0.0000	0.0000	0.0006	0.0033	0.0115	0.0291	0.0477	0.1009	0.1489	0.1934
	8	0.0000	0.0000	0.0000	0.0001	0.0005	0.0024	0.0078	0.0149	0.0420	0.0762	0.1208
	9	0.0000	0.0000	0.0000	0.0000	0.0001	0.0004	0.0015	0.0033	0.0125	0.0277	0.0537
	10	0.0000	0.0000	0.0000	0.0000	0.0000	0.0000	0.0002	0.0005	0.0025	0.0068	0.0161
	11	0.0000	0.0000	0.0000	0.0000	0.0000	0.0000	0.0000	0.0000	0.0003	0.0010	0.0029
	12	0.0000	0.0000	0.0000	0.0000	0.0000	0.0000	0.0000	0.0000	0.0000	0.0001	0.0002
13	0	0.8775	0.5133	0.2542	0.1209	0.0550	0.0238	0.0097	0.0051	0.0013	0.0004	0.0001
	1	0.1152	0.3512	0.3672	0.2774	0.1787	0.1029	0.0540	0.0334	0.0113	0.0045	0.0016
	2	0.0070	0.1109	0.2448	0.2937	0.2680	0.2059	0.1388	0.1002	0.0453	0.0220	0.0095
	3	0.0003	0.0214	0.0997	0.1900	0.2457	0.2517	0.2181	0.1837	0.1107	0.0660	0.0349
	4	0.0000	0.0028	0.0277	0.0838	0.1535	0.2097	0.2337	0.2296	0.1845	0.1350	0.0873
	5	0.0000	0.0003	0.0055	0.0266	0.0691	0.1258	0.1803	0.2067	0.2214	0.1989	0.1571
	6	0.0000	0.0000	0.0008	0.0063	0.0230	0.0559	0.1030	0.1378	0.1968	0.2169	0.2095
	7	0.0000	0.0000	0.0001	0.0011	0.0058	0.0186	0.0442	0.0689	0.1312	0.1775	0.2095
	8	0.0000	0.0000	0.0000	0.0001	0.0011	0.0047	0.0142	0.0258	0.0656	0.1089	0.1571
	9	0.0000	0.0000	0.0000	0.0000	0.0001	0.0009	0.0034	0.0072	0.0243	0.0495	0.0873
	10	0.0000	0.0000	0.0000	0.0000	0.0000	0.0001	0.0006	0.0014	0.0065	0.0162	0.0349
	11	0.0000	0.0000	0.0000	0.0000	0.0000	0.0000	0.0001	0.0002	0.0012	0.0036	0.0095
	12	0.0000	0.0000	0.0000	0.0000	0.0000	0.0000	0.0000	0.0000	0.0001	0.0005	0.0016
	13	0.0000	0.0000	0.0000	0.0000	0.0000	0.0000	0.0000	0.0000	0.0000	0.0000	0.0001

		Probability p										
N	x	0.01	0.05	0.10	0.15	0.20	0.25	0.30	0.33	0.40	0.45	0.50
14	0	0.8687	0.4877	0.2288	0.1028	0.0440	0.0178	0.0068	0.0034	0.0008	0.0002	0.0001
	1	0.1229	0.3593	0.3559	0.2539	0.1539	0.0832	0.0407	0.0240	0.0073	0.0027	0.0009
	2	0.0081	0.1229	0.2570	0.2912	0.2501	0.1802	0.1134	0.0779	0.0317	0.0141	0.0056
	3	0.0003	0.0259	0.1142	0.2056	0.2501	0.2402	0.1943	0.1559	0.0845	0.0462	0.0222
	4	0.0000	0.0037	0.0349	0.0998	0.1720	0.2202	0.2290	0.2143	0.1549	0.1040	0.0611
	5	0.0000	0.0004	0.0078	0.0352	0.0860	0.1468	0.1963	0.2143	0.2066	0.1701	0.1222
	6	0.0000	0.0000	0.0013	0.0093	0.0322	0.0734	0.1262	0.1607	0.2066	0.2088	0.1833
	7	0.0000	0.0000	0.0002	0.0019	0.0092	0.0280	0.0618	0.0918	0.1574	0.1952	0.2095
	8	0.0000	0.0000	0.0000	0.0003	0.0020	0.0082	0.0232	0.0402	0.0918	0.1398	0.1833
	9	0.0000	0.0000	0.0000	0.0000	0.0003	0.0018	0.0066	0.0134	0.0408	0.0762	0.1222
	10	0.0000	0.0000	0.0000	0.0000	0.0000	0.0003	0.0014	0.0033	0.0136	0.0312	0.0611
	11	0.0000	0.0000	0.0000	0.0000	0.0000	0.0000	0.0002	0.0006	0.0033	0.0093	0.0222
	12	0.0000	0.0000	0.0000	0.0000	0.0000	0.0000	0.0000	0.0001	0.0005	0.0019	0.0056
	13	0.0000	0.0000	0.0000	0.0000	0.0000	0.0000	0.0000	0.0000	0.0000	0.0001	0.0009
	14	0.0000	0.0000	0.0000	0.0000	0.0000	0.0000	0.0000	0.0000	0.0000	0.0000	0.0001
15	0	0.8601	0.4633	0.2059	0.0874	0.0352	0.0134	0.0047	0.0023	0.0005	0.0001	0.0000
	1	0.1303	0.3658	0.3432	0.2312	0.1319	0.0668	0.0305	0.0171	0.0047	0.0016	0.0005
	2	0.0092	0.1348	0.2669	0.2856	0.2309	0.1559	0.0916	0.0599	0.0219	0.0090	0.0032
	3	0.0004	0.0307	0.1285	0.2184	0.2501	0.2252	0.1700	0.1299	0.0634	0.0318	0.0139
	4	0.0000	0.0049	0.0428	0.1156	0.1876	0.2252	0.2186	0.1948	0.1268	0.0780	0.0417
	5	0.0000	0.0006	0.0105	0.0449	0.1032	0.1651	0.2061	0.2143	0.1859	0.1404	0.0916
	6	0.0000	0.0000	0.0019	0.0132	0.0430	0.0917	0.1472	0.1786	0.2066	0.1914	0.1527
	7	0.0000	0.0000	0.0003	0.0030	0.0138	0.0393	0.0811	0.1148	0.1771	0.2013	0.1964
	8	0.0000	0.0000	0.0000	0.0005	0.0035	0.0131	0.0348	0.0574	0.1181	0.1647	0.1964
	9	0.0000	0.0000	0.0000	0.0001	0.0007	0.0034	0.0116	0.0223	0.0612	0.1048	0.1527
	10	0.0000	0.0000	0.0000	0.0000	0.0001	0.0007	0.0030	0.0067	0.0245	0.0515	0.0916
	11	0.0000	0.0000	0.0000	0.0000	0.0000	0.0001	0.0006	0.0015	0.0074	0.0191	0.0417
	12	0.0000	0.0000	0.0000	0.0000	0.0000	0.0000	0.0001	0.0003	0.0016	0.0052	0.0139
	13	0.0000	0.0000	0.0000	0.0000	0.0000	0.0000	0.0000	0.0000	0.0003	0.0010	0.0032
	14	0.0000	0.0000	0.0000	0.0000	0.0000	0.0000	0.0000	0.0000	0.0000	0.0001	0.0005
	15	0.0000	0.0000	0.0000	0.0000	0.0000	0.0000	0.0000	0.0000	0.0000	0.0000	0.0000
20	0	0.8179	0.3585	0.1216	0.0388	0.0115	0.0032	0.0008	0.0003	0.0000	0.0000	0.0000
	1	0.1652	0.3774	0.2702	0.1368	0.0576	0.0211	0.0068	0.0030	0.0005	0.0001	0.0000
	2	0.0159	0.1887	0.2852	0.2293	0.1369	0.0669	0.0278	0.0143	0.0031	0.0008	0.0002
	3	0.0010	0.0596	0.1901	0.2428	0.2054	0.1339	0.0716	0.0429	0.0123	0.0040	0.0011
	4	0.0000	0.0133	0.0898	0.1821	0.2182	0.1897	0.1304	0.0911	0.0350	0.0139	0.0046
	5	0.0000	0.0022	0.0319	0.1028	0.1746	0.2023	0.1789	0.1457	0.0746	0.0365	0.0148
	6	0.0000	0.0003	0.0089	0.0454	0.1091	0.1686	0.1916	0.1821	0.1244	0.0746	0.0370
	7	0.0000	0.0000	0.0020	0.0160	0.0545	0.1124	0.1643	0.1821	0.1659	0.1221	0.0739
	8	0.0000	0.0000	0.0004	0.0046	0.0222	0.0609	0.1144	0.1480	0.1797	0.1623	0.1201
	9	0.0000	0.0000	0.0001	0.0011	0.0074	0.0271	0.0654	0.0987	0.1597	0.1771	0.1602
	10	0.0000	0.0000	0.0000	0.0002	0.0020	0.0099	0.0308	0.0543	0.1171	0.1593	0.1762
	11	0.0000	0.0000	0.0000	0.0000	0.0005	0.0030	0.0120	0.0247	0.0710	0.1185	0.1602
	12	0.0000	0.0000	0.0000	0.0000	0.0001	0.0008	0.0039	0.0092	0.0355	0.0727	0.1201
	13	0.0000	0.0000	0.0000	0.0000	0.0000	0.0002	0.0010	0.0028	0.0146	0.0366	0.0739
	14	0.0000	0.0000	0.0000	0.0000	0.0000	0.0000	0.0002	0.0007	0.0049	0.0150	0.0370
	15	0.0000	0.0000	0.0000	0.0000	0.0000	0.0000	0.0000	0.0001	0.0013	0.0049	0.0148
	16	0.0000	0.0000	0.0000	0.0000	0.0000	0.0000	0.0000	0.0000	0.0003	0.0013	0.0046
	17	0.0000	0.0000	0.0000	0.0000	0.0000	0.0000	0.0000	0.0000	0.0000	0.0002	0.0011
	18	0.0000	0.0000	0.0000	0.0000	0.0000	0.0000	0.0000	0.0000	0.0000	0.0000	0.0002
	19	0.0000	0.0000	0.0000	0.0000	0.0000	0.0000	0.0000	0.0000	0.0000	0.0000	0.0000
	20	0.0000	0.0000	0.0000	0.0000	0.0000	0.0000	0.0000	0.0000	0.0000	0.0000	0.0000
25	0	0.7778	0.2774	0.0718	0.0172	0.0038	0.0008	0.0001	0.0000	0.0000	0.0000	0.0000
	1	0.1964	0.3650	0.1994	0.0759	0.0236	0.0063	0.0014	0.0005	0.0000	0.0000	0.0000
	2	0.0238	0.2305	0.2659	0.1607	0.0708	0.0251	0.0074	0.0030	0.0004	0.0001	0.0000

N	x	0.01	0.05	0.10	0.15	0.20	0.25	0.30	0.33	0.40	0.45	0.50
							Probability p					
	3	0.0018	0.0930	0.2265	0.2174	0.1358	0.0641	0.0243	0.0114	0.0019	0.0004	0.0001
	4	0.0001	0.0269	0.1384	0.2110	0.1867	0.1175	0.0572	0.0313	0.0071	0.0018	0.0004
	5	0.0000	0.0060	0.0646	0.1564	0.1960	0.1645	0.1030	0.0658	0.0199	0.0063	0.0016
	6	0.0000	0.0010	0.0239	0.0920	0.1633	0.1828	0.1472	0.1096	0.0442	0.0172	0.0053
	7	0.0000	0.0001	0.0072	0.0441	0.1108	0.1654	0.1712	0.1487	0.0800	0.0381	0.0143
	8	0.0000	0.0000	0.0018	0.0175	0.0623	0.1241	0.1651	0.1673	0.1200	0.0701	0.0322
	9	0.0000	0.0000	0.0004	0.0058	0.0294	0.0781	0.1336	0.1580	0.1511	0.1084	0.0609
	10	0.0000	0.0000	0.0001	0.0016	0.0118	0.0417	0.0916	0.1264	0.1612	0.1419	0.0974
	11	0.0000	0.0000	0.0000	0.0004	0.0040	0.0189	0.0536	0.0862	0.1465	0.1583	0.1328
	12	0.0000	0.0000	0.0000	0.0001	0.0012	0.0074	0.0268	0.0503	0.1140	0.1511	0.1550
	13	0.0000	0.0000	0.0000	0.0000	0.0003	0.0025	0.0115	0.0251	0.0760	0.1236	0.1550
	14	0.0000	0.0000	0.0000	0.0000	0.0001	0.0007	0.0042	0.0108	0.0434	0.0867	0.1328
	15	0.0000	0.0000	0.0000	0.0000	0.0000	0.0002	0.0013	0.0040	0.0212	0.0520	0.0974
	16	0.0000	0.0000	0.0000	0.0000	0.0000	0.0000	0.0004	0.0012	0.0088	0.0266	0.0609
	17	0.0000	0.0000	0.0000	0.0000	0.0000	0.0000	0.0001	0.0003	0.0031	0.0115	0.0322
	18	0.0000	0.0000	0.0000	0.0000	0.0000	0.0000	0.0000	0.0001	0.0009	0.0042	0.0143
	19	0.0000	0.0000	0.0000	0.0000	0.0000	0.0000	0.0000	0.0000	0.0002	0.0013	0.0053
	20	0.0000	0.0000	0.0000	0.0000	0.0000	0.0000	0.0000	0.0000	0.0000	0.0003	0.0016
	21	0.0000	0.0000	0.0000	0.0000	0.0000	0.0000	0.0000	0.0000	0.0000	0.0001	0.0004
	22	0.0000	0.0000	0.0000	0.0000	0.0000	0.0000	0.0000	0.0000	0.0000	0.0000	0.0001
	23	0.0000	0.0000	0.0000	0.0000	0.0000	0.0000	0.0000	0.0000	0.0000	0.0000	0.0000
	24	0.0000	0.0000	0.0000	0.0000	0.0000	0.0000	0.0000	0.0000	0.0000	0.0000	0.0000
	25	0.0000	0.0000	0.0000	0.0000	0.0000	0.0000	0.0000	0.0000	0.0000	0.0000	0.0000
30	0	0.7397	0.2146	0.0424	0.0076	0.0012	0.0002	0.0000	0.0000	0.0000	0.0000	0.0000
	1	0.2242	0.3389	0.1413	0.0404	0.0093	0.0018	0.0003	0.0001	0.0000	0.0000	0.0000
	2	0.0328	0.2586	0.2277	0.1034	0.0337	0.0086	0.0018	0.0006	0.0000	0.0000	0.0000
	3	0.0031	0.1270	0.2361	0.1703	0.0785	0.0269	0.0072	0.0026	0.0003	0.0000	0.0000
	4	0.0002	0.0451	0.1771	0.2028	0.1325	0.0604	0.0208	0.0089	0.0012	0.0002	0.0000
	5	0.0000	0.0124	0.1023	0.1861	0.1723	0.1047	0.0464	0.0232	0.0041	0.0008	0.0001
	6	0.0000	0.0027	0.0474	0.1368	0.1795	0.1455	0.0829	0.0484	0.0115	0.0029	0.0006
	7	0.0000	0.0005	0.0180	0.0828	0.1538	0.1662	0.1219	0.0829	0.0263	0.0081	0.0019
	8	0.0000	0.0001	0.0058	0.0420	0.1106	0.1593	0.1501	0.1192	0.0505	0.0191	0.0055
	9	0.0000	0.0000	0.0016	0.0181	0.0676	0.1298	0.1573	0.1457	0.0823	0.0382	0.0133
	10	0.0000	0.0000	0.0004	0.0067	0.0355	0.0909	0.1416	0.1530	0.1152	0.0656	0.0280
	11	0.0000	0.0000	0.0001	0.0022	0.0161	0.0551	0.1103	0.1391	0.1396	0.0976	0.0509
	12	0.0000	0.0000	0.0000	0.0006	0.0064	0.0291	0.0749	0.1101	0.1474	0.1265	0.0806
	13	0.0000	0.0000	0.0000	0.0001	0.0022	0.0134	0.0444	0.0762	0.1360	0.1433	0.1115
	14	0.0000	0.0000	0.0000	0.0000	0.0007	0.0054	0.0231	0.0463	0.1101	0.1424	0.1354
	15	0.0000	0.0000	0.0000	0.0000	0.0002	0.0019	0.0106	0.0247	0.0783	0.1242	0.1445
	16	0.0000	0.0000	0.0000	0.0000	0.0000	0.0006	0.0042	0.0116	0.0489	0.0953	0.1354
	17	0.0000	0.0000	0.0000	0.0000	0.0000	0.0002	0.0015	0.0048	0.0269	0.0642	0.1115
	18	0.0000	0.0000	0.0000	0.0000	0.0000	0.0000	0.0005	0.0017	0.0129	0.0379	0.0806
	19	0.0000	0.0000	0.0000	0.0000	0.0000	0.0000	0.0001	0.0005	0.0054	0.0196	0.0509
	20	0.0000	0.0000	0.0000	0.0000	0.0000	0.0000	0.0000	0.0001	0.0020	0.0088	0.0280
	21	0.0000	0.0000	0.0000	0.0000	0.0000	0.0000	0.0000	0.0000	0.0006	0.0034	0.0133
	21	0.0000	0.0000	0.0000	0.0000	0.0000	0.0000	0.0000	0.0000	0.0006	0.0034	0.0133
	22	0.0000	0.0000	0.0000	0.0000	0.0000	0.0000	0.0000	0.0000	0.0002	0.0012	0.0055
	23	0.0000	0.0000	0.0000	0.0000	0.0000	0.0000	0.0000	0.0000	0.0000	0.0003	0.0019
	24	0.0000	0.0000	0.0000	0.0000	0.0000	0.0000	0.0000	0.0000	0.0000	0.0001	0.0006
	25	0.0000	0.0000	0.0000	0.0000	0.0000	0.0000	0.0000	0.0000	0.0000	0.0000	0.0001
	26	0.0000	0.0000	0.0000	0.0000	0.0000	0.0000	0.0000	0.0000	0.0000	0.0000	0.0000
	27	0.0000	0.0000	0.0000	0.0000	0.0000	0.0000	0.0000	0.0000	0.0000	0.0000	0.0000
	28	0.0000	0.0000	0.0000	0.0000	0.0000	0.0000	0.0000	0.0000	0.0000	0.0000	0.0000
	29	0.0000	0.0000	0.0000	0.0000	0.0000	0.0000	0.0000	0.0000	0.0000	0.0000	0.0000
	30	0.0000	0.0000	0.0000	0.0000	0.0000	0.0000	0.0000	0.0000	0.0000	0.0000	0.0000

APPENDIX H CRITICAL VALUES FOR WILCOXON'S *T*

Two tails	0.10	0.05	0.02	0.01
One tail	0.05	0.025	0.01	0.005
N				
4				
5	0			
6	2	0		
7	3	2	0	
8	5	3	1	0
9	8	5	3	1
10	10	8	5	3
11	13	10	7	5
12	17	13	9	7
13	21	17	12	9
14	25	21	15	12
15	30	25	19	15
16	35	29	23	19
17	41	34	27	23
18	47	40	32	27
19	53	46	37	32
20	60	52	43	37
21	67	58	49	42
22	75	65	55	48
23	83	73	62	54
24	91	81	69	61
25	100	89	76	68
26	110	98	84	75
27	119	107	92	83
28	130	116	101	91
29	140	126	110	100
30	151	137	120	109
31	163	147	130	118
32	175	159	140	128
33	187	170	151	138
34	200	182	162	148
35	213	195	173	159
36	227	208	185	171
37	241	221	198	182
38	256	235	211	194
39	271	249	224	207
40	286	264	238	220
41	302	279	252	233
42	319	294	266	247
43	336	310	281	261
44	353	327	296	276
45	371	343	312	291
46	389	361	328	307
47	407	378	345	322
48	426	396	362	339
49	446	415	379	355
50	466	434	397	373

SOURCE: The values in this table were obtained from McCornack, R. L. (1965). Extended tables of the Wilcoxon matched pair signed rank test. *Journal of the American Statistical Association, 60,* 864–871. Used by permission of the publisher.

APPENDIX I ONE-TAILED CRITICAL VALUES FOR THE WILCOXON TWO-GROUP TEST

Note: N_1 is the *smaller* group size and N_2 is the *larger*. If the obtained value is less than or equal to the tabled value, there is a significant difference between the groups.

			$N_1 = 1$							$N_1 = 2$				
N_2	0.001	0.005	0.010	0.025	0.05	0.10	0.001	0.005	0.010	0.025	0.05	0.10	N_2
2												—	2
3												3	3
4											—	3	4
5											3	4	5
6											3	4	6
7										—	3	4	7
8						—				3	4	5	8
9						1				3	4	5	9
10						1				3	4	6	10

			$N_1 = 3$							$N_1 = 4$				
N_2	0.001	0.005	0.010	0.025	0.05	0.10	0.001	0.005	0.010	0.025	0.05	0.10	N_2
3					6	7							
4				—	6	7			—	10	11	13	4
5			6	6	7	8		—	10	11	12	14	5
6			—	7	8	9		10	11	12	13	15	6
7		6		7	8	10		10	11	13	14	16	7
8		—	6	8	9	11		11	12	14	15	17	8
9		6	7	8	10	11	—	11	13	14	16	19	9
10		6	7	9	10	12	10	12	13	15	17	20	10

			$N_1 = 5$							$N_1 = 6$				
N_2	0.001	0.005	0.010	0.025	0.05	0.10	0.001	0.005	0.010	0.025	0.05	0.10	N_2
5		15	16	17	19	20							
6		16	17	18	20	22	—	23	24	26	28	30	6
7	—	16	18	20	21	23	21	24	25	27	29	32	7
8	15	17	19	21	23	25	22	25	27	29	31	34	8
9	16	18	20	22	24	27	23	26	28	31	33	36	9
10	16	19	21	23	26	28	24	27	29	32	35	38	10

			$N_1 = 7$							$N_1 = 8$				
N_2	0.001	0.005	0.010	0.025	0.05	0.10	0.001	0.005	0.010	0.025	0.05	0.10	N_2
7	29	32	34	36	39	41							
8	30	34	35	38	41	44	40	43	45	49	51	55	8
9	31	35	37	40	43	46	41	45	47	51	54	58	9
10	33	37	39	42	45	49	42	47	49	53	56	60	10

SOURCE: The values in this table were obtained from Verdooren, L. R. (1963). Extended tables of critical values for Wilcoxon's test statistic. *Biometrika, 50*, 177–186. Used by permission of the Biometrika Trustees.

N_2	$N_1 = 9$						$N_1 = 10$						N_2
	0.001	0.005	0.010	0.025	0.05	0.10	0.001	0.005	0.010	0.025	0.05	0.10	
9	52	56	59	62	66	70							
10	53	58	61	65	69	73	65	71	74	78	82	87	10

df Error	α	\multicolumn{19}{c}{Number of means}																	
		2	3	4	5	6	7	8	9	10	11	12	13	14	15	16	17	18	19	20
1	.05	17.97	26.98	32.82	37.08	40.41	43.12	45.40	47.36	49.07	50.59	51.96	53.20	54.33	55.36	56.32	57.22	58.04	58.83	59.56
	.01	90.03	135.0	164.3	185.6	202.2	215.8	227.2	237.0	245.6	253.2	260.0	266.2	271.8	277.0	281.8	286.3	290.4	294.3	298.0
2	.05	6.08	8.33	9.80	10.88	11.74	12.44	13.03	13.54	13.99	14.39	14.75	15.08	15.38	15.65	15.91	16.14	16.37	16.57	16.77
	.01	14.04	19.02	22.29	24.72	26.63	28.20	29.53	30.66	31.69	32.59	33.40	34.13	34.81	35.43	36.00	36.53	37.03	37.50	37.95
3	.05	4.50	5.91	6.82	7.50	8.04	8.48	8.85	9.18	9.46	9.72	9.95	10.15	10.35	10.52	10.69	10.84	10.98	11.11	11.24
	.01	8.26	10.62	12.17	13.33	14.24	15.00	15.64	16.20	16.69	17.13	17.53	17.89	18.22	18.52	18.81	19.07	19.32	19.55	19.77
4	.05	3.93	5.04	5.76	6.29	6.71	7.05	7.35	7.60	7.83	8.03	8.21	8.37	8.52	8.66	8.79	8.91	9.03	9.13	9.23
	.01	6.51	8.12	9.17	9.96	10.58	11.10	11.55	11.93	12.27	12.57	12.84	13.09	13.32	13.53	13.73	13.91	14.08	14.24	14.40
5	.05	3.64	4.60	5.22	5.67	6.03	6.33	6.58	6.80	6.99	7.17	7.32	7.47	7.60	7.72	7.83	7.93	8.03	8.12	8.21
	.01	5.70	6.98	7.80	8.42	8.91	9.32	9.67	9.97	10.24	10.48	10.70	10.89	11.08	11.24	11.40	11.55	11.68	11.81	11.93
6	.05	3.46	4.34	4.90	5.30	5.63	5.90	6.12	6.32	6.49	6.65	6.79	6.92	7.03	7.14	7.24	7.34	7.43	7.51	7.59
	.01	5.24	6.33	7.03	7.56	7.97	8.32	8.61	8.87	9.10	9.30	9.48	9.65	9.81	9.95	10.08	10.21	10.32	10.43	10.54
7	.05	3.34	4.16	4.68	5.06	5.36	5.61	5.82	6.00	6.16	6.30	6.43	6.55	6.66	6.76	6.85	6.94	7.02	7.10	7.17
	.01	4.95	5.92	6.54	7.01	7.37	7.68	7.94	8.17	8.37	8.55	8.71	8.86	9.00	9.12	9.24	9.35	9.46	9.55	9.65
8	.05	3.26	4.04	4.53	4.89	5.17	5.40	5.60	5.77	5.92	6.05	6.18	6.29	6.39	6.48	6.57	6.65	6.73	6.80	6.87
	.01	4.75	5.64	6.20	6.62	6.96	7.24	7.47	7.68	7.86	8.03	8.18	8.31	8.44	8.55	8.66	8.76	8.85	8.94	9.03
9	.05	3.20	3.95	4.41	4.76	5.02	5.24	5.43	5.59	5.74	5.87	5.98	6.09	6.19	6.28	6.36	6.44	6.51	6.58	6.64
	.01	4.60	5.43	5.96	6.35	6.66	6.91	7.13	7.33	7.49	7.65	7.78	7.91	8.03	8.13	8.23	8.33	8.41	8.49	8.57
10	.05	3.15	3.88	4.33	4.65	4.91	5.12	5.30	5.46	5.60	5.72	5.83	5.93	6.03	6.11	6.19	6.27	6.34	6.40	6.47
	.01	4.48	5.27	5.77	6.14	6.43	6.67	6.87	7.05	7.21	7.36	7.49	7.60	7.71	7.81	7.91	7.99	8.08	8.15	8.23
11	.05	3.11	3.82	4.26	4.57	4.82	5.03	5.20	5.35	5.49	5.61	5.71	5.81	5.90	5.98	6.06	6.13	6.20	6.27	6.33
	.01	4.39	5.15	5.62	5.97	6.25	6.48	6.67	6.84	6.99	7.13	7.25	7.36	7.46	7.56	7.65	7.73	7.81	7.88	7.95
12	.05	3.08	3.77	4.20	4.51	4.75	4.95	5.12	5.27	5.39	5.51	5.61	5.71	5.80	5.88	5.95	6.02	6.09	6.15	6.21
	.01	4.32	5.05	5.50	5.84	6.10	6.32	6.51	6.67	6.81	6.94	7.06	7.17	7.26	7.36	7.44	7.52	7.59	7.66	7.73
13	.05	3.06	3.73	4.15	4.45	4.69	4.88	5.05	5.19	5.32	5.43	5.53	5.63	5.71	5.79	5.86	5.93	5.99	6.05	6.11
	.01	4.26	4.96	5.40	5.73	5.98	6.19	6.37	6.53	6.67	6.79	6.90	7.01	7.10	7.19	7.27	7.35	7.42	7.48	7.55
14	.05	3.03	3.70	4.11	4.41	4.64	4.83	4.99	5.13	5.25	5.36	5.46	5.55	5.64	5.71	5.79	5.85	5.91	5.97	6.03
	.01	4.21	4.89	5.32	5.63	5.88	6.08	6.26	6.41	6.54	6.66	6.77	6.87	6.96	7.05	7.13	7.20	7.27	7.33	7.39
15	.05	3.01	3.67	4.08	4.37	4.59	4.78	4.94	5.08	5.20	5.31	5.40	5.49	5.57	5.65	5.72	5.78	5.85	5.90	5.96
	.01	4.17	4.84	5.25	5.56	5.80	5.99	6.16	6.31	6.44	6.55	6.66	6.76	6.84	6.93	7.00	7.07	7.14	7.20	7.26
16	.05	3.00	3.65	4.05	4.33	4.56	4.74	4.90	5.03	5.15	5.26	5.35	5.44	5.52	5.59	5.66	5.73	5.79	5.84	5.90
	.01	4.13	4.79	5.19	5.49	5.72	5.92	6.08	6.22	6.35	6.46	6.56	6.66	6.74	6.82	6.90	6.97	7.03	7.09	7.15
17	.05	2.98	3.63	4.02	4.30	4.52	4.70	4.86	4.99	5.11	5.21	5.31	5.39	5.47	5.54	5.61	5.67	5.73	5.79	5.84
	.01	4.10	4.74	5.14	5.43	5.66	5.85	6.01	6.15	6.27	6.38	6.48	6.57	6.66	6.73	6.81	6.87	6.94	7.00	7.05
18	.05	2.97	3.61	4.00	4.28	4.49	4.67	4.82	4.96	5.07	5.17	5.27	5.35	5.43	5.50	5.57	5.63	5.69	5.74	5.79
	.01	4.07	4.70	5.09	5.38	5.60	5.79	5.94	6.08	6.20	6.31	6.41	6.50	6.58	6.65	6.73	6.79	6.85	6.91	6.97
19	.05	2.96	3.59	3.98	4.25	4.47	4.65	4.79	4.92	5.04	5.14	5.23	5.31	5.39	5.46	5.53	5.59	5.65	5.70	5.75
	.01	4.05	4.67	5.05	5.33	5.55	5.73	5.89	6.02	6.14	6.25	6.34	6.43	6.51	6.58	6.65	6.72	6.78	6.84	6.89
20	.05	2.95	3.58	3.96	4.23	4.45	4.62	4.77	4.90	5.01	5.11	5.20	5.28	5.36	5.43	5.49	5.55	5.61	5.66	5.71
	.01	4.02	4.64	5.02	5.29	5.51	5.69	5.84	5.97	6.09	6.19	6.28	6.37	6.45	6.52	6.59	6.65	6.71	6.77	6.82
24	.05	2.92	3.53	3.90	4.17	4.37	4.54	4.68	4.81	4.92	5.01	5.10	5.18	5.25	5.32	5.38	5.44	5.49	5.55	5.59
	.01	3.96	4.55	4.91	5.17	5.37	5.54	5.69	5.81	5.92	6.02	6.11	6.19	6.26	6.33	6.39	6.45	6.51	6.56	6.61
30	.05	2.89	3.49	3.85	4.10	4.30	4.46	4.60	4.72	4.82	4.92	5.00	5.08	5.15	5.21	5.27	5.33	5.38	5.43	5.47
	.01	3.89	4.45	4.80	5.05	5.24	5.40	5.54	5.65	5.76	5.85	5.93	6.01	6.08	6.14	6.20	6.26	6.31	6.36	6.41
40	.05	2.86	3.44	3.79	4.04	4.23	4.39	4.52	4.63	4.73	4.82	4.90	4.98	5.04	5.11	5.16	5.22	5.27	5.31	5.36
	.01	3.82	4.37	4.70	4.93	5.11	5.26	5.39	5.50	5.60	5.69	5.76	5.83	5.90	5.96	6.02	6.07	6.12	6.16	6.21
60	.05	2.83	3.40	3.74	3.98	4.16	4.31	4.44	4.55	4.65	4.73	4.81	4.88	4.94	5.00	5.06	5.11	5.15	5.20	5.24
	.01	3.76	4.28	4.59	4.82	4.99	5.13	5.25	5.36	5.45	5.53	5.60	5.67	5.73	5.78	5.84	5.89	5.93	5.97	6.01
120	.05	2.80	3.36	3.68	3.92	4.10	4.24	4.36	4.47	4.56	4.64	4.71	4.78	4.84	4.90	4.95	5.00	5.04	5.09	5.13
	.01	3.70	4.20	4.50	4.71	4.87	5.01	5.12	5.21	5.30	5.37	5.44	5.50	5.56	5.61	5.66	5.71	5.75	5.79	5.83
∞	.05	2.77	3.31	3.63	3.86	4.03	4.17	4.29	4.39	4.47	4.55	4.62	4.68	4.74	4.80	4.85	4.89	4.93	4.97	5.01
	.01	3.64	4.12	4.40	4.60	4.76	4.88	4.99	5.08	5.16	5.23	5.29	5.35	5.40	5.45	5.49	5.54	5.57	5.61	5.65

SOURCE: The values in this table were obtained from *Biometrika Table for Statisticians*, 2nd ed., Vol. 1 (Table 29, pp. 176–177). Used by permission of Cambridge University Press.

Two tails One tail df	0.10 0.05	0.05 0.025	0.02 0.01	0.01 0.005	0.005 0.0025	0.001 0.0005
1	.9877	$.9^2692$	$.9^3507$	$.9^3877$	$.9^4692$	$.9^5877$
2	.9000	.9500	.9800	$.9^2000$	$.9^2500$	$.9^2000$
3	.085	.878	.9343	.9587	.9740	$.9^2114$
4	.729	.811	.882	.9172	.9417	.9741
5	.669	.754	.833	.875	.9056	.9509
6	.621	.707	.789	.834	.870	.9249
7	.582	.666	.750	.798	.836	.898
8	.549	.632	.715	.765	.805	.872
9	.521	.602	.685	.735	.776	.847
10	.497	.576	.658	.708	.750	.823
11	.476	.553	.634	.684	.726	.801
12	.457	.532	.612	.661	.703	.780
13	.441	.514	.592	.641	.683	.760
14	.426	.497	.574	.623	.664	.742
15	.412	.482	.558	.606	.647	.725
16	.400	.468	.543	.590	.631	.706
17	.389	.456	.529	.575	.616	.693
18	.378	.444	.516	.561	.602	.679
19	.369	.433	.503	.549	.589	.665
20	.360	.423	.492	.537	.576	.652
25	.323	.381	.445	.487	.524	.597
30	.296	.349	.409	.449	.484	.554
35	.275	.325	.381	.418	.452	.519
40	.257	.304	.358	.393	.425	.490
45	.243	.288	.338	.372	.403	.465
50	.231	.273	.322	.354	.384	.443
60	.211	.250	.295	.325	.352	.408
70	.195	.232	.274	.302	.327	.380
80	.183	.217	.257	.283	.307	.357
90	.173	.205	.242	.267	.290	.338
100	.164	.195	.230	.254	.276	.321

SOURCE: The values in this table were obtained from *Biometrika Tables for Statisticians*, 2nd ed., Vol. 1 (Table 13). Used by permission of Cambridge University Press.

r	z	r	z	r	z
0.00	0.0000	0.33	0.3428	0.66	0.7928
0.01	0.0100	0.34	0.3541	0.67	0.8107
0.02	0.0200	0.35	0.3654	0.68	0.8291
0.03	0.0300			0.69	0.8480
0.04	0.0400	0.36	0.3769	0.70	0.8673
0.05	0.0500	0.37	0.3884		
		0.38	0.4001	0.71	0.8872
0.06	0.0601	0.39	0.4118	0.72	0.9076
0.07	0.0701	0.40	0.4236	0.73	0.9287
0.08	0.0802			0.74	0.9505
0.09	0.0902	0.41	0.4356	0.75	0.9730
0.10	0.1003	0.42	0.4477		
		0.43	0.4599	0.76	0.9962
0.11	0.1104	0.44	0.4722	0.77	1.0203
0.12	0.1206	0.45	0.4847	0.78	1.0454
0.13	0.1307			0.79	1.0714
0.14	0.1409	0.46	0.4973	0.80	1.0986
0.15	0.1511	0.47	0.5101		
		0.48	0.5230	0.81	1.1270
0.16	0.1614	0.49	0.5361	0.82	1.1568
0.17	0.1717	0.50	0.5493	0.83	1.1881
0.18	0.1820			0.84	1.2212
0.19	0.1923	0.51	0.5627	0.85	1.2562
0.20	0.2027	0.52	0.5763		
		0.53	0.5901	0.86	1.2933
0.21	0.2132	0.54	0.6042	0.87	1.3331
0.22	0.2237	0.55	0.6184	0.88	1.3758
0.23	0.2342			0.89	1.4219
0.24	0.2448	0.56	0.6328	0.90	1.4722
0.25	0.2554	0.57	0.6475		
		0.58	0.6625	0.91	1.5275
0.26	0.2661	0.59	0.6777	0.92	1.5890
0.27	0.2769	0.60	0.6931	0.93	1.6584
0.28	0.2877			0.94	1.7380
0.29	0.2986	0.61	0.7089	0.95	1.8318
0.30	0.3095	0.62	0.7250		
		0.63	0.7414	0.96	1.9459
0.31	0.3205	0.64	0.7582	0.97	2.0923
0.32	0.3316	0.65	0.7753	0.98	2.2976
				0.99	2.6467

NOTE: The table shows positive values; the transformed value takes the sign of the original *r* (e.g., *r* = 0.81 becomes 1.1270, and *r* = −0.81 becomes −1.1270).

SOURCE: The values in this table were computed by the author.

APPENDIX M POWER AS A FUNCTION OF α AND δ

	Alpha for Two-Tailed Test			
δ	.10	.05	.02	.01
1.00	0.26	0.17	0.09	0.06
1.10	0.29	0.20	0.11	0.07
1.20	0.33	0.22	0.13	0.08
1.30	0.37	0.26	0.15	0.10
1.40	0.40	0.29	0.18	0.12
1.50	0.44	0.32	0.20	0.14
1.60	0.48	0.36	0.23	0.17
1.70	0.52	0.40	0.27	0.19
1.80	0.56	0.44	0.30	0.22
1.90	0.60	0.48	0.34	0.25
2.00	0.64	0.52	0.37	0.28
2.10	0.68	0.56	0.41	0.32
2.20	0.71	0.60	0.45	0.35
2.30	0.74	0.63	0.49	0.39
2.40	0.78	0.67	0.53	0.43
2.50	0.80	0.71	0.57	0.47
2.60	0.83	0.74	0.61	0.51
2.70	0.85	0.77	0.65	0.55
2.80	0.88	0.80	0.68	0.59
2.90	0.90	0.83	0.72	0.63
3.00	0.91	0.85	0.75	0.66
3.10	0.93	0.87	0.78	0.70
3.20	0.94	0.89	0.81	0.73
3.30	0.95	0.91	0.84	0.77
3.40	0.96	0.93	0.86	0.80
3.50	0.97	0.94	0.88	0.82
3.60	0.98	0.95	0.90	0.85
3.70	0.98	0.96	0.92	0.87
3.80	0.98	0.97	0.93	0.89
3.90	0.99	0.97	0.94	0.91
4.00	0.99	0.98	0.95	0.92
4.10	0.99	0.98	0.96	0.94
4.20	...	099	0.97	0.95
4.30	...	0.99	0.98	0.96
4.40	...	0.99	0.98	0.97
4.50	...	0.99	0.99	0.97
4.60	...	...	0.99	0.98
4.70	...	...	0.99	0.98
4.80	...	...	0.99	0.99
4.90	...	...	...	0.99
5.00	...	...	...	0.99

SOURCE: The values in this table were obtained from Howell, D. C. (1989). *Fundamental Statistics for the Behavioral Science*. Boston: PWS.

APPENDIX N STATISTICAL PACKAGE ASSUMPTIONS

A program to be used in conjunction with this book should have the features listed as "essential" or "must." Those labeled "should" or "desirable" will make a student's life much easier.

If you are shopping for a program, first determine exactly what kind of computer you will be using and restrict your shopping to only those programs that run on that system. Next, explore the list of features as well as you can, and in particular compare them with the listing below. Note that there are a few features that are so essential that their lack is sufficient to drop the program from consideration, regardless of how well they match other features. (Some of these characteristics include the lack of an internal editor, the inability to obtain printed output of both numeric and graphic information, and lack of graphics capability.) Any program that does not offer a feature that is listed as "essential" should be dropped as a candidate.

Spend as much time with the program as you can before you buy it. Try out the manual. Can you understand it, or are you frustrated with the jargon and the assumptions that it makes about your knowledge? Try the manual's examples. Do you get the same results? Does the manual have an index? Use it to try to locate the critical items below. Does the program feel "comfortable" in use? Is it stable, or does it "crash" when you do something that you think should work? Are the error messages comprehensible and informative?

A. STORE, EDIT, AND RETRIEVE DATA SETS

Note: A few programs rely on an external editor to prepare a data file for analysis. This makes using the program *much* more difficult, especially for a relative novice in computing and statistics. The lack of an internal editor *alone* is sufficient grounds for rejecting the program as your primary data analysis tool.

1. Must allow keyboard input of data
2. Must allow viewing and editing of input or retrieved data
3. Must be able to store and retrieve data files
4. Should permit character as well as numeric variables
5. Should permit named variables and should also apply the labels appropriately to output
6. Highly desirable to have the ability to accept data sets from external editors and sources as well as from internal editors

B. OUTPUT

1. Printed output from all numeric and graphic analyses is essential. (The lack of this feature *alone* is sufficient grounds for rejecting the program.)
2. Desirable to have the ability to select portions of the output from the screen and store it for later processing

C. SELECTION OF CASES FOR ANALYSIS

1. A program must permit a variable to be used as some form of "selector" to specify data to be grouped or chosen from main data set for analysis.
2. The ability to write a logical expression to select data is highly desirable.

D. GRAPHICS

Note: The lack of graphics *alone* is sufficient grounds for rejecting the program.

1. Frequency distributions & histograms
   a. The program must be able to construct a frequency distribution of a set of data.
   b. It is essential that the program have the ability to specify upper and lower bounds and/or midpoints and interval widths.
   c. It is highly desirable that the program have the ability to construct frequency distributions of character (nominal or category) variables as well as numeric variables.
   d. Box plots are highly desirable.
   e. Stem-and-leaf plots are desirable.
2. The ability to form scatterplots of two variables is essential.

E. DESCRIPTIVE STATISTICS

Of course, those listed in point 1 are essential. Beyond that, the more measures of center and spread the better.

1. At an absolute minimum, arithmetic mean, median, N, and standard deviation for each variable must be available.
2. It is desirable that the program have the ability to specify a set of variables and get the same statistics on all variables at the same time.

F. RANDOM NUMBER GENERATION

1. Sampling from at least normal & rectangular distributions is essential.
2. Ability to specify the population parameters is highly desirable.
3. Sampling from other distribution forms is highly desirable.

G. TRANSFORMATIONS AND FUNCTIONS

1. Standard transformations (square root, trigonometric functions, etc.) must be present.
2. The ability to define new variables as combinations and/or functions of existing ones is essential.
3. Sorting and ranking
   a. The ability to sort a numeric variable in ascending or descending order is essential.
   b. The ability to sort one variable and "carry along" other(s) is highly desirable.
   c. The ability to generate ranks is desirable.
   d. The ability to sort character variables is desirable.
4. The ability to generate a "patterned" variable (e.g., 10 1's, then 10 2's, etc.) is highly desirable.

H. CORRELATION & REGRESSION

1. The ability to conduct bivariate correlation and regression is essential.
2. The ability to conduct multiple regression is essential.
3. Automatic computation of predicted values and residuals is desirable; if not available, the transformations capability must be able to produce them.

I. ONE AND TWO SAMPLE TESTS

1. One sample t & Z for arbitrary μ is essential.
2. Two group t & Z for $\mu_1 - \mu_2 = 0$ is essential; for arbitrary $\mu_1 - \mu_2$ is preferred.
3. Statement of exact probability of the obtained statistic is highly desirable.
4. If a two-sample repeated measures test is not provided, the transformations capability must be able to produce a difference variable for use in a one-group test.
5. A small selection of nonparametric tests is highly desirable.

J. FREQUENCY DATA

1. One- and two-way frequency counting is essential.
2. Chi-square in one- and two-way tables is highly desirable.
3. The ability to compute chi-square from an input frequency matrix is desirable.

K. ANOVA

1. One-way ANOVA for equal group sizes is essential.
   a. The ability to conduct unequal group size computations using unweighted means is highly desirable (as is the ability to choose between weighted and unweighted means solutions).
   b. The ability to obtain means and standard deviations for each group is highly desirable within the ANOVA routine itself.
   c. The ability to conduct post hoc tests (Scheffe, Neuman-Keuls, Tukey, etc.) is highly desirable.
   d. The ability to conduct post hoc linear comparisons is highly desirable.

2. Two-way Between Groups ANOVA for equal group sizes is essential.
    a. The ability to conduct unequal group size computations is highly desirable (as is the ability to choose between weighted and unweighted means solutions).
    b. The ability to obtain means and SDs for each group and marginal is highly desirable.
    c. Interaction plotting is highly desirable.
    d. The ability to conduct simple effect tests, post hoc tests, and linear comparisons is desirable.
3. Two-way Within Groups and Mixed ANOVA is very desirable
    a. The ability to conduct unequal group size computations is highly desirable (as is the ability to choose between weighted and unweighted means solutions).
    b. The ability to obtain means and SDs for each group and marginal is highly desirable
    c. Interaction plotting is highly desirable
    d. Post hoc tests and comparisons are desirable
    e. The ability to conduct simple effect tests, post hoc tests, and linear comparisons is very desirable.
    f. The computation of epsilon for repeated measures variables is nice.
4. Statement of exact probability level of obtained statistic is highly desirable. At least significance level is required.

L. GENERAL LINEAR MODEL

These features are optional but useful if they are offered.

M. ACCURACY

It goes without saying that a computer program that purports to do statistical computations should be able to do so accurately. Unfortunately, there are programs that cannot. How can you tell? You can't tell by reading the label and the manual, or by assuming that if it's expensive, then it must be good. So here are four simple tests that you can use. (These are also very good for you to use when you're trying out the program; you can tell a lot about how it will feel to use the program by doing these tests.)

1. Simple accuracy test. Enter these data values: 8000000001, 8000000002, and 8000000003 into a variable. Obtain the mean and the standard deviation. The correct values are $\bar{X} = 8000000002.0$ and 1.0. (If the program happens to use the "population" or "N" form for the standard deviation, the second value should be 0.8164958.) If you don't get the right answers, remove a zero from each data value and repeat until you do. The larger the number of digits, the better.
2. ANOVA algorithm accuracy test. Here is a set of data for a three group experiment. The correct F ratio is 7.411. As before, if you don't get that value, remove a zero from each value and repeat until you do. A program should be able to handle at least five-digit values correctly; all nine is best.

Group 1	Group 2	Group 3
100000016	100000004	100000002
100000018	100000006	100000010
100000010	100000008	100000009
100000012	100000010	100000013
100000019	100000002	100000011

3. Multiple regression test number 1. The tests for multiple regression are slightly more complicated. We provide two here. Enter the data below and use multiple regression to predict the first column from the next three. The regression should fail because the first two predictors are perfectly correlated with the third. The program should issue a warning (perhaps saying something about colinearity) or should give results that clearly look incorrect.

34.49629	40.42189	90.26162	130.68351	1.0
36.81650	37.17093	107.39382	144.56475	1.0
53.55746	38.97025	116.48220	155.45246	1.0
45.35021	54.05939	105.83000	159.88939	1.0
43.00875	57.22742	80.61142	137.83884	1.0
39.25219	44.11581	116.70356	160.81937	1.0
46.63869	67.08172	89.45464	156.53637	1.0

36.11099	42.23770	100.32523	142.56293	1.0
43.29906	62.87395	88.16708	151.04103	1.0
37.00662	32.44350	103.23119	135.67469	1.0
27.83607	56.46697	60.15070	116.61767	1.0
49.35529	68.14403	119.09569	187.23972	1.0
29.12261	45.84262	76.94583	122.78845	1.0
37.05529	59.87797	78.25898	138.13695	1.0
43.15374	40.27851	104.34813	144.62664	1.0
48.54774	56.67289	106.29185	162.96474	1.0
40.97546	42.91610	115.35694	158.27304	1.0
35.18105	42.35466	88.67056	131.02522	1.0

4. Multiple regression test number 2. Using the above data, try to predict the first column from the fourth and fifth. Again, the regression should fail, this time because the fifth column is constant. The program should issue a warning or should give results that clearly look incorrect.

SOLUTIONS TO SELECTED EXERCISES[1]

Chapter 1

1. a. ratio

   b. interval

   c. ordinal

   d. ratio

   e. ratio

   f. ratio

   g. nominal

   h. ordinal (could be interval if you assume equal intervals)

   i. ratio

   j. nominal

   k. ratio

   l. ordinal

   m. ratio

3. It appears to be reasonable if the scale is regarded as interval because summing is a reasonable operation with interval measurements. Deleting the high and low values would eliminate the effect of a possible extreme score.

5. a. To establish the validity using content validity, you would have to show that your test satisfactorily represents the content of the course. You might have an instructor define the content, and compare your test with that definition.

   b. Students who succeed in a statistics course should be expected to do well in certain other courses as well. If your test's predictions agree with the student's performance in those other courses, then you have established construct validity.

7. a. Have everyone line up by height.

b. Ask them to walk, at their own rate, from the psychology building to the library; write down the order in which they arrive.

c. Look at the order in which papers are stacked on the instructor's desk.

d. Ask your classmates to pick one of the following words to describe the temperature: freezing, chilly, nice, warm, hot.

9. a. Use a tape measure or yardstick.

   b. Use a stopwatch.

   c. Use a stopwatch.

   d. Obtain a Kelvin (absolute) thermometer from the physics department. Or use an ordinary Fahrenheit thermometer and then use the conversion formula

$$\left(\frac{5}{9}\right)(F - 32) + 273.15$$

where F is the temperature in Fahrenheit.

Chapter 2

1. a.

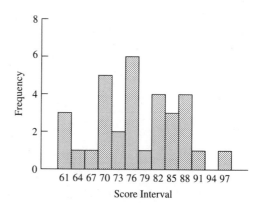

b.

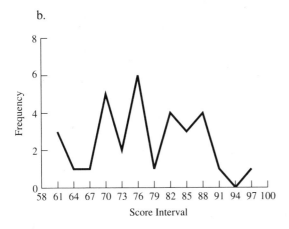

c.

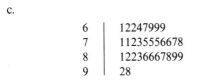

```
6 | 12247999
7 | 11235556678
8 | 12236667899
9 | 28
```

d. (1)

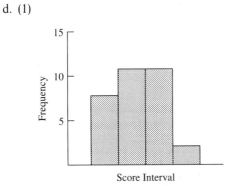

d. (2)

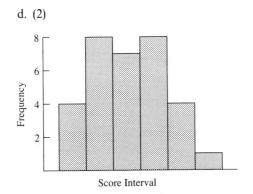

d. (3)

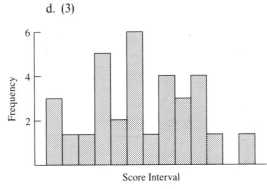

d. (4)

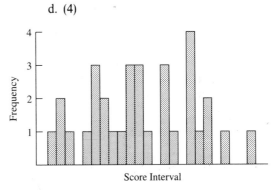

d. (5) The distribution with 6 intervals shows the data to be symmetrical, with a large grouping in the center, while that with roughly 15 indicates a possible outlier at the high end. All in all, the distribution with 6 intervals may be the best for these data.

3. a. (1)

REACTION TIME INTERVAL MIDPOINT	FREQUENCY
12	0
20	9
28	4
36	2
44	1
52	2
60	1
68	0
76	1

84	2
92	2
100	0
108	1
116	1
124	0
132	0
140	0
148	2
152	0

a. (2)

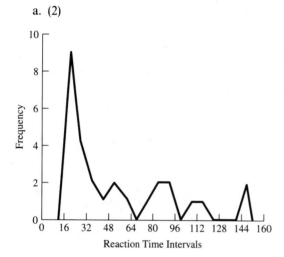

b.

1	789
2	011223568
3	188
4	2
5	35
6	0
7	2
8	329
9	4
10	5
11	9
12	
13	
14	89

c. The data are clustered toward the low end of the scale, indicating a large number of very fast reaction times (around 0.20 sec), with a more or less even spread into the longer reaction times, ranging upward to well over 2 sec.

5.

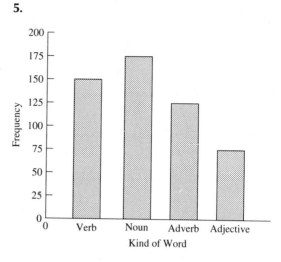

7. a.

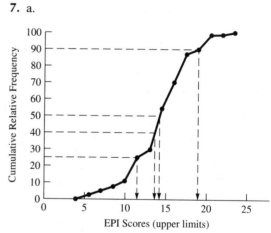

Percentiles are 14, 13.5, 11, and 19.

b.

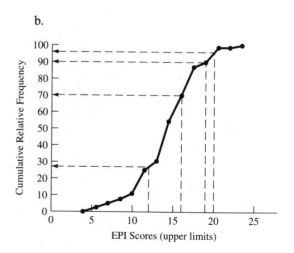

Percentile ranks are 27, 70, 96, and 90.

9. a. (1)

OTHER REFERENCE		SELF-REFERENCE	
SCORE INTERVAL	FREQUENCY	SCORE INTERVAL	FREQUENCY
500	2	500	0
600	0	600	2
700	1	700	0
800	2	800	2
900	5	900	1
1000	0	1000	3
1100	2	1100	2
1200	3	1200	1
1300	2	1300	1
1400	1	1400	1
1500	1	1500	3
1600	0	1600	0
1700	1	1700	2
		1800	0
		1900	0
		2000	1
		2100	1

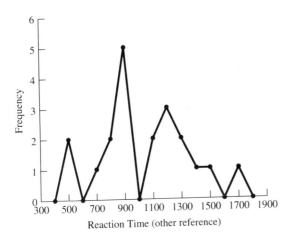

Reaction Time (other reference)

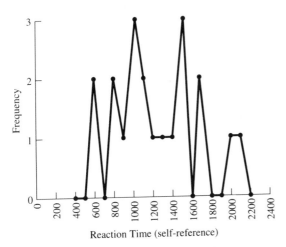

Reaction Time (self-reference)

b.

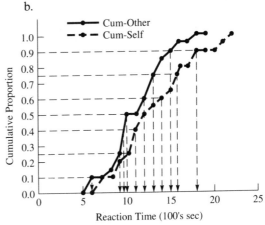

Reaction Time (100's sec)

Percentiles (other reference): 6, 9, 10, 12, 13, 15

Percentiles (self-reference): 7, 10, 11, 12, 14, 18

c. The reaction times seem quite variable for both conditions. On the whole, the response times for other reference words seem somewhat slower than those for self-reference.

11. a. (1)

Number Correct

a. (2)

SCORE INTERVAL	SPACING PHRASE	NORMAL	EVEN
21	0	0	0
29	0	0	1
37	0	1	0
45	0	2	3
53	0	4	1
61	6	5	4
69	2	5	7
77	3	2	3

85	3	5	1
93	2	1	2
101	2	0	0
109	0	0	0

b.

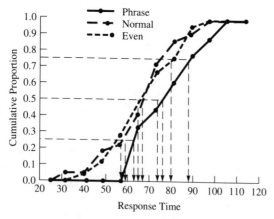

Quartiles (phrase): 63, 75, 88
Quartiles (normal): 55, 65, 80
Quartiles (even): 57, 67, 84

c.

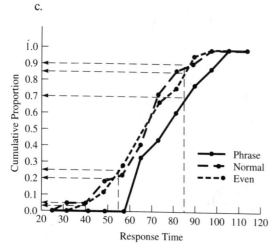

Percentile ranks (phrase): 0, 0, 69
Percentile ranks (normal): 4, 25, 86
Percentile ranks (even): 5, 21, 89

Chapter 3[1]

1. $\bar{X} = 77.22$
Mdn $= 76.00$
$s = 9.53$
$s^2 = 90.76$
$Sk_P = 0.38$

The class's scores are very slightly positively skewed ($Sk_P = 0.38$). The mean and the median are 77.22 and 76.00, respectively. The standard deviation is 9.53.

3. $\bar{X} = 54.18$
Mdn $= 38$
$s = 39.93$
$s^2 = 1594.52$
$Sk_P = 1.22$

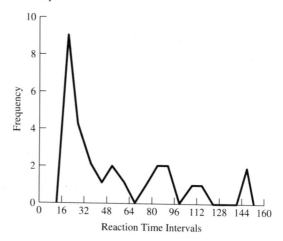

The reaction time data are positively skewed, with a large number of very fast responses, and a much smaller number of long ones. The median is 38, indicating that 50% of the responses occurred in 0.38 sec or less. The mean is 54.18, showing the influence of the extremely long scores made by a few individuals. The standard deviation (39.93) and the variance (1594.52) also illustrate a substantial spread around the mean.

5.

	A	B	C
Mean	46.25	50.50	53.67
Median	42.00	49.50	51.50
Range	53.00	17.00	48.00
Interquartile	6.50	7.50	22.00
MAD	3.00	3.5	10.5
Variance	199.48	30.09	236.06
s	14.12	5.48	15.36

7.

WEEK	MEAN	MEDIAN	s^2	s	IQR
1	44.04	24.85	363.42	19.06	29.00
2	24.85	23.00	74.67	8.64	10.50
3	52.26	52.00	39.12	6.26	9.50
4	43.74	46.00	227.74	15.09	20.00

9.

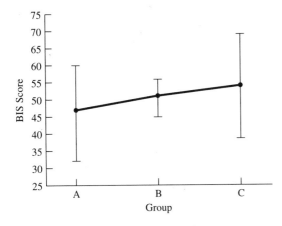

For the original data:

$$\overline{X} = 0.318, \text{Mdn} = 0.293, s = 0.196,$$

$$\text{MAD} = 0.098, \text{Sk}_P = 0.383$$

For the transformed data:

$$\overline{X} = 0.540, \text{Mdn} = 0.541, s = 0.166,$$

$$\text{Sk}_P = -0.018$$

The square root transformation almost completely eliminates the skewness.

15.

	MEAN	MEDIAN	Ss	Sk$_P$
Jingles	3.70	4.00	0.47	−1.91
Nonjingles	2.80	3.00	0.89	−0.67

11.

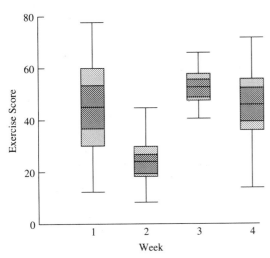

17. a.

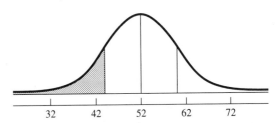

b.

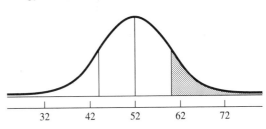

13.

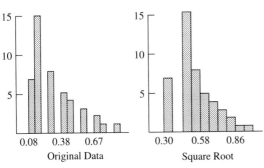

c.

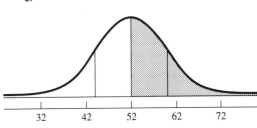

d.

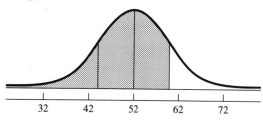

e.

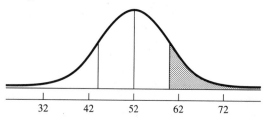

f.

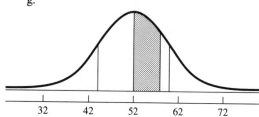

g.

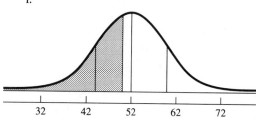

h.

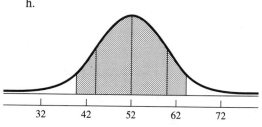

Chapter 4[2]

1. For Test 1   For Test 2

$$z = \frac{62 - 52}{8.5} \qquad z = \frac{62 - 52}{3.6}$$

$$= 1.18 \qquad\qquad = 2.79$$

You did much better on Test 2.

3.

	ORIGINAL	z
Mean	7.00	0.00
Median	8.00	0.45
s	2.20	1.00
Sk_P	−1.36	−1.36

As expected, standardizing the variable changes the mean and the standard deviation, but the skewness does not change because the form of the distribution is unaffected by the z transformation.

5. a.

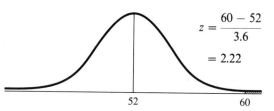

$$z = \frac{60 - 52}{3.6}$$

$$= 2.22$$

From Appendix A, the area to the right of $z = 2.22$ is 0.01321.

b.

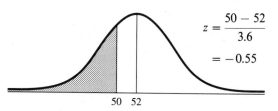

$$z = \frac{50 - 52}{3.6}$$

$$= -0.55$$

From Appendix A, the area to the left of $z = -0.55$ is 0.29115.

[2] The computations and illustrations in this and all following sections were done by computer. Remember that because of rounding and differing computational formulas, your results may not agree down to the last decimals. You should, however, be very close.

c.

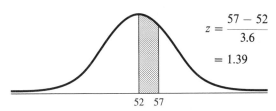

$$z = \frac{57 - 52}{3.6}$$

$$= 1.39$$

From Appendix A, the area between the mean and $z = 1.39$ is 0.41775.

d.

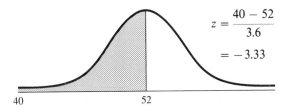

$$z = \frac{40 - 52}{3.6}$$

$$= -3.33$$

From Appendix A, the area between the mean and $z = -3.33$ is 0.42074.

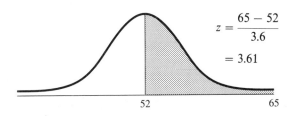

$$z = \frac{65 - 52}{3.6}$$

$$= 3.61$$

From Appendix A, the area between the mean and $z = 3.61$ is 0.49984.
Summing the two areas gives $0.49961 + 0.49984 = 0.99945$.

7. First determine the z values corresponding to the first and third quartiles:

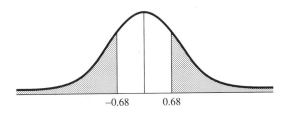

Using the z formula with the known values of -0.68 and 0.68, we find that the upper and lower values are

$$-0.68 = \frac{\text{Lower} - 50}{15}$$

$$\text{Lower} = 50 - 0.68(15)$$

$$= 39.8$$

and

$$0.68 = \frac{\text{Upper} - 50}{15}$$

$$\text{Upper} = 50 + 0.68(15)$$

$$= 60.2$$

Thus the required cut-off values are roughly 40 and 60.

9. -2.02, 0.22, and 1.35

11. -0.90, 0.18, 0.78, and 1.59

13. 0.36, 0.32, 0.16, 0.44, 0.24, 0.12, 0.04, 0.04

15. 0.16601, 0.21770, 0.68729, 0.01564, 0.07493

Chapter 5

1.

	MEAN	MEDIAN	s
Quiz 1	23.50	24.00	4.35
Quiz 2	21.94	23.50	4.58

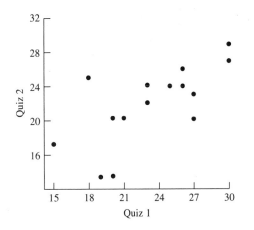

3. a.

	MEAN	MEDIAN	s	Sk_P
Trial 1	22.10	11.00	25.03	1.33
Trial 20	5.52	6.0	2.88	-0.50

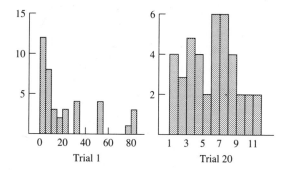

Trial 1   Trial 20

b.

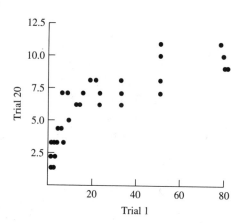

Trial 1

c. $r = 0.82$

d. The correlation is positive, but the relationship seems quite nonlinear.

5. $r_S = 0.84$

7.

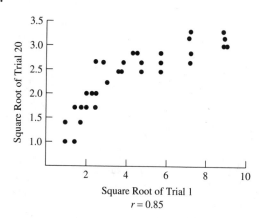

Square Root of Trial 1
$r = 0.85$

The correlation increased slightly after the square root operation, and the scatterplot showed slightly less curvilinearity.

Chapter 6

1. a. $\widehat{Quiz2} = 0.73(Quiz1) + 4.85$

   b. Predicted values are:

   19.39, 26.66, 21.57, 24.48, 21.57, 15.76, 26.66, 19.39, 23.76, 24.48, 18.67, 17.94, 20.12, 23.76, 23.03, 23.76

   c. Residuals are:

   -6.39, 0.34, 0.43, -1.48, 2.43, 1.24, 2.34, 0.61, 0.24, -4.48, -5.66, 7.06, -0.12, 2.24, 0.97, 0.24

   d. $SS_{resid} = 164.8$

   e.

   $$S_{est} = \sqrt{\frac{SS_{resid}}{df_{Error}}}$$
   $$= \sqrt{\frac{164.8}{14}} = 3.43$$

   f.

   $$S_{est} = s_Y\sqrt{1 - r^2}\sqrt{\frac{N-1}{N-2}}$$
   $$= 4.58\sqrt{1 - 0.69^2}\sqrt{\frac{16-1}{16-2}} = 3.43$$

3. a. $\widehat{SSST} = 1.11(EPIE) + 4.35$

   b. Predicted values:

   21.01, 19.90, 11.02, 26.56, 19.90, 19.90, 22.12, 21.01, 17.68, 19.90, 19.90, 19.90, 17.68, 16.57, 17.68, 16.57, 19.90, 8.794, 23.23, 18.79

   c. Residuals:

   -8.01, 2.10, 5.98, 6.44, -1.90, -1.90, 4.88, -8.01, -2.68, 1.10, 7.10, -2.90, -9.68, -3.57, 2.32, -2.57, 1.10, 2.21, 1.77, 6.21

   d. $SS_{resid} = 474.39$

   e.

   $$S_{est} = \sqrt{\frac{SS_{resid}}{df_{Error}}}$$
   $$= \sqrt{\frac{474.39}{18}} = 5.13$$

   f.

   $$S_{est} = s_Y\sqrt{1 - r^2}\sqrt{\frac{N-1}{N-2}}$$

$$= 6.32\sqrt{1 - 0.61^2}\,\sqrt{\frac{20 - 1}{20 - 2}} = 5.14$$

Chapter 7

1. The proportion should be 1/5 or 0.20 for each. Because the animals have no preferences, they are likely to pick any substance, resulting in equal choice. The values are probabilities because they are derived from a theoretical analysis; relative frequencies are summaries of actual data.

3. a. 0.28

b. 0.352

c. 0.768

5. a, b.

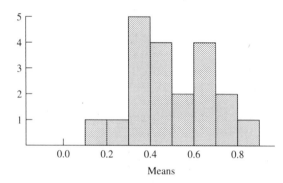

Means

c, d, e. The mean of the sample means is 0.478, which is close to the mean of the population (0.5). The standard deviation of the 20 samples is 0.179. The form of the distribution of the means is unimodal and more or less symmetrical, while the population from which the samples came is rectangular.

7. a. 0.98040

b. 0.53670

c. 0.39726

d. 0.61680

e. 0.1604

f. 0.0356

g. 0.00636

h. 0.1457

9. $\mu = 2.0$, $\sigma_{\bar{X}} = 0.177$
The distribution of the means is symmetrical and unimodal; it becomes more compact be-

cause its standard deviation decreases as the sample size increases.

11. a. about 20

b. probably none

c. about 20

d. 19

e. 1

f. 13 or 14

g. 6 or 7

13. 90%: 5.8 ± 0.231
99%: 5.8 ± 0.361

15. For males: 90%: 6.1 ± 0.119
95%: 6.1 ± 0.141
99%: 6.1 ± 0.186
For females: 90%: 6.0 ± 0.201
95%: 6.0 ± 0.239
99%: 6.1 ± 0.315

Chapter 8

1. The population mean for each sample is 0.5 and $\sigma = 0.289$, so that $\sigma_{\bar{X}} = \dfrac{\sigma}{\sqrt{N}} = \dfrac{0.289}{\sqrt{2}} = 0.204$.

a. (60%)	b. (95%)	c. (99%)
0.4188–0.7627	0.3080–0.8735	0.2192–0.9623
−0.0385–0.3055	−0.1492–0.4162	−0.2380–0.5051
0.2228–0.5667	0.1120–0.6775	0.0232–0.7663
0.4703–0.8143	0.3596–0.9251	0.2708–1.0140
0.2559–0.5999	0.1452–0.7106	0.0564–0.7995
0.3141–0.6581	0.2033–0.7688	0.1145–0.8576
0.1359–0.4799	0.0252–0.5906	−0.0637–0.6794
0.0287–0.3727	−0.0820–0.4834	−0.1708–0.5723
0.5383–0.8823	0.4276–0.9930	0.3387–1.0820
0.4461–0.7901	0.3353–0.9008	0.2465–0.9896
0.3619–0.7058	0.2511–0.8166	0.1623–0.9054
0.3089–0.6529	0.1982–0.7636	0.1093–0.8525
0.2143–0.5583	0.1036–0.6691	0.0148–0.7579
0.5449–0.8889	0.4342–0.9996	0.3453–1.0880
0.1711–0.5151	0.0603–0.6258	−0.0285–0.7146
0.4384–0.7824	0.3277–0.8931	0.2389–0.9820
0.2482–0.5922	0.1375–0.7029	0.0486–0.7917
0.6320–0.9760	0.5213–1.0870	0.4324–1.1760
0.1376–0.4816	0.0269–0.5924	−0.0619–0.6812
0.4395–0.7835	0.3288–0.8942	0.2400–0.9831

3. a. 4.74, 3.87, 3.13, 2.65

b. $\bar{X} = 105$: 97.41–112.58
$\bar{X} = 97$: 89.41–104.58
$\bar{X} = 84.6$: 77.01–92.18

c. 70%: 105.3–111.9
   90%: 103.5–113.7
   95%: 102.5–114.7
   99%: 100.5–116.7

5. Your numbers will probably be slightly different:

INTERVAL	EXPECTED	ACTUAL
60%	12	13
75%	15	17
90%	18	18

7.

	DISTRIBUTION OF MEANS	DISTRIBUTION OF MEDIANS
Mean	19.87	19.50
Std. dev.	1.24	1.36

9. Because $z = -2.694$, reject the hypothesis that $\mu = 2.0$ with $\alpha = .05$. 95% interval is 1.104–1.859.

11. a. The null hypothesis is that the infants look at the pair of videotapes equally, and that the population percent of time that they watch the left video is thus 50.

   b. Because $z = -0.529$, we cannot reject the null hypothesis with $\alpha = .05$ or .01.

   c. A little less than 0.40

13. a. Null: $\mu = 125$. Alternative: $\mu \neq 125$

   b. $\sigma_{\bar{x}} = \dfrac{\sigma}{\sqrt{N}} = \dfrac{3}{\sqrt{28}} = 5.67$

   c. We cannot reject the hypothesis: $z = 1.22$, $p > .05$.

   d. 90%: 122.6–141.3
      95%: 120.8–143.0
      99%: 117.3–146.5

   e. For a 5-point difference, the power is less than 0.17 (because $\delta = 0.88$, and the lowest entry in the table is for $\delta = 1.0$, which has a power of 0.17). For a 10-point difference, the power is about 0.44.

15. a. Null: $\mu = 5$. Alternative: $\mu \neq 5$

   b. $\sigma_{\bar{x}} = \dfrac{\sigma}{\sqrt{N}} = \dfrac{3}{\sqrt{35}} = 0.51$

   c. We reject the hypothesis: $z = 1.978$ $p < .001$. This value is significant at the .10 and the .05 levels, but not at the .01 level.

   d. 90%: 3.166–4.828

95%: 3.003–4.991
99%: 2.689–5.305

   e. At $\alpha = .10$, power is about .64
      At $\alpha = .05$, power is about .52
      At $\alpha = .01$, power is about .28

17. Power was about 0.71.

Chapter 9

1. $t(14) = 1.904$, $p > .05$

3. The results suggest that this group of students is probably not different from the national norms, at least not within the usual significance levels used in testing hypotheses. The confidence intervals suggest there may be a difference, but significance testing with $\alpha > .05$ would be required.

5. The obtained value of t does not permit us to reject the hypothesis that the mean is 5 (the norm for maze-bright animals) at the .01 level.

7. Of the eight scores, two are above the population median of 125 gm. The probability of two or fewer scores falling above the median if the null hypothesis is true is, from Appendix G, 0.14; we conclude that there is no evidence that this group differs from the norm.

9. This set of introversion scores has a mean of 13.00 and standard deviation of 3.528. The hypothesized population mean from which these scores were drawn is 10. We cannot conclude that these scores represent a population with a different mean: $t(9) = 2.689$, $p > .01$.

11. The coefficient does not differ significantly from 0.0 (critical value is 0.90).

13. $r_S = 0.556$. This is significantly different from 0 at $\alpha = .02$ (critical value is 0.520).

15. $r = 0.738$. This is not significantly different from 0.50, $z = 1.65$, $p > .05$.

$$z = \frac{z_r - \mu_r}{\sqrt{\dfrac{1}{N - 3}}} = \frac{0.9505 - 0.5493}{\sqrt{\dfrac{1}{20 - 3}}} = 1.65$$

17. $r = 0.628$. This is significantly different from 0 at $\alpha = .05$ (critical value is 0.423). In contrast with exercise 9.16, this time there is a correlation between the two measures.

Chapter 10

1. a. The mean of paired differences = 3.267, $t(14) = 3.50, p < .05$.

   b. $T = 12$; critical T from Appendix H is 25, so we conclude that the difference is significant, which agrees with the answer in part a.

3. a. The mean of paired differences = 1.450, $t(9) = 1.672, p > .10$.

   b. $T = 7.5$; critical T from Appendix H is 10, so we conclude that the difference is significant, which does not agree with the answer in part a.

5. $z = \dfrac{z_{r_1} - z_{r_2}}{\sqrt{\dfrac{1}{N-3} + \dfrac{1}{N-3}}} = \dfrac{-0.1103 - 0.4356}{\sqrt{\dfrac{1}{10-3} + \dfrac{1}{10-3}}}$

$= -1.00$. Because a z with an absolute value of 1.65 or greater is required for significance at the .10 level, we conclude that the two correlations are not significantly different.

7. a. Males and females differ in their ratings: $t(106) = -2.734, p < .05$.

   b. The 22 female and the 86 male therapists reported mean ratings of 5.636 and 5.209, respectively. The standard deviations for the two groups of ratings are 0.6707 for the males and 0.5811 for the females. These values are so close to equal that the equal variance form of the t test is appropriate. We conclude that there is a significant difference in the ratings of the males and females: $t(106) = -2.734, p < .05$.

9. a. $t(26) = 15.255, p < .01$

   b. $t(26) = 2.974, p < .01$

   c. $r = 0.888$. At $\alpha = .05$, this is significantly different from 0.00. (The sample size of $N = 27$ is not listed in Appendix K, but the obtained r exceeds the critical values for both $N = 25$ and $N = 30$.)

   d. $r = 0.784$. At $\alpha = .05$, this is significantly different from 0.00.

   e. This year's correlation of 0.888 does not differ from last year's, $z = 0.63, p > .05$.

$$z = \frac{z_r - \mu_r}{\sqrt{\dfrac{1}{N-3}}} = \frac{1.4219 - 1.2933}{\sqrt{\dfrac{1}{27-3}}} = 0.63$$

   f. This year's correlation of 0.784 does not dif-

fer from last year's, $z = 1.57, p > .05$.

$$z = \frac{z_r - \mu_r}{\sqrt{\dfrac{1}{N-3}}} = \frac{1.0454 - 0.7250}{\sqrt{\dfrac{1}{27-3}}} = 1.57$$

Chapter 11

1. $\chi^2(4, N = 45) = 16.67, p < .05$

3. The proportion of males in the class (32 of 48, or 66.67%) is significantly different from 50%, $z = 2.31, p < .05$.

5. Your results will vary, of course, but for one set of random values:

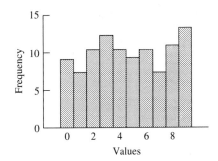

$\chi^2(9, N = 100) = 3.64, p > .05$

7. $C = 0.399, \Phi = 0.434$

9. a. The observed matrix is:

	LEVEL				
	1	2	3	4	TOTAL
Sit	170	516	1355	3	2044
Eat	26	109	531	9	675
Groom	42	100	407	0	549
Locomotion	202	351	660	137	1350
Rest	9	177	488	1	675
Total	449	1253	3441	150	5293

$\chi^2 = 586.63$, df = 12. The value is significant, $p < .01$.

   b. The matrix of standardized residuals follows:

	LEVEL			
	1	2	3	4
Sit	-0.31	1.63	0.54	-9.08*
Eat	-4.23*	-3.76*	2.79*	-2.44*
Groom	-0.68	-2.43	1.66	-4.11*
Locomotion	9.06*	1.78	-5.03*	18.23*
Rest	-6.53*	1.27	1.49	-4.37*

*$p < .01$

The description of the relationship should pay special attention to the significant residuals. Among other things, the ceiling (Level 4) is used for almost nothing other than locomotion; the floor (Level 1) is also used heavily for locomotion. Eating appears to occur primarily on Level 3, and to occur less often than expected on Level 2 (this is especially interesting because both levels are "off the ground"). Finally, Level 3 seems to be a goal rather than a means—it is significantly *not* used for locomotion, and is used for eating and other sedentary activities.

11. $\chi^2(4, N = 8643) = 442.64$, $p < .01$
$C = 0.221$, $\Phi = 0.160$

Chapter 12

1.

GROUP	MEAN	STD. DEV.
90 days	25.57	12.940
120 days	13.21	9.916
150 days	15.21	9.633

SOURCE	df	SS	MS	F	
Age	2	1231.86	615.929	5.1524	$p < .05$
Error	39	4662.14	119.542		
Total	41	5894.00			

The Tukey critical value is 10.05, so that

90 days vs 120 days: $25.57 - 13.21 = 12.36$	significant
90 days vs 150 days: $25.57 - 15.21 = 10.36$	significant
120 days vs 150 days: $13.21 - 15.21 = -2.00$	not significant

3.

LENGTH	MEAN	STD. DEV.
10 items	8.62	5.303
15 items	12.44	4.560
20 items	15.94	7.496
25 items	16.75	6.836

SOURCE	df	SS	MS	F	
Test length	3	668.80	222.932	5.814	$p < .01$
Error	60	2273.06	37.884		
Total	63	2941.86			

The Tukey critical value is 7.06, so that

10 vs 15 items: $8.62 - 12.44 = -3.82$	not significant
15 vs 20 items: $12.44 - 15.94 = -3.50$	not significant

20 vs 25 items: $15.94 - 16.75 = -0.81$	not significant
10 vs 20 items: $8.62 - 15.94 = -7.32$	significant
15 vs 25 items: $12.44 - 16.75 = -4.31$	not significant
10 vs 25 items: $8.62 - 16.75 = -8.13$	significant

5. $H = 7.93$, critical value is 5.991. We reject the hypothesis of equal groups distributions and come to the same conclusion as in exercise 12.1

7. $H = 5.39$, critical value is 5.991. We do not reject the hypothesis of equal groups distributions and come to a different conclusion from that in exercise 12.4.

Chapter 13

1. a.

SOURCE	SS	df	MS	F
Regression	144.196	6	24.033	3.65
Residual	85.604	13	6.585	

VARIABLE	COEFFICIENT
Constant	10.353
SSST	-0.794
BIS	-0.002
V	0.574
I	0.255
TAS	-1.175
ES	1.311

$s_{est} = 2.566$

b, c.

STUDENT	PREDICTED	RESIDUAL	STANDARDIZED RESIDUAL
1	12.96	2.044	0.797
2	12.74	1.256	0.489
3	11.90	-5.898	-2.299
4	18.44	1.564	0.609
5	13.44	0.562	0.219
6	13.61	0.394	0.154
7	13.94	2.062	0.804
8	13.25	1.752	0.683
9	9.04	2.963	1.155
10	14.47	-0.475	-0.185
11	16.37	-2.369	-0.923
12	12.25	1.753	0.683
13	11.33	0.671	0.261
14	9.63	1.367	0.533
15	13.88	-1.883	-0.734
16	13.45	-2.453	-0.956
17	14.14	-0.143	-0.056
18	6.11	-2.109	-0.822
19	17.20	-0.197	-0.077
20	13.86	-0.861	-0.336

5. a, b.

SOURCE	SS	df	MS	F
Regression	1231.86	2	615.929	5.15
Residual	4662.14	39	119.542	

The summary table values are identical to those for exercise 12.1.

The original means are: 25.57, 13.21, and 15.21.

The predicted scores are:

$$25.57$$
$$25.57$$
$$\vdots$$
$$25.57$$
$$13.21$$
$$\vdots$$
$$13.21$$
$$15.21$$
$$\vdots$$

for the three groups.

7. a, b.

SOURCE	SS	df	MS	F
Regression	101.900	3	33.967	3.831
Residual	195.062	22	8.866	

CONDITIONS	DIFFERENCE	SCHEFFÉ	TUKEY-KRAMER	LSD	DUNNETT C
A vs B	2.54	5.04	4.63	2.91	5.04
A vs C	5.21	4.69	4.30	2.71	4.34
A vs placebo	2.91	5.30	4.87	3.06	9.15
B vs C	2.67	4.89	4.49	2.82	4.40
B vs placebo	0.37	5.48	5.04	3.17	4.93
C vs placebo	2.3	5.16	4.74	2.98	4.41

Chapter 14

1.

SOURCE	SS	df	MS	F
Subjects	360.563	11	32.778	
Trial	610.229	3	203.410	29.765
Error	225.521	33	6.834	
Total	1196.313	47		

The means for the trials are 6.75, 10.00, 14.08, and 15.92. To test all six pairs of means and keep the overall α at .10, we conduct each test at $\alpha = .0167$. The table shows the t value (df = 11) and the probability.

	TRIAL 3	TRIAL 5	TRIAL 7
Trial 5	−2.575, $p > .0167$		
Trial 7	−7.260, $p < .0167$	−5.152, $p < .0167$	
Trial 9	−12.803, $p < .0167$	−4.241, $p < .0167$	−1.722, $p > .0167$

3.

SOURCE	SS	df	MS	F
Subjects	11.000	11	1.000	
Trial	7.167	3	2.389	5.699
Error	13.833	33	.419	
Total	32.000	47		

The means for the adjective groups are 2.417, 1.750, 1.500, and 2.333. To test all six pairs of means and keep the overall α at .10, we conduct each test at $\alpha = .0167$. The table shows the t value (df = 11) and the probability.

	HIGHLY POSITIVE	SLIGHTLY POSITIVE	SLIGHTLY NEGATIVE
Slightly Positive	2.602, $p > .0167$		
Slightly Negative	2.930, $p < .0167$	1.149, $p > .0167$	
Highly Negative	0.290, $p < .0167$	−2.244, $p < .0167$	−3.458, $p < .0167$

Chapter 15

1.

SOURCE	df	SS	MS	F
Stimulus	3	5850.00	1950.00	33.312
Species	1	302.50	302.50	5.160
Interaction	3	953.90	317.97	5.432
Error	32	1873.20	58.54	
Total	39	8979.60		

3. A results section should contain the means of each cell in the design, and probably a plot of the interaction similar to the following. It should also point out that the species differ for all stimuli expect for the comfort call.

5.

SOURCE	df	SS	MS	F
Sex at kindergarten	1	0.125	0.125	0.004
Sex at grade 2	1	406.125	406.125	13.531
Sex at grade 4	1	540.250	10.125	0.337
Error	18	1873.20	30.014	

7. Overall analysis:

SOURCE	df	SS	MS	F
Drug	2	349.405	174.702	42.131
Boredom suscept	1	0.865	0.865	0.209
Interaction	2	358.754	179.377	43.258
Error	66	273.678	4.147	
Total	71	982.701		

Simple effects analysis:

SOURCE	df	SS	MS	F
Drug @ low	2	708.120	354.06	85.385
Drug @ high	2	0.038	0.019	0.005
Boredom @ L-dopa	1	65.737	65.737	15.853
Boredom @ placebo	1	39.015	39.015	9.409
Boredom @ haloperidol	1	254.867	254.867	61.463
Error	66	273.678	4.147	

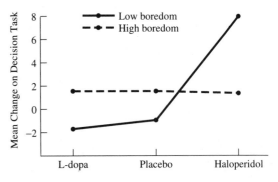

9. The results presentation should include the overall summary table, the table of simple effects, and the interaction plot. Special attention should be given to the large and significant differences between the amounts of the sweet taste consumed by the two groups.

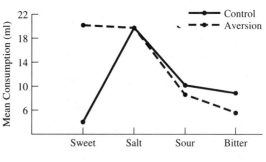

SOURCE	df	SS	MS	F
Aversion @ sweet	1	1238.450	238.450	105.526
Aversion @ salt	1	0.050	0.050	0.004
Aversion @ sour	1	10.513	10.513	0.835
Aversion @ bitter	1	59.513	59.513	4.727
Taste @ aversion	3	14119.248	427.856	33.987
Taste @ control	3	1123.269	374.423	45.629
Error	72	906.400	12.5889	

11.

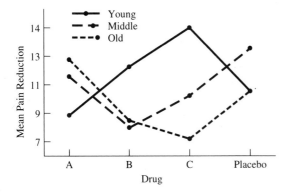

Index

TO THE OWNER OF THIS BOOK

We hope that you have found *Statistics in the Behavioral Sciences: A Conceptual Introduction* useful. So that this book can be improved in a future edition, would you take the time to complete this sheet and return it? We'd really like to hear what you think.

School and address: _____

Department: _____

Instructor's name: _____

1. What I like most about this book is: _____

_____

_____

2. What I like least about this book is: _____

_____

_____

3. My general reaction to this book is: _____

_____

4. The name of the course in which I used this book is: _____

_____

5. Were all of the chapters of the book assigned for you to read? _____

   If not, which ones weren't? _____

6. In the space below, or on a separate sheet of paper, please write specific suggestions for improving this book and anything else you'd care to share about your experience in using the book.

_____

_____

_____

_____

_____

Optional

Your name: _____ Date: _____

May Brooks/Cole quote you, either in promotion for *Statistics in the Behavioral Sciences: A Conceptual Introduction* or in future publishing ventures?

Yes: _____ No: _____

Sincerely,

Richard S. Lehman

FOLD HERE

NO POSTAGE
NECESSARY
IF MAILED
IN THE
UNITED STATES

BUSINESS REPLY MAIL

FIRST CLASS   PERMIT NO. 358   PACIFIC GROVE, CA

POSTAGE WILL BE PAID BY ADDRESSEE

ATT: *Richard S. Lehman* _____

**Brooks/Cole Publishing Company
511 Forest Lodge Road
Pacific Grove, California 93950-9968**

FOLD HERE